THE *GLOSAE SVPER PLATONEM* OF BERNARD OF CHARTRES

Edited with and Introduction by
Paul Edward Dutton

Aristotle, Theophrastus, Cicero, Plutarch, Apuleius, Porphyry, Calcidius, Proclus, Boethius, al-Fārābī, Yaḥyā ibn ʿAdī, al-Razī, William of Conches, Petrarch, Marsilio Ficino, Francis Cornford, and Luc Brisson: the roll of those who have devoted themselves to exploring Plato's *Timaeus* is rich, but far from closed. Of all Plato's dialogues, it is the *Timaeus* that has, in terms of the continuity of its transmission and the difficulty of its doctrine, exercised a far-reaching influence on the history of western philosophy.

Plato's enigmatic work, which the Middle Ages inherited in the translation of Calcidius, was central to that intellectual revival of the early twelfth century often associated with the masters of Chartres. The principal medieval commentary on the work was a magisterial set of glosses composed by William of Conches. But William admitted that he had drawn on the work of other learned glossators. One of these was his own master, the famous Platonist Bernardus Carnotensis who had written an even more popular set of glosses on the *Timaeus*. The case for attributing these *Glosae super Platonem*, which exist in six twelfth-century manuscripts, to Bernard of Chartres depends upon a complex concurrence of palaeographical, codicological, philosophical, and historical evidence. It is demonstrated here in detail for the first time.

The *Glosae* can be divided into eight parts: an *accessus ad auctorem*, glosses on Calcidius' introductory letter, and six sets of glosses on the *Timaeus* itself. Bernard's sources are manifold: Boethius, Macrobius, and Calcidius are the central figures in the gathering of authors and authorities in the glosses. A careful student of all of them, Bernard is nevertheless a resourceful reader, at once deferential, appropriative, and critical toward his *auctoritates*.

Something of Bernard's own metaphysical predilections is refracted in the *Glosae*, too. The work everywhere attests to his profound interest in the filiations between the Platonic Ideas, the archetypal world, and primordial matter. To explain the relationship of the Ideas to primordial *hyle*, Bernard conceived of the *formae natiuae* as the images of the Ideas that enter matter and are found in created things. It was this original notion that John of Salisbury attributed to Bernard of Chartres and to Gilbert of Poitiers.

Yet a truer measure of achievement may lie not in the invention of terms, but in the growth of a particular way of reading. The lineaments of that reading are clear enough: Bernard identifies and examines Plato's main ideas, then turns to the specific difficulties presented by the text. Unexceptional as it may first appear, this pattern of exposition nonetheless reveals what was probably Bernard's own methodological innovation, the comprehensive *glosa*, a genre that conjoins the two traditions of commentary, with its emphasis upon the general meaning or ordering idea of a text, and of glossing, with its detailed unravelling of the *materia* of particular words.

Written between 1100 and 1115, Bernard's glosses served to establish an interpretation of the *Timaeus* that was to shape the very understanding of Plato in the twelfth century. The *Glosae super Platonem* are, finally, not merely another entry in the historiographical dossier on the continuity of the Platonic tradition, but an important historical guide to the proper reading of Plato's secretive, inexhaustible dialogue.

"Hic lege Bernardum et adhuc inuenies"

Oxford, Bodleian Library Auct. F.3.15, folio 9r: the text of *Timaeus* 34b–36a, in an elegant twelfth-century Irish script, with marginal and interlinear glosses from the *Glosae super Platonem* (reproduced by permission of the Bodleian Library, Oxford).

STUDIES AND TEXTS 107

THE
GLOSAE SUPER PLATONEM
OF BERNARD OF CHARTRES

Edited with an Introduction by

PAUL EDWARD DUTTON

PONTIFICAL INSTITUTE OF MEDIAEVAL STUDIES

ACKNOWLEDGMENT

This book has been published with the help of a grant
from the Canadian Federation for the Humanities,
using funds provided by the Social Sciences
and Humanities Research Council of Canada.

CANADIAN CATALOGUING IN PUBLICATION DATA

Bernard, of Chartres.
. The Glosae super Platonem of Bernard of Chartres

(Studies and texts, ISSN 0082-5328 ; 107)
Introduction in English; text in Latin.
Includes bibliographical references.
ISBN 0-88844-107-X

1. Plato. Timaeus. I. Dutton, Paul Edward, 1952- . II. Pontifical Institute of
Mediaeval Studies. III. Title. IV. Series: Studies and texts (Pontifical Institute of
Mediaeval Studies) ; 107.

B387.B47 1991   113   C90-095522-8

PRINTED BY UNIVERSA, WETTEREN, BELGIUM

Contents

Preface

I have taken as my mandate the name of the series in which this book appears, so that the reader will find herein both a Study and a Text. Those who wish to be spared a lengthy introduction should turn immediately to the critical edition of the *Glosae super Platonem* of Bernard of Chartres. The preliminary study, however, supplies the background material that many readers will want before turning to the edition itself. Most important of all in the introduction is the obligation to restate the case for the attribution of this set of glosses on the *Timaeus* to Bernard of Chartres. Issues such as the doctrine of the *formae natiuae* are central to the question of Bernard's authorship and, therefore, are dealt with at some length. Moreover, the life and thought of Bernard of Chartres have not been thoroughly re-examined since Clerval's pioneering reconstruction of them over a century ago. In order to reconsider Bernard's career in detail, it has been necessary to weigh the quality of all the witnesses to it, especially John of Salisbury and the rich and multiform account of Bernard that he supplies in the *Metalogicon*. Lastly, *Timaeus* glosses, particularly in their highly developed, twelfth-century form, require a few introductory words in order to explain their special genre and context.

The individuals and institutions to whom I owe a debt of deep gratitude are numerous. In 1982 the Library of the Pontifical Institute of Mediaeval Studies, under the charge of D.F. Finlay, began to acquire microfilms of glossed manuscripts of the *Timaeus* for my use. One of these led to the uncovering of the *Glosae super Platonem* of Bernard of Chartres. Six libraries in Europe, the homes of the six manuscripts of the work edited below, generously allowed me access to their manuscripts and permission to publish the edition. The staff of the Inter-Library Loan office at Simon Fraser University spent many hours locating books uncommon in our *finibus mundi*.

A Research Fellowship awarded by the Social Sciences and Humanities Research Council of Canada allowed me to examine the manuscripts of the *Glosae* in Europe and to purchase microfilms of virtually all the glossed copies of the *Timaeus* from the Middle Ages. The History Department and Humanities Institute of Simon Fraser University have provided me with constant support throughout the last seven years. My greatest institutional debt, however, must be to the Pontifical Institute of Mediaeval Studies, where my medieval interests were nurtured and this book underwent its difficult parturition in the rare M.S.D. examination.

I am also grateful to the many individuals who have commented on and criticised my work in progress. The first of these is Edouard Jeauneau who over a decade ago introduced me to the study of the *Timaeus* in the Middle Ages. Without his fundamental studies and editions of Latin glosses on Plato, we would today know very little about a rich source of medieval thought. M. Jeauneau was ready throughout the length of this project to help me with problems, to supply suggestions, and to offer encouragement. I thank him for his unswerving support and friendship.

Other Fellows of the Pontifical Institute of Mediaeval Studies also generously assisted me. Brian Stock, in particular, put at my disposal his considerable knowledge of medieval Platonism and the twelfth century. James Reilly reviewed with me the matter of the textual tradition of the *Glosae* and Walter Principe carefully examined a selection of variants. Leonard Boyle, now Prefect of the Vatican Library, considered the palaeographical character of some of the main manuscripts with me early in the course of the project.

Peter Dronke of Cambridge twice supplied me with stimulating questions about the *Glosae* which I have tried to answer in the introduction. D.E. Luscombe of the University of Sheffield urged me to consider some issues in my final revision that otherwise might have been left unaddressed. R.W. Southern of Oxford and Tullio Gregory of Rome also commented on and expressed some interest when I took up this project. I have profited as well from many conversations with James Hankins of Harvard University on the subject of the manuscripts of the *Timaeus*. Lastly, Mary-Ann Stouck of Simon Fraser University kindly reviewed the final typescript. To all of these my heartfelt thanks.

I cannot conclude without thanking my wife Barbara for her patience and our daughters Laura and Kate for moments of peace in which to work.

Abbreviations

Cal., *Comm.*
> Calcidius, *Commentarius*, ed. J.H. Waszink. In *Timaeus a Calcidio translatus commentarioque instructus*, pp. 53-346. Plato latinus, vol. 4, ed. Raymond Klibansky. 2nd ed. London: The Warburg Institute, 1975.

Clerval, *Les écoles*
> Clerval, Alexandre. *Les écoles de Chartres au Moyen-Age.* Chartres: Garnier, 1895; rpt. Frankfurt: Minerva, 1965.

Dutton, "*Illustre ciuitatis*"
> Dutton, Paul Edward. "*Illustre ciuitatis et populi exemplum*: Plato's *Timaeus* and the Transmission from Calcidius to the End of the Twelfth Century of a Tripartite Scheme of Society," *Mediaeval Studies* 45 (1983) 79-119.

Dutton, "The Uncovering"
> Dutton, Paul Edward. "The Uncovering of the *Glosae super Platonem* of Bernard of Chartres," *Mediaeval Studies* 46 (1984) 192-221.

Glosae
> *Glosae super Platonem Bernardi Carnotensis*, edited below, pp. 137-234.

Glose Willelmi de Conchis super Platonem, ed. Jeauneau.
> In Guillaume de Conches. *Glosae super Platonem.* Ed. Edouard Jeauneau. Textes philosophiques du Moyen Age 13. Paris: Vrin, 1965.

Gregory, *Platonismo medievale*
> Gregory, Tullio. *Platonismo medievale: studi e ricerche.* Studi storici, fasc. 26-27. Rome: Istituto storico Italiano per il medio evo, 1958.

Häring, "Chartres and Paris Revisited"
> Häring, Nikolaus. "Chartres and Paris Revisited." In *Essays in Honour of Anton Charles Pegis*, ed. J. Reginald O'Donnell, pp. 268-329. Toronto: Pontifical Institute of Mediaeval Studies, 1974.

Jeauneau, *Lectio*
> Jeauneau, Edouard. '*Lectio philosophorum*': *Recherches sur l'Ecole de Chartres.* Amsterdam: Hakkert, 1973.

PL
> Patrologiae cursus completus: Series Latina. Ed. J.-P. Migne. Paris: 1844-1864.

Southern, "Humanism"
>   Southern, Richard W. "Humanism and the School of Chartres." In
>   R.W. Southern, *Medieval Humanism and Other Studies*, pp. 61-85.
>   New York: Harper Torchbooks, 1970; rpt. Oxford: Blackwell, 1984.

Timaeus
>   Plato. *Timaeus a Calcidio translatus*, ed. J.H. Waszink. In *Timaeus
>   a Calcidio translatus commentarioque instructus*, pp. 1-52. Plato
>   Latinus, vol. 4, ed. Raymond Klibansky. 2nd ed. London: The
>   Warburg Institute, 1975.

Waszink, "Praefatio"
>   Waszink, J.H. "Praefatio." In *Timaeus a Calcidio translatus commen-
>   tarioque instructus*, pp. vii-cxciv. Plato Latinus, vol. 4. Ed. Raymond
>   Kilbansky. 2nd ed. London: The Warburg Institute, 1975.

Nota bene:

In the introduction and edition that follow the *Timaeus* is cited by the standard reference
numbers (for example, 17c). Specific references to Calcidius' translation and commentary
have been cited according to the page and line numbers of Waszink's edition (hereafter W).
Thus W5:11-13 refers the reader to page 5, lines 11-13 of Waszink's edition. Specific
references to Bernard of Chartres's *Glosae super Platonem* are given according to section and
line numbers. Thus 6.34-38 directs the reader to section six, lines thirty-four to thirty-eight
of the *Glosae* edited below.

Introduction

Background

Aristotle, Theophrastus, Cicero, Plutarch, Apuleius, Porphyry, Calcidius, Proclus, Boethius, al-Fārābī, Yaḥyā ibn ʿAdī, al-Rāzī, William of Conches, Petrarch, Marsilio Ficino, T.H. Martin, A.E. Taylor, Francis Cornford, and Luc Brisson:[1] the roll of those who have devoted themselves to exploring the meanings of Plato's *Timaeus* is rich, but far from closed. Of all Plato's dialogues, it is the *Timaeus* that has, in terms of the continuity of its presence and the difficulty of its doctrine, exercised the profoundest influence on the history of western philosophy. The multivalence of the work accounts, in some measure, for its enduring appeal, since it treats of myth and cosmology, history and the human body. In its very structure, the *Timaeus* is a provocatively disjointed dialogue. Though Socrates and his three guests begin their conversation with the recollection of an ideal city similar to the one described in the *Republic* and then turn to discuss the myth of Atlantis (17a-27b), the work is primarily devoted to Timaeus of Locri's account of the workings of the cosmos. Even the great Wilamowitz was unable to smooth out the bumps in the failed design of the old Plato's majestic trilogy of the *Timaeus, Critias,* and *Hermocrates.*[2]

---

[1] For the ancient tradition, see Matthias Baltes, *Die Weltenstehung des Platonischen Timaios nach den Antiken Interpreten,* Philosophia antiqua: A Series of Monographs on Ancient Philosophy 30 (Leiden, 1976); for the Arabic, see Richard Walzer, *Greek into Arabic: Essays on Islamic Philosophy,* Oriental Studies, ed. S.M. Stern and Richard Walzer (Cambridge, Mass., 1962), 1: 5-6, 31, 236-252; for the medieval, see Raymond Klibansky, *The Continuity of the Platonic Tradition during the Middle Ages: Outlines of a Corpus Platonicum Medii Aevi* (London, 1939, rpt. 1950; rpt. with a new preface and four supplementary chapters, 1981). See also T.H. Martin, *Etudes sur le Timée de Platon,* 2 vols. (Paris, 1841; rpt. New York, 1976); A.E. Taylor, *A Commentary on Plato's Timaeus* (Oxford, 1927; rpt. 1962); Francis MacDonald Cornford, *Plato's Cosmology: The 'Timaeus' of Plato Translated with a Running Commentary* (London, 1937); and Luc Brisson, *Le même et l'autre dans la structure ontologique du 'Timée' de Platon: un commentaire systématique du 'Timée' de Platon,* Publications de l'Université de Paris X Nanterre, Lettres et Sciences Humaines: Série A: Thèses et travaux 23 (Paris, 1974).

[2] U. von Wilamowitz-Moellendorff, *Platon,* 2 vols. (Berlin, 1919; rpt. 1959-1962) 1: 592-599 and 2: 255-257. See also Warman Welliver, *Character, Plot, and Thought in Plato's Timaeus-Critias,* Philosophia antiqua: A Series of Monographs on Ancient Philosophy 32 (Leiden, 1977), pp. 1-49.

Whether there can in the end be any final word on what the *Timaeus* means seems unlikely. Cornford admitted as much, but held out "some hope of persuading scholars that a Greek sentence means one thing rather than another."[3] Yet when the sentences are placed one against another, doctrine against doctrine, and dialogue against dialogue, the difficulties of later Platonism explode upon the reader, threatening, as Euripides had in the *Bacchae*, any sense of comfortable certainty. Within Timaeus' speech there is, for instance, a startling shift in perspective, one characteristic of Plato's profound intuitive leaps, but bound to dizzy the student. Midway in the dialogue (47e) the interlocutor shifts abruptly from a top-down consideration of the provident and reasoning worker-god in the act of arranging the world to a bottom-up study of the necessary limitations placed upon his work by the errant nature of the disordered chaos he first surveyed. Perhaps Plato wanted only to provoke his listeners with what he describes as no more than a "likely story" (29d); so much of what Timaeus reports as probable is, after all, outside human ken. The *Timaeus* has engaged the attention of serious minds for two millennia precisely because of its plastic (rather than poetic) quality, for it is a profoundly perplexing work.

Looking over the long list of Timaean commentators one notices a cyclical pattern of interest in the dialogue. The process, begun in the ancient world and repeated once in the Middle Ages, and again in modern times, has been one that moves from occasional comments by a wide number of readers to the systematic and synthetic studies of a few. Thus, in the ancient world Aristotle opened a round of specific, but not systematic, interest in the *Timaeus* that would conclude with the systematic studies of Porphyry, Calcidius, and Proclus. A characteristic feature of the later works in each cycle is their awareness of a prior tradition of comment, their synthesis of acceptable positions and denial of the unacceptable, and their search for some reasonable grounds for consensus. The pattern is still at work, if we may judge from Luc Brisson's criticism of Taylor and Cornford.[4] For a medievalist Brisson's comment is reminiscent of William of Conches's appraisal of his own predecessors:

   [3] *Plato's Cosmology*, p. vii.
   [4] Brisson, *Le même et l'autre*, p. 9: "Certes, en langue anglaise, les remarquables travaux de A.E. Taylor et de F.M. Cornford ont fait date. Toutefois, même s'il demeure indispensable au niveau de l'analyse détaillée du texte, le *Commentary on Plato's Timaeus* de A.E. Taylor repose sur des hypothèses générales dont la fausseté a été démontrée depuis longtemps. Par ailleurs, l'admirable commentaire qui accompagne l'excellente traduction de F.M. Cornford dans *Plato's Cosmology* présente les désavantages de ses avantages: il ne peut être ni systématique, puisqu'il suit de très près le texte, ni exhaustif, puisqu'il considère ce dialogue en lui-même sans chercher à le situer dans le cadre des derniers dialogues, et dans le cours de la tradition platonicienne."

> Etsi multos super Platonem commentatos esse, multos glosasse non dubitemus, tamen quia commentatores, literam nec continuantes nec exponentes, soli sententie seruiunt, glosatores uero in leuibus superflui, in grauibus uero obscurissimi uel nulli reperiuntur, rogatu sociorum quibus omnia honesta debemus excitati, super predictum aliquid dicere proposuimus, aliorum super-flua recidentes, pretermissa addentes, obscura elucidantes, male dicta remouentes, bene dicta imitantes.[5]

These cycles of interpretation moving from the occasional to the systematic are in some sense cumulative, building within the whole tradition upon available and received opinions. Aristotle's insights, for instance, have become a fixture, while Porphyry's, with the loss of his treatise, must remain a subject of conjecture.

Just why a new cycle of interpretation begins is not clear. Most likely a complex set of changing cultural values and the scholarly fashions that reflect them slowly work to focus attention on the text. A long period of relative neglect may precede one of these periods of re-examination, so that some ages must essentially rediscover the importance of the dialogue. In the case of the Middle Ages the *Timaeus* had become by the year 1000 a largely forgotten book. Between Boethius' death and the eleventh century, a period of some five hundred years, there had been little sustained interest in the *Timaeus.* Even the so-called Carolingian renaissance had failed to take it up fully in its reconsideration of ancient Latin books.[6] After the twelfth century another period of relative neglect would set in. Thirteenth-century thinkers, preoccupied with a massive influx of Aristotelian texts and a few newly translated Platonic and Neo-Platonic books, had little time for the familiar *Timaeus.* Nor, in the wake of the wider interest of Ficino and the Platonists of the Italian Renaissance in the entire corpus of Platonic dialogues, did the early modern world puzzle long over the one dialogue that had been known for centuries. Some thinkers in the Middle Ages could ignore the *Timaeus* because of the perceived sufficiency of previous synthetic work, but philosophical vocabularies change over time and the need for new interpretations arises.

Beginning in the eleventh century a new phase of interest in Plato's *Timaeus* began to build in western Europe. One encounters it first in the

---

[5] *Glose Willelmi de Conchis super Platonem,* 1.prol., ed. Edouard Jeauneau, in Guillaume de Conches, *Glosae super Platonem,* Textes philosophiques du Moyen Age 13 (Paris, 1965), p. 57. In this passage "nulli" is to be preferred over "nonnulli," which is printed in the edition: see Edouard Jeauneau, "Plato apud Bohemos," *Mediaeval Studies* 41 (1979) 191 n.102.

[6] There is some doubt, for instance, about the extent to which even Eriugena knew the *Timaeus:* see Maïeul Cappuyns, *Jean Scot Erigène, sa vie, son oeuvre, sa pensée* (Louvain and Paris, 1933; rpt. Brussels, 1964), pp. 389, 392.

increased production of manuscripts of the dialogue and in the sparse
interlinear glosses that frequently accompany them.[7] By late in the century,
Manegold of Lautenbach could already chastise those who would Christia-
nise the *Timaeus*.[8] In Manegold, Lanfranc of Bec, Odo of Tournai, and
Adalbold of Utrecht, one sees eleventh-century thinkers who had studied the
Timaeus, but who touch on it only in passing, in the midst of their other
Neo-Platonic concerns.[9] Thus, the eleventh-century interest in the *Timaeus*
was (in the sense outlined) an occasional one, yet one which was building
towards the synthetic and systematic study of the dialogue that would take
place in the twelfth century.[10]

Read in isolation from the other works of Plato, as it was of necessity in
the Middle Ages, the *Timaeus* must have seemed a most trying text, one that
demanded the intermediary agency of a skilled medieval explicator or
glossator. Late in the second quarter of the twelfth century William of
Conches, relying upon recent work on the *Timaeus*, was able to synthesise
the current interpretations of his day on the meaning of Plato's work in a
large and magisterial set of glosses.

Oddly enough, the *Timaeus* intrigued twelfth-century thinkers like William
precisely because of its paradoxical and puzzling character.[11] To them it was
a book that presented a seemingly rational and straightforward search for
causes in the universe[12] and yet the dialogue remained covered by a complex

---

[7] For an extensive list of the medieval manuscripts of the *Timaeus*, see Waszink, "Praefatio," in *Timaeus a Calcidio translatus commentarioque instructus*, ed. J.H. Waszink, Plato
Latinus, vol. 4, ed. Raymond Klibansky, 2nd ed. (London, 1975), pp. cvi-cxxxi, cxciii-cxciv.
On the basis of the dates of the manuscripts provided by Waszink, a schematisation of their
production by half centuries was produced by R.W. Southern, *Platonism, Scholastic Method,
and the School of Chartres: The Stenton Lecture 1978* (Reading, 1979), p. 14. On the oldest
manuscripts of Calcidius' translation, see Eckart Mensching, "Zur Calcidius-Überlieferung,"
Vigiliae Christianae 19 (1965) 42-56. On the eleventh-century interest in the *Timaeus*, see
Margaret Gibson, "The Study of the *Timaeus* in the Eleventh and Twelfth Centuries,"
Pensamiento 25 (1969) 183-194.

[8] *Liber contra Wolfelmum* 2-3, ed. Wilfried Hartmann, *Monumenta Germaniae Historica:
Quellen zur Geistesgeschichte des Mittelalters*, vol. 8 (Weimar, 1972), esp. pp. 47-51. See also
Tullio Gregory, *Platonismo medievale: studi e ricerche*, Studi storici, fasc. 26-27 (Rome,
1958), pp. 17-30, and Wilfried Hartmann, "Manegold von Lautenbach und die Anfänge der
Frühscholastik," *Deutsches Archiv für Erforschung des Mittelalters* 26 (1970) 58-60, 72-82.

[9] See Gregory, *Platonismo medievale*, pp. 1-51; Gibson, "The Study of the *Timaeus*," pp.
183-194; and the eleventh-century texts edited by R.B.C. Huygens, in "Mittelalterliche
Kommentare zum *O qui perpetua* ...," *Sacris Erudiri* 6 (1954) 373-427.

[10] See M.D. Chenu, *Nature, Man, and Society in the Twelfth Century. Essays on New
Theological Perspectives in the Latin West*, ed. and trans. Jerome Taylor and Lester K. Little
(Chicago, 1968), pp. 49-98, esp. 65-72.

[11] See R.W. Southern, *Platonism, Scholastic Method, and the School of Chartres*, pp. 5-40.

[12] On the *Timaeus* as an impetus towards new ideas on causality in the twelfth century, see
Tullio Gregory, "La nouvelle idée de la nature et de savoir scientifique au XIIᵉ siècle," in *The

literary and mythic envelope of meaning that made necessary new means of explication. One of their interpretative strategies, particular to the twelfth century, but a product of the plasticity of Plato's dialogue itself, was the recognition of the integumental character of the *Timaeus*: that somehow it could be understood on several different levels, and that what it seemed to say could be reconciled with what it ought to mean.[13] Another of what Whitehead would call the 'high generalities'[14] of the *Timaeus* that appealed to the twelfth century was its sense of the wholeness of the world, of the veritable *uniuersitas* of ordered creation.[15] Furthermore, the *Timaeus* accommodated a wide variety of twelfth-century interests. Natural philosophers with their increasing awareness of material nature and physical particulars were fascinated by the concrete account of how the *opifex* or worker-god had assembled the *machina mundi*. Metaphysicians turned to the dialogue for its complex treatment of the archetypal Ideas. Even historians and moralists found in its opening pages a sketch of Plato's conception of a radically different social order, one that caused them to question their high opinion of Plato rather than the design of their own society. Thus, despite (or perhaps because of) its difficulties and multifaceted nature, the *Timaeus* became the most important philosophical text of the early twelfth century.

The set of glosses submitted here to the scrutiny of scholars for the first time is in many ways a modest one, but it played an essential role in the twelfth-century rediscovery of the *Timaeus*. In length the *Glosae super Platonem* is relatively short, containing, with lemmata, just under 25,000 words.[16] William of Conches's glosses, by way of comparison, run to over 50,000 words. In terms of the sources drawn upon, the *Glosae* contains few surprises, its chief sources being those known to men of the early Middle Ages: Boethius, Calcidius, and Macrobius. In terms of doctrine, the *Glosae* is less original than one might have hoped, except on one point where it makes a remarkable contribution to the perplexing Platonic problem of the relation of the Ideas to sensible things. Indeed, aside from Tullio Gregory and the editor, the *Glosae* has received scant attention from scholars, being

---

Cultural Context of Medieval Learning, Boston Studies in the Philosophy of Science 26, ed. J.E. Murdoch and D.E. Sylla (Dordrecht, 1975), pp. 196-200.

[13] See Winthrop Wetherbee, "Philosophy, Cosmology, and the Twelfth-Century Renaissance," in *A History of Twelfth-Century Western Philosophy*, ed. Peter Dronke (Cambridge, 1988), p. 34: "To read the *Timaeus* as philosophy or science requires that one should come to terms with its surface of literary myth."

[14] Alfred North Whitehead, *Adventures of Ideas* (1933; rpt. New York, 1967), p. 12.

[15] On the special sense of the wholeness of the world brought about by the study of the *Timaeus* in the twelfth century, see Chenu, *Nature, Man, and Society*, pp. 67-68.

[16] For the exact size of the treatise and its constituent parts, see pp. 50-51 below.

hidden, one must suppose, amidst a host of anonymous medieval *Timaeus* glosses.[17]

Yet, for all that, the *Glosae* needs to be seen as an important and influential text, not so much for what it contributes to any critical understanding of Plato, as for the crucial position it occupies in a cycle of interpretation. Written before William's glosses, the *Glosae* is systematic, but is not, in William's terms, exhaustive. Nonetheless these glosses can be shown to have influenced William's and, indeed, to have shaped a set of Platonic concerns for the early twelfth century. Moreover, it is the *Glosae* rather than William's glosses that was later reworked in a score of dependent sets of *Timaeus* glosses, a quantifiable indication, as it were, of its considerable influence in the Middle Ages.

The popularity of the *Glosae* can be accounted for in a number of ways: it is a systematic, straightforward, and in some ways simple set of explications of the difficulties of the *Timaeus*. These characteristics define it as a teacher's text or, even, textbook. Indications of oral teaching practices are to be found throughout the work, thus placing it near the very beginning of a *Quaestio* tradition that was to develop in the twelfth century. In its own way, the *Glosae* is a synthetic work, but one that relied upon sources and opinions available around the year 1100.

The chief contribution of the *Glosae* to the medieval study of the *Timaeus* was in some sense a negative one: the partial displacement of Calcidius' commentary. Both Cicero and Calcidius had translated a portion of the *Timaeus*, but what seems to have ensured the popularity of Calcidius' truncated (rather than abridged) translation was that he had added a commentary on the difficult text.[18] One suspects that this commentary had

---

[17] A few extracts from the *Glosae* have been previously edited: see Gregory, *Platonismo medievale*, pp. 66-71, 76 n.1, 88-91, 103, 120-121, who employed two MSS (M and V: for the sigla, see below p. 138); Peter Dronke, *Fabula: Explorations into the Uses of Myth in Medieval Platonism* (Leiden, 1974), p. 89 n.1, who edits one gloss from M; and Dutton, "*Illustre ciuitatis et populi exemplum*: Plato's *Timaeus* and the Transmission from Calcidius to the End of the Twelfth Century of a Tripartite Scheme of Society," *Mediaeval Studies* 45 (1983), pp. 95-96 and nn.62-64, and Dutton, "The Uncovering of the *Glosae super Platonem* of Bernard of Chartres," *Mediaeval Studies* 46 (1984), pp. 202-217, where D, M, O, P, and V were used.

[18] Cicero's translation extends from *Timaeus* 27d to 47b: see the edition of Remo Giomini in *M. Tullii Ciceronis scripta quae manserunt omnia*, vol. 46: *De divinatione, De fato, Timaeus* (Leipzig, 1975). On this translation, see Roland Poncelet, *Cicéron, traducteur de Platon: l'expression de la pensée complexe en latin classique* (Paris, 1957), and Remo Giomini, *Ricerche sul testo del Timeo ciceroniano*, Studi e saggi, vol. 9 (Rome, 1967).

Calcidius' translation and commentary were previously edited by J. Wrobel, *Platonis Timaeus interprete Chalcidio cum eiusdem commentario ...* (Leipzig, 1876). The standard

become a bit of a puzzle by the millennium; not only is it six times the length of Plato's dialogue, but it is filled with an eclectic set of Middle and Neo-Platonic doctrines that are not systematically arranged. If medieval students of the *Timaeus* were to make any significant study of the dialogue, they required a commentary that they could consult either before or, preferably, instead of Calcidius'. What was needed was a systematic treatment of the *Timaeus* that incorporated the useful material from Calcidius' commentary together with the insights culled from other Platonising texts such as those of Macrobius, Boethius, and Martianus Capella. This the *Glosae* furnished, allowing medieval students for the first time to dispense with Calcidius as the necessary intermediary between them and Plato's text. Indeed no substantial medieval tradition of glossing Calcidius' commentary ever arose, I would argue, because it was displaced by the *Glosae*. Unlike Calcidius' complex commentary, these early twelfth-century glosses could be separated out and then re-attached as marginal and interlinear glosses to the appropriate places in a manuscript of the *Timaeus*.

---

edition is now Plato, *Timaeus a Calcidio translatus commentarioque instructus*, ed. J.H. Waszink, Plato Latinus, vol. 4, ed. Raymond Klibansky, 2nd ed. (London, 1975), pp. 1-52.

For comparisons of the translations of Cicero and Calcidius, see Giomini, *Ricerche sul testo del Timeo ciceroniani*, pp. 47-125 and Roland Poncelet, "Deux aspects du style philosophique latin: Cicéron et Chalcidius, traducteurs du *Phèdre* 245c," *Revue des études latines* 28 (1950) 145-167.

Calcidius' commentary (hereafter Cal., *Comm.*) is edited by Waszink, in *Timaeus a Calcidio translatus commentarioque instructus* 2nd ed., Plato Latinus, vol. 4, ed. Raymond Klibansky (London, 1975), pp. 53-346. On the identity of Calcidius, see John M. Dillon, *The Middle Platonists: A Study of Platonism, 80 B.C. to A.D. 220* (London, 1977), pp. 401-408; John M. Rist, "Basil's 'Neoplatonism': Its Background and Nature," in *Basil of Caesarea: Christian, Humanist, Ascetic. A Sixteen-Hundredth Anniversary Symposium*, ed. Paul Jonathan Fedwick, 2 vols. (Toronto, 1981), 1: 151-155; and Waszink, "Praefatio," pp. ix-xvii.

On Calcidius' commentary and philosophy, see Waszink, "Praefatio," pp. xvii-cvi; J.H. Waszink, *Studien zum Timaioskommentar des Calcidius*, vol.1: *Die erste Hälfte des Kommentars (mit Ausnahme der Kapitel über die Weltseele)*, Philosophia antiqua: A Series of Monographs on Ancient Philosophy 12 (Leiden, 1964); B.W. Switalski, *Des Chalcidius Kommentar zu Plato's Timaeus: eine historisch-kritische Untersuchung*, Beiträge zur Geschichte der Philosophie des Mittelalters, 3.6 (Münster, 1902); J.C.M. van Winden, *Calcidius on Matter: His Doctrine and Sources. A Chapter in the History of Platonism*, Philosophia antiqua: A Series of Monographs on Ancient Philosophy 9 (Leiden, 1959; rpt. 1965); Jan Franciszek Sulowski, "Studies on Chalcidius: Anthropology, Influence, and Importance (General Outline)," in *L'homme et son destin d'après les penseurs du Moyen Age. Actes du premier Congrès international de philosophie médiévale, Louvain-Bruxelles 28 Août-4 Septembre, 1958* (Louvain, 1960), pp. 153-161; J. den Boeft, *Calcidius on Fate: His Doctrine and Sources*, Philosophia antiqua: A Series of Monographs on Ancient Philosophy 18 (Leiden, 1970) and *Calcidius on Demons (Commentarius, Ch. 127-136)*, Philosophia antiqua: A Series of Monographs on Ancient Philosophy 33 (Leiden, 1977); and Stephen Gersh, *Middle Platonism and Neoplatonism: The Latin Tradition*, 2 vols., Publications in Medieval Studies, The Medieval Institute, University of Notre Dame 23.1-2 (Notre Dame, 1986), 2: 421-492.

Early in the twelfth century, then, the author of the *Glosae* took stock, making of a seemingly mysterious work of Plato one that was at last approachable by a wider audience of students. To him must go much of the credit for the popularity of the *Timaeus* in the twelfth century. His Platonic concerns were to shape what we generally think of as Chartrian Platonism. There is also a sense in which the author of the *Glosae* confined himself to questions more purely Platonic in nature than those put by the Neo-Platonists of the Middle Ages. However humble the *Glosae* might seem to those who have studied the fuller syntheses of Proclus, Calcidius, and William of Conches, this set of glosses was to be the cornerstone of a renewed medieval interest in the *Timaeus*. It came to occupy a critical place in the culminating phase of a medieval cycle of interpretation.

Authorship and Date of the Glosae super Platonem

The riskiest of all scholarly games to play is attribution of authorship. Without the coincidence of an explicit title page naming the author, *testimonia* that acknowledge authorship, and the recognisable doctrines of a known author, the status of an attribution will always be a matter of some doubt. Even a late medieval library catalogue and a fifteenth-century manuscript that both name Bernard Silvester as the author of a celebrated commentary on the first six books of Virgil's *Aeneid* [19] have not saved a long assumed attribution from being undermined.[20] Often it is much easier to

---

[19] Volume 35 of the extensive poetry holdings of the Collegium Amplonianum of Erfurt contained among other things (according to a book-list of 1410-1412): "... commentum Bernhardi Siluestris super 6 libris Eneidos ... ," ed. P. Lehmann, in [Catalogi], *Mittelalterliche Bibliothekskataloge*, vol. 2: *Bistum Mainz, Erfurt* (Munich, 1928), p. 15.35. The incipit of the copy of the commentary found in Paris, Bibliothèque Nationale, Lat. MS 16246 of the fifteenth century is: "Incipit commentum Bernardi Siluestris super sex Libros Eneidos Virgilii:" see [Bernard Silvester], *The Commentary on the First Six Books of the 'Aeneid' of Vergil Commonly Attributed to Bernardus Silvestris: A New Critical Edition*, ed. Julian Ward Jones and Elizabeth Frances Jones, (Lincoln, Neb., 1977). See, in general, Giorgio Padoan, "Tradizione e fortuna del commento all'*Eneide* di Bernardo Silvestre," *Italia medioevale e umanistica* 3 (1960) 227-240.

[20] In 1972, Brian Stock, in an important footnote, called the attribution into question: see *Myth and Science in the Twelfth Century: A Study of Bernard Silvester* (Princeton, 1972), pp. 36-37 n.42. The most recent editors of the text followed his line: see [Bernard Silvester], *The Commentary on the First Six Books of the 'Aeneid'*, ed. Jones and Jones, pp. x-xi. See also [Bernard Silvester], *The Commentary on Martianus Capella's 'De nuptiis Philologiae et Mercurii' Attributed to Bernardus Silvestris*, ed. Haijo Jan Westra, Studies and Texts 80 (Toronto, 1986), pp. 7-10.

Still in favour of accepting the attribution or, at least, finding no sound reason for overturning the attribution are Peter Dronke, in [Bernard Silvester], *Cosmographia*, ed. Peter

disprove an attribution than it is to make one stick,[21] but if the case is sound
the risks seem worth taking. One marvels still, for example, at the perspi-
cacity of Ravaisson in discerning that Eriugena was the author of an
anepigraphic commentary on the Gospel of John.[22]

It was with eyes open to the difficulties involved in attribution,[23] especially
of an anonymous set of glosses on Plato to a famous medieval figure, that I
first proposed in 1984 to assign to Bernard of Chartres the set of *Glosae
super Platonem* with the incipit "Socrates de re publica decem libris disputauit" (1.1) and the explicit "quod superius promiserat" (8.448).[24] The case
I made there was based on a complex concurrence of appropriate *testimonia*,
codicological and palaeographical information, and philosophical tenets. I
shall refrain here from rehearsing the entire argument, not only because it is
already in published form, but also because the introduction to the critical
edition is a continuous argument for the aptness of the attribution. Nevertheless, some important points need to be reviewed here.

Of the six known manuscripts of the *Glosae*, none possesses a title naming
either the work or its author.[25] One would, in fact, have been happily

---

Dronke, Textus minores 53 (Leiden, 1978), pp. 3-5, and Edouard Jeauneau in a review of
the same in *Medium Aevum* 49 (1980) 112-113. See also Winthrop Wetherbee, *Platonism and
Poetry in the Twelfth Century: The Literary Influence of the School of Chartres* (Princeton,
1972), p. 105; Simone Viarre, "L'interprétation de l'*Enéide*. A propos d'un commentaire du
douzième siècle," in *Presence de Virgile. Actes du Colloque des 9, 11, et 12 Décembre 1976
(Paris E.N.S., Tours)*, ed. R. Chevallier (Paris, 1978), pp. 223-232; and Jean Jolivet, "Les
rochers de cumes et l'antre de Cerbère. L'ordre du savoir selon le *Commentaire* de Bernard
Silvestre sur l'*Enéide*," in *Pascua Mediaevalia. Studies voor Prof. Dr. J.M. De Smet*, ed. R.
Lievens, E. Van Mingroot, and W. Verbeke (Louvain, 1983), pp. 263-276.
Oddly and, indeed, illogically some of the doubters have jettisoned the "Silvester," but
retained the "Bernard" from the same ascription. Among those who have looked for other
Bernards as author of the commentary on the *Aeneid*, see Christopher Baswell, "The Medieval
Allegorization of the *Aeneid*: MS. Cambridge, Peterhouse 158," *Traditio* 41 (1985) 214-215;
Jones and Jones, in [Bernard Silvester], *The Commentary on the First Six Books of the
'Aeneid'*, p. xi; and E.R. Smits, "New Evidence for the Authorship of the Commentary on the
First Six Books of Virgil's *Eneid* Commonly Attributed to Bernardus Silvestris?" in *Non noua,
sed noue: Mélanges de civilisation médiévale dédiés à Willem Noomen*, ed. M. Gosman and
J. van Os (Groningen, 1984), pp. 239-246.
[21] See, for instance, Paul Edward Dutton and Edouard Jeauneau, "The Verses of the *Codex
Aureus* of Saint-Emmeram," *Studi Medievali*, ser. 3a, 24.1 (1983) 75-120, where the
attribution of a group of poems to Alcuin was rejected.
[22] See [Eriugena], Jean Scot, *Commentaire sur l'Evangile de Jean*, ed. Edouard Jeauneau,
Sources Chrétiennes 180 (Paris, 1972), pp. 11-14.
[23] See, for instance, the cautionary words of R.W. Southern on the attempts to identify the
original *sententiae* of Anselm of Laon, in *Platonism, Scholastic Method and the School of
Chartres*, p. 30.
[24] Dutton, "The Uncovering."
[25] On the MSS, see below pp. 108-131.

surprised had such a title existed, since most twelfth-century commentaries, even by well known authors, were published anonymously.[26] Glosses, in particular, were thought to be instruments or aids to understanding a specific treatise: "Nullus enim sibi sed aliis glosare debet," said William of Conches in his *Glosae super Priscianum*.[27] Glossators were teachers and their glosses were a written extension of their teaching. In the early twelfth century glossators seem to have believed that the anonymity of their art was a reflection of self-sacrifice and humility. Pride of place belonged to the ancient authors of the texts being glossed and the words of these giants were writ large on the parchment; the explications of the glossators hang tenuously on the page, cramped between lines and searching for space in the margins where they might be noticed and put to good use. Only rarely, almost incidentally, was a glossator's work granted the dignity of authorial status.

Although an impressive number of medieval glosses on the *Timaeus* bear witness to the influence of the *Glosae*, only one supplies an indication of the identity of its author. Oxford, Bodleian Library Auct. F.3.15 is a manuscript written entirely by Irish scribes of the twelfth century.[28] The text of the *Timaeus* (fols. 1r-19v) was written about 1100 in a large and elegant Irish script (see the frontispiece), possibly by a certain "Salmon" who recorded his name at the end of the text (fol.19vb). In the mid twelfth century, the manuscript of the *Timaeus* was combined with manuscripts of two recently copied works: a treatise *De temporibus* (fols. 21r-30v) and a number of extracts from Eriugena's *Periphyseon* (fols. 31r-68v, but composed of two separate sections: fols. 31r-53v and 54r-68v) which have been extensively studied by Sheldon-Williams.[29]

---

[26] See Nikolaus Häring, "Commentary and Hermeneutics," in *Renaissance and Renewal in the Twelfth Century*, ed. Robert L. Benson and Giles Constable with Carol D. Lanham (Cambridge, Mass., 1982), p. 175: "for authors of the twelfth century it is wise to assume that their commentaries were published anonymously and without what we might call an authentic title or inscription." See especially Häring's arguments on this point, pp. 175-180.

[27] Edited by Edouard Jeauneau, in Edouard Jeauneau, *'Lectio philosophorum': Recherches sur l'Ecole de Chartres* (Amsterdam, 1973), p. 347.

[28] On this MS, see F. Madan et al., *A Summary Catalogue of Western Manuscripts in the Bodleian Library at Oxford*, vol. 2.2 (Oxford, 1937), pp. 666-667 (no. 3511). The MS came to the Bodleian, as an inscription on fol. 1r suggests, by way of Thomas Allen, the mathematician: see Andrew G. Watson, "Thomas Allen of Oxford and His Manuscripts," in *Medieval Scribes, Manuscripts, and Libraries: Essays Presented to N.R. Ker*, ed. M.B. Parkes and Andrew G. Watson (London, 1978), pp. 295 and 310. See also E.A. Lowe, *Codices latini antiquiores*, vol. 2, 2nd ed. (Oxford, 1935), p. 32 (no. 232); Klibansky, *The Continuity*, p. 30; Waszink, "Praefatio," p. cxix; and Dutton, "The Uncovering," pp. 206-207.

[29] I.P. Sheldon-Williams, "An Epitome of Irish Provenance of Eriugena's *De diuisione naturae* (MS. Bodl. Auct. F.3.15)," *Proceedings of the Royal Irish Academy* 58, Section C (1956) 1-16.

The handwriting of one scribe is to be found in all four sections of the manuscript: he corrected the main text of the *Timaeus*, added the glosses to the text, and left comments throughout the other sections of the manuscript. Another scribe noted in Old Irish that his teacher Tuilecnad had been away on a tour of teaching, but had returned on the Feast of Saint Benedict. From this it has been speculated that Tuilecnad (a name that means "Wave of Knowledge") was the director and main scribe of the volume's corrections and glosses.[30] Hereafter, for the sake of convenience, I shall refer to the Irish scribe of the glosses in question as Tuilecnad, despite the fact that the identification is merely a supposition.

In adding glosses to the *Timaeus*, Tuilecnad drew directly from the *Glosae*. He excerpted freely, altered a few glosses, and only departed from it when he added some simple glosses on the opening section of the *Timaeus* (see Appendix 3.4). After repeating, albeit in slightly corrupted form, a long passage from *Glosae* 5.35-44 (significat ... rebus) on *Timaeus* 34c (W26:6), Tuilecnad added the comment: "Lege Bernardum et Calcidium et multas formas inuenies" (see the frontispiece, bottom left).[31] If we read Bernard and Calcidius, the sentence seems to say, we shall find a number of opinions on the world-soul. Alternatively one might take the sentence to mean that we should read more of Bernard in order to find the opinions of Calcidius and others on the world-soul. In fact, if one examines the entire passage in *Glosae* 5.33-85, one does discover a discussion of just such a series of positions on the world-soul, among them that of Calcidius at 5.58-64. Furthermore, the gloss in question does not correspond closely to any specific passage in Calcidius' commentary, so that Tuilecnad can not have meant that one should turn separately to both Bernard and Calcidius for the "multas formas." We should also note that Bernard's name is not mentioned in the body of the Oxford gloss itself. Thus his opinions seem to be quoted rather than discussed by Tuilecnad. In effect, Tuilecnad has provided us with a footnote to his source, the preceding material being a direct extract from the *Glosae*.

---

[30] The Old Irish glosses of the MS were first edited by Whitley Stokes, "Irish Glosses and Notes on Chalcidius," *Zeitschrift für Vergleichende Sprachforschung* 29, Neue Folge 9 (1887) 372-380; they were reedited and translated by F. Shaw, "The Irish Glosses and Marginalia in Bodl. MS. Auct. F.3.15," *Proceedings of of the Royal Irish Academy* 58, Section C (1956) 17-20. The Tuilecnad references and other indications of provenance are found there in items 23, 27-28, pp. 19-20. In the catalogue *A Thousand Years of Irish Script: An Exhibition of Irish Manuscripts in Oxford Libraries Arranged by Francis John Byrne* (Oxford, 1979), pp. 14-15 (no.5), Tuilecnad is identified as the chief scribe and director of the volume. On the Irish character of the MS, see also James F. Kenney, *The Sources for the Early History of Ireland: An Introduction and Guide* (New York, 1929; rpt. 1966), p. 679 (no. 539).

[31] For a transcription and comparison of the two copies of the gloss, see Dutton, "The Uncovering," pp. 207-208.

If the first *testimonium* is open to some degree of interpretation, the second is less so. At *Timaeus* 35b (W27:19) Tuilecnad follows another substantial and exact borrowing from the *Glosae* (5.125-136: *Portio ... distinguntur*) with the comment: "Hic lege Bernardum et adhuc inuenies" (frontispiece, bottom right).[32] Though the sense of "adhuc" here is not absolutely clear, the sentence informs the reader that if he consults Bernard about the *Timaeus* at this point, he will find more of the same passage. In other words, Bernard is the author of the quoted gloss.

No equivocation on the attribution of the passage is implied by Tuilecnad. He is not, for instance, inviting the reader to consult a third set of glosses that lie outside his own copy and those of the *Glosae* on which he is directly drawing. While twentieth-century scholars might engage in careful *Quellen-forschung* and comparative analysis, it is unlikely that Tuilecnad wished to make the sophisticated comparison of sources that this implies. Nor does this seem to have been his point, since he specifies no doctrine at issue and discusses none. Rarely in glossing the *Timaeus* did scribes stop to comment on other medieval authorities on the dialogue. In addition, the "adhuc inuenies" directive of the second testimonial tag—with its invitation to find more of the gloss in Bernard's work—directly ties the quoted gloss to Bernard. Even the use of "inuenies" at the end of the first gloss carries, in this light, the same force, inviting the reader to find more of the quoted gloss (including some mention of Calcidius) in Bernard's work. Note too that in the Oxford manuscript the glosses in question are but a portion of longer glosses found in the *Glosae*, so that there actually is more to read in the *Glosae* than Tuilecnad supplies. The "adhuc inuenies" comment, therefore, is consistent with the known nature of the *Glosae*. To argue that Tuilecnad thought of Bernard's work as a third set of glosses, one would have to ignore the fact that he excerpts directly and only from the *Glosae* (see App. 3.4). He does not seem to rely in his work upon any other set of glosses. Indeed he may even have known of the relevance of Calcidius' position on the world-soul from the *Glosae* and not independently. Yet, if we were to accept that the references to Bernard's work indicates a third set of glosses, we should expect Tuilecnad to be a scribe-glossator with a wide knowledge of the field and there is no evidence that he knew any other glosses on the *Timaeus*. Moreover, the two testimonial tags are not themselves part of the *Glosae*, as if they had been incorporated there and were thence carried over by the scribe. Nor are they repeated in any of the other glosses dependent

---

[32] Again for a transcription and comparison of the two copies of this gloss, see Dutton, "The Uncovering," pp. 208-209.

on the *Glosae* at these points. In short, Tuilecnad is not urging us to consult another set of *Timaeus* glosses, but rather twice identifies the author of the single set that he knows and wishes us to examine.

To repeat this important conclusion: the Oxford *testimonia* are statements tacked on at the end of passages lifted directly from the *Glosae* and they refer pointedly to them, identifying the author of these glosses as Bernard.

While Tuilecnad in the mid twelfth century might not have been in a position to carry out a comparative analysis of recent *Timaeus* commentaries, he does name the one source upon which he was dependent. It is very likely that Tuilecnad was himself the excerpter of the glosses he copied and was not just dependent on an exemplar in which they had already been copied out in the same form. Salmon's main text of the *Timaeus* had been left unglossed, so that it fell to Tuilecnad both to add the glosses and to supply variant readings to the text of the *Timaeus* itself. Perhaps Tuilecnad was in possession of a manuscript that had independent copies of the *Timaeus* and the *Glosae*, as do two of the manuscripts containing the *Glosae* today (P and V). The use of "inuenies" in both of Tuilecnad's ascriptions suggests that he had a complete copy of Bernard's *Glosae* before him as he worked. If so, he knew that it contained longer glosses at these points in the *Timaeus* than he cared to copy or could copy, given the limits of space in the margins of an already inscribed main text. In fact, in both of these cases the glosses run to the ends of columns (fol. 9ra and 9rb respectively), where they conclude with the *testimonia* (see the frontispiece), almost as if the *testimonia* are to make up for stopping short of completing very long passages. Tuilecnad appears to have been reluctant to carry glosses over to another column or folio. The very reason, therefore, for his unusual but fortuitous citation of source may be that he ran out of parchment on which to copy out the two glosses in their entirety. This might also explain why he cites Bernard only twice, though he had excerpted from him throughout: elsewhere he had supplied either all or the important parts of individual glosses, but in these two cases he could not. In lieu of the complete glosses he informed his readers where they might find the rest: not only the double "inuenies," but also the words "Calcidium et multas formas" and "adhuc" suggest this promise of the rest of the truncated glosses, with a hint of the nature of the content in the first statement. Thus both *testimonia* might be loosely understood to mean: "Turn to Bernard for the rest."

The specific nature of the guides left by Tuilecnad for readers of the *Timaeus* suggests that they were 'in-house' references, that either his monastery, cathedral, or school contained in its library a copy of the *Glosae* with an ascription of authorship to Bernard. How exactly this copy had come to denote the authorship of Bernard is likely to remain a mystery. But students, he seems to imply, could turn directly to an available volume, the one he himself was drawing upon, for the remainder of Bernard's glosses. This copy of the *Glosae* was likely written in the second quarter of the twelfth century and probably on the continent in a late Caroline script. The latter may be inferred from the difficulty Tuilecnad had in transcribing some of the abbreviated words in his exemplar: he transformed "attenditur" (5.40), for instance, into the absurd "ait non dicitur." This is not a simple scribal mistake, but one that suggests that the scribe was unfamiliar with the norms of another style of writing. We know that in reversed cases continental scribes often had great trouble in copying Insular manuscripts.

Tuilecnad's efforts, if he was indeed the scribe and compiler of Bodleian MS Auct. F.3.15, were more scribal than scholarly, but his *testimonia* are unique, for they attach a name to our set of *Glosae*. Yet he supplies, perhaps as it existed in his exemplar, only a first name without any clarification of who this Bernard might be.

Three sets of evidence can be brought to bear on the question of the date of the *Glosae*. In the first place, Durham, Cathedral Library MS C.IV.7, fols. 42ra-49va, the oldest copy of the *Glosae*, was written late in the first quarter of the twelfth century.[33] It is a manuscript filled with works composed early in the twelfth century in northern France. In the second, the extensive diffusion of the *Glosae* and its influence seem to begin in the first quarter of the twelfth century.[34] To give but one example: William of Conches in the composition of his glosses on the *Timaeus* in the second quarter of the twelfth century already knows and borrows from the *Glosae* (see App. 3.3).[35] In the third place, whereas William, early in the second quarter of the twelfth century, is one of the first authors to cite such texts as the *Isagoge ad Techne Galieni* of Johannitius and the *Pantegni* translated by Constantine the African, Bernard gives no indication whatsoever of employing these works newly introduced to the west.[36] His sources were those known to scholars at the turn of the century.

---

[33] On D, see Dutton, "The Uncovering," pp. 197-198 and below, pp. 109-112.

[34] See pp. 105-108 below.

[35] On the date of William's set of glosses on Plato, see *Glose Willelmi de Conchis super Platonem*, ed. Jeauneau, pp. 14-15, where it is dated to the second quarter of the twelfth century. Southern, *Platonism, Scholastic Method, and the School of Chartres*, pp. 16-17 and n.17 accepts the sequence posited by Jeauneau, but tends to push the composition of William's works back towards the first quarter of the century. For a demonstration of the dependence, see Dutton, "The Uncovering," pp. 202-206.

[36] See *Glose Willelmi de Conchis super Platonem*, ed Jeauneau, p. 29 and n.3; Southern, *Platonism, Scholastic Method, and the School of Chartres*, pp. 17-18; Peter Dronke, "New Approaches to the School of Chartres," *Anuario de estudios medievales* 6 (1969) 124-127. On the role of William and Chartres in the reception of these texts, see Heinrich Schipperges,

Against the possibility that the *Glosae* might have been composed well before the first quarter of the twelfth century, since this is only a terminal date after which the text could not have been written, one should note that although no set of eleventh-century *Timaeus* glosses reflects the *Glosae*, we can demonstrate a definite use of the *Glosae* in the twelfth century (see App. 3). Internal evidence, in addition, suggests that in terms of doctrine, its striking use of Calcidius' commentary, and its rather precocious development of the *quaestio* method, the *Glosae* belongs to the early twelfth century. Given these indications, it seems likely that the *Glosae* had a fixed publication date sometime in the first quarter of the twelfth century, probably between 1100 and 1115.

The Oxford *testimonia* and the approximate date of composition are pieces of information that help us to narrow the search for the author of the *Glosae*, for they tell us that this set of *Timaeus* glosses issued from a certain Bernard, probably on the continent, early in the twelfth century. The Durham manuscript contains, immediately prior to the *Glosae* and written by the same early twelfth-century scribe, copies of two works on rhetoric by master William of Champeaux, Abelard's famous rival, who was active in and around Paris between 1100 and 1120. The two treatises were probably composed circa 1100.[37] The world of Bernard too seems to have been that of northern France in the first quarter of the twelfth century, where the *Timaeus* and other texts such as those of Priscian, Boethius, and Macrobius were being systematically studied in the cathedral schools. Indeed two of the twelfth-century manuscripts of the *Glosae* (M and V) also contain in subsequent positions works of William of Conches, though this constitutes no proof of a tie with Chartres.[38] William's obvious familiarity with the

---

"Die Schulen von Chartres unter dem Einfluss des Arabismus," *Sudhoffs Archiv für Geschichte der Medizin und der Naturwissenschaften* 40 (1956) 193-210 and *Die Assimilation der arabischen Medizin durch das lateinische Mittelalter*, Sudhoffs Archiv für Geschichte der Medizin und der Naturwissenschaften, Beihefte, Heft 3 (Wiesbaden, 1964), pp. 111-123; Charles Burnett, "The Content and Affiliation of the Scientific Manuscripts Written at, or Brought to, Chartres in the Time of John of Salisbury," in *The World of John of Salisbury*, ed. Michael Wilks, Studies in Church History, Subsidia 3 (Oxford, 1984), pp. 129, 139; and Dorothy Elford, "Developments in the Natural Philosophy of William of Conches: A Study of the *Dragmaticon* and its Relationship to the *Philosophia*" (Ph.D. diss., Cambridge, 1983).

On the texts themselves, see Danielle Jacquart, "Aristotelian Thought in Salerno," in *A History of Twelfth-Century Western Philosophy*, ed. Peter Dronke (Cambridge, 1988), pp. 411-416; Jean Jolivet, "The Arabic Inheritance," in *A History of Twelfth-Century Western Philosophy*, ed. Peter Dronke (Cambridge, 1988), pp. 113-118; [Johannitius], in "Johannicius, *Isagoge ad Techne Galieni*," ed. Gregor Maurach, *Sudhoffs Archiv* 62.2 (1978) 148-174; and Danielle Jacquart, "A l'aube de la renaissance médicale des XIe-XIIe siècles: L'*Isagoge Johannitii* et son traducteur," *Bibliothèque de l'Ecole des chartes* 144 (1986) 209-240.

[37] See below, p. 111.

[38] On M and V, see below pp. 112-114, 124-126.

Glosae does supply a link with Chartres, since he had been a student of Bernard of Chartres (see App. 2.4.A-B and 2.5.F).[39] Even their respective copies of the *Timaeus* in Calcidius' translation share anomalies that bind them together.[40] In addition, the *quaestio* techniques and certain indications of an oral style in the *Glosae* strongly suggest the pedagogy of a cathedral school presided over by a master.

Though the twelfth century is crowded with Bernards,[41] there is only one of any note in the first quarter of the twelfth century who matches the evidence we possess, and that is Bernard of Chartres. From John of Salisbury we have independent witness not that Bernard of Chartres ever published glosses on the *Timaeus*, which would have been a surprising piece of information given the anonymous nature of early twelfth-century glosses, but that he had a keen interest in the text and quite likely lectured on it (App. 2.5.A-C). Indeed Bernard's poem "non dico" contains a specific reference to *Timaeus* 49e (App. 2.2.B1).[42] The strongest proof for the attribution of the *Glosae* to Bernard of Chartres must, in the end, come from the correspondence of its doctrines with those historically associated with his name by John of Salisbury, especially his belief in the Platonic Ideas and the so-called *formae natiuae*.

Though any single piece of evidence so far presented might leave ample room for doubt about such an attribution, the accumulation of pieces argues for the authorship of Bernard of Chartres. In addition, the striking and essential concern of the *Glosae* with the idea of the *formae natiuae* supplies a strong argument for the attribution of the *Glosae* to Bernard of Chartres. John of Salisbury, as we shall soon see, associated this special Platonic concept with Bernard of Chartres. Neither Gilbert of Poitiers, who is also associated with the idea, nor any other set of independent glosses on the *Timaeus* takes up the idea of the *formae natiuae* in a major way. In fact no other twelfth-century composition that I know of except the *Glosae* and John of Salisbury's *Metalogicon* contains a full and substantial treatment of this distinctive concept, a coincidence of concerns that can not easily be ignored.

Given, then, that the *Glosae super Platonem* was composed between 1100 and 1115, probably in northern France, by a Bernard who develops the

---

[39] For a comparison of some of the corresponding passages, see Dutton, "The Uncovering," pp. 203-206.

[40] See pp. 132-134 below.

[41] Nikolaus Häring, "Chartres and Paris Revisited," in *Essays in Honour of Anton Charles Pegis*, ed. J. Reginald O'Donnell (Toronto, 1974), pp. 295-299, reviews the various Bernards active in the twelfth century, but of these only Bernard of Chartres was active in the first quarter of the century.

[42] See below pp. 81-82.

distinctive and rare concept of the *formae natiuae*, the evidence points directly to Bernard of Chartres, "perfectissimus inter Platonicos seculi nostri" (App. 2.2.B1), as the author of the *Glosae*.

Before I can proceed to an examination of the career of Bernard of Chartres, some lingering doubts about the attribution need to be addressed. In *A History of Twelfth-Century Western Philosophy* Peter Dronke tentatively acknowledges the "presence" of Bernard of Chartres's thought in the *Glosae*,[43] particularly in the full gloss on the world-soul partially copied and attributed by the Irish scribe:

> since in the "Socrates de re publica" commentary the gloss for this lemma does in fact have a remarkable allegorical continuation, it would seem that this passage at least represents the work of "Bernardus," and there is no doubt that in the early twelfth century the Bernard most celebrated for his Platonism was Bernard of Chartres.[44]

Dronke, however, wonders whether the whole of the *Glosae* can be attributed to Bernard. But if, as we have seen, Tuilecnad excerpted passages from only one book of glosses on the *Timaeus*, and names the author of portions of it as Bernard, does it not reasonably follow that the whole of the *Glosae* is by Bernard? Why should we assume that Tuilecnad meant to divide off those two quotations as genuinely Bernardine from the rest of the *Glosae*? Moreover, the passages in which Dronke recognises the presence of Bernard of Chartres are similar in both content and style to those spread throughout the *Glosae*, and are not merely confined to the two Oxford excerpts and their continuations.

Dronke is also troubled by the fact that the dependent set of glosses in British Library Royal 12.B.xxii (see App. 3.6) is in a manuscript that has been roughly placed in the period circa 1100, a date very early for a set of glosses to depend on a work of Bernard of Chartres.[45] In fact, the London manuscript has never been scientifically dated on palaeographical grounds and possesses no internal evidence of date. Even to set the date of the manuscript as the beginning of the twelfth century, as do Waszink and Gibson, is only to supply a general indication of a likely time frame for the

---

[43] Dronke, "Introduction," in *A History of Twelfth-Century Western Philosophy*, ed. Peter Dronke (Cambridge, 1988), pp. 14-17.

[44] Dronke, "Introduction," p. 15, and ibid.: "Certain indications that Dutton has given do seem to point to the presence of Bernard of Chartres in this commentary. Its author takes up the distinction that John of Salisbury saw as characteristic of Bernard, between the ideas (*ideae*) as eternal exemplars in the divine mind, and the images of those ideas, the 'forms as born (*natiuae formae*)', which exist in the physical world."

[45] Dronke, "Introduction," pp. 15-16. The dependence of one set of glosses from this manuscript on the *Glosae* was first pointed out in Dutton, "*Illustre ciuitatis*," pp. 95-96 and n.64 and Dutton, "The Uncovering," pp. 199-200 and n.41.

copy.[46] But the manuscript might as easily have been copied around 1125, which I suspect is closer to the mark. Indeed, the copy of the *Timaeus* and its first set of glosses (both written by the same scribe) may seem slightly older than their letter forms and conventions would suggest because the manuscript is in poor condition and the handwriting is frequently illegible. Interestingly, portions of the two glosses excerpted from the *Glosae* by Tuilecnad and acknowledged as Bernardine by Dronke are to be found in the London glosses.

In general, Dronke wonders if the *Glosae* might not be a layered work, containing glosses from Bernard of Chartres alongside earlier eleventh-century speculations on the *Timaeus*.[47] While the *Glosae* may yet reveal some level of dependence upon eleventh-century thought on the *Timaeus*, no deep dependence has as yet been found. Though it is surprising, Bernard appears not to have relied significantly upon any extant eleventh-century glosses on the *Timaeus*, and I compared all of these to the *Glosae* in order to compile the third appendix to this edition. Macrobius, Boethius, and Calcidius were Bernard's major sources, not some putative eleventh-century tradition of commenting on the *Timaeus*. Bernard was setting a new twelfth-century agenda for dealing with the *Timaeus* rather than following an already established eleventh-century one.

Dronke brings to the issue an eleventh-century reference which underlines, rather than undermines the case for the newness of Bernard's approach to the *Timaeus*.[48] Following an observation of Garin, he notes that in the mid eleventh century Papias in his *Elementarium* had already defined the Idea in the following terms:

> idea, exemplar, sicut Plato asseruit condiscipulis: nam tria principia consti-
> tuerunt omnium, id est: deum, ideam, id est exemplar, et materiam, quam Greci
> uocant hilen. Ideas dixerunt ipsas exemplares species que fuerunt in mente
> diuina, cum has natiuas species faceret. Nam illas ideas in mente diuina aut in
> archetipo mundo semper esse dixerunt.[49]

---

[46] Waszink, "Praefatio," p. cxxiii, gives it the date "Saec. XII in." without explanation, and Gibson, "The Study of the *Timaeus*," p. 185, guesses "circa 1100." George Frederic Warner and Julius P. Gilson, *British Museum. Catalogue of Western Manuscripts in the Old Royal and King's Collections*, 2 vols. (London, 1921), 2: 18, date the manuscript simply to the twelfth century. The manuscript was once owned by the astrologer John Dee: see Montague Rhodes James, "List of Manuscripts formerly owned by Dr. John Dee with Preface and Identifications," *Supplements to the Transactions of the Bibliographical Society, 1921-1926* (London, 1926), p. 29.

[47] Dronke, "Introduction," pp. 16-17.

[48] Dronke, "Introduction," p. 16.

[49] The text is printed in Eugenio Garin, *Studi sul Platonismo medievale* (Florence, 1958), pp. 53-54 n.1.

Papias here reveals his direct dependence upon Calcidius, not only for the schematisation of the three principles, but also for the very phrase *natiua species*.[50] For both Calcidius and his imitator Papias, the *natiua species* is something akin to visible or temporal form, a kind of end product of material creation. The term anticipates, as we shall see, little of Bernard of Chartres's concept of the active and essentially mediating nature of the *formae natiuae*. In the works of both Boethius and Calcidius there is an undeveloped sense of the images of the Ideas,[51] but Papias suggests nothing of the kind here. Rather he means to emphasise the immutability of the Ideas which remain tucked away neatly in the divine mind. It would fall to Bernard of Chartres to take the notion of the exemplary images in a new direction, one which can hardly have been a distinctive "talking-point" before he made it so.

Another question about the attribution was put to me by D.E. Luscombe: could the *Glosae* be a first redaction of William of Conches's own glosses on Plato? This issue has been discussed before, under another guise, as scholars have tried to determine the status of the *Timaeus* glosses edited by Toni Schmid from Uppsala, Universitetsbiblioteket MS C. 620.[52] This set of glosses has seemed to some to be an early, primitive, and shorter redaction of William's glosses on Plato, but in fact it contains a mixture of passages extracted from the independent glosses of Bernard, William, and others by a late twelfth or thirteenth-century scribe (see App. 3.2). Thus, the Uppsala glosses make no statement about an earlier stage of William's glosses and, indeed, demonstrate the necessity of separating the glosses of Bernard and William. Though it is not impossible that William had some hand in either recording or circulating his master's *Glosae*, there is no evidence to suggest that he participated in the composition of Bernard's *Glosae*. If the *Glosae* was written in the period between 1100 and 1115, it is too early a date for William to have been the author, since his career was just beginning about 1115 and continued until 1149-1154.[53] His early work, the *Philosophia mundi*, perhaps written circa 1125, does make one isolated reference to *glossulae* on Plato.[54] Jeauneau suggested that this might mean that William

---

[50] See below p. 77 and van Winden, *Calcidius on Matter*, pp. 26-27, 227-228, 231.

[51] See below pp. 74-77.

[52] See below p. 259.

[53] On the dates of William's career, see *Glose Willelmi de Conchis super Platonem*, ed. Jeauneau, pp. 9-10.

[54] *Philosophia mundi* 1.4 (13), ed. Gregor Maurach, in Wilhelm von Conches, *Philosophia* (Pretoria, 1980), pp. 22-23 (also in PL 172: 46c11-47A5): "Anima ergo mundi secundum quosdam spiritus sanctus est. Diuina enim uoluntate et bonitate (quae spiritus sanctus est, ut praediximus) omnia uiuunt quae in mundo uiuunt. Alii dicunt animam mundi esse naturalem uigorem rebus insitum, quo quaedam uiuunt tantum, quaedam uiuunt et sentiunt, quaedam

had written a small set of preparatory glosses on the *Timaeus* prior to his full treatment. If he did, these are now lost or not yet identified. On the other hand, the reference to *glossulae* might be taken as an announcement of a future project, for which there is, as Jeauneau points out, some precedent in the way in which he announced plans for other projects and, of course, there is the extant set of *Timaeus* glosses as fulfilment of the promise. Or it may be that William in revising the *Philosophia* later in his career made a cross-reference to his full set of glosses on the *Timaeus*.[55] If William in his reference to the *glossulae* meant to indicate what specifically was said in these glosses—about the world-soul as the Holy Spirit, as a natural vigour, and why it was wrong to conclude that man possessed two souls—then the *Glosae* can not be that work, since it lacks those particulars (see 5.1-13). If he only meant to indicate that one could find an exposition of the composition of the soul in his *glossulae*, then the statement is a vague one and could apply to almost any set of *Timaeus* glosses from the Middle Ages.

There are still other arguments against identifying the *Glosae* with an early redaction of William's glosses on Plato. In a few cases, for instance, where William indicates that a certain opinion on the *Timaeus* was held by unspecified others and, therefore, did not originate with him, we find that Bernard in the *Glosae* subscribes to the same doctrine.[56] The *Glosae* and William's *Philosophia mundi*, moreover, have few points of striking similarity, despite their dependence on the *Timaeus*. If both works were by the young William one would expect to find a substantial amount of shared material.[57] But the philosophies of the two authors are very different. While Bernard, as we know from both the *Glosae* and John of Salisbury, was a proponent of the concept of the *formae natiuae*, William never mentions the idea, even in his early works, and was never associated with it by his student John. Indeed, it would be true to describe Bernard in the *Glosae* as chiefly concerned with the primary causes of the universe, while William in his is primarily concerned with its secondary causes. Their sources too are different, as

---

uiuunt et sentiunt et discernunt; nec est aliquid quod uiuat et sentiat et discernat, in quo non sit ille naturalis uigor. In homine ergo est illa et propria anima.

Si aliquis concludat: 'Ergo in homine sunt duae animae', dicimus 'Non', quia non dicimus animam mundi esse animam, sicut nec caput mundi esse caput.—Hanc dicit Plato esse excogitatam ex diuidua et indiuidua substantia, ex eadem natura et diuersa. Cuius expositionem si quis quaerat, in glossulis nostris super Platonem inueniet."

On the date of the *Philosophia mundi*, see Dronke, "New Approaches to the School of Chartres," pp. 129-130.

[55] See *Glose Willelmi de Conchis super Platonem*, ed. Jeauneau, pp. 14-15.

[56] Cf. *Glosae* 3.158-161 below and *Glose Willelmi de Conchis super Platonem* 24, ed. Jeauneau, p. 86.24-27.

[57] See pp. 97-99 below.

Bernard drew chiefly on Boethius, Calcidius, and Macrobius, while William was one of the first to employ, as early as 1125 in the *Philosophia mundi* and still later in his actual glosses on Plato, newly available medical texts.[58] The similarities and differences between the two sets of glosses are more easily accounted for if we allow that William of Conches would have been familiar with the teachings of his master Bernard of Chartres, especially on the *Timaeus*, rather than by seeing William as the author of both sets of glosses. William's dependence on the *Glosae* is never slavish (see App. 3.3), but manifests both dependencies and departures from his master. William admitted as much in the prologue to his own glosses on Plato when he said that he had borrowed what was good from other glosses and had rejected what was bad.[59]

The uncertainties and scholarly doubts that frequently surround the attribution of anepigraphic glosses do not, in this case, seem warranted, since an accumulation of evidence supports a single answer to the question "Who wrote the *Glosae*?" It remains, in this light, both reasonable and probable that Bernard of Chartres, that perfect Platonist of the early twelfth century, was the author of the *Glosae super Platonem* edited below. What follows in the rest of the introduction, particularly concerning Bernard's career, methods, and philosophical beliefs, should serve to reinforce the attribution.

Bernard of Chartres

In sketching an outline of the career of Bernard of Chartres, those scholars who have held fast to the portrait provided by John of Salisbury in the *Metalogicon* have always come closest to the truth.[60] We have never, in fact, been able to move very much beyond the rich and sensitively drawn description left by John. Whereas Mabillon, knowing only Otto of Freising's mention of Bernard of Chartres as a master of Gilbert of Poitiers (App. 2.4.C), could but dismiss Bernard as a virtually unknown master, Jean Liron in 1719 was able, through a reading of the *Metalogicon* and *Policraticus*, to furnish the readers of the first volume of the *Bibliothèque générale des auteurs de France* with an essentially correct and important new entry on the career of Bernard of Chartres.[61] From the *Metalogicon* Liron derived that exalted

---

[58] See n. 36 above.
[59] See p. 3 above.
[60] See *Metalogicon*, ed. Clement C.J. Webb (Oxford, 1929) and App. 2 below.
[61] Vol. 1: *La bibliothèque chartraine ou le traité des auteurs et des hommes illustres de l'ancien Diocèse de Chartres* (Paris, 1719; rpt. as *Bibliothèque chartraine*, Geneva, 1971), pp.

image of Bernard which has become so much a part of the tradition; Bernard
was, he said, "un des plus grands hommes de son temps, et le maître de
presque tous les Sçavans du XII. siècle."[62]

Within a half century the *Histoire littéraire de la France* had already
subsumed under the name of Bernard of Chartres the poet we now know as
Bernard Silvester.[63] From there the idea of Bernard of Chartres as the Latin
poet of the *Cosmographia* and the Platonic philosopher and teacher of
Chartres began to spread.[64] When Victor Cousin, with his vast knowledge of
early twelfth-century thinkers, accepted this conflation as true it achieved
some currency.[65] In 1872-1873 the growth of Bernard's reputation peaked
with the publication of Demimuid's *De Bernardo Carnotensi grammatico
professore et interprete Virgilii* and an address by Hauréau to the Académie
des Inscriptions et Belles-Lettres.[66] In the latter, Hauréau argued that to fit
the facts the Breton Bernard of Chartres must have been the younger brother
of Thierry of Chartres and have followed him in the office of chancellor of
Chartres. As if two Bernards rolled into one were not enough, Hauréau
added a third: Bernard of Moëlan, later Bishop of Quimper. One suspects
that what drove eighteenth and nineteenth-century scholars to the creation
of this fantastical Bernard, who was at once superior teacher, sublime poet,
and Platonic philosopher, and whose career spanned some fifty years, was

---

48-50. Liron, p. 50, seems to have believed that Bernard actually wrote a book in which he
reconciled Aristotle with Plato.

[62] Ibid.

[63] Vol. 12 (Paris, 1763; rpt. Paris, 1869), pp. 261-274.

[64] Reginald Lane Poole, *Illustrations of the History of Medieval Thought in the Departments
of Theology and Ecclesiastical Politics* (London, 1884), p. 114 n.9: "The *Histoire littéraire*,
12.261, rightly points out all the facts related of Bernard of Chartres and his opinions agree
with the writings bearing the name of Bernard Sylvester. The accord indeed is too exact to
make anything but an identification possible." Alexandre Clerval, "Bernard de Chartres," *Les
lettres chrétiennes* 4 (1882) 390 and n.2 points out that it was Brial who first lumped together
the two Bernards. It is odd that R.W. Southern, "Humanism and the School of Chartres," in
R.W. Southern, *Medieval Humanism and Other Studies*, (New York, 1970; rpt. Oxford,
1984), p. 61, should say that the authors of the 1814 volume of the *Histoire littéraire* "knew
nothing, or almost nothing, of the School of Chartres," when it was in the *Histoire littéraire*
that one of the cornerstones of the conception of the school of Chartres was first put into
place.

[65] See *Fragments philosophiques: philosophie scholastique* 2nd ed. (Paris, 1840), pp.
173-177, 336-367, and the same in Victor Cousin, *Fragments de philosophie du Moyen Age*,
2nd ed. (Paris, 1856), pp. 138-142, 265-291.

[66] Mauritius Demimuid, *De Bernardo Carnotensi grammatico professore et interprete Virgilii*
(Paris, 1873) and B. Hauréau, "Bernard de Chartres et Thierry de Chartres," *Académie des
Inscriptions et Belles-Lettres. Comptes rendus des séances de l'année 1872*, 3e serie, 1 (Paris,
1873) 75-85. See also Hauréau, "Mémoire sur quelques maîtres du XIIe siècle, à l'occasion
d'une prose latine publiée par M. Th. Wright," *Académie des Inscriptions et Belles-Lettres,
Paris. Mémoires* 28.2 (Paris, 1876) 223-238, which contains essentially the same position.

John of Salisbury's *Metalogicon*. There readers are led to think great things of the old man of Chartres.

Over the next thirty years, amid considerable controversy, this cunningly constructed image of a larger-than-life Bernard was to be disassembled. By 1884, Hauréau had had second thoughts, and now distinguished between Bernard of Chartres, Bernard Silvester, and Bernard of Moëlan. Nevertheless many of the details of his new account of Bernard of Chartres remained confused, especially the supposed relationship and chronologies of the Breton brothers, Bernard and Thierry of Chartres.[67] Hauréau still believed that Thierry had preceded his brother as chancellor, but he now maintained that Bernard had moved to Paris late in his life and there, at some point between 1136 and 1141, had taught John of Salisbury. Charles Langlois, in a forceful and less-than-delicate article of 1893, reasserted the thesis that Bernard of Chartres and Bernard Silvester were one and the same individual, casting back on Hauréau his own arguments of twenty years before.[68] Hauréau, in a restrained reply to Langlois, defended his thesis of 1884 against confounding the Bernards.[69]

In a little-noticed article of 1882 Alexandre Clerval set right much of the career of Bernard of Chartres.[70] Supporting his argument with information gathered from the cartularies of Chartres, Clerval sketched a career for Bernard that ran from the last decade of the eleventh century until his death in 1124; he had in his time been a subdeacon, master, and chancellor of Chartres. Clerval rejected a series of widespread assumptions about Bernard of Chartres: that he was to be identified with either Bernard Silvester or Bernard of Moëlan, that he had taught John of Salisbury, and that Thierry was his brother. His treatment of the documentary details of Bernard's career in this article was, in fact, more careful than it was to be in the famous work that followed. In 1895 in his monumental *Les écoles de Chartres au Moyen Âge* Clerval incorporated most of his earlier article, though he now argued that Thierry had been Bernard's brother, and supplied an analysis of Bernard's thought and his place in the development of the cathedral school of Chartres.[71] Clerval's argument about Bernard of Chartres was a much needed reconciliation of the documentary and chronological facts with John of Salisbury's literary description. The argument was simple, but tremen-

---

[67] "Mémoire sur quelques chanceliers de l'église de Chartres," *Académie des Inscriptions et Belles-Lettres, Paris. Mémoires* 31.2 (Paris, 1884) 77-104.

[68] "Maître Bernard," *Bibliothèque de l'Ecole des chartes* 54 (1893) 237-247.

[69] "Maître Bernard," *Bibliothèque de l'Ecole des chartes* 54 (1893) 792-794.

[70] "Bernard de Chartres," *Les lettres chrétiennes* 4 (1882) 390-397.

[71] Alexandre Clerval, *Les écoles de Chartres au Moyen Age (du Ve au XVIe siècle* (Paris, 1895; rpt. Frankfurt, 1965), pp. 158-163, 248-254.

dously influential. Poole, who had earlier accepted the composite Bernard, now changed his mind, though he deeply regretted the separation of the Bernards.[72]

Even the controversy over the status of the school of Chartres which broke out in the mid 1960s with Southern's essay on "Humanism and the School of Chartres" left Clerval's picture of Bernard of Chartres largely untouched.[73] The people around Bernard were almost all called into question—was Thierry his brother, were Richard the Bishop and William of Conches his students—as was the institution from which he drew his claim to fame, but Bernard of Chartres's career as described by Clerval was left intact.[74]

In fact, even Clerval's 1895 sketch of Bernard of Chartres deserves examination, for it is less solid than it seems. Clerval tended to exaggerate in 1895 the modest claims he had made about Bernard of Chartres in 1882, perhaps in response to those who had come to expect so much more of the great Chartrian. He suggests, for instance, that there is extensive cartulary evidence for Bernard's career, when there is surprisingly little; that Bernard regularly signed charters as the *magister scolae*, when there is only one such document extant and its epithet warrants further scrutiny; that Bernard and Thierry witnessed a charter together, when no such document exists; and that Bernard wrote a prose treatise on Porphyry from which John of Salisbury derived his specific knowledge of Bernard's philosophy.[75] Nevertheless, Clerval's main solution to the puzzle of Bernard's career remains a remarkable achievement.

---

[72] Cf. Reginald Lane Poole, *Illustrations of the History of Medieval Thought in the Departments of Theology and Ecclesiastical Politics*, pp. 114-123 and Poole, *Illustrations of the History of Medieval Thought and Learning* 2nd rev. ed. (London, 1920; rpr. New York, 1960), pp. 101-106. Also see Poole, "The Masters of the Schools at Paris and Chartres in John of Salisbury's Time," *The English Historical Review* 139 (1920) 328, where he comments on the separation of the Bernards that: "This is the more to be regretted since all that John of Salisbury tells us about the opinions of his Bernard corresponds closely with those expressed in the *Cosmographia* of the other Bernard; even the verses quoted by John from the one might easily be believed to be taken from the other." This study is also reprinted in R.L. Poole, *Studies in Chronology and History* (Oxford, 1934), pp. 223-247. See the expression of the same regret in Poole, *Illustrations of the History of Medieval Thought and Learning*, p. viii.

[73] The sequence of publications in this controversy was "Humanism," (1965), printed in R.W. Southern, *Medieval Humanism* (New York, 1970), pp. 61-85; Peter Dronke, "New Approaches to the School of Chartres," published in 1969; Häring, "Chartres and Paris Revisited," which appeared in 1974; Southern, *Platonism, Scholastic Method and the School of Chartres* printed in 1979; and R.W. Southern, "The Schools of Paris and the School of Chartres," in *Renaissance and Renewal in the Twelfth Century*, ed. Robert L. Benson and Giles Constable with Carol D. Lanham (Cambridge, Mass., 1982), pp. 113-137.

[74] See Southern, "Humanism," p. 68.

[75] See Clerval, *Les écoles*, pp. 160-163, 248-254.

In the second appendix I have gathered together, for ease of consultation, those extant documents that refer to Bernard of Chartres. Before turning to the content of these, we need to examine the epithets applied to Bernard of Chartres in this collection. Of the appellations, *Bernardus Carnotensis* is the most specific and least open to debate; it is employed nine times, eight by John of Salisbury in the *Metalogicon* and once by Otto of Freising in the *Gesta Friderici I imperatoris*.[76] Given that these are both works of the late 1150s, we may wonder whether *Bernardus Carnotensis* was simply a name coined for the sake of convenience, one used in the mid century to distinguish this Bernard from the other Bernards still or recently active. Was *Bernardus* called *Carnotensis* in his own time? Perhaps not, but his students, Gilbert of Poitiers, William of Conches, and Richard the Bishop, probably identified him in this way to their own students in places like Paris. Once in the *Metalogicon*, John speaks of *Carnotensis senex Bernardus*, so that there should be no doubt about the identity of the *senex Carnotensis* twice cited in the *Policraticus*.[77] Though again it is possible that at least one of Bernard's students described him as the old man of Chartres in lectures heard by John of Salisbury, we have no guarantee that this usage was not John's own invention. In the *Policraticus* Bernard is cited just twice, both times as the *senex Carnotensis*. Given the specificity of the *Metalogicon* references, it may be that even John did not expect that the readers of the *Policraticus* would immediately know or, perhaps, care who this old man of Chartres was. Both *Bernardus Carnotensis* and *senex Carnotensis* seem to have been mid-twelfth-century usages. In Chartres itself there can have been little need to describe someone as "of Chartres" and it would likely have been deemed disrespectful to refer to a still living Bernard as "the old man of Chartres."

In his own time, according to the charters which he witnessed, Bernard called himself *subdiaconus* twice, *magister* twice, perhaps *scolae magister* once, and *cancellarius* twice.[78] These are titles to which, by virtue of the documents on which they exist, we need to add the understood *Beatae Mariae Carnotensis*. Each of the titles in the cartularies exists in isolation from the others, but we can confidently connect *subdiaconus* and *cancellarius* because this is the manner in which the two versions of the necrology of Chartres describe Bernard.[79] Nothing, however, can move us with absolute

[76] See App. 2: 2.B1; 3.B; 3.D; 4.A; 4.B; 5.A for two examples; 5.C, all supplied by John; 4.C by Otto.

[77] See App. 2: 3.C; 2.A2; and 3.A. Even the mild caution of Jeauneau—"'Vieillard de Chartres'-Bernard de Chartres, selon l'opinion commune"—seems unwarranted: see Edouard Jeauneau, "Jean de Salisbury et la lecture des philosophes," in *The World of John of Salisbury*, ed. Michael Wilks (Oxford, 1984), p. 85.

[78] See App. 2.1.

[79] See App. 2.6.

certainty from one title to the next, chronology being the only string to bind up this parchment career. *Magister Bernardus*, for instance, was only signed twice in charters, a third time if *scolae magister* is counted.[80] *Magister* does, however, gain some support from additional witnesses: there are two letters to Chartres, one mentioning, and another addressed to, *magister B.*; a letter from another at Chartres who identifies himself to his father as a student of *dominus magister Bernhardus*; and the report of a student about a specific point on which William of Conches disagreed with *magister Bernardus*.[81] We know, furthermore, from the accounts of John of Salisbury and Otto of Freising, that Bernard of Chartres was certainly a *magister*, their evidence of the context of his teaching career being considerably stronger than that culled from the charters.

The final epithet is Hugh of Saint-Victor's vague reference to a *sapiens quidam* as the author of a set of verses. This epithet would be utterly useless were it not clarified by John of Salisbury's subsequent identification of the poet of the same set of verses as the *senex Carnotensis*.[82] Similarly the two references to *Bernardus* by Tuilecnad would be too vague to identify Bernard of Chartres were it not for their special historical and philosophical context.[83] Lastly the isolated use of *Carnotensis*, which does not occur anywhere in the collection of reasonably secure *testimonia*, is of dubious value in identifying Bernard of Chartres.[84] If Bernard of Chartres published anything in his

---

[80] See App. 2: 1.C; 1.D; 1.E.

[81] See App. 2: 4.D; 4.E; 5.F.

[82] See App. 2.1.A1-2.

[83] See App. 2.5.D-E.

[84] Such a case is the one recently turned up by Smits, "New Evidence for the Authorship of the Commentary on the First Six Books of Virgil's *Eneid* Commonly Attributed to Bernardus Silvestris?" Helinand of Froidmont (ca. 1160-1229) in his *Chronicon* 8.71 employs an excerpt from the Virgil commentary and says: "Carnotensis autem aliam interpretationem ponit de ramo aureo, sed ut mihi uidetur incongruam," (in Smits, p. 239). Smits speculates that this might suggest that Bernard of Chartres was the author of the famous commentary (see above, p. 8 and nn. 19-20). Actually, it seems more likely that Helinand meant to indicate John of Salisbury here, rather than any Bernard. In the first place, Helinand knew the Virgil Commentary exclusively from John's *Policraticus*, deriving this specific passage from *Policraticus* 8.24-25, ed. Clement C.J. Webb, 2 vols. (Oxford, 1909) 2: 415.15-421.13. Since John had already reworked the passage once and Helinand had reworked it again, it seems unlikely that Helinand knew the commentary itself, but likely that he quotes an opinion extracted directly from the *Policraticus*. Moreover, nowhere in the *Policraticus*, which Helinand did know, does John state that the commentary is by a Bernard or by anyone else. It is doubtful if Helinand had even heard of Bernard of Chartres, given Bernard's limited fame by the late twelfth century. John of Salisbury does not mention Bernard by name in the *Policraticus* and his *Metalogicon*, where Bernard was a prominent figure, was an extremely rare book in the Middle Ages, one Helinand seems not to have read. Helinand must, therefore, have assumed that the opinion he was quoting was by John of Salisbury himself. By *Carnotensis*, "The

lifetime under his own name, he may simply have signed as *Bernardus,* as Tuilecnad seems to have known him. His glosses for the most part would have circulated anonymously. If *Bernardus* was the personal name by which he was known in his own time, and if he was addressed by his title when serving in an official capacity, then it fell to others after his death to give him the distinctive name by which we now know him.

In organising the surviving witnesses to the career of Bernard of Chartres in the second appendix, I have placed those that derive directly from Bernard at the beginning. In fact only the charters which he signed bear witness to direct and datable actions, and even they are preserved not in original copies, but in cartulary copies (App. 2.1). The verse (App. 2.2) and dicta (App. 2.3) represent apparently genuine products of Bernard's career, but they have passed to posterity through other witnesses. After that, with the exception of the three letters (App. 2.4.D-F) and the necrology (App. 2.6), everything is in some sense hearsay, mere reports on Bernard's career, often recorded long after his death.

The information to be gathered from the charters preserved in three cartularies connected with Chartres and an additional early manuscript is thin and not without problems as to dates and titles, but it is also invaluable. Since we know from the necrology of Chartres (App. 2.6) that Bernard was a subdeacon of Notre-Dame of Chartres, it is likely that, before he held any official office in the cathedral, he would have signed his earliest documents simply as *Bernardus subdiaconus.* In fact, a document preserved in the cartulary of Saint-Jean-en-Vallée of Chartres includes a subdeacon Bernard as one of its witnesses in 1108 (App. 2.1.A). This document, not published until after Clerval's 1895 study, provides a date some seven years earlier than any other yet advanced for connecting Bernard with Chartres. In the past it was merely assumed that Bernard's career at Chartres must have stretched back to the first decade of the twelfth century, otherwise his datable career at Chartres would have run only from 1115 to 1124, too short a time for him to have accomplished anything of significance, certainly not the establish-

---

Chartrian," he evidently meant to designate someone familiar and important, a description and dignity that probably suited a bishop much better than it did a half-forgotten subdeacon and master of nearly a century before. Poole, "The Masters of the Schools," p. 331, notes that though John of Salisbury was bishop of Chartres for only a few years he was still known as the "holy Carnotense" in the fifteenth century. See also Edouard Jeauneau, "Berkeley, University of California, Bancroft Library MS. 2 (Notes de lecture)," *Mediaeval Studies* 50 (1988) 452-454 and Amnon Linder, "The Knowledge of John of Salisbury in the Later Middle Ages," *Studi Medievali* ser. 3a, 18.2 (1977) 318, 362.

Equally suspect seem to me the arguments set forward in Hermann Heimpel, "Reformatio Sigismundi, Priesterehe und Bernhard von Chartres," *Deutsches Archiv für Erforschung des Mittelalters* 17 (1961) 526-537.

ment of a tradition of teaching.[85] Given the paucity of early twelfth-century charters in any of the extant cartularies of Chartres, it is not surprising that Bernard does not appear in the documents until 1108. He was probably at Chartres long before that date. A document of 1115 (App. 2.1.B) does confuse the issue of the identity of subdeacon Bernard, since it lists two subdeacons by that name, the second "of Poitiers."[86] While it is not impossible that Bernard of Chartres was this subdeacon, the lack of *Pictauensis* in all other *testimonia* to his career supports the assumption that Bernard identified himself early in his career simply as a subdeacon of Chartres.

Unfortunately the only information we have about Bernard's life before 1110 must be inferred from his subdiaconal status. The subdiaconate at Chartres during Ivo of Chartres's episcopacy was still a minor order, but one which was, with the increasing demands of chastity and office, in transition towards greater status. If Bernard followed the normal practices set out in Ivo's *Decretum* and *Panormia*, then he would not have been ordained before he was fourteen years old and might have been much older.[87] In his ordination he would have received not the laying on of hands, but the empty paten and chalice from the bishop and a cruet and ewer of water, a towel,[88] and possibly a maniple and tunicle from the archdeacon of Chartres. His function as subdeacon would have been to assist the deacons in the celebration of mass, not to carry or distribute the host, but to ready the empty vessels, to elevate the paten, and to read, where necessary, the Epistles.[89] Perpetual chastity in Bernard's time was an important obligation of the subdiaconate.[90] Bernard of Chartres remained throughout the rest of his career, as we know from the necrology of Chartres (App. 2.6), a subdeacon, an indication, Clerval believed, of his abiding humility.[91].

---

[85] Clerval, *Les écoles*, p. 160.

[86] In another document, no. 8 from 1108, in the *Cartulaire de Saint-Jean-en-Vallée de Chartres* (see App. 2.1.A), which the subdeacon Bernard signed, the signature of a certain "Bernardus monachus Pictaviensis" is also found. Note that Bernard of Chartres should not be confused with the "Bernardus capicerius" who appears in a number of documents during and after Bernard's career at Chartres; he was a different individual.

[87] See Ivo, *Panormia* 3.32, PL 161: 1136D13-1137A1.

[88] See Ivo, *Decretum* 6.14, PL 161: 447D2-8; 6.9, 445B1-6; *Panormia* 3.35, PL 161: 1137B6-10. On the office of subdeacon, see J.A. Jungmann, *The Mass of the Roman Rite. Its Origins and Development (Missarum Sollemnia)*, trans. F.A. Brunner, revised by C.K. Riepe (London, 1959), pp. 268, 472-473.

[89] See Ivo, *Decretum* 2.43, PL 161: 170A5-11; 2.79, 178B4-6; 3.105, 221B9-13; 6.8, 445A9-11.

[90] See Ivo, *Decretum* 6.8, PL 161: 445A12-16; 6.119, 474C3-8; 6.221, 492B12-C12; *Panormia* 3.89-90, PL 161: 1150D11-1151B4; 3.99, 1152C4-D1; 3.102-104, 1153A1-B8.

[91] Clerval, "Bernard de Chartres," p. 397: "Pour terminer, signalons un détail intéressant. Bernard ne fut jamais que sous-diacre. Ce fait nous est une preuve de sa modestie, comme le

Between 1115 (or perhaps five years earlier) and 1119 Bernard signed two
charters as *magister Bernardus* (App. 2.1.C-D). The second of these two
charters was securely dated to 29 November 1119 by Merlet. From the fact
that the first concerns an action of Bishop Ivo of Chartres we can conclude
that it had been Ivo himself who had appointed Bernard the master of the
cathedral school. That this appointment occurred before 1115 is corrobo-
rated by another source. Gilbert of Poitiers studied under a series of great
men, first Hilary of Poitiers, next Bernard of Chartres, and finally the
brothers Anselm and Ralph of Laon (App. 2.4.C). If the sequence of
Gilbert's education given by Otto of Freising is exact, then Gilbert must
surely have been a student of Bernard at some point between 1110 and 1115,
since Hilary of Poitiers was active between 1105 and 1113 and Anselm of
Laon died around 1117 while Gilbert was still his student. Probably the best
guess is that Gilbert studied under Bernard at Chartres at some point
between 1112 and 1114. On the basis of John of Salisbury's statement that
William of Conches and Richard the Bishop had formed their own students,
including John, "ad huius magistri formam" (App. 2.4.A), it is now generally
accepted that they too were the direct students of Bernard.[92] When William
and Richard studied at Chartres is not known, though it was quite likely in
the period after Gilbert's departure for Laon, probably for several years
between 1115 and 1124.

The one charter in which Bernard has the epithet *scolae magister* (App.
2.1.E) presents some problems. In *Les écoles de Chartres*, Clerval states that
between 1115 and 1119 Bernard had regularly signed as *magister scolae* after
Vulgrin's signature as chancellor.[93] In fact, no document supports this
assertion. According to Clerval, Bernard became chancellor after Vulgrin's
retirement to Saint-Jean in 1119. In this new capacity he signed at some

---

surnom de *Senex Carnotensis* témoigne de la respectueuse affection dont il était entouré. On
est touché de voir ce vénérable et savant vieillard restant aux degrés inférieurs de la hiérarchie
ecclésiastique, et n'acceptant que très tardivement la dignité de chancelier. Sa chaire suffisait
à son ambition, ses élèves faisaient le plaisir de sa vie; grâce aux talents qu'il leur avait
communiqués, ceux-ci devenaient évêques et archevêques: pour lui, il se contentait de les avoir
formés."

[92] Southern, "Humanism," p. 71 registered some mild doubt about the assumption that
William of Conches was Bernard's student. Dronke, "New Approaches to the School of
Chartres," p. 121 strongly defended the connection, arguing that the words "ad huius magistri
formam" left little room for doubt. Southern, *Platonism, Scholastic Method, and the School
of Chartres*, p. 16 n.16, now seems ready to grant the point. The argument in favour is further
reinforced when we realise that Gilbert of Poitiers was, according to the reliable witness of
Otto of Freising, a student of Bernard of Chartres, yet John of Salisbury nowhere mentions
the fact. Hence the phrase "ad huius magistri formam" is a very strong and definite statement
in the *Metalogicon*, one that directly links William and Richard to their master Bernard.

[93] Clerval, *Les écoles*, p. 160.

point between 1119 and 1124 the charter which became a part of what Clerval and Merlet called the *manuscrit chartrain* of the Bibliothèque municipale de Saint-Etienne (Loire). With Merlet, Clerval edited this manuscript which, after the destruction of much of the cathedral library of Chartres during the Second World War, was returned to Chartres.[94] In fact it is only in this charter that Bernard takes the title *scolae magister* and in it Vulgrin is still chancellor.[95] Merlet and Clerval date this isolated copy of the oath of the canons of Chartres to the period 1119 to 1124, specifying 1121 as the most likely date.[96] In the case of Bernard, at least, the dating is a circular argument, since here the document is partially dated on the basis of the putative chronology of his career, while in *Les écoles de Chartres* the chronology of his career is partially based on the date of the same document.

More worrisome still is the copy of Bernard's signature. Merlet and Clerval leave us with the impression that Bernard himself signed as *scolae magister* immediately under the chancellor's signature, and this has long been accepted as evidence of Bernard's special place in the changing educational structure of the cathedral school of Chartres.[97] Southern called it the "most important document for Bernard's career at Chartres."[98] But the scribe of the copy of the oath recorded titles for only the first three of the oath-takers and then continued with a simple list of first names. Another scribe in a different ink added in minuscule letters above each name the titles and epithets that Merlet and Clerval took to be part of the original.[99] Perhaps the scribe of the main text asked an assistant to provide the titles which he had purposely omitted, but what could have prompted him to omit them in the first place? There was ample space on fol. 130v to continue with the fuller list and it would have been a curious way to treat a significant legal document being inserted into an important manuscript. Hence, one might speculate that at some later date a scribe of Chartres independently identified the people

---

[94] René Merlet and Alexandre Clerval, *Un manuscrit chartrain du XIe siècle* (Chartres, 1893). I should like here to thank the Bibliothèque municipale de Chartres for sending me a photograph of fol. 130v of the manuscript. Häring, "Chartres and Paris Revisited," pp. 269-271, reexamines Clerval's treatment of documents in *Les écoles*.

[95] Merlet and Clerval, *Un manuscrit*, pp. 195-196.

[96] Merlet and Clerval, *Un manuscrit*, p. 197.

[97] Ibid.

[98] Southern, "Humanism," p. 68 n.1 and see Southern, "The Schools of Paris and the School of Chartres," p. 135. See also Jean Châtillon, "Les écoles de Chartres et de Saint-Victor," in *La scuola nell'occidente latino dell'alto medioevo*, in Settimane di studio del Centro Italiano di studi sull'alto medioevo 19.2 (Spoleto, 1972), pp. 799-800 and n.12.

[99] Points of difference in the scripts are the formation of the letter *d* which has a straight ascender in the first hand, curved in the second; the letter *g* which is closed in the first, open in the second (as, for instance, in the word *magister*); and the tall *s*.

named in the oath. If this were true, it would mean that no document survives in which Bernard of Chartres calls himself *scolae magister*.

There is, in fact, no *testimonium* that surely demonstrates that the subdeacon Bernard and master Bernard were one and the same individual, nor is there one that ties together the master and the chancellor. But, in light of Bernard's obituary notice (App. 2.6), one must conclude that the same subdeacon Bernard became *magister* and *cancellarius*. Bernard was chancellor by 1124, since he signed one document *Bernardus cancellarius* in that year (App. 2.1.F) and another that can be roughly assigned to the period between 1119 and 1126 (App. 2.1.G). These documents along with the necrology notices are the only witnesses to Bernard as chancellor.

From this skimpy set of documents, a rather grandiose and momentous scheme of events has been deduced: that Bernard's career was a pivotal one in transforming Chartres into a cultural centre of the first order. Says Klibansky:

> in 1115 a change in the organization came about: the chancellor whose function it had been previously to deputize for, and assist, the bishop, now took complete charge of the teaching, while the bishop withdrew altogether from taking any immediate part in the life of the school and confined himself to being its patron. Those functions which the chancellor had formerly fulfilled were now handed over in turn to the so-called *magister scholae*, the schoolmaster. This change of organization in the teaching hierarchy is associated with Bernard of Chartres, whose principles and methods gave to the school its particular stamp.[100]

The documents, unfortunately, do not allow us to construct an argument about a fundamental change in the institutional structure of Chartres based on Bernard's career. Had very much actually changed in the scholastic structure of Chartres since Fulbert's day?[101] The relationship between the offices of master and chancellor at Chartres in the early twelfth century is not discussed in any extant documents. Nor was the succession from one office to the other standard, since the chancellor after Bernard had not previously been the master of the school. The specific meaning of Bernard's official titles is, therefore, unknown.[102] And though John of Salisbury provides a wonderful

---

[100] "The School of Chartres," in *Twelfth-Century Europe and the Foundations of Modern Society*, ed. M. Clagett, G. Post, and R. Reynolds (Madison, 1966), pp. 5-6.

[101] See *The Letters and Poems of Fulbert of Chartres*, ed. and trans. Frederick Behrends (Oxford, 1976), pp. xvii, xxviii-xxxvi. On the type of cathedral school that Chartres was, see Châtillon, "Les écoles de Chartres et de Saint-Victor," pp. 796-804.

[102] For some general reservations on the use of the terms *magister* and *magister scholae*, see Roberto Giacone, "Masters, Books and Library at Chartres According to the Cartularies of Notre-Dame and Saint-Père," *Vivarium* 12 (1974) 33-40.

account of how Bernard actually taught (App. 2.4.A), he tells us almost nothing about Bernard's institutional function as *magister*: how he was appointed, how students joined his class, who they were, how long they spent with him, and whether Bernard had assistants. Nor does Southern's argument about the institutional significance of whether the word *magister* precedes or follows a name fit Bernard's case.[103] If, as chancellor in his last years, Bernard still supervised the cathedral school of Chartres, we have no specific witness to the fact. We are more in the dark about Bernard's place in the institutional structure of the cathedral of Chartres than Clerval and his interpreters would lead us to believe.

The year of Bernard of Chartres's death can not be precisely determined. Whereas Gilbert of Poitiers had appeared as *canonicus* in the 1124 document which Bernard had signed as *cancellarius* (App. 2.1.F), he signed himself as "Gillebertus cancellarius" in one charter assigned to the period 1116-1124 by its editor and in another firmly dated on 27 November 1126.[104] Oddly Gilbert seems to have signed another document merely as *canonicus* on the same day.[105] Now Clerval assumed that Gilbert became chancellor when Bernard died, even though Vulgrin's example suggests that a chancellor might retire from office. Thus, for Clerval, Bernard must have died between 1124 and 1126. Merlet and Clerval added to this argument the evidence of the early necrology of Chartres contained in the *manuscrit chartrain*, but again the argument is somewhat circular as they also date the last necrology entries on the basis of the presumed date of Bernard's death.[106] The first version of the obit (App. 2.6.A1) records that Bernard, subdeacon and chancellor of the cathedral of Chartres, died on 2 June and left his books to the church. The later necrology from the cartulary of Notre-Dame of Chartres, written after 1130, specifies that Bernard had given twenty-four volumes of books to the church on his death (App. 2.6.A2). Clerval believed the later entry reflected the incorporation of Bernard's library into that of Chartres, whereas the former had been inscribed hurriedly in 1124 immediately after Bernard's death.[107] If the reasoning seems simplistic and the difference in the two entries open to other interpretations, perhaps the conclusion is still basically correct. Despite Clerval's arguments Poole

---

[103] See Southern, "The Schools of Paris and the School of Chartres," pp. 134-135.

[104] See *Cartulaire de l'abbaye de Saint-Père de Chartres*, vol. 2, ed. B. Guérard, Collection des cartulaires de France 2 (Paris, 1840), 2: 2.1.doc.7, pp. 266-267 and 2.1.doc.53, pp. 306-307.

[105] See *Cartulaire de l'abbaye de Saint-Père de Chartres*, 2: 2.1.doc.4, pp. 263-64.

[106] Merlet and Clerval, *Un manuscrit*, p. 140.

[107] Clerval, *Les écoles*, p. 161.

rounded off Bernard's death-date to 1130,[108] so that three dates have traditionally been associated with Bernard's demise: 1124, 1126, and 1130. In truth, all that we can say with absolute certainty is that Bernard of Chartres was alive in 1124 (App. 2.1.F) and that there is no proof whatsoever that he was still alive after 1126.

The fact that Bernard left to his church a bequest of twenty-four volumes of books is information that should help us to identify the chancellor of Chartres with master Bernard. The bequest was not an insignificant one, especially when compared with the mere four volumes left to Chartres by its great bishop Ivo.[109] Saint-Père of Chartres possessed, by way of comparison, about a hundred volumes in the eleventh century.[110] Bernard's collection, then, was extensive, but one might have expected an active teacher of Bernard's sort to have had personal copies of the works he lectured on. Bernard, Gilbert, Thierry, and John of Salisbury were all to enrich the library of the cathedral with bequests of books, so that the cathedral of Chartres must have possessed one of the most splendid libraries in all of twelfth-century Europe.[111] The size of Bernard's personal collection also suggests that he was a man of some means at the cathedral, a fact that corresponds with what we know of his high office.[112]

In the end we know less than we might have hoped about the dates and offices of Bernard's career at Chartres, but we do know something. We know that he was a subdeacon of the cathedral in the first decade of the twelfth century and remained so until his death; that he was appointed *magister* by Ivo of Chartres, presumably by 1112, and remained master until at least 1119; that in 1124 he was *cancellarius*; and that he probably died soon afterwards, leaving his personal collection of books to the cathedral. However, the connections between the offices, the meanings of those offices, and the exact dates of his career remain obscure.

Bernard's reputation depends not on the documentary traces of himself he left behind at Chartres, but on the impression he made upon his students.

---

[108] Poole, "The Masters of the Schools," pp. 326-327.

[109] See Giacone, "Masters, Books and Library at Chartres," pp. 42-44.

[110] See Lucien Merlet, "Catalogue des livres de l'abbaye de Saint-Père de Chartres, au XIe siècle," *Bibliothèque de l'Ecole des chartes* 15 (1853-1854) 263-270.

[111] See *Cartulaire de Notre-Dame de Chartres*, ed. E. de Lépinois and L. Merlet, 3 vols. (Chartres, 1862-1865), 3: 167-168, 206, 201-202, for the bequests of Gilbert, Thierry, and John. See also Giacone, "Masters, Books and Library at Chartres," pp. 42-46 and Häring, "Chartres and Paris Revisited," p. 292.

[112] On the substantial income of the masters of Chartres, see J. Châtillon, "Les écoles de Chartres et de Saint-Victor," pp. 800-801 and Emile Lesne, *Histoire de la propriété ecclésiastique en France*, vol. 5: *Les écoles de la fin du VIIIe siècle à la fin du XIIe* (Lille, 1940), p. 478.

Peter Dronke has suggested that Bernard would be thought of today as a "charismatic teacher" and he is doubtless right.[113] Still, a good deal of romanticism has surrounded Bernard's reputation as saintly scholar and sage,[114] and this despite the fact that we possess very few direct references to him by his students. The most important of these is the letter preserved in the so-called Chartres Letter-Book from a certain student G. to his master B. at Chartres (App. 2.4.E). The letter is filled with the unrestrained admiration of a devoted disciple for his master. In his salutation the student hopes that all will embrace philosophy and offers thanks that he himself has been instructed by so great a master. He confesses that he has been thinking of his master frequently of late, because he too is now in charge of a school, in Aquitaine, and greatly regrets being separated from such a distinguished doctor. Indeed, he longs to rejoin his master B. in penetrating things that had, before his teacher had begun to study them, been utterly hidden in the secret folds of philosophy. To drink unceasingly from the pure and inexhaustible fountain of his master's wisdom (*nitidus atque inexhaustus tue sapientie fons*) is G.'s highest hope. Though physically separated from his master, he feels intellectually at one with him, since the human mind has the capacity to join disjointed things. In concluding the letter, the student vows to attribute whatever good fortune, prosperity, or knowledge God had already or would grant him and, indeed, whatever he might achieve in his life, to God and his master.

It is generally agreed that the addressee is Bernard of Chartres, but Southern registered a mild protest against automatically plumping for Gilbert

---

[113] Dronke, "Thierry of Chartres," in *A History of Twelfth-Century Western Philosophy*, ed. Peter Dronke (Cambridge, 1988), p. 359.

[114] Representative of this romantic view of Bernard of Chartres is R.R. Bolgar, *The Classical Heritage and Its Beneficiaries: From the Carolingian Age to the End of the Renaissance* (London, 1954; rpt. New York, 1964), pp. 174-175: "While the students of Paris were crowding the lectures of Abelard, a man of remarkable attainments had appeared on the Chartrain scene. The patience, the habit of petty authority, the systematic orderliness which are the necessary attributes of a good schoolmaster, shrivel the spirit. Few teachers, supremely competent in the daily performance of their tasks, are able to pursue simultaneously with such tasks some original and creative line of thought. Fewer still have that unstinted emotional power which characterises the natural leader. In the personality of Bernard of Chartres these incompatible virtues were successfully united. An excellent pedagogue, adept at working out programmes and unflagging in their application (he could apparently teach the whole of Latin grammar within a single year), an original philosopher, expert in the unfamiliar as well as the familiar aspects of his subject, a man of charming piety who valued faith above learning and whose spiritual peace sustained and enriched all around him, he exercised an enormous influence over his many pupils. He wrote little by all accounts, and his few writings have not survived. But contemporary references afford ample proof of his formative role. This man, with his almost magical power over the minds of the young, was unfashionably a Platonist; or would Neoplatonist be a more correct description?"

of Poitiers as the author of the letter.[115] The letter is, as he put it, wildly enthusiastic. But is it unexpectedly so? Gilbert had, according to Otto of Freising, gone looking for the teaching of the greatest men in his youth and had trusted in their authority (App. 2.4.C). It was against this almost boundless respect for the authority and person of the old masters that Abelard reacted. But both Gilbert and Abelard wanted to be masters themselves; they simply chose different ways to achieve it, one by reverence and imitation, the other by usurpation. Moreover, Gilbert was an ambitious man, who in the years prior to 1124 found himself far removed from what he must have considered to be the intellectual centre of Europe. The letter to his old master may be fawning to a fault, but a point lurks behind it: would they not, master and loyal disciple, be better off together, continuing their studies in philosophy? Was Gilbert, then, gently reminding Bernard of his continued affection and respect and, at the same time, requesting a recall to Chartres? What effect the letter had we do not know, but it may not be a mere coincidence that Gilbert was back in Chartres as a canon in 1124 and succeeded Bernard as chancellor in 1126. Perhaps the letter to his old master had more than a little to do with the promotion of his career.[116]

The letter itself is not without interest, for we see reflected in it the respect for Bernard that would reappear in John of Salisbury's *Metalogicon*. Of the three students of Bernard who taught him—Gilbert of Poitiers, William of Conches, and Richard the Bishop—John of Salisbury may well have derived his sharpest impression of Bernard from Gilbert. The *fons sapientiae* metaphor employed by Gilbert in the letter is one which John repeats in describing Bernard as "exundantissimus modernis temporibus fons litterarum in Gallia ..." (App. 2.4.A). Indeed the very hyperbole, so uncharacteristic of John, might be rooted in Gilbert's limitless esteem for his master. Moreover, it was probably Gilbert rather than William of Conches who supplied John with a working knowledge of the concept of the *formae natiuae*. The implications of the letter run deeper still, for Gilbert's phrase, "animus disiuncta coniungit," is a specific evocation of Boethius' commentary on the *Isagoge* of Porphyry.[117] Not only does this reinforce the case for Gilbert's

---

[115] See Hauréau, "Mémoire sur quelques chanceliers," pp. 92-93; Poole, "The Masters of the Schools," pp. 325-326; Clerval, *Les écoles*, p. 164; Southern, "Humanism," pp. 70-71; and Häring, "Chartres and Paris Revisited," pp. 300-301.

[116] A suggestion made by Häring, "Chartres and Paris Revisited," p. 301. Häring, p. 300, notes that Gilbert would have been over forty years old when he wrote this 'enthusiastic' letter to his old master. On Gilbert's early career, see also N. Häring, "Zur Geschichte der Schulen von Poitiers im 12. Jahrhundert," *Archiv für Kulturgeschichte* 47 (1965) 23-47.

[117] Boethius, *In Isagogen Porphyrii commenta: editio secunda* 1.11, ed. S. Brandt, Corpus scriptorum ecclesiasticorum latinorum 48 (Vienna, 1906), p. 165.3-4: " ... at uero animus, cui potestas est et disiuncta componere et composita resoluere ... ." This was a favourite

authorship of the letter, but it also underlines the shared interest of Gilbert
and his revered master in authors such as Boethius. There is too, in the letter,
a suggestion of the *lectio philosophorum*, Bernard's systematic teaching of the
difficult treatises of the philosophers, particularly Porphyry's *Isagoge* and
Plato's *Timaeus*. Both Calcidius and Bernard (1.60-2.2) recognised that the
latter was a work which, because of its difficulty, few had cared to tackle or
been strong enough to explain. Nonetheless, said Bernard, friendship and
love could overcome every difficulty (2.11-15). In fact, the very words with
which Gilbert concludes his letter, that whatever good or prosperity should
come his way he owes to God and Bernard, echo closely Bernard's own gloss
on the *causa totius prosperitatis* (W5:2). All good and all prosperity, as much
inner as outer, derive from virtue, claims Bernard (2.16-20).[118] Perhaps
Gilbert, who had doubtless studied the *Timaeus* under Bernard, could not
resist at the end of his letter flattering his old master with an allusion familiar
to them both.

The earliest reference to Bernard, apart from the charters and letters, is in
Hugh of Saint-Victor's *Didascalicon*, written about 1125-1127. There he
includes a certain wise man's three hexameters *de disciplina*, on the so-called
Six Keys of Learning. Some thirty years later in the *Policraticus* John of
Salisbury attributed the same poem to Bernard of Chartres (App. 2.2.A1-2).
While John praises Bernard's advice on how to live as a philosopher, he
laments Bernard's rough verse and makes little more of the poem. Hugh, in
contrast, constructs an entire section of his book around the Six Keys,
expanding on the implications of each.[119] It is interesting that the student
who wrote home to his father seeking financial assistance should have
explained that he was at Chartres, "ubi ego sub disciplina domini magistri
Bernhardi dego ..." (App. 2.4.F). Bernard's *disciplina* may well have been
a formalised teaching programme which he explained to his students in terms
of the Six Keys. Moreover, Bernard's conception of the significance of
disciplina was probably grounded in his reading of the *Timaeus*. Thus, he

---

expression of William of Conches as well: *Glose Willelmi de Conchis super Platonem* 59, ed.
Jeauneau, p. 129: "ut ait Boetius 'uis est intellectus coniuncta disiungere et disiuncta
coniungere'." See also *Glose Willelmi de Conchis super Platonem* 104 and 170, ed. Jeauneau,
pp. 259 and 280.

[118] Cf. also *Glose Willelmi de Conchis super Platonem* 8, ed. Jeauneau, p. 64.1-2.

[119] See *Didascalicon* 3.12; 3.13 "De humilitate"; 3.14 "De studio quaerendi"; 3.16 "De
quiete"; 3.17 "De scrutinio"; 3.18 "De parcitate"; 3.19 "De exsilio," ed. C.H. Buttimer, in
Hugonis de Sancto Victore Didascalicon De studio legendi: A Critical Text, Studies in Medieval
and Renaissance Latin 10 (Washington, 1939), pp. 61-69. See also Stephen C. Ferruolo, *The
Origins of the University. The Schools of Paris and their Critics, 1100-1215* (Stanford, 1985),
pp. 38-39.

glossed "*amatorem intellectus et disciplinae*" (W43:19-20) with "id est eum qui amat ita docere ut plene intelligatur ..." (7.351-352). Bernard's love of teaching and the fame that spread about his pedagogy in his own lifetime were such that he attracted students of the quality of Gilbert of Poitiers, William of Conches, and Richard the Bishop to Chartres for the express purpose of studying under him (as Otto of Freising said Gilbert had done). To have one of his poems commented upon shortly after his death was also an extraordinary compliment for one of the *moderni*.

Bernard's dicta have achieved singular fame, largely through the unique account of them preserved by John of Salisbury. Four dicta survive, though one is a mere Virgilian commonplace (App. 2.3.A). His famous metaphor of the moderns as dwarfs seated on the shoulders of the giants of antiquity (App. 2.3.B) has achieved a popular place in western thought and was repeated without attribution by William of Conches, as Jeauneau has so brilliantly shown in his history of the figure.[120] In the image Bernard of Chartres expressed his deep respect for the ancients in whose tradition he and the moderns were like dwarfs, seeing farther because they were carried aloft on gigantic backs. It was an ideal suitable not only for a master whose system was the reading of ancient texts, but also for the humble glossator of an ancient text.

Two other poems of Bernard (App. 2.2.B-C), two other dicta (App. 2.3.C-D), and the general outlines of his teaching practices and his Platonic philosophy can be set aside until later more appropriate places in the introduction, but John of Salisbury must be discussed here since so much has always depended on his testimony. John studied under a series of masters in and around Paris and possibly at Chartres between 1138 and 1147. Among his many teachers were three who had been students of Bernard of Chartres: William of Conches, Richard the Bishop, and Gilbert of Poitiers.[121] Doubtless it was from them that he heard accounts of Bernard: of his manner of

---

[120] See Jeauneau, *Lectio*, pp. 58-60. See Jeauneau, *Lectio*, p. 53 n.1 for the extensive literature on the metaphor and see also the discussion that followed Jeauneau's "Nains et géants," in *Entretiens sur la renaissance du 12ᵉ siècle*, ed. M. de Gandillac and Edouard Jeauneau (Paris, 1968), pp. 21-52. See also the discussion in John Howle Newell, "The Dignity of Man in William of Conches and the School of Chartres in the Twelfth Century," (Ph.D. diss., Duke University, 1978), pp. 43-46.

[121] See the remarkably clear and helpful article of Olga Weijers, "The Chronology of John of Salisbury's Studies in France (*Metalogicon* 2.10)," in *The World of John of Salisbury*, ed. Michael Wilks (Oxford, 1984), pp. 109-116. Note also that John corresponded with Richard the Bishop: see letter 201, ed. W.J. Millor and C.N.L. Brooke, in *The Letters of John of Salisbury*, vol. 2: *The Later Letters (1163-1180)*, (Oxford, 1979), pp. 292-94. From the high praise of Anselm of Laon in this letter, one can not help but wonder whether Richard like Gilbert of Poitiers had also travelled to Laon to study under its famous master.

teaching, of the short poems and pithy remarks that adorned his lectures, and of the notable features of his Platonic philosophy. But Bernard had already been dead for over a decade by the time John first learned of him, and he was not to publish the reports of his career until nearly thirty-five years after his demise. The phrase *senex Carnotensis* as John uses it, for instance, probably possesses several meanings. On the one hand, it reflects the reverential description of the aged master of Chartres that John had derived from his own teachers. On the other, it may contain another meaning in the context of the *Metalogicon* and *Policraticus* where John characterises "the old man of Chartres" as a figure from a simpler and philosophically more primitive time in European intellectual history. John's description of Bernard frequently possesses these two sides: a core of factual information that must derive from his teachers, and what this information means in the context of his two books. So dependent are we on John's account of Bernard's career and so much of it is believable and reasonable at first sight that we need, if we wish to arrive at a truer portrait, to weigh one against the other.

The ground might be relatively solid under our feet were it not that John of Salisbury has a polemical thesis to expound in the *Metalogicon*. In the much longer *Policraticus*, apparently also completed in 1159, Bernard of Chartres is almost totally neglected and is never mentioned by name. But in the *Metalogicon* John sets out to combat the unidentified Cornificius and a new breed of students who are lazy, insincere, and disrespectful towards the old methods of learning. In book one, he argues at length for the necessity of a solid education in grammar before any useful study of the higher disciplines can begin. In the twenty-fourth chapter he constructs his argument on a concrete modern example, that of Bernard of Chartres's method of instruction (App. 2.5.1). He who aspires to become a philosopher, John says at the outset of the chapter, must take up *lectio*, *doctrina*, and *meditatio*, as well as the performance of good works.[122] Bernard had achieved just this at Chartres: his teaching was a systematic introduction to grammar through the imitation of ancient authors and it was infused with a strong moral character. In the *Metalogicon*, Bernard of Chartres stands not only for the old and fundamental ways of learning, but also as a countertype to Cornificius himself. Moreover, he represents John's own tradition, the one that had moulded three of his teachers. Two of these, William and Richard, had recently abandoned teaching when students under the spell of Cornician indolence had balked at learning in the onerous old way. It is not without design, therefore, that Bernard is portrayed in John's polemical book as the

---

[122] *Metalogicon* 1.24, ed. Webb, p. 53.21-22.

ideal master of the early twelfth century: serious, methodical, moral, and brilliant.

But how reliable is John's description of Bernard's method? Has he perhaps inferred this method from the way in which he himself was taught and adorned it with some remembered anecdotes about Bernard? In the past one might have automatically assumed that John's account was entirely faithful, but we now know much more about John's creative use of classical materials.[123] If John was prepared to play with, alter, improve, and even invent ancient quotations and whole works, what assurance can we have that he did not treat contemporary oral sources in a similar manner? Even if John did not falsify any part of Bernard's method, his account is specifically directed to a certain end: the refutation of the Cornificians. Yet, in his own day, Bernard can hardly have been the reactionary and conservative figure that he appears to be in John's polemic. Perhaps Bernard was not nearly as rigorous or methodical in real life as he seems to be in the pages of the *Metalogicon*. In the *Glosae*, for instance, Bernard is not as principled about borrowing from Calcidius as John would have us expect of a master who disapproved of the theft of classical materials by his students. But then John does acknowledge that Bernard reproached them gently for their plagiarism, and his own senior students Gilbert and William were borrowers too.[124] All three could lift whole passages, if it suited their purposes, and William, in the case of the dwarfs and giants metaphor and the *Glosae*, borrowed extensively from Bernard himself.[125] In John's quest for the perfect anti-Cornifician hero, he may have neglected to describe a more ordinary Bernard, one who less brilliantly used to invoke Virgil when fortune turned sour (App. 2.3.A) and whose doctrines his students occasionally dismissed (App. 2.5.F).

The very continuity of method and masters which John presents in chapter twenty-four of the *Metalogicon*, where wisdom is seen to flow from Bernard to his students and so down to John, cannot be reconciled with the partial abandonment of Bernard's philosophical tenets by his students and with the

---

[123] See Hans Liebeschütz, "John of Salisbury and the Pseudo-Plutarch," *Journal of the Warburg and Courtauld Institutes* 6 (1943) 33-39 and *Mediaeval Humanism in the Life and Writings of John of Salisbury*, Studies of the Warburg Institute 17 (London, 1950), pp. 23-26; Janet Martin, "John of Salisbury as Classical Scholar," in *The World of John of Salisbury*, ed. Michael Wilks (Oxford, 1984), pp. 179-202; and Rodney Thomson, "John of Salisbury and William of Malmesbury: Currents in Twelfth-Century Humanism," in *The World of John of Salisbury*, pp. 118-119.

[124] See below, p. 67 and n. 204.

[125] See Jeauneau, *Lectio*, pp. 58-60 and Dutton, "The Uncovering," pp. 202-205. Elford, "Developments in the Natural Philosophy of William of Conches," pp. 145, 235-236, speaks of William's "straightforward plagiarism" of Seneca in the *Dragmaticon*.

total absence of comment on Bernard in the extensive published works of
William of Conches. How convenient for John that Bernard belonged almost
exclusively to a domain of fading memories, whence he could construct the
superior master we observe at work early in the *Metalogicon*. By the end of
the book, we need to remember, Bernard has become a Platonic philosopher
with whom John strongly disagrees (App. 2.5.A-C), and in the *Policraticus*
he is the largely neglected old man who wrote rough poetry and invoked
Virgilian commonplaces. Indeed of the two main portraits of Bernard
provided in the *Metalogicon*, that of the teacher and that of the philosopher,
the latter may be more trustworthy, given John's open disagreement with
Bernard's Platonism,[126] and the former less trustworthy in that Bernard was
merely another weapon in John's battle against the Cornificians. The point
here is not to repudiate John of Salisbury's *Metalogicon*, for we must still rely
on it as our major source of information on Bernard of Chartres, but to issue
a necessary *caveat lector*.

On the perplexing problem of whether Bernard of Chartres and Thierry
of Chartres were brothers, so much has been written that it may not be
necessary to say a great deal.[127] John of Salisbury has nothing to contribute
to the subject and this in itself is curious, since he had also been a student
of Thierry and might have found the fraternal bond of two of Chartres's
famous masters worthy of comment. The case in favour has mainly rested on
Otto of Freising's statement, in introducing Abelard to his narrative, that
Brittany has produced learned men, ones especially gifted in the arts such as
the two brothers Bernard and Thierry.[128] But Otto is less than specific about
the exact identity of the two brothers. He does not state, for instance, that
the Bernard he names here is the Bernard that he will introduce later as

---

[126] Liebeschütz, *Mediaeval Humanism in the Life and Writings of John of Salisbury*, pp.
75-76: "As we know from the *Metalogicon* and the greater *Entheticus*, John was interested in
noting down metaphysical disputes both among the ancient, and contemporary, thinkers. But
usually he does not take sides. For instance, he gives us a very clear account of how Bernard
of Chartres established the relation between God, idea and matter in eternity and time by
combining the Latin *Timaeus* and St. Augustine with the argument of Porphyrius' introduction
to logic. That was the origin of the Christian Platonism of the School of Chartres."

[127] See Southern, "Humanism," pp. 69-70; Häring, "Chartres and Paris Revisited," pp.
296-297; and the thorough survey of the issues in J.O. Ward, "The Date of the Commentary
on Cicero's *De inventione* by Thierry of Chartres (ca. 1095-1160?) and the Cornifician Attack
on the Liberal Arts," *Viator* 3 (1972) 263-266.

[128] *Gesta Friderici I imperatoris* 1.49, 3rd. ed., ed. G. Waitz, in Monumenta Germaniae
Historica: Scirptores rerum Germanicarum in usum scholarum (Hanover, 1912), p. 68:
"Petrus iste ex ea Galliae prouincia, quae nunc ab incolis Brittania dicitur, originem trahens—
est enim predicta terra clericorum acuta ingenia et artibus applicata habentium, sed ad alia
negotia pene stolidorum ferax, quales fuerunt duo fratres Bernhardus et Theodericus, uiri
doctissimi ... ."

Gilbert's master (App. 2.4.C). In fact, his language would lead us to assume the opposite. On the one hand, Otto recognises the cleverness of the Bretons, but thinks Peter and his countrymen dullards in almost all matters except the arts, and, on the other, he holds Gilbert of Poitiers and his succesive masters in the highest esteem. Otto labours to distinguish Peter Abelard and Gilbert of Poitiers and their two groups precisely on these grounds: that Gilbert had sought out the careful and sober instruction of great men like Bernard of Chartres, whereas Peter and his Breton countrymen Bernard and Thierry had trusted in their own cleverness and had concerned themselves with superficial things. Otto would not likely have used the same Bernard as an example of unbridled Breton intellect and as the very figure of the exemplary teacher, one who supplied Gilbert with solid and moral instruction. Some have thought that Otto's reference to the two Breton brothers is supported by a vague mention of two brothers, who are not specified either by name or place of origin, in Abelard's *Theologia christiana*, but the evidence is weak.[129] Otto writing in the mid twelfth century must have assumed that his contemporary readers would know that he was referring, in fact, to two different Bernards.

No other source speaks of Bernard of Chartres as a Breton, though Bernard's Breton background has always been widely assumed. In fact there was a famous *Bernardus Brito* flourishing in the mid twelfth century in Thierry's company. William of Tyre names him as a master, an auditor of Thierry of Chartres, and later Bishop of Cornouailles.[130] The *Metamorphosis Goliae* places this Bernard in the midst of other mid-century theologians.[131] Scholars now agree that this celebrated mid-twelfth-century theologian was Bernard of Moëlan.[132] Hence there was a well known Breton Bernard

---

[129] *Theologia christiana* 4.80, ed. E.M. Buytaert, in Corpus Christianorum: Continuatio Mediaevalis 12 (Turnhout, 1969), p. 302: "Nouimus et duos fratres qui se inter summos connumerant magistros, quorum alter tantam uim diuinis uerbis in conficiendis sacramentis tribuit, ut a quibuscumque ipsa proferantur aeque suam habeant efficaciam, ut etiam mulier et quislibet cuiuscumque sit ordinis uel conditionis per uerba dominica sacramentum altaris conficere queat. Alter uero adeo philosophicis innitatur sectis, ut profiteatur Deum priorem per existentiam mundo nullatenus esse." Poole, *Illustrations of the History of Medieval Thought in the Departments of Theology and Ecclesiastical Politics*, p. 115, who apparently learned of the identification from Rémusat, was not completely convinced. Buytaert and others have assumed it: see Abelard, *Theologia christiana*, ed. Buytaert, pp. 47-48, who proceeds to date the redactions of Abelard's work on the presumed connection with Bernard of Chartres. For an opinion to the contrary, see *The Latin Rhetorical Commentaries by Thierry of Chartres*, ed. Karin M. Fredborg, Studies and Texts 84 (Toronto, 1988), pp. 4-5.

[130] See R.B.C. Huygens, "Guillaume de Tyr étudiant: un chapitre (19.12) de son *Histoire* retrouvé," *Latomus* 21 (1962) 822-825.

[131] *Metamorphosis Goliae* 50, ed. in R.B.C. Huygens, "Mitteilungen aus Handschriften. III: Die Metamorphose des Golias," *Studi Medievali* ser. 3, 3 (1962) 771.197-200.

[132] Ward, "The Date of the Commentary," p. 264; Häring, "Chartres and Paris Revisited," pp. 323-327; and John F. Benton, "Philology's Search for Abelard in the *Metamorphosis*

associated with Thierry with whose reputation Otto of Freising must have been familiar. Bernard of Moëlan's career would, as well, fit the chronology of Thierry's life much better than that of Bernard of Chartres. It has always seemed odd that Thierry died some thirty-five years after the demise of the "old man" of Chartres, their careers puzzlingly out of step if indeed they were brothers. The evidence for Thierry's career in the 1120s while Bernard was still alive is almost non-existent: he signed no extant charters with his brother as Clerval had claimed, and Luscombe has doubted whether the Thierry at Abelard's trial in 1121 was Thierry of Chartres.[133] If Thierry can not be convincingly connected with Chartres in Bernard's day, and if Otto meant to indicate another Bernard as Thierry's brother, then the entire support for the argument in favour of Bernard of Chartres and Thierry as brothers collapses.

The implications of separating Bernard and Thierry of Chartres are important for understanding the career of Bernard of Chartres. Bernard apparently had a brother at Chartres with him, if the other letter to Chartres is to be believed (App. 2.4.D), but we no longer know his name. Nor can it be maintained without additional proof that Bernard of Chartres was a Breton. That he was not a native to the region of Chartres may be implied by the sixth key to learning—that students should accept it as their lot to study in foreign lands—but it is impossible to guess where his original home might have been. Separating the two scholars might seem at first to undermine some of the perceived unity and continuity of the school of Chartres, but it will also allow us to forgo the forced chronologies of scholars like Hauréau and Clerval. The one felt justified in thinking that Bernard of Chartres had gone to Paris in the 1130s and 1140s, there to live a little longer in Thierry's world, meet John of Salisbury, and be immortalised in verse, and the other thought he saw in the charters a young and brilliant Thierry at the feet of his older brother, the mighty chancellor of Chartres.

The bald facts of Bernard of Chartres's career make a decidedly dry tale and yet, without doing violence to the facts, much more can be said or guessed at. Since Bernard died near the end of the first quarter of the twelfth century, it is reasonable to suppose that he was born circa 1060. He may have

Goliae, _Speculum_ 50 (1975) 208-209. On Bernard of Moëlan's career, see Häring, "Chartres and Paris Revisited," pp. 297-298. Ironically the _Histoire littéraire de la France_ vol. 13 (rpt. Paris, 1869), pp. 376-381 made the case that it was Bernard of Moëlan who was Thierry's brother.

[133] See Clerval, _Les écoles,_ p. 160; Southern, "Humanism," pp. 69 and 70 n.1; and D.E. Luscombe, _The School of Peter Abelard: The Influence of Abelard's Thought in the Early Scholastic Period,_ Cambridge Studies in Medieval Life and Thought, new series 14 (Cambridge, 1969), pp. 57-58. See also Châtillon, "Les écoles de Chartres et de Saint-Victor," p. 800 n.2, and [Thierry of Chartres], _The Latin Rhetorical Commentaries,_ ed. Fredborg, pp. 4-5.

been at Chartres for much of his life, but he only surfaces in written records during the episcopate of the great Ivo of Chartres. He was appointed *magister* by Bishop Ivo himself (d. 1115), who believed that bishops ought to employ masters of the liberal arts in their schools and whose obituary notice succinctly stated "Scolas fecit".[134] Nonetheless, Bernard's rise to high office at Chartres must have been painfully slow. Gilbert of Poitiers seems to have moved much faster up the ecclesiastical ladder than ever his master did.

The height of Bernard's teaching career was reached in the second decade of the twelfth century when he taught local boys the rudiments of Latin and lectured on texts such as the *Isagoge* of Porphyry and the *Timaeus* of Plato to more advanced students who had come to Chartres in order to study under him. Such were Gilbert of Poitiers, William of Conches, and Richard the Bishop. These men were doubtless attracted to Chartres by Bernard's fame, which we see reflected in Hugh of Saint Victor's reference to him as "sapiens quidam." Bernard offered these students not only the services of a superior grammarian, according to John of Salisbury, but also those of a Platonic philosopher, according to both John and Gilbert of Poitiers. The sheer excitement of studying with Bernard came from the feeling, as Gilbert suggested, that together they were unlocking the treasures of philosophy, hitherto hidden away in difficult texts. With the *lectio philosophorum* Bernard brought gifted students like William of Conches face to face with a series of ancient books that would forever after lie at the heart of their learning. His legacy to them was, in the end, a method for approaching texts, especially complex ones. A foundation in confident critical thinking was excellent preparation for European thinkers on the eve of the first substantial reception of recently translated ancient texts. William, for instance, never avoided newly available books, but confidently put them to good use when they came into his possession.

Bernard belongs to the time of the great masters of Europe, men who had acquired their knowledge slowly and carefully, whose manner was sober and upright, and whose teachings were weighty and demanded respect. The contemporaries of Bernard of Chartres are familiar names—Anselm of Laon, William of Champeaux, and Roscellin—but we know of only one contact with them, and it was not scholarly in nature. On 29 November 1119 master Bernard and William of Champeaux, then Bishop of Chalons-sur-Marne, together signed a document at Chartres drawn up by the chancellor Vulgrin.[135] Though the renowned masters of Bernard's day were under attack,

---

[134] Ivo, *Decretum* 4.214, PL 161: 311c10-D5. *Cartulaire de Notre-Dame de Chartres,* ed. Lépinois and Merlet, 3: 225, and Merlet and Clerval, *Un manuscrit,* p. 185.

[135] See the document cited in App. 2.1.D, which also contains: "Ego Willelmus, Cathalaunensis episcopus, subscripsi."

to use Abelard's martial language, no ambitious student seems to have sought to unseat the old master of Chartres.[136] Fortunately for Bernard, Abelard did not seek him out when he began his assault on the old magisterial tradition, since it is unlikely that Abelard would have been any kinder in Chartres than he had been in Paris and Laon. At the council of Soissons in 1121 Geoffrey, the bishop of Chartres, in rising to defend Abelard before the assembled bishops, granted that not only the fame of Abelard's masters, but even the fame of their own (and in his case this could only mean Bernard) had been eclipsed by Abelard, but then this praise of Abelard was preserved by none other than Abelard himself.[137] As far as we know, Bernard was relatively free of controversy in his career and his *Glosae* are not controversial. But, as we shall see, there is some suggestion in the *Metalogicon* that Bernard may have been forced at some later point in his career to clarify his Platonic language, especially where it seemed to compromise the omnipotence and eternity of God.

By the early 1120s Bernard's career was drawing to a close. The chancellorship of Chartres which he held by 1124 was the crowning achievement of a career, but he did not retain the office for very long and the record of his tenure is confined to the charters. Of these there are very few, a further indication that Bernard was chancellor for only several years. John of Salisbury and Bernard's own students do not seem to have thought of him as the chancellor of Chartres, but as the master of the school. Yet the fame of Bernard of Chartres, no matter how deeply he had impressed his students, was fragile. Had John of Salisbury not taken a sabbatical from his ecclesiastical duties in the late 1150s to write the *Metalogicon*,[138] we would know so little about Bernard of Chartres that he would scarcely warrant a footnote in histories of twelfth-century thought. But we need to go beyond the sparse facts, to pay tribute to the insightful character of John's sketch and to recognise, at the same time, that John's own considerable genius informs the portrait. To think for a moment about the image we would have of Socrates

---

[136] On the competitive nature of early twelfth-century cathedral schools in which ambitious students occasionally attempted to unseat their masters, see the case of Rupert of Deutz and his master Anselm of Laon in Chenu, *Nature, Man, and Society*, pp. 270-272; the case of Hugh of Marchiennes and his master Alberic of Rheims, in Southern, "The Schools of Paris and the School of Chartres," pp. 117-118; and finally on Abelard, see Peter Abelard, *Historia calamitatum*, ed. J.T. Muckle, in "Abelard's Letter of Consolation to a Friend (*Historia calamitatum*)," *Mediaeval Studies* 12 (1950) 176-182.

[137] *Historia calamitatum*, ed. Muckle, p. 194, that Abelard: "magistrorum tam suorum quam nostrorum famam maxime compressisse ... ."

[138] See Christopher Brooke, "John of Salisbury and His World," in *The World of John of Salisbury*, ed. Michael Wilks (Oxford, 1984), pp. 8-9.

if only Xenophon's account had survived is to grasp in miniature what Bernard's almost magical reputation owes to John of Salisbury.

Nevertheless, John seems to have thought that Bernard belonged to an age very different from his own, a quieter, less controversial time at the century's beginning. There is more than a little nostalgia in the *Metalogicon* when John turns to his description of Bernard in confident control of his classroom, lecturing and enlightening even the dullest of his charges. Yet in a way that John of Salisbury never suspected, since he looked back upon Bernard as a stalwart and conservative upholder of an older educational tradition, Bernard of Chartres was a watershed figure in the intellectual history of the Middle Ages. Though his learning belonged to the early Middle Ages and was the culmination of the careful study of texts that had been known for half a millennium, his method belonged to the twelfth century and marked a new approach to the *lectio philosophorum*.

The Glosae: *Character, Structure, and Style*

Turning to the *Glosae*, we should first ask in what form the work has been preserved. Is the *Glosae* only a *reportatio*, a student record of Bernard's lecture on the *Timaeus*, or is it a composition that came directly from Bernard's pen?

In dealing with medieval glosses we need to realise just how complicated their descent might be: the glossator might produce several versions of what were essentially his lecture notes, the master might begin the circulation of these or students might make their own copies, and lastly other students and scribes might alter and add to the received copy.[139] Despite the potential for a chaotic and complex tradition of glosses, the *Glosae* of Bernard of Chartres breaks down into two basic patterns of descent: the main manuscript tradition which began in the early twelfth century, and a score of dependent, but edited, sets of glosses (App. 3). The dependent glosses are neither as full nor as doctrinally consistent as the main manuscript tradition; nor do they establish anything like a single common text amongst themselves, but all look to the *Glosae* as if to a mother text. The *Glosae* is, moreover, a complete treatment of the *Timaeus*, having none of the gaps, confusions, or student interventions that one occasionally finds in *reportationes*.[140] It is both stylisti-

---

[139] See Anthony Kenny and Jan Pinborg, "Medieval Philosophical Literature," in *The Cambridge History of Later Medieval Philosophy from the Rediscovery of Aristotle to the Disintegration of Scholasticism, 1100-1600*, ed. Norman Kretzmann, Anthony Kenny, and Jan Pinborg (Cambridge, 1982), pp. 34-38, and Peter Dronke, "Thierry of Chartres," p. 364.

[140] See, for instance, the problems evident in the various extant versions of the glosses on

cally and doctrinally consistent; on occasion it refers readers back to
definitions given previously (see, for instance, 7.49). Important issues such
as the Platonic Ideas and *formae natiuae* are treated gradually and coherently
within the work as a whole. Moreover, the consistent use of a specific set of
glossing techniques throughout also argues for the hand of a single author.
In many ways the *Glosae* is a polished treatise, though it does retain
something of an oral or classroom style. Thus from three points of view—that
of textual transmission, doctrine, and methodology—it is likely that the
Glosae is a text that depends directly upon a particular set of lecture notes
on the *Timaeus* composed by Bernard of Chartres. It is unlikely that it was
the sole or even the fullest lecture that he ever gave on Plato, but it is the one
that began to circulate in his own time and that was associated, according to
the evidence of Tuilecnad, with his name.

That Bernard of Chartres was an author—in the early twelfth-century sense
of that word—should not surprise us. The old masters of Bernard's day—
Manegold of Lautenbach, Ivo of Chartres, William of Champeaux, and
Anselm of Laon—were all authors, but they do seem to have published in
different and sometimes less distinct ways than authors of the mid twelfth
century. Works of Manegold and William, for instance, have been identified,
but we are still unsure how much of Ivo's work was a product of his own
labour, and Anselm's *sententiae* have proved difficult to distinguish from the
general output of Laon.[141]

From John of Salisbury's statement, "Vt enim ait in expositione Porphirii"
(App. 2.5.C), Clerval and others have assumed that Bernard of Chartres
wrote a treatise on Porphyry.[142] But the matter is ambiguous, since John
might have meant either that in expounding on Porphyry Bernard had said
something which his teachers had informed him of, or that Bernard had
actually left a work of his explanations of Porphyry which he knew of or had
seen. Of the two possibilities, the former seems more likely. John rarely cites
the specific works of twelfth-century authors in the *Metalogicon* and, as we
have seen, compositions in Bernard's day, particularly glosses, often circu-

---

Juvenal attributed to William of Conches: in Guillaume de Conches, *Glosae in Iuvenalem*, ed.
Bradford Wilson, Textes philosophiques du Moyen Ages 18 (Paris, 1980), pp. 17-47.

[141] See above pp. 4 n. 8, 9 n. 23. See also Marcia L. Colish, "Another Look at the School
of Laon," *Archives d'histoire doctrinale et littéraire du Moyen Age* 53 (1986) 7-22.

[142] Clerval, *Les écoles*, pp. 248-254; Maurice de Wulf, *History of Mediaeval Philosophy*, vol.
1: *From the Beginnings to Albert the Great*, trans. Ernest C. Messenger (New York, 1926),
p.151; Max Manitius, *Geschichte der lateinischen Literatur des Mittelalters*, vol. 3: *vom
Ausbruch des Kirchenstreites bis zum Ende des zwölften Jahrhunderts* (Munich, 1931) 3: 197;
and Haijo Jan Westra, "Bernard of Chartres," in *Dictionary of the Middle Ages* (New York,
1983) 2: 190.

lated anonymously.[143] To repeat: it would have been surprising had John actually supplied the title of a work by Bernard, for it is doubtful if in his own time he could have identified any such writing. At the very least, John confirms what kind of work we should expect from Bernard, for the *expositio* in the technical sense was the explication of a text that followed on the *accessus*.[144] We should, therefore, expect Bernard to have been a practitioner of that art of close textual analysis which at Chartres was called the *glosa*.

William of Conches leads us to expect as much of one of his masters. In his glosses on Priscian, while clarifying the comprehensive nature of the *glosa*, he said:

> Primi enim magistri discipulos paterno affectu diligentes, quia non poterant in omnibus aliorum dubitationibus esse presentes, quaedam scripta illis composuerunt in quibus quicquid ab illis presentibus audirent, oculis aspicerent et que uice magistri consulerent. Nullus enim sibi sed aliis glosare debet.[145]

William here provides an argument for the necessity of masters to gloss texts, something that the first masters did out of love for their students, so that they might always assist them even when absent. Thus, William stressed the utility of the written gloss in theory, as we know he did in practice. These magisterial glosses were at the disposal not only of students, but of other masters. Yet one should note the tone that William strikes here, for these compositions of the first masters seem somehow more casual than his own. They were composed in a specific setting and answered the immediate needs of a master's own students first. These early glosses were not, it would seem, designed for wider publication, but were at once more immediate and more familiar, a kind of 'work in progress' on a particular text. Part of their meaning derived from the classroom setting in which they were composed and brought to bear on the analysis of a book, a context that William feared was being lost in his own time. He proceeded in his Priscian gloss to lament the breakdown in the relationship in his day between masters and students.[146]

---

[143] But see the rare mention in *Metalogicon* 4.3, ed. Webb, p. 167.18-20: "quo quidem uitio Anglicus noster Adam michi pre ceteris uisus est laborasse in Libro quem Artem Disserendi inscripsit."

[144] See G. Paré, A. Brunet, P. Tremblay, *La renaissance du XIIe siècle: les écoles et l'enseignement*, Publications de l'Institut d'Etudes Médiévales d'Ottawa 3 (Paris, 1933), pp. 113-119.

[145] Edited in Jeauneau, *Lectio*, p. 347.

[146] "Sed nos miseri magistri, quid in districto examine dicturi sumus, qui nostras lectiones, uel nouitate uerborum uel ordine, ut discipuli parum uel nichil intelligant, turbamus, quod illis proficiat nichil scribimus uel, quando scribimus, decisse obscure hoc facimus, uel ut paruos diu circa nos ad ostensionem pompe retineamus? Inde duo mala proueniunt. Aliquando enim propter nostre doctrine obscuritatem artes odio habent. Quidam enim quibus est innatus amor sciendi ad illud tarde et cum summo labore perueniunt, ad quod, si diligenter legeremus

He believed that masters had grown too novel and prolix in their language
and method to be understood by many; now they only confused their
students. The schools in which the glosses of the first masters had been
meaningful had, in this way, lost their purpose. William may have wondered
if the *glosa* form suited the new age in which he found himself, but he seems
to have looked back with some warmth on an earlier time when masters and
students were bound together by their love for each other and the common
bond of the gloss by which their attention was firmly fixed on the text at hand
in the classroom.

Bernard too, in the *Glosae* stresses that it was love and friendship that had
allowed Calcidius to overcome the difficult task of working on the *Timaeus*,
but he refers his students to the liberal arts of the trivium and quadrivium as
those which strengthen a man (2.35-38). Though he has nothing to say on
the subject of the *glosa* proper, he does note that Calcidius, after translating
the *Timaeus*, had commented on it, "non ubique nec continue, sed ubi opus
fuit" (2.6-7), which recalls William's own criticism of commentators in the
prologue to his *Timaeus* glosses.[147] Bernard seems to imply that one of the
reasons he has taken up the *Glosae* is to treat systematically of the whole of
the translated *Timaeus*. Calcidius' commentary was not sufficient, since it
was neither comprehensive nor systematic. Behind this thinking lay the
Chartrian idea of the superiority of the *glosa* over all other forms of textual
commentary, for, as William repeatedly said, the *glosa* is more comprehensive.[148] It treats both the individual words (the *littera*) and the deeper
meaning (*sententia*) of a text, whereas glossators, sticking too closely to the
text, had either been too cursory in simple matters or too obscure in deep
ones, and commentators had served sense alone, not treating the text
thoroughly. This new and richer Chartrian conception of the *glosa* genre
should not be confused with a tradition of sparser and less structured glosses
that had dominated in the previous century.

Bernard's theory of *ingenium* (see App. 2.3.C) is the best illustration of
the *glosa*'s advantages. There were, he thought, three kinds of intellectual
abilities: one that flits about on high, but can hold on to nothing firmly; one
at the bottom that can rise to nothing important and so can make no
advancement; and one in the middle that can both hold on to something

---

et scriberemus, cito et sine difficultate erant peruenturi." Edited in Jeauneau, *Lectio*, p. 347.
On the passage and its possible Cornifician context, see J.O. Ward, "The Date of the
Commentary," pp. 236-237. On William of Conches's attitude towards masters and students,
see Jeauneau, *Lectio*, pp. 356-357.

[147] *Glose Willelmi de Conchis super Platonem* 1.prol., ed. Jeauneau, p. 58. For the text, see
above p. 3.

[148] See Jeauneau, *Lectio*, pp. 346-349.

firmly and yet rise to important things. Only the middle way, Bernard thought, could lead to steady progress and its practice was most suitable for those philosophising. This is just the kind of theory that must have been behind the Chartrian justification of the comprehensive *glosa*. If commentators had soared too high above their texts and simple glossators had become too mired in the *littera*, the practitioner of the Chartrian *glosa* pursued a middle way which joined the best of both traditions. His work was grounded in a specific text, which he treated systematically and comprehensively, but within the structure of the *glosa* form he was able to rise to the discussion of more important matters. There is good reason to think that in the *Glosae* we have one of the first and formative uses of this comprehensive *glosa* type at Chartres.

As a genre the *glosa* reached its fullest development at Chartres in the mid twelfth century and received from Bernard and William of Conches its theoretical underpinnings. In their devotion to old and profound books, glossators were committed to an expression of cultural continuity and their glosses are essentially conservative in character. Bernard's dwarfs and giants metaphor affirms explicitly what the *glosa* genre conveys implicitly: that true learning is cumulative and that the great thinkers of the past deserve an abiding respect. Indeed glosses became such a popular instrument of higher learning at the end of the early Middle Ages, because they belonged to the genre that was best suited to the intensive explication of the few philosophical books that were available. The rules for studying treatises change, in other words, if one has only twenty significant books to read over and over again and not two hundred; if the former situation leads to the detailed glosses of William of Conches on a handful of books in the twelfth century, the latter leads to the synthetic *summae* of Thomas Aquinas in the thirteenth. Ironically, the intensive attention to a delimited body of writings in the early twelfth century may have given rise to the dialectical spirit of Abelard's *Sic et non* and Ivo of Chartres's collections of sorted canons.[149]

The *Glosae* is strictly speaking a literal commentary,[150] though Bernard and William would have thought of it more particularly as an example of the comprehensive *glosa*. From a codicological viewpoint, that is, how the work appears on the actual page, the manuscript tradition of the *Glosae* is in the form of what I have called a lemmatic commentary: the *Glosae* is not, in other

---

[149] See Richard McKeon, "The Organization of Sciences and the Relations of Cultures in the Twelfth and Thirteenth Centuries," in *The Cultural Context of Medieval Learning*, ed. J.E. Murdoch and E.D. Sylla, Boston Studies in the Philosophy of Science 26 (Dordrecht, 1975), p. 166 and the discussion that followed, as recorded on pp. 184-186.

[150] See Kenny and Pinborg, "Medieval Philosophical Literature," pp. 29-30.

words, written alongside the *Timaeus* in its margins and between the lines of the text, but stands on its own with lemmata excerpted from the *Timaeus* to indicate the word or passage being glossed. The archetype of the *Glosae* was probably in this form as well, since no copy exists in which the *Glosae* consists of marginal or interlinear glosses attached to a copy of the *Timaeus.* The reader or student needed, therefore, to have a copy of the *Timaeus* before him in order to employ the *Glosae*, for it was essentially an aid to understanding the text. In his use of lemmata, Bernard frequently changed the text of the *Timaeus* in minor ways to suit the needs of his own exposition. In place of the enclitic *-que*, for example, he generally substitutes *et* (which will be found italicised in the edition). Occasionally he changes the case of the word being glossed in order to satisfy the grammatical needs of his own sentence (these are not italicised in the edition: see, for instance 3.43, 6.179, and 8.428-429). Sometimes the entire word order of a sentence was altered so that he might gloss certain words in a particular sequence.[151] Bernard did not mind, as the author of a modern dictionary might, reworking the words from a sentence of the *Timaeus* in order to explain that sentence, because he was attempting to demonstrate both what the sentence meant and how it worked as a grammatical unit. Frequently he also reuses words from a prior sentence of the *Timaeus* to explain the present one (these words from already glossed passages are not italicised, since properly speaking they are no longer lemmata). Whatever we may think of the circularity of this kind of glossing, its purpose was to heighten the student's awareness of continuity in the text as new glosses fell back on old ones and the Platonic vocabulary already acquired was reinforced. These careful interweavings of words from the Latin *Timaeus* with Bernard's glosses and the new lemmata must have given students a sense of growing familiarity with the *Timaeus* ; each passage was designed to be the teacher of the next.

In structure, the *Glosae* can be divided into three main sections: the front matter, which contains the *accessus* and the glosses on Calcidius' letter; the glosses on the first book of the *Timaeus*; and the glosses on the second. The glosses on each book can, in turn, be divided into three essential units, so that the structure and size of the *Glosae* can be schematised as follows:

	WORD COUNT	
STRUCTURE OF THE *'GLOSAE'*	BERNARD'S	LEMMATA
1. Accessus	613	
2. Glosae super prooemium Calcidii	571	118

---

[151] See, for instance, *Glosae* 2.43 where W5:10-11 was changed from "Et quamquam ipse hoc cum facilius tum commodius facere posses" into "*Et quamquam facere posses facilius* ex sapientia, *commodius* ex gratia ... ."

Glosarum super Timaeum Platonis liber primus

3. Recapitulatio Socratis et Narratio Critiae	2402	338
4. De constitutione mundi	3511	492
5. De anima mundi	3408	514

Glosarum super Timaeum Platonis liber secundus

6. De quattuor generibus animalium	2461	376
7. De humano corpore	3896	680
8. De primordiali materia	3926	686
	20788	3204

23992

Though there are no section titles present in the *Glosae*, the divisions are justified by the substantial breaks in the *Glosae* and the introductions provided to each section by Bernard.

Bernard seems to have been the first medieval glossator to have employed this basic division of topics in the *Timaeus*. Calcidius' commentary, in contrast, possessed twenty-seven topical titles, only thirteen of which are actually treated in his study.[152] There is a certain symmetry to Bernard's presentation of the *Glosae*, as each book of glosses is balanced by three topically discrete units. The sizes of these give us a rough idea of Bernard's interests, for though the *Recapitulatio Socratis et Narratio Critiae* occupies a quarter of the Latin *Timaeus*, it receives just over a tenth of Bernard's glosses. The *De primordiali materia* part of the Latin *Timaeus*, on the other hand, occupies approximately one sixth of the dialogue, but receives one fifth of the total glosses. Bernard was more interested in explaining the philosophical issues raised by the *Timaeus* than in treating its mythological and historical material. He shows little interest in such puzzling matters as the myth of Atlantis. Section 3, in fact, has more than its fair share of simple glosses, but this may be due to a greater concentration of unusual names and events in *Timaeus* 17a-27b.

But if the structure of the *Glosae* is basically symmetrical, what happened to the front matter? Here there are only two sections, though one might have expected three. What seems to be lacking is a prologue by the author. Such a prologue exists in the first position in William's set of glosses, thus giving his work the perfectly symmetrical appearance of three sets of three. It is not impossible that the *Glosae* originally had such a structure as well and that Tuilecnad knew Bernard's name because he had seen an extra bit of front

---

[152] See Cal., *Comm.* 7 (W60:4-61:9).

matter in his copy of the *Glosae*. But the material at the front of a codex—title
page, prologue, and preface—was always vulnerable to destruction and
damage. Only three of the eight manuscripts of William's glosses employed
by Jeauneau in his edition retained the prologue.[153] Thus, it may be that the
early copy of the *Glosae* from which all the manuscript copies descend had
already lost a prologue and perhaps title page, or it may be, given the
tendency to circulate glosses anonymously, that they simply never existed. In
either case, it was Bernard's structured approach to the *Timaeus* that William
of Conches adopted.

The *Accessus ad Timaeum* of Bernard of Chartres is shorter than William's
and not as concerned with categories of causes and branches of philosophy,[154] but it is not unsophisticated in its own right. Bernard begins with an
opening statement in which he treats the standard topics of the *accessus*—
materia, intentio, modus, and *utilitas*—but does not name them (1.1-39).[155]
His language here is thick with allusions to Calcidius, Cicero, Horace, and
Boethius. At 1.40-43, for any who might have missed the *accessus* topics
buried in his opening statement, Bernard summarises, this time supplying the
appropriate terms. Next (1.44-55) he considers two other opinions about the
principal subject matter of the *Timaeus,* for some think it is the administra-
tion of the state, and support their position with reference to Macrobius,
while others hold that it is the generation of the sensible world.

For Bernard, the principal subject matter of the *Timaeus* is natural justice.
Indeed, the *Glosae* stands very near the start of that rather intense twelfth-

---

[153] See *Glose Willelmi de Conchis super Platonem* 1.prol., ed. Jeauneau, pp. 57-58. Of the
three partial copies of the *Glose Willelmi de Conchis super Platonem* discovered in Czechoslo-
vakia by Jeauneau only one contains the prologue: see Jeauneau, "Plato apud Bohemos," pp.
189-196. Nor does the fragment from Salamanca, Biblioteca Universitaria MS 2322, fols.
190v-191r contain the prologue: see Paul Edward Dutton and James Hankins, "An Early
Manuscript of William of Conches' *Glosae super Platonem*," *Mediaeval Studies* 47 (1985)
487-494.
[154] *Glose Willelmi de Conchis super Platonem* 2-6, ed. Jeauneau, pp. 58-62. On the *accessus
ad auctores*, see Edwin A. Quain, "The Medieval *Accessus ad auctores*," *Traditio* 3 (1945)
215-264, esp. 243-254; R.W. Hunt, "The Introductions to the 'Artes' in the Twelfth Century,"
in *Studia mediaevalia in honorem admodum reverendi patris Raymundi Joseph Martin ordinis
praedicatorum S. theologiae magistri LXXum natalem diem agentis* (Bruges, 1948), pp.
85-112 and rpt. in R.W. Hunt, *The History of Grammar in the Middle Ages: Collected Papers*,
ed. G.L. Bursill-Hall (Amsterdam, 1980), pp. 117-144; *Accessus ad auctores. Bernard
d'Utrecht, Conrad d'Hirsau, Dialogus super auctores*, ed. R.B.C. Huygens (Leiden, 1970); J.O.
Ward, "The Date of the Commentary," pp. 247-261; and Edouard Jeauneau, "Gloses et
commentaires de textes philosophiques (IXᵉ-XIIᵉ s.)," in *Les genres littéraires dans les sources
théologiques et philosophiques médiévales: définition, critique, et exploitation: Actes du Colloque
international de Louvain-la-Neuve, 25-27 mai 1981* (Louvain-la-Neuve, 1982), pp. 121-122.
[155] On various examples of the *accessus ad Timaeum*, see Gregory, *Platonismo medievale*,
pp. 59-73.

century interest in the definition of justice, both natural and positive.[156] Natural justice, according to Bernard, was made manifest in the just *constitutio mundi*; that is, in the just arrangement of worldly parts and the proper separation of celestial and non-celestial things (1.32-39). Out of love the creator gave to each part of his creation what naturally (or properly) belonged to it (1.35-36); here Bernard gives the classical definition of justice (1.11) a cosmic twist. The very foundation (*fons et origo*: 1.22) of positive or human justice was, therefore, grounded in the natural justice of divine dispensation. After the creation of mankind, the creator promoted virtuous behaviour among men, especially in the first age when natural justice flourished. Even now, Bernard says, the creator urges us to take up natural justice (1.36-39). In contrast with this extended treatment of the *materia* of the *Timaeus*, William of Conches said simply that the subject matter of the *Timaeus* was "naturalis iusticia uel creatio mundi."[157]

Next (1.56-63) Bernard considers what parts of philosophy the *Timaeus* belongs to. In its different aspects he thinks the dialogue concerns ethics, logic, and physics. This Stoic division of the fields of philosophy, perhaps derived from Augustine, was later repeated by Gilbert of Poitiers and John of Salisbury, though not by William of Conches.[158] Since, for Bernard, the *Timaeus* touches on almost all the arts, it is a work designed not for beginners, but for those already far along in the study of the quadrivium (1.60-62).

If we are to believe the report of one of William's students, William later expanded this introductory statement of the branches of philosophy treated by a book to include the philosopher himself (App. 2.5.F).[159] Bernard apparently rejected the notion that an author like Plato could be subsumed in a part of philosophy. It was simply not an issue that applied to authors since they themselves were not parts of philosophy and did not treat philosophy in terms of its parts. This, Bernard must have felt, is the task of the glossator as he objectively analyses a work after its composition. In the *Glosae* Bernard holds to this position and names only the parts of philosophy that the *Timaeus* touches upon. But, then, this too was generally William's

---

[156] See Stern Gagnér, *Studien zur Ideengeschichte der Gesetzgebung* (Uppsala, 1960), pp. 210-267.

[157] *Glose Willelmi de Conchis super Platonem* 3, ed. Jeauneau, p. 59.17-18.

[158] Augustine, *De civitate dei* 8.4, ed. B. Dombart and A. Kalb, Corpus christianorum: Series Latina 47 (Turnhout, 1955), pp. 219-220. See also James A. Weisheipel, "The Nature, Scope, and Classification of the Sciences," in *Science in the Middle Ages*, ed. David C. Lindberg (Chicago, 1978), p. 469. And see below p. 63 and n. 193.

[159] On this passage, see Guillaume de Conches, *Glosae in Iuvenalem, Accessus ab auctore incerto*, ed. Bradford Wilson, pp. 28-29 and J.O. Ward, "The Date of the Commentary," p. 248 n.79.

practice, even in the *Glosae in Iuuenalem* where the student's report occurs.[160] There is one noticeable difference between the two authors in their treatment of the *accessus*: Bernard holds off his consideration of the title of the work until he glosses the first use of the name Timaeus in the dialogue (3.12-20), whereas William advances it to the *accessus* proper.[161]

Bernard glosses the dialogue in a regular pattern that moves from the general to the specific.[162] At each important passage or main break in the text of the *Timaeus*, he begins with a general commentary in which he surveys the main issues about to be treated by Plato. These commentaries are often, though not always, introduced with a lemma so that the reader or student might find the proper place to begin reading in the *Timaeus*. Next the glossator descends to a consideration of the continuity of the passage, its links with what has preceded and with what will follow. These connecting glosses are frequently introduced by the word *Continuatio*, but occasionally by other connectives such as *Vel sic continua*, *Vel sic*, and *Quod uero sic incipit*.[163] Finally the glossator turns to a consideration of sentences, phrases, and individual words. This more detailed examination of passages generally begins with the formula *Et hoc est*, a shortened form of *Et hoc est quod ait*, which brings the glossator down to the level of the words in the treatise. If the passage does not need to be linked with what has preceded, as in the opening gloss on Calcidius' letter (2.1-11), Bernard moves directly from his introductory comment to the formula *Et hoc est*. In individual glosses the use of *Et hoc est* at the end of an analysis often has a probative function, returning the reader or student from the glossator's interpretation to Plato's own words.

Though this method of glossing texts has ancient roots,[164] Bernard of Chartres may have helped to systematise it. Jeauneau thought, for instance, that the use of the *Continuatio* and *Et hoc est* formulae was so characteristic of William of Conches's style of glossing that it was a strong argument in favour of attributing the *Glosae super Priscianum* to him.[165] Thus, William once again reveals his indebtedness to Bernard of Chartres, this time for the basic tools of the glossator. Bernard's system of glossing belongs to the Chartrian development of the comprehensive *glosa*, for it combines the

---

[160] *Glosae in Iuvenalem, Accessus ab auctore incerto*, ed. Wilson, pp. 89-91.

[161] *Glose Willelmi de Conchis super Platonem* 6, ed. Jeauneau, p. 62.

[162] See, in general, Jeauneau, "Gloses et commentaires," pp. 122-126.

[163] For examples of *Continuatio*, see 4.5; 4.62; 4.121; 4.133; 4.245; 5.29; 5.86; 5.278; 6.210; 7.35; 7.417. For *Vel sic continua*, see 4.241; for *Vel sic*, see 4.376; and for *Quod uero sic incipit*, see 3.21.

[164] See Jeauneau, "Gloses et commentaires," pp. 123-124.

[165] Jeauneau, *Lectio*, pp. 340-342.

commentator's interest in the general sense of the treatise with the glossator's attention to details that might otherwise confuse students. Calcidius had commented, as Bernard says, "nec ubique nec continue."

Other technical phrases are employed by Bernard in the *Glosae*. The most common of these is *Quasi diceret*—and its abridgement *Quasi*—by which the glossator denotes a statement that could be substituted for the one being glossed. The glossator strives to be faithful to Plato's meaning in these substitutions. But the fact that he several times emphasises his agreement with a specific substitution should alert us to the possibility that he did not always concur (see 3.70-72). *Bene dicit* is a phrase employed to mark the glossator's acceptance of a particular expression of Plato as translated by Calcidius (see 4.92, 7.423, and 8.134). In drawing inferences, Bernard used expressions such as *Conclusio extra* (4.91) and *Illatio talis est* (5.250). Repetition in the dialogue was noted by *Repetitio* and *Ideo repetit* (see 4.105 and 4.210). When he wished to indicate other interpretations of a passage, or perhaps that he was unsure of the correct interpretation, he frequently used such phrases as *Vel sic, Vel ita, Vel aliter, Aliter*, and *e conuerso* to introduce the second of these explanations. Many of these technical formulae are to be found not only in William of Conches's glosses, but also in those of Gilbert of Poitiers.

From a methodological standpoint the most interesting development in the *Glosae* is the emergence of an incipient *Quaestio* form of disputation.[166] Phrases such as *ne quis contenderet* and *ne quis uellet* suggest that Bernard had begun to anticipate the difficulties and questions of students and to answer them in his glosses. *Obicitur, Potest quaeri, Sed potest quaeri, sed tunc quaeretur*, and *sed opponitur* are answered in the *Glosae* by *R<espondendum>* and *Ad quod r<espondendum>*. Once *Sed potest quaeri* is answered by a sentence that begins with *Patet*.[167] Four of these instances are located in the *Tractatus de primordiali materia* of the last section of the glosses where Bernard takes great pains to clarify positions, including his own. Thus, Bernard in his classroom at Chartres may stand close to the beginning of a tradition of the scholastic question-and-answer method that was to figure so prominently in the universities of the next century. On the development of this critical approach to texts in the twelfth century, Chenu said:

> Henceforth the professor, as *lector*, would not only be an exegete, but a master who, according to the usage which developed, "determined" the questions. To

[166] On the origins, development, and importance of this pedagogic technique, see Martin Grabmann, *Die Geschichte der scholastischen Methode* 2 vols. (1909-1911; rpt. Graz, 1957), esp. 1: 234-257; Chenu, *Nature, Man, and Society*, pp. 291-300; Kenny and Pinborg, "Medieval Philosophical Literature," pp. 24-26.

[167] See 4.52-53; 7.215-220; 8.11-13; 8.264-265; 8.276; and 8.298-305.

do this, he no longer marshaled old authorities who left one's understanding empty—even if obedient and confident—but he searched out and displayed "reasons" that got to the root of things ... . The masters of Chartres, readers of the *auctores*, of the *Timaeus*, of Boethius, of the Bible, were surely the ones who got the new method going.[168]

Perhaps at Chartres in the first decade of the twelfth century, as Ivo established the comparative topics for his collection of canon law texts and Bernard began to ask questions about the *Timaeus*, a more systematic kind of disputation was being born. Indeed, in the debate about whether the *disputatio* method derived from the canonistic treatment of texts or from the *lectio philosophorum*, we should probably reconsider the case of Chartres under the influence of Ivo and Bernard where the two traditions were complementary.[169] The specialness of this scholastic development, even if the first steps were hesitant ones, should not be underestimated.[170]

What must lie behind the questioning that begins to surface in the *Glosae* is the cathedral school. One senses that a classroom of *auditores* was the real audience of Bernard's *Timaeus* glosses. He must stop from time to time, for instance, to specify where he is in the text: "Vel ibi incipe uersum *multo maior*" he says at one point (7.40) and in another he is forced to warn his students that he has had to jump ahead in the text (4.260). His style is made more immediate by the frequent omission of *est* and *sunt* and, indeed, by the incomplete sentences that were always a part of the glossator's method. Imperatives fill the *Glosae*, particularly *Nota* and *Et nota*, but others such as *intellige* (2.37-38; 5.205), *accipe, recte accipe, Hic accipe* (4.11, 5.204, 5.379), *hoc refer* (2.38), *Sic construe* (6.73), and *Sic lege litteram* (7.351) abound. Gentler subjunctives such as *consideres* (3.34) and *Videamus* (4.262) work to engage the attention of the student or reader. Finally questions are put to students throughout, such as *Et unde hoc?* (2.27) and *Quibus?* (3.128). The overall impression created by these stylistic features is of a set of glosses that is less polished than William's, but is in some ways livelier. It was William himself who had suggested that the works of the first masters had been more casual, for they had belonged to a tight circle of master and students.

[168] Chenu, *Nature, Man, and Society*, pp. 292-293.
[169] See esp. Grabmann, *Die Geschichte der scholastischen Methode*, 1: 240-246 and Kenny and Pinborg, "Medieval Philosophical Literature," p. 26.
[170] Here I would disagree with Wetherbee's comment in "Philosophy, Cosmology, and the Twelfth-Century Renaissance," p. 33: "Bernard of Chartres, in many ways the father of the group, has been called the last of the Carolingian grammarians, and in what we know of his teaching there is little that differs from the methods of glossing curriculum authors that had been used by Eriugena and Remigius of Auxerre."

Bernard's concern with the moral development of boys in the *Glosae* may also reflect the preoccupation of a pedagogue. Five times in his discussion of the newly incarnated soul (43a-b), Bernard talks about boys, drawing a parallel between their immaturity and the inexperienced nature of the new soul.[171] The new soul is drawn to form false opinions, he says, just as a boy often thinks that to touch a piece of charcoal will bring good luck or bad (7.19-20).[172] Boys, trusting too much in their senses, like the immature soul, believe that the best things are those that please them (7.111-112). Ever the Platonist, Bernard sought to lead minds away from overmuch reliance on the senses, just as he must have tried to remind the boys of Chartres who passed under his care that there were higher things than sensual pleasures.

The road that led beyond the entanglement of sensual pleasure, at least at Chartres, was Bernard's *disciplina*, his special system of instruction. Hence the student who wrote home to his father for more money spoke of being "sub disciplina domini magistri Bernhardi" (App. 2.4.F). From the so-called Six Keys, described as "De disciplina" by Hugh of Saint-Victor, we have a good idea of the essential desiderata of Bernard's educational philosophy: a humble mind, a desire to learn, a tranquil life, silent scrutiny, freedom from riches, and a foreign land (App. 2.2.A). The true lover of *intellectus et disciplina*, according to Bernard, was one who loved to teach in the hope of being fully understood (7.351-352). The methodical manner in which he daily lectured the students of Chartres on the rudiments of Latin casts another light on Bernard's science of instruction (App. 2.4.A). The moral values that Bernard sought to inculcate in his hearers may have derived directly from Christianity, but they were reinforced by the central tenets of his Platonic metaphysics.

For Bernard the relationship of Socrates and Plato was one of *magister* and *discipulus*. We need to remember that, since Bishop Fulbert's time, Socrates had been a much admired figure at Chartres.[173] Bernard speculates that the dialogue had been named after Timaeus because Plato had not wished to attach his own name to the book, lest he seem to go against or even

---

[171] In addition to the cases discussed here, see also 7.29-30 and 7.38-42.

[172] A point made by the Pseudo-Bede and echoed by the Third Vatican Mythographer seems related, but different: see Pseudo-Bede, *De mundi celestis terrestrisque constitutione*, ed. and trans. Charles Burnett, Warburg Institute Surveys and Texts 10 (London, 1985), p. 60: "Quod patet in stultitia puerorum qui carbone lucente lesi decipiuntur."

[173] Early in the eleventh century, Adelman of Liége had spoken of the school of Chartres and Fulbert in these terms: "In academia Carnotensi sub nostro illo uenerabili Socrate ... ": see PL 143: 1289A. On the reputation of Socrates in the late ancient and early medieval worlds, see Ilona Opelt, "Das Bild des Sokrates in der christlichen lateinischen Literatur," in *Platonismus und Christentum: Festschrift für Heinrich Dörrie*, ed. H.D. Blume and F. Mann, Jahrbuch für Antike und Christentum 10 (Münster, 1983), pp. 192-207.

be preferred to his master Socrates. With his public reverence for Socrates still intact, therefore, Plato assumed the place of his disciple *Timaeus* who was not really up to the challenge of undertaking the discourse (3.15-18). Again when trying to account for the missing fourth person, the one who had been present at the previous day's conversation, Bernard mentions that some think that the fourth was Plato himself who had withdrawn out of respect for his master, so that no one might believe that he preferred himself to Socrates if he supplied what his master could not in the discussion (3.40-42). William of Conches interestingly follows Bernard in neither of these explanations,[174] but for Bernard the relationship of Socrates and Plato was an exemplary one grounded, as he says, "reuerentia magistri Socratis."

Yet Bernard's attitude towards authority is not altogether what one would expect from an early twelfth-century master.[175] He does not generally speak of authority and quotes few such authorities in his set of glosses. On one occasion he seems rather arbitrarily to invoke Augustine as an authority on the nature of unformed matter or hyle: "Cum ergo auctoritas dicat eam esse informem et neget esse corpus, sic accipe." (8.278-279) Almost immediately, however, he qualifies this statement, since he proceeds to argue that hyle can be called, in a certain sense, a body. Bernard's attitude, which he perhaps perceived in Plato's own use of authorities, is that great authorities deserve a hearing (see 6.94-95). To be sure, Plato is the highest authority in the *Glosae*, but we find in Bernard none of the adulation of Plato, of "nos Platonem diligentes," that is in William's books.[176] Bernard is all business when it comes to analysing the text at hand. On a matter where Plato and Macrobius might be at odds, or at least where Macrobius claimed more than Plato did, he does not state that Plato is right: "Sed sufficiat interim ea quam Plato docet." (4.286-287) With Calcidius who did not have the status of *auctor*, but commentator, he was prepared to disagree openly (see, for instance, 8.254-259).

Bernard was also ready, on some of the social issues raised early in the *Timaeus*, to disagree with Plato or, at least, to interpret him favourably despite the apparent meaning of the text. Bernard notes that certain of Socrates' proposals for the republic are called remarkable, because no one,

---

[174] See *Glose Willelmi de Conchis super Platonem* 6, ed. Jeauneau, p. 62, and 13, p.72.

[175] On authority, see M.D. Chenu, *La théologie au douzième siècle* 3rd ed., Etudes de philosophie médiévale 45 (Paris, 1976), pp. 353-357 and Nikolaus Häring, "*Auctoritas* in der sozialen und intellektuellen Struktur des zwölften Jahrhunderts," in *Soziale Ordnungen im Selbstverständnis des Mittelalters*, 2 vols., ed. A. Zimmermann, Miscellanea Mediaevalia 12 (Berlin, 1980) 2: 517-533.

[176] *Glose Willelmi de Conchis super Platonem* 119, ed. Jeauneau, p. 211.

for instance, believes that soldiers lack possessions (3.75-76). It was, however, the doctrine of the community of women and children that most deeply disturbed Bernard.[177] He thinks that this proposal, whereby women would be held in common and children would not know the identity of their parents, is neither a just nor honest arrangement of the republic (3.76-81):

> Dicamus igitur per inuolucrum hoc esse dictum: quod innuit, dicens contra *consuetudinem* hoc dici. Quando enim egit Socrates *de communibus nuptiis et de communi prole*, aliud dixit et aliud intendit. Ac si diceret, non accipio istud in re carnaliter, sed in sola affectione, remota turpitudine ... . (3.81-85)

The notion that Socrates said one thing and meant another—which is not an unfair description of the experimental programme announced in the *Republic*—is for Bernard a way of reconciling Plato with his own beliefs about society: "Haec ordinatio ad litteram potest intelligi, et etiam ad integumentum" (3.94-95). Thus, through the use of the Chartrian techniques of *inuolucrum* and *integumentum*, Bernard was prepared to look beyond the simple letter of the text and its apparent meaning to the deeper truths taught by Plato. Though the words *inuolucrum*, *integumentum*, and *fabula* are used sparingly in the *Glosae*,[178] they were to have such an extensive fortune in the twelfth century that it is interesting to find them used so early and in a manner consistent with other Chartrian texts.[179] If Bernard was prepared to give Plato the benefit of the doubt in interpreting his seemingly radical social scheme, he was not blind to its implications. He would only accept the idea of a community built on common affection, not common lust as the one proposed by Socrates seemed to promote. Here Bernard aligned himself with the doctrines of the prelates of the church and, perhaps mistakenly, invoked Augustine to support his position (3.87-88). Both Abelard and William of

---

[177] On this theme in twelfth-century authors, see Stephan Kuttner, "Gratian and Plato," in *Church and Government in the Middle Ages: Essays Presented to C.R. Cheney on his 70th Birthday*, ed. C.N.L. Brooke, D.E. Luscombe, G.H. Martin, and Dorothy Owen (Cambridge, 1976), pp. 93-118, esp. 107-108. The article was reprinted in Kuttner, *The History of Ideas and Doctrines of Canon Law in the Middle Ages* (London, 1980).

[178] For *per inuolucrum*, see 3.1; 3.81-82; 5.50; and 5.180. For *ad* and *per integumentum*, see 3.94-95; 5.34; and 5.126. For *fabula*, see 3.154 and 6.134. Note, by way of comparison, that William of Conches in his glosses on Plato does not use *inuolucrum*, but does employ *integumentum* ten times, seven of those when dealing with the world soul: see Southern, *Platonism, Scholastic Method, and the School of Chartres*, p. 22 n.26.

[179] See Jeauneau, *Lectio*, pp. 125-192; Peter Dronke, *Fabula*; Haijo Jan Westra, ed., *The Commentary on Martianus Capella's 'De nuptiis'*, pp. 23-33; Wetherbee, "Philosophy, Cosmology, and the Twelfth-Century Renaissance," pp. 32-37; and Tullio Gregory, "The Platonic Inheritance," in *A History of Twelfth-Century Western Philosophy*, ed. Peter Dronke (Cambridge, 1988), pp. 57-61.

Conches similarly rejected Socrates' proposal, if he really meant to encourage sexual promiscuity.[180]

Bernard looked upon the *Timaeus* as a moral text, one that taught ethics (1.56-57). Again the twelfth century's image of Socrates looms large here, for from Augustine's *De civitate dei* they had learned that Socrates was the inventor of ethics and the first moral philosopher.[181] The chief matter of the *Timaeus* is, as Bernard claims in his *accessus*, natural justice, which teaches one to show respect towards God and greater ones, piety towards parents, and love towards loved ones (1.13-14). Indeed, natural justice, which is common to both God and man, proceeds from love (1.16-17) and God's very justice towards man arises from his love (1.35-36). Plato's intention in the *Timaeus* is precisely to instruct us in the practice of natural justice (1.40-42). All good fortune, both inner and outer, according to Bernard, comes from virtue, which makes impossible things possible (2.16-22). There are, throughout the *Glosae*, numerous references to the vices and virtues, which Bernard seeks to understand in terms of the operating principles of the world. There is, in short, a moral purpose enmeshed in the very structure of things. The seven principal vices as irrational motions of the soul, for instance, are related to the irregular motions of the seven planets (5.215-222). Thus the ability to see is essential to morality:

> Ad quae uisus est necessarius, quia per uisum notamus rationabilem motum aplanos, qui et se ipsum mouet sine errore et planetarum erraticos motus contemperat. Quod notantes debemus aplanon nostrae mentis ita instituere, ut se ipsum sine errore moueat et erroneos motus uitiorum refrenet, quae morum correctio ualet in publicis et priuatis rebus. (7.389-394)

Our mind is a firmament that should be ordered like the cosmos, in order to avoid the irrational motions of the vices and to lead to the reform of our morals in public and private life. Hearing too was given to man so that through music our morals might be reformed (7.438-443). Although Bernard was never able to read *Timaeus* 90a-d, here he seems to have intuited from what he did know of the dialogue (47c-d) Plato's final moving

---

[180] See Abelard, *Theologia christiana* 2.46-48, ed. Buytaert, pp. 150-151 and *Glose Willelmi de Conchis super Platonem* 18, ed. Jeauneau, p. 78. See also Tullio Gregory, "Abélard et Platon," *Studi Medievali* ser. 3a, 13 (1972) 539-562.

[181] Augustine, *De civitate dei* 8.3, ed. Dombart and Kalb, pp. 218-219. See also Conrad d'Hirsau, *Dialogus super auctores* 1793-1795, ed. Huygens, in *Accessus ad auctores*, p. 129; Hugh of Saint-Victor, *Didascalicon* 3.2, ed. Buttimer, p. 50; Abelard, *Theologia christiana* 2.3, ed. Buytaert, p. 145; and John of Salisbury, *Policraticus* 7.5, ed. Webb, 2: 105.12-16. And see Gagnér, *Studien zur Ideengeschichte*, pp. 213-214.

appeal for men to order their souls in conformity with the regular motions of the universe.[182]

Yet despite its strong moral character, the *Glosae* is not formally concerned with the promotion of Christianity. Christ, in fact, is mentioned just once in the entire treatise (2.29-30). The few references to Christian practice occur early in the *Glosae*[183] and there are but a handful of Biblical allusions.[184] It is Plato, in the context of the *Timaeus*, who labours to prepare us for religion (8.95). There need be no contradiction between Bernard's general lack of interest in inserting Christianity openly into his treatment of Plato and his Christian morality. Bernard was apparently more interested in glossing the *Timaeus* directly than he was in making the kind of overt Christian interpretation or rejection of the *Timaeus* that Manegold of Lautenbach and Abelard did.[185] In matters philosophical, Bernard was prepared to consider the issues on their own terms.[186]

Liebeschütz thought that Bishop Ivo and Bernard of Chartres, though working in different fields, shared a complementary programme:

> When we observe Ivo distinguishing by newly-developed dialectic methods between the spiritual and secular functions and powers comprised in the bishop's office, and when we see his keen interest in defining exactly the sphere to which different human actions refer, we shall not take it as mere coincidence that in the later years of Ivo's pontificate we find Master Bernard lecturing at the Cathedral school on the contrast between the eternal reality of the world and its sensual appearance.[187]

To go further, one might say that in the *Glosae* Bernard's morality is grounded in his metaphysics, for he looked beyond the appearances of this flawed world to the principles on which it was established by its good author. The search for some correspondence between the higher truth of things and the imperfection of this world and the men who live in it was the shared programme of the ecclesiastical reformer and the Platonic philosopher of Chartres. The way in which, in two different fields, they wedded their moral concerns to new methods of inquiry has far-reaching implications for our understanding of that early twelfth-century methodological revolution in learning usually credited to Abelard.

[182] See Gregory, "The Platonic Inheritance," pp. 62-63.
[183] See the references to martyrdom (2.29-30), to prelates (3.87), and to monks (3.99-101).
[184] See 6.150-151, 6.167, 6.252-253, and 7.400-401.
[185] See Gregory, *Platonismo medievale*, pp. 17-30 and "Abélard et Platon," pp. 539-562.
[186] On William of Conches's similar attitude, see Poole, *Illustrations of the History of Medieval Thought in the Departments of Theology and Ecclesiastical Politics*, p. 358.
[187] *Mediaeval Humanism in the Life and Writings of John of Salisbury*, p. 87.

The old man of Chartres was without doubt a moralist: he looked to Plato for many truths, but particularly for those that would lead wise men and even school boys to moral improvement. To succeed, however, his *disciplina* would have to be based on the serious study of a specific text. Bernard taught his students how to approach not only the *Timaeus*, but texts in general. His *Glosae* is a structured and, in its own way, systematic study of the *Timaeus*, one designed to answer the questions students might pose when reading this difficult book. It is as well an early and, thus, formative example of the comprehensive *glosa* genre. Most of its techniques for glossing texts were handed over to and refined by glossators like Gilbert of Poitiers and William of Conches. As such Bernard's *Glosae* contributed, in its own small and incipient way, to the twelfth century's legacy of methodological inventiveness to western civilisation.

Sources

If the *Glosae* is methodologically precocious, it contains few surprises as to sources. Bernard cites by name relatively few authors. Among them are Horace (1.18), Virgil (5.8), Macrobius (1.46, 1.49, 4.238, 4.286), Augustine (3.88, 3.142), the apostolic author of the Epistle to the Hebrews (3.15), Aristotle (5.72, 7.87, 8.269), Plato and Calcidius, of course, and a number of Greek authors mentioned in Calcidius' commentary.[188] Phrases such as *Dicunt quidam, Alii uero dicunt*, and *Item quidam philosophi* may hide other direct references, but some of these can be traced back to the controversies recorded by Calcidius in his commentary. It is what is absent in the *Glosae* that seems peculiar: no explicit mention of Boethius, Porphyry, Apuleius, Priscian, or even Isidore.

Moreover, the extent of Bernard's debt to Augustine is not at all clear. On the one hand, he seems to call Augustine an *auctoritas* in alluding to an opinion from the *Confessiones* (see 8.278-279), and yet, on the other, his two explicit references to Augustine are curious, since neither can be located in Augustine's works.[189] Bernard claims that Augustine accounted for the controversial doctrine of holding women in common by asserting that Socrates meant here to indicate that they would be held in common affection and not lust (3.87-88). William of Conches, who expresses the same idea,

---

[188] The specific citations for the sources mentioned here can be located in the edition.

[189] See Pierre Courcelle, *Late Latin Writers and their Greek Sources*, trans. Harry E. Wedeck (Cambridge, Mass., 1969), pp. 170-171 and Harald Hagendahl, *Augustine and the Latin Classics*, 2 vols., Studia Graeca et Latina Gothoburgensia 20.1-2 (Goteborg, 1967), 1: 112-138 and 2: 535-253, 586-587.

does not attribute it to Augustine, but simply takes it as a given that Plato had not commanded lust for his state, but common affection among its members.[190] Although it is not impossible that there is a source for this opinion, perhaps some authorial confusion led to the misleading citation of Augustine. Bernard would not have been able to reconcile the dangerous immorality suggested in the *Timaeus* with the portrait of the highly moral Socrates found in Augustine's *De civitate dei.* The second citation (3.142-143) is almost as odd: an etymology in which the word *caerimonium* is said, on the authority of Augustine, to derive from Cerimonides, the founder of the rite. In the *Retractationes* Augustine stopped to comment on the meaning of the word, but did not supply this specific explanation.[191] Once again William of Conches also gives Bernard's gloss without the attribution to Augustine.[192] Perhaps Bernard had here drawn a conclusion based on the etymological procedure followed by Augustine in the first half of the *De civitate dei*, where he argues that pagan religious practices and gods have human origins. Another reflection of Augustine's great tome may lie in Bernard's division of philosophy into ethics, logic, and physics (1.55-60). Although a commonplace Stoic distinction, Bernard may have thought it genuinely Platonic because Augustine takes great pains to associate Plato with its original formulation.[193] Later in the *Glosae* Bernard would follow Calcidius in dividing one of the branches of philosophy into theology, physics, and logic (7.377-383). Whatever the source of these Augustinian citations and their confusions, they suggest that Bernard probably had a long-standing knowledge of Augustine, but did not draw directly from him when composing the *Glosae*.

The *Glosae* does not, in fact, give the impression of being a researched set of glosses on the *Timaeus*. Perhaps this was an intentional strategy designed not to distract students with material not directly bearing on the dialogue. As Chenu has suggested, the new masters of the twelfth century were turning away from overmuch reliance on authoritative statement and towards ques-

---

[190] *Glose Willelmi de Conchis super Platonem* 18, ed. Jeauneau, p. 78.

[191] *Retractationes* 2.37 (63), ed. Almut Mutzenbecher, Corpus Christianorum: Series Latina, 57 (Turnhout, 1984), p. 121.

[192] *Glose Willelmi de Conchis super Platonem* 23, ed. Jeauneau, p. 84.

[193] See p. 53 and n. 158 above. Given Bernard's dependence on the Stoic division of philosophy associated with Plato by Augustine in *De civitate dei* 8.4 and his similar treatment of Socrates, it is not unlikely that at some stage in his career Bernard had been a careful reader of Augustine's treatment of Plato in *De civitate dei* 8.3-4. On Augustine's view of Plato, see Frank Regen, "Zu Augustins Darstellung des Platonismus am Anfang des 8. Buches der Civitas dei," in *Platonismus und Christentum: Festschrift für Heinrich Dörrie*, ed. H.D. Blume and F. Mann, Jahrbuch für Antike und Christentum 10 (Münster, 1983), pp. 208-227, esp. 217-218 on the division and its sources.

tions and reasons. The *accessus* to the *Glosae* does provide a suggestion of the depth of the author's learning, as he mentions Macrobius and Horace explicitly, clearly employs Calcidius, and strikes verbal parallels with Cicero, Boethius, and Horace again.

For the most part, Bernard does not directly cite authoritative statements to support or adorn his glosses. The editor is left, therefore, with the difficult task of identifying allusions without creating them. For example—again on the doctrine that women ought to be held in common—Bernard, quoting Lucan's *Pharsalia*, notes that Cato is said to be the father of Rome and married to her (3.90-92). This passage had been similarly interpreted by Priscian in his *Institutiones* and Bernard seems to allude to the passage with his use of the word *utilitas*, but the reference is not specific enough to allow us to make the connection with absolute certainty. Among some of the other unnamed sources from which Bernard definitely drew were Virgil's *Aeneid* (3.60), Horace's *De arte poetica* (3.165), Isidore's *Etymologiae* (see 3.68-69), Priscian's *Institutiones* (8.69-70, 8.147-148), and Martianus Capella's *De nuptiis Philologiae et Mercurii* (3.157, 4.350-351).

The chief sources of the *Glosae* are three: Macrobius, Boethius, and Calcidius, in order of increasing influence. Each of these, we should note, had written about the *Timaeus*, so that Bernard's chief authorities on Plato were late ancient Latin writers. Though each of them opened up windows, as it were, on ancient Greek sources, the picture provided was extremely fragmented. Perhaps no coherent sense of ancient opinion on the *Timaeus* ever emerged for Bernard or, for that matter, for his students. Nonetheless, they were the only relevant sources Bernard could lay hold of and he incorporated what he could.

Bernard may have known Macrobius' *Saturnalia* (see 3.227), but it is the commentary on the *Somnium Scipionis* that he acknowledges in the *accessus* as an important source of opinion on the *Timaeus* (1.44-49). The commentary particularly influenced his treatment of the astronomical, geometrical, and mathematical questions raised in *Timaeus* 31b-40d. Though his characterisation of the elements was derived from Isidore,[194] Bernard drew on Macrobius for information about their qualities and how they joined together (4.284-286). From Macrobius, he also learned about the role of the

[194] See Isidore, *De natura rerum* 11.1, ed. Jacques Fontaine, in Isidore de Seville, *Traité de la nature*, Bibliothèque de l'Ecole des Hautes Etudes Hispaniques, fasc. 28 (Bordeaux, 1960), p. 213. As Fontaine stresses elsewhere, Isidore was probably influenced by Calcidius, so that for medieval readers these two writers reinforced similar positions: see Jacques Fontaine, *Isidore de Seville et la culutre classique dans l'Espagne wisigothique* 2 vols. (Paris, 1959) 1: 406-411, 2: 657-670.

number seven in the conception and procreation of children, the ages of men, and the course of the stars (5.135-136), the length of time it took for the moon to complete a revolution (5.331-335), and the nature of the great year (5.384-387). The vocabulary of Macrobius' commentary seems also to have influenced Bernard's: the words *elimata* (5.193) and *seminarium* (5.189) may have entered Bernard's philosophical vocabulary from the commentary.

Bernard never cites Boethius by name, but employs a number of his works throughout his glosses on the *Timaeus*.[195] He seems to have known the *De trinitate* (8.129-130) and perhaps the *Contra Eutychen* (8.389-392) of the *Opuscula sacra*. The *Philosophiae consolatio* played a more definite role in the glosses, providing him in one case with examples of metempsychosis (6.272-273) and in another with an idea about the movement of reason toward things universal (4.18-19). From the *De institutione arithmetica*, he derived basic definitions of number (3.30), unity (5.127-128), circle (5.362-363), point (6.63-64), and other types of numbers (4.262-275). The *De institutione musica* is behind much of Bernard's thought on the *anima mundi* (see 3.26-29), but its specific influence on the *Glosae* is not as great as that of the *De institutione arithmetica*. Lastly it is through Boethius that Bernard came into contact with Aristotle, Porphyry, and a tradition of logic. Bernard does make allusions to the *Isagoge* of Porphyry (4.213-214), Aristotle's *Categoriae* in Boethius' translation (8.268-275), and Boethius' commentary on the same (4.367-368, 8.264).

Except for the direct quotations of the poets (Horace, Lucan, and Virgil, but apparently not Ovid), Bernard cites nothing and borrows nothing holus-bolus; all is allusion until we reach the case of his deep dependence on Calcidius. Here Bernard lifts striking Calcidian phrases such as "ueneranda puritas nullius corporis contagione uiolatur" (5.76-77), draws directly on Calcidius' illustrations (see 6.238-241, 7.123-125), and cites his sources.[196] Although Calcidius' influence on Bernard stretches from the opening lines of the *accessus* (1.1-4) to the final lines of the *Glosae* (8.447-448), his most substantial contribution falls in the final two sections: the *Tractatus de humano corpore* and the *Tractatus de primordiali materia*. On matters musical, arithmetical, astronomical, and cosmological, Bernard preferred Boethius and Macrobius; on matters medical and material, he turned to Calcidius.

---

[195] On the presence of Boethian works at Chartres, see Chenu, *La théologie au douzième siècle*, pp. 142-144.

[196] See the references to Trasimachus (1.3); Isocrates (2.14-15); Hesiod (6.65-67); Pythagoras (6.160-161, 6.262-263); Aristotle (7.87), Anaxagoras (7.394-396), and the Stoics (8.203).

In a number of instances Bernard begins with a Calcidian schematisation of some idea, but edits and expands it to suit his own needs. In this fashion he treats the motions of the soul (7.139-145), the birth of desire (6.241-245), and the nature of sight (7.72-224). Bernard follows the general outline of Calcidius' demonology, but changes some of its essential terms (6.105-127). Often he departs from Calcidius, inserting, for instance, a distinction about his definition of the senses (6.231-235). Where Calcidius posits a five-fold classification of dreams, Bernard returns us to a more Platonic classification based on the three powers of the soul (7.240-250).[197] He ignores, in addition, Calcidius' lengthy discussions of harmony, the motions of the planets, arithmetic, fate, and fortune. As one glossing *ubique et continue*, Bernard treats other matters either not fully explained by Calcidius or not touched upon at all.[198]

Yet Bernard of Chartres was to be a most influential transmitter and shaper of some Calcidian leads. Two striking examples can be given. At 17c in the *Timaeus* Socrates vaguely sketches the division of society found in the *Republic* (412a-417b).[199] Without Calcidius' commentary the Platonic formulation of this tripartite division of society—into wise men who live high up in the city, soldiers who live below them in the middle of the city, and workers who live in the lowest parts of the city—would have been largely unknown to the Middle Ages. But Calcidius schematised the orders of men and drew parallels with the cosmos, the functions of its orders, the human body, and its faculties.[200] Bernard of Chartres took this scheme, removed the cosmic parallel, retained its tripartite shape, and employed some of its specific Calcidian vocabulary, including the word *sellularii* (3.51-56, 7.148-154).[201] From Calcidius and Bernard this tripartite scheme passed to William of Conches and the thinkers of the twelfth century.[202] Though not central to the main concerns of the *Timaeus*, for Bernard and other Chartrians the scheme came to stand for the connectedness of the political,

---

[197] Cf. Cal., *Comm.* 256 (W264-265) and J.H. Waszink, "Die sogenannte Fünfteilung der Träume bei Chalcidius und ihre Quellen," *Mnemosyne* new series 3 (1942) 65-85.

[198] Cf. 7.155-171 and Cal., *Comm.* 234-235 (W247:13-248:14).

[199] On the following issue, see Dutton "*Illustre ciuitatis.*"

[200] Ibid., pp. 79-86.

[201] Ibid., pp. 95-96.

[202] Ibid., pp. 86-119. Georges Duby, *The Three Orders: Feudal Society Imagined*, trans. Arthur Goldhammer (Chicago, 1980) neglected, in his consideration of the vast medieval ideology of the three orders, to take account of the influence of the *Timaeus*. Since my article was written some other evidence has been added: see G. Dahan, "Une introduction à la philosophie au XIIe siècle: le *Tractatus quidam de philosophia et partibus eius*," *Archives d'histoire doctrinale et littéraire du Moyen Age* 49 (1982) 177-179, 190-191, and Gregory, "The Platonic Inheritance," p. 62.

and physical lives of man. Thus as human justice derives from a divinely created natural justice, so the human social order reflects the underlying pattern of the cosmos itself.

In another striking case Bernard reworks the entire passage where Calcidius drew his distinction between the works of God, of nature, and of man imitating nature (4.32-47).[203] Again Bernard endeavours to simplify and explain what he must have considered to be an essential insight of Calcidius. Where Calcidius was less than clear about what was meant by nature, Bernard supplies a definition: "Natura quidem est uis et ratio gignendi" (4.33-34). Early in his treatment Bernard deals with the central issue: that the world is not a work of man, but of God, and hence bears a likeness to the eternal nature that its archetype, the intelligible world, possesses. Here too he must make a series of terminological distinctions sketched by Calcidius about whether this world suffers diminishment: the world flows within its elements (*fluere, influere, defluere*), but the elements do not depart (*effluere*) from the world. Instead its worn-out parts are recreated or remade in something like a steady state of flux. Bernard is more dependent upon Calcidius in this passage than almost anywhere else in the *Glosae*, probably because he deemed it of such great importance. Indeed it was quite likely Bernard who first drew the attention of early twelfth-century thinkers to the significance of what was to become one of the cornerstones of their metaphysics.[204] Calcidius' tripartition of works allowed them to separate out and explain priority among causes and effects.

What, then, are we to make of Bernard's direct dependence on Calcidius? Since Calcidius' long commentary accompanied a great many medieval manuscripts of the translated dialogue, it was the most readily available source of interpretation on Plato's dialogue and, in particular, on the variety of opinions its doctrines had engendered. Yet eleventh-century glossators on

---

[203] Gregory noted that a gloss in Vienna, Österreichische Nationalbibliothek MS 278 (which is one of those dependent, as it turns out, on the *Glosae*) depended heavily on Calcidius in this case: see the demonstration with parallel columns in Gregory, *Platonismo medievale*, pp. 88-91.7.

[204] Cf. Cal., *Comm.* 23-25 (W73-76); Hugh of Saint-Victor, *Didascalicon* 1.9, ed. Buttimer, p. 16.7-8; Gilbert of Poitiers, "Note super Johannem," ed. M.D. Chenu, in "Découverte de la nature et philosophie de l'homme à l'école de Chartres au XIIᵉ siècle," *Cahiers d'histoire mondiale* 2 (1954) 317 n.5 and Chenu, *Nature, Man, and Society*, pp. 40-41; *Glose Willelmi de Conchis super Platonem* 37, ed. Jeauneau, pp. 104-105; and William of Conches, *Glosae super Boetium*, ed. [in part] J.M. Parent, in J.M. Parent, *La doctrine de la création dans l'école de Chartres*, Publications de l'Institut d'Etudes Médiévales d'Ottawa 3 (Paris, 1938), p. 128.1-17. See also Gregory, *Platonismo medievale*, pp. 54-55, esp. n.1 and Tullio Gregory, "L'idea della natura nella scuola di Chartres," *Giornale critico della filosofia italiana* 4 (1952) 433 and Joseph Moreau, "'Opifex, id est Creator': Remarques sur le platonisme de Chartres," *Archiv für Geschichte der Philosophie* 56 (1974) 41-43.

the *Timaeus* give little indication of any profound study of Calcidius. Their thin glosses are instead concerned with points of grammar and etymology. Bernard took account of Calcidius' commentary in a way that his predecessors had not, extracting the good and pruning away the rest, to employ William of Conches's imagery. Something of the nature of this exercise is hinted at by the *Notae Platonicae* (see App. 1) which follow the *Glosae* in half of the extant codices. These notes consist, for the most part, of extracts from Calcidius' commentary. They were bits of Calcidius' study that could, in this separated form, be more effectively brought to bear on perplexing passages in the *Timaeus*. In the one incident where Bernard reworks an extensive passage from the commentary—the *opera Dei, naturae, et hominis* sequence—we might imagine Bernard in his classroom, directing the attention of students to a particularly significant distinction he had discovered in Calcidius' commentary. From there the modified Calcidian interpretation might have become incorporated both in his lecture and in the *Glosae*.

Bernard's set of glosses appears not to draw deeply on any known or still surviving tradition of medieval glosses on the *Timaeus* and I was able to consult virtually all of these glosses when compiling the third appendix. How much Bernard owed either to eleventh-century thought or to that of his early twelfth-century contemporaries is an open question. He shares several terms with the eleventh-century *De mundi celestis terrestrisque constitutione* of the so-called Pseudo-Bede, but these are of a fairly general nature.[205] The recent editor of the Pseudo-Bede treatise does not, incidentally, count as part of the original work the Platonic note shared by the uncritical and expansive Migne edition of the work and the *Notae Platonicae* (see App. 1.1). Adelard of Bath in his *De eodem et diuerso* and Bernard in the *Glosae* (4.21-24) share only one interesting, if again general and differently worded, insight: that sense perception fails us in gauging the magnitude of the heavens or the smallness of an atom.[206] In the *Glosae* Bernard acknowledges intellectual debts to his ancient giants, but not once to the fellow dwarfs with whom he shared an intellectual world; his practice was consistent with his metaphor.

---

[205] Cf. 6.54-57 and Pseudo-Bede, *De mundi celestis terrestrisque constitutione* 1.20, ed. Burnett, p.18 on the pole/axis as an intellectual line and cf. 6.108 and Pseudo-Bede, *De mundi celestis terrestrisque constitutione* 1.160, p. 130 where both employ "calodemones."

[206] Adelard, *De eodem et diuerso*, ed. Hans Willner, in *Des Adelard von Bath Traktat De eodem et diuerso*, Beiträge zur Geschichte der Philosophie des Mittelalters, 4.1 (Münster, 1903), p. 13.4-9: "O peruersa rerum conuersio, cum nihil ratione certius, nihil sensibus fallacius! Primum quia nec in maximis nec in minimis rerum sensus uigent. Quis enim unquam caeli spatium uisu comprehendit? Quis sonum eiusdem caelestemque concentum auribus clausit? Quis item atomi paruitatem oculo distinxit? Quis sonum eisdem atomis collisis creatum aure notauit?"

The few references to unnamed others whose positions are generally stated can not, for the most part, be identified, just as they also defy identification in William of Conches's glosses.[207] While it may be that some of these imprecise references hide specific citations, Kenny and Pinborg have suggested that vague citation was a technique of the incipient *disputatio*, one that allowed the author to state anonymous or general positions.[208] In favour of this argument, it is worth noting that these references in Bernard's glosses are collective ones, always to 'others' and not to 'another'. In the case of the *Glosae*, in fact, many of these vague citations serve to set up and support Bernard's own positions. In one instance, the unnamed "alii philosophi" can be identified as Calcidius alone (5.75-79). Several times Bernard credits these anonymous others with a certain opinion, as though to give it credibility, but later presents it as his own without qualification (cf. 8.6-9 and 8.200-202). He first introduces the doctrine of the *formae natiuae* without attribution, as though it were his own or genuinely Platonic (4.192), but he later seems to give it wider support by invoking anonymous supporters.

When reading the *Glosae*, we are near the beginning of a new systematic approach to the *Timaeus* that belongs to the twelfth century. Bernard had simplified a complex commentary tradition and its heavy burden of authorities in order to allow the dialogue itself to speak to medieval readers. Bernard's students, trained in the trivium and quadrivium and familiar with Macrobius and Boethius, now possessed in the *Glosae* an explication of the *Timaeus* that specifically suited their needs. Calcidius' commentary had become something of an obstacle to the meaningful study of the *Timaeus* by the twelfth century. His commentary simply did not suit the needs of the classroom, where the text to be studied was the *Timaeus* and not a lengthy commentary on it. Furthermore, it must have been awkward for medieval students to locate Calcidius' specific explanations of difficult passages in the *Timaeus* since his commentary does not proceed systematically. Even when these students identified the appropriate interpretations, they must have found much that was perplexing in Calcidius' eclectic commentary.

In terms of sources, therefore, Bernard's greatest accomplishment was to make Calcidius' commentary less relevant and necessary. Bernard's students and successors were able, with the aid of his glosses, to by-pass Calcidius and go directly to the dialogue. Jeauneau wondered, for instance, about William

---

[207] The following are some of the general references to "others": 3.205 "Dicunt quidam aliter"; 4.79 "Legunt etiam quidam"; 4.110 "Dicunt quidam"; 4.112 "Alii e conuerso"; 5.9 "Dicunt tamen quidam"; 5.50 "Alii uero dicunt"; 5.67 "Item quidam philosophi"; 5.75 "Alii autem philosophi dicunt"; 8.42 "Quidam enim dicunt"; and 8.47 "Alii dicunt."

[208] "Medieval Philosophical Literature," p. 32.

of Conches's negligible use of Calcidius: "On peut même se demander si, en tous les passages des *Gloses* où l'influence de Chalcidius est reconnaissable, Guillaume depend directement de cet auteur ou s'il se contente de le citer à travers les glossateurs anonymes qu'il utilise."[209] Calcidius' commentary doubtless did not lose its utility for gifted readers like Gilbert of Poitiers, but by the second quarter of the twelfth century students across Europe were turning to the glosses of Bernard and William when they wanted to understand the *Timaeus*. Bernard's *Glosae* may not, therefore, be full of newly translated materials,[210] but in its own way it was a pioneering synthesis of sources, one necessary for the advancement of the study of the *Timaeus* in the Middle Ages.

The Birth of the Concept of the Formae Natiuae

Of all the ideas associated with Bernard of Chartres his putative Platonic exemplarism and the novel idea of the *formae natiuae* have stirred the most interest.[211] Indeed, Bernard has generally been regarded as the last great Platonist of the Middle Ages before an onrush of newly translated Aristotelian texts swept over the schools of the twelfth century. The label stuck to Bernard by John of Salisbury—"perfectissimus inter Platonicos seculi nostri" (App. 2.2.B1 and 2.5.C)—sealed his reputation as a figure representative of Platonism at the end of the early Middle Ages. We have hitherto known of Bernard's thought almost entirely from John of Salisbury's *Metalogicon* (see App. 2.5),[212] but too infrequently have we reminded ourselves that this is but

---

[209] *Glose Willelmi de Conchis super Platonem*, ed. Jeauneau, p. 27.

[210] See Dutton, "The Uncovering," pp. 205-206 and Marie-Thérèse d'Alverny, "Translations and Translators," in *Renaissance and Renewal in the Twelfth Century*, ed. Robert L. Benson and Giles Constable with Carol D. Lanham (Cambridge, Mass., 1982), pp. 422-426. See also p. 14 and n. 36 above.

[211] See especially Clerval, *Les écoles*, pp. 248-254; Clemens Baeumker, "Der Platonismus im Mittelalter" (1916), rpt. in *Platonismus in der Philosophie des Mittelalters*, ed. W. Beierwaltes, Wege der Forschung, vol. 197 (Darmstadt, 1969), pp. 15-16; Etienne Gilson, "Le platonisme de Bernard de Chartres," *Revue néo-scholastique de philosophie* 25 (1923) 5-19; Maurice de Wulf, *History of Mediaeval Philosophy*, 1: 151-153; J.M. Parent, *La doctrine de la création dans l'école de Chartres*, pp. 45-48, 84-85; Eugenio Garin, *Studi sul Platonismo medievale*, pp. 50-53; Tullio Gregory, *Anima mundi: la filosofia di Guglielmo di Conches e la scuola di Chartres*, Pubblicazioni dell'istituto di filosofia dell'universita di Roma, vol. 3 (Florence, 1955), pp. 76-79 and *Platonismo medievale*, pp. 113-115; Wetherbee, *Platonism and Poetry in the Twelfth Century*, pp. 22-23; John Marenbon, *Early Medieval Philosophy (480-1150): An Introduction* (London, 1983), p. 146.

[212] I say almost entirely because many inferences have been drawn from the works of his students: see, for instance, Gilson, "Le platonisme de Bernard de Chartres," pp. 5, 16.

an account of his philosophy and not the philosophy itself.[213] For the first
time we are in a position to consider some aspects of Bernard's philosophy
as they are revealed in his own words in the *Glosae*. A word of caution is in
order here: glossators were engaged in explaining a text and would only
occasionally stand self-consciously aside from that task. Bernard's role,
therefore, was to interpret Plato's philosophy as he had received it, and not
to put forward his own, though the two seem to have coincided. After
examining Bernard's glosses we shall be in a better position to judge the truth
of John of Salisbury's report.

Bernard begins the *Tractatus de constitutione mundi* with a series of
perfectly Platonic distinctions: that what truly exists is that which always
exists (4.6), for it lacks generation (4.6-7), is an essence (4.7), and is
immutable (4.13), but what takes up existence by being born is sensible and
does not always exist (4.7-8). The former he thinks of as the archetype (4.6),
the latter as sensible things. After God everything is either born or unborn
(4.8-9). He recognises that to say that whatever exists is either creator or
creature is another interpretation, but he notes that this distinction is not
necessary to the argument Plato makes (4.9-11). Our very knowledge of
something born is, at best, conjectural, since it derives from *opinio* joined to
sense perception. Together these two faculties allow us to regard bodies
(4.16-17). But sense, which is called irrational, is deceived in the perception
of things and neither comprehends the greatest nor the least of things. For
no one can comprehend by sense perception either the smallness of an atom
or the magnitude of the heavens (4.21-24). Thus, Bernard expresses an
essentially Platonic insight in the *Glosae*: that the sensible world is less real
in being, eternity, and immutability than that which truly exists as its cause.

After an interesting discussion of the Calcidian distinction of three types
of works and the eternity of the world, Bernard demonstrates his exemplarism. Here, however, he faced a terminological dilemma of some complexity.
Calcidius, both in his translation and commentary, had freely interchanged
exemplum and *exemplar*, with the former being the standard word for the
archetypal model or *species principalis*.[214] For both Bernard and William,
dependent as they were on Calcidius' vocabulary, the *exemplum* took
precedence, but they recognised that the terms were frequently, though
improperly, interchanged.[215] Despite this confusion of terms, which Bernard

---

[213] But Jeauneau, *La philosophie médiévale*, p. 47: "S'il est assez périlleux de tenter la
reconstitution de son 'platonisme' à partir des maigres renseignements que nous possédons,
sa méthode pédagogique nous est, par contre, bien connue."

[214] Cf. *Timaeus* 28a (W20:12-21:3), 31b (W24:2-4), and Cal., *Comm.* 337 (W230:5-10).

[215] See 4.110-113 and *Glose Willelmi de Conchis super Platonem* 38, ed. Jeauneau, p.
105.19-21.

does not entirely escape,[216] his meaning is clear: this world is made to the likeness of an immutable model (4.102, 4.109-110) which is the archetype (4.44-45, 4.65). Thus, ironically, Bernard's exemplarism overcomes the occasionally awkward philosophical vocabulary he was forced to adopt.[217]

But how does the Platonic order conceived by Bernard operate, and how does it relate sensibles and exemplars? Bernard identifies three Platonic principles: the first is God, the maker of all things; the second, the Ideas, the original forms of all things which are never mixed in with creatures; and the third, hyle, the matter of bodies (4.235-237).[218] Let us examine these one by one.

Deus, omnium opifex. If the Demiourgos of the *Timaeus* is a worker-god, literally a craftsman and perhaps a setter of physical and even aesthetic standards in the universe,[219] it is not surprising that Bernard conceived of him as the Christian *deus*.[220] The argument for their one and sameness is simply put: because the world is made, therefore it has a maker, and since it can have no other, it has God (4.94-96). Though Plato may have thought of the Demiourgos as a fashioner and orderer, one who begins to fashion and order already existing but disordered matter, Bernard's *deus* is the *creator* (1.35, 4.10). Though he acknowledges the Platonic term *opifex* (4.97-101), Bernard customarily speaks simply of *deus*. This assumption, so revealing of the Chartrian conviction of the true identity of the Demiourgos in the *Timaeus*, leads to the displacement of the craftsman-*opifex* by the creator-*deus*.[221] The implications for God's role are crucial: the Platonic *opifex* is an artisan who works with already available materials, whereas the Christian *deus* created from nothing.[222] Bernard also identifies the *auctor* or author of

---

[216] See 4.97-104. See also 4.67-68; 4.223; 4.229; and 4.231.

[217] Another example of Calcidius' loose use of terms is the lack of sharp distinction in his commentary between *sensibilis* and *sensilis*.

[218] Cf. 8.401-402 and see p. 89 below on various formulations of the Platonic principles.

[219] On the Demiourgos, see Gregory Vlastos, *Plato's Universe* (Seattle, 1975), p. 26 and Luc Brisson, *Le même et l'autre*, pp. 29-106. On the thesis of the Demiourgos as setter of standards, see Richard D. Mohr, *The Platonic Cosmology*, Philosophia antiqua: A Series of Monographs on Ancient Philosophy 42 (Leiden, 1985), pp. 1-52. On whether the Demiourgos was irrational or sane, see David Keyt, "The Mad Craftsman of the *Timaeus*," *The Philosophical Review* 80 (1971) 230-235 and Richard D. Mohr, "Plato's Theology Reconsidered: What the Demiurge Does," in *Essays in Ancient Greek Philosophy III: Plato*, ed. John Anton and Anthony Preus (Albany, 1989), pp. 293-307.

[220] On the Chartrian reconciliation of *deus* with the Platonic Demiourgos, see Parent, *La doctrine de la création dans l'école de Chartres*, pp. 35-40 and Gregory, *Anima mundi*, pp. 49-50.

[221] See Gregory, "The Platonic Inheritance," p. 61.

[222] See Moreau, "'*Opifex, id est creator*': Remarques sur le platonisme de Chartres," pp. 37-41.

the world as God, the *actor* or chief mover who establishes those things that always exist (4.105-106).[223] The will (*uoluntas*) of God is the cause or reason why he made the world and, because he led things from disorder into order, he truly wished all things to be ordered like him (4.179-182). Nevertheless, though some creatures are more perfect and some less perfect than others (4.175-178), the less perfect are not evil (4.183-184). In his demonstration of the eternal world Plato proceeded by an examination of its best author, beautiful example, best cause, and worthy material (4.241-244). It remains the measure of Bernard's faithfulness to the literal meaning of Plato and the *Timaeus* that he can recognise that the philosophers say that God had not made the world from nothing, but had only adorned (*exornasse*) or arranged it from nothing (4.194-195).[224] Later he will state again that the confused matter in hyle was created from nothing or lacks a beginning (8.13-14).[225] What this implied about God's power and the limitations placed upon it by pre-existing matter, Bernard never directly addresses. If, as Chenu suggests, the substitution of *deus* for *opifex* threatened to unbalance the three principles of the *Timaeus*, Bernard was able to restore some semblance of a balance by restricting most of his talk about God to the early part of the *Tractatus de constitutione mundi* and by insisting upon the essential place of the Ideas and of hyle in the Platonic scheme of true being.[226] Moreover, by leaving the issue of the creation *ex nihilo* unresolved, a certain tension persists in Bernard's *Glosae*, one that worked to focus attention on the critical roles played by the other two first principles in the arrangement of the world.

Ideae, originales formae omnium quae numquam admiscentur creaturis. Bernard is careful to make two essential distinctions about the Ideas: one, in this sentence, that they are not mixed in with creatures, and therefore stand apart from created things. The second, which immediately follows (4.238-239), is, as it were, a distinction at the other end: that the Ideas are in the mind of God which is inferior to God. Bernard derived the distinction between God and his mind from Macrobius. Thus, the Ideas are from God and reside in his mind, but neither the Ideas nor his mind are identical with God. Are the Ideas, then, also creations of God? John of Salisbury's account

---

[223] See M.D. Chenu, "Auctor, actor, autor," *Bulletin du Cange (Archivium Latinitatis medii aevi)*, 3 (1927) 81-86.

[224] On the theme of the *exornatio mundi* at Chartres, which arose from a reading of *Timaeus* 52d (W51:6-7), see *Glose Willelmi de Conchis super Platonem* 174-176, ed. Jeauneau, pp. 287-289. And see Parent, *La doctrine de la création dans l'école de Chartres*, pp. 42-43.7.

[225] See below p. 86 on the *ex nihilo* issue.

[226] *Nature, Man, and Society*, p. 68.

suggests just this, for he says that Bernard believed that the divine mind makes (*facit*) one of its two works out of itself and contains it in itself (App. 2.5.C). This thing made by the divine mind is the Idea.

For Bernard, an archetype is a collection of Ideas, but it is *diuersus* or different from God because of its multiplicity (4.32-34). It is inferior to God, since it is in the mind of God and the mind of God is inferior to God (4.38-39). Nevertheless, the archetype (4.44-45, 4.32-33) and the Ideas (8.229-230) are eternal, having neither beginning nor end. Early in the *Glosae*, in language reminiscent of Eriugena, Bernard calls the Ideas reasons (*rationes*).[227] These reasons of the world exist at two levels (4.114-115). At the level of the archetype they are so related to the archetype that they cannot be comprehended by man. As the archetype, for instance, is eternal, so are its reasons (4.115-118). At the level of the sensible world, Plato was unable to demonstrate the firm reasons of things, because this world varies and is inconstant (4.117-120). Unable, therefore, to supply the reasons, Plato intended at least to determine the differences between their natures (4.120-121).

Bernard thinks that the *genera* and *species* of all things are Ideas in the intelligible world, that is, things which exist with a true reason as pure archetypes in the mind of God (see 4.138-140, 6.9-11, 8.350). They do not vary in their universal being (5.46-47), and as Ideas they do not pass from one nature into another (8.384-385). Thus Bernard believed in the Ideas as universals *ante rem*; they have true being or they truly exist, but outside of things and before them. The Ideas themselves do not in any way inhere in things, for as exemplary Ideas they stand apart from the corruptible and transitory. The Ideas, according to Bernard, have no contact with our senses (8.377-378) nor are they predicable species, but sensibles exist in their likeness (8.315-317, 4.215-218). The Ideas, then, are inferior to God and are not mixed in with creatures, but this sensible world in some way reflects the archetypal world of the Ideas.

Hyle, materia corporum. The third principle is hyle, the matter of bodies, but since Bernard spends his entire last and longest chapter on matter we shall only be able to set down a few of its characteristics. Hyle is a word

---

[227] See, for instance, [Eriugena],*Periphyseon* 1, ed. I.P. Sheldon-Williams with Ludwig Bieler, in *Iohannis Scotti Eriugenae Periphyseon (De diuisione naturae)*, Scriptores latini Hiberniae 7 (Dublin, 1968), p. 46.13-16, and cf. p. 114.18-19: "Omnia enim unum et idipsum immobile erunt quando in suas immutabiles rationes omnia reuersura sunt." Despite Paolo Lucenti, *Platonismo medievale: contributi per la storia dell'Eriugenismo* 2nd ed. (Florence, 1980), p. 50, there seems to be no clear allusion in Bernard to Eriugena's philosophy. On the *rationes* in Chartrian philosophy, see Gregory, "L'idea della natura nella scuola di Chartres," pp. 436-437.

that does not occur in the translated part of Plato's *Timaeus*,[228] where the third principle is effectively space or the spatial field, not matter.[229] Ironically, the *Timaeus* tells the Platonic story of the concretisation of creation.[230] Hence it is not surprising that, under the impress of the Aristotelian understanding or transformation of this Platonic concept of space into matter (as conveyed by Calcidius),[231] Bernard should conceive of the third principle as both material and spatial: hyle is not only the *materia corporum*, but also *locus* (8.354, 8.397). Whereas Plato with his spatial principle had preferred to think of hyle as that place in which (*in qua*) bodies come into existence, Calcidius confused the issue by speaking of hyle both as that in which (*in qua*) and that out of which (*ex qua*) bodies come into being. Bernard, however, generally prefers the "out of which" (*ex qua*) or material formula.[232]

Hyle proves a most difficult thing to define (8.87-89) and, in fact, takes on a number of auxiliary descriptions: necessity, fraud, receptacle, nurse, and bosom.[233] As the universal is perceived through the individual, so hyle is felt and understood through bodies (8.244-245), but only by a certain kind of bastard reasoning (8.366-368). Hyle, in fact, defies categorisation (8.264-299), since it like the Ideas can not be predicated in a normal way. Hyle's particular problems of predicability are that it is neither a substance nor an accident, neither a singular nor a universal. It is not a singular because it is whole in diverse bodies and is not a universal since there is no individual through which it exists in actuality (8.271-274). Nonetheless, hyle is one of those truly existing things that always remains the same in its own nature (8.372-373) and that is worthy of being designated by a pronoun

---

[228] But the word was used in the untranslated part of the *Timaeus* at 69a.

[229] See David Ross, *Plato's Theory of Ideas* (Oxford, 1951; rpt. 1963), p. 222.

[230] See J.N. Findlay, *Plato: The Written and Unwritten Doctrines* (London, 1974), pp. 302-325.

[231] On the Platonic use of the term hyle and the Aristotelian qualification of it, see J. Reginald O'Donnell, "The Meaning of 'Silva' in the Commentary on the *Timaeus* of Plato by Chalcidius," *Mediaeval Studies* 7 (1945) 2-4. See, in general, Dietrich Joachim Schulz, *Das Problem der Materie in Platos 'Timaios'*, Abhandlungen zur Philosophie, Psychologie, und Pädagogik 31 (Bonn, 1966). And see the monumental study by Heinz Happ, *Hyle. Studien zum aristotelischen Materie-Begriff* (Berlin, 1971), pp. 95-130 on matter in the *Timaeus*, pp. 85-208 on the material principle according to Plato's thought, and pp. 273-277 on the word hyle.

[232] See 8.4-6, 8.17-19, 8.176-179. And see van Winden, *Calcidius on Matter*, pp. 31-32. On the nature of the problem, see Brisson, *Le même et l'autre*, p. 236.

[233] On Calcidius' Latin terms and their influence, see van Winden, *Calcidius on Matter*; O'Donnell, "The Meaning of 'Silva'," pp. 1-20; Etienne Gilson, "Note sur les noms de la matière chez Gilbert de la Porrée," *Revue du Moyen Age Latin* 2 (1946) 173-176. On Chartrian concepts of matter, see Parent, *La doctrine de la création dans l'école de Chartres*, pp. 40-43 and Heinrich Flatten, "Die *materia primordialis* in der Schule von Chartres," *Archiv für Geschichte der Philosophie* 40 (1931) 58-65.

(8.160-161). Without hyle it would be impossible for any corporeal thing to exist, and, therefore, hyle is called necessity (8.5-6). But hyle in or by itself remains confused and disordered (4.191). Hyle is additionally called an erratic cause because of its fluctuation (8.39-40). In hyle's chaotic state there is, in actuality, no motion, that is, until the contrary natures of the elements began to struggle against each other (8.416-424). Hyle is, in some sense, passive or inert; its existence does not and can not explain the existence of particular concrete things.

In the *Timaeus* Plato produces a story of the universe that is suggestive, but its principles are never fully explained. Calcidius, in his extensive chapter on matter (*De silua*), follows the most static aspects of the Platonic world-order.[234] In his study God, the Ideas, and matter stand apart from each other without a principle of motion. Their separated existences will not explain the appearance of sensible, particular things. Calcidius' system, if it may be called that, given its eclecticism, is one in which the principles are locked in almost immobile rigidity, unable to commence the motion that will lead to creation. For Calcidius the first two principles are God and matter, a Stoic position that he weakly attempts to refute.[235] The place of the Ideas or exemplary forms in the Platonic scheme is grudgingly acknowledged by Calcidius, but they never assume their full and important Platonic role.[236] The all-important question left to be answered, then, by medieval readers of the *Timaeus*, who saw in it the promise of a fully rounded metaphysics, was how this world and its particular things were related to hyle and the Ideas residing in the divine mind.

Here Bernard of Chartres arrived at a satisfying solution: he created the concept of the *formae natiuae*. The problem was, on the one hand, to insure that the Ideas were fully separate from and not mixed in sensible things and, on the other, to discover a principle of imitation of those exemplars that was in and yet, at some level, separable from sensible things. Thus, the concept of the *formae natiuae* came to account for the relationship of the Ideas and hyle (unformed matter) to bodies (things formed) (8.194-197). The Ideas, after all, could not mix with hyle, but their images could. If the sensible world was the child and hyle the mother, then the *formae natiuae* acted as the father of the sensible world (8.198-202).

---

[234] See, for instance, Cal., *Comm.* 330 (W324-325) and van Winden, *Calcidius on Matter*, p. 245.

[235] See Cal., *Comm.* 297 (W299:5-7). On the Stoic division into two first principles, see Michael Lapidge, "The Stoic Inheritance," in *A History of Twelfth-Century Western Philosophy*, ed. Peter Dronke (Cambridge, 1988), p. 106.

[236] See Cal., *Comm.* 304 (W305-306) and 307 (W308:14-315:2). On the weakness of the exemplary principle in Calcidius' commentary, see van Winden, *Calcidius on Matter*, pp. 142-143.

In both Calcidius' commentary and Boethius' *De trinitate* there is a certain, though undeveloped, recognition that the images of the Ideas must somehow be present in *res formatae*.[237] But Calcidius and Boethius worked, as it were, on opposite ends of the problem, Calcidius stressing the necessity of matter's existence, and Boethius emphasising the immutability and incorruptibility of the first forms or Ideas. In both authors the issue seems an incidental one which arose from their consideration of other matters. Bernard's conception of the *formae natiuae* must have emerged from his reading of these sources, but he chose to extend to the intermediary forms a more central and, indeed, critical function in creation.

We seem to see the first formulation of the very term *formae natiuae* in the *Glosae* and this is why, I think, we can legitimately speak of Bernard of Chartres's creation of the concept. In closely studying Calcidius, Bernard encountered the distinction between the *intelligibilis species* and the *species natiua*;[238] he understood the first to be the Idea and for the second substituted the phrase <*formae*> *natiuae*:

Calcidius, *Comm.* 347 (W339:1-6)	Bernard, *Glosae* 233.3-5
Diuisa ergo a se sunt tria illa separatimque examinata, et est idea quidem intelligibilis species, utpote quae puro intellectu comprehendatur, species uero natiua opinione percipibilis proptereaque opinabilis, silua porro neque intellegibile quid neque opinabile, quia neque intellectu neque sensu comprehendatur, uerum est suspicabilis, suspicio autem spuria quaedam ratio est atque adulterina.	Nota hylen, id est siluam, nec intelligibile quid esse, ut ideae sunt, nec opinabile, ut natiuae, sed suspicabile. Suspicio uero est adulterina ratio.

Notice that Bernard in the simple epistemological distinction here has provided his own equivalent of not just one, but two Calcidian terms. Thus he acknowledges that hyle is also called *silua*, a distinctly Calcidian usage, and substitutes <*formae*> *natiuae* for Calcidius' *species natiua*. The omission of *formae* in the passage does not affect this interpretation, since Calcidius elsewhere states "quippe secunda species, id est natiua"[239] and

---

[237] See Cal., *Comm.* 349 (W340:21-341:7), *Comm.* 344 (W336:4-13), and Boethius, *De trinitate* 2, in *Opuscula sacra*, ed. Peiper, in *Anicii Manlii Severini Boetii Philosophiae consolationis libri quinque accedunt eiusdem atque incertorum Opuscula sacra* (Leipzig, 1871) pp. 152-154.

[238] See Cal., *Comm.* 337 (W330:7-18) and *Comm.* 344 (W336:4-13). See also the definition of Papias printed above, pp. 18-19.

[239] Cal., *Comm.* 344 (W336:6-7).

Bernard identifies this second form specifically with the *formae natiuae* (8.351-352). On those two or three occasions in the *Glosae* when Bernard refers to the opinions of certain unnamed others about the *formae natiuae* he may either be marshalling fictive support for his own position or he may be thinking of Calcidius as a general proponent of the concept. Indeed, Bernard conceived of the term *formae natiuae* from a close reading of Calcidius' commentary, as Gregory had suspected.[240] We are, therefore, very close in the *Glosae* to the moment of its first formulation, though it would soon have a life of its own and its inception in Calcidian terminology would be forgotten.

But Bernard does with the concept of the *formae natiuae* what Calcidius was never able to do with his *species natiua*; he makes the *formae natiuae* the active intermediary principle of his metaphysical system. We need to remember here that the exemplary principle had been weak in Calcidius' system, but Bernard from the start of his study of hyle insists on restoring the Ideas to their powerful and incorruptible place in the Platonic scheme of things. Where Calcidius had likened the Idea to the father and matter to the mother in the Platonic metaphor,[241] Bernard found this unsatisfactory since it violated the integrity of both. For Bernard the Ideas and matter had never come into contact with each other and never would. Instead, said Bernard, although one might speak of the archetypal world as obtaining the place of the father, it is the *formae natiuae* that actually enter matter (8.198-202). Better still to say that the *formae natiuae* obtain the place of the father, because just as the seed of the father makes a child in the womb of the mother, so the *formae natiuae* entering hyle generate bodies (8.6-9). In this way, in Bernard's philosophy, the Ideas remain properly speaking outside the corporeal metaphor; he will not allow their purity and immutability to be compromised even by language. The *formae natiuae* introduce into the Platonic cosmos an active or generative force, one that like the seed of the father in the womb of the mother sets life in motion. It is not, therefore, hyle, but the *formae natiuae* that are the chief cause of this sensible world (8.50-52). Calcidius had anticipated little of this, his *species natiua* being more truly a label for visible and temporal form.

The concept of the *formae natiuae* is central to the metaphysical scheme presented in the *Glosae*. The phrase itself or the implied <*formae*> *natiuae* is employed nineteen times and the use of the implied *formae* <*natiuae*>

---

[240] *Anima mundi*, pp. 195-196; *Platonismo medievale*, pp. 114-116. Also see Gregory, "Note sul platonismo della scuola di Chartres: la dottrina delle *specie native*," *Giornale critico della filosofia italiana* 32 (1953) 358-362.

[241] Cal., *Comm.* 330 (W324:19-23).

many more times. The *formae natiuae* are, according to Bernard, like the Ideas because they proceed from the likeness of the Ideas into substance (5.69-70). He describes them as the "formae natiuae, quae sunt imagines idearum" (8.201-202) and as the *simulacra idearum* (8.191-192, 8.251-252).

The *formae natiuae* are associated with hyle because they are incorporated and changed there, as if in hyle (5.71). Before hyle was formed or, rather, when it was unformed, a nursery of bodies existed in flux in it. Though it was not yet a body, it had the potential to be formed, and stood ready to receive forms (4.188-191). Thus, according to Bernard, God formed that nursery of hyle with or by means of the *formae natiuae* (4.191-192). The confused matter in hyle was created from nothing or lacked a beginning, but when the *formae natiuae* were taken up, matter first passed into the *eliquata* or separated elements and, then, those having been assumed, passed into elementary things (8.13-16, 4.191-195). Hyle, in short, has no form of its own, but receives all forms (8.181-182). The forms entering hyle beget those visible things which are called the *simulacra* or semblances of the Ideas (8.251-252). Bernard even corrects Calcidius who had maintained that pure fire, that is, the pure archetype of fire, was made from the combination of the *intelligibilis species* and hyle. For Bernard this could not constitute a definition of the pure archetype, since even pure fire was the result of the joining of hyle and the *forma natiua* and, therefore, could not be the immutable Idea of Fire itself (8.254-259). Hyle, for Bernard, is *locus* or space because into it the *formae natiuae* descend, but should they recede from it hyle does not perish (8.354-355). The *formae natiuae* reflect the eternal character of their Ideas; although some perish, others succeed them, and they are said to remain throughout the ages on account of the archetypes which are their Ideas (8.230-232). Before the creation of the world all the *formae natiuae* that would afterwards come into hyle existed potentially in it. But those *formae natiuae* that were to form hyle to produce the four elements of the world actually already existed in hyle before the adornment or arrangement of the world. Still Bernard stressed the point that the *formae natiuae* were subsequent, in order not to posit more first principles than the three: God, hyle, and the Ideas (8.397-402). In the composition of the soul, the *formae natiuae* also play a role. The soul is composed of different substances, each of which looks to its own nature. Thus, the soul is said to be composed of undivided substance while it thinks of God and his mind; of divided substance when it looks to hyle and the *formae natiuae*; of intermediate substance when it studies the Ideas; of the same nature while it studies *genera* and *species*, which do not vary in their universal being; of diverse nature while it studies the properties of the accidents; and of mixed nature while it studies individual things (5.43-48). Some philosophers (and here again Bernard was probably thinking of Calcidius) think that Plato understood by the undivided substance of the soul the Ideas; by the divided, hyle; and by these two mixed together, the *formae natiuae* through which the soul is observed to possess sense and intellect (5.67-69). Worthily, says Bernard, is the soul said to exist out of the *formae natiuae* because, according to Aristotle, the soul is *endelichia*, that is the form of the body which informs the body by enlivening it in a certain way (5.71-74).[242]

That Bernard of Chartres should have taken up the Aristotelian term *endelichia* is an interesting comment on his more general debt to Aristotle, because in fact the very concept of the *formae natiuae* as presented in the *Glosae* is an accommodation of the differing demands of Platonism and Aristotelianism. If the medieval reader of the *Timaeus* could find a means of granting the absolute separation of the immutable and eternal Ideas and yet find a mechanism by which particular sensible things imitated those Ideas without participating in them, he would have gone some way towards a reconciliation of the Platonic and Aristotelian positions stated by Boethius:

> Sed Plato genera et species ceteraque non modo intellegi uniuersalia, uerum etiam esse atque praeter corpora subsistere putat, Aristoteles uero intellegi quidem incorporalia atque uniuersalia, sed subsistere in sensibilibus putat; quorum diiudicare sententias aptum esse non duxi, altioris enim est philosophiae.[243]

Bernard was not unaware of the nature of the problem, since he was a reader of available Aristotelian materials: the *Categoriae*, Porphyry's *Isagoge*, and Boethius' translations and commentaries. From Calcidius' commentary, indeed, he knew that Aristotle held out three principles of material things: hyle, *species* or form, and privation.[244] Moreover, for Bernard, as a reader of Calcidius' translation and commentary, hyle was already conceived in terms partially Platonic and partially Aristotelian. Bernard's conception of the problem involved was, therefore, already touched unavoidably by the Aristotelianism of the Neo-Platonic books he read. He thought, for instance, of the form as similar to a cause (see 4.166-168). The *formae natiuae*, as we have seen, were deemed to be the cause of bodies, bringing their active nature to bear on inert hyle. Since the *formae natiuae* belong properly to generation (8.397), they could be found joined to matter in things made.

---

[242] On the term *endelichia* in *Timaeus* glosses, see Gregory, *Platonismo medievale*, pp. 136-138.

[243] Boethius, *In Isagogen Porphyrii commenta: editio secunda* 1.11, ed. Brandt, p. 167.12-17.

[244] Cal., *Comm.* 283 (W286:2-3).

Bernard of Chartres's special contribution to the medieval understanding of the *Timaeus* lay in a bold, if simple, insight: that one could reconcile the Platonic intuition of the Ideas with a practical Aristotelian emphasis upon the forms and causes of this world by envisaging the *formae natiuae* as the intermediating images of the Platonic Ideas. Bernard departed from Calcidius and Boethius not only in his fuller development of the concept, but also in his fundamental conception of the metaphysical implications of the exemplary images. If they had chiefly employed the notion of the images of the Ideas as a way of describing the form that inheres in sensible objects, Bernard was more interested in an earlier stage of the process: the moment when and the reasons why matter and the images of the Ideas merge. He was driven to this by his special conception of the *formae natiuae* as the active intermediary force in creation, the one that explained how, despite the absolute separateness of the Ideas and hyle, sensibles could come to exist. He thought of the *formae natiuae* as causative agents; hence he likened them to a father, hyle to a mother, and the sensible world to their offspring (8.199-202). Calcidius and Boethius had thought of the inhering images in terms of an end product of creation, as the incorporated sensible form that human beings encounter in daily life. In a sense, therefore, theirs was an epistemological problem: how were the Ideas known? Perhaps they thought these images could only be talked about when they existed in an incorporated form, but Bernard was quite prepared to talk about them before or even as they entered hyle. Thus, he distinguished between all the *formae natiuae* that existed potentially in hyle *ante constitutionem mundi* and those first *formae natiuae* that actually existed in hyle *ante mundi exornationem* in order to produce the four elements (8.397-401). Unlike Calcidius and Boethius, Bernard wanted to understand how the *formae natiuae* fitted into the universal scheme of things and what relation they had with hyle in particular. Though they were not a fourth principle, for Bernard the *formae natiuae* were essential, for only their existence could explain how the sensible world achieved its material form.

Before we turn to John of Salisbury, we should say something about the light cast by the *Glosae* on some of Bernard's philosophical poetry and sayings. The famous poem which begins "Non dico" (see App. 2.2.B1) is a case in point. In the first two lines of the poem Bernard denies that there is being or a truly existing nature in that which, gathered together in twinned part, contains form interwoven with matter. The form referred to here is the *forma natiua* which together with hyle produces sensible things. He insists on the "gemina parte" in order to draw attention to the original separateness of the *forma natiua* and matter and to stress the necessity of both in the generation of sensible things. Bernard denied that a *res formata* possessed true being in the manner of the three first principles (God, the Ideas, and hyle). In the third line of the poem the word "una" poses a certain problem. It can not be identified with "forma" as McGarry translated it, for the *forma natiua* is not the Idea of line four.[245] Rather, the Idea and hyle of the last line need to be related to their dependent numbers in the second line: form and the matter in sensible things. For proper scansion as well the "una" must be taken as an ablative and the whole sentence must mean that Bernard admits that there is being or a truly existing nature "in the one" (*una*) that corresponds to each of them. That is, that the Idea is related to the *forma natiua*, while hyle is related to sensible matter.

In the fourth line of the poem he says that the Achaean (Plato), called "this" the Idea and "that" hyle. Hyle was not, we need to note, a word that Plato used in the translated part of the *Timaeus*, but was one that Bernard took up as his own in the *Glosae*. Calcidius, however, had consistently and purposely employed *silua*.[246] The use of hyle in the poem and in the *Glosae* should, therefore, be viewed as a specific and, perhaps, distinctive feature of Bernard's philosophical vocabulary. More significant still, it has not been generally realised that the poem's fourth line refers specifically to *Timaeus* 49d-50a: *hoc* and *illud* are lemmata and ought, following convention, to be italicised. The second witness to this poem discovered by Jeauneau in a set of glosses at the Vatican (see App. 2.2.B2) is precisely a marginal gloss attached to *Timaeus* 49d-50a of the same folio.[247] In the *Glosae* at 49d Bernard introduces a theme he will reiterate in the following glosses: things that lack stability are not worthy of being designated by pronouns. Then, alluding to a point made in Priscian's *Institutiones*, he notes that it is the function of pronouns to point out pure substance alone (8.147-148). Mutable things are not worthy, he argues, of being designated by pronouns. Hyle, however, deserves to be named by a pronoun because it always exists immutably and uniformly in its own nature, has no proper quality of its own, and merely allows for the release and passing away of individual bodies according to the variation of forms (8.155-161). Thus, *hoc* and *illud* in the poem "Non dico" are pronouns heavy with Platonic meaning, designating two unchanging natures: the Ideas and hyle.

[245] See *The Metalogicon of John of Salisbury. A Twelfth-Century Defense of the Verbal and Logical Arts of the Trivium*, trans. Daniel D. McGarry (Berkeley, 1962), p. 259.

[246] Calcidius contrasted his own use of the term 'silua' with that of Plato's students who had employed 'hyle': see Cal., *Comm.* 273 (W278:1-2); van Winden, *Calcidius on Matter*, p. 47; O'Donnell, "The Meaning of 'Silva'," pp. 6-7. Nonetheless, Calcidius uses the term hyle three times: see *Comm.* 123 (W176:6), *Comm.* 268 (W273:15-16), and *Comm.* 278 (W282:5). Only once, at *Glosae* 8.336, does Bernard acknowledge *silua* as another term for hyle.

[247] See Jeauneau, *Lectio*, pp. 199-200 and pl. 13.

If the poem and the *Glosae* reveal Bernard to be a philosopher with a grammatical bent, so does the exemplum of the white virgin (App. 2.3.D). In a chapter of the *Metalogicon* devoted to the utility of the *Categoriae*, a work with which, as we know from the *Glosae*, Bernard was fully familiar, John of Salisbury produces an account of Bernard's illustration of the parallelism between ontology and grammar.[248] Thus, Bernard likened the word *albedo* or "whiteness" to an uncorrupted or pure virgin; *albet* or "is white" to the same woman in the act of entering the bedroom and lying on the bed; and *album* or "white" to the same lady, but now corrupted. As Bernard explained it, *albedo* denotes the quality itself, namely the species or form of the colour, simply and without the participation of a subject. *Albet* indicates the same quality, but now with the accidental participation of a subject or person who is contained in the verb. Lastly *album* signifies the same quality, but now spread on and joined together with substance, and in this way still more corrupt. Thus, Bernard set up parallels in his metaphor between grammar, ontology, and ethics:

	1	2	3
1	substantive noun	colour itself	pure virgin
2	verb	the colour active in a subject	the woman in the act of surrendering her virginity
3	adjective	the colour mixed in the substance of a subject	the defiled woman

This is essentially the threefold descent found throughout Bernard's ontological system. Being descends from the Ideas to their images, the *formae natiuae*, which in contact with hyle make particular corporeal things. For Bernard, in the *Glosae*, this is certainly a process of corruption. There he likens the agency of the *formae natiuae* to the semen entering a woman's womb to produce a child (8.7-9), thus associating a descent in being to sexual generation. Moreover, Bernard knew from Plato that colour itself, when joined to substance, was a kind of infection (8.207-208), and he was aware that Calcidius spoke of the presence of a substantial body as a kind of contagion (5.76-77).

In the *Timaeus* (48b; W45:25) Plato, playing upon the double meaning of elements and letters in the Greek word στοιχεῖα, remarked that the

---

[248] See especially Chenu, *La théologie au douzième siècle*, pp. 95-96 and Jean Jolivet, "Eléments pour une étude des rapports entre la grammaire et l'ontologie au Moyen Age," in *Sprache und Erkenntnis im Mittelalter*, ed. Jan P. Beckmann et al., Miscellanea mediaevalia 13.1 (Berlin, 1980), pp. 136-139.

elements did not deserve to be ranked as low as syllables. Calcidius approached the statement as a simple piece of logic: since the elements of the
word are the letters, and syllables fall in second place, then the four basic
elements of the world cannot be ranked as syllables. Rather he thought that
the first element of the world was *silua*, shapeless matter without quality.[249]
Bernard, for his part, found in this passage another opportunity to strike a
correspondence between ontology and grammar. Here, drawing upon the
component parts of speech in Priscian's *Institutiones*, Bernard constructs a
complete set of parallels (8.69-72):

Elementa	*Constitutio uocis*	*Constitutio huius mundi*
1 primum	littera	hyle
2 secundum	sillaba	quattuor pura <elementa>
3 tercio loco	dictio	quattuor mixta <elementa>

In associating the four pure elements with the syllables of human speech,
Bernard would seem to run directly counter to Plato's remark. Perhaps he
thought that Plato had wished to eschew a simple comparison of the elements
to the syllables or that the specific comparison given by Plato was somehow
flawed. His introductory words do suggest some measure of uncertainty about
Plato's meaning (8.69). But he could not resist demonstrating once again the
parallel between ontology and grammar, for we proceed in his example from
higher to lower, from simple to complex, and from uncorrupted to corrupted.
There was for Bernard a language of the universe, an idea that must have
arisen from his parallel reading of Plato and Priscian.

The other poem by Bernard recorded in the *Metalogicon* (App. 2.2.C)
touches on that Calcidian passage about the distinction between the works
of God, of nature, and of man imitating nature which Bernard had reworked
and popularised.[250] All things in time (*in tempore*), according to Bernard in
the *Glosae*, are born and die and, therefore, are called temporal things. But
the works of God are not temporal, because they have neither a beginning
nor an end in time. Instead they are called causative, because they have causes
known before the existence of time (*ante tempus*) to God alone, not to us.
These works of God do not suffer from the things that time introduces,
namely death and sickness, and are *sine necessitate incommodi* (4.37-44).[251]

The poem sharply mirrors this treatment of Calcidius' scheme in the
Glosae. In the first two lines of the poem Bernard asserts that neither time

[249] Cal., *Comm.* 272 (W276:8-11).
[250] See p. 67 and n. 204 above.
[251] The phrase "extra omnem necessitatem incommodi" is used at 4.326 in the *Glosae* and
hyle was identified as Necessity at 8.5.

(*aetas*) nor old age wreck or demolish the *principium* or foundation for which the divine will (*uoluntas*) alone was responsible. Thus, Bernard holds in the poem, as he did in the *Glosae*, that the work of God (*principium*) can not be touched by temporal effects. According to the third and fourth lines of the poem, time (*tempus*) works to dissolve those temporal things it produces, if not now, then whenever the necessity (*necesse*) exists. Thus, "necessity" in both the poem and the *Glosae* captures Bernard's sense of the compulsory nature of the process of temporal dissolution. Note that Bernard does not speak of time, even in a negative sense, as causative, since causes belong to God and the principles. Instead time brings forth mere appearances, which are also dissolved in it. One of the definitions of temporal, sensible, particular things in the *Glosae* is that they are dissoluble (4.27-28). Bernard then remarks in the poem's last two lines that anyone who laments this state of things, that is, the perishable nature of this world, does so with little or no reason. *Ratio* here is the power of the intellect that turns toward the consideration of universal things, and no true *ratio* is weak (4.18-19). For Bernard, those who lack this profound insight into the true nature of higher things must always dwell at the level of things trapped in time and, therefore, lack reason.

Immediately prior to this poem, John of Salisbury reports a remark of Bernard, apparently about the *Isagoge* of Porphyry (App. 2.5.C).[252] Bernard seems to have said that the work of the divine mind is double or twofold: one work that it creates out of subjected matter (or out of matter that is created simultaneously with it), and another that it makes from itself and contains in itself, needing no external support. John himself explains Bernard's observation, by saying that, thus, the divine mind had made the heavens in its intellect (Ps. 135:6) from the beginning, and that these divinely conceived heavens required neither matter nor external form. Again, then, we find ourselves faced with Bernard's persistent distinction between the immutable and eternal Ideas contained in the divine mind and the created sensible world.

The first line of the explanation is particularly intriguing: "alterum quod de subiecta materia creat aut quod ei concreatur." The use of *de* here recalls Bernard's specific arguments in favour of employing "out of which" (*ex qua*), rather than "in which" (*in qua*), to explain how bodies proceed from hyle. Moreover, matter is *subiecta* when (or as) it is formed. In this way Bernard maintains, in his comment on Porphyry, that the divine mind creates sensible things out of hyle (chaotic matter) subjected to the *formae natiuae*. But Bernard introduces a qualification or restatement of the first work, prefaced

---

[252] On the question of the meaning of "in expositione Porphirii," see above pp. 46-47.

by "or, rather" (*aut*). Here he employs a word, "to create simultaneously" (*concreare*), never used in the *Glosae*. If the divine mind is the subject of the verb "creat," it can not be the subject of "concreatur," since the divine mind is not created with creation. It seems reasonable to think, therefore, that Bernard means to qualify his statement about matter through the use of the the conjunction *aut*. Thus, he claims that the divine mind creates one work out of subjected matter or, rather, out of matter created simultaneously with (or for) the work. The statement as a whole continues Bernard's equivocation on the question of a creation *ex nihilo*. If the words "de subiecta materia creat" allow for the possible pre-existence of matter before creation, then "aut quod ei concreatur" quickly asserts that matter is created simultaneously with creation. The former is consistent with Bernard's understanding of the *Timaeus*, the latter with Genesis. In the *Glosae*, as we have already seen, Bernard retains the same equivocation (8.12-16).

Taken altogether the lines on Porphyry are bound to puzzle us, in part because Bernard considers the Ideas in two different spheres (that of the two different works).[253] The second work, which one would expect him to treat first, may most profitably be thought of as the archetype, that collection of Ideas which is the model of the sensible world. The pure, incorruptible, and sufficient Ideas are preserved by their existence in the divine mind, separated there from all necessity (hyle). In the other work (the one actually named first), the "subiecta materia" must include the *formae natiuae* since hyle is, by definition, unsubjected matter. The divine mind could be said to create the sensible world out of this subjected matter because, according to the *Glosae* (4.191-192), God himself sowed hyle, that nursery of forms, with the *formae natiuae*. The thrust of Bernard's maxim, therefore, is to separate the Ideas in the divine mind from sensible creation, and yet to acknowledge God's omnipotence in the creative process. Still it was this kind of conceptual problem—how the separated Ideas relate to hyle—that led Bernard to the concept of the *formae natiuae*, for they function in a mediating capacity that was forbidden, in Bernard's terms, to the Ideas, and they possess an active, ordering character that was lacking in passive and disordered hyle.

With an examination of Bernard's genuine verse and dicta in hand, we are now in the rare position of being able to turn the tables on John of Salisbury, to test his account of Bernard's philosophy against the *Glosae*. John introduces Bernard almost incidentally in his treatment of the discussions of his day

---

[253] See Garin, *Studi sul Platonismo medievale*, p. 52 and Stephen Gersh, "Platonism—Neoplatonism—Aristotelianism: A Twelfth-Century Metaphysical System and Its Sources," in *Renaissance and Renewal in the Twelfth Century*, ed. Robert L. Benson and Giles Constable with Carol D. Lanham (Cambridge, Mass., 1982), p. 522 n.50.

on *genera* and *species* (see App. 2.5.A). He tells us that Walter of Mortagne, having emulated Plato, and in imitation of Bernard of Chartres, now supported the doctrine of the Ideas: he held that *genera* and *species* were nothing except Ideas.[254] This, as we saw in the *Glosae* (6.9-11), was Bernard's belief, since the Ideas are the *genera* of all things. In their universal being *genera* and *species* do not vary (5.46-47), but are properly intelligible and separated (8.348-350). Intelligible creatures (that is, the Ideas of creatures) are, therefore, the *genera* of those creatures, and, though they are not predicable *genera* or *species*, sensible creatures are made in their likeness (4.215-218, 8.315-317). Plato teaches, according to the *Glosae*, that this world is made similar to a general, rather than specific, nature, and, thus, it derives its perfection from its likeness to its *genus* (4.212-213). Bernard supports Plato's argument with the observation, probably derived from Porphyry, that *genus* is more perfect than *species* because it is more connected or contained (4.213-214).

After a discussion of the position of those in general who believe that universals are the Ideas—eternal exemplars, incorruptible, immutable, fixed in number, and separated from things—John returns immediately to Bernard of Chartres. For though Aristotle had disagreed with the doctrine of the Ideas, Bernard and his students had worked with great energy to reconcile the teachings of Aristotle with those of Plato. At this point, John introduces his famous joke, that he thought it far too late in the day and a vain exercise for Bernard and company to attempt a reconciliation of two men who, while they were alive, had always disagreed. John's witticism with its clever irony does not, of course, seek to explain the essential thrust of Bernard's programme, which was, as we have seen, to identify Aristotelian forms as the images of the Platonic Ideas. The reconciliation of Aristotelianism with Platonism was a persistent feature of Bernard's school and one that has something of a Boethian mandate to it. Moreover, the drive towards a synthesis of the outstanding differences between the two ancient philosophers was not tied to a single doctrinal insight. Gilson, for instance, observed that in Gilbert of Poitiers' philosophy we see another form of reconciliation: a mix of metaphysical realism and Aristotelian abstraction.[255] But John of Salisbury was far from sympathetic towards what he considered to be Bernard's own heavy-handed use of Aristotle, especially in the exemplum of the white virgin (see App. 2.3.D)

---

[254] See below p. 102 n. 296 on Walter's earlier position.
[255] "Le platonisme de Bernard de Chartres," p. 16.

Still, John must have known something of the specific nature of Bernard's attempted reconciliation, since immediately after the joke he enters into a brief discussion of the *formae natiuae*. The sentence that begins, "Porro alius, ut Aristotilem exprimat, cum Gilleberto ..." (App. 2.5.A), refers not to some anonymous other, but to the aforementioned other, Bernard of Chartres.[256] In it John reports that in an attempt to explain Aristotle this other had laboured to identify the universals with the *formae natiuae*, as Gilbert of Poitiers still did. It was Bernard, as John had established with the joke and as he would later reinforce with the exemplum of the white virgin, who was keen to force Aristotle into agreement with Plato and with his own philosophy. It was also Bernard who attributed universality to the *formae natiuae*, as is apparent from later remarks in the *Metalogicon* (App. 2.5.C) and from the *Glosae*. Moreover Gilbert of Poitiers is set in a subordinate position in this very important sentence. He appears dependent on the other proponent of the concept, and labours with him to establish the similarity of the *formae natiuae* and the universals. It is hard to imagine Gilbert dependent on anyone except one of his four great masters, and the only one of these who was ostensibly concerned with Platonic doctrine, according to John, was Bernard of Chartres. In addition, the verb *laborat* echoes the use of *laborasse*, which John had employed to emphasise the futility of Bernard's programme of reconciliation. Gilbert is, thus, portrayed as the continuator of Bernard's philosophical plan. The most reasonable explanation of John's statement, therefore, is that the *alius* is Bernard of Chartres, the great Platonic predecessor of Gilbert of Poitiers.

John next provides his definition of the *forma natiua*: it is an original example and does not exist in the divine mind, but rather inheres in created things. The Greeks called this inhering form an *idos*, which stands in relation to the Idea as the example does to the exemplar. Indeed, says John, the *forma natiua* is sensible in sensible things, but insensible as conceived by the mind. Furthermore, it is singular in singular things, but universal in all

---

[256] But see the different interpretation of the sentence by McGarry, *The Metalogicon of John of Salisbury*, p. 115. Most, however, have taken the general statement to refer to the combined efforts of Bernard and Gilbert: see Clerval, *Les écoles*, pp. 251, 262; Garin, *Studi sul Platonismo medievale*, pp. 52-53; Gregory, *Anima mundi*, pp. 78-79 and *Platonismo medievale*, p. 113. It has been generally assumed because of John's description here that Bernard of Chartres was the inventor of the concept of the *formae natiuae*: see Gilson, "Le platonisme de Bernard de Chartres," p. 12; Charles Homer Haskins, *The Renaissance of the Twelfth Century* (1927; rpt. New York, 1957), pp. 344-345; David Knowles, *The Evolution of Medieval Thought* (New York, 1962), p. 132; and David Luscombe, "Bernard of Chartres," in *The Encyclopedia of Philosophy* (New York, 1967) 1: 305. Gregory also thinks, from the evidence of the *Metalogicon*, that Bernard employed the term, though John never directly and unambiguously says so: see "Note sul platonismo della scuola di Chartres: la dottrina delle *specie native*," p. 360.

universal things. For Bernard in the *Glosae*, the *formae natiuae* do not exist in the divine mind, but rather inhere in things as they are created. On many points John's description of the *formae natiuae* seems to go well beyond the verifiable opinions of Bernard of Chartres: the word *idos*, for instance, does not appear in the *Glosae*; Bernard does not specifically employ the illustration of the exemplar/example in this regard, though it is implied by his description of the *formae natiuae* as the images of the Ideas; he speaks in his glosses more about the *formae natiuae* as a generative force than about their specific place in individuals; he applies the singular/universal question in the *Glosae* to the special case of hyle, but not to the *formae natiuae*; and lastly Bernard says simply that whereas the Ideas are *intelligibile* and hyle is *suspicabile*, the *formae natiuae* are *opinabile* or conjectural in the human mind (8.366-367). One suspects that John of Salisbury must have known a slightly later and perhaps more systematic formulation of the *formae natiuae* than the one we find in the *Glosae*. His best source of information about the concept, after all, was probably Gilbert of Poitiers. The great virtue of the *Glosae*, however, is to reveal the idea of the *formae natiuae* to us very near the moment of its conception, before some of the more sophisticated questions about it had even been asked. Moreover, John was not at all sympathetic towards notions of the Platonic Ideas or the *formae natiuae*, which he said must be abandoned if one wished to follow Aristotle (App. 2.5.B). Chapter 20 of the second book of the *Metalogicon* is, in fact, a lengthy review and outright rejection both of the Ideas and of opinions other than Aristotle's on the question of universals.[257]

We do not meet Bernard's Platonic philosophy again until very near the end of the *Metalogicon* (App. 2.5.C). There, after a fairly standard description of the medieval set of Platonic doctrines, John notes that for Plato: "Hanc autem ueram existentiam partiebatur in tria, que rerum principia statuebat; Deum, scilicet, materiam, et ideam." Plato himself, however, never states this specifically in the *Timaeus*, though it is implied. Calcidius, like the Stoics, tended to talk of *Deus* and *silua*, and only once set out that: "Sunt igitur initia deus et silua et exemplum."[258] Apuleius, in his *De Platone et eius dogmate*, had written: "Initia rerum tria esse arbitratur Plato: deum et materiam rerumque formas, quas ideas idem uocat."[259] A number of other

---

[257] *Metalogicon* 2.20, ed. Webb, pp. 97-116. And see Brian Hendley, "John of Salisbury and the Problem of Universals," *Journal of the History of Philosophy* 8 (1970) 289-302 and Michael Wilks, "John of Salisbury and the Tyranny of Nonsense," in *The World of John of Salisbury*, ed. Michael Wilks (Oxford, 1984), pp. 263-286.

[258] Cal., *Comm.* 307 (W308:14-309:1).

[259] 1.5, ed. Paul Thomas, in *Apulei Platonici Madaurensis opera quae supersunt* vol. 3: *De philosophia libri* (Stuttgart, 1970), p. 86.

formulations of this Platonic commonplace may have been known to both
Bernard and John of Salisbury,[260] but it is not impossible that John depended
on the medieval schematisation that derived from Bernard. Thus, in the
Glosae, Bernard held fast to the idea that there were no more than "principia
prima ... tria: scilicet deus, hyle, et idcac" (8.401-402). But John's discussion
of the differences between the three first principles—that the first is in all
respects immutable, while the other two are *immobilia*, though they vary
from each other in effects—again states more than Bernard does in the
Glosae.

In the following sentences John speaks of the forms as the Ideas. When
the forms enter matter, they dispose it, rendering it susceptible to movement
or change. But the encounter of the forms with matter makes both mutable.
John notes that Boethius, however, had denied that the Ideas were mixed
with matter or were subject to movement. Instead, states John, from these
Ideas proceed the *formae natiuae*, namely the images of the exemplars which
are created simultaneously with particular things in nature. Next John quotes
an opinion of Boethius from the *De trinitate*. Now John's discussion of the
forms here has always been taken as an identification of the source of the
concept of the *formae natiuae*: that Bernard and Gilbert had derived the
concept directly from Boethius. In fact, it seems, from the evidence of the
Glosae, that Bernard had conceived of the *formae natiuae* not from reading
Boethius, but Calcidius. Indeed, we can watch Bernard in the *Glosae*
substitute his own term for the Calcidian one. Why then did John of Salisbury
mistakenly believe that the concept came from Boethius? Probably he had
learned about the *formae natiuae* from Gilbert of Poitiers, whose own
investigations had led him to consider the concept in terms of Boethius'
thought. Thus, John probably heard of the specific Boethian background of
the *formae natiuae* in Gilbert's classroom. John was once again, then, in
contact with a later interpretation of the *formae natiuae* than the one we meet
in the *Glosae*.

At this precise point in his account John returns directly to Bernard of
Chartres, thus tying him inextricably to the doctrine of the *formae natiuae*.
In introducing the poem "Non dico," John calls Bernard the "perfectissimus
inter Platonicos seculi nostri." Some have wondered whether John meant to

---

[260] By way of contrast, cf. the earlier formulations edited by Huygens, in "Mittelalterliche
Kommentare zum *O qui perpetua...* ," p. 386.100-106 and the later formulations in Moreau,
"'*Opifex, id est Creator*': Remarques sur le platonisme de Chartres," p. 38 n.21. The three
principles were a fairly consistent commonplace of the Platonic, Neo-Platonic, and Middle
Platonic traditions: see Stephen Gersh, *Middle Platonism and Neoplatonism: The Latin
Tradition*, 1: 244-246, 2: 436-437.

compliment Bernard with this extravagant title. Perhaps he thought that Bernard had carried the doctrine of the Platonic Ideas too far and that his Platonism was simply old-fashioned by the mid twelfth century.[261] A more generous interpretation might be that John thought of Bernard of Chartres as the most accomplished representative of Plato's teachings in recent memory. Others like William of Conches may have glossed the *Timaeus* more systematically and thoroughly, but their positions were less purely Platonic. John may have thought of Bernard as the most faithful and outstanding disciple of Plato in the early twelfth century, especially in his strict adherence to Platonic doctrines such as the Ideas with which John disagreed. But John also doubtless associated Bernard with a specific inter-pretation of the *Timaeus* that had been given almost historical status in the classes he attended. We have been so convinced of the many Platonisms of the Middle Ages and of the uncritical eclecticism produced by them,[262] that we forget that there were attempts to deal with Plato on his own terms. Perhaps the *perfectissimus* of the title was merely an acknowledgement of Bernard's orthodoxy and integrity in sticking to the doctrine of the text. Indeed, a certain pointedness would seem to be one of the distinguishing characteristics of Bernard's approach to texts in general.[263] In the *Glosae*, for instance, Bernard refused to force the *Timaeus* into a Christian straitjacket. Unlike William of Conches and Abelard, he did not apparently ever entertain the idea that the *anima mundi* was the Holy Spirit.[264] Instead, he confidently approached the *Timaeus* on its own terms, even though this meant that Bernard occasionally had to fit a square peg of Christian doctrine into the round hole of his Platonic philosophy.

John remarks that Bernard maintained, with all those who philosophise correctly, that neither the Idea nor matter is coeternal with God. He assented to the opinion of the Fathers of the church, including Augustine, that God, in making all things from nothing, had created the matter of all things.

---

[261] See Wetherbee, *Platonsim and Poetry in the Twelfth Century,* p. 23; Dutton, "The Uncovering," p. 212; and Wetherbee, "Philosophy, Cosmology, and the Twelfth-Century Renaissance," p. 34.

[262] See esp. Chenu, *Nature, Man, and Society,* pp. 49-98 and Gilson, *History of Christian Philosophy in the Middle Ages* (New York, 1955), p. 144.

[263] Wetherbee, "Philosophy, Cosmology, and the Twelfth-Century Renaissance," p. 32 came to the same conclusion: "... I would argue that it is largely their willingness to engage an ancient source, directly and as nearly as possible on its own terms, that distinguishes the work of Thierry, Bernard of Chartres, and William of Conches from that of their contempo-raries."

[264] See Gregory, *Anima mundi,* pp. 133-139 and Dorothy Elford, "William of Conches," in *A History of Twelfth-Century Western Philosophy,* ed. Peter Dronke (Cambridge, 1988), pp. 326-327.

Nevertheless, according to John, Bernard continued to assert that the Idea was eternal, for he pointed as proof to the eternity of divine providence in which God made all things once and for all, setting out near himself all the things that would come to be in time and those that would abide throughout eternity. The Idea, however, could not claim equality with the Trinity, for in its nature it was posterior to the Trinity and was a certain effect subsisting in some secret mystery of the divine mind, not needing any external cause. In this sense, then, Bernard was said to have restricted coeternity to the three persons of the Trinity, because he scrupulously distinguished between God and the divine mind. The Ideas belong to the latter, but only God could be identical and coeternal with himself. And so Bernard of Chartres was prepared to call the Idea eternal, but would never refer to it as coeternal with God.

Of all of John of Salisbury's observations on Bernard's Platonism this one may be the most historically significant. In the *Glosae* Bernard recognises that the philosophers say that God had only adorned or arranged (*exornasse*) the universe from nothing, but had not created it from nothing (4.194-195). Nonetheless he offered two opinions of his own: either the confused matter in hyle was created from nothing or, lacking a beginning, it passed (once the *formae natiuae* had been taken up) into the separated elements and then into elementary things (8.13-16). Though the Ideas are said to exist eternally (8.229-230), Bernard carefully avoids the issue of the eternity of matter.[265] Hyle is said to remain *semper* in its own nature (8.157-158) and its matter, as we have seen, may have lacked a beginning (8.14). *Semper*, Bernard noted early in the glosses, refers to *tempus*, not *aeuum* (4.11). Later, he added that *aeuum* is coeternal with the intelligible world (5.301), while *tempus* is coequal with this world (5.310) and the visible heavens by which time is noted (5.306, 5.310-311). The question was whether things preceded the beginning of time or not: the works of nature and man follow time, while those of God precede it (4.73-79). Early in the *Glosae* Bernard makes his essential distinction on this point: "Nec dicimus aeternum quod careat principio, sed intelligimus perpetuum et indissolubilem" (4.61-62). In this way Bernard can speak of the first principles hyle and the Ideas as effectively eternal, and yet mean by this that they were eternal in the sense of being perpetual and indissoluble. Nonetheless, they were subsequent to God and inferior to his eternal nature. Following in the footsteps of Boethius, Bernard began that Chartrian preoccupation with

---

[265] On the difficult questions posed by the problem of the eternity of matter in the twelfth century, see Parent, *La doctrine de la création dans l'école de Chartres*, pp. 40-43.

correct talk about time.[266] Later in the *Glosae* when he says that the archetype has neither beginning nor end and nevertheless is diverse and inferior, he quickly explains why he maintains such a view. The archetype is diverse because it collects in itself the Ideas of all things; it is inferior because, according to Macrobius, the Ideas are in the mind of God which is inferior to God (4.232-239). This is the argument, then, that allowed Bernard to restrict coeternity to the persons of Trinity, for even the Ideas of the divine mind were in some sense subsequent to God. Only twice in the *Glosae* does Bernard employ the term coeternity, once when he notes that Plato taught the doctrine of the birth of the soul lest anyone contend that the soul was coeternal with God (5.27-29), and the second time when he remarks that *aeuum* is coeternal with the intelligible world (5.301). The first instance suggests that Bernard's position was that only God could be coeternal with himself, while the second suggests that Bernard regarded the very term "coeternal" as a comparative, rather than absolute unit. John of Salisbury's account of this problem in Bernard's philosophy is interesting because it suggests, with the phrases "cum illis qui philosophantur," "Adquiescebat enim Patribus," and "Ideam uero eternam esse consentiebat," that Bernard of Chartres was criticised in his own day for leaning too far in favour of a Platonic position on a point in conflict with Christian authority. In the end, "coeternity" was a distinction that allowed Bernard to reconcile the theological demands of his time with Plato's emphasis upon the eternity of the Ideas, hyle, and the intelligible world.

As one might have suspected, John of Salisbury's summary history of Bernard of Chartres's philosophy is coloured, in the Platonic sense, by some contaminating influences. The first of these was his own ostensible Aristotelianism in the *Metalogicon*, which had been less pronounced in the *Entheticus*.[267] John was probably not predisposed to treat Bernard's Platonism

---

[266] Cf. Hugh of Saint-Victor, *Didascalicon* 1.6, ed. Buttimer, pp. 12.25-13.3: "Sunt namque in rebus alia quae nec principium habent nec finem, et haec aeterna nominantur, alia quae principium quidem habent, sed nullo fine clauduntur, et dicuntur perpetua, alia quae et intimum habent et finem, et haec sunt temporalia." William of Conches, *Glosae super Boetium*, ed. [in part] Parent, in *La doctrine de la création dans l'école de Chartres*, p. 125: "Notandum est in hoc loco cum perpetuum sit quod habet principium sed caret fine, discurrens de preterito in presens de presenti in futurum ut est anima; eternum uero est quod utroque caret scilicet principio et fine cui nichil preteritum nichil futurum immo omnia presentia; cur diuinam rationem cui nichil preteritum uel futurum perpetuam uocat non eternam? Sed dicendum est quod unam particulam pro alia posuit scilicet perpetua pro eterna."

On distinctions about time in Chartrian thought, see Parent, *La doctrine de la création dans l'école de Chartres*, pp. 95-106; Chenu, *Nature, Man, and Society*, pp. 57-60; and Gregory, *Anima mundi*, pp. 50-59 and *Platonismo medievale*, pp. 81-82.

[267] See Rodney Thomson, "What is the *Entheticus?*" in *The World of John of Salisbury*, ed. Michael Wilks (Oxford, 1984), p. 300.

sympathetically and seems not to have been in a position to study it fully. Thus, another qualification of John's sketch is that it was apparently not based on primary materials, but on hearsay. There is no clear indication in the *Metalogicon* that he had ever consulted the *Glosae*, though much of what he knows about the *Timaeus* derives from a tradition of interpreting Plato that had begun with Bernard. A good deal of what John knows about Bernard had come by way of Gilbert of Poitiers, especially his understanding of the very rare doctrine of the *formae natiuae*. Indeed, the only substantial accounts of the concept are to be found in the *Glosae* and the *Metalogicon*, and only the *Glosae* provides an example of the *formae natiuae* as a working philosophical concept.[268]

John of Salisbury's portrait of Bernard as a Platonic philosopher is particularly intriguing because of its suggestion of further development to Bernard's thought after he had composed the *Glosae*. Words like *concreare*, twice used by John in *Metalogicon* 4.35, imply that Bernard later refined his Platonic language. Bernard may have been searching with words such as *concreare* and *coaeternum* for terminological solutions to apparent conflicts between the doctrines of Plato and Christian doctrine. Whereas in the *Glosae* Bernard straddles the fence on issues like the creation *ex nihilo* of matter, in John's account he is presented as one ready to clarify further his talk about some of these troubling matters. Everything else in John's final summary of Bernard's philosophy, *mutatis mutandis*, fits comfortably enough with the doctrines presented in the *Glosae*. John of Salisbury remains, then, in the end, as he had been in the beginning, a precious witness to both the career and thought of Bernard of Chartres.

Bernard's most original contribution to the study of the *Timaeus* in the Middle Ages was the conception of the *formae natiuae*. The marvel of the *Glosae*, though it is too brief a text to satisfy fully, is that we can observe the concept of the *formae natiuae* forming out of the incidentals of Calcidius' unwieldy commentary. Thus, on one level, Bernard employed the concept in his search for a resolution to a perplexing problem in the history of philosophy. But, on another, the concept of the *formae natiuae* reflects Bernard's underlying belief that the study of this world can be grounded in an examination of the inhering, if imperfect, reflection of the Ideas in sensible things. For Bernard the point was to go beyond the mere appearances of material things to their causes, the Ideas. "For by those things which are

---

[268] Gregory seems to suggest that other glosses contain references to the *formae natiuae*, but he is actually referring to the *Glosae* in manuscripts M and V: see Gregory, "The Platonic Inheritance," p. 74 n.64. There are some interesting remarks on the *formae natiuae* in glosses demonstrably dependent on the *Glosae*: see in particular App. 3.11.

visible," he wrote, "we are led to understand invisible things" (7.400-401). Moreover, the universal is understood through the singular (8.244-245). Bernard thought that he had discovered in Plato's *Timaeus* and in the doctrine of the *formae natiuae* an inherent connection between the imperfect and perfect, between this world and its archetype, and between creature and creator.

We need to remember that, unlike modern commentators on Plato, Bernard was not dispassionately seeking to take the measure of the historical Plato and his profound book, but to understand a newly relevant Plato. If the ninth century had in a very real sense rediscovered Martianus Capella's *De nuptiis* for the Middle Ages, it fell to Bernard of Chartres and the early twelfth century to do the same for the *Timaeus*. For his part, Bernard sought from Plato a reasonable and working explanation of the universe, intellectual and physical, in which he lived. This was, whatever we might think of it, a living Platonism, deeply felt and thought to be at work in the world.

Bernard was more faithful in his explication of the text than were many medieval glossators. His attitude in this was a remarkably text-bound one and in his role as glossator he must have believed that he was simply stating and restating Plato's own positions. Nonetheless, there are significant departures from Plato or, at least, from a modern interpretation of the *Timaeus*. These are not without interest, because they reveal medieval assumptions about the dialogue. One wonders, in fact, whether Bernard was aware that he differed on many points from the ancient author he was attempting to explain. Bernard assumed, as we have seen, that the worker-god of the *Timaeus* was a creator-God, and this shift instilled a persistent tension into his Platonism. Hence, Bernard was quick to seize on the *uoluntas dei* as the primary, if unexplanatory, reason for creation, whereas Plato's *opifex* entered at a slightly later stage as the arranger of already available, but chaotic matter. Bernard also preferred to think of hyle as matter rather than as spatial field and this had significant implications for his doctrine of the *formae natiuae*, for it implied that the *formae natiuae* and hyle had something like equal parts to play in creation. If Plato had spoken of hyle as both Necessity and the Errant Cause, Bernard emphasised the former and downplayed the latter; perhaps the reason was that Bernard could understand the principle of material imperfection in Necessity, but not the limitation seemingly placed on God's omnipotence by the idea of an Errant Cause. The phrase *necessitas incommodi*, which denotes this material corruption, is found in the *Glosae* and the same sense of Necessity is captured in one of the poems. Ironically, Bernard is more the Platonist than Plato on a few occasions. Whereas Plato seems, albeit metaphorically, to envisage the merging of the Ideas and matter (*Timaeus* 50d), Bernard remains a rigorist, maintaining the absolute separateness of the Ideas and matter. His *formae natiuae* concept was born of the need to explain the mechanics of creation in spite of the absolute isolation of the Ideas and hyle from each other.

Also striking is Bernard's persistent moralism: he read the *Timaeus* on one level as an explanation for the moral nature of creation and for the very existence of the vices and virtues. Bernard could not, therefore, believe that Socrates would promote sexual promiscuity among the members of his republic, and so he resorted to an integumental leap over the problem. For Bernard, the *Timaeus* was quite simply a moral text; this was the ethical side of the dialogue that he had identified in his *accessus* (1.56-57). He was inclined to identify the *Timaeus* with what he knew of the Socratic mission to improve human character. As such the *Timaeus* was doubtless a very personal book for the old master of Chartres who had a moral mission of his own.

We should probably not think that the *Glosae* contains Bernard's final word on Plato, but rather regard these simple glosses as one expression of a Platonic philosophy that was still developing. But, until his death, Bernard apparently remained a Platonist, the most complete Platonist of them all according to John of Salisbury. Perhaps Bernard died believing that there were three everlasting principles in the universe—God, the Ideas, and hyle—and that, even as he breathed his last, *formae natiuae* were entering into hyle to make yet other bodies that could be seen and felt, and that implied yet higher realms of real existence.

Influence and Diffusion

So much of a general nature has been written about Bernard of Chartres's influence that here we must search out and stick fast, I think, to specific cases. The doctrines of the *Glosae*, for example, can be compared to those of other thinkers who are known to have come into contact with Bernard's thought. For instance, much of Hugh of Saint-Victor's teaching on the *Timaeus* is consistent with Bernard's, but it is also of a very general nature.[269] His formulation of the three principles is identical with Bernard's,[270] and among his many definitions and classifications of philosophy Hugh notes that some divide it into physics, ethics, and logic, a distinction found in Bernard's *accessus*.[271] Whether Hugh knew Bernard's work on the *Timaeus* or not is

---

[269] See, for instance, *Didascalicon* 1.1, 1.6, 1.9, ed. Buttimer, pp. 4.14-17, 13, and 16.

[270] *Didascalicon* 2.5, ed. Buttimer, p. 29.21-23, and see p. 72 above.

[271] *Didascalicon* 2.16, ed. Buttimer, p. 35.8-11 and cf. *Glosae* 1.56-60. Cf. John of Salisbury, *Metalogicon* 2.2, ed. Webb, pp. 62-63, 2.13, pp. 84-85, and *Policraticus* 7.5, ed.

open to question, but he certainly knew of Bernard (see App. 2.2.A) and had an early twelfth-century interest in the *Timaeus*.

It remains surprising that neither William of Conches nor Gilbert of Poitiers ever mentions Bernard in their voluminous writings. They certainly spoke of him in their own classrooms, as the student author of the *accessus* to the *Glosae in Iuuenalem* (App. 2.5.F) records and as we can infer from John of Salisbury's own experience. Perhaps, as the character of the *Glosae* suggests, they learned more of method than doctrine from Bernard: William's style of glossing is essentially Bernard's. The three step approach of general comment and survey, *continuatio*, and *et hoc est*, specifically recalls Bernard's system of the comprehensive *glosa*. William's student, in fact, seems to confirm that William still thought of Bernard as one who had grounded him in the mechanics of approaching a text. The master also seems to have focused the attention of his students on some important passages, such as Calcidius' "Omnia enim quae sunt uel dei opera sunt uel naturae uel naturam imitantis hominis artificis."[272] This passage, which Bernard had carefully reworked, became the common property of those who had come into contact with him. Indeed, the very popularisation of the *Timaeus* that took place in the early twelfth-century was the same kind of enterprise, drawing the attention of students to the more profound and stimulating aspects of Plato's dialogue. Moreover, what Bernard instilled in the mind of William was an abiding interest in a certain group of authors: Macrobius, Boethius, Plato, and Priscian.

The young William seems to reflect something of Bernard's teachings, but these appear for the most part to have been the remembered incidentals of Bernard's lectures and not the crux. Thus, in William's early work, the *Philosophia mundi*,[273] one finds a comparable definition:

Bernard, *Glosae* 6.54-56	William, *Philosophia* 2.8 (21)
Polum accipit lineam intelligibilem, quae ab arctico per diametrum ad antarcticum polum protenditur, quae dicitur uadens per omnia et continens, quia et terram et omnes circulos penetrat.	Axis uero est linea intelligibilis de polo ad polum per medium terrae directa, circa quam uoluitur firmamentum.[274]

Webb, 2: 107-108. See also Cal., *Comm.* 264-65 (W270:6-25). See also Gregory, *Anima mundi*, pp. 270-273.

[272] Cal., *Comm.* 23 (W73:10-12). On the use of this text by William, Gilbert, and Hugh of Saint-Victor, see p. 67 and n. 204 above.

[273] On the date of the work, see p. 19 n. 54 above.

[274] In Wilhelm von Conches, *Philosophia*, ed. Maurach, pp. 48-49, or PL 172: 61D13-15.

Both generally reflect the *Timaeus* and Calcidius' commentary,[275] but the
specific formulation of the pole or axis as an intelligible or notional line was
an interest pursued by Bernard's school (see App. 1.3).

Again in the classification of vision we see Bernard acting as a kind of filter
through which William received a simplified Calcidian scheme:

Bernard, *Glosae* 7.263-270	William, *Philosophia* 4.23 (42)
Quia cepit ostendere naturam uisus, ostensa tuitione, uult docere intuitionem et detuitionem. Hi sunt enim tres modi uisus. Tuitio est quando uisus dirigitur ad aliquod tale corpus, unde non reuerberatur, ita ut ex eo imago uultus appareat, ut lapidem uel tale quid inspiciamus. Intuitio est cum aliquid tale inspicimus, in cuius superficie imago uultus apparet, ut speculum uel aliquod aliud corpus bene detersum et leuigatum. Detuitio est cum tale quid inspicimus, ubi non in superficie, sed interius imago uidetur apparere, sicut uitrum nigrum uel obscurum stagnum.	Visus autem species sunt tres: Contuitio, detuitio, intuitio. Et est contuitio, quando aliquid uidemus nullo in eo occurrente simulacro. Sed ostendentes, qualiter uisus fieret, de ea satis diximus. Intuitio est, quando aliquid uidemus, in cuius superficie aliquod occurrit simulacrum. Detuitio uero est, quando non in superficie, sed in profundo apparet, ut in aqua, diciturque detuitio quasi deorsum tuitio.[276]

Both of these have their ultimate source in Calcidius,[277] but they are much
closer in content and expression to each other than they are to Calcidius.

In yet another case, William defines *calodaemones* and *cacodaemones* as
had Bernard (see 6.108-127):

> Qui differunt ab aliis daemonibus in hoc, quod duo primi ordines dicuntur
> calodaemones, id est bonum scientes, calos enim est bonum, daemon sciens;
> isti uero dicuntur cacodaemones, id est malum scientes, cacos enim malum est,
> ne abhorreas nomen, quod isti et illi dicuntur daemones quasi scientes, cum isti
> et illi angeli dicantur, unde dicitur bonus angelus et malus.[278]

Though William speaks elsewhere as if Plato himself had referred to the
calodaemones, this relatively rare word is neither in the Latin *Timaeus* nor

---

[275] *Timaeus* 40b-c (W33:19-21); Cal., *Comm.* 122 (W166:3-10).

[276] In Wilhelm von Conches, *Philosophia*, ed. Maurach, pp. 108-109, or PL 172: 96c8-D2.

[277] See Cal., *Comm.* 239 (W251-252).

[278] In Wilhelm von Conches, *Philosophia* 1.5 (15), ed. Maurach, p. 24, or PL 172: 47c13-D5.

in Calcidius' commentary.[279] Later in his glosses on the *Timaeus*, William would drop the names for the two types of *daemon*, but early in his career they may have been a kind of trace element registering recent learning.[280] In all probability a full investigation of William's glosses on Macrobius and Boethius would uncover more evidence of the influence of the *Glosae*.

The grounds for comparison with Gilbert of Poitiers are different, chiefly because he was a theologian and did not comment directly on the quadrivium. Yet we have been led to believe by John of Salisbury that Bernard and Gilbert shared a basic metaphysics. Indeed, both commented on the three Platonic principles of things, though Gilbert was less than fully comfortable with the formula.[281] Gilbert's use of the word *natiua* in the commentaries on the *Opuscula sacra* of Boethius holds some importance for our re-examination of Bernard of Chartres's influence. Notwithstanding the prevailing assumption that Gilbert actively promoted the concept of the *formae natiuae*, he never actually employs the phrase in his commentaries, but rather speaks of the *natiuum* or *natiua*.[282] Are Gilbert's *natiua*, in fact, to be equated with Bernard's *formae natiuae*? Once he does refer to the "natiuorum inabstractae formae," or solid forms of these *natiua*.[283] But he seems to think of these concrete wholes (*natiua*) as things born or created (from *natiuitas*) and also as *naturales*. The *natiua* are concrete, solid, and in motion.[284] For Gilbert, the *natiua* are in part a way of speaking about and conceiving of created natures:

---

[279] See Wilhelm von Conches, *Philosophia* 1.6 (18), ed. Maurach, p. 25, or PL 172: 48B14-c3. See also Cal., *Comm.* 132-136 (W173-177) and J. den Boeft, *Calcidius on Demons (Commentarius Ch. 127-136)*, Philosophia antiqua: A Series of Monographs on Ancient Philosophy 33 (Leiden, 1977).

[280] See *Glose Willelmi de Conchis super Platonem* 110, ed. Jeauneau, pp. 199-201. See also Garnerius, bishop of Langres, *Sermo (IV) in aduentu Domini*, PL 205: 598D11-13: "Sed illi (angeli) qui bona nuntiant, calodaemones; qui autem mala, cacodaemones nuncupantur."

[281] See "Expositio in Boecii librum De trinitate," 1.4.65, in *The Commentaries on Boethius by Gilbert of Poitiers*, ed. Nikolaus M. Häring, Studies and Texts 13 (Toronto, 1966), p. 128 and "Expositio De bonorum ebdomade," 1.2.30, ibid., p.195. See also L.O. Nielsen, *Theology and Philosophy in the Twelfth Century. A Study of Gilbert Porreta's Thinking and the Theological Expositions of the Doctrine of the Incarnation during the Period 1130-1180*, Acta Theologica Danica 15 (Leiden, 1982), p. 71.

[282] Gilbert's belief in the *formae natiuae* has been assumed on the basis of John of Salisbury's testimony and the presence of the word *natiua* in the commentaries. For an example of this line of reasoning, see Aimé Forest, "Le réalisme de Gilbert de la Porrée dans le commentaire du 'De hebdomadibus'," *Revue néo-scholastique de philosophie* 36 (1934) 102-110.

[283] "Expositio De trinitate," 1.2.30, ed. Häring, p. 84.

[284] See "Expositio Contra Euticen et Nestorium," 1.82 and 85, in *The Commentaries on Boethius by Gilbert of Poitiers*, ed. Nikolaus M. Häring, Studies and Texts 13 (Toronto, 1966), p.260, and "Expositio De trinitate," 1.2.26, ibid., p.83.

Que uero in ea ratione natiua sunt quod natiuorum subsistentium esse sunt et
eis adeo insita ut aut in eis perpetuo maneant aut suo abscessu illa corrumpant,
proprius et usu plurimo dicuntur "nature."[285]

Natiua nanque per aliquam sui uel efficientem uel efficiendi proprietatem
concipiuntur: ut album per albedinem et albedo per naturam faciendi album.[286]

This last argument with its three stages of conceptual abstraction and the
illustration of *albedo*, *albet* (in effect), and *album* recalls Bernard of
Chartres's dramatic example of the white virgin. But Gilbert here means to
distinguish the *quod est* from the *quo est*, the concrete whole from the cause
which renders it conceivable. Primordial matter, incomprehensible in itself,
becomes intelligible because of the *natiua* made by God, whom he calls
"natiuorum omnium Opifex."[287] Gilbert sharply contrasts the corruptible and
corporeal *natiuum* with the incorruptible and incorporeal *genuinum*:[288]

Et natiua quidem eorum quibus aliquid sunt: ficta uero eorum, quibus aliquid
esse finguntur, amminiculis concipiuntur. Genuina uero que sunt natiuorum
principia—Deus scilicet et primordialis materia—longe aliter. Non enim sunt
aliquid huiusmodi subsistentiis uel quantitatibus uel qualitatibus quibus uel
natiua uere sunt aliquid uel, que neque sunt aliquid neque sunt, tamquam
aliquid sint finguntur.[289]

Thus, the *natiua* lie absolutely outside their real principles and (to reverse the
same observation) the principles are in no way confused with the *natiua* or
their accidents.[290]

The closest parallel to Bernard's doctrine of the *formae natiuae* occurs in
Gilbert's commentary on the *De trinitate*:

Tercia uero speculatio que omnia natiua transcendens in ipso eorum quolibet
principio—scilicet uel Opifice, quo auctore sunt, uel idea, a qua tanquam
exemplari deducta sunt, uel yle in qua locata sunt—figit intuitum, per excel-
lenciam "intellectualis" uocatur.[291]

In this passage Gilbert characterises a process in which the *natiua* are things
made by the Platonic worker-god, but are derived from the Idea, their
exemplar, and are located in hyle. If Gilbert's notion of the *natiua* was born

[285] "Expositio Contra Euticen," 1.85, ed. Häring, p. 260.
[286] "Expositio Contra Euticen," 1.16, ed. Häring, p. 245.
[287] See "Expositio Contra Euticen," 1.26, ed. Häring, p. 247 and 1.32, ed. Häring, p. 248.
[288] "Expositio Contra Euticen," 1.66, ed. Häring, p. 256: "Sicut enim omne genuinum incorruptibile sic omne natiuum est corruptibile." On the corporeal nature of the *natiua*, see "Expositio Contra Euticen," 1.67, ed. Häring, p. 256.
[289] "Expositio Contra Euticen," 1.23, ed. Häring, pp. 246-247.
[290] See "Expositio Contra Euticen," 1.84, ed. Häring, p. 260.
[291] "Expositio De trinitate," 1.2.34, ed. Häring, p. 85.

of some contact with Bernard of Chartres's philosophy, it became something very different, both in terminology and meaning. The casual use of "in which" (*in qua*) here ran against Bernard's arguments about the nature of the contact beteeen the *formae natiuae* and hyle. Moreover, the special and rather tense relationship between the *formae natiuae* and the Ideas sketched by Bernard in the *Glosae* has been relaxed here in order to relate the *natiua* equally to all three principles. Moreover, Gilbert tends to blur the distinction between the inherent forms as the images of the Ideas and the actual concrete wholes, probably because he thought of the relationship between the *natiua* and the exemplars as one of weak imitation.[292] If Gilbert identifies the universal at all, it is not with the *formae natiuae*, as John of Salisbury would have us believe (App. 2.5.A), for *forma natiua* is a phrase and doctrine not employed by Gilbert in his extant writings. Gilbert more likely attached universality to his *quo est* distinction, but the *quo est* is not the image of the exemplary Idea in Gilbert's thought.[293]

Remarkably, twice in the same commentary Gilbert perpetuates a Calcidian confusion, at least according to Bernard's understanding of Calcidius' position. Interestingly Gilbert is commenting here on the sentence of Boethius where John of Salisbury thought the doctrine of the *formae natiuae* was first propounded:

> *Ex his enim formis que sunt preter materiam* id est ex sinceris substanciis: igne scilicet et aere et aqua et terra—non utique his que in yle mutuam habent concrecionem sed que sunt ex silua et intelligibili specie que sunt idee sensilium—*iste forme que sunt in materia et* ei, quod est esse materie, aduenientes *corpus efficiunt* quadam exempli ab exemplari suo conformatiua deductione *uenerunt.* Ac per hoc ille sincere idee id est exemplares et uero nomine "forme" uocantur.[294]

Either Gilbert has here confused the *species intelligibilis* with the *species natiua* or (as seems more likely) he has opted for that Calcidian position in which the pure archtypes of the elements are formed from the contact of the Idea (*species intelligibilis*) and hyle.[295] In order to preserve their simple purity and immutability, Bernard had rejected outright the notion that the Ideas and matter ever merged, even at the level of the archetypal elements.

---

[292] See Nielsen, *Theology and Philosophy in the Twelfth Century*, pp. 72-73.

[293] See John Marenbon, "Gilbert of Poitiers," in *A History of Twelfth-Century Western Philosophy*, ed. Peter Dronke (Cambridge, 1988), pp. 342, 351 and n.107.

[294] "Expositio De trinitate," 1.2.97, ed. Häring, p. 100. See also "Expositio De trinitate," 1.2.17, ed. Häring, pp. 80-81.

[295] See Nielsen, *Theology and Philosophy in the Twelfth Century*, p. 74 and Marenbon, "Gilbert of Poitiers," pp. 349-350 and n.102.

Thus, even with respect to his most important contribution to Platonic metaphysics, Bernard's legacy was not a particularly influential one. Walter of Mortagne in the mid twelfth century was known to be an outright imitator of Bernard's philosophy of the Platonic Ideas, but whether this included the *formae natiuae* we are not told (App. 2.5.A). If, as John reports, Walter changed his mind on the universals in mid-career, perhaps even he was unable to establish a tradition of interest in Bernard's Platonism.[296] John of Salisbury himself knew enough of the original doctrine, probably from Gilbert, to provide a basic description of it, but Gilbert in his commentaries on the *Opuscula sacra* does not faithfully imitate his master's special metaphysical doctrine, nor does he make it the linchpin of his own metaphysics. William of Conches neglected the concept of the *formae natiuae* entirely, preferring to speak in general of forms in a more Aristotelian sense and only once calling the Ideas forms.[297] Though Bernard's students may have carried on something of his method, they seem to have turned away from his specific philosophical tenets. This is not to suggest that the underlying method of Bernard's approach to such problems as the *formae natiuae* did not find a receptive audience in his students, for it probably did.[298] But William of Conches and Gilbert of Poitiers were not ordinary students, who might have been expected to bind themselves exclusively to their master's teachings. Bernard had taught them how to think, not what to think. Said William, perhaps in tribute: "Etenim principium a magistro, sed perfectio debet esse ab ingenio."[299]

---

[296] See *Metalogicon* 2.17, ed. Webb, p. 93.9-14: "Partiuntur itaque status, duce Gautero de Mauritania, et Platonem, in eo quod Plato est, dicunt indiuiduum; in eo quod homo, speciem; in eo quod animal, genus; sed subalternum; in eo quod substantia, generalissimum. Habuit hec opinio aliquos assertores; sed pridem hanc nullus profitetur."

A certain treatise, now referred to as the *Tractatus 'Quoniam de generali'*, possesses something like Walter's first position and has been attributed to him by B. Hauréau, ed., in *Notices et extraits de quelques manuscrits latins de la Bibliothèque Nationale* 5 (Paris, 1892), pp. 298-325. On Walter, see Nikolaus Häring, "A Hitherto Unknown Commentary on Boethius' *De hebdomadibus* Written by Clarenbaldus of Arras," *Mediaeval Studies* 15 (1953) 214 and n.10. On Walter's first position on universals, see Martin M. Tweedale, "Logic (i): From the Late Eleventh Century to the Time of Abelard," in *A History of Twelfth-Century Western Philosophy*, ed. Peter Dronke (Cambridge, 1988), pp. 221-222.

[297] *Glose Willelmi de Conchis super Platonem* 56, ed. Jeauneau, p. 126. On William of Conches and the concept of the *formae natiuae*, see Gregory, *Platonismo medievale*, pp. 115-116.

[298] See Dronke's interesting suggestion about how William of Conches might have applied Bernard's type of distinction to his own work on the elements: "New Approaches to the School of Chartres," pp. 131-132.

[299] In Wilhelm von Conches, *Philosophia* 1.7 (26), ed. Maurach, p. 29, or PL 172: 50D14-15.

The students of Bernard's students reflect the further dissolution of Bernard's philosophical bequest. John of Salisbury, as we have seen, knew the doctrines of the Ideas and *formae natiuae* as propounded by Bernard, but denied that there was universality in either. In the *Entheticus*, which was written before the *Metalogicon*, John, as if to complicate matters, actually once employs the phrase *forma natiua*:

> Omne, quod est uerum, conuincit forma uel actus;
>   Nec falsum dubites, si quid utroque caret.
> Forma suo generi quaeuis addicta tenetur,
>   Et peragit semper, quicquid origo iubet.
> Ergo quod in forma natiua constat, agitue,
>   Quod natura manens in ratione monet,
> Esse sui generis, uerum quid dicitur; idque
>   Indicat effectus, aut sua forma probat.[300]

His emphasis here, however, is Aristotelian in its practical concern with the meaning of form and has little to do with the metaphysical concept by means of which Bernard described the mediating relationship of the *formae natiuae* to the Ideas and primordial matter. To underline the point, we might note that later in the *Entheticus*, when he treats of Plato's philosophy proper, John makes no mention of the *formae natiuae*.[301] John, in some sense, meant by *natiua* what Gilbert of Poitiers had, that is, a natural thing.

Otto of Freising owed the same debt to Gilbert. His portion of the *Gesta Friderici I imperatoris* (for it was continued by his secretary Rahewin) is roughly contemporary with the *Metalogicon*. Otto had been a student in Paris for five years, beginning about 1128. He seems to have heard Gilbert lecture, for he expends some energy in trying to explain Gilbert's complex and controversial thought. Indeed, his own philosophical and theological excursus near the start of the *Gesta* reveals the profound influence that Gilbert had had on his thought:

> Quicquid est aut genuinum est aut natiuum. Sicut autem genuinum non potest esse non simplex et, ut ita dixerim, non singulare, non solitarium, ita natiuum non potest esse non compositum, non conforme, non concretum. Primo ergo uideamus, quid genuinum, quid natiuum appelletur, ut exhinc horum sensus

---

[300] *Entheticus Maior* 1.Par.29, lines 397-404, in *John of Salisbury's Entheticus Maior and Minor*, vol. 1, ed. Jan van Laarhoven, Studien und Texte zur Geistesgeschichte des Mittelalters 17, ed. Albert Zimmerman (Leiden, 1987), p. 131. See also Roland E. Pepin, "The *Entheticus* of John of Salisbury: a Critical Text," *Traditio* 31 (1975), pp. 148-149. On the work, see also Thomson, "What is the *Entheticus*?" pp. 287-301.

[301] *Entheticus Maior* 2.Par.64-67 lines 937-994, ed. Laarhoven, 1: 167-171.

uerborum facilius appareat. Genuinum dicitur tamquam generans et non genitum, id est carens generatione: natiuum uelut natum aut genitum, descendens a genuino. Unde Plato: "Est igitur, ut mihi uidetur, in primis diuidendum, quid sit quod semper est, carens generatione, quid item quod gignitur nec est semper." Et Boetius: "Qui tempus ab euo/ Ire iubes." Generationem uero large accipimus pro ingressu in quamlibet proprictatem uel, ut manifestius loquar, pro quolibet ingressu de non esse ad esse. Unde Aristotiles: "Ex oppositis fiunt generationes." In omni enim natiuo negatio prior est affirmatione. Genuinum est igitur carens generatione, carens principio, quale aput nos unum tantum inuenitur, eternitas uidelicet, soli diuinitati accommoda. Non enim tria aput nos, quae Plato posuit, inueniuntur principia, sed unum tantum, "Deus pater, ex quo omnia," Deus filius, "per quem omnia," (1 Cor.8:6) Deus spiritus sanctus, in quo omnia. Et hi tres, sicut nec tres dii, ita nec tria principia nec tria aeterna, sed unum principium et unum aeternum.[302]

The distinction made by Otto between *genuinum* and *natiuum* derives from Gilbert's commentaries on Boethius. The *natiuum* is composite, multiple (in sharing likenesses with other things), and concrete. It is the exact opposite of the *genuinum*, which is simple, single, and separate. Whereas the *genuinum* begets, but is not begotten, the *natiuum* is born or begotten, descending from the *genuinum*. Otto restricts eternity to divinity, the *genuinum* that alone lacks a beginning. Furthermore, he denies Plato's scheme of the three principles, rejecting outright the notion that they are like the Trinity or are eternal.[303] Otto's *natiuum* is quite simply a natural thing: created, sensible, and particular. The properties of the *natiuum* are the properties of sensible and accidental things. There are forms in these *natiua*, but the *natiua* themselves are not differentiated forms; they are informed.[304]

Otto's obvious interpretation of Gilbert's concept of the *natiuum* as a natural or created thing supports our earlier contention that Gilbert himself did not espouse the doctrine of the *formae natiuae*. As early as the late 1120s, then, Otto had heard Gilbert speak of the *natiuum* as a created, concrete whole. Had Gilbert already retreated from his master's particular metaphysical construct by the time of Otto's participation in his class? If so, perhaps Gilbert merely related anecdotes and historical information about the philosophical beliefs of Bernard of Chartres to his students Otto of Freising and John of Salisbury. Bernard's special Platonic philosophy was quietly being put aside soon after his death, relegated by his students to a

---

[302] *Gesta Friderici I imperatoris* 1.5, ed. Waitz, pp. 16.11-17.3.

[303] On other twelfth-century thinkers who rejected the idea of three Platonic principles, see Chenu, *Nature, Man, and Society*, pp. 56-57 and Gregory, *Anima mundi*, pp. 47-48.

[304] See *Gesta Friderici I imperatoris* 1.5, ed. Waitz, pp. 17.3-22.20.

small chapter in the history of philosophy. By the time of the generation of students once removed from him, his specific teachings had been so corrupted as to be devoid of any central meaning, or else they had been reduced to the status of half-remembered oral accounts. Otto did not subscribe to the philosophy of the Ideas and went so far as to reject the very existence of the three Platonic principles: God, the Ideas, and hyle. He had picked up the essential term *natiuum* from Gilbert of Poitiers, but it meant for him just a created thing and had little or nothing to do with the concept of the *formae natiuae*. By the mid twelfth century, as John of Salisbury implies in the *Metalogicon*, the concept of the *formae natiuae* had largely been abandoned; Bernard's metaphysics had been undone. And while the memory of Bernard lived on in the classrooms of his students, it faded with a new generation that had never been exposed to Bernard's masterful teaching and that had ceased to speak of his wisdom. Though John of Salisbury preserved a precious account of Bernard, his *Metalogicon* was a rare and neglected book in the following centuries.[305] The Middle Ages, so full of intellectual ferment by the late twelfth century, soon forgot the old man of Chartres.

But if the fame of Bernard's personality and doctrines was soon eclipsed, his *Glosae* achieved a remarkable success. The third appendix to the edition below is devoted to listing all of those instances so far found in which other sets of glosses on the Latin *Timaeus* demonstrate a dependence on the *Glosae* of Bernard of Chartres. Every lemmatic commentary or glossed copy of the *Timaeus* from the Middle Ages hitherto identified has been compared to Bernard's. With this appendix we can begin to document the extensive diffusion of the *Glosae*.

Apart from the six twelfth-century manuscripts which contain copies of the *Glosae*, three commentaries on the *Timaeus* reflect its influence. William of Conches's set of glosses on Plato is the most important of these, but the points of similarity and difference between the two call for a study of their own. William's work shows an unmistakable dependence on Bernard's (App. 3.3),[306] much greater in fact than can be demonstrated by a simple list of shared phrases and ideas. They both had, as we shall see, similar, though not identical, copies of Calcidius' translation of the *Timaeus*. Interestingly William tends to gloss the same words from the *Timaeus* as Bernard, though the choice of these was in some sense arbitrary and was not to be repeated by other independent glosses on the *Timaeus*. They share an odd etymology or two, insert lines from the *Aeneid* at the same points in their glosses, and

[305] See Linder, "The Knowledge of John of Salisbury," pp. 318, 362.
[306] See Dutton, "The Uncovering," pp. 203-206.

on occasion employ identical metaphors.[307] But philosophically William was moving in another direction. In his own *accessus*, with its identification of the efficient, formal, final, and material causes, William alerts us to his greater concern with the secondary causes of things.[308] His master had been almost exclusively concerned with the primary causes of things, and this more than anything may explain their different approaches.

The so-called Sigtuna commentary on the *Timaeus* from Uppsala, Universitetsbiblioteket MS C. 620, edited by Toni Schmid, was thought by many to be an early redaction of William's glosses.[309] As previously stated, this set of glosses actually contains a mixture of passages extracted from Bernard, William, and others (App. 3.2).[310] It is relatively easy to imagine how this might have happened: the scribe of the Uppsala glosses or its exemplar was probably in possession of a copy of the *Timaeus* that possessed marginal glosses taken from both Bernard and William. British Library, Add. MS 22815 contains just such a copy of the *Timaeus* with glosses extracted from Bernard, William, and unidentified others (see App. 3.8).[311] Such glosses, perhaps layered at different times and by different scribes in the exemplar, would then be transformed into a lemmatic commentary containing a jumble of undifferentiated glosses. The difficulty of this task for a scribe and the inevitable confusions introduced into the commentary go some way towards explaining the corrupt nature of the Uppsala glosses.

A twelfth-century lemmatic commentary on the *Timaeus* has been found in Leipzig, Universitätsbibliothek, Lat. 1258, fols. 1r-8v.[312] Its glosses, as can be seen from the list of dependent passages (App. 3.1), heavily rely on those of the *Glosae*. Moreover, this manuscript contains one of the *Notae Platonicae* (App. 1.7 and cf.1.1). Thus, William of Conches and the compilers of

---

[307] Cf. 2.51-52 and *Glose Willelmi de Conchis super Platonem* 10, ed. Jeauneau, p. 66.27-28 and note a. For the shared *Aeneid* citations, see *Glosae* 3.60 and 5.8 and *Glose Willelmi de Conchis super Platonem* 16 and 71, ed. Jeauneau, pp. 76.3 and 145.2. For the shared metaphor, see 4.382-383 and *Glose Willelmi de Conchis super Platonem* 70, ed. Jeauneau, p. 144.3-4.

[308] *Glose Willelmi de Conchis super Platonem* 4, ed. Jeauneau, p. 60.

[309] Toni Schmid, "Ein Timaioskommentar in Sigtuna," *Classica et mediaevalia: Revue Danoise de philologie et d'histoire* 10 (1949-1951) 220-266. For a variety of positions on the relation of these glosses to William's, see Southern, *Platonism, Scholastic Method, and the School of Chartres*, p. 16 n.17 and pp. 22-23; Gagnér, *Studien zur Ideengeschichte der Gesetzgebung*, p. 229; Gregory, *Anima mundi*, pp. 15-16; *Glose Willelmi de Conchis super Platonem*, ed. Jeauneau, pp. 13-14; Jeauneau, *Lectio*, p. 150 n.1; and see above p. 19.

[310] See the parallel texts supplied in Dutton, "The Uncovering," pp. 201-202.

[311] See Edouard Jeauneau, "Extraits des *Glosae super Platonem* de Guillaume de Conches dans un manuscrit de Londres," *Journal of the Warburg and Courtauld Institutes* 40 (1977) 212-222 and Dutton, "The Uncovering," p. 200.

[312] I should like to thank James Hankins for first drawing my attention to this set of glosses.

the lemmatic commentaries in the Sigtuna and Leipzig manuscripts were all readers of the *Glosae* of Bernard of Chartres.

The wider diffusion of the *Glosae* among glossed manuscripts of the *Timaeus* is even more striking. Seventeen sets of dependent glosses have been identified (App. 3.4-20).[313] None of these is identical with another in its choice of extracted glosses, though some reveal a similar selection of specific glosses, and none repeats any more than a small portion of the complete *Glosae*. Nor is any of these dependent sets of glosses as early in date as the manuscript tradition of the *Glosae*. For these reasons, we can reasonably refer to these other glosses as derivative or dependent.

In a number of cases these manuscripts reflect an almost entirely scribal reception of the *Glosae*, as scribes copied directly from it, although in shortened form (see App. 3.1, 4-8). In a number of other cases, glossator-scribes apparently reworked Bernard's individual glosses, often providing new introductions, conclusions, and partially rewritten sentences (see App. 3.2, 9-15). Indeed the last examples in the appendix (App. 3.16-20) doubtless reflect only a distant and indirect influence of the *Glosae*, one probably filtered through other intermediary glosses. The diffusion of Bernard's Timaean glosses belongs, at this level at least, to an 'open' tradition. Scribes, glossators, and students must have excerpted freely, altered where they felt the need, and added glosses frequently.

In the hands of medieval students the *Glosae* proved, at the very least, to be a highly useful aid to understanding the *Timaeus*. But, to go further, Bernard's influence in shaping an essential medieval reading of the *Timaeus* was vast, given that the list in the third appendix contains almost one third of all the extant glossed copies of the *Timaeus* from the Middle Ages. By date the dependent glosses include fifteen twelfth-century examples, two from the thirteenth century, two from the fourteenth, and one from the fifteenth. The preponderance of dependent glosses and manuscript copies of the *Glosae* from the twelfth century is in itself a striking feature. Today these dependent glosses are to be found in manuscripts located in libraries across Europe. The teachings of Bernard of Chartres were, therefore, widely diffused, albeit anonymously.

---

[313] In *Platonismo medievale*, pp. 88-91, Gregory noted the correspondence between the *Glosae* and the glosses contained in Vienna, Österreichische Nationalbibliothek MS 278, fols. 1r-84v and Vatican City, Biblioteca Apostolica Vaticana, Vat lat. 2063, fols. 1r-68v (see App. 3.14-15). There was, it should be noted, an understandable tendency in Gregory's pioneering book to blur the distinction between these dependent glosses and the *Glosae*.

In Dutton, "*Illustre ciuitatis*," pp. 95-96, 97 n.67, four other sets of dependent glosses were identified and in the "The Uncovering," pp. 198-200, another six. One of these, the glosses in London, British Library Arundel MS 339, fols. 110v-120r of the thirteenth century, I now leave off the list because the dependency was limited to only one, albeit identical, passage.

That one out of every three glossed copies of the *Timaeus* should depend to some degree on the *Glosae* testifies to the magnitude of Bernard's formative role as an interpreter of Plato for his century. We should not underestimate the impact that a single, sound interpretation of a difficult book could have on subsequent readers in the Middle Ages. The twelfth was to be the century of the *Timaeus'* greatest popularity in the Middle Ages, in part because Bernard had revealed a new way both to approach and to understand this profound book. The *Glosae* sets down a basic, if relatively simple, reading of the *Timaeus* on which other medieval commentaries could build. Just as Fulbert's massive crypt lies below the soaring cathedral of Chartres today, defining and supporting the structure of the magnificent building above, so Bernard of Chartres laid down and defined a foundation for the twelfth-century's inspired reception of the *Timaeus*. *Sic quoque Bernardus Carnotensis.*

B: The Text

Description of the Manuscripts

All six of the known copies of the *Glosae super Platonem* have been utilised in the critical edition that follows.[314] Five of the copies (D, M, O, P, and T) are complete, though two have suffered varying degrees of physical damage at the end: P sustained water damage on its last half folio and two thirds of the last folio of T was torn away with the resultant loss of approximately two columns of writing. The sixth copy, V, ends abruptly at *Glosae* 6.261 with a gloss on the word *Acturis* (*Timaeus* 42b; W37:10). The copies of the *Glosae* were all written in the twelfth century: D dates from the first quarter of the twelfth century, O and V from the middle of the century, M and P from closer to the fourth quarter, and finally T from the end of the century.[315]

In each of the following codicological descriptions the reader will find first a brief statement of the main content, date, and provenance of each codex; followed by lengthier treatments of its physical character (number of folios,

---

[314] For a table of the sigla, see below p. 138. In 1884 Hauréau informed Delisle that the *Glosae* in O were the same as those in V: see Léopold Delisle, "Notice sur plusieurs manuscrits de la Bibliothèque d'Orléans," *Notices et extraits des manuscrits* 31.1 (1884) 391 n.1. The shared text of three other manuscripts was announced by Klibansky, *The Continuity*, pp. 30, 52, and 55. Finally the copy of the *Glosae* in T was announced by Raymond Klibansky, "Report by the General Editor on the Progress of the Corpus Platonicum Medii Aevi," in *University of London. The Warburg Institute Annual Report 1956-1957* (London, 1957), p. 13.

[315] See Dutton, "The Uncovering," p. 198.

size of page and writing frames, collation, and binding) and provenance; a detailed list of contents; and finally a summary differentiation of the scripts in the codex. I have three reasons for supplying longer manuscript descriptions than is usually the custom. In the first place, it was the model established by my predecessor Edouard Jeauneau for the only other book-length edition of *Timaeus* glosses. In the second, all six manuscripts come from the twelfth century and are, therefore, especially valuable witnesses not only to the text of the *Glosae*, but also to its diffusion and reception in Bernard's own century. Lastly, the long descriptions spring from my conviction that codices themselves deserve a full hearing, whether all of their material seems pertinent to the edition being made or not. Part of our problem, after all, with sorting out the *Timaeus* glosses of the Middle Ages has been a lack of detailed information about the manuscripts in which they occur. Waszink's cursory description of extant *Timaeus* manuscripts, though perfectly reasonable in the context of his large project, has not helped scholars to explore the complex manuscript traditions of the glosses themselves.

The reader only casually interested in the codices of the *Glosae* will find most of the information he needs about each manuscript in the opening statement of each description.

D
D = Durham, Cathedral Library C.IV.7

Glosses of William of Champeaux on Cicero's *De inuentione* and the *Rhetorica ad Herennium*; Bernard of Chartres's glosses on Plato's *Timaeus*; *Notae Platonicae*; anonymous glosses on Boethius' *De institutione arithmetica*; and some anonymous notes. First quarter and middle of the 12th century.[316] In Latin, on parchment, written by several early and mid-twelfth-century scribes, probably at Durham.

PHYSICAL CHARACTER

ii + 68 + ii. Blank folios of parchment at front and back serve as guards, placed there when the volume was rebound. Fly-leaves counted as folios 1 and 70 are folded single leaves and measure approximately 210 × 250 mm.: they are written in an eighth-century majuscule script studied by Lowe and

---

[316] On the date of D, see R.A.B. Mynors, *Durham Cathedral Manuscripts to the End of the Twelfth Century* (Oxford, 1939), p. 58 (no. 79), who places it in the first half of the century; N.R. Ker, *Medieval Libraries of Great Britain. A List of Surviving Books* 2nd ed. (London, 1964), p. 71, "s. xii in."; and Dutton, "The Uncovering," p. 198.

Mynors and contain fragments of Leviticus (fol. 1: Lv. 26:5-28 *adprehendet ... plagis* and fol. 70: Lv. 14:46-15:16 *Qui ... coitus*).[317] Foliation, beginning at 2, is modern and consistent. Page size: 235/225 × 150/145 mm. Frame of writing: 190/180 × 120/110 mm. Two columns. Fols. 2-49 contain 67-75 lines, ruled with lead; fols. 50-69 contain 42 lines, ruled with dry-point. Collation: 1-4[10], 5[8] (wants 2 after fol. 49), 6-7[10]. Two items listed in the fourteenth-century table of contents on fol. 1r are now missing: a *Prima rethorica* before fol. 2 and a *Tractatus super Macrobium* immediately after fol. 41. Gathering marks in 1-4 (11v *primus*; 21v *secundus*; 31v *tertio*; 41v *quarto*) may, therefore, date from the point when the codex was reassembled and the two other treatises separated off. The original volume with both the extant and two lost pieces existed until 1392-1417. Some initial letters in red, often wanting illumination. Binding: leather with clasp, early modern with a coat of arms of the cathedral of Durham on the first pastedown.

PROVENANCE

Durham.[318] In the *Catalogi Veteres* (from 1392 and 1395) of Durham found under *Libri Tulii*: "F. Prima Retorica. Glosa super Retorica. Tractatus super Macrobium. Glosa super Platonem. Tractatus super Artem Metricam. II fo., 'quadam'."[319] The same is repeated in the Spendement Inventory of 1417.[320] On fol. 1r of D another list of contents was written in a fourteenth-century script: "prima rethorica/ Glose super rethoricam/ tractatus super macrobium/ Glose super platonem/ tractatus super arismeticam." Beside the first two items in a later hand, "Tullii Ciceronis," and beside the last, "incomplete." It is upon this fourteenth-century list of contents that the 1392 cataloguer must have relied, transforming *arismeticam* into *Artem metricam*. It should be noted that a twelfth-century Durham catalogue vaguely listed a volume with "Rhetoricae III."[321]

---

[317] See E.A. Lowe, *Codices latini antiquiores* vol. 2, p. 11 (no. 154), and Mynors, *Durham Cathedral Manuscripts*, p. 00 (no.10).

[318] See Mynors, *Durham Cathedral Manuscripts*, p. 58 (no. 79) and Ker, *Medieval Libraries of Great Britain*, p. 71.

[319] *Catalogi Veteres librorum ecclesiae Cathedralis Dunelm. Catalogues of the Library of Durham Cathedral at Various Periods from the Conquest to the Dissolution ...* , ed. James Raine, Publications of the Surtees Society 7 (London, 1838), p. 31.

[320] *Catalogi Veteres*, p. 108.

[321] *Catalogi Veteres*, p. 4. The same twelfth-century catalogue lists a copy of the *Timaeus* among Durham's holdings (p. 4). On the library of Durham Cathedral, see S.L. Greenslade, "The Contents of the Library of Durham Cathedral Priory," in *Transactions of the Architectural and Archaeological Society of Durham and Northumberland* 11.5-6 (1965) 347-369, and A.J. Piper, "The Libraries of the Monks of Durham," in *Medieval Scribes, Manuscripts, and Libraries: Essays Presented to N.R. Ker*, ed. M.B. Parkes and Andrew G. Watson (London, 1978), pp. 213-249.

CONTENTS

1. Glosses of William of Champeaux on Cicero's *De inuentione*[322]
   fol. 2ra: GLOSAE SVPER RETHORICAM CICERONIS. In primis materia et intentio huius rethoris, scilicet Ciceronis ...
   fol. 30vb: ... quae restant in reliquis libris dicemus quod forsitan fecit.
These glosses and the next item were composed by William around 1118, according to Dickey, around 1100, according to Fredborg.[323]

2. Glosses of William of Champeaux on the *Rhetorica ad Herennium*
   fol. 30vb: LIBER I AD HERENNIUM ... Cum Tullius de quinque partibus rethoricae se tractaturum promiserat, inuentione prima parte exposita ...
   fol. 41vb: Et hoc est quod dicit acute et cito reperiemus. Explicit.

3. *Glosae super Platonem* of Bernard of Chartres
   fol. 41ra: (1.1) <S>ocrates de re publica decem libris disputauit ...
   fol. 41rb: (3.1) <P>lato per inuolucrum cuiusdam conuiuii tractat praedictam materiam ...
   fol. 43rb: (4.1) Est igitur. Timaeus, plene pro posse hominis tractaturus ...
   fol. 49va: ... quattuor principalium corporum, quod superius promiserat. (8.448)

4. *Notae Platonicae* (see App. 1)
   fol. 49va: (1) Nota tres figuras in compositione animae ...
   fol. 49vb: (2) Nota Platoni consentire Hebraicam philosophiam ...
      (3) Nota in omni rotundo ...
      (4) Nota caelum diuerso modo ...
      (5) Nota dum planetae ...
      (6) Nota uertentem annum ...
      (7) Platonica sententia est ignem interiorem ...

5. Anonymous Glosses on Boethius' *De institutione arithmetica*
   fol. 50ra: <I>ncipiunt arithmeticae Anicii Manlii Seuerini Boetii ... Aresmetica interpretatur uirtus. Rithmus numerus ...

[322] See R.W. Hunt, "Studies on Priscian in the Eleventh and Twelfth Centuries," *Mediaeval and Renaissance Studies* 1 (1941-43) 207 n.3 and rpt. in R.W. Hunt, *The History of Grammar in the Middle Ages: Collected Papers*, ed. G.L. Bursill-Hall (Amsterdam, 1980), pp. 1-38; Mary Dickey, "Some Commentaries on the *De inventione* and *Ad Herennium* of the Eleventh and Twelfth Centuries," *Mediaeval and Renaissance Studies* 6 (1968) 5, who discusses D under the shelf-mark of another Durham MS; and Karin Margareta Fredborg, "The Commentary on Cicero's *De inventione* and *Rhetorica ad Herennium* by William of Champeaux," *Cahiers de l'Institut du Moyen-Age Grec et Latin* 17 (1976) 1-39.
[323] Dickey, "Some Commentaries," p. 15 and Fredborg, "The Commentary," pp. 4-5.

fol. 66rb: Contra quod dicitur: hemitonium non esse sonum secundum musicam, sed semitonus. Explicit.

6. Diagrams and lines of verse

fols. 66v-68r are blank.

fol. 68v, top: diagram of the four elements with legends, "Conexio elementorum," "Concordia elementorum," and "Discordia elementorum." Eight lines of verse, beginning: "Ignea uis terrae conectitur ariditate."

fol. 68v, bottom: Diagram of the four elements, humours, seasons, and ages of man. The text surrounding it begins: "Tu triplicis quidam philosophorum animam mundi..." and ends fol. 69ra: "... in zodiaco circulo explet cursum suum."

fol. 69ra (third of the way down) to 69vb (end): blank.

SCRIPTS

Items 1-4 are written in the same, small, early twelfth-century handwriting. Items 5 and 6 are in a larger script, possibly from the mid twelfth-century. From the change of scripts, number of lines per column, and style of ruling, items five and six would seem to belong to a different and, perhaps, later booklet. Items 2-4 and, quite likely, the two lost treatises were the product of the same scribe, probably working at Durham late in the first quarter of the twelfth century.

M
M = Munich, Bayerische Staatsbibliothek, Clm. 540B.

Bernard of Chartres's glosses on Plato's *Timaeus*; *Notae Platonicae*; fragments of William of Conches's glosses on the *Timaeus*. Fourth quarter of the 12th century. In Latin, on parchment, written by two different scribes, probably in Germany.

PHYSICAL CHARACTER

44 folios. Page size: 200 × 140/135 mm. Frame of writing: 120/110 × 160/135 mm. Foliation modern and consistent, in ink. Fols. 1r-39r contain 24-27 lines, fols. 40r-43r contain 31-34 lines. Prickings on edges, ruled in ink. Collation: 1-5^8, 6^4. Decoration: only on fol. 1r, initial letters in red, fol. 3r <*P*> *lato* wants illumination. Binding: leather over board with metal clasp, by 1487 since the pastedown inside the front cover gives this date.

PROVENANCE

The monastery of Saint Vitus of Prüll, near Regensburg.[324] On fol. 1r upper, the possession mark: "Liber Sancti Viti in prül." In 1487 Dr. Hartmann Schedel, the Nuremberg humanist, exchanged a book of theology for this volume with the Carthusian monks of Prüll, as noted on fol. 44v of the manuscript: "Pro isto libro dedi Cartusiensibus in prül prope Ratisponam librum theologie. Anno etc. 1487."[325] In Schedel's library the book seems to have been catalogued as "Commentarium in Thimeum Platonis; in pergameno," a title that is also found on the present front cover.[326] The manuscript, along with the rest of Schedel's library, was purchased by J. Fugger of Augsburg in 1552 and was, in turn, sold to Duke Albert V of Bavaria in 1571, whence it entered the ducal collection and came to the Bayerische Staatsbibliothek.[327]

CONTENTS

1. *Glosae super Platonem* of Bernard of Chartres
   fol. 1r: (1.1) Socrates de re publica decem libris disputauit ...
   fol. 3r: (3.1) <P>lato per inuolucrum cuiusdam conuiuii tractat predictam materiam ...
   fol. 8r: (4.1) Est igitur. Thimeus pro posse hominis plene tractaturus ...
   fol. 38v: ... quattuor principalium corporum quod superius promiserat. FINIT. (8.448)

2. *Notae Platonicae*, the first six. (see App. 1)
   fol. 38v: (1) Nota tres figuras in compositione animae ...
   (2) Nota Platoni consentire Hebraicam philosophiam ...
   fol. 39r: (3) Nota in omni rotundo ...

---

[324] On the library of Prüll, see Paul Lehmann, *Mitteilungen aus Handschriften 5*, Sitzungsberichte der bayerischen Akademie der Wissenschaften: philosophisch-historische Abteilung 4 (Munich, 1938), p. 50 and Bernhard Bischoff, *Die südostdeutschen Schreibschulen und Bibliotheken in der Karolingerzeit*, vol. 1: *Die bayerischen Diözesen* (Wiesbaden, 1960), pp. 261-262.

[325] See Richard Stauber, *Die Schedelsche Bibliothek. Ein Beitrag zur Geschichte der Ausbreitung der italienischen Renaissance, des deutschen Humanismus und der medizinischen Literatur*, Studien und Darstellungen aus dem Gebiete des Geschichte 6.2-3 (Freiburg, 1908), pp. 56, 108.

[326] See [Catologi], "Katalog der Bibliothek Hartmann Schedels," ed. Paul Ruf, in *Mittelalterliche Bibliothekskataloge Deutschlands und der Schweiz*, vol. 3: *Bistum Augsburg* (Munich, 1932), p. 811.7-8.

[327] See Karl Felix von Halm and G. Laubman, *Catalogus codicum latinorum Bibliothecae regiae monacensis*, vol. 1.1: *Codices num. 1-2329 complectens* (Munich, 1868), p. 44 and *Glose Willelmi de Conchis super Platonem*, ed. Jeauneau, p. 42, where a full description of the manuscript is supplied.

(4) Nota celum diuerso modo ...

(5) Nota dum planetae ...

(6) Nota uertentem annum ...

fol. 39v: ... que fuit in initio MVNDI.

3. Three fragments of William of Conches's glosses on the *Timaeus*

fol. 39v: (A) Hucusque de causis et creatione mundi egit ...

fol. 43r: ... nosse cupientem nostra docebit phylosophia.

A on *Timaeus* 34b-36b (W26:17-28:9-10), in *Glose Willelmi de Conchis super Platonem* 71-87, ed. Jeauneau, pp. 144-168.

fol. 43r: (B) De somniis. Somniorum quaedam causae sunt exteriores ... uel contrarium, quod futurum est insinuatur.

B on *Timaeus* 45e (W42:11), in *Glose Willelmi de Conchis super Platonem* 141, ed. Jeauneau, pp. 242-243.

fol. 43r: (C) De materia primordiali. Materia est quod, accepta forma ...

fol.43v: ... hic tractat P<lato> per dissolutionem rerum.

C on *Timaeus* 47e (W45:9), in *Glose Willelmi de Conchis super Platonem* 154-55, ed. Jeauneau, pp. 258-260.

fols. 43v-44r: blank

fol. 44v: Schedel possession mark top, the rest blank.

SCRIPTS

A variation in the appearance of the writing at various places in the first 38 folios (cf. fols. 1r-11r and 15v-19r) suggests that two late twelfth-century scribes worked on the manuscript.

O

O = Orléans, Bibliothèque municipale 260 (216)

Dialectica of Garland of Besançon; anonymous glosses on the *Philosophiae consolatio* of Boethius; Bernard of Chartres's glosses on Plato's *Timaeus*. Middle of the 12th century. In Latin, on parchment, written by one scribe, perhaps at the Benedictine monastery at Fleury-sur-Loire.

PHYSICAL CHARACTER

108 folios. Pagination modern, but the first page (recto) is not numbered, nor is the blank verso after p. 146; therefore the pagination begins on the first verso and numbers 214 in total. 180 × 110/105 mm. Frame of writing: 175/155 × 100/85 mm. Pp. 1-83 contain 43 lines per page; pp. 84-173, 50-57 lines; pp. 175-214, 40-44 lines. Lines pricked and ruled with

dry-point. Collation: 1-4⁸, 5¹⁰, 6-10⁸, 11⁶, 12-13⁸, 14⁴. Pp. 86/87 and 96/97, 149/150 and 159/160, 153/154 and 155/156, and 167/168 and 169/170 are not continuous, but half-sheets. A fly-leaf, now missing, contained some lines of verse. A copy of Macrobius' *Somnium Scipionis* and a fragment of a commentary on the Gospel of Matthew were separated off and are now apparently in the Mediceo-Laurenziana at Florence in Cod. Ashburnhamiani 36 (100ˣ) fragment B.[328] The *Glosae* in O has also suffered some minor physical damage from worm holes and trimming. Binding: leather over wooden boards.

PROVENANCE

Fleury-sur-Loire, monastery of Saint Benedict. On the unnumbered first recto a note, written in what de Rijk calls a twelfth-century hand: "Ex libris Monasterii Sancti Benedicti Flor."[329] Below this a fourteenth-century note: "Incipiunt regulae magistri Gerlandi de dialectica" and a *probatio pennae*. The manuscript is now MS 260 (formerly 216) of the Bibliothèque municipale of Orléans.[330]

CONTENTS

1. *Dialectica* of Master Garland of Besançon, called Compotista
   p. 1: Incipiunt regulae Magistri Gerlandi super dialecticam. Cum prolixitas et difficultas ...
   p. 83: ... si diligenter inquirantur. EXPLICIT TRACTATVS YPOTE-TICORUM SILLOGISMORUM.
This treatise was first edited by de Rijk, who argues that Garland was the late eleventh-century master of Besançon.[331]

2. Anonymous glosses on Boethius' *Philosophiae consolatio*
   p. 84: Iste Boethius hic ponit miserum hominem materiam partim ...
   p. 146: ... anime ut homicidium. LIBER QVARTVS. (bottom blank and unnumbered verso blank)

---

[328] See *Catalogue général des manuscrits des bibliothèques publiques de France. Départements* (Octavo series). vol. 12: *Orléans* (Paris, 1889), p. 125 and *Indici e cataloghi*, vol. 8: *I codici Ashburnhamiani della R. Biblioteca Mediceo-Laurenziana di Firenze*, vol. 1.1, ed. Caesare Paoli and Enrico Rostagno (Rome, 1887), pp. 55-56.

[329] See Garlandus of Besançon, *Dialectica*, in Garlandus Compotista, *Dialectica*, ed. L.M. de Rijk (Assen, 1959), p. xlv and pp. xliv-xlv on O.

[330] See Léopold Delisle, "Notice sur plusieurs manuscrits de la Bibliothèque d'Orléans," pp. 390-391.

[331] See Garlandus of Besançon, *Dialectica*, in Garlandus Compotista, *Dialectica*, ed. de Rijk, pp. xlii-xlv and see also A. Cordoliani, "La *Logica* de Gerland de Besançon," *Revue du Moyen Age Latin* 5 (1949) 43-47.

p. 147: LIBER QVARTVS INCIPIT. <H>ec cum philosophia. Sicut
in secundo ...

p. 173: ... qui spectat diuersos actus cunctorum. EXPLICIT.

A partial edition of this anonymous set of glosses, which exists in six
manuscripts, was made by A. Wilmart.[332]

3. Anonymous passage on the lyric

p. 173: Quoniam liber iste diuersis uocabulis apellatur ...

p. 174: ... a uiciis debeamus. (ends after five lines, the rest of the page
is blank)

4. *Glosae super Platonem* of Bernard of Chartres

p. 175: (1.1) Socrates de re publica decem libris disputauit ...

p. 177: (3.1) Incipit Timeus Platonis. Plato per inuolucrum cuiusdam
conuiuii tractat predictam materiam ...

p. 182: (4.1) Est igitur. Thime<u>s, plene pro posse hominis tractatus
...

p. 214: ... quattuor principalium corporum, quod superius promiserat.
FINIT LIBER. (8.448)

Hauréau alerted Delisle to the existence of the same commentary in V.[333]

SCRIPTS

The same mid twelfth-century scribe seems to have been responsible for the
entire extant volume, though there is evidence in a few places in item 4 of
another scribe's work: on p. 185, for instance, lines 11-20 are written in a
larger more cursive script that ignores the regular pattern of lines and frame
of writing.

P

P = Pommersfelden, Gräflich Schönborn'sche Bibliothek 76 (2663)

Plato's *Timaeus* in the Latin translation of Calcidius, glossed; Bernard of
Chartres's glosses on Plato's *Timaeus*; various notes. Last quarter of the
12th century. In Latin, on parchment, written by a single late twelfth-century
scribe, with some later additions, probably in Germany.

---

[332] *Analecta Reginensia*, (Città del Vaticano, 1933), pp. 259-262, and see Pierre Courcelle,
La consolation de philosophie dans la tradition littéraire. Antécédents et Posterité de Boèce
(Paris, 1967), pp. 410-411.
[333] See p. 108 n. 314 above.

PHYSICAL CHARACTER

ii + 60 + ii. Folded sheets of paper at front and back act as fly-leaves. Foliated twice in Arabic numerals: in a dark brown ink one set of early modern folio numbers effectively begins fol. 1 at the actual fol. 2, while another set begins with the first folio and continues throughout the volume. There has been some confusion caused by these two sets of numbers: Waszink lists the copy of the *Timaeus* in P as fols. 1r-39v, when it is in fact 1r-38v.[334] The second and more modern foliation is to be preferred. Size of pages: 215 × 130/120. Frame of writing: fols. 1-40, 165 × 60; fols. 41-60, 200/185 × 110/105. Fols. 1-40 contain 19-20 lines of main text with ample room left between the lines for interlinear glosses; pages pricked and ruled with dry-point. Fols. 41-48 and 55-60 pricked and ruled with dry-point for a single column of text without marginal glosses. Fols. 49-54, the eighth gathering, were pricked and dry ruled for two columns of writing, which the scribe followed on 49r, but abandoned afterwards. Fols. 42-48 contain 36-39 lines; fols. 49-58r, 40 lines; fols. 58v-59r, 51 lines. Double columns on fols. 40 and 49r; the rest of the volume is inscribed in single columns. Fol. 60 was originally missing a rectangular piece of parchment measuring 105 × 45 mm. along bottom outer edge. The top of fol. 60v is water damaged. Collation: 1-4⁸, 5⁶, 6² 7⁸, 8-9⁶. Some initial letters are decorated in red ink. A copy of Calcidius' commentary possibly separated off after fol.40 (see below under provenance). Binding: brown leather over pressed paper sheets, with the Schönborn coat of arms both back and front. Pastedown of coloured paper with design.

PROVENANCE

Germany, Erfurt. In September 1232 a certain Morellus traded some other books for this volume with Quinandus, as is noted on fol. 1v: "Morellus clericus emit Platonem istum a Quinando clerico et dedit pro eo flores ethimologiarum grecarum, que incipiunt Latinorum sollercia philosophorum, scriptas in bono uitulino et intitulatas colore iacinctino et rubeo, et duos quaternos Prisciani de constructione et quosdam uersus differentiam glossatos, in quibus erat barbarismus. Anno gratie MᵒCCᵒ Tricesimo secundo mense Septembri."[335] The manuscript next appears in the library of the Collegium Amplonianum of Erfurt. In the college's catalogue of books from

---

[334] Waszink, "Praefatio," p. cxxii, where a brief description of the MS is given.

[335] Edouard Jeauneau informed me that copies of the work *Flores ethimologiarum graecarum* are to be found in Douai, Bibliothèque municipale MS 751 and Valenciennes, Bibliothèque municipale MS 397.

1410-1412, Metaphysica 8 was: "Item duo libri Platonis in Thymeo, optime glosati et bene distincti cum prologo Calcidii; commentum Calcidii super libris Thimei Platonis." Lehmann and others have assumed this volume to be identical to P,[336] but can it be? P now has no copy of Calcidius' commentary, though a twelfth-century scribe wrote at the bottom of fol. 40v: "Incipit prologus Calcidii in Timeo Platonis. Osio suo Calcidius salutem." Fol. 40va-b also contains a list of the chapter headings of Calcidius' commentary. Two explanations seem possible for the discrepancy: a basic misidentification was made by a scribe who thought the *Glosae* was Calcidius' commentary or Calcidius' commentary once accompanied the Erfurt volume, but has since been separated off. In 1725 Lothar Franz von Schönborn, in the act of assembling one of Europe's great private libraries, had the opportunity to buy all the manuscripts of the Collegium Amplonianum; he found the price for the lot (1000 fl.) exorbitant, and instead purchased individual items.[337] Thirty-nine of these, including P, were installed in his collection in the Palace of Weissenstein near Pommersfelden. Upon entering the library of Lothar Franz von Schönborn, P was rebound (the gathering marks of the rebinding are evident) and numbered 2663 and later 76.

CONTENTS

1. Notes and Diagrams on Platonic Material
    fol. 1r: Diagram of the tones (12th century);
    "Tymeus platonis" inscription (14th century)
    fol.1v: Diagram of the planets in red and black ink
    the "Morellus clericus" inscription from 1232 in the left margin
    Notes on Plato in a late twelfth-century hand at bottom:
        (1) Intentio Platonis est tractare de naturali iusticia ...
        (2) Calcidius mittens epistolam Osio amico suo ...
        (3) Virtus redigit ad possibilitatem impossibilia ... impossibilium pene etc.

---

[336] See [Catalogi], in *Mittelalterliche Bibliothekskataloge Deutschlands und der Schweiz*, vol. 2: *Bistum Main, Erfurt*, p. 42 and 2:6: "Metaph.8 = Pommersfelden 76 (2663)." For the dependent identifications, see Klibansky, *The Continuity*, pp. 30, 52; and Waszink, "Praefatio," p. cxxii.

[337] On this incident, see Eva Pleticha, *Adel und Buch. Studien zur Geisteswelt des fränkischen Adels am Beispiel seiner Bibliotheken vom 15. bis zum 18. Jahrhundert*, Veröffentlichungen der Gesellschaft für fränkischen Geschichte, Reihe IX, Darstellungen aus der fränkischen Geschichte 33 (Neustadt, 1983), pp.157-58, 262-264.

2. Plato's *Timaeus* translated by Calcidius, with interlinear and marginal glosses

> fol. 2r: Prohemium Calcidii in Thymeum Platonis. (14th-century inscription) Socrates in exhortationibus suis uirtutem ... (W5:1)
>
> fol. 3r: Vnus, duo, tres. Quartum de numero ... (*Timaeus* 17a; W7:1)
>
> fol. 13v: Est igitur, ut mihi quidem ... (*Timaeus* 27d; W20:15)
>
> fol. 23r: Et iam fere cuncta ... (*Timaeus* 39e; W32:15)
>
> fol. 39v: ... admonitione perspicuo. (*Timaeus* 53c; W52:6) EXPLICIT THIMEVS PLATONIS

3. Miscellaneous Texts

> fol. 40ra: (1) Ylen uocauerunt philosophi necessitatem ... et uariis formis uestita.
>
> (2) DE SEPTEM GRADIBUS ANIMAE. I. Anima igitur gradu primo corpus hoc ...
>
> fol. 40va: ... memoria dum membra uegetat anima, anima.
>
> fol. 40va: (3) Plato eruditionis gratia in Egiptum ... in dialogum transtulit quem scripsit de uirtute
>
> (4) Plato dum litteras toto fugientes orbe ... Plato fuit maior uendente pirata.
>
> (5) Queritur primo de genitura. II. De ortu animae. III. De modulatione ...
>
> fol. 40vb: XXVII. De intelligibili deo. (for item 3.5, see Cal., *Comm.* 7, W60:5-61:8)
>
> (6) Primas etas infancia ... LXV partibus.
>
> (7) As deunx ... (a short text on mass weights)
>
> fol. 40va-b, bottom: (8) Incipit prologus Calcidii in Timeo Platonis. Osio suo Calcidius salutem.
>
> fol. 41r, top of: a diagram of the *diatessaron* and *diapente* and a *probatio pennae*
>
> fol. 41v: Ciuibus Traiectensibus de Bonlerat salutem ... semper studere incommodo. (perhaps a thirteenth-century *probatio pennae* based on a letter); several other *probationes pennae* in the same dark black ink.

4. *Glosae super Platonem* of Bernard of Chartres

> fol. 42r: (1.1) <S>ocrates de re publica decem libris disputauit ...
>
> fol. 43r: (3.1) Plato per inuolucrum cuiusdam conuiuii tractat predictam materiam ...
>
> fol. 45v: (4.1) Est igitur. Thymeus, plene pro posse suo[uel hominis] tractaturus ...
>
> fol. 60v: ... quattuor principalium corporum, quod superius promiserat. (8.448)

5. A Short Note

    fol. 60v: Si deuias equalia ab equalibus tunc remanent equalia ... ordine probabilium. (A brief note written below *promiserat* of the *Glosae*.)

SCRIPTS

The same late twelfth-century scribe seems to have written items 1, 2 (both the *Timaeus* and the glosses), 3.1-5, 3.8, and 4. This scribe was, in some sense, the architect of "Platonem istum" as the volume was called in 1232. He corrected his copy of the *Glosae* both at the time of original transcription (in a light brown ink) and later (in a darker ink). Items 3.6, 3.7, 5 were written by different thirteenth-century scribes.

T

T = Paris, Bibliothèque Nationale, MS Nouvelles acquisitions latines 281

A collection of material from nine manuscripts: hymns, a treatise on rhetoric, glosses on Paul's letters, Hugh of Saint-Victor's *Didascalicon*, sermons, a short piece on simony, theological questions and glosses on Virgil's *Aeneid*, canon law texts, and Bernard of Chartres's glosses on Plato's *Timaeus* with the *Notae Platonicae*. Tenth to thirteenth centuries. In Latin, on parchment, written by many scribes.

PHYSICAL CHARACTER

i + (i) + iv + 131 + i. At the front of the volume, after a paper guard contemporary with the binding (and matched at the end of the volume), some nineteenth-century paper additions: a folded piece of lined paper, loose, with notes in Italian on the manuscript and another set of two sheets, four folios, with information on the manuscript written in Latin. Foliation is modern and consistent. Page size: 205/200 × 135, some trimming evident. Frame of writing and lines per page vary from section to section. Collation: $1-3^8$, 4^7 (wants one after fol. 31), $5-9^8$, $10-11^2$, $12-13^8$, 14^{10}, 15^8, 16^{10}, 17^5 (wants one after fol. 120), 18^7 (wants one after fol.131). The manuscript is made up of nine discrete booklets: 1. fols. 1-31; 2. fols. 32-39; 3. fols. 40-47; 4. fols. 48-73; 5. fols. 74-75; 6. fols. 76-83; 7. fols. 84-91; 8. fols. 92-124; and 9. fols. 125-131. Binding: brown leather on boards, no clasp, with the stamp of the Bibliothèque Nationale.

PROVENANCE

Italy. Between 1877 and 1880 the Duc de la Trémoïlle (hence the siglum T) donated forty-nine manuscripts to the Bibliothèque Nationale in Paris.[338] T had been number 49, the last volume of his collection. It became Bibliothèque Nationale, MS nouv. acq. lat. 281 and was briefly described by Ulysse Robert in 1882.[339] Delisle in his *Catalogue des manuscrits du fonds de la Trémoïlle* counts T among "Trente-deux manuscrits d'origine italienne."[340] Delisle had likely obtained this information from the Duke himself, who was, as Delisle said, an avid collector of things medieval. It may be that the Duc de la Trémoïlle had purchased thirty-two medieval manuscripts in Italy. The loose leaf, nineteenth-century description of the manuscript in Italian, which is today inserted at the start of the volume, might lend credence to this specualtion. In addition, certain orthographic peculiarities of T's copy of the *Glosae* (*mistis* for *mixtis*, *iusta* for *iuxta*, and *extimat* for *estimat*) suggest that it at least was transcribed in Italy.

CONTENTS

1. *Hymni de tempore et de sanctis*, with marginal and interlinear glosses
   fol. 1r: Materia istius libri in hoc opere est laus Dei ... (the first hymn begins in the middle of this recto) "Primo dierum omnium ..."
   fol. 31v: ... ut carnis estus frigeat.
Script of the twelfth century. Frame of writing: 150 × 57 mm., 19 lines per page with many glosses inserted in the ample margins and between the lines.

2. Anonymous, *Tractatus de rhetorica*
   fol. 32ra: <C>um a natura nobis sit datum nostris sermonibus ...
   fol. 39vb: ... quibus rebus beniuolentia comparens.
Written in two columns in a twelfth-century script. Frame of writing: 185 × 110, 41 lines per column.

3. Anonymous, *Glosule super epistolas Pauli*
   fol. 40ra: GLOSULE SVPER EPISTOLAS PAULI. <S>icut in ueteri testamento post legem Moysi ...
   fol. 47vb: ... per Adam et Euam. Nam pecc.
Written in two columns in a twelfth-century script. Frame of writing: 170 × 110 mm. with 44 lines per page.

---

[338] See Léopold Delisle, *Catalogue des manuscrits du fonds de la Trémoïlle* (Paris, 1889), p. 5.
[339] Ulysse Robert, *Le cabinet historique: Moniteur des Bibliothèques et des Archives*, new series 1, 28th year (Paris, 1882), p. 66.
[340] Delisle, *Catalogue des manuscrits*, p. 5.

4. Hugh of Saint-Victor's *Didascalicon*

> fol. 48ra: Tribus modis res subsistere habent: in actu, in intellectu, in mente diuina ... et fecit deus ad actum rerum. (see the appendix to the *Didascalicon*, ed. Buttimer, pp.134-135)
>
> fol. 48rb: Multi sunt quos ipsa adeo natura ... (*Didascalicon*, praefatio, ed. Buttimer, p.1)
>
> fol. 73rb: ... ad puram et sine animalibus cenam. (*Didascalicon* 6.13, ed. Buttimer, p.130)
>
> fol. 73v: (some faint lines and a poem of 27 lines beginning) Deus enim publicam parat ultionem ...

Written in two columns in a twelfth-century script. Frame of writing: 175 × 105 mm. with 39 lines per page.

5. Sermons

> fol. 74r: SERMO IN NATIVITATE DOMINI. Verbum caro factum est ...
>
> fol. 75v: ... que pertinent ad salutem.

Written in one column early in the thirteenth century. Frame of writing: 175 × 110 mm. with 50 lines per page.

6. Fragment of a tractate on simony

> fol. 76ra: Expositis in prima parte diuinis officiis ...
>
> fol. 83vb: ... in quadruplum post annum non competit accio simpli in/

Written in two columns in a script from the early thirteenth century. Frame of writing: 145 × 100 mm. with 34 lines per column.

7. Miscellaneous theological texts; glosses on the *Aeneid*

> fol. 84r: blank
>
> fol. 84va: (1) <Queri>tur de illo qui patenter commisit adulterium ...
>
> fol. 85vb: ... ignorantia uere dicitur esse/ (end of theological fragment)
>
> fol. 86ra: (2) ... etc. hodie dicti thema proponimus ... *Arma uirumque cano. Arma* id est bella metonomicos *et uirum* quod bella gessit. Vel cano arma et uirum id est uires et ingenium ...
>
> fol. 89rb: ... *cum domus Assaraci* id est similia Troiana/ (a fragmentary set of glosses on the first 284 lines of Virgil's *Aeneid*)
>
> fol. 89v: blank
>
> fol. 90ra: (3) /peccatum quod sit criminalis et sic dicitur ...
>
> fol. 90va: ... Dicit autem quod unusquisque/ (fragment of a theological text)
>
> fol. 91ra: Dicit autem unusquisque resurget in etate XXX annorum ...
>
> fol. 91rb: ... sed similiter. (end of theological fragment)
>
> fol. 91v: (4) /inimicum ... Incipit ad fatiendum catecuminum ... Nunc ergo prom/ (fragment of a ritual)

7.1 is written in two columns in a late twelfth-century or early thirteenth-century script. Frame of writing: 175 × 120 mm. with 42 lines per page. 7.2 is written in two columns in a late twelfth-century script. Frame of writing: 180 × 102 mm. with 42-47 lines per page. 7.3 is written in two columns in a late twelfth-century script. Frame of writing: 170/180 × 120/130 mm. with 36-42 lines per page. 7.4 is written in a single column of 32 lines in a twelfth-century script. Frame of writing: 160 × 115.

8. Canon law texts
  fol. 92r: /tra patientia mansuetudine ...
  fol. 94v: ... id est annum/
  fol. 95r: /pluuia et nebula. Error ...
  fols. 121r-124v: (capitula of the canons)
  fol. 124v: CCCVIII De completis.
Item 8 consists of fragments of two manuscripts in confused order. One part is described by the *capitula* on fols. 121r-124v, whose parts are found on fols. 95-98, 102-109, 111-118, 120-124. The other, a penitential, also has a list of *capitula*, but on fol. 101v. Both were written in one column, the former 180 × 110 with 22 lines per page, the latter 175 × 105 with 23 lines. The handwriting of the former may be late tenth-century and of the latter early tenth-century. Delisle who attempted to sort out much of this thought they might be Italian fragments.[341]

9. *Glosae super Platonem* of Bernard of Chartres and the *Notae Platonicae* (see App. 1)
  fol. 125ra: (1.1) <S>ocrates de re publica decem libris disputauit ...
  fol. 125rb: (3.1) Plato per inuolucrum cuiusdam conuiuii tractat predictam materiam ...
  fol. 126ra: (4.1) Est igitur. Timeus pro posse hominis plene tractaturus ...
  fol. 131vb: ... quattuor principalium corporum, quod superius <promisera>t. (8.448)
  Notae Platonicae
  fol. 131vb: (1) Nota tres figuras in corporee ...
    (2-4, 6: present but damaged, see App.1 for specific readings).
Item 9 in T is a separate booklet. Page size: fols. 125-126, 195/185 × 132 mm.; fol. 127, 160/150 × 132; fols. 128-129, 175/170 × 132; fol. 130, 175/160 × 125. Frame of writing: 175/145 × 120/115 mm. Two columns of writing. Folio 131 has been torn away, totally removing fol. 131rb and 131va, but leaving a portion of the columns in fol. 131ra and 131vb. Lines

---

[341] Delisle, *Catalogue des manuscrits*, pp. 49-51.

per page vary between 61 on fol. 125 and 53/54 on fol. 127. One scribe wrote all of item 9 late in the twelfth century in a tiny, but legible script.

Since Delisle's catalogue of the Fonds de la Trémoïlle, it has been suspected that this was a commentary on Plato's *Timaeus*.[342] The work in question was identified as the *Glosae* by Klibansky, but, unfortunately, news of the identification never worked its way into the general literature on medieval *Timaeus* glosses.[343]

V

V = Vienna, Österreichische Nationalbibliothek 2376

Plato's *Timaeus* in the Latin translation of Calcidius, with numerous glosses; Bernard of Chartres's glosses on Plato's *Timaeus*; William of Conches's *Philosophia mundi*. Middle of the 12th century. In Latin, on parchment, written by one scribe, possibly in Germany.

PHYSICAL CHARACTER

i + 64 + (2) + i. At front and back of the volume a sheet of paper acts as the guard. In addition to the 64 folios there are two unnumbered parchment inserts. Foliation is modern and consistent. Page size: 265/270 × 155/160 mm. Frame of writing: in fols. 19-26, 210 × 110 mm; fols. 27-31, 210 × 130; the remainder 215 × 115. Pricked and ruled with a dry-point. Collation: 1^8 (wants one after fol. 2, another after fol. 7), 2^8, 3^2 (wants two after fol. 18), 4^8, 5^5 (wants three after fol. 31), $6\text{-}8^8$, 9^9 (one added at end). After fol. 9 a small parchment insert, not foliated, and another after fol. 17. Fol. 64 is a half-sheet glued to 63. Gatherings 6 through 9 have medieval catchmarks: at the bottom of fol. 32r, *I*; 40r, *II*; 48r, *III*; 56r, *IIII*. Perhaps this portion of the manuscript once stood separately. Binding: probably early modern, parchment over cardboard with raised spine. Stickers on the spine: upper, "IN TIMAEVM PLATON. COMMENT." and lower, "COD.MS. PH/L N

---

[342] Delisle, *Catalogue des manuscrits*, p. 51: "Fragments mutilés d'un ouvrage philosophique, peut-être un commentaire sur le Timée de Platon."

[343] Klibansky, "Report by the General Editor," p. 13. Despite this announcement, Klibansky did not incorporate this manuscript into the list of the *Glosae* copies printed in *The Continuity* which was reissued in 1981. Thus, P.O. Kristeller, *Iter Italicum accedunt alia itinera. A Finding List of Uncatalogued or Incompletely Catalogued Humanistic Manuscripts of the Renaissance in Italian and Other Libraries*, vol. 3: *(Alia itinera 1) Australia to Germany*, (London, 1983), p. 278, still listed the work in 1983 as an unidentified commentary on Plato, and I was lucky enough, following Kristeller's lead, to reidentify the work in 1986, independent of Klibansky's earlier identification.

CCLXX." Coat of arms in the middle of cover, front and back. Front cover, letters in gold: upper, "E.A.B.C.V." and lower, "17*G*L*B*V*S*B*55." Some decoration of intitial letters in red throughout.

PROVENANCE

Medieval place of origin and home unknown. In the bottom margin of fol.64v: Q 4681. This was the number assigned to the volume by the imperial librarian Hugo Blotius of Vienna in the second half of the sixteenth century.[344] Blotius speculated that the volume might contain "Alcionius in Thimaeum Platonis." The markings on the cover indicate that the book was rebound in 1755 and came: E<x> A<ugustissima> B<ibliotheca> C<aesarea> V<indobonensis>. Thus, the book has a firm history in Vienna since the sixteenth century and is now codex 2376 of the Österreichische Nationalbibliothek.[345]

CONTENTS

1. Plato's *Timaeus* in the translation of Calcidius, with glosses[346]
  fol. 1r: Socrates in exortacionibus suis uirtutem ... (W5:1)
  Vnus, duo, tres. Quartum e numero ... (*Timaeus* 17c; W7:1)
  fol. 5v: Est igitur, ut mihi quidem ... (*Timaeus* 27d; W20:15)
  fol. 10r: Et iam fere cuncta ... (*Timaeus* 39e; W32:15)
  fol. 18r: ... admonitione perspicuo. (*Timaeus* 53c; W52:6)

2. Miscellaneous Platonic Materials.
  A. after fol. 9, an unnumbered parchment insert (147 × 160 mm.):
    Timeus Platonis et a ueteribus ... tegerentur. (Cal., *Comm.* 1-4, W57:1-58:24)
  B. after fol. 17, an unnumbered parchment insert (48 × 160 mm.):
    Duo sunt motus in celestibus. Motus firmamenti ... celestium ordinem contemplantes id est uite modo atque constant. (anonymous)
  C. at the end of the end of the *Timaeus*, fol. 18r, immediately after

---

[344] See Hermann Menhardt, *Das älteste Handschriftenverzeichnis der Wiener Hofbibliothek von Hugo Blotius 1576. Kritische Ausgabe der Handschrift Series nova 4451 vom Jahre 1597 mit vier Anhängen*, Österreichische Akademie der Wissenschaften, philosophisch-historische Klasse, Denkschriften 76 (Vienna, 1957), p.82.

[345] See *Tabulae codicum manu scriptorum praeter graecos et orientales in Bibliotheca palatina Vindobonensi asservatorum*, vols. 1-2 *(Cod. 1-2000-3500)*, (Vienna, 1864-68; rpt. Graz, 1965), 2: 65. Note that it is incorrect to refer to V as 2376,1 and 2376,2 as Gregory does throughout *Platonismo medievale*, for while he meant to separate out items in the same manuscript, others have assumed that this implied two different manuscripts.

[346] See the description in Waszink, "Praefatio," p. cxxvi.

"admonitione perspicuo.": Alii philosophi dixerunt indiuiduam substantiam esse ydeas ... Mediam dicebant hominum animam quae intelligere diuinam. (anonymous)

fol. 18v: blank

3. *Glosae super Platonem* of Bernard of Chartres

fol. 19r: (1.1) Socrates de re publica decem libris disputauit ...

fol. 20r: (3.1) Plato per inuolucrum cuiusdam conuiuii tractat predictam materiam ...

fol. 23r: (4.1) <E>st igitur. Thimeus plenae pro posse hominis tractatus ...

fol. 31v, 10 lines down: ... rediens eterna fruitur beatitudine./

The copy of the *Glosae* in V, therefore, ends abruptly at 6.261 with a gloss on *Acturis* (*Timaeus* 42b; W37:10). Since the remainder of fol. 31v is blank and three folios are wanting after fol. 31, perhaps the scribe of V was in possession of an incomplete exemplar of the *Glosae*.

4. *Philosophia mundi* of William of Conches[347]

fol. 32r: *probatio pennae*: manus domini tetigit me, manus mee fecerunt t<e>

also a poem of eleven lines which begins: aurum sedusum nisi deducatur in usum ... (beside the last two lines of the poem, in the left margin, in another hand): Abel/ Cain

fol. 32v: INCIPIT PROLOGVS IN PHYLOSOPHYA WILLEHELMI. Quoniam ut ait Tullius in prologo Rethoricorum eloquencia ... (prologue, ed. Maurach, p. 17 or PL 172:D8-9)

fol. 33r: Philosophia est eorum quae sunt ... (1.1, ed. Maurach, p. 18 or PL 172:B13)

fol. 64v: ... compendia diximus ratione operis terminemus. (4.33, ed. Maurach, p. 116 or PL 172:A5-7).

fol. 64v, after a gap of three lines: Quattuor genera dampnationis erant Rome ... nec aliquid suorum amittebat. (a passage on the types of exile from the city of Rome).

SCRIPTS

Except for a few scattered later notes V is the product of a single mid-twelfth-century scribe.

---

[347] See A. Vernet, "Un remaniement de la *Philosophia* de Guillaume de Conches," *Scriptorium* 1 (1946-1947) 254, where the copy of the *Philosophia* in Vernet's list is no. 63 and he gives it a twelfth-century date. The article has been reprinted in A. Vernet, *Etudes médiévales* (Paris, 1981), pp. 143-159.

The Descent of the Manuscripts

The common text of the *Glosae* contained in the six manuscripts is remarkably uniform. Though one of the manuscripts certainly comes from England, one from France, two from Germany, and two less certainly from Austria and Italy, and the dates of the manuscripts range from early to late twelfth century, the degree of textual variation between the manuscripts is small. There are no major textual disagreements between them. The text of the *Glosae* would seem, therefore, to descend from a single archetype (ω) that must have existed in the first quarter of the twelfth century. Appended to this archetype or one of its early copies was quite likely a copy of the *Notae Platonicae* 1-6, and possibly 7, as the same sequence of notes is found in D, M, and T. Two examples of sentence-long transpositions suggest that early in the tradition two scribes of hyparchetypes interpreted differently where these passages belonged in the lemmatic commentary. D and P agree with one of these hyparchetypes (α), while M, O, and V agree with the other (β). T, late in the century, depended on a manuscript in which the less severe of these transpositions had been corrected.[348] That this kind of anomaly is not more common in the manuscripts of the *Glosae* suggests that the archetype too was in the form of a lemmatic commentary, as scribes independently transforming marginal and interlinear glosses into a lemmatic commentary would have introduced many more transpositional anomalies. Aside from the two transpositions, the hyparchetypes must have been very similar, for from them descend all the manuscripts and the differences between these are not great.

Since none of the extant copies of the *Glosae* repeats the homoeoteleutons or additions of another, it seems safe to assume that none of these manuscripts is a direct copy of one of the other surviving manuscripts. We, therefore, have six separate witnesses to the manuscript tradition of the *Glosae*. All the manuscripts have been employed in the critical edition because each provides at least one good reading independent of the others. The two most corrupt manuscripts, P and T, are amongst the last copied and share a certain number of anomalies (for instance, *gloriosum* at 2.23 for *generosum*). Nonetheless both independently offer a few good readings (P has *finitum* at 8.357 and T *Reuocabuntur* at 7.125) and provide some other

---

[348] In the first and less severe transposition, M O V placed "Vel probat ... discrimina" (3.251) after "Neque enim" (3.250), in which position the *Vel* is meaningless. D P T presented the sentences as they stand in the present edition. In the second transposition, M O T placed "Ideo ... nuntiantes" (7.74-77) after "palpare possunt" (7.89). Again the sense of the passage suggests that the order of D P as presented in the edition is to be preferred.

good readings in common (*uoluntas* at 2.52). O and V possess a number of conjunctive variants, as does M with V and O, and D with P. T is the odd player in the tradition, agreeing here and there with manuscripts representing both hyparchetypes. Among the variant readings we find the following examples of the textual tradition:

3.193	*D M P T* instituit] iustis *O V*
3.260	*D M T* otiosum] omne *O P V*
5.86	*P T* principali iure] principali *D* : principem iure *M V* : propria cum iure *O*
5.213	*D P T V* diuisa] diuersa *M O*
5.243	*D M P T* intelligibilibus] intellecti *O V*
6.8	*D P V* addebat] et idem *M O* : addidit *T*
6.82	*D O P T* colorem] calorem *M V*
6.139	*D O P V post* ad] homines *exp. M V*
6.193	*D M O V* mentem] hilen *P T*
6.242	*D P T V* uoluptate] uoluntate *M O*
7.49	*D P T* supra data] supradicta *M O*
7.189	*D M O* interior] exterior *P T*
7.392	*M O T* instituere] instruere *D P*
8.92	*M O T* imaginariis] magnis *D P*

These readings tend to support the idea suggested by the two transpositions of two hyparchetypes, one from which D and P descended and another from which M O V ultimately descended.

   T, however, is an example of how complex these traditions could be and should caution us against oversimplification. Not only does it straddle the issue of the major transpositions, but it agrees and disagrees across the board with the other manuscripts. In fact, glosses, especially those preserved in interlinear and marginal form, may not be the best candidates for the recensionist technique, since their textual traditions are rarely closed. The relationship of such manuscripts of glosses is made complex and confusing by the presence of simple scribal additions, subtractions, and alternative readings, and by the more difficult to distinguish layers of student glosses. As long as they were studied, glosses belonged to a constantly changing textual tradition that was rarely fixed.

   But the glosses preserved in the form of a lemmatic commentary are a different matter, and their textual traditions tend to be more closed. Since they were not in direct contact with the treatise commented upon, lemmatic commentaries tended to be copied straight out by scribes. The inclination of students was to add glosses in the margins of a copy of the *Timaeus*, not to make notes to a set of glosses in the form of the more removed lemmatic commentary. None of the copies of the *Glosae* possesses such added notes.

It is not impossible that twelfth-century authors were aware of the potential contamination to which their glosses would be exposed if they circulated in an interlinear or marginal form, and so chose the form of the lemmatic commentary as a somewhat safer vehicle of transmission.

There is, nonetheless, some evidence in the textual tradition of the *Glosae* of a small degree of 'contamination.' In the case of the lemmata, to which we shall turn in a moment, M and T seem to have relied on manuscripts that had fuller and perhaps better readings of the *Timaeus*, probably drawn from an available copy of Calcidius' translation by a scribe or student. Other 'contamination' must, for the most part, be scribal in nature. Both M and P, for instance, contain corrections, but of widely varying quality. The scribe of P copied portions of the *Glosae* with a batch of bad ink and returned later to erase, correct, and add alternative readings in a darker ink. But he was not the best of scribes or his exemplar may have been seriously flawed, for many absurd, if isolated and minor, errors remain in his manuscript. Not all of these have been printed as variants to the edition. The scribe of M also inserted corrections in his manuscript, apparently of a speculative kind and not ones based on readings encountered in another copy of the *Glosae*.

Let me provide but one striking example of the questions that these alternative readings give rise to:

> 5.293 *V* fore nec fuisse] erit ^{fore} nec ^{nec} fuit ^{fuisse} *D* : erit nec fuit *M*: erit fore nec fuit fuisse *O P T*

D, thus, possesses the correct reading but as an alternative written above the line; M, representative of the other hyparchetype, the less good reading; and O P T have in some way incorporated both readings into the main text. Does this mean that the archetype equivocated too and that we see in D a more faithful copy of the early tradition? If one were to imagine that a number of lost manuscripts of the *Glosae* also possessed these on the spot corrections, alternative readings, and speculative readings, one would not have been surprised to discover an extremely complex textual tradition. Moreover, given the potential for a textual tradition of marginal or interlinear glosses to 'open up' continually, it has been comforting to find that the lemmatic commentary edited here does not do so, but remains fairly true to a common text.

The following, therefore, was my working *stemma codicum* and should not be construed as anything like a true recreation of the descent of the manuscripts. After all, dozens of copies of the *Glosae* have been lost, a fact we can infer from the extensive influence of the *Glosae* on other dependent sets of glosses (see App. 3). Even with just six manuscripts, the number of possible *stemmata codicum* is over 10,000.[349] T, because it shows some 'contamination' has been left out of the *stemma*, but not the edition.

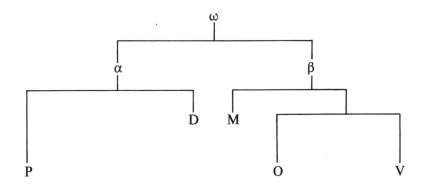

D, the earliest manuscript, and M, one of the later ones, vary less than 5% from the common text, while the others range as high as 10% in the case of P. Both D and M generally supply excellent readings and, since they seem tó stand dependent on different hyparchetypes, it has been my policy to seek agreement among them where that is possible. They have the incidental advantage of being complete copies of the *Glosae*, whereas V is incomplete and P and T are slightly damaged. Where D and M disagree, it has been necessary to seek wider consensus amongst the witnesses. In only a few cases was it actually necessary to propose an emendation, often of lemmatic lacunae.

The orthography employed throughout the edition is that either expressed in or implied by D which regularly uses *ae* or *e* cedilla, but does not employ *oe* in words such as *cepit*. Upper case *U* and *V* are both represented by *V*, while lower case *u* and *v* both take *u* in the medieval fashion. Differences in orthography and word order in the manuscripts have not been indicated in the variants. Glosses are not the easiest of texts for an editor to punctuate, partly because the lemmata can often be read as grammatical units apart from the glosses. Both D and M supply medieval punctuation for the text, which, while not always consistent, tends to separate glosses from lemmata and clauses from each other. My policy has been to accede to the rhythm of their medieval reading of the text, but to bear in mind Jeauneau's general model

---

[349] See the figures provided by Paul Maas, *Textual Criticism*, trans. Barbara Flower (Oxford, 1958), pp. 44-47.

for punctuating William of Conches's glosses. Many of the seemingly absurd readings of P and T are printed because of the basic belief that in considering such glosses we need to remember that these traditions were often 'open', and that something of the witness of these two manuscripts and their potential influence on dependent glosses would be lost if we did not. Waszink, working with a much larger collection of Calcidian manuscripts, produced a more classically formatted edition, one with a sparse list of strictly significant variants, and hence not as helpful to the medievalist interested in tracing textual traditions in which a scribal bit of nonsense may be as telling as another good reading.

Bernard of Chartres's Copy of the Timaeus

We should probably imagine the use of lemmatic commentaries in two settings. The individual reader might sit with two open manuscripts before him, the lemmatic commentary and a copy of the Latin *Timaeus* in Calcidius' translation. The reader would keep his finger on the manuscript of the *Timaeus* as he moved from passage to passage, turning to the commentary for its explanation of each. In the classroom, students must have gathered around a single text of the *Timaeus* as a lemmatic commentary was employed by a master to explain its meanings. In both cases, for the lemmatic commentary to be useful it must be brought directly to bear on a copy of the text commented on. In the edition of the *Glosae* the italicised lemma might, therefore, be understood as the place where the student or reader's finger has stopped under a word or passage from the *Timaeus*, holding, as it were, his spot. Words taken from prior passages in the *Timaeus* and reworked in a gloss are not, therefore, italicised because the *lectio* continues forward. The reader of the following edition will also find it necessary to read the Latin *Timaeus* alongside the *Glosae*. Since it has been my policy to italicise only lemmata taken directly from the *Timaeus*, a number of unitalicised lemmatic references will be spotted by the reader who follows the main text with the aid of the reference numbers provided in the margin or whose attention is alerted to these references by Bernard's use of such words as "dicit" and "uocat."

But if students and readers required a copy of the *Timaeus* to make sense of the commentary, scribes did not. Indeed in only two of the manuscripts (P and V) of the *Glosae* is a copy of the *Timaeus* also present. Scribes could copy the *Glosae* without consulting the *Timaeus*, with the result that the lemmata often became badly garbled over time. Removed from direct contact with the text commented on, scribes simply copied and frequently misread the highly abbreviated lemmata in their exemplars. The case could be made that the textual tradition of the *Glosae* proper and its lemmata can be considered separately, since the latter is apt to be more corrupt. Often the scribes of the *Glosae* cannot have known what it was they were copying when they repeated a string of letters, each denoting a word in the *Timaeus*. Not all of their attempts to copy these lemmata, which are frequently unintelligible, have been printed in the list of variants. A good example of how a lemma might break down in the descent of the manuscripts is the case of *locauit* at 5.100 (W27:10). Whereas D M P possessed the truncated form *lo.*, O wrote *et c.*, T *et oc.*, and V *et o.* Some early scribe seems to have read an *l* for an *et* sign and the mistake was repeated. In the example found at 5.258 (W29:13) *accidunt* was truncated as *ac.* in M and T, *acci.* in O, *hac.* in D and P, and finally *haec* in V. At precisely the point where scribes decided to expand abbreviated and truncated lemmata, errors and anomalies were frequently introduced into the tradition. There is also evidence of a tradition of underlining the lemmata in the *Glosae*. While no single manuscript is trustworthy in this regard, the underlinings indicate something about the nature of the archetype and have been taken into consideration in the edition.

In the matter of the lemmata two manuscripts, M and T, reveal a degree of 'contamination.' Most likely at some point in the traditions that they follow, a scribe or student seeking clarification of an abbreviated lemma turned to an available copy of the *Timaeus* and corrected or expanded a lemma in the *Glosae* from the reading of his *Timaeus*. M and T both occasionally expand lemmata, though not the same ones, adding more words from the *Timaeus* than were apparently in the lemmata of the archetype of the *Glosae*. That most of these expansions were not in the archetype is likely, since both M and T add words inappropriately or in the wrong sequence. At 3.178, for instance, M added *monimentorum* after *Nutrit perseuerantiam* (W14:20-21), even though the word is glossed by itself a few words later and it was apparently not the practice of Bernard, who was economical in his use of lemmata, to confuse a gloss in this fashion. Similarly at 5.267 after the lemma (W29:19), T supplies an additional seven words of the *Timaeus*, but one of these words is glossed again a few words later. The occasionally fuller lemmata of M and T may not, therefore, have their source in the archetype of the *Glosae*, but in exemplars whose lemmata were 'contaminated.' The tradition of the lemmata of the *Glosae* would seem, therefore, to be more 'open' than the main text of the glosses.

Despite the frequently corrupt and 'contaminated' character of the lemmata of the *Glosae*, it is possible to draw some conclusions about Bernard of Chartres's copy of the *Timaeus* as translated by Calcidius. In the first place it was very like, though not identical with William of Conches's copy of the

Timaeus. At *Timaeus* 19a Socrates ends a sentence with " ... *alendos.*," Timaeus adds "*Id ipsum.*," and Socrates begins again with the word "*Ceteros* ... " (W9:26-10:1). Both Bernard and William apparently had copies of the *Timaeus* in which the sequence was reversed: " ... *ceteros.*," Timaeus, "*Id ipsum.*," Socrates, "*Alendos.*"[350] Waszink lists among his variants no manuscript that possesses this reading, though many manuscripts reveal some confusion at just this point. Both Bernard and William also read *famae* instead of *fama* (W22:8), *uniuersitate* instead of *uiuersitate* (W27:24), *nam facto* instead of *unde facto* (W30:1), *motus* instead of *metus* (W34:8), *emittendi* instead of *omittendi* (W41:6), *pauidos* instead of *probatos* (W41:18), *in aplano* instead of *aplanem* (W44:22), and *intensio* instead of *intentio* (W45:2).[351] Some of these conjunctive variants are significant[352] and may point to the character of the twelfth-century text of the *Timaeus* available at Chartres.[353]

Bernard's lemmata indicate some separative variants, ones that separate his copy from Waszink's standard edition of the *Timaeus* and from the copy of the *Timaeus* presumably owned by William of Conches:

BERNARD'S COPY OF THE *TIMAEUS*	CALCIDIUS' TRANSLATION AND WILLIAM'S READINGS
4.94 *Ergo*	*Igitur* (W21:11)
4.97 *Porro*	*Certe* (W21:13)
4.175 *similiter*	*consequenter* (W22:19)
4.317 *his*	*isdem* (W25:4)
5.253 *etiam*	*item* (W29:12)
5.381 *fit miranda*	*sit admiranda* (W32:5-6)
6.83 *sol et certae stellae*	*solet—certae stellae* (W34:5)
6.131 *igitur credamus*	*credamus ergo* (W34:15)
6.137 *His ergo*	*His igitur* (W35:7)
6.154 *igitur*	*ergo* (W36:6)

[350] *Glosae* 3.102-104 and *Glose Willelmi de Conchis super Platonem* 20, ed. Jeauneau, p. 80.

[351] For these readings, see *famae* 4.156 and *Glose Willelmi de Conchis super Platonem* 46, ed. Jeauneau, p. 115; *uniuersitate* 5.149, *Glose Willelmi* 81, p. 160; *nam facto* 5.282, *Glose Willelmi* 95, p. 177; *motus* 6.86, *Glose Willelmi* 109, p. 198; *emittendi* 7.162, *Glose Willelmi* 135, p. 235; *pauidos* 7.190, *Glose Willelmi* 138, p. 239; *in aplano* 7.429, *Glose Willelmi* 151, p. 255; and *intensio* 7.444, *Glose Willelmi* 153, p. 257.

[352] On the significance of the *motus* reading, for instance, see *Glose Willelmi de Conchis super Platonem*, ed. Jeauneau, p. 198 note b.

[353] By the nineteenth century before the destruction of most of the library of the cathedral in the Second World War, Chartres possessed no manuscript of the *Timaeus*: see *Catalogue générale des manuscrits des bibliothèques publiques de France. Départements* (Octavo Series), vol. 11: *(Chartres)* (Paris, 1890).

6.271 *discedentibus*	*desciscentibus* (W37:13)
7.209 *aliquid*	*quid* (W42:1)
7.237 *ipsa*	*illa* (W42:9)
7.301 *renidet*	*recidet* (W43:2)
8.27 *constat*	*constitit* (W45:12)
8.183 *remanet*	*manet* (W48:5)
8.202 *illi uero*	*illi autem* (W48:16)

While most of these are minor anomalies, easily explained away as variants either in the archetype of the *Glosae* or as ones that crept into the manuscript tradition of the *Glosae*, some may have existed in Bernard's copy of the *Timaeus*.

Almost all of the lemmatic variants of the *Glosae* can be located either in William of Conches's lemmata or in the combined readings of two twelfth-century manuscripts of the *Timaeus*: Brussels, Bibliothèque Royale MS 5093, fols. 13v-26r and Florence, Biblioteca Nazionale MS Conv. soppr. J.2.49, fols. 1r-27v.[354] Hence, on Waszink's impressive *Stemma codicum translationis* Bernard's copy of the *Timaeus* might reasonably be placed in the χ sub-group of family β.[355] In this sub-group Waszink also places the copy of the *Timaeus* in P. Note too that another manuscript assigned to the same sub-group, Florence, Biblioteca Nazionale MS Conv. soppr. J.2.49, is one of those whose glosses on the *Timaeus* seem most dependent on the *Glosae* (see App. 3.5).

The Notae Platonicae

The first six notes edited in the first appendix are all to be found immediately after the *Glosae* in D, M, and, in much damaged form, in T.[356] A copy of the first note, which was probably meant to accompany diagrams, was added, most likely in the twelfth century, to a copy of the Pseudo-Bede's *De mundi celestis terrestrisque constitutione*.[357] It is not unlikely that it was added to the

[354] On these MSS, see Waszink, "Praefatio," pp. cx, cxiv.

[355] See Waszink, *Praefatio* after p. clxvi and, on the family, pp. clvii-clviii.

[356] On the copy of the *Notae Platonicae* in M, see Gregory, *Platonismo medievale*, pp. 66-67 n.1 and *Glose Willelmi de Conchis super Platonem*, ed. Jeauneau, p. 41.

[357] Garin, *Studi sul Platonismo medievale*, pp. 33-46 pointed out the Chartrian character of the Pseudo-Bede, *De mundi celestis terrestrisque constitutione*. But the edition of Charles Burnett, in Warburg Institute Surveys and Texts 10 (London, 1985) should call this assumption into question. He dates the Pseudo-Bede text to the eleventh century, but divides off as later additions everything in the Migne edition from PL 90: 904A11 forward. Thus the first note of the *Notae Platonicae* (App. 1.1) falls immediately after the genuine text as a later addition. Indeed what follows in the Migne edition, PL 90: 904A11-910A2—on the three diagrams, the harmonic proportions, elements, hyle, virtues, and arts—may well have a Chartrian character, but the former is earlier in date and more encyclopedic in tone.

copy of the work printed by Migne by a scribe-compiler who had come into contact with the *Notae Platonicae*. The lemmatic commentary on the *Timaeus* in Leipzig, Universitätsbibliothek 1258, fols. 1r-8r, which possesses not only extracts from the *Glosae* (App. 3.1) and a copy of the seventh note (App. 1.8), also reflects a similar debt to this note (App. 1.1). Notes 2, 4, 5, and 6 are all extracts from Calcidius' commentary. Note 2, in fact, was also internalised at 7.272 in the copy of the *Glosae* found in O. From this one might suspect that O descended from a particular manuscript tradition in which some enterprising scribe had taken note 2 from the end of a copy of the *Glosae* and had inserted it in the *Glosae* where it seemed to him relevant. Thus, the internalised note in O suggests that it too descended from a manuscript tradition of the *Glosae* that once had a copy of the *Notae Platonicae*. Notes 1 through 6 were, therefore, most likely in the archetype of the *Glosae* manuscript and stood as a kind of appendix to it.

The status of note 7 is more problematic. It is only found in one of the *Glosae* manuscripts (D) and there it falls at the end of the rest of the notes. It also begins not with *Nota* as do the others, but with *Platonica sententia*. Unless it was dropped very early in the manuscript tradition of the *Glosae*, it seems unlikely that it too existed in the archetype of the *Glosae* manuscript.

Did Bernard have anything to do with collecting together the *Notae Platonicae*? The first and third notes are the most interesting in this regard, since they do not have their direct source in Calcidius' commentary. Indeed, the third note bears some relation to Bernard's own gloss on *polus* (6.54-57). None of the other notes seems to have deeply influenced Bernard's individual glosses, but they may still have held some importance for his school. Bernard and his students were seriously interested in some aspects of Calcidius' commentary on the *Timaeus*. That four of the *Notae Platonicae* are direct extracts from Calcidius and that note 1 essentially describes three diagrams from the commentary might underline the nature of Bernard's enterprise: to plumb Calcidius for what was valuable and to leave the rest aside.

\<BERNARDI CARNOTENSIS\>

GLOSAE SVPER PLATONEM

Sigla

In the edition of the *Glosae* the first column of numbers in the left-hand margin refers to the standard *Timaeus* edition of Henri Estienne (Stephanus) of 1527, while the second identifies the page and line numbers of Waszink's edition of Calcidius' translation of the *Timaeus*. The abbreviations and sigla found in the critical apparatus are those recommended by Dondaine and the Leonine Commission for the editions of philosophical texts of the Middle Ages.[358] The sigla of the manuscripts are:

D = Durham, Cathedral Library C.IV.7, fols. 41ra-49va

M = Munich, Bayerische Staatsbibliothek, Clm. 540B, fols. 1r-38v

O = Orléans, Bibliothèque municipale 260 (216), pp. 175-214

P = Pommersfelden, Gräflich Schönborn'sche Bibliothek 76 (2663), fols. 42r-60v.

T = Paris, Bibliothèque Nationale, MS Nouvelles acquisitions latines 281, fols. 125ra-131vb

V = Vienna, Österreichische Nationalbibliothek 2376, fols. 19r-31v.

---

[358] Antoine Dondaine, "Abbréviations latines et signes recommandés pour l'apparat critique des éditions de textes médiévaux," *Bulletin de la Société internationale pour l'étude de la philosophie médiévale* 2 (1960) 142-149 and "Variantes de l'apparat critique dans les éditions de textes latins médiévaux," *Bulletin de la Société internationale pour l'étude de la philosophie médiévale* 4 (1962) 82-100.

<1>

<ACCESSVS AD TIMAEVM>

Socrates de re publica decem libris disputauit. Ad quem tractatum incidenter
descendit, scilicet ut determinaret quid posset et quibus maxime prodesset
iusticia, de qua quaestio erat. Trasimachus enim orator dicebat eam magis
prodesse his qui plus possent; Socrates e contra his qui minus possent. Quod
ut confirmaret, elegit uim iusticiae assignare non in priuata re alicuius, sed   5
in quadam ciuili re publica. Quam cum iusticia administratam, id est bonis
moribus, rectis institutis et legibus, iocundam et felicem fore cognouit;
remotis illis, exiciabilem et miseram. Vrbem igitur talem sibi adumbrauit,
cuius exemplum in mundo inuenire non potuit, in qua plene uim iusticiae
positiuae quaesitam inuenit.   10

   Est autem iusticia qua datur cuique quod suum est. Huius alia species
positiua, id est consuetudinaria, pertinens ad hominum instituta, tam scripta,
quam non scripta; alia naturalis, quae docet reuerentiam deo et maioribus
exhibere, parentibus pietatem, <et> dilectionem diligendis communicare.
Positiua spernenda fugit, mores instruit, maxime ex timore, scilicet ex   15
meritis poenas pensans et praemia. Naturalis, deo communis et hominibus,
ex dilectione magis operatur, fugiens fugienda, petens petenda. De qua
Horatius:

         "Oderunt peccare boni uirtutis amore."

---

1 Socrates] ocrates *rub. om. D P T*   Ad quem tractatum] a quo tractatu ad hunc *V*   2
scilicet] id est *M*   maxime] magis *T*   3 magis] maxime *V*   4 his² *om. O*   minus]
minime *T*   6 ciuili *om. O*   7 moribus *om. P*   legibus] legis *V*   9 inuenire] uenire
P: reperire *T*   11 autem *om. V*   cuique] unicuique *P T V*   *post* species] est *add. O*
13 quam non scripta *om. T*   *post* maioribus] et minoribus *add. O*   14 <et>] omnes
codices def.: scrips.   diligendis communicare] diligentibus communicat *T*   15 fugit]
fugere *V*   instruit] instituit *M*   maxime] magis *T*   17 fugiens *om. O*

1-6 Cf. Cal., *Comm.* 5 (W59:3-8); Plato, *Republic* 338c-340d.   8-10 Cf. Cal., *Comm.*5-6
(W59-60); Dutton, "*Illustre ciuitatis,*" p. 83.   11 Cf. Macrobius, *Comm.* 1.8.7 (ed.
Willis, p. 38.14-15): "iustitiae seruare uni cuique quod suum est."; *Rhetorica ad Herennium*
3.2.3 (ed. Marx et Trillitzsch, p. 74): "Iustitia est aequitas ius uni cuique re tribuens pro
dignitate cuiusque."   13-14 Cf. Cicero, *Partitiones oratoriae* 22 (78): "iustitia dicitur eaque
erga deos religio, erga parentes pietas ..."   17 Cf. Horatius, *Serm.* 1.2.75 et 1.3.114: "non
fugienda petendis."   19 Horatius, *Epist.* 1.16.52.

Cum ergo Socrates rem publicam adumbratam tum positiua iusticia tum aliis   20
recte administrari decem libris docuisset, superesset uero naturalis inquisitio
iusticiae, quae fons et origo est positiuae. Reputans hoc ipse Socrates sibi
onerosum, simul fatigatus praedicta librorum serie, aliis illud inuestigandum
reseruauit.

   Plato autem quod magister dimiserat supplere uolens, de naturali egit   25
iusticia, non tamen statim ab ea incipiens, sed commodum faciens descen-
sum, de positiua praemittit, quam plene exerceri in ueteribus Athenis fir-
mauit. Quam urbem exemplum urbis a Socrate effigiatae in actu esse repperit.
Item, ut euidens faciat totum quod diximus, Plato inducit Socratem collo-
quentem quibusdam philosophis et statum rei publicae sibi depictae memo-   30
rantem paucis. A quibus etiam exigit eius exemplum actu reperiri et de
naturali iusticia suppleri, quod in parte non translata aperitur. Et quia Plato
de naturali iusticia plene agere uoluit, a genitura sensilis mundi cepit, in cuius
creatione et iusta partium ordinatione, caelestium et non caelestium discre-
tione, naturalis uim iusticiae docuit, qua creator erga creaturam usus est, ex   35
sola dilectione tribuendo cuique quod suum erat naturaliter. Deinde creatis
hominibus eos moribus instruit, uirtutibus exornat, sic ostendens quando
naturalis iusticia maxime uiguit in hominibus, prima scilicet aetate. Et per
haec omnia nos inuitat ad naturalis exercitium iusticiae.

   Materiam igitur habet naturalem iusticiam; quod enim de positiua inserit   40
incidens est. Intentio eius est tractare de ea, scilicet instruere nos ad cultum
naturalis iusticiae. Modus est quem praenotauimus. Vtilitas: scire quid ualeat,
quid conferat usus naturalis iusticiae.

---

21 recte om. V   administrari] administrare O   22 hoc] hic O: om. V   23 post simul]
etiam add. V   25 dimiserat] dimisit D   28 repperit] reperit M O P T   29 euidens]
euidentius P   Plato inducit] p. inducit D V: praeinducit M O P T   31 actu] actum O
32 Et] sed ut vid. in cod. T   33 cepit] incepit O   34 et iusta om. V   post
ordinatione] et add. V   35 ex om. O   36 sola om. P   cuique] unicuique T   erat]
est V   37 exornat] ornat O   38 super iusticia] iusticia add. V   maxime] magis T
hominibus] omnibus P   scilicet om. P   40 post enim] primum add. O   41
Intentio eius est tractare] Intentionem tractare D: Intentio tractare P: Intentio est tractare
O T   ea] ethica P   42-43 Modus ... iusticiae hom. D   42 post Vtilitas] est add. P T
scire] uero V

20-24 Cf. Cal., Comm. 6 (W59:14-18)   22 fons et origo] cf. Boethius, Phil. consol. 4,
metrum 6.36 (ed. Bieler, p. 85); Huygens, "Mittelalterliche Kommentare zum O qui perpetua ...," Sacris erudiri 6 (1954) p. 412.70 et 84.   28 Cf. Cal., Comm. 5 (W59:8-13), 6
(W59:18-60.3), 233 (W246:24-247:2); Dutton, "Illustre ciuitatis," p. 83.   33 Cf. Cal.,
Comm. 7 (W60:5)   35-36 Cf. 1.11 supra.   42 praenotauimus] cf. 1.22-39 supra.

Ponunt alii materiam rem publicam, de cuius diligenti administratione tum
per naturalem (et principaliter) tum per positiuam iusticiam dicunt eum 45
laborare. Quod etiam firmant per Macrobium dicentem: "Inter Platonis libros
quos de re publica scripsit, etc." Secundum quod intendit docere nos qualiter
sciamus administrare rem publicam. Finis est assequi fructum quem promittit
Macrobius rectoribus et conseruatoribus rei publicae.

Vel, secundum alios, principalis materia est generatio sensilis mundi, in 50
qua inuestigatur naturalis iusticia, per quam dii concordant inter se, et hic
mundus et quae eius sunt ab eis reguntur concorditer. Nam licet elementa
quasdam habeant contrarias qualitates, numquam tamen una in officium
transit alterius. Est autem, secundum hos, naturalis iusticia rerum omnium
concordia, genus scilicet positiuae.   55

Supponitur uero ethicae, secundum quod de naturali iusticia uel de
ordinatione rei publicae agit. Respicit logicam, cum per aliorum sententias
suas firmat rationes. Ad phisicam tendit, cum de planis figuris et solidis
corporibus, de incorporatione animae mundi et aliarum, earumque motu
perpetuo, de stellarum discursibus ratis et errantibus loquitur. Vnde seruata 60
omnium artium fere ratione, hoc opus non rudibus, sed in quadruuio
promotis elaboratum est, ut si quae quaestiones de musica et aliis oriuntur,
domesticis rationibus, scilicet musicis, arithmeticis, et ceteris, sopiantur.

---

44 tum] tunc *M O*   45 principaliter] principalem *V T*   tum] tunc *M O*   iusticiam *om.*
P   eum] eam *M*   46 etiam *om. T*   firmant] firmatur *P*: confirmat *T*: firmat *V*   *post*
Platonis] et Ciceronis *add. P*   47 de re] ut dicitur *P*   scripsit] in<scripsit> *P*
Secundum quod] Sed quia *O*   docere] docens *V*   49 conseruatoribus] seruatoribus
O   51 hic] iste *O*   52 eis] illis *M O P T V*   reguntur] regere *O*: regi *T*: regitur *V*
53 una] unum *P*   57 ordinatione] ordine *V*   58 firmat] confirmat *O T*: firmant *V*
tendit] concordat *V*   cum de *om. V*   59 mundi] mundanae *V*   mundi et aliarum
earumque] sensilem mundum uiuificantis et aliorum eorumque *T*   *post* motu] omnium *add.*
P   60 de] et *V*   62 elaboratum] elaborandum *P*   de] in *V*   *post* et] in *add. V*
63 *post* musicis] et *add. P T*   et ceteris] et aliis *D*: *om. T*   sopiantur] soluantur *V*

46-47 Cf. Macrobius, *Comm.* 1.1.1 (ed. Willis, p. 1.1-2): "Inter Platonis et Ciceronis libros,
quos de re publica uterque constituit ..."; 1.5.1 (ed. Willis, p. 14.8-9): "Sed iam quoniam inter
libros quos de re publica Cicero quosque prius Plato scripserat ..."   48-49 Cf. Macrobius,
Comm. 1.4.3-4 (ed. Willis, p. 13.16-23).   49 rectoribus et conseruatoribus] cf. Cicero,
Somnium Scipionis 1.3.1 (ed. Willis, p. 157.11-12); Macrobius, *Comm.* 1.8.2 (ed. Willis, pp.
36.30-37.2).   56-60 Cf. Augustinus, *De ciuitate dei* 8.4 (ed. Dombart et Kalb, *Corpus
Christianorum: Series latina* 47, p. 220.24-33); Cal., *Comm.* 2 (W58:3-5).   62-63 Cf.
Cal., *Comm.* 2 (W58:6-8).

<2>

<GLOSAE SVPER PROOEMIVM CALCIDII>

Quare liber iste difficilis apud antiquos habitus est, nec a multis probatus?
Quia pauci in his quaestionibus explicandis ualebant. Fuit etiam intranslatus
usque ad tempus Osii Hispaniae episcopi, qui uidens utile esse latinis si
transferretur, a Calcidio archidiacono seu amico suo hoc obtinuit. Qui,
difficultatem operis attendens, primam partem libri tantum apud Graecos   5
transtulit, et in eamdem commentatus, non ubique nec continue, sed ubi opus
fuit.

W5:1   Misit eam domino et amico suo cum hac epistula *Isocrates etc.*, in qua
reddit eum beniuolum commendando amicitiam dum comparat eam uirtuti,
attentum dum difficultatem perhibet, docilem dum primam partem libri   10
Platonis se transtulisse memorat. Et hoc est: *Isocrates etc.* Quasi diceret:
rogas me tui causa suscipere hoc opus, quod faciam, licet sit difficile, quia
difficultatem amor transcendit. Quod ostendit a simili, quia sicut uirtus omne
difficile superat, ita amicitia. Quod autem uirtus difficilia superet, probat
auctore Isocrate. Et hoc est: *Isocrates in exhortationibus*, id est in scripturis 15
W5:2-3   quibus hortatur homines ad uirtutem, *cum diceret penes eam*, id est circa
species eius uirtutis, *consistere causam etc.*, id est diceret ab ea procedere
omne bonum et omnem prosperitatem, tam extrinsecam quam intrinsecam,
addidit eam *solam*, id est praecipuam, *esse quae res* quasi *impossibiles*, uel
impossibiles sine uirtute, *redigeret ad facilitatem possibilem* per uirtutem.   20
W5:4   *Quid enim*: uirtus uere redigit ad possibilitatem impossibilia, quia incepta et
non incepta. Et hoc est: *Quid enim pigeat aggredi*, id est incipere, *generosam
magnanimitatem*, id est uirtutem, reddentem de ignobili generosum, *uel* quod

---

2 pauci *om.* P   explicandis *om.* D   3 Hispaniae] Hispaniensis *V*   6 eamdem] eadem
M O P V: eodem *T*   *post* commentatus] est *add. O   post* non] inquam *add.* P   8 eam]
eum *P*   8-11 Isocrates ... est *hom.* D   8 Isocrates etc. *om.* T   Isocrates] Socrates *M*
9 eum *om.* T   eam *om.* P   11 Et hoc est *om.* T   est *om.* V   Isocrates] Socrates
M   etc. *om.* T   13-14 omne difficile] difficilia *P*   14 superet] superat *O*: superat *corr.*
V   15 auctore] auctoritate *V*   Isocrate] Socrate *M*   Et hoc est *om.* T   Isocrates]
Socrates *M*: qui *T*   scripturis] scriptis *O P T V*   16 hortatur] exhortatur *M*   eam *om.*
P   17 etc. *om.* M   *post* id est] cum *add.* T   19-20 uel impossibiles *om.* M P   20
redigeret *om.* T   facilitatem] facultatem *M*: *om.* O   21 uere *om.* P   23 generosum]
gloriosum *P T*

1-2 Cf. Cal., *Comm.* 1 (W57:1-6); 142 (W181:13-19).

ceptum est tam difficile, cui succumbat prae difficultate? Quasi diceret:
uirtuosum nil quod sit honestum piget incipere uel perficere.   25

W5:5-6   *Eadem est.* Quasi diceret: quia per uirtutem superantur tam difficilia, ergo
per amicitiam. Et unde hoc? Quia *eadem uis*, id est idem feruor faciendi, *est*
utrique, scilicet amico et uirtuoso, hoc in minus grauibus, et *par extricatio*,
in grauioribus, *paene*, quia uix pro amico aliquis uellet pati quod multi pro

W5:6-8   fide Christi passi sunt, sicut decollationem et similia. *Cum alter.* Vere   30
extricatur res per amicitiam, quia per utrumque amicum, hoc est *cum alter
adminiculetur effectui*, id est sustentet effectum, *operis complaciti*, id est quod
placet utrique, et hoc non superbe iubendo, sed cum *religione*; *alter adminiculetur*, non timore uel ex tristitia parendo, sed solo *uoto*.

W5:8   *Conceperas.* Quia ita est inter alios quod amicitia superat omnia difficilia,   35
igitur nostra amicitia superabit quod tu *conceperas* in *animo florente*, id est
ualente, *omnibus studiis humanitatis*, id est in quibus homo ualere potest—in-

W5:9   tellige liberalibus, hoc refer ad triuium—*et ingenio excellenti*, in quadruuio.
Conceperas, inquam, *spem operis prouenturi*, id est latinis profuturi, *dignam*,
tua scientia, uel dignam, dum sperabas me dignum hac translatione; *intemp-*   40
tati a latinis.

W5:10-12 *Et quamquam.* Statueras hoc opus conferre latinis, in quo tu sufficiebas.
Et quamquam facere posses facilius ex sapientia, *commodius* ex gratia, *credo
etc. Verecundiam* dicit, quia uerecundabatur laudari si transferret; *admirabi-
lem*, quia mirum erat uitare laudem in tanto opere.   45

W5:13   *Possemne.* Quasi diceret: cum attenderem me esse quasi te, id est tecum
unum per amicitiam et morum concordiam, licet alterum in persona, igitur

W6:1-2   *possem etc.* Quasi diceret: non potui me honeste *excusare, de quo* tam bene
senseras et quem tantum honorabas. *Et qui.* A minori probat. Quasi: uere non
possum me excusare de hoc munere, quia *numquam* recusaui tibi in minori   50

---

24 prae difficultate] per difficultatem *T*   Quasi diceret *om. T*   27 Et *om. O   post*
eadem] est *add. P*   idem *om. O T*   28 minus] minis *P*: uel minus *superscr. P*   29
post uellet] mori uel *add. V*   30 decollationem et similia] mortem *T*   31 res *om. T*
post amicum] et *add. O P*   32 quod] qui *O*   33 non *om. T*   34 timore uel ex
tristitia] ex timore uel tristicia *P*   35 *post* Conceperas] animo *suppl. P*   36 in *om. M*
37 ualente] ualentem *V*   humanitatis *om. O V*   37-38 intellige] intelligere *D*   38
refer] refert *V*   39 spem] sperendi *O*   profuturi] profiteri *P*   40-41 intemptati]
intemptatum *M*   41 a *om. P*   42 in quo tu sufficiebas *om. T*   43 *post* quamquam] ipse
hoc *suppl. M*   facere] facilius *M*: *om. D*   47 unum] ante *O*   48 honeste *om. T*   49
tantum] tam *O*: tamen *V   post* qui] numquam *suppl. M*   50 numquam] non *O*   tibi]
uel *M*   minori] maiori *O*

36-38 Vide Jeauneau, *Lectio*, pp. 359-360 n. 89.

obedire. Sollon commune uel multum dicitur, inde sollemnis, id est communis. Solon singulare quasi a sole, inde sollemnis uoluntas, id est singularis et priuata.

W6:3-4   *In quo.* Quia sic eramus unanimes, ut dictum est, igitur non debui declinare a petitione. Et hoc est: *in quo,* id est in qua re, *declinatio speciosi*   55
muneris, id est si declinarem a specioso munere mihi iniuncto, *callida excusatione ignorationis,* id est ignorantiam meam excusando callide simula-
W6:5   rem me esse sapientem. *Itaque.* Quia nolui tibi recusare, igitur *parui. Non sine diuino*: quasi dii uellent per me naturalem latinis reuelari iusticiam, qua fruuntur in regendo se et mundum hunc. *Propterea,* quia speraui deos   60
W6:6   adiutores. *Primas* secundum ordinem, scilicet primum librum decem librorum, uel primas, id est praecipuas, scilicet quae digniora uidebantur. Res
W6:8   latinis recondita fuit liber Platonis. *Simulacrum* eius: hoc opus translatum,
W6:9   quod *obscurius* est, quia in alia lingua ita proprie exprimi non potuit. *Causa,*
W6:10   scilicet cur partem transtulit, partem dimisit, *fuit etc.*   65

51-52 Sollon ... communis *hom. T*   52 uoluntas] uoluptas *D M O V*: uel uoluntas *superscr. man. al. M*   54 *post* quo] declinatio *suppl. M*   non *om. V*   55 declinare] inclinare *P*   55-56 petitione ... a *hom. T*   55 *post* petitione] ut dictum est *add. P*   56 callida *om. T*   56-57 callida excusatione ignorationis] callida esset excusatione ignorationis scientiae futura stimulatio *suppl. M*   58 Itaque *om. T*   recusare] excusare *P*: resistere *T*   igitur] itaque *P T*   *post* parui] Certus *suppl. M*   59 reuelari] reuelare *O P T V*   60 speraui *om. P*   63 eius *om. P*   63-64 translatum quod obscurius] translatum est quia obscurus *D*   64 ita *om. T*   65 fuit etc. *om. T*   *post* fuit] operis prolixitas *suppl. M*

---

51 Sollon commune uel multum dicitur] vide Ernout et Meillet, *Dictionnaire étymologique de la langue latine: histoire des mots,* Editio quarta (Paris, 1959), pp. 632-634; *Glose Willelmi de Conchis super Platonem,* ed. Jeauneau, p. 66 n.a   52 Cf. Varro, *De lingua latina* 5.68 (ed. Goetz et Schoell, p. 22); Macrobius, *Comm.* 1.20.4 (ed. Willis, p. 79); Martianus Capella, *De nuptiis* 2.188 (ed. Willis, p. 52), 8.835 (ed. Willis, p. 315); Isidorus, *Etymologiae* 3.71 (ed. Lindsay).

\<GLOSARVM SVPER TIMAEVM PLATONIS\>

\<Liber Primus\>

\<3\>

\<RECAPITVLATIO SOCRATIS ET NARRATIO CRITIAE\>

Plato per inuolucrum cuiusdam conuiuii tractat praedictam materiam. Volens enim per positiuam iusticiam accedere ad naturalem de qua intendit, inducit Socratem magistrum suum pridie Timaeo cum quibusdam aliis dedisse epulum, id est tractatum de positiua iusticia, hoc pacto ut sequenti die epulum illud recompensarent in reinueniendo rem publicam, quam depinx-   5
erat, et de naturali supplendo iusticia. Et memorat per propria uerba sententias Socratis de ordine rei publicae habitas. Inducit etiam sub dialogo Timaeum et alios Socrati respondentes et debitum ei conuiuium soluentes. Quos non habet ueritas sic disputasse.

Sed cum sint tria genera poematum—enarratiuum quando ex propria   10
persona auctor loquitur, actiuum quando per introductas agit, commune quando per utrasque—hic Plato insistit actiuum genus. Inscripsit etiam hoc opus nomine Timaei discipuli pro more philosophorum, uitando scilicet arrogantiam. Vel ideo ne per appositionem nominis sui aemulos contra se incitaret, sicut Apostolus tacet nomen suum in epistula ad Hebreos. Vel etiam   15
ne Socrati magistro contraire uel praeferri uideatur, qui non Platoni sed Timaeo hoc iniunxerat. Sed quia Timaeus non sufficiebat tanto operi, Plato

---

1 *ante* Plato] Incipit Timeus Platonis *add. O V*   Plato] lato *rub. om. D M*   2 naturalem de qua] quam *O*   4 *post* ut] in *add. O*   *post* die] idem *add. D*   5 illud *om. D* recompensarent] recompensando *corr. P*   in *om. P*   6 Et memorat] commemorat *O*: Et memorando *V*   7 Inducit] In dialogo ducit *O*   8 *post* alios] discipulos *exp. P*   ei conuiuium soluentes] conuiuium exoluentes *D*   11 auctor] actor *O*   *post* introductas] personas *add. M V*   12 *post* hoc] ergo *add. T*   13 discipuli pro more philosophorum *om. T*   *post* discipuli] sui *add. O P*   pro more philosophorum *om. P*   14 arrogantiam] arrogandam *D*   ideo ne per appositionem] ne appositione *P*   15 in epistula *om. V*   etiam *om. T*   16 *post* magistro] suo *add. O P*   uel praeferri *om. V*

locum et personam gerit discipuli, salua reuerentia magistri Socratis. Vel
dicitur liber iste Timaeus, id est animalis, quia de generatione mundi, quod
est maius animal, agit.   20

17a W7:1   Quod uero sic incipit *Vnus, duo, tres,* innuit ipsos philosophos pridie
refectos a Socrate suo die conuenisse ad soluendum Socrati conuiuium. Vnde
Socrates, numerans illos qui suo interfuerant conuiuio, requirit unum quem
sentit abesse, non forsitan realiter, sed sub significatione. Nam subtracto
quarto, remanent partes quae coniunctae faciunt primum perfectum nume- 25
rum, id est sex, et ideo a perfecto incipit, ut notet perfectionem operis. Vel
ideo quartum uoluit abesse, quia tractaturus erat de anima, quae ex tribus
primis consonantiis primo loco figuratur constare, scilicet diatessaron,
diapente, diapason. Vel ideo quia in his tribus numeris magna uis perpendi-
tur, unitas enim fons est omnium numerorum: binarius et ternarius primi sunt 30
qui in se ipsos et alter in alterum multiplicati firmam faciunt conexionem,
sicut bis bini bis, ter terni ter, bis bini ter, ter terni bis. Quae tam firma et
solida conexio praesenti operi de mundi genitura agenti bene conuenit, quod
per tres auditores notatur. Si uero Socratem cum tribus consideres, quattuor
sunt, in quo numero omnes musicas consonantias uel proportiones inuenies. 35
Duo enim ad unum duplus est, scilicet diapason; tres ad duo sesquialter, id
est diapente; quattuor ad tres sesquitercius, id est diatessaron; ad unum idem
quattuor quadruplus, id est bis diapason. Quibus simphoniis mundi fabricam
constructam esse docebit. Non sine causa ergo quartus auditor subtractus est.
Hunc quartum dicunt fuisse in re Platonem, qui pro magistri reuerentia se 40
subtraxit, ne uideretur se illi praeferre, si suppleret quod magister non
poterat. Sed totum in significantia melius uidetur esse dictum.

---

18 et personam gerit] peragit *V*   *post* magistri] sui *add. O*   magistri Socratis] magistro
Socrati *V*   21 uero *om. P*   22 conuenisse] uenisse *T*   23 illos *om. V*   28 primis
om. M O   30 omnium *om. T*   binarius et ternarius] binarius ternarius *D M P V*: duo
tres *O*   31 conexionem] complexionem *O*   32 sicut] sic. *D M O T*   bis bini bis] VIII
superscr. P   ter terni ter] XXVII *superscr. P*   bis bini ter] XII *superscr. P*   ter terni
bis] XVIII *superscr. P.*   35 proportiones] portiones *V*   37 quattuor ... diatessaron *om.
O*   sesquitercius] sexquitercia *M*   *post* idem] id est *add. P*   38 diapason] diapente *V*
simphoniis] consonanciis *P*   39 esse] eam *O*   docebit] docebat *P*   42 significan-
tia] significatione *M*

25-26 Cf. Macrobius, *Saturnalia* 7.13.10 (ed. Willis, p. 445); Macrobius, *Comm.* 1.6.12 (ed.
Willis, p. 20); Martianus Capella, *De nuptiis* 7.736 (ed. Willis, p. 264); Cal., *Comm.* 38
(W87:15-16); 5.140-141 infra.   26-29 Cf. Boethius, *De institutione musica* 1.1 (ed.
Friedlein, p. 180.3-5), 1.16 (ed. Friedlein, pp. 201-203).   30 unitas] cf. Boethius, *De
institutione arithmetica* 1.3 (ed. Friedlein, p. 13.11-12): "Numerus est unitatum collectio, uel
quantitatis aceruus ex unitatibus profusus."   36-39 Cf. Macrobius, *Comm.* 2.2.18-19 (ed.
Willis, pp. 102-103).   39-42 Cf. 3.12-18 supra.

W7:2   Epulum, id est conuiuium, dicitur disputatio philosophorum per simile, quia sicut in conuiuio multa habentur fercula, ita in eorum disputatione multae et uariae tractantur sententiae. Mos enim erat philosophorum ut in 45 conuentu de rebus necessariis dissererent, quod in conuentu isto factum est.

7b W7:10   *Normulam* uocat rem publicam, quam depinxit secundum positiuam iusticiam.

7c W8:1   *Cardo hesternae disputationis,* id est materia circa quam uersatur intentio, ut ostium circa cardinem. 50

W8:4   *Quid illud,* id est ordinationem illam, qualem esse iudicatis, quae facta est ad similitudinem hominis? Cuius res publica a deo sic ordinata est. In arce enim capitis, id est in cerebro, uersatur sapientia; sub arce, id est in corde, iracundia, quasi uigor iuuentutis; concupiscentia in inferioribus, scilicet circa lumbos, cui illa superiora dominantur. Ita in superiori parte urbis potentes, 55 in medio ciues honesti, in suburbiis sutores et ceteri similes locati sunt.

W8:4-5   Ceteros dicit sutores *et ceterarum artium professores* quorum natura aliud expetit, aliud pugnantium.

d W8:10-11   Agere *mitibus quidem iudiciis etc.,* id est ut scirent:

"Parcere subiectis et debellare superbos." 60

Vel solis dico entibus *mitibus iudiciis.* Et existentibus *asperis etc.*

a W8:12   *Biformi.* Et iniunximus illos debere *praeditos biformi natura,* scilicet ut essent mites et feroces.

W8:16   *Huius ancipitis,* id est duplicis, *naturae.* Quasi: ita nutriendi sunt tutores patriae, ut prompti ad laborem et affabiles sint obedientibus. Quod prompti 65 sint per exercitium, scilicet cursum, uenatum, et ludos gymnasii; quod mites et affabiles, per delinimenta praeparatur musicae, quae per sonorum conue- nientiam morum docet concordiam. Gymnos, nudus: inde gymnasium, certamen in quo nudi agebant se. Palin. lucta: inde palestra.

---

43 *post* philosophorum] quae *add. O*   simile] similitudinem *V*   44 in² *om. T*   45 enim *om. V*   philosophorum] philosophis *V*   46 *post* conuentu¹] suo *add. M T* conuentu² *om. V*   52 Cuius] eius *O*   55 Ita *om. V*   56 ceteri similes] ceteros ciues *T*   58 expetit] exigit *D*   59-61 Agere ... etc. *in marg. sinist. P*   59 quidem *om. D O P V*   id est *om. T*   61 iudiciis] in iudiciis *D P T*: inde iudiciis *M*: ut uidere *O*   62 Et *om. T*   praeditos] praedictos *P*   62-63 biformi ... feroces *in marg. sinist. P*   64 *post* Huius] autem *add. P*   *post* ancipitis] naturae *suppl. M*   *post* duplicis] naturae *om. M*   Quasi] qua *P*   nutriendi] tutandi *M*: uel nutriendi *superscr. M*   sunt] sint *O*   65 ut] et *P*   66 ludos] ceteros ludos *P T*   68 nudus] id est ludus *P*   69 Palin lucta] Palam luctam *O*

51-58 Cf. Cal., *Comm.* 233 (W247:2-12); Dutton, "*Illustre ciuitatis.*"   60 Virgilius, *Aeneid* 6.853.   64-65 Cf. Dutton, "The Uncovering," pp. 199-200 n.41.   68-69 Cf. Isidorus, *Etymologiae* 18.17.1-2, 18.24 (ed. Lindsay).

18b W8:23   *Exhibentibus.* Quasi diceret: et etiam praediximus, ut essent quasi solidarii   70
rei publicae, aliis exhibentibus illis mercedem de communi, ita ut sufficeret
eis, in nullo laborantibus nisi in militia.

18c W9:4   *Quid de procreandis etc.?* Quasi: multa quae sunt contra consuetudinem.
Procreandos uocat naturales filios, suscipiendos adoptiuos.

W9:5   *Cetera* dicit esse miranda. Quae dicta sunt, quia nemo aestimat milites   75
propria possessione carere. Communes nuptias dicit in re, scilicet ut quicum-
que ad quamcumque uellet libere accederet, sicut ad propriam, quae ei
assideret in domo, et cuiusque filium suum aestimaret, et quemque maiorum
auum uel patrem uel quoquo alio modo sibi iunctum crederet, et sic communi
affectione omnes sibi iungerentur. Sed secundum hoc nec iusta nec honesta   80
uideretur ordinatio rei publicae a Socrate depicta. Dicamus igitur per inuolu-
W9:6-7   crum hoc esse dictum: quod innuit, dicens contra *consuetudinem* hoc dici.
Quando enim egit Socrates *de communibus nuptiis et de communi prole*, aliud
dixit et aliud intendit. Ac si diceret, non accipio istud in re carnaliter, sed
in sola affectione, remota turpitudine, quasi in omni re publica uellem esse   85
ut quisque ita diligeret alium ut filium, uel fratrem, uel patrem, et uxorem
alterius ut suam, sequendo in hoc praelatorum doctrinam. De hoc loco dicit
Augustinus quod Socrates hic inducit affectionem, non turpitudinem. Vel
potest intelligi communes nuptias, quod ducerent uxores non pro delecta-
tione, sed pro communi utilitate, scilicet pro rei publicae defensione. Vnde   90
dicitur de Catone:

"... urbi pater est, urbique maritus."

70 etiam *om. D*   quasi *om. V*   73 etc. *om. T*   74 *post* suscipiendos] id est *add. T*
75 Cetera] Cuncta *T*   aestimat] existimat *O*   76 possessione carere] profusione
carente re *O*   76-82 Communes ... dici *om. T*   76-77 quicumque] unusquique *O*:
quisque *P*: quiscumque *V*   78 aestimaret] existimaret *O*   quemque] quemcumque *P V*
maiorum] maiorem *P*: maiorum uel *M*   79 quoquo] quo *O*   et *om. O*   80 hoc]
haec *M P*: *om. D*   81 uideretur] uidetur *O*   depicta] facta *D*   igitur] ergo *D*   84
intendit] intellexit *D T*   diceret] dicat *P*   istud *om. T V*   in re *om. T*   carnaliter]
carnali *P*   85 affectione] dilectione *T*   *post* turpitudine] alter non uidetur honesta
ordinatio rei publicae a Socrate depicta *add. T*; *cf. 2.80-81 supra*   86 et] uel *M P*   88
quod] quia *M O P V*   hic *om. T*   89 intelligi] legi *O*   communes nuptias quod] n.
T   uxores *om. T*

87-88 Locus non inventus. Vide pp. 62-63 supra.   92 Lucanus, *Bellum ciuile* 2.388; cf.
Priscianus, *Institutiones grammaticae* 18.23-24.23-26 (ed. Hertz, in *Grammatici Latini* 3, p.
218): "Lucanus in II: 'urbi pater est urbique maritus', id est 'ad utilitatem urbis et pater fieri
passus est maritus.'"

W9:14   *Quid illud?* Quasi diceret: hanc ordinationem, qualem esse iudicatis? *Quod sine odio etc.* Haec ordinatio ad litteram potest intelligi, et etiam ad integumentum. Constituit enim ut uir unus uiris praeficeretur, et mulier mulieribus,   95 quorum iussione et obedientia ad eas quas sibi eligerent sine inuidia accederent. Quae enim inuidia, ubi quisque quam desideraret sibi conuenientem haberet? Per hoc autem quod illi duo in utroque sexu praeficiuntur aliis, non aufertur illis communis libertas, sed conseruatur accedendi religio, ut nihil sine obedientia et iussione praefectorum faciant, sicut monachi, licet omnia 100 sint eis communia.

W10:1   *Ceteros,* id est ignobiles, constituit esse alendos minori cultu. Sed, ante-
W9:21 quam Socrates posset dicere *"alendos,"* interrupit uerba eius Timaeus,
W9:22 dicens: *"Id ipsum."*

W10:2   Et promulgaui *nihilo remissiore <cura>* quam de nutritura *notanda* esse 105
W10:3 etc. Et hoc ideo: ut ignobiles, si probi fuerint, *prouehantur* et obtineant locum nobilium, nobiles uero, si degeneres sint, deprimantur.

W10:5   *Et quid?* Quasi: in hac nostra replicatione hesterni epuli de positiua iusticia uideor satisfecisse uestrae receptioni, quam debetis reddere de naturali iusticia.   110

W10:9   *Scis <ne> igitur?* Quia nichil uis addi, igitur scis, et nonne scis?

W10:12-17   *Vt si quis.* Ordo est: qui depinxi rem publicam, *deposco* mihi ostendi a uobis, uel ab aliis, in re *populum* realiter *agentem,* id est ita ordinatum et educatum, ut docui in hac pictura rei publicae, *ut* sit *si quis* uidens picturam equi uel tauri uel aliorum pulchram *desideret spectare* talem equum currere 115 uiuentem et talem taurum certare.

W10:17   *Quippe.* Ideo deposco, quia per me non sufficio maxime ad inueniendum naturalem iusticiam, unde positiua procedit.

W10:18   *Nec mirum, si tantam indolem non possim laudare,* quia nec auctores nec
W10:20 poetae possunt. Nec ideo dico hoc ut *contemnam poeticam nationem,* id est 120
W10:21 poetas, sed potius dico quia confido eos *perfecte posse aemulari,* id est
W11:1 tractare et laudare, *ea quorum usum et experientiam habeant ab ineunte,* id

---

93 diceret] et *D M P T V*   Quod] quia *O*   94 intelligi] legi *O*   94-95 etiam ad integumentum] alter *T*   95 ut *om. T*   97 ubi] ut *M*: si *V*   98 aliis] ceteris *T*   99 accedendi] accendentia *V*   100 praefectorum] perfectorum *P*: praedictorum *V*   faciant] facerent *M*   102 *post* alendos] sed *add. T*   102-103 minori ... alendos *in marg. dext. P*   104 Id] ad *V*   105 Et *om. O*   <cura>] *cf. W10:2*   106 etc. *om. D*   prouehantur] promoueantur *P*: prouebant *O*   107 sint *om. T*   108 hac *om. V*   nostra *om. T*   epuli] poculi *V*   111 Scis<ne>] *cf. W10:9*   Scis ... scis *in marg. dext. P*   et nonne scis *om. T*   112 quis] quisque *D*   depinxi] depinxit *O*   112-113 a uobis *om. O*   113 in re *om. P*   114 pictura] depictum *P*: picta *T*   114-115 ut sit ... equi *om. V*   115 spectare] speciem *M*: postea *O*   117 Quippe] Qua propter *O*   119 *post* si] eam *add. O*   possim] possum *V*   120 contemnam] contra *D O*   id est *om. O*   122 ab ineunte] lab. me. *V*: *om. O*

W10:21 est transacta, *aetate*: illos, dico, *peritos imitandi* id tantum *quod* est *euidens*
W10:20 *et perspicuum*, scilicet circa ethicam. Phisica enim ad phisicos magis pertinet.
W11:2 Vel *euidens* dicit quod est uel fuit sensui notum. *At uero.* Facile est poetis 125
19e W11:4 quod dixi, sed confido *difficilem esse imitationem*, sicut est de re hac quam
depinxi, *effictam* a me *oratione, uersibus* ab alio. Vel difficilis disserere
oratione et uersibus. Quibus? Scilicet *praeclaris etc.*

W11:5 *Vagi* localiter; *palantes*, per incertas deceptionis uias discurrentes.

W11:9 *Superest igitur.* Quia nec ego nec historiographi nec alii sufficimus, igitur 130
uos deposco.

20a W11:10 *Siquidem*: probat de singulis quod sunt nutriti *publica cura.*

W11:15 *Rebus de quibus*, scilicet de positiua et naturali iusticia.

20b W11:16-17 Quia uos adeo ualetis, *ideo parui et facile*, quia sciebam uos reddituros mihi
uicem. *Reliquas.* Post positiuam, scilicet de naturali. 135

W11:19-20 *Mutuum*: ut mihi uicem redderetis, quod facere debetis, quia hoc *munus*
a me suscepistis, quod me dare imperastis.

20c W12:2-3 *Namque.* Vere non est ratio excusandi, quia reddere possumus. Quod inde
patet, quia de hac re post egimus.

20e W12:11 *Huius urbis*, scilicet Athenae. 140

21a W12:13 *Quo tam penes*, id est ut tibi placeat et Mineruae.

21b W12:16 Teste Augustino: Cerimonides fuit quidam qui instituit ritum qui uocatur
cerimonium.

W12:17-18 *Nos pueros inuitare*, uel ut antiqua eis memoriae reduceremus, uel ut quae
dicebantur memoriter teneremus. 145

W12:20 *Vt quae.* Quasi: Solonis carmina comparatione aliorum noua erant, et ideo
magis grata.

21c W13:1-4 *Igitur senex.* Quia Solonem ita laudauit, *inquit senex*: "*Quid si non*

---

124 perspicuum] perfectum *corr. P*   scilicet *om. M O*   phisicos] philosophos *V*   126
difficilem] difficile *M*   esse *om. D O P T V*   imitationem] una *D O P V*: *om. M*   hac
om. P V   quam] qua *V*   127 depinxi] prae depinxi *O*   oratione] orationem *D O P*
uersibus *om. V*   128 oratione] orationem *D O P*   et] ut *O*   uersibus] uersum *D*:
uersus *O*   praeclaris] periculis *V*   *post* praeclaris] praestantibus ingeniis *suppl. M*
129 incertas] disputas *superscr. P*   130 igitur^2] ergo *O T*   132 quod] qui *O*   sunt
om. V   133 *post* Rebus] his *suppl. M*   134 uos] nos *O*   ualetis] ualentes *O*   facile]
scilicet *T*   sciebam *om. O*   136 mihi uicem redderetis] inuicem reddetis *T*   137
suscepistis] accepistis *T*   139 post] prius *D P*   141 penes *om. M*   *post* penes] nos
add. V   143 cerimonium] certamen *T*   144 inuitare *om. M P*   eis] eius *O P*
reduceremus] reducemus *M V*   145 memoriter] memorie *T*   146-148 et ... Solonem
in marg. sinist. P   148 *post* laudauit] ita *add. O*   Quid] qui *O*: *om. P*

142-143 Cf. Augustinus, *Retractationes* 2.37 (63), (ed. Mutzenbecher, in *Corpus Christianorum: Series latina* 57, p. 121), sed non inuenitur ipsa sententia quae hic a Bernardo ponitur;
cf. p. 63 supra.

perfunctorie," id est transitorie et imperfecte, cepit enim, sed non perfecit. Hic innuit Solonem in Egypto aliquid insigne didicisse, quod *reuersus,* 150 scribere incipiens, explere non potuit, ciuili discordia occurrente, quod ideo subdit, ne pigritiae uel negligentiae causa uideatur Solon dimisisse quod cepit.

W13:3   *Mi Aminander*: nomen est fabulae quam incepit. Vel duae partes sunt, ut
W13:6   dicatur: o *mi Aminander. Et ille* Aminander ait ueteri Critiae uel ille Socrates 155 ait minori.

W13:11   *Delta*: nomen est figurae d; cui Δ graeco similis erat in situ illa regio.

W13:13   Variari dicunt nomen conditoris eius ciuitatis masculino genere et femi-
W13:14   nino, dum dicitur ΘHYC *Athena,* ut diuersas potestates sapientiae notet, quae in perfectis masculino, scilicet ΘHYC, in minus perfectis feminino, 160 scilicet Athena, id est immortalis, dicenda est. Haec uero sapientia, licet in aliis locis perfecte pro modo ipsorum suscipiatur, ipsa tamen eadem manens condidisse illas ciuitates perhibetur, quia ibi a pluribus et studiosius colebatur.

W13:17-14:2   *Referebat* Solon *se irrisum.* Et referebat auus meus *Solonem* fuisse *percon-*
W14:3-4   *tatum cur hoc diceret* sacerdos et referebat sacerdotem respondisse:*"Quia* 165 *rudi..."*

W14:8   Filius *solis* dicitur calor, qui genitus a sole paulatim crescendo et humori praeualendo exurit subdita. Et nota hoc dictum ad similitudinem rotae molendini, quae postquam conterit cardinem in quo uoluitur, axis eius propior fit aquae et uicinior terrae, sed cum renouatur cardo, altius ipsa rota 170

---

149 perfunctorie] perfunctoriae *M*   enim] autem *M*: enim *superscr. man. al. M*: *om. T* sed] et *P V*   150 *post* Solonem] scilicet *add. O*   insigne *om. P*   152 uideatur] iudicatur *O*   154 Mi Aminander] Minam. *D O P T V*   est *om. T*   155 Aminander²] Aminandum *D*: Animandus *O*   ueteri] seni *T*   Socrates] Socrate *O*   156 minori] iuniori *M*: iuueni Critiae *T*   157 *om. T*   d] Δ *M*   Δ] in *O*: Λ *P*: a *V*   graeco] graecae *D*   regio] religio *O*   158 *post* conditoris] et *add. P*   genere *om. O*   159 dicitur] dicerent *O*   ΘHYC] ΘHCYC *D*: *om. V*   Athena] scilicet *V*   160 in perfectis] in *M   post* perfectis¹] in *add. P*   scilicet *om. D*   scilicet ΘHYC *om. P T* ΘHYC *om. V*   perfectis²] imperfectis *P   post* feminino] reponatur *superscr. P* 163 et *om. O*   studiosius] studiose *O*: studiosis *T*   164 Referebat ... irrisum *om. P post* se] ibi *add. T*   Et *om. T*   165 cur hoc diceret sacerdos] sacerdotem *T* diceret *om. D*   166 *post* rudi] etc. *add. M*   168-172 Et nota ... facit *om. T* 169-171 axis ... uoluitur *in marg. sinist. O*   170 aquae] atque *corr. P*   renouatur] remouetur *D*

---

157 Cf. Martianus Capella, *De nuptiis* 6.675 (ed. Willis, p. 239.19-21).   158-161 Cf. *Glose Willelmi de Conchis super Platonem* 24 (ed. Jeauneau, p. 86.24-27): "Quidam conantur reddere causam quare Pallada masculino et feminino nomine designauit, quia sapientia quam designat Pallas et in perfectis est masculina et in minus perfectis feminina."   160-161 Cf. *Mythographus Vat.* 2.39 (ed. Bode, pp. 87.42-88.1); Isidorus, *Etymologiae* 8.11.71 (ed. Lindsay).   161-163 Cf. Isidorus, *Etymologiae* 19.20 (ed. Lindsay).

uoluitur: sic axis solis tunc tantum quando sol cum totis uiribus est exustio-
nem facit.

22d W14:12   *Tunc igitur*, quia fit inflammatio. Aliis nocet calor, sed apud nos non
   W14:13   potest praeualere humori. Et hoc est: *nobis etc.*

   W14:15   *Item.* Quasi diceret: sicut pereunt apud uos per ignem, ita per diluuium 175
humore paulatim crescente et praeualente calori.

22e W14:19   *Superne*, id est desuper, quia nulla uel rara est ibi pluuia, Nilo satisfaciente.
   W14:20-21   *Quae causa*, scilicet humoris et caloris temperati, *nutrit perseuerantiam*, id
est perpetuam memoriam, *monumentorum*, id est librorum continentium

23a W15:1   publica facta et priuata. Apud nos remanet *fama*, sed *apud uos* non est cana 180
   W15:2-3   memoria, et apud *ceteros* de aliis nationibus, quia *aedes nunc* sunt *plane*, id
est nouiter, destructae praecedente diluuio, et constructae iterum pereunt.

23b   Litteras publicas uocat communiter notas, uel publica facta notantes.

   W15:5   *Nouam* sicut fecit Carmentis mater Euandri.

        Qua ratione, diluuii scilicet et exustionis, sequitur ut uestra et aliorum facta 185
ignoretis. Et ea de historiis Athenarum, quae tu putas antiqua, ut de
Phoroneo et Nioba uxore eius, sint puerilia.

23c W15:10   *Publicam cladem* dicit submisionem insulae cum innumeris Atheniensibus.
Quae paulo post explicabitur.

   W15:11   *Fuit enim.* Bene dixi optimum, nam *fuit etc.*   190

23d W15:14   *Tum* referebat auus meus *Solonem admiratum etc.* Et referebat *illum*
   W15:15-16 sacerdotem *respondisse*: "*mos est gerundus tibi*" ut hospiti. *Educauit*:
   W15:18   conditam auxit; *instituit* praeceptis informando *uestram* urbem *priorem*
23e   nostra *annis mille fere*, quasi parum (forsitan plus uel minus fuit), annis dico
ductis, id est incipientibus, *ex indigete*, id est a natiuitate Erictonii, uel finem 195
habentibus in eadem natiuitate, quod non ualet, quasi tempore quo natus est

---

171 sic] sicut *P*   tantum] tamen *V*   174 etc. *om. T*   175 Item] Ita *T*   diceret] dicat
T   ignem] calorem *T*   177 *post* pluuia] nisi *add. V*   satisfaciente] satis inundante *P*
178 et] uel *P*   temperati] temperata *M*   nutrit perseuerantiam] monimentorum
perseuerantiam *M*   180 facta] fata *T*   remanet fama *om. M*   fama] infinita *V*
cana] causa *corr. V*   181 nunc sunt *om. T*   plane] planatae *M*   183 publica *om.*
T   184 fecit] factam *T*   185 et[1] *om. M*   186 historiis Athenarum] historia Athenorum
P   187 Nioba] Niobe *P*   189 explicabitur] explicabuntur *P*: explicabimus *T*   190 etc.
om. T   191 Tum] Tunc *M O*   auus] animus *O*   illum *om. T*   192 hospiti] hosti
V   Educauit] Edidit *M*: Edem *O P*: Eadem *T*   193 conditam] condita *D T*   instituit]
institutis *M*: iustis *O V*   informando] informandam *V*   uestram] nostram *O*   194
mille *om. M*   uel minus] minusue *T*   195 id est[1]] et *P*   *post* indigete] a<gro> *suppl.*
V   196 natiuitate ... quo *in marg. sup. P*

179-180 Cf. Macrobius, *Comm.* 2.10.14 (ed. Willis, p. 127); Isidorus, *Etymologiae* 1.41.2
(ed. Lindsay).   184 Cf. Virgilius, *Aeneid* 8.335-336; Hyginus, *Fabulae* 277 (ed. Rose, pp.
170-171).

Erictonius condidit Pallas Athenas, ex quo mille anni fuerunt usque ad
constitutionem Sais. Vel e conuerso: a tempore conditarum Athenarum
usque ad ortum Erictonii, quo tempore condita est Sais, fuerunt mille anni.
W15:19   *Hanc nostram posteriorem*: nostram condidit, *octo milibus annis* transactis   200
W15:21   *post* eius, scilicet secundae, constitutionem. Et sic erant *nouem milia anno-*
rum ex quo Athenae ceperunt institui usque ad hanc narrationem sacerdotis.
Ante cuius constitutionem multi *uixerunt*, qui post eam conditam habitaue-
runt. Vel *ante* quod sequitur pro 'antea' lege, supplens 'infra', uel tale quid;
et sic bene procedit haec sententia. Dicunt quidam aliter, scilicet quod   205
Athenae priores fuerunt conditae mille annis, additis octo milibus annorum
qui sequuntur, ut sint nouem milia a tempore quo Athenae ceperunt fieri
usque ad tempus quo ciuitas sacerdotis condita fuit. Nec obest tamdiu uixisse
Mineruam, quae immortalis est, ut dea sapientiae.
W15:18   *Indiges ager* dicitur, quasi naturalis, quia Erictonius de eo ut de matre   210
natus est. Nam Pallade coitum Vulcani abnuente, semen in terra effusum est,
quod Pallas pede conculcauit, unde Erictonius creatus est. Ex parte terrae
serpentinos pedes habuit, ex parte hominis in superioribus homo fuit. Qui
post, rex eiusdem ciuitatis, prior currus dicitur iunxisse, pro celanda pedum
turpitudine. *Eris* interpretatur lis, quia in tali lite Vulcani et Mineruae fuit   215
creatus.
W16:2   *Leges* dicit, quod unicuique officio proprius locus deputatus est.
W16:10   *Prudentiae.* Cetera apud nos sunt sicut apud uos, nam de studio sapientiae et religionis non est dubium.
W16:12-14   *Nonne?* Quod apud nos est *diuinatio etc.* Et uere *instinctu* illius, quia *hac*   220
exornatione etc.

---

199 ortum] tempus *T*   est *om. V*   200 nostram¹] uestram *P V*   nostram²] uestra *M*
O V: uestram *T*: *om. P*   condidit] condita fuit *V*   milibus *om. T*   202 *post* Athenae]
primum *add. P*   ceperunt] cepit *O P T*   institui] constitui *O*   203 post eam] postea
O   204 sequitur pro *om. V*   lege] legem *O*   206 Athenae priores fuerunt
conditae] Athena prior fuit condita *D M O P T*   207 *post* tempore] ex *add. T V*
ceperunt] cepit *M O P T*   208 usque ad tempus] a tempore *P*   fuit *om. T*   209
ut] utpote *T*   210 Indiges ager] Lugides ag. *D*: Indiges agit *O*: Ludi gessat *V*   ut] et
V   211 coitum] scortum *P*   Vulcani] Vulcano *P V*   abnuente] obiciente *P*   effu-
sum] profusum *O*: fusum *T*   212 conculcauit] occultauit *P*   unde] inde *O*   creatus]
natus *V*   est *om. D P T*   *post* est] et *add. O*   terrae *om. M*   213 habuit] habens
T   in superioribus] inferioribus *T*   214 *post* post] primus *add. P*   iunxisse pro
celanda] intrasse ad celandam *T*   217 quod] quia *D*   proprius] prius *V*   218 Cetera]
Cuncta *M P T*: certe *V*   220 Nonne? Quod] Numquid *O*: Non quidem *M*: Non quid *P*
Nonne ... etc. *om. T*

208-209 Cf. *Mythographus Vat.* 1.124 (ed. Bode, p. 39.40-41); *Mythographus Vat.* 2.39 (ed.
Bode, p. 87.32-88.2); Fulgentius, *Mitologiae* 2.1 (ed. Helm, p. 38.11-13).   210-216 Cf.
Fulgentius, *Mitologiae* 2.11 (ed. Helm, pp. 51-52); Hyginus, *Fabulae* 166 (ed. Rose, pp.
116-117); *Mythographus Vat.* 2.37 (ed. Bode, p. 86.32-87.19).

W16:17   *Sui similes*, id est praecellentes omnium fertilitate, sicut ipsa regio est
ceteris fertilior.

24d W16:17-20 *His ergo*, quia *nobilitati* erant *his legibus* praemissis, ergo *eruditi, utpote*
germani diuinae prosapiae, scilicet nati de Erictonio. *Captum*, id est intellec- 225
tum uel appetitum, id est ultra quam humana gloria posset capere.

24e W16:21-22 Mane bonum, inde immanis non bonus *iniuriis* qui omnibus iniurius est.
Et inexpugnabilem, quia tot erant quod expugnari non poterant.

W17:1   *Ex Atlantico mari*, id est ex insula cui imminet Atlas et Calpe, qui duo
montes prius iungebantur, sed fretum oceani eos interrumpens mare Mediter- 230
raneum fecit, quod Hispanos dirimit ab Africa. Atlas in fine sedet Africae
supra oceanum, Calpe ex altera parte in Hispania. Et dicuntur Gades
Herculis, quia ibi posuit aereas columnas in signum. Sciendum quod illa
magna insula tota erat in mari, ex omni parte circumfluente oceano, et huic
magnae aliae adiacebant paruae insulae. In defectu, id est in fine, quarum erat 235
quoddam fretum, id est aestus et ingressus oceani, ubi facit Mediterraneum,

25a W17:6-7 et ubi est *initium terrae continentis*, id est solidae, hoc est ubi primo inuenitur
portus ab illis qui insulis egrediuntur. Et ita illis de magna insula *patebat*
commeatus, id est transitus, ad alias gentes, eundo per alias insulas usque ad

W17:7-8 illam extremam, cui erat terra contigua, et quae *uero mari*, id est oceano, erat 240
uicina. *Quippe*. Vere mare illud habet insulam in introitu, quia *hoc fretum*, ens

W17:8-9 *intra os* (id est Herculis) *diuiditur a continenti*, id est a terra contigua illi
W17:9   insulae, uel a solido mari, *angusto litore*, id est perangustum litus. *At uero*.
W17:10   Quasi: istud fretum est quoddam falsum mare, at oceanus est *uerum mare*.

Igitur. Quia inde patebat transitus ad ceteras gentes et inexpugnabilis erat 245
illa manus *in hac* etc.

25b W17:14 *Quae quidem*. Quasi: haec manus Egyptum et Graeciam deleuisset, nisi
uestri Athenienses eis gloriose restitissent.

25c W17:19-21 *Communem custodiam* dicit publicam *libertatem*.

---

222 Sui] Cui *O*   omnium] omni *P*   224 eruditi *om. V*   225 scilicet] id est *P: om.*
O V   226 id est *om. T*   227 *post* Mane] id est *add. P*   est] erat *P*   229 mari
om. P   231-232 Atlas ... Hispania *in marg. dext. P*   233 posuit] imposuit *T*   quod]
quia *M V*   234 erat] fuit *P*   235 In defectu] In deflectu *V*   236 et *om. P*   237 hoc]
id *T*   inuenitur] inuenerunt *O*   238 qui] quod *D V*: quidem *T*   insulis] de insulis *M*
P   patebat] patet *M T*   239 commeatus id est] enim *V*   240 terra ... erat *superscr.*
V   241 Quippe] Quod pe. *O*   242 intra] inter *M P*: in terra *D*   id est[1] *om. M*   244
quoddam *om. M T*   mare[1] *om. V*   oceanus est] oceanus *O*   mare[2] *om. M O P V*
245 Igitur] Et *D*   patebat] patebit *O*   ceteras] cunctas *M T*   gentes] gressus *V*
post et] ideo *add. O*   erat] fuit *V*   247 *post* Quasi] dicat *add. P*   248 restitissent]
restituissent *O*   249 custodiam] custodit *O*

---

227 Mane] cf. Varro, *De lingua latina* 6.2.4 (ed. Goetz et Schoell, p. 58); Macrobius,
Saturnalia 1.3.13 (ed. Willis, p. 12).

W17:22   *Neque* enim tunc, inquam, enituit nam paulo post periit et *terrae motu et* 250
diluuio. Vel probat quod per summa discrimina.

5d   W18:6   *Sed cum.* Quasi diceret: uix recolui illam rem publicam Atheniensium,
cum audiui te depingere tuam rem publicam.

W18:10   *Reticui tamen.* Quasi: licet aliquantulum recordarer, tamen nolui inprae-
meditatus respondere quae ab auo audieram, sed malui singula prius reducere 255
ad memoriam.

a   W18:12   *Ex quo.* Quia mecum illud prius uolui tractare *ex quo etc.*

W18:14   *Itaque.* Quia imperio tuo parere uolebam, diu in hac recordatione laboraui.
Hermocrates *dixit* supra. Mox conuentu soluto tractatum habuimus non
otiosum. 260

b   W18:19   Nec scio quare, *nisi* quod *in illa aetate.* Vel hoc facit frequens et aperta
c   W18:21   relatio aui. *Meracam* uocat quasi meram potionem.

W18:22   *Quare?* Quia singula memoraui, *quare paratus sum.*

d   W19:5   *Imperato.* Paratus, inquam, sum, sed sub hac conditione: si socii mihi non
defuerint. 265

e   W19:8-9   *Aestima fieri* tibi *remuneratione*; tu, dico, *contentus* hac remuneratione.

W19:10-11   Ferias uocat dies festos Mineruae, quibus huic disputationi uacabant. Hoc
approbo et aestimo *magnificum etc.*

W19:13   *Quare?* Quia imprimis bene uobis successit, quare *pergite* accedendo ad
W19:14   naturalem iusticiam. *Attonito*, id est attento. 270

W19:16   *Si est commoda*, id est si bene recompensamus quod debemus.

W19:17   *Placuit enim.* Vere est commoda, quia Timaeus, primum ferculum in hoc
conuiuio ponens, ut qui in phisica praeeminet, producet sermonem usque ad
W19:19   generationem hominum, incipiens *a constitutione sensibilis mundi.* Quos
formatos eius sermone ego secundi uice ferculi suscipiam, instruendo eos 275

---

250 inquam] in qua *V*   250-251 terrae motu et diluuio] in terrae motu et in diluuio *V*
251 *post* discrimina] etc. *D*   252 *post* cum] praeterito *suppl. M*   diceret] dicat *M*
illam *om. P*   254 Quasi *om. T*   257 illud prius uolui tractare] uolui illum re-
tractare *T*   *post* quo²] factum *suppl. M*   259 Hermocrates dixit] Vt hic id est Ermocrates
dixit *T*; *cf. W18:14*   dixit] dicit *M*   soluto tractatum] solutum tractauit *V*
260 otiosum] omne *O P V*   261-263 nisi ... Quare *hom. V*   261 aetate] est *D*
263 memoraui] commemoraui *M*: commemoraui *O*   quare paratus sum *om. T*   264
Imperato] Imperate *O T*   mihi non] me non *P*: uel mei non *superscr. P*   265 defuerint]
deficiunt *O*: defereruerint *corr. P*   266 fieri] si *P T V*   tu dico] iudico *V*   contentus]
contemptus *D*   267 disputationi] disputatio *T*: dispositioni *V*   uacabant] uacabat *D*:
uocabat *T*   267-268 Hoc approbo] Hic approprio *V*: Hoc proprio testimonio *P*: uel hoc
approprio *superscr. P*   268 magnificum] magno *V*   269 imprimis] primum *V*   *post*
quare] fortuna prosperante *suppl. M*; *cf. W19:13*   270 naturalem] talem *O*   attento]
attentum *T*: attento silentio *M*; *cf. W19:14*   271 recompensamus] te compensamus *O*:
recompensauimus *T*   272 enim *om. M*   quia] quae *V*   273 praeeminet] praeeminet
omnes codices: *scrips.*   *post* praeeminet] et *add. D*   274 sensibilis] sensilis *M T*   275
formatos] informatos *P*   secundi *om. T*

moribus et uirtutibus. Et hoc tam primae creationis homines quam succeden-

27b   W20:1   tis, descendendo usque ad Athenienses, *fama Egyptiorum* celebratos, quos
sub ciuili iure descriptos constituam ante Timaeum et Hermocratem, ut inde
iudicent.

W20:3   *Ne*, id est certe *ego etc.*   280

27c   W20:6   *Nam*. Vere inuocandum est in hoc maiore negotio, quia etiam in minoribus
hoc seruatur.

27d   W20:10-12   *Sit igitur*. Inuocatio ut dicamus *quae deo placeant* et *ut* a *nobis* nec
dissideamus nec a nostro *proposito*.

---

276 hoc] *om. D*: enim *O*   277 celebratos] celebrandos *V*   278 constituam] construam
V   280 certe *om. P*   etc. *om. T*   281 Vere] est *V*   282 hoc *om. V*   seruatur]
obseruatur *M P*   283 Sit] Sint *M*   Inuocatio] Inter *V*   et *om. O*   284 nostro] meo *T*

\<4\>

\<TRACTATVS DE CONSTITVTIONE MVNDI\>

Est igitur. Timaeus, plene pro posse hominis tractaturus de naturali iusticia, incipit a generatione mundi. Quem, quia dixit sensilem, id est omnia quae fiunt sentientem, uel sensibus inuestigabilem, ne uideretur additio illa superflua, innuit alium mundum esse, scilicet archetipum, et hos duos ostendit differre, diuidendo eos a se imprimis. Continuatio. Quia inuocaui deum, ut congruum est, igitur dicam *quid sit* idem *quod semper est,* id est archetipus, et quia semper, ideo caret *generatione,* et quid, id est quae essentia sit; *idem quod gignitur,* id est sensilis, et quia *gignitur, non est semper.* Hic innuitur haec diuisio: quicquid est post deum uel est genitum uel ingenitum. Posset etiam intelligi: quicquid est uel creator uel creatura, sed sequentia non requirunt hoc. *Semper* accipe non aeui, sed temporis.

Alterum. Exsequitur membra diuisionis sub expositione, dicens: *Alterum,* id est quod caret *generatione, semper* est *idem,* id est immutabile, quod inde patet, quia *perceptibile* est *intellectu* et ratione inuestigata ducente nos ad illud uel ad intellectum.

Porro alterum, id est genitum, est *opinabile, opinione* iuncta *cum sensu,* quae utraque circa corpora uersantur. Opinio uero, quando certa est, sensus purgatus est. Ratio circa uniuersalia, quae tunc certa est, quando purgatur animus, licet proprie nulla ratio infirma dicatur. Intellectus circa diuina tantum, qui tunc purgatus est, quando nulla rerum imagine impeditur. Et est

---

1 hominis] suo *P*: uel hominis *superscr. P*   tractaturus] tractatus *O V*   2 sensilem] sensibilem *corr. V*   3 fiunt] sunt *P*: uel fiunt *superscr. P*   4 alium] alterum *O* mundum *om. M*   scilicet] id est *T*   ostendit *om. T*   5 diuidendo] ostendendo *O* *post* Continuatio] est *add. P*   ut] et *corr. P*   6 est[1]] fuit *V*   quid] quod *D*   idem *om. V*   7 *post* semper] est *add. P*   quid] qui *O*: quae *V*   quae *om. V*   8 sensilis] sensibilis *O*   quia gignitur] quia ginnuntur *O*   innuitur] innuit *P*   9 haec] illa *V* haec diuisio *om. T*   9-10 diuisio ... creator uel *hom. O*   9 est[2] *om. T*   *post* genitum uel] est *add. P V*   9-11 Posset ... hoc *om. T*   10 *post* est uel] est *add. P*   11 requirunt] requiretur *corr. V*   *post* accipe] est *add. O*   aeui] eius *V*   12 *post* Alterum[1]] id est *add. V*   membra] membrum *M*   sub] super *O*   14 inuestigata] inuestigante *M*   15 uel] id est *M*   16 alterum] ab. *D*: ah. *V*   opinione *om. P*   18-20 Ratio ... impeditur *om. T*   19 proprie] propriae *V*   20 qui] quae *D*   purgatus est] purgata est *D*: certus est et purgatus *O*   *post* quando] purgatus est animus sic ut *add. V*   imagine] imaginatione *V*   impeditur] impeditus est *O*: impediatur *V*   est[2] *om. O*

16-19 Cf. Boethius, *Phil. consol.* 5, *prosa* 4.34 (ed. Bieler, p. 97); 5, *prosa* 5.4-7 (ed. Bieler, pp. 99-100).

aliud hic opinio quam imaginatio. Fit enim opinio *cum sensu,* illo quiescente sensu qui dicitur irrationabilis, quia fallitur in rerum perceptione, et quia nec minima nec maxima comprehendit. Nullus enim paruitatem atomi uel magnitudinem caeli sensu comprehendit.

W20:18-20   *Propterea*: quia sensu capitur, *nascens et occidens,* sed *incertum,* id est   25
effluendo per partes; et quia incertum, ideo non *perseuerans etc.*

W20:20   *Omne.* Plato ostensurus mundum sensilem esse factum, quia corporeum, cum omne quod factum est in sui natura sit dissolubile, ipse uero dicturus sit eum indissolubilem (quod est contra omnium opinionem), prius propagare uult eum aeternitati. Quod facit quattuor modis, scilicet docens a quo, et ad   30
cuius exemplum, et ex quibus partibus, et qua causa factus sit. Per auctorem probat mundum aeternum, cum dicit a deo factum. Omne enim quod fit, uel est opus dei, uel naturae, uel hominis artificis imitantis naturam. Natura quidem est uis et ratio gignendi. Hominis autem opus patet non esse mundum, nec naturae. Opera naturae sunt quae habent semina in uisceribus   35
terrae ad arbores et segetes et cetera procreanda, uel quae habent semina in genitalibus membris ad fetus animalium, quae omnia in tempore nascuntur et occidunt, et ideo dicuntur temporalia. Est igitur mundus opus dei. Opera uero dei non sunt temporalia, quia nec principium nec finem habent in tempore. Vocantur quidem causatiua, quia habent causas, ante tempus soli   40
deo et non nobis cognitas, quae ita sunt fundamenta dei operum, sicut semina naturae operum naturalium, et ideo nihil patiuntur ex his quae infert tempus, scilicet nec morbum nec senium nec similia, sed sunt sine necessitate incommodi. Per exemplum quoque propagatur mundus aeternitati, quia, cum archetipus qui est eius exemplum sit aeternus, ex ipso similitudinem aeterni-   45
tatis trahit. Sicut enim aeternitatem ille habet semper manendo, ita iste fluitando. Ille semper est; hic fuit, est, et erit semper.

---

21 illo] illa *D P T V*   22 qui] quae *O*   et *om. T*   23 *post* comprehendit] sensu *exp.*
T   23-24 Nullus ... comprehendit *in marg. dext. P*   25 sed *om. T*   incertum]
inconstanti *M*: incertum est *P*   26 incertum] uincunt *O*: incertum est *P*   ideo *om. V*
27 *post* Omne] autem *add. T*   28 cum] quia *O*   in sui natura] uisibile *V*   sui] sua
T   29 indissolubilem] indissolubile *V*   30 scilicet *om. T*   ad *om. P*   33-35 uel
hominis ... naturae[1] *hom. O*   34 quidem] quod *V*   opus *om. V*   35 nec] hec *P*
post Opera] enim *add. O*   36 cetera] certa *ut uid. in codd. M T*   37 quae omnia]
quaedam *T*   38 occidunt] accidunt *O*   dicuntur] dicunt *V*   opus *om. D M P V*   40
quidem] quaedam *V*   quia] quae *V*   *post* tempus] et *add. T*   41 et *om. P*   *post*
cognitas] sed *add. D*   operum] operis *P*   42 operum] operis *corr. P*   ex his *in marg.*
sinist. P   infert] inferunt *D*   43 scilicet *om. M*   *post* scilicet nec] tempus *add. V*
nec morbum nec] morbum uel *T*   nec similia] *om. O*: et similia *T*   44 mundus *om. T*
45-46 aeternitatis *om. T*   46 trahit] habet uel trahit *M*   47 fuit] finitus *O*   est[2]
om. T

---

28 dicturus] vide *Timaeus* 32c (W25:8-10).   32-59 Cf. Cal., *Comm.* 23-25 (W73-76).

Per ea ex quibus constat propagatur aeternitati, quia confectus est ex
quattuor integris corporibus sine ulla diminutione, scilicet ex quattuor
elementis; et quia totum frigus totum calorem habet, non patitur importuna   50
accessione frigoris uel caloris. Inde enim corpora nostra patiuntur, quia non
sunt ex integris. Obicitur: cum mundus constet ex corporibus quorum natura
sit semper defluere, mundus semper in fluxu debet esse. R⟨espondendum⟩:
non sequitur. Licet enim mundus in partibus suis patiatur defluxum, quia
non patitur effluxionem, ideo non patitur corruptionem. Sola enim effluxio   55
infert corpori corruptionem. Mundus uero non effluit, sed influit. Nam, cum
terra soluatur in aquam, aqua in aerem, aer in ignem tenuetur, et e conuerso
ignis spissetur in aerem, aer in aquam, aqua in terram, haec influxio non est
corruptio, sed fatigatarum partium recreatio. Propagatur etiam mundus aeternitati per causam, quia, cum uoluntas dei mundi causa sit, quae aeterna est,   60
ipsa quoque eum aeternum facit. Nec dicimus aeternum quod careat principio, sed intelligimus perpetuum et indissolubilem. Continuatio. Omne quod
est uel est genitum uel ingenitum, sed *omne quod gignitur* habet legitimam,
id est rationabilem, causam.

W20:20

Operi. Respicit ad exemplum. Quasi diceret: non solum quod genitum est   65
habet causam, sed etiam *fortunam*, id est euentum permanendi felicem uel
infelicem, honestum uel inhonestum: honestum, cuius exemplar aeternum
est, minus honestum, cuius exemplar natum est. Et hoc est: *quippe etc.*

W20:22

Omne igitur. Quia omne quod est aut semper est aut ortum, *igitur mundus*,
qui est *omne*, id est omnia in se continens, uel *omne caelum*, id est omnes   70
caelestes circuli. Et quia per hoc non habebat terram et alia, ideo corrigit: *uel*

8b W21:4

---

50 habet] haberet *P*   importuna] importunam *T V*   51 accessione] accessionem *V*: *om.*
T   post accessione] corporis et *add. O*   52 Obicitur] Obicient *V*: Hic solet opponi
scilicet *O*   53 *post* mundus] quoque *add. T*   in fluxu] in fixu *O*   debet *rep. V*
54 non sequitur *om. T*   enim *om. T*   in] *exp. P*: uel cum *superscr. P*   defluxum]
defluxionem tamen *T*   55 corruptionem] confluxione concorruptionem *V*   55-56 Sola
... corruptionem *om. T*   56 corpori *om. V*   sed influit *om. T*   57 aqua ... tenuetur
om. T   57-58 aer ... aquam *in marg. infer. P*   58 aer in aquam, aqua in terram] etc. *T*
59 fatigatarum] defatigatarum *T*   mundus *om. T*   60 dei *om. T*   sit *om. T*   61
quod] quia *T*   62 indissolubilem] indissolubile *T*   63 uel[1] *om. O V*   est[2] *om. D O*
P T V   65 est *om. D*   66 sed *om. V*   fortunam] sortem *O*   66-67 uel infelicem
om. O   67 exemplar] exemplum *V*   67-68 aeternum ... natum est *in marg. sinist. P*
69 Quia *om. T*   *post* ortum] est *add. T*   igitur] ergo *O*   70 qui] quod *O T*
71 caelestes] celestis *V*

61-62 Cf. Boethius, *Phil. consol.* 5, *prosa* 6.14 (ed. Bieler, p. 102): "Platonem sequentes deum
quidem aeternum, mundum uero dicamus esse perpetuum."

mundus seu quo alio dignatur nomine, id est dignus sit uocari, *considerandum*
W21:6-7   *est fueritne semper citra exordium temporis,* id est an ceperit esse post tempus,
scilicet praecedenti tempore, *an sit originem etc.,* id est an ceperit esse cum
tempore. Vel aliter: an habeat originem non ex tempore, sed cum tempore,   75
an ex tempore, ita quod habeat aliquam notam temporis quo cepisset esse.
Operibus enim dei non conuenit esse ex tempore, sed cum tempore; operibus
uero naturae et hominis non conuenit cum tempore, sed ex tempore, quia ea
praecedunt tempus, haec sequuntur. Legunt etiam quidam *citra* pro 'ante', et
est dicere: an ante tempus, an cum tempore fuerit, uidendum est.   80

W21:4-5   *Faciendum enim.* Ideo sic determinaui caelum uel mundum, quia hic
faciendum est quod ubique, scilicet quo nomine dicatur, et *quid sit de quo*
W21:5-6   *agitur. Item,* sicut scilicet *in omni tractatu, mundus etc.*

W21:7-8   *Factus est.* Quod dixit considerandum esse modo soluit, subiungens: esse
factum. Quod probat cum dicit: *corporeus.* Incorporea enim non dicuntur   85
fieri, sed simpliciter esse. Et quod corporeus sit, probat cum dicit: *qui*
uideatur et tangatur.

W21:8-9   *Siquidem.* Dixit mundum uideri et tangi. Sed quod est *huius modi,* id est
quod uidetur et tangitur, est *sensilia* et ita *corporeae naturae.*

   Sensibilis. Dixit mundum sensibilem esse, sed omnia sensibilia facta sunt,   90
quod probat per partem, cum dicit: generata sunt. Conclusio extra: scilicet
28c   W21:10-11   igitur mundus factus est. Bene dicit opinionem praesumere, quia praesump-
tuose iudicat illud, sed quod sibi incertum est.

---

72 quo alio] quod animal *D*   dignus] indignus *O*   73 fueritne *om. V*   citra] an ceperit
M   74 praecedenti] procedenti *T*   74-75 an sit ... sed *hom. P*   74 originem] ortum
M: omni *O V*   75 non *om. V*   *post* cum] habeat an *add. V*   76 cepisset esse] cepisset
T   77 conuenit esse] conuenit *O*   79 praecedunt] praecedit *O*   *post* quidam] quod
add. P   81 determinaui] determinauit *P V*   82 faciendum est] factus est *M*: facit *V*
de quo] de *D*   83 *post* scilicet] est *add. T*   *post* mundus] est *add. T*   84 *post* est]
etc. *add. V*   85 Quod] quia *P*   corporeus *om. T*   Incorporea] in corpora *V*   87
uideatur] uidetur *M O T V*   et tangatur] etc. *M T*   88 mundum ... modi *in marg. sinist.*
P   89 et tangitur] etc. *D*   sensilia] sensibilia *M*   et ita corporeae naturae *om. T*
corporeae] corporeum *M*   naturae] enim *P V*   90 Sensibilis] Sensilis *T*   sensibi-
lem] sensilem *O T*   sensibilia] sensibus *O V*: sensilia *T*   91 partem] partes *P*   dicit]
dixit *V*   scilicet] sed *V*: si *P*: *om. O*   92 Bene dicit] bene *O*: bene dixit *T*   93 sed
om. M   *post* sed] illud *rep. O*

72-79 Cf. Macrobius, *Comm.* 2.10.9 (ed. Willis, p. 126.10-12): "sed mundum quidem fuisse
semper philosophia auctor est, conditore quidem deo, sed non ex tempore; si quidem tempus
ante mundum esse non potuit cum nihil aliud tempora nisi cursus solis efficiat."; Augustinus,
De ciuitate dei 11.6 (ed. Dombart et Kalb, in *Corpus Christianorum: Series latina* 48, p.
326.16-17): "procul dubio non est mundus factus in tempore, sed cum tempore."   81-82
Cf. Macrobius, *Comm.* 2.11.12 (ed. Willis, p. 129.24-25): "mundus proprie caelum uocatur";
Cal., *Comm.* 98 (W151.3): "caelum quoque usurpantes mundum omnem uocamus."
85-86 Cf. Boethius, *Contra Eutychen et Nestorium* 6 (ed. Peiper, p. 208.63-72).

Ergo opificem. Et quia mundus factus est, igitur habet opificem et, cum alium non habeat, deum habet. Vel quia omnia facta habent opificem, ergo   95 mundus.

W21:13   *Porro.* Ostenso quod habeat opificem excellentem, docet quod habeat
W21:14   exemplum et quale, scilicet immutabile; *fundamenta,* scilicet quattuor elementa.

9a W21:15   *Nam si.* Probat mundum factum esse ad immutabile exemplar, quia ipse   100
W21:16-19   est pulcher et opifex eius optimus. *Sin uero.* Si mundus pulcher est et *fabricator eius optimus,* habuit immutabile exemplum. Sed si nec hoc nec illud est, tunc *molitio,* id est institutio mundi, est facta *ad elaboratum exemplum.*

W21:20-23   *Quippe hic* mundus etc. Repetitio est probationis. Et *ille auctor,* id est deus,   105 est actor *in constituendo his quae semper existunt,* id est respexit ad intelligibilem mundum, in *ratione et prudentia,* id est in rationabili et prudenti compositione, *sui operis,* id est sensilis mundi.

W21:23   *Imago.* Et quia hic mundus factus est ad exemplum immutabile, ergo est *imago alterius,* id est archetipi. Dicunt quidam exemplum esse ad cuius   110 similitudinem aliquid fit, exemplar quod ad alterius simile fit, et tamen improprie posita pro se inueniuntur. Alii e conuerso uolentes Platonem improprie exemplum pro exemplari posuisse.

b   *Et quoniam.* Dixit hunc mundum esse imaginem archetipi, uellet autem aliquis sibi reddi rationes utriusque. Plato uero ostendit de archetipo se non   115 posse reddere rationes, quia cum omnium rerum rationes rebus ipsis cognatae sint — sicut archetipus aeternus est, ita eius rationes aeternae sunt — et ideo hominum ingenio nequunt comprehendi. De sensili autem, si non satis firmas

---

94 Ergo] Igitur *T*: Et *V*   Et *om. T*   factus *om. V*   igitur] ergo *M*   *post* opificem] ergo mundus *add. V*   95 habeat] habet *V*   98 scilicet quattuor] sunt quattuor *M O T V*   101 opifex ... et *om. T*   est² *om. P*   102 eius *om. M O T V*   optimus *om. M* 103 molitio] moles *M*   105 hic mundus *om. M*   etc. *om. M T*   probationis] proposicionis *P*   auctor] actor *D O*   106 actor] auctor *M*   *post* actor] id est *O* constituendo] constitutione *corr. O*   id est *om. M*   106-107 respexit ... in rationabili *hom. O*   107 in¹ *om. T*   in rationabili] irrationabili *O V*: rationabili *T*   prudenti] prudentia *M*   108 compositione] positione *O V*: ratione *D*: uel ratione *superscr. P*: *om. M*   sensilis] sensibilis *O*   109 *post* Imago] est *suppl. T*   110 *post* exemplum] eius *add. O*   111 fit¹ *om. P*   quod] quid *O*   ad *om. O*   simile] similitudinem *M*   tamen] tantum *V*   112-113 Alii ... posuisse *om. T*   114 autem] etiam *O*   118 hominum] horum *O*

105-106 Cf. M.D. Chenu, "Auctor, Actor, Autor," *Bulletin du Cange (Archivium Latinitatis medii aevi)* 3 (1927), 81-86.   110-112 Cf. *Glose Willelmi de Conchis super Platonem* 38 (ed. Jeauneau, p. 105.19-22): "Et est exemplum id iuxta cuius similitudinem fit aliquid, exemplar uero id quod fit ad similitudinem alterius rei. Sed sepe unum pro alio ponitur. Vnde in hoc loco proprie exemplum dicitur diuina sapientia ad cuius similtudinem omnia sunt facta."

rationes afferat, docet non esse mirandum, cum ipse mundus uarietur inconstanter. Et cum nequeat dare rationes, uult saltem inter eos ponere differentiam per eorum naturas. Continuatio. Ille est origo huius, sed *ratione etc. Et* 120
quoniam, hoc est: *distinguendae sunt etc.* Naturas idem uocat quod causas, scilicet proprietates archetipi et sensilis, quarum quaedam certae et stabiles ut archetipum, quaedam uagae et incertae ut sensilis. Vel naturas dicit ipsum archetipum et sensilem mundum, causas rationes quae sequuntur utrumque. 125
Nam de re incerta et instabili non habetur ratio certa et stabilis, licet uera interdum habeatur. Nam cum dico corpus album esse, antequam rationem illam finiam, potest fieri nigrum. Item si dicam "hoc est tangibile," quia in hac proprietate uariatur—modo enim tangitur ut durum, modo ut molle—ideo ratio ipsa uidetur instabilis. Etiamsi dicam hunc mundum constare ex 130
quattuor elementis, ratio talis dicitur instabilis propter partium uariationem, dum effluunt et influunt.

Continuatio. *Naturae imaginis et exempli distinguendae sunt.* Supple: per causas. Quae causae, id est quae rationes, sunt *consanguineae,* id est similes earum rerum quae sunt, quia ita est in omnibus. *Itaque.* Quia omnium rerum 135
rationes consanguineae sunt ipsis rebus, igitur idem reperitur in ratione intelligibilis mundi. Et hoc est: *itaque constantis.*

Et ratio, id est rationabilis causa, *generis,* id est archetipi, et uere *constans,* quia *stabilis,* et uere stabilis, quia *rei perspicuae intellectui et prudentiae,* non sensui, sicut sensilis mundus *reperitur etc. At uero.* Ratio archetipi constans 140
est, sed *ratio eius rei,* quae *facta est ad similitudinem constantis et perpetuae,* id est intelligibilis mundi, *mutuatur similitudinem perfunctoriam,* id est non perfectam, quia non ostendit mundum sensilem impermutabilem, sed transitorium, cum ratio intelligibilis mundi ostendat illum mundum impermutabilem aeternum, *utpote imaginaria,* id est comprobatoria, *imaginis,* id est 145

Marginal sigla: W22:1-2 · W22:3 · W22:3-4 · W22:5 · 29c W22:5-6 · W22:6-7

---

121 *post* sed] sine *add. O*   ratione] rationem *O P*   122 hoc] hic *M*   distinguendae] disiungendae *M*   sunt *om. O T*   etc.] *om. O:* imaginis exemplique naturae *suppl. M*   124 *post* archetipum] et *add. V*   uagae *om. M*   127 rationem] orbem *V*   128 nigrum] nigredo *P: om. D*   129 ut[1]] ubi *V*   130 Etiamsi] etiam *D:* et si *T:* non si *P*   130-131 dicam ... instabilis *om. D*   131 propter] per *O*   133 imaginis] unaquaeque res *M*   134 similes] consimiles *T*   136 rationes] creationes *M*   sunt *om. D*   rebus] rerum *M*   137 constantis] etc. *T: om. V*   138 Et *om. T*   constans] constat *P*   139 et[2] *om. P*   *post* prudentiae] id est *add. M*   140 sensui] sensim *D*   141 eius *om. T*   est[2] *om. O*   *post* constantis] rei *suppl. T*   *post* perpetuae] rei *suppl. M*   142 perfunctoriam id est] perfectam et *O*   id est[2] *om. V:* inde *M*   142-143 non perfectam] inperfectam *M:* non inperfectam *P*   143 sensilem] sensibilem *corr. P*   143-145 sed ... impermutabilem *hom. T*   144 ostendat] ostendit *O: om. D*   *post* impermutabilem] et *add. T*   145 imaginis] imago *M*

127-128 Cf. Aristoteles, *Categoriae. Translatio Boethii* 5 (ed. Minio-Paluello, p. 12.10-13); 10 (ed. Minio-Paluello, p. 34.23-24).

sensilis, qui est imago intelligibilis; et ideo ipsa ratio huius mundi est *simulacrum rationis* quae probat intelligibilem mundum. Vel aliter: sicut sensilis est imago intelligibilis, ita ratio sensilis mundi est imago illius uerae rationis quae habetur de intelligibili, et sic dupliciter est imago: quia et imaginatur, id est designat sensilem, de quo habetur, et est imago illius 150 rationis, quae habetur de intelligibili. Nam sicut illa certa est quae uere imaginatur certum, ita incerta est illa quae imaginatur imaginarium, id est incertum.

W22:7-8 *Quantoque.* Adaptat similitudinem, quia *quanto essentia,* id est intelligibilis, *est melior generatione,* id est dignior sensili qui gignitur, *tanto ueritas,* id 155 est ratio illius essentiae, est *praestantior incerto famae et opinionis,* id est ratione sensilis mundi, quae est quasi fama et opinio incerta comparatione intelligibilis mundi.

W22:9 *Quare?* Quia omnes res habent rationes similes sibi, quia sunt uel uerae uel
W22:10-11 imaginariae; ergo *ne miremini* si de incertis do incertas, et de certis certas, 160 non incertas de certis, et e conuerso.

⁾d W22:12 *Memento enim.* Vere non est mirum, quia res est uariabilis, et ideo etiam quia ego et uos homines sumus.

W22:16 *Leges certaminis sacri:*

"Primo ne medium, medio ne discrepet imum." 165

Vel ut, dato initio, ducat opus ad finem. Vel leges dicit causas rerum et formas: quae dicuntur leges, quia sicut cuique rei lex est imposita et distincta, ita causa et forma. Hoc certamen dicit sacrum, quia cum alii dicant dissoluendum, iste probat numquam dissolui mundum.

W22:17 *Dicendum igitur.* Quia omne quod gignitur ex aliqua causa gignitur, ergo 170 et qua causa genuerit mundum, et quare tam optimum fecerit, dicendum est.
W22:17-18 Et hoc est: *omne hoc etc.*

---

146 *post* sensilis] mundi *add. P*   146-148 et ideo ... intelligibilis *hom. O*   148 sensilis¹] sensibilis *D*   sensilis²] sensibilis *D V*   149-150 quia ... imago *in marg. sinist. P*   149 quia] que *T*   et² *om. O*   152 ita ... imaginatur *in marg. dext. P*   incerta] incertum *V*: certa *O*   illa *om. O*   imaginatur² *om. T*   imaginarium] imaginariam *M P T*: id est imaginaria *O*: imaginaria *V*   155 generatione *om. T*   156 essentiae *om. V*   158 intelligibilis] sensilis *corr. M P*   160 miremini] mirum *M V*   160-162 do ... mirum *in marg. sinist. P*   160 certas] certis *T*   161 et e conuerso *om. V*   162 enim *om. M* etiam *om. P*   164 Leges certaminis sacri] Leges *M*: *om. V*   165 medio *om. O*   ne discrepet imum] etc. *T*   imum] imo *O*   166 initio] initium *V*   167 cuique] unicuique *P*   imposita] incomposita *V*   168 dicit] dicitur *M*   169 dissoluendum] soluendum *T*   170 *post* Dicendum] est *add. O T*   170-171 ergo et] igitur ex *T*   171 mundum *om. M*   fecerit] fecit *O*   172 omne] et *V*

---

165 Horatius, *De arte poetica* 152.

29e W22:18   *Optimus.* Recte fecit optimum, quia ipse *optimus erat*; quod inde apparet, quia non inuidit facturae suae suam communicare beatitudinem.

W22:19   *Itaque.* Quia optimus erat, *similiter*, id est per rationem, *uoluit effici cuncta* 175
W22:19-20 *similia sui*, non tamen uno modo, sed *prout natura cuiusque poterat esse capax beatitudinis*, quia in creaturis sunt perfectiora ut homo, quaedam minus perfecta ut asinus.

W22:20   *Quam quidem.* Hic habemus uoluntatem ipsius esse causam quare fecerit mundum.   180

30a W22:22   *Volens.* Vere uoluit cuncta effici similia sui, quia ex inordinatis fecit ordinata.

W22:23   *Prout eorum.* Quia licet non sint perfecta quaedam, non tamen sunt dicenda mala.

Omne. Non reliquit *propaginem*; immo malum, id est non perfectum, 185
W23:1-2 *redegit* ad bonum qualiscumque perfectionis. Et hoc est: *redegit in ordinem omne uisibile et corporeum*, et hoc, dando proprias formas singulis.

Fluctuans, id est in modum fluctuum se commiscens. Hoc ideo dicit, quia in hyle antequam formaretur, iactabatur seminarium corporum, non quod adhuc esset corpus, sed formandum erat, et ideo nitebatur ut formas accipe- 190
ret. In qua hyle ipsa confusio erat, quasi fluctuatio et incerti motus. Illud uero seminarium natiuis formis deus formauit, per quas discreta a se ipsis quattuor elementa, liquida et elimata, inuenta sunt, nondum sensu comprehensibilia, et inde dicunt philosophi non ex nihilo deum fecisse mundum, sed tantum exornasse. Seminarium etiam animae uolunt quidam in hyle prius iactari, et 195
post formatum apposito intellectu. Quod si dicunt hylen materiam esse animae, ex qua fit, non est ratio; si materiam, in qua fit, potest ferri. De hac uero hyle quid sit, in sequenti nos qualitercumque docebit, quousque et nos de ea differamus.

---

173 *post* Optimus] erat *add. P*   *post* fecit] mundum *add. M*   175 erat *om. D* similiter] simul *V*   176 tamen] tantum *M*: *om. O*   natura cuiusque] natus *V*   177 creaturis] creatis *O*   *post* creaturis] quaedam *add. V*: est aliqua *add. T*   quaedam] quia *V*   179 Quam quidem] Quamquam *O V*: Quamquam igitur *P*   183 *post* Prout eorum] natura fert *suppl. M*   licet *om. V*   tamen] tantum *V*   185 propaginem] propagandum *P*   non perfectum] imperfectum *P*   187 *post* omne] inordinatum *add. M*   singulis] singulas M   188 Fluctuans] fluctus *O V*   id est *om. D*   dicit *om. V*   190 esset] esse *M*   et *om. O*   191 qua *om. V*   192 discreta] discretas *O*   ipsis] ipsa *D M P V*   193 et ... sunt *in marg. sinist. P*   194 tantum] tamen *P*   195 *post* quidam] etiam *add. D*   prius] *om. D*: post *V*   196 hylen] hyle *D M P*   197 *post* fit[1]] et *add. V* si] sed *D O T*   materiam] materia *D*   ferri] fieri *D O V*   197-199 De ... differamus *om. T*   198 sit in] fit se *O*

---

191 Cf. Macrobius, *Comm.* 1.12.10-11 (ed. Willis, p. 49.27-31).   193 elimata] cf. Macrobius, *Comm.* 1.12.17 (ed. Willis, p. 51.14).   194-195 Cf. Cal., *Comm.* 354 (W344-345).

W23:3   *Nec uero.* Quasi: probabile est eum redegisse in ordinem, quia *nec erat etc.* 200

b W23:4   *Eratque.* Et quod pulchrum uoluit facere, ex hoc potest probari, quia *erat certum tantae diuinitati,* quam nihil latet, *nihil eorum quae sentiuntur,* id est

W23:5   nullum sensibile, *dumtaxat hebes,* id est carens ratione, quia *nec intelligens.* Hoc, inquam, erat certum non *esse melius intelligente,* sed peius, quasi uidit illa sensibilia digniora esse, quibus per animam proueniret intellectus, et 205 intelligens melius sentiente. Et quia hoc erat certum, cum pulchrum uellet

W23:8   opus facere, fecit *mundum sensibilem* et intelligibilem, intellectu dato animae, anima data mundo, per quam rationabiliter mouetur.

W23:10   *Hoc ita.* Dixit mundum animatum. Consequens est ergo ostendere *ad*
W23:10-11 *cuius animantis similitudinem* factus sit. Ideo repetit quod praedixit de 210 exemplo, ut addat hunc sensilem unum esse, sicut illud est unum animatum.

W23:11   *Speciali.* Ideo dicit hunc mundum factum similem generali, non speciali naturae, ut ex generis similitudine doceat eum esse perfectum. Genus enim perfectius est specie, quia continentius.

W23:13-14   *At uero.* Speciali non fecit similem, sed fecit similem *eius in quo continen-* 215 *tur genera intelligibilium animalium,* id est intelligibilia animalia, quae sunt genera horum animalium, non genera praedicabilia, sed ad quorum similitudinem haec fiant.

W23:16   *Ergo intelligibili.* Quia fecit hunc mundum similem intelligibili, qui est unus, igitur et istum constituit unum similitudine illius. Et sicut ille continet 220 conuenientia suae naturae, id est intelligibilia, sic iste continet conuenientia suae naturae, id est uisibilia.

W23:22   *Id enim.* Probat quod exemplum sit unum, quia non sunt duo diuersa.

W23:23   *Vtrum enim.* Vere non sunt duo intelligibiles, quia nec aequales nec inaequales. Duo aequales non, quia tunc unus superfluus esset. Nec duo 225

---

200 probabile] probabit *P*   in ordinem] inordinata *M*   erat] erant *V*   201 quod] quia *M*   uoluit] uolunt *O*   ex] et *V*   203 sensibile] sensile *T*   204 peius] pro eius *corr.* *P*   206 sentiente] sentientem *V*: sentit *O*   certum *om. O*   207 sensibilem] sensilem *M T*   et intelligibilem *om. V*   210 sit] est *T*   praedixit] dixit *P*   211 sensilem] sensibilem *P*   unum] uerum *O*   *post* animatum] sicut illud *add. D O V*: sic illud *add. P*   212 *post* hunc] sensilem *add. P*   214 specie] simile speciae *V*   215 sed fecit] sed *P*   215-216 continentur] contra *M*: *corr. in marg. sinist. T*   216 *post* animalium] i.a. *add. O*   219 Ergo intelligibili] Ergo intellectus *M*: Quo intellectus *O*: Quo intelligibili *V*: Continuatio *T*   220 unum *om. V*   similitudine] similitudinem *V*: ad similitudinem *P*   ille *om. V*   221 continet *om. O T*   222 naturae *om. M V*   id est] scilicet *O P T V*   224 Vtrum] Verum *O*   225 Duo aequales] Duo inequales sunt *O*   superfluus esset] superflueret *D*

213-214 Cf. Porphyrius, *Isagoge. Translatio Boethii* 15.15 (ed. Minio-Paluello, pp. 23.24-24.2); Boethius, *In Isagoge Porphyrii. Editio secunda* 5.7 (ed. Brandt, pp. 304-305).

inaequales, quia alter eorum minus esset continens et imperfectus, quod non
conuenit.

W24:1   *Nec esset.* Alia causa cur duo intelligibiles esse non poterant: quia iam *nec
esset simplex initium,* id est unum exemplum.

31b W24:2-4 *Vt igitur.* Et quia plures intelligibiles non erant, igitur sensilis *unicus factus* 230
est, ut per unitatem etiam *exemplari* suo conueniret. Incongruum enim erat
deum aliquid superfluum uel imperfectum creare. Nota archetipum nec
principium nec finem habere, et tamen secundum philosophos diuersum esse
a deo et inferiorem. Diuersus est, quia colligit in se omnium rerum ideas,
quae sunt unum de tribus principiis a Platone consideratis: est quippe unum 235
deus, omnium opifex, alterum ideae, id est originales formae omnium quae
numquam admiscentur creaturis, tercium hyle, materia scilicet corporum.
Inferior est, cum Macrobius dicat ideas esse in mente dei, quae inferior est
deo.

W24:5   *Et quia.* Dictum est deum inordinata ordinasse. Quomodo ordinauerit et 240
quas partes operi suo dederit, hic explicat. Vel sic continua. Proposuit
superius ostendere mundum aeternum, et hoc per optimum auctorem, per
pulchrum exemplum, per optimam causam, per ualentem materiam. Et quia
de ceteris egit, restat de materia, de qua incepit: *et quia corpulentus.*
Continuatio. Vnicus factus est mundus, et hoc, iactis duobus primis funda- 245
mentis, scilicet igne et terra: terra ideo, quia *corpulentus futurus erat,* et uere
corpulentus, quia *contiguus* (nihil enim tangitur sine corpore; dicit tamen
contiguum propter media); igne ideo, quia *uisibilis erat futurus* (nihil autem
uidetur uel illuminatur nisi corpulentum).

          Merito dicit. Quia facturus erat homines ad cognitionem sui conditoris, qui 250
non starent sine solido, nec sine igne alter alterum uideret, nec rationabilem

---

226 alter] unus *T*   228 esset] etiam *T*   duo *om. O*   iam *om. D*   229 initium *om.*
M   230 Et *om. T*   sensilis] sensibilis *T*   232 creare] creasse *P T*   233 philoso-
phos] sophos *M O*   234 est *om. O*   in se *om. V*   *post* rerum] naturas *exp. D*   235
unum] unus *O*   237 tercium] initium *O*   *post* hyle] id est *add. V*   238 cum] quod
V   esse *om. T*   *post* est] a *add. O*   240 ordinauerit] ordinauit *V*   241 quas] qua
V   Proposuit] quia posuit *O*   242 ostendere mundum] mundum esse *T*   auctorem]
actorem *D O V: corr. P*   243 Et *om. T*   244 ceteris] certis *T*   *post* corpulentus] etc.
O T   245 Continuatio *om. O*   246 et[1] *om. D P T V*   corpulentus] corpus *M*   247
corpulentus] corpulentis *D*: corpulentum *M*   contiguus] contra *M P V*: tangit *T*   tamen]
tantum *M O*   *post* tamen] tam *add. T*   248 igne] ignem *T*   ideo] iam *V*   uisibilis]
tu *O*   autem] enim *D*   250 dicit] dixit *T*   conditoris] creatoris *M*   qui] quia *P*

236-237 Cf. Macrobius, *Comm.* 1.2.14 (ed. Willis, p. 6.25-26).   238-239 Cf. Macrobius,
Comm. 1.2.14 (ed. Willis, pp. 6-7); 1.6.8 (ed. Willis, pp. 19-20); 1.6.20 (ed. Willis, p. 22);
1.14.6 (ed. Willis, p. 56); 1.14.15 (ed. Willis, p. 58); 1.17.12 (ed. Willis, p. 69).

motum aplanos inspiceret, unde creatorem laudaret, et motus suae animae illi similes componeret, ideo posita sunt soliditas et ignis. Hic accipit solidum quasi durum. Ignem et terram uocat prima fundamenta, quia in omni sua proprietate sunt contraria, ita dico si secundum cubos iungantur. Nam terra 255
est corpulenta, obtusa, immobilis; ignis subtilis, acutus, mobilis; et ex his proprietatibus conficiuntur media.

W24:8 *Quoniamque.* Dixit deum duo fundamenta iecisse, quae ex toto sunt
W25:3 diuersa. Et quia duo diuersa sine medio iungi non possent, *idcirco mundi opifex etc.* Hoc longe inferius. Sed praemittit probationem, quod medium 260
necessarium fuit, et non unum, sed duo, quia non planum sed solidum opus uolebat facere. Videamus igitur in numeris qualiter planum uno egeat medio et solidum duobus. Plani numeri sunt qui duas habent dimensiones, ut bis bini, ter terni. Omnis enim numerus per se acceptus est linearis, ut bis et ter. In se ductus superficialis est, ut bis bini, ter terni; et iunguntur isti uno medio 265
sumpto ex extremitatibus utriusque, ut bis ter, ter bis. Verbi gratia: quattuor, nouem. Hi duo quadrati plani sunt et generantur: quattuor a binario in se ducto, ut bis bini; nouem a ternario triplicato, ut ter terni. Habent autem medium quo iunguntur, scilicet sex et hunc tantum. Nam sicut senarius se habet ad quattuor, scilicet quod est ei sesquialter, ita nouem ad sex, et sic 270
eadem proportione iungit medium duo extrema. Cubici numeri sunt qui habent tres dimensiones, ut bis bini bis et ter terni ter. Qui iunguntur duobus mediis sumptis ex duobus extimis, ita ut unum medium duo brachia extendat ad unum extimum, tercium ad alterum, et ponatur iuxta illud cuius habet duas partes, ut bis bini ter et alterum similiter, et dicatur, ter terni bis.   275

251-252 nec rationabilem ... laudaret *in marg. sup.* P   252 laudaret] laudarent *O*   253 componeret] componerent *O*: conficeret *T*   *post* soliditas] terra et uisibilis *add. T   post* ignis] et *add. O*   254 *post* durum] et *add. D*   255 proprietate] potestate *T*   iungantur] iunguntur *M T*   256 his *om. O*   257 conficiuntur] constituuntur *O T*   258 Quoniam-que] Quoniam quidem *M*   260 Hoc *om. V*   261 fuit] sit *T*: fuerit *V*   262 facere] efficere *V*   264 et *om. D*   265 est *om. D*   iunguntur] iungentur *P*   uno *om. V*   266 ex] ab *M*: *om. T   post* extremitatibus] et *add. T*   ter bis] bis *O*   267 quadrati] numeri *V*   generantur] generatur *M V*   269 quo iunguntur scilicet *om. D* iunguntur] iungantur *O*   270 scilicet *om. T*   271 *post* iungit] unum *add. O* extrema] extima *M*   272 et *om. M O   post* iunguntur] de *add. M*   273 ex] a *P* extimis] extremis *P*   274 extimum] extremum *P*   275 bis[1] *om. O*

---

255 Cf. Boethius, *De institutione arithmetica* 2.25 (ed. Friedlein, p. 111).   255-257 Cf. Isidorus, *De natura rerum* 11.1 (ed. Fontaine, p. 213).   262-266 Cf. Macrobius, *Comm.* 1.5.12-18 (ed. Willis, pp. 17-18).   262-275 Cf. Boethius, *De institutione arithmetica* 2.46 (ed. Friedlein, pp. 149-151).   271-272 Cf. Macrobius, *Comm.* 1.5.10 (ed. Willis, p. 16).

Verbi gratia. Sint duo cubi, VIII et XXVII, differentes per omne latus. Hos
iungunt XII (qui sumit bis bini, id est longum et latum ab VIII et ter, id est
altum, a XXVII) et XVIII (qui sumit ter terni a proximo, bis a remoto), et
iunguntur omnes in sesquialtera habitudine. Sicut ergo inuenitur in cubicis
numeris, ita deus, communicando qualitates terrae et ignis aeri et aquae   280
mediis, fecit solidam conexionem. Aqua enim a terra, cui proxima est, duas
recipit, scilicet quod corpulenta, quod obtusa; ab igne, quod mobilis. Aer
uero ab igne duas recipit, scilicet mobile et subtile; terciam a terra, quod
obtusus, unde aues pendent in aere. Similiter, secundum planos, posset fieri
conexio, licet non sic firma, dando duas qualitates duobus extimis easque   285
altrinsecus medio communicando uel mediis, quam facit Macrobius. Sed
sufficiat interim ea quam Plato docet.

31c W24:9-10   *Nexu enim.* Bene dixi "non cohaerent," quia *est opus* nexu et non
qualicumque, sed firmo. *Ille uero firmissimus est, qui et se etc.*, hoc est: se
cum extimis in eadem proportione coniungit, ut quattuor, sex, nouem.   290

W24:11   *Hoc*, id est nexum, *efficit modus*, ut in qualitatibus elementorum, *et
mensura partium*, ut in numeris et molibus, ut quanto medius primum, tanto
ultimus medium superet. *Congrua* dicit, quia quanta parte sui quattuor
uincitur a sex, scilicet media, tanta sex a nouem; et qua parte sui nouem
superat sex, scilicet tercia, eadem sex superat quattuor. Quae partes et similes   295
dicuntur congruae.

W24:11   *Cum enim.* Probat per medium extima iungi, quia ita est in *numeris* et
W24:12   *molibus*, id est in ponderibus, scilicet in nolis, in cimbalis, et in ponderibus,
W24:12-13   id est in qualitatibus ut elementorum. *Quadrare* dicit concordare, unde

---

276 Verbi gratia. Sint duo cubi] Vt hi cubici *T*   et *om. O P V*   277 sumit] sunt *T*   ab]
ad *V*   VIII] III *O*   id est[2] *om. T*   278 altum] alterum *M*   post et[1]] similiter *add.*
T   sumit] sunt *T V*   post terni a] XXVII *add. T*   post proximo] et *add. T V*   post
bis] ab VIII *add. T*   279 post sesquialtera] proportione uel *add. M*   Sicut] Sic *O*
280 communicando] continuando *superscr. P*: communiendo *V*   282 post scilicet
quod] est *add. T*   corpulenta quod] corpulenta est et *O*: corpulenta et *T*   post mobilis]
est *add. O T*   283 scilicet] id est *V*   mobile et subtile] quod corpulenta est scilicet
mobilis et subtilis *add. O*   285 firma dando] firmando *M*: formando *T*   286 altrinsecus]
extrinsecus *corr. O*: extrinsecus *V*   quam] quod *D*: qua *O*   facit] fecit *V*   287 interim]
in Timeo *T*   ea *om. T*   quam] quae *T V*   289 firmissimus] firmus *M T V*   hoc
est] id est *T*   290 extimis] extima *T*   291 id est] est *V*   293 medium] medius *V*
quanta] qua *T*: quota *O*   294 uincitur] *om. M*: iungitur *O*   a[1]] ad *O*   tanta] tota
D M O P V   sex] III *O*   post sex] uincitur *add. T*   a[2] *om. O*   et *om. T*   295
post superat] enim *add. M*   Quae partes et] qua parte *T*   296 post dicuntur] et *add. M*
P   297 iungi] coniungi *O*   ita *om. O*   est *om. P*   post et] in *add. O P V*   298
molibus] medio *O*   in ponderibus[1]] ponderibus *D P T*   in nolis in cimbalis] in nolis
cimbalis *M*: in nolis id est in cimbalis *P*: in molibus et in cimbalis *T*   299 concordare]
conuenire *V*

284-286 Cf. Macrobius, *Comm.* 1.6.23-28 (ed. Willis, pp. 22-23).

<table>
<tr><td>2a</td><td></td></tr>
</table>

2a   quadrati lapides melius iunguntur. *Medietas* ut sex, *imo* ut quattuor, *summitas*   300
ut nouem, omnes sesquialtero modo conectuntur.

W24:14-15   *Rursus.* Extima dicit reduci *ad conditionem medietatis*, quia unum sesquialterum, alterum subsesquialterum, sicut medium.

W24:16   *Medietas* enim recipit *uicem extimorum*, quia est sesquialtera et subses-
quialtera sicut extima. Vel extima reducuntur ad conditionem medietatis, si   305
ipsa extima in se multiplicata idem reddunt, quod medietas in se multiplicata,
ut quater nouem uel nouies quattuor, idem est quod sexies sex, et sic in
ceteris. Et cum hoc totum sit: *fit, opinor, ut tota materia*, id est illa tria sibi
W24:17-18   collata, *societur eadem ratione*, id est proportione, et *effectis membris unis*,
id est secundum proportionem coniunctis terminis, *erit unum*, id est sibi   310
consentiens.

W24:19-21   *Quare?* Quia omnibus planis sufficit una medietas, propter duas tantum
dimensiones quas habent. Quare mundano corpori *una sufficeret, si crassitu-*
W25:1-3   *dinem*, id est alto careret. Sed quia *soliditate opus erat* ad maiorem perfectionem, *solida porro ⟨numquam⟩ duabus medietatibus uinciuntur*, quia tres   315
habent dimensiones, scilicet longitudinem, latitudinem, altitudinem, idcirco
W25:4   in se duo media, scilicet *aera et aquam*, et hoc fecit *libratis his* partibus,
scilicet ut quanto est leuior ignis aere, tanto aer aqua, tantoque aqua terra;
et quanto est grauior terra quam aqua, tanto aqua aere, et aer igne, ita ut tota
terra toti aquae comparetur, et sic in ceteris.   320
    Salubri modo dicit, quia ex hoc tendit tempus ad aeternitatem.
W25:8   *Amica partium aequilibritatis ratione*, id est conuenienti proportione in
ponderibus *sociatam*, ut dictum est, secundum leuitatem et grauitatem.
W25:8-10   *Quo immortalis.* Quasi: ideo aequilibrauit partes mundi, ut per hoc etiam
mundus esset aeternus, et *indissolubilis aduersum omnem casum*, id est   325

---

300 imo ut] uno ut *M T*: uno *V*   302 medietatis] medium *O V*: medii *M P*   303
subsesquialterum] sesquialterum *O*   304-305 sesquialtera et subsesquialtera] sesquialterum
T   304 et *om. D*   305 conditionem] cognitionem *O*   medietatis] medii *D*: mediam
M: mediorum *P*: medietatem *T*   307 idem est] id est *V*   308 fit *om. P*   opinor]
opinio *M*   sibi] sint *O V*   309 *post* societur] una et *suppl. T*   *post* et] ipsa *add. T*
unis] numeris *ut vid. in cod. D*   310 id est[1] *om. O V*   secundum *om. T*   312 Quia
om. V   tantum] tamen *O*   314 careret] caret *O P*   314-315 perfectionem] perfectio-
rem *M*   315 solida] scilicet *O*   porro *om. V*   ⟨numquam⟩] *scrips.: cf. W25:2*
uinciuntur] et non *O*   316 scilicet] sed *O*   longitudinem] longe *O*: longum *V*
latitudinem] lata *O*: latum *V*   altitudinem] alta *O*: altum *V*   317 his *om. M O T V*
318 est] cum *V*   319 *post* tanto aqua] et *add. V*   320 in] de *V*   322
aequilibritatis ratione] equitate *M*: aequi. *O*: *om. T*   id est *om. P T*   conuenienti] in
conuenienti *D O P*   proportione] in proportionem *T*   323 sociatam] sociata *M*   324
ideo] tam *P*   aequilibrauit] librauit *T*

312-314 Cf. Macrobius, *Comm.* 1.5.9 (ed. Willis, p. 16); 2.2.6 (ed. Willis, p. 100).
314-317 Cf. Boethius, *De institutione arithmetica* 2.4 (ed. Friedlein, pp. 88.28-89.3; Cal.,
Comm. 8 (W61:10-15); Cal., *Comm.* 38 (W87-88); Isidorus, *Etymologiae* 3.12.1 (ed.
Lindsay).

positus extra omnem necessitatem incommodi, *excepta uoluntate sui fabrica-*
toris, qua sola potest dissolui. Nam quicquid habet causam compositionis,
habet causam dissolutionis, etsi non soluatur. Et quia hoc, quod mundus
esset indissolubilis, contra opinionem omnium erat, medendum erat mundo;
et ideo quattuor modis praedictis eum aeternitati propagauit.   330

W25:11   *Igitur quattuor*, scilicet ut esset indissolubilis, *integra* dicit secundum
qualitates, *sine delibatione*, id est diminutione naturae.

W25:12   *Ex omni*. Vere sine delibatione, quia si aliter, posset laedi *importuna*
W25:16-17 *accessione*. Vel uere integra, quia ex toto.

32d W25:15-16   *Hoc amplius* fecit ex integris, ut dictum est, ideo ut esset perfectus amplius   335
hoc, id est potius propter hoc ut *foret* aeternus.

33a W25:16   *Videbat enim*. Ideo fecit ex integris, quia si quid extra dimitteret, eius
W25:17-18 accessione laedi posset. *In magna potentia* dicit esse calorem, obtunsionem,
acumen, et similia.

W25:18-19   *Quo consilio*, id est ut incolumis esset, et *qua reputatione*, quia facile   340
poterat ei noceri importuna accessione, *unum perfectum etc. citra senium*, id
est ut numquam contingat senium.

33b W25:20-21   *Formamque dedit ei congruam*, scilicet *globosam et rotundam*, *quippe*
animali (id est mundo) *regesturo animalia*. Regerit enim mundus animalia
alia in ignem, uel in humum, uel in cinerem, etc., et cum animalibus *formas*   345
eorum. Nota tale quid esse globosum, quod non est rotundum et e conuerso,
ut lapis quadratus est globosus et non rotundus, hasta uero rotunda et non
globosa. Hoc uero rotundum et globosum est, quod ex omni parte rotundum
est, nihil habens concauum.

W25:22-23   *Quae a medietate*, id est ipsa sperica forma *distat* a medio, id est a terra   350
aequaliter ex omni parte. Quae terra est quasi centrum in mundo.

---

327 qua] quare *V*   habet] habeat *T*   causam] causa *O*   328 causam] et *M*
soluatur] dissoluatur *O*   Et quia hoc *om. T*   hoc] hic *P*   330 modis] in omnis
V   praedictis] supradictis *P*   eum] cum *M V*   aeternitati] aeternitate *P*: uel ‹aeterni-
tat›i *superscr. P*   332 id est *om. T V*   333 aliter] dicitur *T*   336 aeternus] compos
aeternae incolumitatis *suppl. T*   337 enim] al. *P*: *om. T*   *post* integris] ut dictum est
add. T   dimitteret] dimitteretur *O*   338 obtunsionem] obtusionem *M O P T*   339
acumen] acutum *P T*: acuitum *in marg. sinist. M*   340 id est] *om. M*: scilicet *T*   *post*
reputatione] id est *D*: scilicet *T*   341-342 id est *om. T*   342 senium] sene *T*   343
ei *om. O*   globosam] globosum *P*: globum *O*   *post* rotundam] et *add. V*   344
regesturo] regit *O V*   *post* regesturo] cuncta *suppl. T*   Regerit] Regeret *M T*: Regit *P*:
Redigit *O*   *post* animalia²] cetera *add. O*   345 in² *om. V*   347 *post* non²] quadrata
add. O   349 est nihil habens] nihil habet *P*   350 Quae] Quod *M*: Qua *O*   aˡ *om. O*
post sperica] perfecta *ut uid. in cod. O*   351 aequaliter] aequabiliter *O P T V*   Quae]
quia *P*   mundo] medio *exp. D*: medio *corr. P*

350-351 Cf. Martianus Capella, *De nuptiis* 6.599 (ed. Willis, p. 210); 8.814 (ed. Willis,
p. 309).

W25:23   *Quo totus.* Quasi: uidebat res ex omni parte consimiles in rotunditate meliores esse dissimilibus.

W25:24   *Leuem.* Rotundum fecit et leuem, id est planum, *undique*, id est ex omni parte, scilicet ut seruaretur aequalitas.   355

W26:1   *Siquidem.* Ideo extra planum fecit, quia non erant ei necessarii oculi uel cetera instrumenta animalium.

W26:5   *Liquore posito.* Ideo dicit quia humor cibi per uitalia diffunditur, faex ipsius cibi digeritur. Stomachus enim naturalis olla est, in qua cibus decoquitur, et inde faex ut spuma eicitur. Liquor uero qui ibi remanet per uenas et uitalia 360 diffunditur ad corroborandum corpus.

W26:6   *Sed corruptela.* Non comedebat, unde ergo uiuebat? *Corruptela partium*, scilicet quod quaedam in eo franguntur ut lapides, ligna; quaedam incinerantur ut cadauera et similes mutationes. Haec cibant eum, ita ut quicquid partes agant uel patiantur, per ipsas idem mundus agat et patiatur eadem.   365

W26:10   *Nec pedes.* Septimus motus proprius est animae, qui est rationalis, scilicet in eodem loco orbiculariter uolui. Non enim mouetur per alios sex, scilicet per ante et retro, sursum, deorsum, dextrorsum, sinistrorsum, sed circulariter per corpus, quia tota uadit, tota remanet, certa lege in se rediens. Cardo firmamenti est centrum, id est terra, quae fixa est et immobilis.   370

W26:12-13   *Propterea.* Quia *fixo* uoluitur *cardine*, id est rationabiliter, quod non habent planetae, ideo *eius agitatio est rata*. Et quia hoc habent planetae, certo enim tempore finiunt cursum suum, subdit: *et inerrabilis*.

W26:14   *Haec igitur.* Ponit partem in libro unde inferat, ut sic dicatur, quia uoluit
W26:14-16   eum *futurum deum*, id est aeternaliter mansurum, iuxta hoc quod res nata 375 poterat esse capax aeternitatis, fecit *eum leuem etc.* Vel sic: quia fecit eum talem, ut diximus, igitur *progenuit* eum similem archetipo. Et *haec* est *prospicientia*, id est prouidentia, *aeterni dei*. *Progenuit* hoc firmamentum *iuxta natiuum*, id est naturalem, scilicet archetipum mundum, et *umquam*, id

---

353 meliores] meliora *O*   354 undique] mundum *V*   355 scilicet *om. O*   356 ei *om.*
P   358 diffunditur *om. O*   359 digeritur] egeritur *P T*: degeritur *corr. M*   enim *om.*
O   naturalis] nature *V*   *post* olla] nature est *add. V*   est *om. O*   360 uero] enim
O   ibi] inde *V*   363 quod] quia *P*   *post* ligna] quod *add. O*   364 mutationes] in
utero esse *O*   ita *om. V*   365 et] uel *O*   patiatur] patiantur *V*   366 qui] quae *V*
rationalis] rationabiliter *O*   367 mouetur] moueretur *O*   368 *post* dextrorsum] et
add. T   369 *post* uadit] et *add. T*   370 firmamenti] firmamentum *O*   371 fixo]
fixa *V*   uoluitur cardine] est *T*   quod] quae *V*   habent] habeant *V*   372 *post*
agitatio] inerrabilis *suppl. T*   quia] per *D*   375 hoc *om. M*   376 eum[2] *om. V*
377 eum similem] consimilem *M*   378 prouidentia] prudentia *O*   dei *om. T*   379
scilicet] id est *M*   umquam] numquam *V*

367-368 Cf. Boethius, *In categorias Aristotelis* 4 (PL 64: 289D-290B).   369-370 Cf.
4.350-351 supra.

est semper, *futurum deum*, id est immortalem. Et repraesentat qualem fecit 380
eum, scilicet *leuem*, id est leuiter mobilem, *et aequiremum*, id est aeque,
scilicet in omni parte se mouentem. Hoc dicitur ad similitudinem nauis, quae,
si habeat aequos remos, ex utraque parte aequaliter promouetur.

34b W26:15-16   *Indecliuem*, id est non pendentem oblique, *et a medietate* sui ipsius
undique uersum, id est aeque a terra distantem uel arcuatum, *aequalem*, id 385
est expositum.

---

381 eum *rep. V*   id est[1] *om. V*   id est[2]] scilicet *M P*   aeque *om. M*   382 scilicet
om. M T V   in] ex *M P*   383 habeat aequos remos] habeatur qui nos *O*: habeat pares
remos id est equos *P*   utraque] utroque *O*   promouetur] mouetur *M T*   384 non *om.*
D   a medietate] ad medietatem *O*   385 uersum *om. T*   arcuatum] acutum *V*:
aromatum *corr. P*

<5>

<Tractatvs de anima mvndi>

4b W26:17 *Animam.* Mundum ita constituit; et *animam in medietate eius locauit,* id est
uitalem motum temperandarum rerum. Non quod per medium hic accipias
terram uel solem, qui secundum quosdam cor mundi et medius planetarum
dicitur, sed ideo dicit animam in medio locatam, ut per hoc innuat animam
per omnes partes mundi diffusam aequaliter. Sed quia quaedam corpora   5
magis idonea suae naturae inueniebat, quaedam minus, in eis magis uel minus
uim suam exercet. Vnde Virgilius:

"quantum non noxia corpora tardant."

Dicunt tamen quidam animam mundi per illas tantum partes diffusam,
quae cum mundo ceperunt, scilicet per quattuor elementa, non per ani-   10
malia quae post orta sunt. Sicut enim uermis, qui intra corpus huma-
num mouetur, sua non hominis anima mouetur, ita se habent cuncta animalia in mundi uentre reposita. Sed de his alias.

W26:18   *Quo tectis.* Ideo animam in medio posuit, ut *tectis,* id est protectis,
W26:19   *interioribus partibus* mundi *ambitu animae extima quoque etc.,* id est ut extra   15
et intra animaretur.

Atque. Et quia omnes partes mundi ambit anima, tam exteriores quam
W26:20   interiores, ideo *orbem teretem,* id est ipsum firmamentum, *uoluit conuerti in*

---

1 ita] itaque *M*   medietate] medio *O P*   eius *om. P*   2 motum] modum *D*
temperandarum] temporalem *corr. O:* temperandam *V*   Non quod] Numquam *O*
accipias] accipiamus *T*   3 *post* terram] uel terram *add. O*   et] id est *M*   4 dicitur]
uocatur *T*   innuat] insinuet *M*   5 quaedam *om. M*   corpora] corporea *V*   7 uim
suam] uira sua *P*   8 corpora] eorum *V*   corpora tardant] etc. *T*   9 tamen] inde *O:*
tantum *V*   mundi *in marg. sinist. M*   diffusam] diffusas *O*   *post* diffusam] esse *add.*
T   11 post] postea *O*   orta] exorta *M*   12 *post* ita] etiam *add. D*   *post* habent]
est *add. T*   13 Sed ... alias *om. T*   14 ut] quo *V*   15 *post* ambitu] id est *add. V*   id
est *om. T*   17 tam] tamen *T*   exteriores] retexiores *V*   17-18 quam interiores *om.*
T   18 ipsum *om. V*

3-4 Cf. Cicero, *De diuinatione* 2.91 (ed. Ax, p. 103); Cicero, *Somnium Scipionis* 4.2 (ed.
Willis, p. 159); Macrobius, *Comm.* 1.19.1 (ed. Willis, p. 73), 1.19.14-15 (ed. Willis, pp.
75-76); Martianus Capella, *De nuptiis* 8.820 (ed. Willis, p. 311).   8 Virgilius, *Aeneid*
6.731; cf. Macrobius, *Comm.* 1.14.15 (ed. Willis, p. 58.2); *Glose Willelmi de Conchis super*
Platonem 71, (ed. Jeauneau, p. 145 et n.b).

orbem, id est in orbicularem motum, qui proprius est animae, et *in ambitum*
W26:21 *suum*, id est sibi conuenientem, orbem dico *solum praecipuum*, inter alios 20
orbes, *qui sufficeret propriae conciliationi*, id est motu suo semper sibi
conueniente; et hoc *praestantia uirtutum*, id est quia plures habet uirtutes
quam ceteri orbes, quia eos contemperat et a nullo contemperatur, hoc ibi
W26:22 *nec extraordinario etc. amicum semper sibi*, id est sibi concordantem.

W27:1 *Nec tamen.* Ostensa origine mundi, quia ostensurus erat etiam originem 25
animae, dicit se praepostere agere, cum anima dignior sit corpore et prius
genita. Animae genituram ideo docet, ne quis eam fuisse deo coaeternam
contenderet, et ne homo suam generationem attendens aestimet eandem esse
animae, scilicet caducam. Continuatio. Licet praemiserim generationem
mundi, non tamen fuit ante animam. 30

34c W27:2 *Neque enim.* Vere anima non est iunior corpore, quia regit corpus et non
W27:3 *decebat etc.*

W27:6 *Itaque.* Docet Plato compositionem animae, non quod anima ex his
materialiter componi intelligatur, sed per integumentum loquens eius diuersas uires et potentias significat. Secundum quosdam uero triplicem animae 35
substantiam, scilicet indiuiduam, diuiduam, mediam, et triformem naturam,
eandem scilicet, diuersam, mixtam considerat: quae sex tandem miscet in
efficientia animae. Indiuiduae substantiae dicitur anima in prima creatione
attenta, scilicet ante incorporationem; diuiduae, secundum quod distrahitur
ad incorporandum; mediae, secundum quod attenditur incorporata. Eiusdem 40
naturae putatur, secundum quod tractat de diuinis; diuersae, dum appetit
haec caduca; mixtae, secundum quod utrorumque habens noticiam, praefert
haec illis uel illa istis. Et ita substantia ad esse animae respicit; natura ad
discretionem quam habet in rebus. Vel indiuiduae dicitur substantiae, dum
cogitat de deo et eius mente; diuiduae, dum respicit hylen et natiuas formas; 45
mediae, dum tractat de ideis; eiusdem naturae, dum generibus et speciebus

19 in¹ *om. O T*   orbicularem] orbiculatum *M*   proprius] prius *O V*   20 *post*
praecipuum] id est *add. P*   inter] ante *V*   21 propriae *om. O*   22 habet] habent *T*
23 et *om. T*   24 sibi¹ *om. M*   id est] et *O*   sibi² *om. M*   25 etiam] et *M*   27
ideo] iam *O*   docet] dicit *M*: docetur *V*   28 contenderet] contendat *T*   29 animae
om. M   scilicet] id est *P*   30 tamen] tantum *V*   *post* fuit] compositus *add. P*   31
corpore] corpori *M*   *post* quia] qui *add. D*   33 compositionem] constitutionem *O*
post quod] ita *add. V*   34 materialiter componi intelligatur] naturaliter componatur *M*
per integumentum] id est per figu<ram> *superscr. O*   *post* eius] et *add. M*   34-35
diuersas *om. V*   36 indiuiduam] indiuidiam *V*   diuiduam] diuidiam *V*   *post* diui-
duam] et *add. T*   37 sex] quia *O*   39 incorporationem] corporationem *T*   *post*
diuiduae] scilicet *add. O*: id est *add. P*   *post* secundum] hoc *add. O*   40 quod *om. T*
Eiusdem] Eidem *O*   41 putatur] *om. O*: reputatur *V*   42 utrorumque] utrorum *D*:
utrumque *O T*   43 respicit] tendit *D*   45 *post* mente] noys *add. T*   diuiduae] diuersae
D M O P T   46 *post* dum] de *add. M P T V*

quae in uniuersali esse non uariantur; diuersae, dum de accidentium proprietatibus; mixtae, dum de indiuiduis. Secundum hanc lectionem imprimis leges *tercium* pro 'triplex'. Sequentia satis consonant.

W27:7

Alii uero dicunt Platonem per inuolucrum quattuor tantum attendisse in compositione animae, scilicet diuiduam et indiuiduam substantiam quas commiscuit deus, et ei mixturae addidit eandem et diuersam naturam mixtas inter se. Per mixturam indiuiduae et diuiduae substantiae notantur duae uires animae, scilicet sensus et intellectus: per indiuiduam, intellectus, quia anima solo intellectu concipit diuina; per diuiduam, sensus, quia sensibilia solo sensu percipiuntur. Per eandem et diuersam naturam tercia potentia animae, id est ratio, significatur.

Calcidius tamen per indiuiduam substantiam uult intellexisse Platonem diuinas substantias, cuius generis sunt omnia aeterna; per diuiduam uero corporum essentiam in hyle, quae in multis eadem inuenitur; per eandem naturam, genus, in quo diuersae species eaedem sunt; per diuersam, species, quae generis naturam, quae eadem est, diuersificant; per eandem etiam naturam notantur uirtutes, quae similes sunt ipsi animae; per diuersam, uitia, quae dissimilia sunt animae. Et ideo per idem et diuersum in anima ratio significatur, quia ea per rationem et uniuersalia concipit et discernit inter uitia et uirtutes, scilicet ut uitet uitia et imitetur uirtutes.

Item quidam philosophi dicunt Platonem intellexisse per indiuiduam substantiam, ideas; per diuiduam, hylen; per haec duo mixta, natiuas formas, per quas idem notatur anima sensum habere et intellectum. Natiuae enim ideis similes sunt, quia ex earum similitudine in substantia processerunt. Affines etiam sunt hyle, quia incorporantur et ibi mutantur, sicut hyle. Merito uero dicitur anima constare ex natiuis formis, quia secundum Aristotelem anima est endelichia, id est forma corporis, quae corpus uiuificando quodammodo informat.

50

55

60

65

70

---

47 de *om. M*   49 pro] per *O P*   50 uero *om. P*   52 ei] eidem *M*   mixtas] mixtis *O*   53 mixturam] mixtam *P*   uires *om. O*   54 scilicet *om. M T*   55 solo² *om. M O P T V*   56 percipiuntur] concipiuntur *O*   tercia] terciam *O V*   potentia] potentiam *O*   59 uero *om. T*   60 quae] quod *O*   61 *post* diuersam] naturam *add. P*   62 est *om. V*   62-63 etiam naturam notantur uirtutes] eterna notantur *O*: naturam hortantur uirtutes *V*   63 similes] similia *O*   63-65 uitia ... inter *hom. V*   64 *post* sunt] ipsi *add. O P T*   in anima *om. O*   65 et¹ *om. T*   68 hylen] yle *V*   70 earum] eorum *O T* substantia] substantiam *V*   71 et ibi mutantur] *om. O*: inmutantur *V*   72 uero *om. V* natiuis] naturali *V*   quia *om. V*

58-59 Cf. Cal., *Comm.* 27 (W78:4-6).   72-74 Cf. Macrobius, *Comm.* 1.14.19 (ed. Willis, p. 58); Cal., *Comm.* 222 (W236:5-13, 237:2), 223 (W237:11-16), 225 (W240:3, 240:11-241:1).

Alii autem philosophi dicunt Platonem intellexisse per indiuiduam sub- 75
stantiam ideam animae, quae est purus intellectus et mens, cuius ueneranda
puritas nullius corporis contagione uiolatur; per diuiduam, illam animam,
quae non solum brutis animalibus, sed etiam plantis et arboribus uitalem
praebet uigorem. Ex quarum commixtione, cum admixtione eiusdem et
diuersae naturae, uoluit Plato tercium genus animae, id est animam rationa- 80
lem, deum composuisse. Et hanc mixturam fecit, ut ex idea notaretur in
anima rationali intellectus, quo sciret suum recognoscere conditorem. Ex
sensibili anima habet rationalis anima cognoscere haec sensibilia et his
prouidere. Et quamuis anima sensibilis nondum esset, seminarium tamen
eius, ex quo ista commixtio fieret, secundum quosdam in hyle semper erat. 85

W27:5-7 Continuatio. Quia *uoluit* animam *esse dominam et principali iure* dominari
circa id quod tuetur, igitur ex tam digna materia composuit eam. Et potest
accipi *tercium genus* diuersis modis, scilicet uel tercium genus compositionis,
id est mixtam substantiam unde anima componitur, uel animam tercii
generis, id est rationalem, quae tercia est inter intelligibilem et sensualem. Vel 90
aliter. Vnum genus est animae, quod numquam incorporatur, ut anima
intelligibilis mundi; secundum, quod numquam sine corpore est, ut irrationalis; tercium, quod nunc in corpore est nunc absque eo, id est rationalis anima.
Vel *tercium genus* dicit quantum ad praedictam diuisionem, in qua duo
membra posuit: unum scilicet quod caret generatione, alterum quod gignitur. 95
Nunc ponit animam tercium genus, quod nec omnino caret generatione, nec
gignitur ut corpus, sed inter utrumque consideratur.

---

75 philosophi] per hilen *O*   75-76 substantiam *om. O*   76 animae *om. V*   quae] quia
P   78 etiam *om. M O P V*   79 praebet] praebent *V*   Ex quarum] ex qua *O*: quarum
V   cum admixtione *om. V*   admixtione] admixtionem *O*   81-82 deum ... rationali
in marg. sinist. P   82 recognoscere] cognoscere *V*   conditorem] auctorem *D*   83
rationalis] rationabilis *O*   cognoscere] recognoscere *O*   86 principali iure] principali
D: principem iure *M V*: propria cum iure *O*   87 digna *om. D*   89 mixtam substantiam]
substantia mixta *V*   animam] anima *V*   89-90 tercii generis] tercium genus *O*
90 sensualem] sensibilem *V*   91 quod] que *M*   anima *om. O*   92-93 irrationalis]
irrationabilis *O*: rationalis *V*   93 nunc] modo *O*   in] cum *V*   absque eo] extra corpus
V: absque corpore *T*   94 diuisionem] diuinationem *corr. O*   95-96 alterum ...
generatione *om. V*   96 animam] anima *O*   quod] quae *O*   nec omnino] necessario
T   97 utrumque *in marg. dext. T*

75-85 Cf. Cal., *Comm.* 29-30 (W79-80).   76-77 cuius ... uiolatur] Cal., *Comm.* 29
(W79:15-16).   77 contagione] cf. *Timaeus* 40c (W34:3); Cal., *Comm.* 237 (W250:12),
272 (W275:22), 345 (W337:8); Boethius, *Phil. consol.* 3, *prosa* 12.1 (ed. Bieler, p. 60.3):
"corporea contagione".

W27:7-10 *Ex indiuidua.* Ostendit unde fiat illud tercium genus compositionis uel
tercium genus substantiae, scilicet ex indiuidua et diuidua substantia, et illud
inde *mixtum locauit medium inter utramque,* scilicet quia respicit utramque. 100

W27:10-13 *Eodemque modo.* Sicut coniunxit tercium ex duabus substantiis, ita *ex
gemina natura,* id est eadem et diuersa, *tercium genus commentus,* quod
scilicet mixtum ex utraque natura, *locauit medium inter indiuiduam et
diuiduam substantiam.* Vnde intelligitur quod, commixta substantia, eam
locauit: quam inter utramque substantiam locauerat. Diuiduam docet, cum 105
dicit *coniugatione corporea,* id est cum multis corporibus coniuncta. Eadem
et diuersa natura dicuntur commisceri, non quod unum faciant, sed quod
eadem ui animae, id est ratione, percipiuntur, quia considerantur incorporari
et sine corpore, genera scilicet et species.

W27:13-15 *Triaque haec,* id est mixtam substantiam et eandem et diuersam naturam, 110
permiscuit omnia in unam speciem, id est ut omnia unum efficerentur *diuersa
natura,* id est speciali, uel uitiorum, *repugnante concretioni generum.* Repug-
nant enim diuersae species unum prorsus fieri cum generum identitate; uel
diuersitas uitiorum repugnat idem fieri cum identitate uirtutum; et ideo licet
dicantur permixtim diuersa, tamen remanent eadem et diuersa natura. Ex hoc 115
patet quod magis ratio laboret ad comprehendendam specialem naturam,
quam generalem. Licet enim specialis propior sit sensibus, tamen pro
multiplicitate difficilius ratione percipitur. Nota sex accipi quasi pro tribus,
duo commixta quasi unum, duo indiuidua unum, duo diuidua similiter unum.

W27:15-16 *Quibus,* id est eadem et diuersa natura, *cum substantia mixtis, et redactis* 120
in unum, id est in unam massam, *hoc totum etc.*

W27:16-18 *Quo singulae.* Quasi: ita *diuisit competenter,* ut *singulae partes* sumptae de
illa massa *constarent ex substantia et gemina natura,* id est diuersa et eadem,
instaurans diuisionem hactenus, id est iuxta hanc rationem.

---

98 Ex indiuidua] Ex inde. *M P V*   illud] istud *O*   99 tercium] tercie *O*   *post* tercium]
compositionis uel tercium *add. V*   100 locauit] c. *O*: et oc. *T*: et o. *V*   utramque¹]
utrumque *M T*   utramque²] utrumque *M*: utraque *O*   101 Eodem<que> modo *rep. O*
102 et] in *P*   *post* commentus] est *suppl. T*   quod *om. O V*   105 quam] quod
V   substantiam *om. P*   106 corporea *om. V*   coniuncta] coniunctam *V*   107
commisceri] misceri *T*   faciant] faciat *M V*   quod] quia *O T*   108 incorporari] in
corpore *P*   110 Triaque] Tamque *O*   substantiam *om. D*   111 speciem *om. M*   id
est ut] ut inde *O*   unum *om. O V*   *post* efficerentur] et *add. T*   113-114 cum ... fieri
hom. O   113 cum generum *in marg. sinist. P*   *post* generum] inde *add. V*   113-114
identitate ... cum *hom. M*   115 permixtim] permixti *M*: permisceri *corr. P*: permisceri *T*
diuersa tamen] diuersatum *ut uid. in cod. M*   remanent] permanent *T*   117 quam
generalem *om. O*   specialis *om. D*   pro] quod *O*   118 multiplicitate] multiplicate *P*
accipi quasi] accipi *T*   119 commixta] coniuncta *M*   similiter *om. T*   120 natura
om. D   121 id est *om. M*   *post* massam] ex tribus *suppl. T*   122 diuisit] diuise *M*
ut] quo *T*   sumptae] assumpte *M*   123 *post* eadem] natura *suppl. T*   124 iuxta]
mixta *D*

W27:19   *Portionem.* Proprie dicitur de rebus incorporeis, in quibus non est uere 125
pars, sed instar partis. Pars proprie est in rebus corporeis. Per integumentum
huius diuisionis, notantur diuersae uires et actus animae. Per unitatem in
principio positam, quae uicem puncti obtinet, et est eadem et indiuisibilis.
Notatur anima consimilis uerae identitati, quia aeterna est, et ab eo creata,
a quo procedunt omnia etiam uariabilia. Per lineares, superficiales, et cubicos 130
numeros qui subduntur, notatur animae et corporis coniugium, scilicet quia
ipsa penetratura erat corpus, in quo longum, latum, altum consideratur; et
ideo anima ex longo, lato, et alto componi dicitur, quia similibus similia facile
iunguntur. Septem limites ideo ponit, ut per septenarium puritatem et
dignitatem animae notet. Septenario enim conceptio puerorum, et procrea- 135
tio, et aetas hominum, et cursus siderum, et multa alia distinguntur. Puritas
etiam animae per septenarium habetur, quia septenarius a ueteribus dictus est
Minerua, quia sicut illa sine matre et prole est, ita septenarius infra denarium
nec gignit nec gignitur. Qui denarius perfectus dicitur, quia quod eum
sequitur non est numeratio, sed replicatio numeri. Item per sex interualla 140
septem limitum perfectio animae notatur, quia senarius perfectus est. Item
inter septem partes omnes musicae consonantiae considerantur, per quod
armonia animae naturaliter insita denotatur. Et per haec omnia scientia
quadruuii intelligitur, in quo est perfectio scientiae per numeros: arithmetica
per hoc quod lineares, superficiales, cubici sunt numeri; geometria per 145

---

125 Portionem] Proportionem *D M*   125-126 in ... corporeis *in marg. dext. P*   126 est
om. O   in] de *M*   127 uires] uirtutes *P*   animae *om. T*   129 anima] animam *T*
uerae *om. M*   quia] quae *V*   *post* eo] posita *add. M*   130 uariabilia] inuariabilia
O T   *post* lineares] et *add. O*   132 consideratur] considerantur *V*   133 *post* longo]
et *add. T*   alto] alta *O*   quia *om. V*   similibus] similitudinibus *M*   134 iunguntur]
coniunguntur *M*   Septem limites *om. V*   ideo *om. T*   ponit] potest *V*   135
dignitatem] indignitatem *P*   notet] notaret *P*   puerorum] paruulorum *M*   136
distinguntur] designantur *V*   137 etiam] enim *V*   septenarius] septimus *M*   138 *post*
et] sine *add. O T*   prole] patre *V*   septenarius] septimus *M*   139 Qui] quia *P*: quod
T   *post* perfectus] numerus *add. P*   quod] super *T V*   140 sequitur *om. T V*   141
senarius] septenarius *P*   142 considerantur] notantur *M*   143 armonia] armoniam *T*
insita] *om. P*: insitam *T*   denotatur] denotantur *D P*   *post* haec] etiam *add. P*
144 intelligitur] intelligi *T*

125-126 Cf. Cal., *Comm.* 33 (W82:18-19).   127-128 Cf. Boethius, *De institutione
arithmetica* 2.4 (ed. Friedlein, p. 87.13-14): "Est igitur unitas uicem obtinens puncti, interualli
longitudinisque principium."   130-134 Cf. Boethius, *De institutione arithmetica* 2.4 (ed.
Friedlein, p. 89.9-15), 2.5 (ed. Friedlein, p. 90).   135-136 Cf. Macrobius, *Comm.*
1.6.16-17 (ed. Willis, p. 21), 1.6.62-66 (ed. Willis, pp. 30-31), 1.6.67-76 (ed. Willis, pp.
31-33), 1.6.47-48 (ed. Willis, pp. 26-27); Martianus Capella, *De nuptiis* 2.108 (ed. Willis,
p. 31), 7.738 (ed. Willis, pp. 266-267).   136-140 Cf. Cal., *Comm.* 36 (W85:14-18);
Macrobius, *Comm.* 1.6.11 (ed. Willis, p. 20.15-22); Martianus Capella, *De nuptiis* 7.738 (ed.
Willis, p. 267.3-6).   140-141 Cf. 3.25-26 supra.

consonantias proportionaliter notatas; musica et astronomia, in qua de
musico concentu sperarum agitur.

35c W27:23-24 *Quibus ita diuisis,* scilicet illis septem limitibus, *consequenter etc. Ex
uniuersitate* dicit, id est ex eadem mixtura unde primae partes erant sumptae.
Hic innuitur alia figura animae, in cuius uertice est sex, deinde in duplo latere   150
duodecim, interpositis duobus mediis, scilicet octo et nouem: quorum prior,
36a W27:26 id est octo, *quota parte* senarii uincit eundem senarium, scilicet tercia parte,
eadem parte duodenarii superatur a duodenario. *Altera* uero medietas, id est
nouem, in quot superat senarium, in tot superatur a duodenario, scilicet per
ternarium. Similiter in triplo latere inter sex et octodenarium, triplum scilicet   155
suum, interponuntur nouem et duodenarius: quorum prior medietas, id est
nouem, quota parte senarii superat ipsum senarium, eadem parte octodenarii
superatur ab ipso, scilicet eius medietate. Duodenarius uero quota parte
superat senarium, id est per sex, eadem summa superatur a octodenario, id
est sex. Et hoc totum nota ibi: *medietatum etc.*   160

W28:3   *Natis itaque.* Quia tales ponebantur medietates, quarum prima qua parte
minoris superabat minorem, eadem parte maioris superabatur a maiore, et
alia medietas eadem parte sui superabat et superabatur, igitur nati sunt
sesquialteri, et sesquitercii limites, et etiam epogdoi: inter duplos enim media
posita faciunt ad se epogdoam proportionem. Nam sicut inter triplos medii   165
ad se sunt sesquitercii, ad extremos uero, scilicet unusquisque ad sibi
proximum sesquialteri, ita inter duplos limites medii ad se sunt sesquioctaui,
et cum ipsis limitibus duplis, scilicet unusquisque cum sibi proximo sesquitercii.

---

146 musica] musicae *D M O P T*   in qua *in marg. dext. M*   148 scilicet] de *V*   illis
om. T   consequenter etc.] et se complebat *T*   149 uniuersitate] uniuersis *M V*   *post*
uniuersitate] scilicet *add. V*   ex *om. T*   150 sex] VII *corr. M*: VII *O*   152 id est]
scilicet *M*   *post* eundem] numerum *add. M*   153 eadem parte *om. O*   duodenarii] IX
V   superatur] superat superatur *O*: uincitur *V*   154 *post* senarium] scilicet *add. P*
156 interponuntur] interponitur *V*   157 senarii *om. M V*   157-160 octodenarii ...
medietatum] quia superat ipsum senarium eadem paritate qui superatur ab ipso scilicet eius
medietate duodecim uero quota parte superat interponuntur et XXV quorum prior medietas
id est IX quota parte superat VI id est per sex eadem summam superatur a VIII id est sex id
est hoc totum nota ibi: medietatum *corr. in marg. sinist. O*   157 *post* parte] qui *add. O in
marg. sinist.*   octodenarii *om. O in marg. sinist.*   158 medietate] dimidietate *in marg.
sinist. O*   quota] qua *T*   159 id est per sex *om. T*   159-160 id est sex] *om. M*: scilicet
VI *P*   160 medietatum] medietatem *V*   161 itaque] ita *M*   Quia *om. V*   162
superabat] superat *V*   163 *post* sui] et *add. M O P T V*   164 epogdoi] podoi *O*   165
inter *om. V*   *post* triplos] limites *add. V*   167 *post* proximum] sunt *add. T*

---

148 sqq. cf. Boethius, *De institutione musica* 1.16 (ed. Friedlein, pp. 201-203); Boethius, *De
institutione arithmetica* 2.2 (ed. Friedlein, pp. 80-81), 2.40 (ed. Friedlein, pp. 137-138); Cal.,
Comm. 41-43 (W89-92).   150 figura] cf. Cal., *Comm.* 40 (W90).

36b   W28:6-7   *Ex his nexibus,* id est sesquialteris et sesquiterciis, *complebat prima spatia,*   170
duplorum et triplorum, et idem opifex *complebat interualla omnium epitrito-*
rum, id est sesquiterciorum. *Epogdoi* uel *ex his nexibus,* id est ex epogdois,
complebat prima spatia, scilicet *interualla omnium epitritorum* prima uocat
epitrita spatia, quantum ad epogdoa media. *Ita* complebat ut, continuatis
   W28:7-8   duobus epogdois, *deesset aliquid epitrito,* id est duo epogdoi continuati non   175
perficiunt epitritum sine additione minoris semitonii. Et hoc est: *ita ut ad*
perfectam etc.

   W28:9-10   *Et iam fere.* Quasi: parum restabat de illa massa, scilicet distinctio limatis.
   W28:11   *Tunc hanc.* Ordinatis partibus animae dicit illam *seriem* protendi *in*
longum, et post diuidi: quod item per inuolucrum dicitur. Protensio enim   180
significat quod per desiderium incorporandi anima a simplicitate, quasi a
puncto unitatis, discedit, sicut binarius ab unitate per alternitatem. Per
diuisionem significantur duo motus animae: unus rationalis, alter irrationalis.
Rationalis consideratur in aplano, qui sine uagatione uel regradatione uertitur
ab oriente per occidentem, iterum in orientem. Eodem modo anima rationa-   185
biliter mouetur, cum incipit cogitare de suo oriente, id est conditore, et
transiens per occidentem, scilicet cogitans de terrenis, reuertitur ad ipsum
conditorem. Irrationalis motus est in planetis, qui ab occidente per orientem
uoluuntur et redeunt in occidentem. Similiter anima mouetur irrationabiliter,
quae incipiens cogitare de terrenis, interdum sui recordatur conditoris, sed   190
tamen defigit intuitum in terrenis. Et hoc est: *hanc seriem* proportionum, id
est has partes sic ordinatas diduxit in longum, et hoc longum in *duas* lineas
secuit, de quibus duos orbes fecit, scilicet aplanos et inferiorem, quem post
secuit in septem orbes planetarum.

---

170 *post* his] de *add. T*   nexibus *om. D*   171-172 et idem ... sesquiterciorum *om. O*
171 idem] iam *M*   171-173 complebat ... scilicet *om. P*   172 ex² *om. T V*   173
omnium epitritorum] epogdois *O*   174 quantum] quantam *O*   ut *om. T*   175 aliquid]
alia *O*   176 additione] additionem *D*   178 *post* iam] omne *suppl. T*   *post* illa] materia
uel *add. T*   180 longum] longitudinem *M O*   dicitur] dicit *O*   181 per *om. V*
desiderium] desideria *D*   182 unitatis] imitantis *P*   discedit] discedat *T*   unitate]
unitatem *D*   183 *post* rationalis] et *add. M*   184 aplano] aplanos *M*   qui] quam *O*
post uagatione] id est *add. O*   185-186 per ... oriente *hom. V*   185 iterum *om. M*
Eodem modo] Eo dum *O*   186 incipit] incipiens *T*   *post* est] a *add. V*   188
Irrationalis] Irrationabilis *M O T*: Item rationabilis *P*   est *om. O*   189 uoluuntur]
inuoluuntur *O*   191 proportionum] proportionem *O V*   192 has *om. O*   diduxit]
deduxit *T*   *post* hoc] est *add. V*   longum] longitudinem *M V*   193 de quibus *om. V*
quem post] quem prius *D*: quae post *O*: quae *V*   194 septem] VIII *O*

180-182 Cf. Macrobius, *Comm.* 1.12.5-7 (ed. Willis, pp. 48-49).

6c W28:14   *Alter* orbis, id est aplanos, rotatur *circuitu aduerso* planetis, quia cursum   195
eorum remoratur. *Alter,* id est planetarum, rotatur *obliquo circuitu,* quia non
uadunt recta linea contra firmamentum, sed faciunt spirulas. Vel obliquus
dicitur, quia sicut zodiacus obliquatur per mediam zonam, ita orbes planetarum qui sub eo sunt.

W28:15   *Exterioris.* Imponit nomina ipsis orbibus, uocans hunc rationabilem, illum   200
irrationabilem. Aplanos *eundem,* quia semper uno motu mouetur, et in
eodem loco planetarum, *diuersum,* quia nec eodem modo semper mouetur,
nec eodem loco.

W28:16   *Atque exteriorem.* Recte accipe sinistram et dextram in aplano sicut in
homine. Vel per dextram intellige orientem, quia inde nobis omnia oriuntur,   205
et ideo potior plaga est.

W28:18-19   *Per diametrum* dicit, quia licet zodiacus obliquetur, tamen per medium
diuidit firmamentum.

d W28:20   *Vnam.* Duas fecerat series unam, scilicet quam dederat firmamento,
dimisit *indiuisam,* quia ea debebat totum corpus aplanos mouere et omnium   210
inferiorum cursus temperare.

W28:20-21   *Interiorem,* scilicet circulum planetarum, *scidit sexies.* Vbi enim sex
diuisiones sunt, ad minus septem sunt diuisa; et hoc ideo quia septem
corpora planetarum mouere debebat. In hac septenaria diuisione septem
principalia uitia notantur, per quae anima irrationabiliter agit.   215

W28:21   *Septemque impares orbes,* id est septem motus irrationabiles, *fabricatus
est,* distantes *iuxta dupli etc.,* non quod in motibus ipsis haec distantia
notetur, sed in globis, per quos planetae discurrunt, qui illis septem motibus

W28:22 animae mouentur. *Orbesque,* id est illos septem motus, *iussit ferri agitatione
contraria* sibi et aplano. Dicunt septem prima uitia conuenire secundum   220
duplam et triplam proportionem; quae a ratione temperantur, sicut planetae
ab aplano.

W28:24   *Impari,* quantum ad quantitatem circulorum; *dissimili,* quantum ad ueloci-
tatem, secundum uisum nostrum.

W29:1-2   *Igitur.* Quia recto ordine processit constitutio animae, igitur nata est anima   225
pro uoluntate patris. Et cum hoc esset, *aliquanto post* constitutionem animae

---

197 uadunt] uadit *D*   200 Imponit] id est ponit *V*   uocans] uocatans *O*   201
irrationabilem] irrationalem *P*   eundem] eandem *D*: est eundem *O*   202 modo] loco
P   *post* modo] nec *add. O*   mouetur *om. T*   203 nec] nec in *M*: in *O*   loco] modo
P   204 Atque exteriorem] Ad exterioris *V*   in aplano] et in aplano *D*: in plano *O*: *om.*
T: firmamenti *V*   205 Vel *om. T*   quia inde nobis omnia] unde cuncta *T*   omnia
om. M   210 indiuisam] idem *T*   212 Interiorem] Intentionem *M*   213 ad minus *om.*
T   diuisa] diuersa *M O*   215 agit] agitur *corr. D*: agitur *V*   217 non quod] non
quidem *P*: numquam *V*   haec distantia *om. O*   218 discurrunt] currunt *M*   220
aplano] aplanos *O*   222 ab *om. V*   225 nata] constituta *M*

omne corporeum etc. Hic notatur praeposteratio, scilicet post animam corpora facta esse. Vel corrigit quod supra contra naturalem ordinem praemisit constitutionem corporis mundi. Cum dicit *medium applicans mediae*, notat animam per omnes partes aeque diffusam. *Apto modulamine* 230 dicit, quia sicut in corpore erat longum, latum, spissum, ita haec etiam in anima per numeros posita erant.

Ast illa anima ui rationis *complectens caeli ultima*, non tantum ex una parte, sed extra et intra, *auspicata est diuinam originem*, id est bonam fortunam adepta est ab origine sua, quae diuina est, scilicet ab ipsa mente dei, 235 et inde est *indefessae uitae*, quia non fatigatur mouendo aplanon, *et sapientis*, quia cum ratione mouet.

Et corpus. Quia dixerat constitui animam et diuidi in partes, et egerat de ea, ut de re corporea, uideretur alicui corporea et uisibilis, sicut mundus. Quod remouet cum dicit: *ipsa uero inuisibilis.* 240

Rationis tamen. Hoc subdit, quia sententia quorundam stultorum erat nihil habere rationem praeter corporea. Cum dicit *compos modulaminis*, notat animam scientiam omnis simphoniae. Anima *praestantior* est omnibus *intelligibilibus*, id est cacodemonibus, quantitatibus, et similibus.

Vt igitur. Dixit animam constare ex indiuidua et diuidua substantia, et 245 eadem et diuersa natura, quae omnium rerum sunt initia. Indiuidua substantia est principium, ut deus et archetipus mundus; diuidua, ut hyle. Eadem et diuersa natura sunt principium, quia omnia uel sunt eiusdem uel diuersae naturae. Et quia talis est compositio animae, ostendit animam esse scientiam tam initiorum quam eorum quae sequuntur initia. Illatio talis est: quia cunctis 250 intelligibilibus est praestantior, *igitur facile recognoscit quid sit eiusdem naturae*, ut uirtutes uel genera, *quid indiuiduae* substantiae, ut diuina, *quid etiam diuersae naturae*, ut uitia et specialia, *quid dissolubilis* substantiae, ut sensibilia. Dico *recognoscit, cum offenderit*, id est cogitando inuenerit, *dissi-*

---

228 corpora *om. D*   corrigit] colligit *V*   229 constitutionem] constitutione *D*   Cum]
eum *V*   230 diffusam] diffusa *D*   231 haec *om. T*   232 erant] est *T*   233 tantum]
tamen *T*   234 intra] infra *T*   auspicata est] auspicata *P T*   235 fortunam] formam
T   scilicet] id est *T*   *post* ipsa] diuina *add. O*   236 est *om. T*   *post* indefessae] et
sapientis *suppl. T*   non *om. T*   238 Et *om. V*   in partes *om. V*   egerat] egeat *V*
239 alicui *om. O*   241 Hoc] est quod *M*   quorundam stultorum *om. T*   erat] fuit
M   242 rationem *om. O*   *post* dicit] et *add. V*   notat] uocat *O T*   243-244
intelligibilibus] intellecti *O V*   245 diuidua] indiuidua *V*   246 omnium] omnia *O*
initia] uitia *O*   247 est *om. O P*   et[1]] ut *D: om. T*   diuidua] diuiduam *V*   248
natura *om. O*   *post* sunt[1]] ut *add. O*   uel sunt] prosunt *T*   249 est *om. P*   esse
scientiam tam] scientem *O*   250 Illatio talis est] Continuatio *T*: Illud talis est *V*   252
uel] et *V*   indiuiduae *om. D*   *post* substantiae] est *add. T*   diuina] diuidua *O*   253
naturae *om. T*   specialia] spiritualia *O*   *post* substantiae] est *add. T*   254 inuenerit]
inuenit *M*: inuenitur *O*: inueniet *P*: inueniunt *T*

pabilem substantiam uel indissipabilem, utpote res *coaugmentata*, id est 255
composita, *ex eiusdem etc.* Ipsa, dico, *reuertens in se*, id est in suam originem,
indigete, id est naturali, *motu etc.*

W29:13-14   *Causasque.* Hoc est: initia *uidet, et ex his quae accidunt*, id est ex praeteritis
et praesentibus, *metitur quae sint futura.*

W29:14   *Motusque.* Per motum accipimus hic rationem large, scilicet quodlibet 260
iudicium animae de quocumque discernat. Si autem iudicat de eisdem prout
sunt, nascitur in anima intellectus et uera scientia. Sin iudicet de sensibilibus
W29:15-16 prout sunt, scilicet sensu uera *nuntiante*, nascitur in anima opinio digna credi,
sed nondum uera scientia. *Circulus diuersi generis.* Accipit hic iudicium
animae habitum de rebus sensibilibus. Per intimum motum accipit puram 265
rationem.

W29:19   *Quae quidem omnia*, id est opinionem, rationem, intellectum, *insigniri*,
quasi per imaginem imprimi a deo.

W29:19-22   *Quam cum moueri simulacrum etc.* Anima dicitur simulacrum *immortalis
diuinitatis*, id est ideae suae, uel diuinae mentis, *hilaratus impendio*, id est 270
ualde adaucta laeticia, *impendio* dicitur gaudere, qui uni laeticiae impendit
aliam. *Specimen aemulae similitudinis*, id est sensilem mundum, qui esset
similis animae in immortalitate.

W29:22-24   *Vt igitur.* Quia censuit, igitur *constituit sensibilem mundum immortale
animal ut* (id est sicut) ipsa anima immortalis est. 275

W29:24   *Sed animal.* Vult accedere ad genituram temporis, ut ostendat quod sicut
mundus intelligibilis est aeuo coaequaeuus, ita hic sensibilis tempori, et sicut
hic mundus est imago illius, ita tempus est imago aeui. *Continuatio.* Immortalem genuit sensilem mundum, cuius natura non aequatur aeuo, *sed natura*

---

255 substantiam *om. T*   indissipabilem] indissolubilem *P*   256 ex *om. O*   reuertens]
reuersa *O T*: rerum *V*   *post* id est] ex *add. O*   258 Hoc est] id est *T*   et *om. O*
accidunt] hac *D P*: haec *V*   259 et *om. T*   sint *rep. O*   260 *post* motum]
rationabilem *add. T*   261 eisdem] his *T*   261-262 prout sunt] prorsus etiam *T*   262
Sin] Si *T*   de *om. T*   263 scilicet *om. V*   nuntiante] pronunciante *O*: renunciante *T*
264 Circulus] Circulum *D O P T V*   265 accipit] accepit *P*   265-266 puram
rationem] puras rationes *T*   267 Quae quidem] Quaeque *V*   *post* omnia] in anima fieri
eidemque insigniri palam est *suppl. T*   269 moueri] modo *D*   *post* moueri] ut *add. D*
M O P T   Anima dicitur] Animam dicit *T*   270 hilaratus] hile *O*   id est[2] *om. V*
271 adaucta] adacta *D O*: aucta *T*   272 *post* aemulae] id est *add. T*   qui] quod *O*
esset] etiam *D*   273 in *om. T V*   275 anima *in marg. dext. D*   276 quod] quia
T   277 coaequaeuus] coaeternus *D*   sensibilis] sensilis *O V*   278-279 Continuatio ... aeuo *in marg. dext. P*   279 mundum] in *D O*

274-275 Cf. Macrobius, *Comm.* 2.13 (ed. Willis, pp.133-135).   278 Cf. Cal., *Comm.* 105
(W154:14).

animalis, id est *animal, quod generale,* id est intelligibilis mundus, *aeuo,* id　280
W30:1　est aeternitati, *exaequatur.*

Nam facto. Vere aeuum intelligibili mundo exaequatur, *nam facto,* id est sensili, non congruit.

W30:2　*Quapropter.* Scilicet quia aeuum non aequatur sensili, ideo *imaginem eius,* id est aeui, fecit, quam sensili adaequaret. Tempus dicit mobile, quia de futuro　285 transit in praesens, de praesenti in praeteritum, serpens *numero* secundum
W30:4　partes, scilicet *dies, noctes etc.* Progreditur enim semper, suam inconstantiam pro aeternitate habens.

37e　W30:6-7　*Nosque* has *partes,* scilicet praeteritum, praesens, et futurum, *cum assignamus aeuo,* dicentes "istud est in aeuo," "fuit," uel "erit in aeuo," *non*　290 *recte fingimus partes,* id est aeui, quod est indiuiduum; nec etiam pars esse temporis recte dicitur de aeuo, immo esse quod est semper. Nota in quadam sententia nec fore nec fuisse proprie esse partes etiam temporis, cum aequaliter semper tempus existat, quantum ad se, sed hoc ad uarietatem nostrarum actionum et motuum caeli et planetarum referimus, ut transitoria　295 et inconstantia sic distinguamus. Et dicitur tempus, quod omnes res temperat, ordinando et distinguendo eas.

38a　W30:11-13　*Ergo.* Quia mansio aeui est perpetua, *ergo neque iunior se,* quantum ad futurum, *neque senior,* quantum ad praeteritum, sed *haec omnia,* id est 'fuit', 'erit', *sunt uices,* id est uarietates etc.　300

38b　W30:15-16　*Tempus.* Aeuum coaeternum est intelligibili, *tempus uero caelo.* Hoc inducit contra quosdam uolentes probare tempus non esse, quia nec praeteritum est, nec futurum, nec praesens uidetur esse propter paruitatem. *Si modo etc.:* quaecumque enim habent legem compositionis, habent etiam dissolutionis, si placet conditori: *ratio* ad homines, *fasque* ad deos.　305

---

280 generale] genuit *T*　　282 Vere ... facto *hom. V*　　283 congruit] conuenit *V*　　284 quia *om. V*　　aequatur] coaequatur *M*　　ideo] id est *P*　　285 id est *om. M*　　286 praesenti in] praesenti ad *V*　　serpens numero] semper *T*　　287 etc.] et ceteris *D: om. T* inconstantiam] constantiam *O*　　288 pro aeternitate] per eternitatem *T*　　289 Nosque] Vosque *O*　　scilicet] id est *T*　　290 dicentes] discedentes *O*　　293 fore nec fuisse] erit nec fuit *D M:* fore nec fuisse *superscr. D:* erit fore nec fuit fuisse *O P T*　　etiam *om. D T: rep. O*　　294 semper *om. M T*　　existat] consistat *T*　　*post* hoc] quam *add. T*　　296-297 temperat] temperet *M T*　　298 perpetua] proprie *D O*　　299 quantum *om. T*　　id est *om. D*　　300 id est *om. O*　　uarietates] uarietate *O:* uarietas *V*　　301 Aeuum] Aeuo *V*　　coaeternum] quo eternum *P*　　303 nec praesens ... paruitatem *om. O*　　paruitatem] uarietates *T*　　304 etiam] et *D O P T V*

292-293 Cf. Cal., *Comm.* 106 (W155:5-9); vide 5.302-303 infra.

Simul. Ideo tempus coaequaeuum est caelo, quia *una orta, una dissoluan-*
W30:16-17 *tur,* et *simul.* Ideo coaequaeuum est, ut *uterque mundus similis esset* hic in
exemplo ens *aeuitatis,* id est in tempore, quia sicut hic est per tempus, ita ille
est per aeuum. Et hoc est: *archetipus etc.*

W30:17-21 *Hac ergo.* Quoniam deus fecit tempus coaequaeuum mundo, ideo fecit ea 310
per quae tempus notaretur. *Reditus:* intelligit quando sol uel alia planeta,
peracto cursu suo, ad idem punctum redit. *Anfractus* ascensus et descensus
per diuersos ortus et occasus diuersos. Per quae omnia tempus distinguitur.

W30:23 Vitales motus uocat animas datas planetis, quarum impulsu nituntur contra
aplanon. 315

W31:1-3 *In eo motu qui concurrit,* id est conuenit, *solstitiali,* id est solari, *circuitioni.*
Per hoc notat quod fere eodem tempore hi tres complent cursum suum, ita
ut parum distent in celeritate et tarditate. *Contraria tamen circumfertur*
agitatione. Quia secundum quosdam modo citius, modo tardius perficiunt
cursum, uel secundum alios illae stationariae et retrogradae, sol numquam. 320
Aliter *qui concurrit solstitiali,* id est fere aequaliter currit cum circulo solis ea
parte qua est solstitialis, ubi scilicet ipse sol ascendendo uel descendendo
currit ad Cancrum et Capricornum, quae duo signa solstitialia dicuntur, in
quibus sol stare dicitur, cum nec infra nec ultra procedat.

W31:3 *Quare?* Quia luna est in primo globo et alia ordinatim super eam. *Quare* 325
fit ut comprehendant etc. Inferiores quidem comprehendunt eas quae supra
se sunt, dum eas assequuntur, et eas transeuntes uidentur comprehendi a
superioribus quae sequuntur, sicut luna, dum sequitur solem, quod fit usque
ad plenilunium a reascensione, uidetur eum comprehendere, dum uero
praecedit, quod fit usque ad reascensionem a plenilunio, comprehendi 330
uidetur ab eo. Vel comprehendit eum in ipso momento reascensionis, quia

306 una *om. V*   306-307 dissoluantur] dissoluentur *D M V*: dissolueretur *O*: dissoluuntur
T   307 simul] similis *P V*   coaequaeuum] coaeternum *D*   ut *om. T*   308 ens *om.*
V   ita *om. D P*   311 quando] quia *D T*   312 *post* Anfractus] redi *add. P*   313
diuersos² *om. T*   314 quarum] quorum *M*   nituntur] nititur *O*   315 *post* aplanon]
etc. *T*   317 notat quod] uocat quia *T*   318 distent] disserat *T*   320 *post* cursum]
suum *add. M T*   illae] illi *O*: iste *P*   sol numquam] solitum quam *T*   321 concurrit]
currit *T*   fere *om. T*   322 ubi] ut *T*   scilicet *om. O*   uel] et *M*   323 et] uel ad
O   quae] qui *V*   325 Quia *om. V*   *post* est] in prima *add. O*   globo et] loco *T*
super] supra *V*   326 *post* ut] he *suppl. T*   quidem] quod *D*: *om. T*   comprehendunt eas *om. V*   eas *om. O*   328 dum sequitur] consequitur *M*: dum assequitur *T*
329 plenilunium a reascensione] penultimam reascensionem *O*   eum] eam *T*
329-330 uero praecedit] non procedit *V*   331 in *om. M*   quia] quod *T*

322-324 Cf. Macrobius, *Comm.* 1.12.1 (ed. Willis, pp. 47-48).   331-335 Cf. Macrobius,
Comm. 1.6.48-53 (ed. Willis, pp. 27-28); Martianus Capella, *De nuptiis* 8.865 (ed. Willis, pp.
327-328).

tunc eum assequitur, quod fit post XXVIIII dies et XII horas et paulo plus.
Per totum aliud spatium cursus sui comprehenditur ab eo, scilicet et in XXVII
diebus et VIII horis et parum plus, in quo spatio redit ad idem punctum ubi
erat quando recessit a sole, et in reliquo spatio donec apprehendat solem.   335

W31:4   *Ceteros.* Hic agitur de aliis planetis tantum, uel et de planetis et de fixis.

38e   W31:6   *Opere ipso*, id est principali tractatu, *erit plus* id *quod operis gratia sumitur*,
id est tractatus de exornatione stellarum, qui incidens est.

W31:7   *Ad id de quo agitur*, id est ad genituram temporis.

W31:7-11   *Igitur.* Quia luna posita est prima et ceterae deinde, igitur singulae sunt   340
locatae, et uniuersae, id est omnes, et *his*, tam erraticis quam fixis, locatae
quae consequens, id est conueniens, *erat prouenire tempore*, scilicet ut
facerent annos suos, et *ubi corpora constricta uitalibus nexibus*, id est
animalibus, *facta sunt etc. Per directum*, id est per speras suas, quae habent
eundem motum cum aplano, uel *per directum*, id est contra directum motum   345
aplanos.

39a   W31:13   *Citius.* Quasi: quae habent breuiores globos, id est circulos, citius, quae
ampliores tardius perficiunt cursum suum.

W31:14-16   *Qua de causa.* Quia alii habent breuiores, alii laxiores circulos, et qui
laxiores uiciniores sunt aplano, unde magis ab eo retardantur. Quare fit *ut ex*   350
conuersione ipsius aplanos planetas retorquente, illi planetae qui citius
currerent, cum sint *comprehendi* superiores quos in suo cursu naturali
consequuntur, *uiderentur* ab ipsis superioribus comprehendi per reuolutio-
nem aplanos. Vt si aliqui se sequentes currant contra uehementem impetum
uenti, cogente ipso impetu repelluntur, ita ut qui praecedebat sequatur, et e   355
conuerso.

---

332 eum] eam *D*   post *om. V*   333 scilicet et] scilicet *P T V*   XXVII] XXVIII *O*
334 et parum] etiam parum *O*: parum *P*: et paulo *V*   334-335 ubi erat] de quo fuerat
progressa *V*   335 apprehendat] rediret *exp. M*: apprehendant *superscr. M*: comprehendat
T   336 agitur] aggreditur *V*   fixis] infixis *P*   337 quod] quam *M*   338 exorna-
tione] ornatione *P*   qui] quod *M*: que *P*   est *om. O*   339 agitur *om. D T*   340
Igitur] Ergo *P*   342 consequens] sequens *T*   conueniens *om. T*   343 facerent] faciant
T: faceret *V*   et *om. T*   344 *post* directum] item *add. T ut uid. in cod.*   345 directum¹]
item. *T*   *post* id est] per directum *add. T*   motum²] in *M*   347-349 citius² ... circulos
hom. V   348 perficiunt] perficient *P*   349 alii habent] habent *D*   laxiores] latiores
O   qui] quia *T*   350 ab eo *om. T*   Quare fit] Quare si *O*: si *V*   ex *om. P*   351
post conuersione] in *add. V*   aplanos] aplanes *M*   352 currerent] current *O*   352-353
cum ... consequuntur *in marg. sinist. P*   352 sint] sit *V*   comprehendi] comprehendit
M O   suo] loco *V*   353 uiderentur] uidentur *M P T V*   353-354 reuolutionem]
reuelationem *V*   354 aliqui *om. D*   se *om. T V*   sequentes *om. T*   currant] *om.*
M: currunt *V*   uehementem] uenientem *T*   355 ut] et *T*   sequatur] sequebatur *T*

W31:16-20   *Omnes*. Ideo *uniformis conuersio* facit, ut quae comprehendant comprehendi uideantur, quia hoc facit prae celeritate sua, ut quaedam a se tardius
recedendo, ut Iuppiter et Saturnus, *semper*, id est diu, *ex consecutione*, id est
quando se consequuntur, *proxima* esse uideantur. *Conuersio*, dico, *uertens*   360
circulos in spiram, id est efficiens, ut circuli reuolutorum cum firmamento
fiant *in spiram*. Circulus est linea ad punctum unde procedit reducta,
aequaliter undique distans a centro. Spira est linea non rediens ad idem
punctum, nec aequaliter distans, sed parum ascendens uel descendens. Hanc
facit sol cum in naturali die circumductus a firmamento, quia naturali cursu   365
interim parum ascendit uel descendit, non redit ad idem punctum, sed parum
extra uel intra. Haec uero spira fit, quia feruntur planetae *gemino motu*, id
est naturali, et aplanos. Qui sunt contrarii. Achantus est flos in modum spirae
circumductus.

b W31:20-24   *Atque*. Quasi diceret: ut omnia haec recte notarentur, illuminauit corpus   370
solis, ut per solem *extaret*, id est appareret, *numerus animantium*, dum
exeunt mane uel redeunt uespere greges etc., uel animantium superiorum et
inferiorum.

c W31:25   *Hinc ergo*. Quia igniuit solem, *ergo factus ortus noctis*, per absentiam solis,
diei, per illuminationem, scilicet utrumque metiendo *ex eodem etc*. Integer   375
enim motus aplanos diem naturalem, id est diem et noctem, complectitur.

W32:3   Anfractus uocat diuersos ortus et occasus, quos facit ascendendo et descendendo.

W32:3-5   *Ceterarum*. Hic accipe uel ceteros planetas uel omnia sidera. Si de
omnibus agatur, *errores* ad planetas, *discursus* refer ad infixos.   380

---

357 comprehendant] comprehendat *D*   358 *post* quia] etiam *add. D P T*   prae] pro
T   quaedam] quae *V*   359 *post* Saturnus] qui *add. V*   360 se *om. O*   consequun-
tur] secuntur *T*   proxima esse] proximare *T*   361 cum] a *M P T V*   362 unde] unum
P   reducta] adducta *T*   363 undique] unumcumque *T*   Spira] Spera *D*   364 *post*
distans] a centro *add. T*   365 cum *om. V*   naturali] natali *V*   366 parum² *om. V*
367 motu *om. T*   368 spirae] spere *D: om. T*   370 Atque] Itaque *D*   371 ut *om.*
D M O P T   extaret] extat *D M O P T*   *post* extaret] numerus animantium *suppl. V*
appareret] apparet *M O P T*   372 uespere *om. T*   372-373 et inferiorum] uel
inferiorum *M: om. O*   374 igniuit] igneum *M: om. T*   *post* solem] fecit *add. M*   *post*
ergo] fu. *add. M*   375 *post* scilicet] per *add. P*   377 *post* Anfractus] circuli *add. P*   et
occasus *om. T*   ascendendo et] ascendendo *M:* ascendendo uel *T*   379 planetas *om. T*
380 refer] refert *T*   infixos] fixas *T:* infixas *V*

362-363 Cf. Boethius, *De institutione arithmetica* 2.30 (ed. Friedlein, pp. 121.21-122.1): "Est
enim circulus posito quodam puncto et alio eminus defixo illius puncti, qui eminus fixus est,
aequaliter distans a primo puncto circumductio et ad eundem locum reuersio, unde moueri
coeperat."; Macrobius, *Comm.* 1.20.14-15 (ed. Willis, p. 81); Martianus Capella, *De nuptiis*
6.711 (ed. Willis, pp. 252-253).   368-369 Cf. Cal., *Comm.* 116 (W161:10-12).

39d　W32:5-6　　　*In quo* tempore, scilicet peracto magno anno, *fit miranda uarietas prouen-*
　　　　　　　　tuum, id est significantur mirabiles et uarii prouentus.

　　W32:7　　　　*Est tamen.* Licet homines non attendant omnium stellarum cursus, *tamen*
　　　　　　　　facile est *intellectu etc.* Perfectus annus dicitur quando omnes stellae redeunt
　　　　　　　　ad idem punctum unde ceperunt moueri, peractis scilicet XV milibus anno-　　385
　　　　　　　　rum. Vnam circumactionem dicit omnium fixarum VII planetarum, alteram
　　W32:10　　　circumactionem dicit quando reincipiet mundanus annus. *Motus* aplanos
　　　　　　　　dicitur hoc metiri, quia omnes alii motus fiunt in eo uel sub eo.

　　W32:10-14　　*Quam ob causam,* id est propter magnum annum perficiendum, *cetera*
　　　　　　　　astra, id est fixa, *nata sunt.* Quae *habent conuersiones* motu naturali, uel cum　　390
　　　　　　　　retrograda uel stationaria fiunt, et ideo nata sunt, ut iste sensilis perfectus
　　　　　　　　esset, sicut intelligibilis in quo ideae istarum erant stellarum. Quod exponit
　　　　　　　　cum subdit: et ut *natura socia temporis,* id est quicquid est sub tempore,
　　　　　　　　nancisceretur etc.

---

383 homines] omnes *O*　　385 idem] illum *V*　　unde] unum *P*　　386 circumactionem]
circuitionem *O*　　fixarum] figurarum *corr. M*: fixorum *O*: stellarum *V*　　VII] unam *V*
alteram] altera *D*　　387 circumactionem] circuitionem *O*　　quando] quia *D*
reincipiet] recipiet *O*　　388 fiunt *om. P*　　post eo²] sunt *add. P*　　389 perficiendum]
proficiendum *O*　　390-393 Quae ... socia *om. D*　　392 sicut] sic *V*　　erant *om. P*
393 id est *om. V*　　394 nancisceretur etc. *om. O*　　post etc.] Explicit Liber Primus Thimei
Platonis *add. P*

383-385 Cf. Macrobius, *Comm.* 2.11.9-10 (ed. Willis, pp.128-129).　　384-386 Cf. Cal.,
Comm. 118 (W162:14-163:2).　　385-386 Cf. Macrobius, *Comm.* 2.11.11-15 (ed. Willis,
pp. 129-130).

\<Liber Secundus\>

\<6\>

\<Tractatvs de qvattvor generibvs animalivm\>

9e W32:15-16 *Et iam.* Constitutis mundana anima, sensili mundo, et tempore, restabat creare quattuor genera animalium, scilicet caeleste, inuisibile, etc., ad quorum genituram nunc accedit. Ipse iungit, dicens: *et iam cuncta fere etc.*, id est cuncta temporalia genita erant, praeter quattuor genera animalium. Quod aperit, subdens: *composita ad germanam*, id est ut perfecte omnia essent in   5
hoc sensili, quorum ideae continentur in intelligibili. *Nisi quod etc.*

W32:18 *Hoc igitur.* Quia nondum hic mundus continebat omnia animalia, *igitur deus addebat*, ut nihil esset imperfectum.

W32:18-20 *Atque ut mens* hominis *contemplatur genera idearum*, id est ideas, quae sunt genera omnium rerum *in intelligibili mundo*, sicut sensu comprehende-   10
remus ea quae sunt *in hoc sensili. Deus etc.* Caeleste animal: aliud uisibile ut stellae, aliud non ut calodemones et cacodemones.

)a W33:4 *Et diuini.* Hic docet plene constitutionem caelestis animalis, repetens in parte supradicta. *Speciem diuini generis* uocat siderum corpora, quae ideo dicuntur *ex maxima parte*, igne polita, quia plus habent de igne quam de aliis   15
elementis. Vel *ex maxima parte*, dicit, quia luna minus habet de igne quam ceterae stellae.

---

1 *ante* Et iam] Incipit Secundus Liber *add. O*: Liber Secundus *V*: Et iam fere in alio quaternione queris: secundus liber sit *ut vid. in cod. P*   sensili] et sensibili *T*   restabat *om. P*   2-4 scilicet...animalium *hom. D*   3 accedit] accedens *O*   iungit] subiungit *O* id est] et *T*   4 Quod] quidem *P*   5 subdens] dicens *M O*   7 Hoc igitur] Hoc ergo *T*: Hic igitur *V*   omnia *om. T*   8 addebat] et idem *M O*: addidit *T*   9 ut *om. O P* id est *om. T*   10-11 comprehenderemus] comprehendemus *D*: conciperemus *T*   11 sensili] sensibili *O*   12 stellae] stella *T*   non] inuisibile *D T*   ut] et *T*   13 diuini] diuinum *O*: diuiduum *V*   14 *post* Speciem] est *add. P*   siderum *om. O*   15 maxima] magna *V*   16 maxima] magna *V*

9-10 Cf. Ioannes Saresberiensis, *Metalogicon* 2.17 (ed. Webb, p. 93.14-16): "Ille ideas ponit, Platonem emulatus et imitans Bernardum Carnotensem, et nichil preter eas genus dicit esse uel speciem."; cf. App. 2.5.A infra.   16-17 Cf. Macrobius, *Comm.* 1.19.9-10 (ed. Willis, pp. 74-75).

W33:6   *Figuram porro etc.*, id est talem dedit eis figuram, qualis est figura intelligibilis, scilicet rotundam: per quod notatur perfectio.

W33:7   *Indeclinabiliter euenustabat.* Quia splendor numquam minuetur in eis, 20 quantum ad naturam eorum dico, non quantum ad uisum nostrum, quia quandoque nube impeditur.

W33:7-10   *Totumque eum* deum, scilicet planetas et stellas fixas, quas omnes simul accipit pro uno deo, *posuit in gremio prudentiae caeli.* Ideo caelum prudens dicitur, quia et se ipsum rationabiliter mouet, et aliorum cursus temperat. 25 Omnes dicuntur positae in gremio caeli, quia secundum uisum nostrum omnes putantur infixae. *Stipans eum*, scilicet deum eundem, pulchris *ornamentis*, quasi unamquamque stellam circumdedit multis aliis, *et conuegetans ad aeternitatem*, id est animando fecit aeternas, et *commentus est motum eius conuenientem circulis*, id est circularibus et rotundis eorum corporibus, sed 30 redire ad idem punctum, et *pro natura cuiusque*, quia quaedam stellae contra firmamentum currunt, ut planetae, quaedam cum firmamento, ut fixae.

W33:10-11   *Alterum* determinat de fixis quae moueantur circulariter et in anteriora *eadem deliberantem*, id est quod ab eadem orbita non deuiet, nec in dextram, nec in sinistram, nec sursum, nec deorsum, quod exponit cum subdit *de* 35 *eisdem ratiocinantem*, id est contemperando se rebus eiusdem naturae.

40b   W33:12-15   *Alterum* motum dedit eis in anteriora, *intra obiectum* dicit, quia obicit se aplanos, ne umquam possint exire, quantumcumque procedant. *Quinque* erraticos motus uocat hic: sinistrorsum, dextrorsum, sursum, deorsum, ab ante in retro, et ideo motus illos erraticos abstulit eis, *ut uterque circulus*, 40 scilicet motus proprius, id est circularis et a retro in ante, *esset in optimo beatissimoque statu* mouendi. Vel utrumque circulum uocat motum aplanos et motum cuiusque stellae proprium, qui uterque est circularis.

W33:15-17   *Qua ex causa*, id est quia uterque motus eorum est in beato statu, ideo *facti sunt etc.* <*Nullos*>*errores* dicit, quia non nituntur contra firmamentum, 45 *exorbitationesque*, quia numquam deuiant.

W33:18   *At uero.* Infixi ignes non aberrant, sed planetae errant, *causamque erroris habent*, quia contra firmamentum nituntur, et quia fiunt stationariae uel retrogradae quaedam ex his. Vel distinctio temporis est causa.

---

18 etc. *om. T*   20 euenustabat] euenit *P*   minuetur] minuitur *M*   22 impeditur] impediuntur *V*   24 *post* prudentiae] deus *add. V*   25 rationabiliter] rationaliter *O* temperat] imperat *T*   29 id est *om. V*   *post* fecit] eas *add. M*   commentus] contentus *P*   30 id est circularibus *om. O*   sed] scilicet *P*   33 determinat] determinauit *O*   moueantur] mouentur *T V*   34 id est *om. T*   ab] de *P*   35 in sinistram *om. O*   38 Quinque *om. T V*   40 in] et *O P*   et *om. P*   illos *om. V*   41 scilicet] id est *T*   42 beatissimoque *om. D M T*   44 eorum] earum *superscr. M*: earum *O* beato] optimo *T*   facti] facta *M*   45 <Nullos>: *scrips.: cf. W33:16*   quia *om. P* 47 aberrant] oberrant *O*   errant] aberrant *M*

W33:19   *Terram.* Cum ordine post diuinum animal de aliis esset agendum, quia   50
terra locus est terrestris animalis, omnis uero locus prius est in se locato,
saltem cogitatione, ideo de terra praemittit quaedam. Terrena uocat hominem
et similia, quia plus habent de terra quam de ceteris elementis, et ex ipsa terra

40c   W33:21   trahunt alimenta, et eam habitant. Polum accipit lineam intelligibilem, quae
ab arctico per diametrum ad antarcticum polum protenditur, quae dicitur   55
uadens per omnia et continens, quia et terram et omnes circulos penetrat. Cui
lineae terra constricta, id est alligata, facta est immobilis. Limites uocat hic
arcticum et antarcticum polum; sunt etiam limites oriens et occidens, sed
nihil ad praesens illi.

W33:21   *Custodem diei et noctis* bene dicit terram, quia ipsa semper manet in   60
eodem loco, et, ueniente die, non deperit nox, sed a terra custoditur;
W33:22   accedente nocte, dies conseruatur. *Deam* dicit, cum totum mundum dixerit
deum. *Antiquissimam* dicit, quia locum puncti tenet terra; punctum uero
principium obtinet ad ceteras omnes magnitudines. Vel ideo *antiquissimam*,
quia semper in quiete est, et omnis quies prior est motu. Vel, secundum   65
Hesiodum, prior facta est quam cetera terra:

      "Primo enim fuit caligo, dehinc post terra creata est."

W33:23   *Stellarum.* Licet genera terreni animalis de terra praemiserit, tamen quasi
oblitus redit ad diuinum animal, ut quasi excusando se et ostendendo se nihil
dicturum de stellarum diuersa potentia, quae et in parte est ostensa et ab   70
oculis remota, callide innuat se dicturum de terreno animali, cuius proprietas
nec tam infinita est, nec a noticia nostra remota.

W34:9   Sic construe. *Persequi ratione et orationibus choreas stellarum,* id est
W33:23-24   ordinationes, quae choreae dicuntur propter consonantias quas inter se
reddunt; *et applicationes* persequi, id est adiunctiones, uel quadratas, uel   75

---

50 animal *rep. P*   51 prius] prior *T*   53 habent *om. V*   terra quam de ceteris] terrenis
M   54 accipit] uocat *O*   55 diametrum] diametron *M*   ad] in *T*   56 uadens]
uidens *P*   et terram] terra *T*   57 id est] et *T*   uocat hic *om. V*   58 sunt] sed *O*
60-61 bene...non *in marg. sinist. P*   60 semper *om. T*   62 accedente] antecedente
V   Deam] Dea *O*   dicit] dixit *T*   63 deum *om. T*   Antiquissimam] Antiquissimum
V   64 ceteras *in marg. sinist. M*   antiquissimam] antiquissimum *V*   65 quiete est]
quiete *T*   66 *post* Hesiodum] quia *add. T*   quam cetera terra] quia cetera terra *P*:
terra quam terra quam cetera *V*   67 post] prior *D*: prius *M O P V*: *om. T*: *scrips.: cf. Cal.,
Comm. 123 (W167:3)*   creata] facta *D*   69 animal *om. O*   ostendendo] dicendo *T*
70 de stellarum] *om. M*: esse de stellarum *T*   et in] in *O*   71 innuat] *om. T*: innuit
V   72tam] tamen *P*   73 choreas] chorum *M P T*   74 propter] per *O*   75
quadratas]

54-57 Cf. App. 1.3 infra.   63-64 Cf. Boethius, *De institutione arithmetica* 2.4 (ed.
Friedlein, p. 89.25-29).   67 Hesiodus, *Theogonia* 116-117 secundum Cal., *Comm.* 123
(W167:3): "Prima quidem haec caligo, dehinc post terra creata est."

triangulas, uel aliarum figurarum; et persequi *uarios gyros*, id est circumactio-
nes, quae ampliores, quae strictiores; persequi *etiam accessus et recessus*, id
est quantum liceat uni ad aliam accedere et quantum recedere; et persequi
quales conditiones, id est cuiusmodi euentus significent *ex contagione sua*, id
est ex affinitate, scilicet *cum fiunt sibi contiguae*, id est cum in eadem linea   80
sunt sibi supra positae; et persequi *quam qualitatem*, id est qualem euentum
et cuiusmodi colorem, *ex uaria designatione*, id est dispositione secundum
diuersas figuras *nanciscantur*; et persequi *quae significent sol et certae stellae
cum operiuntur*, id est cum latent quando apparere deberent; et persequi *quae
portendant mox*, id est in proximo, uel *aliquanto post*, id est in longinquo   85
futura; uel persequi *quantos motus*, id est mutationes, *denuncient*, cum in
consueto tempore apparent. Haec et alia huiusmodi *persequi nihil agentis etc.*
Ideo se excusat Plato de his agere, quia et ignota sunt multis et magis
pertinent, teste Calcidio, ad astronomiam quam ad philosophiam.

Quapropter. Quia nihil agentis est, igitur *habeant finem.*   90

At uero. Egit de caelesti animali uisibili, modo cum agendum esset de
inuisibili. Dicit illud intolerabile humano ingenio, et tamen, ne constitutio
sensilis mundi imperfecta sit, facit inde mentionem ponendo sententias
Orphei et aliorum, non quod ipse eas credat uel nobis credere persuadeat,
sed ut ostendat magnorum auctoritatibus uirorum esse credendum. Licet   95
autem hic nihil ex se dicat, in libro tamen qui dicitur Philosophus docet unde
orta sit haec superstitio, ut qui non essent dii pro diis haberentur. Ibi enim
dicit quod priscorum genus hominum, siluicolae et pastores, rationes et
potentias a deo hominibus ad usum uiuendi datas, ut agriculturam et similia
pro diis colebant. Deinde poetae pro lucro et fauore membratim effigiaue-   100
runt, et propriis nominibus assignauerunt, scientiam colendi agros uocantes
Cererem, scientiam colendi uineam Bacchum, turpes etiam actus hominum

The left margin contains: W34:2-9 (near line 77), 40d W34:11 (near line 90), W34:13 (near line 91).

---

76 triangulas] triangulatam *T*   et *om. O*   76-77 uarios...etiam *om. P*   78 *post*
recedere]* nitunt *add. T ut uid. in cod.*   79 id est *om. V*   82 colorem] calorem *M V*
84 deberent] debent *P*   85 portendant mox] portenta mox *M*: mox *T*   *post* proximo]
futura *add. V*   86 uel] et *T V*   mutationes] motiones *V*   87 *post* agentis] est *add.*
T   88 et¹ *om. M T*   91 *post* uisibili] restat *add. V*   cum *om. V*   esset *om. V*   92
post inuisibili] sed *add. V*   93 sensilis] sensibilis *M P*   sit] esset *D*   inde mentionem]
condemnationem *O*   94 eas] *rep. M*: *om. V*   credat] crederet *M*   *post* credat] non
quod *add. D*   credere *om. P*   96 in libro] Iulius *V*   *post* tamen] inde *add. M*   98
quod] quia *P*   99 a deo] ideo *P*   datas] datos *P*: *om. T*   102 *post* uineam] uocantes
add. T   Bacchum *om. P*   etiam] et *P*

88 Vide *Timaeus* 40d (W34:11-12).   88-89 Cf. Cal., *Comm.* 127 (W170:7-12).   92-95
Cf. Cal., *Comm.* 127 (W170-171).   96 Philosophus] id est *Epinomis* Platonis secundum
Calcidium.   96-101 Cf. Cal., *Comm.* 128 (W171).

deos appellantes, ut luxuriam Venerem, et ita loco religionis nata est
superstitio.

In eodem etiam libro dicit quinque esse regiones rationabilibus animalibus 105
inhabitatas: unam supremum aetherem, aliam imum, terciam supremum
aerem, quartam humectum, quintam terram, in qua dicit habitare homines.
In summo aethere calodemones: quod genus summa sapientia praeditum
semper assistit summo pontifici. Et sic describitur: animal rationale, immortale, impatibile. Animal, quia coniuncti sunt ex anima et corpore, licet 110
inuisibili; rationale, quia utitur ratione; immortale, quia non corpus mutat;
impatibile, quia nullo affectu inferiorum tangitur. Inter haec duo extrema sunt
tria genera ex natura extremorum confecta, quae habent pati cum hominibus,
immortale, cum illis superioribus commune. Quorum qui habitant summum
aerem et inferiorem aetherem, custodes dati hominibus, summam diligentiam 115
humanis rebus impertiuntur, quia et preces nostras et indigentiam ad deum
ferunt, et inde eius uoluntatem ad nos referunt; et dicuntur angeli ob
assiduum officium nuntiandi. Qui sic diffiniuntur: animal rationale, immortale, patibile, diligentiam hominibus impertiens. Quod ideo dicitur patibile,
quia affectum erga nos habent, scilicet bonis nostris congratulantur et malis 120
compatiuntur, qui nec tantum habent de igne quod uideri possint, nec tantum
de terra quod tangi. Tercium uero genus, quod in humecto aere manet,
cacodemones dicuntur, qui nec adeo probabiles, nec omnino inuisibiles sunt,
et sunt punitores scelerum nostrorum. Quod genus sic diffinitur: animal
rationale, immortale, patibile, humectum aerem habitans. Quod dicitur 125
patibile, quia gaudet de malis nostris et dolet de bonis. Demon interpretatur
'sciens'; calo 'bonum'; caco 'malum'.

W34:14-19   *Igitur compendium.* Quia *rationem praestare maius est quam hominis* ferat
ingenium, igitur sumatur compendium, id est breuis tractatus, *ex credulitate,*

---

105 rationabilibus] rationalibus *D P V*   108 summa] suprema *O*   110 coniuncti]
coniuncta *V*   ex *om. D*   111 mutat] mutant *T*   112 inferiorum] uitiorum *O: om. P*
113 ex natura *om. D*   114 summum] superiorem *M*: summum *superscr. M*   115
inferiorem] superiorem *T*   116 indigentiam] diligentiam *M*   *post* indigentiam] nostram
add. V   117 ad nos *om. V*   ob] ad *O*   119 diligentiam] curam *T*   120 congratu-
lantur] gratulantur *M*   122 *post* genus] est *add. T*   124 et sunt] suntque *T*   125
habitans] inhabitans *T*   Quod] Qui *P V*   126 *post* quia] etiam *add. O*: et *add. P*   127
calo...malum *om. T*   128-129 ferat...tractatus] ualeat ingenium ferre id est summamus
compendium id est breuem tractatum *T*

105-107 Cf. Cal., *Comm.* 129 (W171-172).   109-110 Cf. Cal., *Comm.* 135
(W175:16-18).   109-116 Cf. Cal., *Comm.* 135 (W175:18-176:3).   116-118 Cf. Cal.,
Comm. 132 (W174:5-8).   122-123 Cf. Cal., *Comm.* 135 (W176:5-6).   126-127
Demon] cf. Macrobius, *Saturnalia* 1.23.7 (ed. Willis, p. 124); Isidorus, *Etymologiae* 8.11.15
(ed. Lindsay); Cal., *Comm.* 132 (W174:2).

id est secundum quod antiqui crediderunt. Et quia sumendum est compen- 130
dium, *igitur credamus his etc.* Rationes dicit incongruas, quantum ad uerita-
40e   tem, quia, mundo pereunte diluuio, sapientes et eorum libri destructi sunt,
solis pastoribus remanentibus in montanis, et sic unius dei noticia periit.
W34:20 Poetae uero, inducti blanditiis fabularum, figmenta locuti sunt. Necessarias
W35:3-4 dicit, quantum ad auctoritatem. Hic accipiuntur Iuppiter, Saturnus, et ceteri, 135
neque corpus stellarum, nec homines, sed quaedam diuinae potentiae.
41a W35:7   *His ergo.* Quia tam uisibilia quam inuisibilia diuinitatem obtinebant, igitur
iniungit illis ut faciant cetera animalia.
W35:9-10   *Dii deorum.* Hic conuertit se tantum ad demones, *opifex,* quantum ad
creationem, *pater,* quia consulit eis ad beatitudinem. Hic reddit eos beniuolos 140
sibi, et attentos ad id quod petit.
41b W35:12   *At uero.* Dissolubiles quidem estis, sed non *dissoluemini,* quia estis opus
meum—non naturae, nec hominis—modis firmis et consonis proportionibus.
W35:15   *Quia uoluntas.* Quasi: hanc aeternitatem non habetis ex nexibus materiali-
bus uestris, sed ex mea uoluntate. 145
W35:17-19   *Iubendi ergo.* Quia tales uos feci, igitur hac causa iubeo uobis istud;
uniuersitati, id est sensili mundo.
41c W36:2   *Proximam diuinitati fortunam,* scilicet rationem et intellectum et dignitatem, secundum parem appellationem, quia homines dicuntur dii. Hic notat
dignitatem humanae compositionis, cum homini docet conuenire consortium 150
diuinitatis.
W36:3   *Quapropter.* Quia uolo esse plenam substantiam uniuersi generis, *quapropter etc.*
W36:5-7   *Imitantes igitur.* Quia ego iubeo, igitur *iuxta uestrum effectum,* id est
secundum quod uos feci, perfectos *imitantes etc. Extricate* ab hyle. 155

---

130 crediderunt] credebant *M*   131 incongruas] incongruis *V*   133 noticia] noticiam
O   134 sunt *om. O*   137 tam *om. O*   diuinitatem] dignitatem *O*   igitur] ergo *T*
138 iniungit] coniungit *O*: iniunxit *T V*   faciant] facerent *T*   139 tantum] tamen
V   *post* ad[1]] homines *exp. M T*   140 pater] operatur *O*   quia] quantum ad hoc quod
T   consulit] consuluit *M*   ad *om. M*   141 sibi et attentos] sunt et attentius *P*   petit]
beat. *M*   142 opus *om. V*   143 modis] modus *O*: modum *P*   144 Quia] Et *D M O
P T*   144-145 materialibus] naturalibus *T*   145 uestris *om. P*   147 sensili mundo]
sensibili mundo *M P*: sensilium *O*   148 scilicet] secundum *P*   rationem] ratione *M V*
intellectum] intellectu *M V*   148-149 dignitatem] dignum *O*: dignitati *V*   149
parem] patrem *P*: partem *O*   150 compositionis] condicionis *M*: compositionis *superscr.
M*   152 substantiam] superbiam *P*   154 igitur[1]] *om. O*: ergo *T*   ego *om. V*
effectum *om. V*   id est] et *D*   155 *post* imitantes] igitur *add. V*

132-134 Cf. Cal., *Comm.* 128 (W171:10-18).   135-136 Cf. Macrobius, *Comm.*
1.19.18-19 (ed. Willis, p. 76).   140-141 Cf. Cal., *Comm.* 139 (W179:9-10).   149 Cf.
Macrobius, *Comm.* 2.12.5-6 (ed. Willis, p. 131).   150-151 consortium diuinitatis] cf. 2
Pet. 1:4.

W36:8-9   *Erit.* Quasi diceret: et haec erit uobis utilitas, quia uobis obsequendo colent *iusticiam.*

1d W36:9-12   *Huius ego.* Quia tale debet esse, ut colat iusticiam, igitur ego *faciam sementem,* id est animam *uniuersi generis,* id est omnium hominum, secundum Calcidium, uel omnium animalium, secundum Pythagoram, sed non in 160 omnibus exercentem rationem, quia corpora impediunt. *Immortalem caelestemque naturam,* id est animam rationalem, *ambiatis mortali textu,* id est corpore, *et iubeatis nasci,* textum ipsum uel animam quae uidetur nasci, quando incipit uegetare et alere corpus suum. *Cibum et incrementa.* Ad litteram uel artes quibus uiuant doceatis; uel per *cibum,* ethicam, per *incre-* 165 *menta,* logicam et phisicam. *Faenus* uocat animam creditam corpori, afferentem iusticiae fructum. Secundum Calcidium haec iussio dei, quam facit demonibus, màxime uersatur circa inferiores animae potentias. Quasi diceret: ego edificabo animam humanam secundum rationem; uos apponite iram, ut malis irascatur; concupiscentiam, ut bona concupiscat, quod tantum faciet 170 adiuta ratione et uirtutibus, sed eis deserta inclinabitur per illas uires ad uitiosa. Vnde uocat eas mortalia, quia in coniunctione corporis nascuntur et in separatione pereunt. Vbi ergo dicitur *tradam uobis sementem,* intellige: ponam in animam rationem per quam diuina conspiciat et, si obtunditur mole corporis, doctrina excitetur. Vos *ambiatis* animam *mortali textu,* id est 175 appetitu, scilicet ira et concupiscentia, quae ad caduca possunt inclinari.

W36:14   *Reliquias* dicit, quia non erat dignum, ut tanta uis rationis inesset humanae, quanta mundanae animae.

W36:15   *Craterem* uocat diuinam prouidentiam, et per hoc intelligendum in cratere superius concretionem illam commixtam.   180

---

156 haec] hoc *D T V*   utilitas] utilitatis *V*   quia] quod *T*   158 tale] talis *O*   159 id est[1] *om. P*   id est[2] *om. P*   160 uel] ut quod *T*   omnium] hominum *P*   163 iubeatis] iubeo *T*   164 Cibum et incrementa] Cibumque et uidetur *T*   165 per cibum] cibus *T*   166 creditam] conditam *O P*: creditam *superscr. P*   167 fructum *om. P* facit] fecit *V*   168 demonibus maxime] de moribus magis *T*   animae] animi *D* 169 iram] terram *O*   170 concupiscentiam] concupiscentia *T*   quod] quae *M* tantum] terra *M*: tamen *O V*   171 adiuta] adiuncta *T*   inclinabitur] inclinabiliter *O* 172 eas] ea *P*   173 ergo] igitur *T*   dicitur *om. O*   intellige] *om. D*: intelligit *O P*   174 conspiciat] concupiat *O*   176 *post* et] cum *add. O*   possunt] possit *V* 178 quanta] quantum *V*   179 Craterem] Creatorem *V*   180 *post* superius] et *add. V*   concretionem] creationem *O*: concreationem *P*: congregationem *T*   commixtam] contextam *O*

159-160 Cf. Cal., *Comm.* 13 ('179-180).   167 iusticiae fructum] cf. Phil. 1:11; Iacob. 3:18.   167-168 Cf. Cal., *Comm.* 188 (W212-213), 137-139 (W177-180).   179-180 Cf. Cal., *Comm.* 140 (W180:5-7).

Eodem propemodum. Quia ex eodem et diuerso hanc concretionem factam
ut superiorem diuisit in duas uirgulas, et eas in duos orbes curuauit, inferiorem uero septem orbes principalium septem uitiorum. Sed *propemodum* hoc
fecit, quia nec tantum sapientiae quantum ad diuina, nec tantum prudentiae
quantum ad caduca, hic apposuit.   185

W36:16   *Eadem ratione*, hoc ad numeros.

Nec tamen. Licet eodem modo commisceret, *nec tamen exoriebatur puritas
eadem*, sicut in anima mundi, quia in tali corpore non poterat anima tam
W36:17-18   puram rationem uel intellectum exercere, sed *secundae dignitatis*, quantum
ad iram, *terciae*, quantum ad concupiscentiam. Ratio enim primo loco sedet 190
in capite; ira circa cor, qui locus secundus est; concupiscentia circa renes, qui
locus tercius est. Vel *secundae* quantum ad ideas, *terciae* quantum ad
mentem.

W36:18-19   *Coaugmentataque mox*, id est semente, *uniuersae rei etc.* Stellae dicuntur
competentia uehicula animarum, quia sicut anima aeterna est, ita competens   195
est, ut uehiculum aeternum esset. Vel sicut anima in motu est semper, ita
competens est, ut uehiculum eius tale esset, quod semper moueretur.

41e W36:20   *Iussit spectare naturam*, ut non possint excusare se, si incorporatae male
uiuant.

W36:21   *Legesque.* Lex est ius uel iussum honesta sanciens, inhonesta prohibens,   200
quam ipse multipliciter exponit. Immutabile decretum uocat necessitatem
incorporationis uel fatum, quod est ordo et lex aeternarum rerum temporali-
ter progredientium. Prima generatio animae est quando ipsa simpliciter
generatur, in qua sunt omnes eiusdem pulchritudinis, sed in corporibus
degenerant. Secunda generatio est quando incorporatur.   205

W36:22-23   *Ne cui.* Ecce una lex in qua potest notari homini esse datum liberum
arbitrium. Quasi diceret: ideo omnes fecit eiusdem dignitatis, *ne a se* auctore

---

181 Eodem] Ex de *O*   propemodum] prope motu *M*: *om. T*   concretionem] concreationem *O*: creationem *P*: congregationem *T*   182 eas] easdem *T*   182-183 curuauit...orbes *om. O*   inferiorem] inferiores *P*   183 *post* uero] in *add. D*   septem²
om. T   Sed] scilicet *P*   *post* propemodum] nondum *add. V*   187 tamen¹] tantum *P
T*   modo] genere *T*   commisceret] commiscetur *O*   tamen²] tantum *P*   189 uel]
et *O*   dignitatis] dignum *D*   193 mentem] hilen *P T*   194 Coaugmentataque]
coagmentataque *W36:18*   etc. *om. T*   196 aeternum esset] aeternum sit uel esset *P*
196-197 aeternum...uehiculum *hom. T*   197 eius tale esset quod] aeternum sit qui *P*
moueretur] mouetur *P*   198 excusare] excusari *D*   incorporatae] in corpore *O*
200 iussum] iustum *V*   sanciens] sentiens *P*   201 *post* decretum] id est *add. M*
204 generatur] genera sunt *O*: est generata *P*   205 est *om. M*   incorporatur]
incorporantur *D P V*   206 *post* cui] competens *suppl. T*

190-192 Cf. Cal., *Comm.* 232 (W246:20-23); Dutton, "*Illustre ciuitatis,*" pp. 83-102.

iusticia alicuius *minueretur*, scilicet ne quis culpam suae iniusticiae posset in auctorem refundere.

W36:21-24   *Oportebat.* Alia lex. Continuatio. Vere docuit *eas* legem *immutabilis* 210 *decreti*, quia hanc, scilicet quod *oportebat eas* sic *satas*, id est incorporatas,
W37:1   *afferre frugem*, id est fructum, *animalium piae nationis*, id est quem hic fecissent animalia pie et sancte uiuentia, quam frugem afferrent *certis uicibus temporum*, scilicet quaedam prius, quaedam posterius; *quae* frux uel *quae* animalia *suspiciant deum praeter ceteras animantes.* Hoc ideo dicit, quia 215 aplanos solum intelligibilem mundum suspicit; stellae uero aplanon et intelligibilem; homo stellas et cetera superiora.

W37:1-2   *Esse autem.* Tercia lex est distinguendi meliora. Est enim melior uirilis sexus, non quantum ad animam, sed ad corpus. Mulier enim inferior est et calidior, quod patet in partu. Et hoc est: oportebat *esse naturam hominis* 220 *geminam*, scilicet masculum et feminam.

W37:2-5   *Cumque.* Quarta lex, quam solam cum prima quidam attendunt, postponentes duas medias. *Necessitate decreti* dicit munus incorporationis ad regendum corpus et usum traiciendi cibos et digerendi; *corporeaque supellex*, ut cibus, potus, calor, frigus, et cetera huiusmodi, *uarie mutabitur quibusdam* 225 *labentibus* de *membris*, ut id quod egeritur per diuersos meatus, tam uisibiles, quam latentes, *aliis succedentibus* per comestionem, potum, etc. Oportebat *primo excitari sensum ex uiolentis passionibus.* Violentas passiones uocat quaecumque ita tangunt corpus, uel leniendo uel exasperando, ut ad animam permeent. Quaedam enim sic tangunt corpus leuiter, ut in nulla motio ad 230 animam perueniat, ut pluuia uel aliquid tale. Sensus uero hic non accipitur pro aliquo sensu corporis, sed est quaedam commotio in anima, quae etiam potest dici sensus, sed non ille quem Calcidius sic diffinit: " Sensus est passio

208 alicuius *om. V*   210 Oportebat] Oportet *M O P*: Oportebit *T*   legem] leges *T*
211 quod *om. V*   eas *om. O*   211-212 id est...frugem *hom. P*   212 id est fructum
om. T   quem] quae *G T V*   213 quam frugem afferrent] qua frugem afferet *T*   certis]
ceteris *D*   214 temporum scilicet *om. O*   215 *post* animalia] suscipiens uel *add. V*
216 aplanon] aplanos *P V*   et *om. T*   217 *post* homo] uero *add. D*   218
distinguendi] distinguendo *V*   219 *post* sed] quantum *add. P*   est *om. P*   222 *post*
lex] est *add. T*   223 medias] medietates *O*   dicit *om. V*   munus] mundus *O V*
224 digerendi] diligendi *V*   226 id] idem *T*   228 Violentas] Voluntas *M*   229
ita *om. V*   corpus *om. O*   exasperando] aspernando *V*   ad *om. O*   230 permeent]
permeant *D*: permeentur *V*   sic] ita *T*   *post* corpus] uel leniendo uel exasperando *add.*
P   231 animam] illam *M*   232 commotio] commixtio *fort. corr. D*   etiam *om. T*
233 sic] ita *M*: sic *superscr. M*   Sensus est] Est ergo sensus *Cal., Comm. 194*
(*W216:14*)

218-220 Cf. Cal., *Comm.* 191 (W215:3-10).   226-227 Cf. Cal., *Comm.* 192
(W215:18-20).   233-235 Cal., *Comm.* 194 (W216:14-15).

corporis a quibusdam extra positis et uarie pulsantibus, eadem passione
commeante usque ad sedem animae." 235

W37:5-6   *Post quem* sensum oportebat *nasci cupidinem mixtam ex uoluptate etc.* Ex
sensu enim, scilicet ex commotione illa quae fit in anima uel ex palpatione
uel exasperatione, in ipsa anima quaedam cupiditas fit interdum, quae dicitur
amor; et sic legem sentiendi sequitur lex amandi. *Cupidinem* dicit *mixtam* ex
utraque, quia efficit utramque. Si enim habeat spem fruendi quod amat, 240
nascitur uoluptas, si desperationem, fit dolor.

42b   W37:6   *Tum uero.* Quasi: ex uoluptate supra modum crescente nascitur metus,
quia timemus amittere quae amamus. Ex eadem uel ex dolore nascitur
iracundia, quae est immoderata ira, nam ira est naturalis quidam uigor
animae, qui immoderate crescens transit in iracundiam. 245

W37:7   *Ceterasque perturbationes.* Oportebat nasci *pedissequas earum,* id est
praedictarum passionum. Voluptas et dolor communes habent pedissequas:
aemulationem, obtrectationem, inuidiam. Voluptas sola habet gaudium in
alienis malis: uanam gloriam, iactantiam. Metum sequuntur formido animi,
trepidatio corporis, et fuga. Iracundiam sequuntur saeuitia, feritas, nimius 250
calor.

W37:8   *Quas* passiones, *si frenarent.* Quia non coronabitur, nisi qui legitime
W37:9-10   certauerit, oportebat *fore iustam* in praesenti, *lenem* in futuro. *Et uictricibus,*
oportebat *patere etc. Contubernium* est locus in quo antiqui in expeditionibus
simul hiemabant, et inde dicuntur contuberniones. 255

W37:10-11   *Acturis* non ad horam, sed *deinceps,* id est post terciam incorporationem,
uitam, perpetuo, *beatam:* dicitur enim, quia licet anima in prima incorporatione, si bene egerit, redeat ad comparem stellam, tamen post mille annos
iterum incorporatur, et post alium millenarium, tercio, et deinde, si bene
militauit deo in corpore, rediens ad comparem stellam aeterna utitur beatitu- 260
dine.

---

234 a] ex *V: om. Cal., Comm. 194 (W216:14)*   237 commotione] motione *V*   237-238
uel...anima *hom. P*   238 exasperatione] ex exasperatione *D:* asperatione *V   post* fit] in
anima *add. T*   240 quia] quae *V*   quod] qui *D O P*   241 nascitur] fit *D*   242 Tum]
Tunc *M O*   uoluptate] uoluntate *M O*   crescente] concrescente *O*   243 quae] quod
T   245 qui] quae *T V*   248 aemulationem] aemulationes *P*   249 sequuntur]
obsequuntur *P*   formido] formidatio *O*   250 corporis *om. T*   252 *post* coronabitur]
quis *add. D*   254 patere *om. T*   257 perpetuo] perpetuam uitam *D*   dicitur] dicuntur
P   259 incorporatur] incorporabitur *M:* incorporaretur *O:* incorporetur *P   post om. T
post* millenarium] et *add. T*   260 militauit] militauerit *V*   in] a *V*   ad comparem
stellam *om. V*   utitur] fruitur *V*   260-261 *post* beatitudine *def. V*

238-239 Cf. Cal., *Comm.* 194 (W216:23).   240-241 Cf. Cal., *Comm.* 194 (W216:22-23).
247-251 Cf. Cal., *Comm.* 195 (W217:15-19).   252-253 Cf. 2 Tim. 2:5: "Nam et qui
certat in agone, non coronatur nisi legitime certauerit."

W37:11   *Victas* uero ab illis passionibus *mutare sexum*. Sententia Pythagorae fuit
quod realiter animae hominum in alia animalia transirent. Sed Plato, teste
Calcidio, hanc mutationem incorporationis noluit, immo quod in eodem
corpore diuersa animalia uiuerent, ut si quis molliter uiuat, mulierem uiuat,   265
si immunde, porcum et similia. Et, secundum hanc Platonis sententiam,
dicuntur bruta animalia non habere animam, nisi quamdam uitalitatem quae,
pereuntibus ipsis, redeat ad uniuersitatem. Secundum Platonem, secunda
generatio dicitur decidere de uitio in uitium.

W37:12-13   *Nec a uitiis*. Licet iam satis punita uideantur in secunda incorporatione,   270
W37:13-15 tamen illis non *discedentibus a uitiis*, oportebat *non cessare* poenas etc., etiam
in tercia incorporatione. *Formas* dicit *congruas meritis et instituto*, scilicet ut
qui uixit rapaciter, lupus, qui stulte, asinus fiat, et similiter alia.

W37:15-17   *Pausamque*. Hoc est: *non prius* cessabit poena in illis, quam ratio *deterserit*
omnia uitia, quaecumque ex corpore contraxerant. Rationem notamus per   275
hoc, quod dicit *eadem mundi circumactio*, corpus cum dicit *contracta ex igne*
et ceteris, minora *uitia* intelligimus cum dicit *omnem illuuiem*, et omnibus
W37:19-20 illis uitiis detersis, *ad antiqui uultus etc.*, id est fiant iterum homines. In
praedictis ostensum est malum ex decreto dei uel uoluntate hominibus non
prouenire, sed eorum imprudentia uel prauitate.   280

W37:21   *Ne qua*, id est ideo omnia patefecit eis, ne possent imputare auctori quod
aliquando peccarent. Quod possent, si leges suas reticuisset.

W38:1-2   *Partim in terra*, posuit animandis, scilicet primis hominibus, quae tamen
descenderant a compari stella, et iam poterant esse tutela corporum; *partim*

---

263 quod realiter animae hominum] quia animae bonum *O*   animalia *om. T*   264 in]
cum *T*   265 mulierem] ut mulier *T*   266 *post* immunde] uiuat *add. P*   Platonis]
Platonicam *D*   268 ad *om. P*   269 *post* generatio] hic *add. O P T*   decidere *om. O*
270 *post* punita] esse *add. M*   in *om. O*   271 tamen] item *O*   non cessare] in
cessare *P*   etc. *om. T*   etiam] et *O P*   272 meritis *om. M*   et *om. P*   instituto]
iusti. *D O*: isti *P*   273 qui *om. O*   fiat et similiter] uiuat et similia *O*   274 cessabit]
cessabis *P*   deterserit] deserit *O*   275 contraxerant] contraxerat *P*   notamus]
mutamus *M*   275-276 per hoc quod dicit *O*: cum dicit *T*   277 et[1] *om.*
P   cum] dum *D O P*   *post* dicit] esse *add. D*   omnem *om. D*   *post* et[2]] ex *add.*
P   277-278 et omnibus illis *om. T*   278 fiant] fiunt *O*   279 uel] et *M*: uel ex *O*
280 prouenire] peruenire *P*   *post* sed] ex *add. O*   eorum] horum *T*   uel] et *P*
281 ideo] omnino *O*   omnia *om. D*   ne] nec *P*   auctori] actori *D O*   282
reticuisset] reticuissent *O*   283 terra] terram *D T*   quae] qui creata uel *T*   284
descenderant] descendant *P*

262-263 Cf. Cal., *Comm.* 196-197 (W217-219).   263-269 Cf. Cal., *Comm.* 198 (W219),
196 (W217-218).   264-266 Cf. Boethius, *Phil. consol.* 4, *prosa* 3.15-21 (ed. Bieler, pp.
71-72); Isidorus, *Etymologiae* 11.18-19 (ed. Lindsay).   272-273 Cf. Cal., *Comm.* 198
(W219:8-9); Boethius, *Phil. consol.* 4, *prosa* 3.17-19 (ed. Bieler, p. 71).   278-280 Cf. Cal.,
Comm. 199 (W220:8-9).

in luna, eas scilicet quae nouiter erant incorporandae; *partim in ceteris,* 285
planetis, *exordia humani generis* dicit animas.

W38:2-3   *Ea porro*, artes scilicet uiuendi, ut scire arare, et similia, *quae sementem*
sequuntur, id est animam.

W38:4   *Ac si qua*, scilicet praecipit eis ut apponerent animae appetitum, memoriam, et si qua essent addenda.   290

42e W38:7   *Proque uiribus*. Non efficientium, sed eorum quae efficiebantur. *Exceptis*
W38:8   *improsperitatibus*, id est perturbationibus uitiorum, quas dii non fecerunt in
hominibus, sed ipsi homines per liberum suum arbitrium.

---

285 nouiter] nouerit *D*   287-288 Ea...animam *om. T*   287 porro...sementem *om. D*
289 si qua] sic qui *O*   apponerent] apponeret *O*   290 essent] erant *O*   291
Proque] Propeque *P*   quae] qui *M*   292 dii] diu *O*

291-292 Cf. Cal., *Comm.* 201 (W221:6-7).

<7>

<TRACTATVS DE HVMANO CORPORE>

W38:10   *In proposito.* Propositum enim creatoris est omnibus consulere ad beatitudinem: diuinis ad aeternitatem, natiuis ad perpetuitatem.

W38:12-15   Immortale initium dicit animam. *Elementarium faenus* uocat corpus, quia post dissolutionem reddetur elementis quod suum erat, scilicet redibit corpus in eadem elementa unde constat. Et *ea quae acceperant,* id est elementa,   5
conglutinabant, id est coniungebant, sed non tam firmis *nexibus,* sicut sua corpora, *sed aliis gomphis inuisibilibus,* non quia corpora non sint, sed *ob incomprehensibilem breuitatem.* Gomphi proprie dicuntur quaedam instrumenta ferrea, quibus adhaeret ostium recurua, ut hami. Hic uero dicit gomphos quaedam colligamenta partium corporis, scilicet coaceruationem   10
minorum corpusculorum proportionaliter in corporibus dispositam.

W38:16-17   *Itaque.* Ita, ut dixi, colligabant per gomphos elementa, et illi *materia itaque apparata circumligabant circuitus animae immortalis.* Circuitus uocat intellectum et opinionem, quae materia est fluidum corpus et irriguum, uel *circumligabant* regendo irriguum et fluidum corpus. Hic notat corpus puerile,   15
W38:18   quod irrigatur ex frequenti infusione et fluit prae nimia egestione. *Sed ui*
W38:18-19   *ferebant,* quia anima uiuificabat corpus et ei incrementum praebebat. *Vi ferebantur,* quando ad aliquos illicitos motus trahebatur a corpore ipsa anima, scilicet ad falsas opiniones. Putat enim saepe puer carbonem tangere bonum esse, et dampnum commodum, et similia. Vnde patet in puerili anima   20
otiosum esse intellectum et opinionem, sed minus opinionem, quia haec

---

1 Propositum *om. P*   creatoris] cantoris *P*   omnibus] hominibus *P T*   3 initium *om.*
T   *post* initium] id est *add. O*   uocat corpus *om. P*   4 dissolutionem] solutionem
M   reddetur...scilicet *hom. O*   redibit] redit *O*   5 unde...elementa *hom. O*   unde]
tamen *P*   6 tam] tamen *P*   7 *post* sed[2]] in *add. M*   9 ut] ubi *T*   dicit] dixit *T*   10
coaceruationem] coaceruatio *O*   11 in *om. P T*   corporibus *om. T*   dispositam]
disposita *O*   12 colligabant] colligebant *M*   15 et *om. T*   16 infusione] confusione
O   17 incrementum] crementum *O*   17-18 Vi ferebantur] inferebantur *T*   18
trahebatur] trahebantur *D P*   19 Putat] Putant *D*   puer] pueri *D*   20 commodum]
comode *T*   puerili] pueri *P*   21 esse *om. O*   quia] quando *D*

1-2 Cf. Cal., *Comm.* 201 (W221:13-16).   10-11 Cf. Cal., *Comm.* 203 (W222:11-12).
15-16 Cf. Cal., *Comm.* 203 (W223:2-3).   19-22 Cf. Cal., *Comm.* 208 (W225:14-226:6).

procedens ex sensibus quinque non fallitur, scilicet quando sensus sunt
ueridici.

43b W38:19   *Vt totum animal,* id est secundum corpus et animam, *moueretur* in
praecipitatione. Hic ostenditur amentia puerilis.   25

W38:20   *Quippe.* Probat inordinate animal moueri, quia raptatur *sine ratione etc.*
Motum sursum habet corpus ab igne, cuius est alta petere; deorsum a terra,
cuius est infra esse; ceteros quattuor ab aere et aqua, quae similiter habent
W38:20-22 fluitare. *Vltro et citro,* id est ante et retro. Et quia his *motibus sine ratione*
mouetur puer, inde *oberrans.* Et subdit quare oberrans: quia *immenso gurgite*   30
irrigante per infusionem et *immoderate effluente.* Quasi diceret: inordinata
ingurgitatio influxionis et effluxionis est causa huius raptionis.

W38:22   *Ex quo.* Quia ostendant corpus moueri intrinsecus per ea quae infunduntur
et egeruntur. Ne quis uellet per interiora corpus tantum uexari, ostendit etiam
per exteriora illud uexari. Continuatio. Ita per influxionem et effluxionem   35
raptatur animal imprimis, sed ex eo tempore *ex quo cibus,* panis, *et alimenta,*
W39:1-2   carnis et huiusmodi, *comparabantur, multo turba,* id est seditio, *uexabat*
corpus *extrinsecus,* scilicet *cum incurrisset offensionem ignis.* Puer enim
saepe cadit in ignem uel etiam *complosionem terrenam,* id est quando ad
W38:23   terram cadens eliditur. Vel ibi incipe uersum *multo maior.* Quasi diceret: ex   40
quo puer sugit lac, sic uexatur, ut dixi, sed cum separatur a lacte et incipit
ire, *multo maior etc.*

W39:3   *Hisque interpellationibus etc.* Quasi: his passionibus sensuum interpellatur
et excitatur anima, *stimulata* uoluptate uel dolore per influxionem amari uel
dulcis.   45

43c W39:4-5   *Qui quidem aestus,* id est perturbationes et passiones, *propterea,* id est quia
ipsae per corpus usque ad animam commeant, *initio sensus cognominantur.*
Et initio cognominantur, id est quando nouiter incorporatur anima, *et nunc*

---

22 ex] a *O*   non *om. T*   quando] quinque *O*   24 secundum corpus et animam] sensus
et anima *T*   24-25 in praecipitatione] in praecipitationem *M P*   26 etc. *om. M O*   27
a terra] altera *P*   29 citro] citra *M T*   31 infusionem] effusionem *D*   32 influxionis
et effluxionis] infusionis *T*   raptionis] raptationis *D O P T*   33 intrinsecus] extrinsecus
T   34 etiam] et *P*   36 ex² *om. M*   *post* cibus] et *add. M*   37 carnis et] carnis et
alia *D*: carnis *P*   comparabantur] operantur *M T*: spera *O*: corpora *P*   40 eliditur]
illiditur *D*   41 sugit] suggerit *T*   43 interpellationibus] interpretatur *O*   etc. *om. P*
T   44 per influxionem] in perfluxionem *P*   46 et passiones *om. P*   47 commeant]
contingant *M*: meant *O*: contineant *T*

---

25 Cf. Cal., *Comm.* 205 (W224:2).   27-28 Cf. Cal., *Comm.* 205 (W224:4-5); Boethius,
Phil. consol. 3, *prosa* 11.26 (ed. Bieler, p. 58); Boethius, *De trinitate* 2 (ed. Peiper, p.
152.8-9); Boethius, *Contra Eutychen et Nestorium* 1 (ed. Peiper, p. 190.40-42); et cf.
8.419-420 infra.

W39:5-7 *usque.* Et hic potest notari diffinitio sensus supra data. Sensus, dico, *cientes* *maximos et uiolentos motus* ut inuidiam, detractationem, etc., quae superius 50
pedissequas diximus, quod contingit cum *quatiunt circuitus animae,* id est
intellectum et opinionem, *naturali deriuatione etc.,* id est per immoderatam
influxionem et effluxionem. Quae sunt quasi turbines.

d W39:7-10 *Illum quidem.* Circuitus animae quatiunt, sed diuersis modis, quia *illum* *prouidum motum eius* animae, scilicet intellectum, *statuentes,* id est cessare 55
et otiari facientes, ita quod cum sit eiusdem naturae, id est rationabilis et
perfectus, non attendat quod suum est. *Et contra.* Et uere quatiunt falsi sensus
rationem, quia operantur contrario modo *quam illa* moueatur, dum *eius*
imperium respuunt.

W39:10-11 *At uero.* Intellectum prorsus statuunt ut nihil operetur, sed motum *diuersi* 60
circuli, id est opinionem, non prorsus statuunt, quia famulantur falsae
opinioni, nuntiantes ei falsa. Intellectus uero numquam falsus. Et tamen
famulantes diuersis motibus opinionis, quatiunt ipsam animam uel opinionem
usque adeo ut diuersis, id est diuersis modis uexent et fatigent animam,
W39:14-16 scilicet *distrahentes* eam *motibus sibi inuicem aduersis,* id est contraria 65
intuentibus et ea falsa, et distrahentes *totam eius* animae *substantiam,* id est
intellectum et opinionem in tantum, *ut una feratur* anima *cum nexibus suae*
confirmationis, id est cum ratione et opinione feratur, inquam, sed *sine*
ratione, id est sine certo animae iudicio, ut *discordantibus motibus,* scilicet
W39:17 rectis et non rectis, et *illecebra etc.* Testimonio enim sensuum credit tantum, 70
postposita ratione. Ideo dixi diuexant et non destruunt, quia anima non
potest dissolui, nisi a suo conditore, tam firmis nexibus proportionum
W39:11 compacta, qui expositi sunt in coniunctione animae mundi. Et hoc est: *quia*
limites duplicis etc. Ideo probauit opinionem non penitus destrui, quia uidetur
penitus destrui, nisi intellectus destrueretur, qui dignior est. Motus falsae 75

---

49 supra data] supradicta *M O*   cientes] scientes *P*   50 etc.] et contraria *P*   51 quod
contingit] quae contingunt *M*: quia contigit *P*: et haec contigit *T*   cum] dum *O*   52 id
est *om. T*   54 *post* quidem] et *add. M*   55 prouidum] que *P*: *om. T*   intellectum]
intellectus *M O*   statuentes] statim *M*: stant *P*   56 quod cum] quaecumque *P*   sit]
sint *M*   naturae] materie *P*   57 Et uere] uere *M*   58 operantur] oporteantur *P*   59
respuunt] respiciunt *D*: despiciunt *T*   60 Intellectum] Intellectus *T*   statuunt] quatiunt
O: statuitur *T*   60-61 ut...statuunt *hom. P*   64 id est *om. P*   65 sibi *om. M P*   66
ea falsa et] *om. D*: eam falsam *P*   animae *om. T*   67 cum nexibus] conexit *O*   68
post sed] non *add. O*   69 certo] certae *D*   ut] et *P*   70 rectis[1] *om. M*   illecebra]
illecebris *P*   tantum] tamen *O*   71 postposita ratione] postpositam rationem *O*   72
nexibus *om. D*   73 coniunctione] coniunctionem *M O*: compositione *T*   quia] qui *M*
74 duplicis] duplorum *M*   penitus] prorsus *D*   *post* destrui] ubi intellectus destruitur
add. O   uidetur] uideretur *D P*   75 nisi] ubi *M O P T*   destrueretur] destruitur *O*

---

49 Vide 6.231-232 supra.   50-51 Vide 6.247-248 supra.

opinionis dicit diuersos a uera opinione et incertos, id est nihil certum nuntiantes.

W39:10   Aliter. *At uero.* Quasi: non solum intellectus quatitur ab illis sensibus, sed *diuersi circuli*, id est ipsa ratio et opinio quatiuntur. Illi, dico, *famulantes diuersis motibus* falsorum sensuum, dum intellectus fit otiosus et opinio adeo   80 perturbatur, ut anima adhuc puerilis credat sensibus nuntiantibus bonum esse, quod est malum; uerum, quod est falsum. Famulantur, dico, *diuersis motibus* sensuum, *usque adeo ut* ipsi sensus diuexent intellectum et opinionem, sed non destruant, quia tam firmiter infixa sunt animae, quod ea remanente destrui non possint, quantumcumque a sensibus uexentur. Nota   85 quod opinio falsa non tantum pueros, sed plerosque usque ad ultimam aetatem, comitatur. Hos Aristoteles senes pueros uocat, non discernentes inter indiuiduam et diuiduam substantiam, credentes ea tantum quae oculis subiacent, quae palpare possunt.

43e W39:17-18   *Propterea.* Et quia illecebra deprauat rectum iter et anima credit testimonio   90 falsidicorum sensuum, *propterea* contingit *existere uarias inclinationes*, id est diuersas deriuationes et uere uarias, quia *obliquas*, id est aliquantulum deuiantes, non tamen aberrantes, et *contrarias*, quando quod subiacet sensibus. Contrario modo opinatur a uia prorsus recedens, *et similes resupinis casibus*, quando id quod uere est *idem* diuersum putant. Vel cum ea quae   95 laedunt dicunt commoda et quae prosunt noxia.

W39:19   *Vt si quis.* Si aliquis stet rectus et alius ante eum capite fixo in terra oppositus ei, unicuique eorum uidebuntur partes dextrae alterius sinistrae, et sinistrae dextrae, sicut si uterque rectus esset, quod falsum est. Vel sic. Ita ille contra naturam agit, quem illecebra sensuum impedit, sicut ille faceret qui 100 contra naturae ordinem sic incederet. Et hoc est: *ut si quis etc.*

W39:22-23   *Id ipsum*, id est similem inordinationem, *patiuntur circuitus animae*, id est intellectus et opinio.

44a W40:1-2   *Nec habet certum ducem*, id est intellectum uel ueram opinionem, *talis peragratio*, id est motus erraticus, quia ratio otiosa est et opinio seducta.   105

---

77 *post* nuntiantes] id est *add. P*: uel *add. T*   79 id est *om. P*   80 sensuum *om. P*   81 credat] condat *O P*   82 quod est[1]] quod *M*   *post* malum] et *add. O*   84 destruant] destruatur *O*: destruunt *T*   86 falsa *om. O*   87 comitatur] commitantur *O*   90 Propterea. Et] Proptereaque *T*   illecebra deprauat] illecebre deprauant *T*   91 propterea contingit] propter eam contigit *P*   existere] existens *O*   92 aliquantulum] aliquantum *M* 93 *post* quando] id *add. P*   quod *om. M*   96 dicunt] dicent *P*   97 Vt] At *P* quis] quisque *T*   Si aliquis *om. P*   fixo] flexo *O*   in terra] in terram *O T*   98 eorum *om. O*   uidebuntur] uideretur *M*   99 est] esset *P T*   Ita *om. T*   100-101 naturam...contra *hom. P*   101 sic] sicut *D*   102 inordinationem] inordinatione *O* 104 *post* habet] ullum *suppl. T*   uel] et *O*

87-88 Cf. Cal., *Comm.* 209 (W226:13-14).

W40:3   *Cumque etc.* Quasi: ita deprauata sunt opinio et intellectus, quod cum
putant se donari sensibus; potius seruiunt.

W40:5-6   *Eademque* anima *passionibus* est *aegra et initio* incorporationis et *quamdiu*
perinde afficietur, id est quamdiu credit ita testimonio sensuum, quod maxime
inuenitur in quibusdam senibus qui, iudicantes bonum quicquid eos delectat,   110
non discernunt inter bonum et malum, sicut pueri putant summa bona esse
quaecumque sibi placent.

4b W40:6-7   *At postquam.* Dum tantus meatus influit et effluit, turbantur omnes animae
circuitus. *At postquam*, crescente homine, cessat illa influxio, sedantur motus
animae et discernunt inter uitia et uirtutes, ut uitia uitent, uirtutes sequantur.   115
Et eodem modo de sensibus postquam uitiorum uoluptas cessat, conuales-
cunt ratio et intellectus.

W40:12   *Ac si.* Quasi diceret: duo illi circuli, id est ratio et opinio, tuebuntur
hominem, sed multo plus si adest doctrina ad illustrandam rationem et uirtus
ad gubernandam opinionem uel iram et concupiscentiam. Vel ita: nutricatio   120
corporis sedat motus, sed si conuersabitur cum bonis, tunc magis sedabuntur
W40:14   et illustrabuntur. Perturbatio ad animam, aegritudo ad corpus referatur.

4c W40:14-15 *Si negleget* utraque curare corpus, scilicet et animam uel intellectum et
opinionem, mancus erit, si alterum claudus, et magis claudus si animam
neglexerit uel intellectum. Reuocabuntur, dicit, quia inde uenerunt, unde   125
Pluto dicitur sator animarum.

4d W40:16   *Sed haec.* Quasi: haec differunt, ne possint dicere se anticipatos.

W40:16-19 *Nunc uero.* Ostensa constitutione hominis in toto et deuiatione ex
consensu sensuum, nunc membratim. Sicut in constitutione mundani corporis fecerat, de eo agit, causasque et utilitatem membrorum sic in hominis   130
corpore dispositorum aperit, et de sensibus unde conficiantur persequitur
ipsemet et iungit, dicens: *nunc conuenit spectari pensum*, id est consideratio-

---

108 *post* initio] id est *add. M*   109 ita *om. D*   maxime] magis *T*   110 senibus]
sensibus *D M O P*: senibus *superscr. M*   iudicantes] uidentes *O*   111 sicut...bona *om.*
P   112 quaecumque] quicquid *T*   placent] placet *P T*   113-114 Dum...postquam
hom. O   113 omnes *om. P*   114 crescente] consentiente *M*: consente *P*   115
discernunt] discernit *O*   ut...uirtutes *om. P*   uitent] uitentur *D*   *post* uitent] et *add.*
T   116 de *om. T*   uoluptas] uoluntas *D*   116-117 conualescunt] conualescere *P*
118 Quasi diceret *om. O*   opinio] intellectus *D*   tuebuntur] tuentur *M*: tenebant *O*
119 hominem] homines *P*   120 *post* gubernandam] rationem *add. O*   121 tunc]
multo *T*   122 referatur] refertur *T*   123 curare *om. O*   scilicet] sed *P*   124 mancus
erit] manseret *M*: manserit *superscr. M*   125 neglexerit] neglexerint *M*   Reuocabuntur]
Reuocabunt *D M O P*   inde uenerunt] inuenerunt *P*   127 differunt] differuntur *M P*:
differantur *T*   possint] possent *D*   129 constitutione] constitutionem *M P*   130
utilitatem] utilitates *T*   sic] sicut *O P*   131 corpore *om. T*   132 ipsemet] ipsam *M*
et iungit] iungit *D P T*: subiungit *O*

123-125 Cf. Cal., *Comm.* 211 (W227:20-228:2).   128-132 Cf. Cal., *Comm.* 212 (W228).

nem et consilium, *diuinae prouidentiae*, ipsorum quibus iniunctum erat facere
hominem, et unde spectari, *ex rationabili conformatione membrorum*, quae
membra *apparabat caelestis prospicientia suscipiendo uitali uigori*, id est   135
animae.

W40:19   *Principio.* Orditur a capite ut a principaliori parte, sic *figuram*, id est
formam, *capitis*, fecerunt rotundam, qualis est forma aplanos, quia in capite
W40:21-22 sedet ratio. *Eidem* capiti *innexuerunt duos circuitus* animae, scilicet uim
intelligentem et opinantem. Diuiditur ratio laxe accepta, scilicet certum   140
animae iudicium, in uim intelligentem et in opinantem. Vis intelligens in
sapientiam et scientiam: sapientia de diuinis, scientia de humanis et aliis
essentiis. Vis opinatrix diuiditur in prudentiam et opinionem ueram: prudentia de dispositione rerum nostrarum, uera opinio uerus conceptus sensibi-
lium.   145

W40:22   *Est autem.* Rotundam formam dedit capiti, eique posito in eminentiori
loco, dedit dominium supra cetera membra, sicut aplanos dominatur inferioribus circulis. Potest uero notari in regione humani corporis dispositio rei
publicae, quia sicut in eminentiori loco ciuitatis habitant maiores, ita in capite
maior uis animae, id est ratio. Et sicut in medio ciuitatis milites habitant qui   150
defendunt ciuitatem, ita in medio hominis, id est in corde, est naturalis uigor
animae, scilicet ira per quam malis irasci debemus. Et sicut in ciuitate circa
extremos habitant opifices, id est sellularii et ceteri seruiles, qui semper
cupiunt adquirere, ita in homine circa posteriora habitant concupiscentiae.

W41:1   *Iure subiecta*, quia sedes principalis est uirtutis, id est rationis, *merito*, quia   155
caput regit cetera membra.

W41:1-3   *Ne sine.* Ideo positum fuit caput eminentius, ne *offensiones procliuitatis
incurreret*, scilicet in ascensu ubi minor est offensio, *et decliuitatis*, in
descensu ubi maior est offensio, si esset positum *in imo*, quia necesse esset
ei omnibus motibus uti propter regimen corporis.   160

---

134 spectari] spectaret *O*   137 a *om. T*   138 capitis] corpori *corr. D*: corpori *O*
139 circuitus] uenerandae diuinitatis *suppl. T*   animae *om. T*   *post* scilicet] uim iuditium
in *add. O*   140 intelligentem] intelligibilem *O*   140-141 opinantem...et *hom. O*   140
certum] circuitus *T*   141 intelligentem] intelligibilem *D M P T*: *scrips.*: *cf. 7.140 supra*
in[2] *om. T*   opinantem] opinabilem *D*   *post* opinantem] uel oppinabilem *T*   142
sapientia] scientia *P*   143 Vis] Vix *D*   147 loco *om. O*   147-148 inferioribus] ceteris
T   149 sicut] sic *P*   149-150 habitant... milites *hom. O*   151 defendunt] defendant
P   153 sellularii] sellarii *D M O P T*: *scrips.*   seruiles] similes *O*   155 quia[1]] qui *M*
157 offensiones] offenderetur *D M P T*: offenderet *O*: *scrips.*: *cf. W41:2*   158 incurreret
om. D O P T   160 regimen] regnum *P*

137-138 Cf. Cal., *Comm.* 213 (W228:14).   139-140 Cf. Cal., *Comm.* 213 (W228:18).
148-154 Cf. Cal., *Comm.* 232-233 (W246-247); Dutton, "*Illustre ciuitatis*".

44e W41:4   *Hac igitur causa,* scilicet ne offenderetur.

W41:4-5   *Addita.* Quasi: brachia data sunt propter usum *tenendi et emittendi,* crura ut possit homo progredi et resistere.

45a W41:7   *Progrediendi.* Causa est cur pedibus data est anterior pars, potius ante quam retro, scilicet quia secundum motum rationabilem *commodius* est ire 165 ante quam recessim ad modum aplanos.

W41:9   *Priores.* Causa est quare facies sit posita ante potius quam retro uel ad dextram seu ad sinistram, quia anteriores partes digniores sunt *posterioribus.*

W41:11   Vultus ideo dicitur persona, quia ibi sunt *instrumenta* omnium sensuum et ideo uultum apposuerunt capiti, ut praesto haberet ratio instrumenta per quae 170 operaretur.

45b W41:13   *Duae sunt.* Ostendit quomodo claritas oculorum seruiat rationi et opinioni, scilicet iuncta cum claritate solis: *edax* exterior, scilicet solis qui edit et exsiccat humorem, *mulcebris* interior, scilicet oculorum. Vel reddit causam quare dati sunt oculi, scilicet ut ignis interior, id est animae cuius natura est 175 mulcere corpus et non consumere, exiret per oculos, cui exeunti associaretur iste exterior. Et illi duo ignes coniuncti insimul tenderent usque ad aliquod corpus cuius formam capientes redirent ad oculum, et ibi exterior haereret, interior intraret, renuntians animae praedictam formam. Et sic efficeretur passio quae dicitur uisus. 180

W41:14-16   *Huic igitur.* Quia duae sunt uirtutes ignis quae iunctae possunt se iuuare, igitur *diuinae potestates commentae sunt corpus oculorum familiare,* id est consimile huic igni, id est exteriori. Et hoc est: *ex qua* uirtute *panditur lux.* In hoc simile est corpus oculorum igni exteriori, quod lucidum et clarum est ut ignis. 185

45c W41:16-19   *Intimum.* Ideo commentae sunt corpus oculorum familiare igni exteriori, quia *uoluerunt* inter ignem exire per oculos ipsos. Qui intimus ignis cognatus

---

161 Hac] Hanc *D O*   offenderetur] offenderent *O*   163 progredi] regredi *T*   164 *post* Progrediendi] enim *add. T*   *post* pars] corporis *add. P*   165 quia secundum *om. O* 166 ad modum] moueri *T*   167 *post* sit] pedibus *add. T*   potius *om. M*   169 ideo] ratio *P*   ibi] tibi *P*   169-170 omnium... instrumenta *hom. M*   170 apposu- erunt] apparuerunt *P*   173 scilicet solis] scilicet *O*   edit] dedit *D*   174 exsiccat] siccat *T*   mulcebris] mulcit *P*   175 scilicet] sed *P*   interior *om. O*   id est] scilicet *M* 176 exiret] exire *O*   177 tenderent] procederent *T*   usque *om. M*   178 exterior] exteriorum *D*   *post* haereret] et *add. O*   179 interior] *om. D:* intencior *P*   181 sunt *om. T*   iunctae possunt] coniuncte possent *M*   182 sunt *om. T*   184 simile] consimile *T*   184 *post* exteriori] et *add. P*   184-186 quod...exteriori *hom. M*   186 *post* sunt] corpus et *add. O*   familiare igni] simile ignis *O T:* famulus igni *P*   exteriori] exterioris *T*   187 inter] ut *D*   Qui] quia *T*   cognatus *om. O*

---

174 sqq. cf. Cal., *Comm.* 244-245 (W255-256).

est sereno liquori, id est igni exteriori. Et ideo uoluerunt exire, ut per *orbes luminum* exiret ignis interior, orbes dico *leues*, id est planos et *congestos*, id est globosos, *et tamquam pauidos firmiore soliditate*, quia quanto sibi plus 190 cauent, tanto magis durant.

W41:19-20   *Quorum tamen*. Licet dixerim quod uoluerunt illum ignem per oculos fluere, non tamen in toto accipias, sed tantum per *medietatem*, scilicet per pupillam quae est quoddam subtile in medio oculorum.

W41:20-22   *Itaque*. Quia sicut erat ille interior ignis, ut statutum est, igitur interior 195 iungitur exteriori, et *cum diurnum iubar*, scilicet solis, *applicat se uisus fusioni*, id est igni interiori exeunti per uisum, id est per oculos. Tunc illi duo ignes similes iuncti *cohaerent in speciem*, id est in formam, *unius corporis*, comprehendendam, id est comprehendunt aliquod corpus quadratum esse uel alterius formae.   200

W41:22-24   *Quo concurrunt*, id est ad quam formam, *concurrunt acies oculorum*, id est illi duo ignes emissi per illos orbes, et in quo corpore *repercutitur acies intimae fusionis*, id est interioris ignis, *occursu contiguae imaginis*, id est formatae rei contiguae.

W41:24   *Totum igitur*. Et quia interius et exterius lumen repercutitur occursu 205 imaginis, *igitur hoc totum*, id est utrumque lumen coniunctum, *sortitum eandem passionem*, id est corporis repercussione, ibi enim utrumque patitur W42:1-2   et sortitur, *effectum eiusdem passionis*, id est eiusdem formae corporis, *ob indifferentem similitudinem*, id est quia ualde sunt similes. *Cum aliud aliquid tangit*, scilicet corpus ad quod dirigitur, *uel ab alio tangitur*, contingit enim 210 dum dirigimus oculos ad aliquid uidendum uel auis uel aliquid se interponat, tunc illud totum *motu tactuum*, id est corporis repercussione, diffundit se per W42:3-4   totum *corpus* oculi, et tunc ignis interior *porrigens sensum per corpus* pupillae *usque ad animam efficit sensum* in anima *qui uisus uocatur*.

Potest quaeri de igne interiori quid sit: substantia scilicet an accidens? 215 Quod si substantia, an eadem cum anima, an aliud? Sed neutrum horum est.

---

188 Et *om. T*   188-189 ut per orbes luminum] per orbes fluere *T*   189 interior] exterior *P T*   191 magis] amplius *D*: magis plus *O*   192 tamen *om. D*   illum *om. P*   illum ignem *om. T*   193 accipias] accipiamus *T*   194 pupillam] pupulam *P*   quae] quidem *M*: quod *P T*   195 sicut] ita *M*: sic *O P*   ille *om. P*   erat] ex. *P*: *om. T*   ut statutum est] ut statum est *O*: exit ut supradictum est *T*   196 *post* iungitur] in *add. P*   197 interiori] exteriori *O*: in exteriori *P*   198 in formam] formam *D P*   200 alterius] alius *M P*   201 ad *om. P*   *post* formam] et *add. T*   id est² *om. D*   203 id est interioris ignis *om. T*   id est² *om. M*   204 formatae] conformate *O*   205 *post* Totum] hoc *suppl. T*   et²] uel *M*: *om. P*   repercutitur] percutitur *P*   207 eandem *om. T* repercussione] repercussionem *O P*   209 *post* ualde] sibi *add. M*   similes] dissimiles *O*   aliquid] aliquod *D P*   210 alio] alia *O*   210-212 enim...illud *om. P*   211 auis] animus *O*   uel...interponat *om. O*   aliquid] aliquod *D*   213 interior] anterior *O* 215-224 Potest...dialectica *om. T*   215 interiori] exteriori *corr. M*   quid] quod *D O P*   216 Quod *om. M*   *post* Sed] si *add. O*

Nec accidens esse uidetur, nullum enim accidens indiuiduum eodem tempore diuersa omnino occupat substantia, nec suum deserit, ut ad aliud transeat, quod uidetur facere ignis ille cum per oculum transiens ad corpus exterius dirigitur. R<espondendum>: ignis quidem ille qualitas est quae sic porrigitur 220 extra ut animam non deserat, nec aliud subiectum inficiat. Porrigitur, inquam, uel per discretionem, scilicet dum discernit formas exteriores, manens semper in anima uel sumens quoddam sui incrementum, uel non obseruabitur hic eadem natura accidentium quae in dialectica.

45d   W42:4-5   *At postquam.* Hic docet aperte utrumque efficere uisum, scilicet exteriorem 225 et interiorem ignem, quia si absit exterior, interior non faciet uisum, sed *hebet,* utpote uiduatus *auxilio* exterioris ignis.

W42:5-8   *Vt quippe.* Non mirum, si hebet, quia *ad dissimile,* id est obscuratum aerem, *procedens, immutatum,* id est ualde mutatus ipse ignis intimus, *extinguitur,* id est non habet effectum uidendi, quia *non habens ullam* 230 *communicationem naturae cum proximo aere,* id est cum obscurato, et ideo *desinit uidere* aliquod *factum,* sic superueniente *illecebra somni* uel facta *illecebra somni* uel tactum *illecebra somni.*

W42:8-11   *Etenim.* Probat quod dormiant, quia ad hoc datae sunt palpebrae, ut coopertoria. Vt enim commodius fieret somnus, fecerunt dii oculis conue- 235 nientia opercula, ne uisus assidue uexaretur corporum obiectu. *Quibus obductis coercetur ignis coniuentia,* id est coniunctione palpebrarum, et *ipsa uis ignis* sic *compressa fundit se per membra* et tunc illis membris *mollitis conualescit quies.*

W42:11-12   *Quae* quies. Quia naturam uisus plene uult exsequi, ostendit quam naturam 240 habeat uisus, etiam in somnis. Quae somnia diuersis modis fiunt, quia sicut tres sunt uires animae—ratio, ira, concupiscentia—ita sunt tria genera natura- lium somniorum. Si quis enim incipiens cogitare de honestis et utilibus sic obdormierit, ex *reliquiis* cogitationum somnia quae procedunt sunt in eodem loco in *quibus* et reliquiae, scilicet in capite, quod est sedes rationis. Si uero 245 cogitans de ultione uel alia re, quae ad iram pertinet, obdormierit, reliquiae

---

217 esse...accidens *hom. P*   accidens *om. D*   220 quidem *om. P*   221 subiectum] superbum *P*   224 hic] haec *O*   225 efficere *om. D*   226 sed] si *O*   228 Vt] At *P* 231 naturae *om. T*   id est *om. P*   232 aliquod] aliqua *O T:* aliud *P*   factum *om. T*   232-233 uel facta illecebra somni *om. O*   234 quod] quia *M*   dormiant] dormiunt *O*   235 fecerunt] fecerant *M*   237 coniuentia] coniunct. *M*   238 compressa] comprehensa *O*   et *om. P*   239 conualescit] et ualescit *M*   240 Quae *om. T*   241 etiam] et *M O P*   242 *post* animae] scilicet *add. D*   244 ex reliquiis] reliquie *P* somnia quae procedunt *om. P*   245 quibus] quo *M O*   et *om. P*   scilicet] sunt *D*

---

224 Cf. Martianus Capella, *De nuptiis* 4.347 (ed. Willis, p. 112).   242 Cf. Cal., *Comm.* 249 (W259:23-260:4).

cogitationum et somnia quae inde procedunt, scilicet de uindicta uel aliquo
tali, sunt circa cor, qui locus est irae. Si autem cogitans ex libidine aliqua
obdormiat, reliquiae cogitationum et somnia quae inde procedunt sunt in
W42:11-13 loco concupiscentiae, scilicet circa posteriora. Et hoc est: *quae* quies *cum est* 250
uehementior, id est firma, *nascentur simulacra*, id est imagines, *somniorum*
de reliquiis motuum, id est recordationis et cogitationis quae sunt motus
animae, *cuius modi*, secundum quantitatem, *paria*, secundum qualitatem, id
est quantae et quales, *erunt* reliquiae, et in eisdem *locis in quibus* sunt
reliquiae.   255

Reliquiae motuum proprie dicuntur intercisae recordationes et cogitatio-
nes animae. Contigit enim ut anima recordans diuersorum, ut dictum est, in
medio talis cogitationis et recordationis in quiete laxetur. Somnia uero quae
non procedunt ex cogitationibus non sunt naturalia. Calcidius tamen uidetur
uelle quod altior quies nihil certitudinis afferat per somnia, dicit enim: 260
"cumque erit altior quies crassiore facto naturali spiritu, nihil aut leue
quiddam et incertum somniamus."

46a W42:14   *At uero.* Quia cepit ostendere naturam uisus, ostensa tuitione, uult docere
intuitionem et detuitionem. Hi sunt enim tres modi uisus. Tuitio est quando
uisus dirigitur ad aliquod tale corpus, unde non reuerberatur, ita ut ex eo 265
imago uultus appareat, ut lapidem uel tale quid inspiciamus. Intuitio est cum
aliquid tale inspicimus, in cuius superficie imago uultus apparet, ut speculum
uel aliquod aliud corpus bene detersum et leuigatum. Detuitio est cum tale
quid inspicimus, ubi non in superficie, sed interius imago uidetur apparere,
sicut uitrum nigrum uel obscurum stagnum.   270

Apparent autem diuersis modis imagines in diuersis generibus speculorum.
Si enim speculum planum sit, quod facimus dextra manu repraesentat imago
sua sinistra, et e conuerso, quia tunc unusquisque oculus obtinet in speculo

---

247-248 scilicet...tali *om. T*   248 *post* sunt] in loco ire scilicet *add. T*   qui] quod *O*
ex] de *O T*   249 *post* obdormiat] et *add. M*   et...procedunt *om. T*   251 firma]
confirma *M*   253 quantitatem] iniquitatem *P*   paria] parca *corr. M*   254-255 et
in...reliquiae *hom. O*   258 quiete] quietem *T*   260 quod] quia *O*   261 altior *om. P*
262 quiddam et incertum] incertumque *P et Cal., Comm. 249 (W259:19)*   *post*
incertum] Nota Plato...panduntur *add. O*: *vide App. 1.2 p. 236 infra*   somniamus *om. O*
263 uisus *om. P*   docere] *om. D*: ostendere *O*   264 *post* uisus] uel *add. P*   *post*
quando] ipse *add. T*   265 tale *om. T*   *post* unde] corpus *add. O*   non *om. P*   ita
om. T   267 inspicimus] inspiciamus *P*   apparet] apareat *T*   268 uel] ut *T*   270
nigrum *om. M*   272 sit] fuerit *M T*   273 conuerso] contrario *P*

259-262 Cal., *Comm.* 249 (W259:18-20).   264-268 Cf. Cal., *Comm.* 239 (W251:11-13).
268-270 Cf. Cal., *Comm.* 242 (W253-254).   271-279 Cf. Cal., *Comm.* 239-240
(W251-253).

partem sibi directe oppositam. Si autem concauum sit speculum et oblongum
in modum imbricis uel nauis, tunc apparebunt partes dextrae dextrae et 275
sinistrae sinistrae, quia si inspiciens aliquid faciat dextra sua, idem faciet
imago dextra manu sua, et idem in sinistra. Si idem concauum speculum ita
conuertat, ut unum latus superius ponat, alterum inferius, tunc uultus inspicientis apparebunt resupini, scilicet caput inferius et mentum superius.

Est alia natura speculorum: scilicet si quis unum speculum ante aliud retro 280
ponat, ita tamen quod corpus non ita obiciat, quin possit lumen transire de
uno ad aliud, uidebit homo occiput suum. Item si quis inspiciat se in speculo
in medio globoso, tunc facies eius apparebit lata et deformis, quantumcumque
tamen per se pulchra sit, et quod faciet inspiciens dextra manu, reddet imago
sua sinistra, ut in primo dictum est.   285

W42:15-18 *Siquidem.* Ostendit quod *facilis* sit *assecutio,* quia *resultant simulacra ex*
conspectu, id est reuerberatione, *leuigati,* id est plani, *corporis et formati in*
multas figuras, quia secundum quod diuerso modo formantur, secundum hoc
diuersas repraesentant figuras. Et hoc fit: *concursu utriusque ignis.*

b W42:18-22 *Dextrae.* Hic docet naturam plani speculi et rotundi, ubi uisus suo loco non 290
potest haerere prae nimia planitudine, sed de uno latere relabitur in aliud
latus. Cum dicit *imago gesticulatur,* id est repraesentat motus inspicientis, *ex*
aduerso partis eius unde fit motus ab inspiciente, id est si inspiciens faciat
aliquid dextra manu, imago repraesentat eundem motum sua sinistra, quae
est dextrae inspicientis recta linea opposita. Et hoc dicit fieri *insolito more,* 295
quia uideretur quasi solitum, quod dextra pars uisus remaneret in dextra parte
speculi, et sic in sinistra. Sed hic cum uisus iacitur in dextrum latus speculi,
relabitur in sinistrum, et e conuerso.

W42:22
W43:1-2 *At uero.* Ostendit naturam oblongi et caui speculi, ubi nulla transmutatio
est partium. Coitum *uisus et splendoris* accipit coniugationem exterioris et 300
interioris ignis, ex quo *coitu renidet,* id est reuerberatur, *corpulentior conglo-*
bata imago, quia in fundo coadunata est, quasi in hoc speculo conglobatur
uisus in medio et non relabitur in aduersa latera.

---

275 *post* partes] et *add. O*   dextrae dextrae] dextre *P*   276 sinistrae sinistrae]
sinistre *P*   277 idem] tunc *O*   in *om. P*   280 speculum *om. T*   281 ponat]
componat *T*   284 tamen *om. M*   287 et *om. P T*   288 figuras *om. M*   secundum[1]
om P   289 concursu] cursu *D M O P*   290 docet] ostendit *T*   291 relabitur] labitur
M: relabuntur *P*   293 motus *om. P*   si inspiciens] suspiciens *T*   294 aliquid *om. D*
296 uideretur] uidetur *O*   remaneret] remanetur *O:* remanet *P:* remanent *T*   297
iacitur] nascitur *T*   298 relabitur] labitur *P*   299 caui] concaui *O T*   300 et[1] *om. P*
splendoris] speculi *O P*   coniugationem] coniunctionem *T*   301 corpulentior]
corpulenta *T*   301-302 conglobata] et globata *D M O P:* et globosa *T: scrips.: cf. W43:1*
post globata] et *add. O*   302 in hoc] nichil *P*   303 relabitur] labitur *P*   latera *om. O*

280-285 Cf. Cal., *Comm.* 241 (W253).

46c W43:2   *Quod fit,* id est quae coniunctio utriusque ignis.

              Quotiens etc. Hic docet unde sit quod dextra remaneat dextra et sinistra 305
sinistra, quia qui uisus dirigitur in dextram partem in sinistram speculi
deicitur, et ibi figitur, et eodem modo sinistra in dextram transit. Ne intelligas
quod hic uidetur dicere, scilicet ut uisus in contrarias partes ex toto transeat,
sed remanet in medio ibique spissatur, et inde fit ut lineamenta corporis recto
ordine repraesentet. 310

W43:4-6   *Cuius speculi,* id est oblongi et concaui, si latera conuertantur, *resupini
uultus* inspicientis *apparebunt,* quod quomodo fiat ostendit, cum subdit,

W43:7   *splendore luminis,* id est oculorum deiecto ex superiore latere, *ad inferiora
et ipso capite,* deiecto, *cum summis partibus,* uultus, *ad inferiora deiectis.
Similis porro,* id est talis tunc apparet imago, ut si mentum et genae *ad* 315
superiora sint sublatae.

W43:9   *Qui quidem.* Quia uisus et alii sensus, qui per instrumenta corporea
exercentur, sensus dicuntur corporis, ideo uideretur quibusdam quod ipsa
instrumenta sentirent per se, quod remouet, docens corpora ex se non
sentire, sed per solam animam, et esse instrumenta sensuum. 320

              Vel quia uisum corporeis nominibus appellauit, scilicet ignem et lumen,
uellet aliquis hunc sensum sicut alios sine anima ministrari, quod remouet,
dicens: *qui quidem sensus,* id est oculi et cetera instrumenta sensuum,
famulantur actibus dei, id est animae, *molientis speciem,* id est animam,
summam per iram, et *primariam* per rationem. Actus animae dicit sensus, 325

46d W43:10 quamuis famulentur animae, tamen *uulgo etc.* Anima est causa eorum quae
fiunt per instrumenta sensuum, et instrumenta sequuntur animam.

W43:13-16   *Licet enim.* Ostendit quod multum differant causa et ea quae causas
sequuntur, quia instrumenta corporea sunt, anima quae causa est incorporea
est, et ea *sentit,* non corpora. Quae *recipiunt* passiones, *non sentiunt.* 330

---

304 quae] quia *M*   305 sit] fit *D*: fiat *T*   remaneat] remanet *T*   sinistra *om. P*   306
post sinistra] sinistra *add. O*   qui] quod *M*: *om. O*   *post* partem] quia *add. D*: speculi
add. T   *post* sinistram] partem *add. P*   307 ibi figitur] *om. O*: in figuris *P*   *post*
modo] qui in *add. T*   transit] transilit *D*   Ne] Nec *D*   308 quod] quia *M*   uidetur]
uideretur *P*   ex toto *om. M*   309 et inde] et ideo *M*: inde *P*   311 id est] scilicet *T*
312 cum subdit] *om. O*: cum dicit *T*   313 inferiora] inferunt *O*   314 uultus]
similiter *T*   deiectis] deiecto *O*: *om. T*   315 Similis] Similiter *O*   id est *om. O T*
apparet] apparebit *O*: apparuit *P*   317 Quia *om. P*   317-318 qui...sensus *hom. P*   318
ideo] iam *P*   uideretur] uidetur *O P*   quod] quia *P*   319 quod] idem *T*
docens] dicens *D*: *om. T*   319-320 corpora ex se non sentire] quod corpora non
sentiant per se *T*   320 solam *om. O*   et esse instrumenta sensuum] corpus uero esse
instrumentum sensuum *T*   322 *post* sicut] et *add. D O P T*   323 cetera] omnia *T*
sensuum] sensuum et instrumenta *D*: *om. T*   324 *post* actibus] opificis *suppl. T*   *post*
animae] dei dico *add. T*   id est¹] in *P*   325 *post* rationem] est *add. P*   326 fa-
mulentur] famuletur *T*   tamen] tunc *O*   327 fiunt *om. O*   et...animam *om. T*
328 causas] causam *O*   329 *post* sunt] et *add. T*   330 est *om. M*   ea] eam *O*

W43:16-17   *Nec uero.* Nec sentiunt corpora, nec *sciunt* agere intellectualiter uel
rationabiliter *in rebus agendis ratione* uel *prudentia*: ratio de diuinis, prudentia de humanis. Vel sic: uere illorum quinque corporis instrumentorum non
est sentire, sed animae, quia scire et intelligere est tantum animae. Et hoc est:
nec sciunt, illa quinque corporea instrumenta, *rationem et intellectum, in*   335
rebus agendis, id est in illis quinque sensibus rationabiliter regendis.

W43:19   *Oportet autem.* Quia longe distant causae et ea quae causam sequuntur
obediendo ei, ut anima et instrumenta corporea, igitur qui de ipsis uult agere
prius debet agere de digniore, id est anima, post de corpore. Et non solum
anima prius consideranda est quam corpus, sed si quis tractet de potentiis   340
animae prius debet de principaliori agere, deinde de secundaria. Principalis
quidem uis in anima est rationalis intellectus, quia ipse a nullo mouetur et
mouet appetitum, id est iram et concupiscentiam. Appetitus secunda potentia
est animae, quia et mouetur a ratione et ipsa mouet corpus, et hi duo motus
sunt animae; corporis octo, duo quorum sunt loculares: translatio scilicet et   345
circumlatio. Translatio habet sex partes: ante, retro, sinistrorsum, dextrorsum, sursum, deorsum. Duo alii sunt motus corporis: secundum quantitatem,
augmentum scilicet et diminutio; secundum qualitatem duo, concretio et
discretio, scilicet qualitatis cum corpore coniunctio et disiunctio. Reliqui duo
sunt secundum substantiam: generatio, corruptio.   350

W43:19-22   Sic lege litteram: *amatorem intellectus <et> disciplinae,* id est eum qui
amat ita docere ut plene intelligatur, *oportet* prius *inquirere principalem*
causam, id est rationem, *prudentissimae naturae,* id est animae, *non admini-*
cula principalis causae, id est iram et concupiscentiam, quae sunt quaedam
instrumenta rationis, quia ea mouet et per ea corpus mouetur. *Illas uero,* id   355
est iram et concupiscentiam, *existimandum* est esse *secundas.*

W43:22-23   *Nobis quoque.* Quia ita ordo exigit et omnes amatores disciplinae hoc
faciunt, *igitur nobis est disserendum de utroque genere causarum,* id est de
ratione et appetitu, quorum utrumque causa est motus corporum.

331-332 uel rationabiliter] probabiliter *P*   332 uel] et *T*   333 instrumentorum] instru-
mentis *P*   335 corporea] corpora *O*   335-336 in rebus] rebus *O P T*   337 Quia]
Quod *P*   338 corporea igitur] corporis *T*   339 agere *om. O*   *post* id est] de *add. O*
340 consideranda *in marg. sinist. M*   341 prius] post *P*   principaliori] potentialiori
O: principali *P*: principalibus *T*   secundaria] secundariis *T*   343 id est] ut *T*   344
et[1] *om. M T*   a ratione *om. O*   ipsa *om. O*   corpus *om. D*   motus] moti *D*   345
octo] VII *O*   345-346 translatio...circumlatio *hom. O*   346 sex] quia *O*   *post* ante]
et *add. T*   350 secundum *om. O*   351 intellectus] intellegendi *P*   <et>] *om. D M O*
P T: scrips.: cf. W43:19   disciplinae *om. M P*   352 plene *om. M*   354 causae *om.*
D   355 per ea] propterea *P*   uero *om. T*   356 secundas] secundam *D*   358 nobis]
nichil *O*

341-342 Cf. Cal., *Comm.* 262 (W268:16-17).   344-347 Cf. Cal., *Comm.* 262
(W268:19-21).   347-350 Cf. Cal., *Comm.* 262 (W268:21-269:1).

W43:23-24   *Sed separatim*, de utroque est dicendum; *sed separatim*, id est prius per 360
se, *de optimis*, id est de ratione intelligenti et opinatrice, *cum intellectu*,
quantum ad diuina, *cum prudentia* in humanis et terrenis.

W43:25   *Seorsum uero*, per se post ea, *de his*, id est ira et concupiscentia, *quae
cassae*, id est priuatae, *mente*, id est intellectu, *et prudentia*, id est non

W44:1   obedientes intelligenti uel opinatrici, *confusa et inordinata relinquunt quae* 365
faciunt, quae uero rationi obediunt, ordinate agunt.

W44:1-2   *Et de oculorum*. Quod interposuit de potentiis animae incidens fuit, nunc
uero redit ad instrumenta corporea, ut eorum doceat utilitatem. Ministerium
oculorum est dirigere aciem ad aliqua exteriora; causa huius ministerii est ut
animae renuntiet exteriorum imagines.   370

W44:3   *De praecipua tamen*. Licet posset sufficere quod diximus de natura uisus,
tamen de praecipua utilitate etc.

47a W44:4   *Visus enim*. Vere utilitas operis oculorum est praecipua, quia confert nobis
philosophiam. Et hoc est: *causa est maximi commodi*, id est philosophiae
non omnibus, sed *institutis ob id* agendum de quo *nunc agimus*, id est propter 375
philosophiam inuestigandam.

Nota duo esse officia philosophiae: considerationem scilicet et actum.
Consideratio est assidua contemplatio diuinorum et immortalium. Actus est
in tuendis conseruandisque rebus mortalibus progressus secundum rationabilem animae deliberationem. Vtrique uero officio uisus necessarius. Quod per 380
singula uideamus. Consideratio in tria diuiditur, in theologiam, phisicam,
logicam: theologia de diuinis, phisica de rerum naturis, logica de rationabili
ordinatione tum aliorum, tum temporum. Ad theologiam necessarius est

W44:6-7   uisus, nullus enim aspiraret ad cognitionem diuinitatis, *nisi uisis stellis* et
ceteris operibus dei, uel edoctus ab eo qui uiderit. Nec aliquis attenderet 385

---

360 separatim¹] semper autem *P*   de...separatim *hom. O*   361 intelligenti] intelligendi
P T   362 quantum *om. M*   363 quae] quia *P*   365 intelligenti] intellectui *O   post*
opinatrici] rationi *add. T*   inordinata reliquunt *lac. in D*   366 ordinate] inordinate *T*
367 animae *om. O*   368 Ministerium] Misterium *O*   369 *post* causa] est *add. O*
ministerii est] misterii *O*   370 animae] diem *P*   renutiet *om. O*   371 *post*
praecipua] est *add. P*   tamen] tantum *O*   de natura *om. P*   373 operis *om. T*   374
causa est] causa *T*   375 propter] *om. O*: per *P*   378 diuinorum] diuinarum *D*   379
progressus] congressus *P*   secundum *om. P*   380 officio uisus necessarius] offitium uisus
est necessarium *T*   382 theologia] theologiam *D P   post* theologia] est *add. O*
phisica] phisicam *D*   logica] logicam *D P T*   382-383 rationabili ordinatione]
rationali ordine *T*   383 aliorum] alliorum *corr. M*: locorum *O*   temporum] ipsorum *T*
384 aspiraret] aspirat *O*   cognitionem] cogitationem *M*

373-376 Cf. Cal., *Comm.* 264 (W269:21-24).   377-383 Cf. Cal., *Comm.* 264
(W269:23-270:11).   382-383 tum aliorum, tum temporum] cf. 1.57-58 supra et
7.398-400 infra.

rerum naturas, nisi res ipsas uideret, nec *quaereret* rationem dispositionum mensium, annorum, et similium, nisi uiderit solem et alia, quorum uolutione haec metimur. Actus uero consideratur in moralitate. Moralitas est in publicis et priuatis rebus: in priuatis, domesticis, et familiaribus. Ad quae uisus est necessarius, quia per uisum notamus rationabilem motum aplanos, qui et se   390 ipsum mouet sine errore et planetarum erraticos motus contemperat. Quod notantes debemus aplanon nostrae mentis ita instituere, ut se ipsum sine errore moueat et erroneos motus uitiorum refrenet, quae morum correctio ualet in publicis et priuatis rebus. Inde etiam Anaxagoras, cum ab eo quaereretur, cur natus esset, fertur respondisse: "ad horum omnium contem-   395 plationem."

W44:6   *Neque enim.* Vere uisus iuuat ad philosophiam, quia ad utrumque officium, scilicet ad considerationem et actum, et prius de consideratione, quia sine uisu non potest cognitio diuinitatis uel naturae rerum uel ordinationis temporum haberi. Per ea enim quae uisibilia sunt ad intelligenda inuisibilia   400 ducimur.

W44:7-9   *Ac diei.* Hic docet quod uisus ualeat ad rationem ordinationis, quae est in logica. Et hoc est: *diei et noctis insinuata nobis,* per uisus, *alterna uice nati sunt menses,* et alia tempora, et existit nobis *dinumeratio eorum* temporum per uisum, *et ex dinumeratione perfectus numerus,* ut annus mundanus et   405 similia.

W44:9-10   *Tum temporis.* Per uisum enim recordamur praeteriti temporis, quae *recordatio docuit quaeri naturam uniuersae rei* factae sub tempore. Per recordationem enim praeteritorum temporum quaerimus naturam praeterita-rum rerum et ex praeteritis perpendimus praesentia et futura.   410

W44:14   *Minora.* Non solum usus uidendi prodest ad considerationem philosophi-cam et actum, sed etiam ad minora officia, scilicet seruilia, ut ad artem

---

386 rationem *om. T*   387 alia] aliam *P*   uolutione] uolutionem *P*   388 consideratur] considerantur *M*   moralitate] mortalitate *M*   est] autem *O*   391 contemperat] temperat *T*   392 mentis ita] menti *O*   instituere] instruere *D P*   393 erroneos] erraticos *O T*   refrenet quae *om. P*   morum] quorum *P*   394 Anaxagoras] Anaxaras *D*   395 quaereretur] quaeretur *M*   natus] uel superatus *O*   399 rerum] rei *T* ordinationis] ordinis *P T*   400 temporum] eorum *O*   402 Ac diei] Hac diei *P*: At nunc *T*   403 nobis *om. T*   404 existit] existat *O*   dinumeratio eorum] diuinorum *P* 405 ut] et *D*   407 Tum] Tunc *O*   408 recordatio *om. T*   docuit *om. M O*   409 naturam] naturas *D*   411 *post* Minora] praetereo *suppl. T*   usus] uisus *O*   411-412 considerationem philosophicam] philosophiam *O*

386-388 Cf. Cal., *Comm.* 264 (W270:12-14).   388-389 Cf. Cal., *Comm.* 265 (W270:21-25).   394-396 Cf. Cal., *Comm.* 266 (W271:5-7).   400-401 Cf. Rom. 1:20.

sutoriam et similia quae sine uisu non possunt haberi, sed ea *praetereo quibus
etc.*

W44:15　　　*Nobis uero.* Ostenso quomodo uisus ualeat ad considerationem, ostendit 415
quomodo ualeat ad actum, in quo est praecipua utilitas oculorum, secundum
quosdam. Continuatio. Non tantum ualet uisus ad considerationem, sed
W44:16-17　etiam ad actum. Diuinum munus accipit oculos: *deum*, puto, *dedisse oculos
etc.* Hoc est: ideo dati sunt oculi *hominibus*, ut *notantes* motum firmamenti
W44:18-20　conficerent *similes* motus *suae mentis*, scilicet rationabiles. Qui motus, id est 420
opinio et ratio, *uocantur animaduersiones*, dum decipiuntur a sensibus, *seu
deliberationes*, dum non deuiant.

47c　W44:21　　*Perturbatos* bene dicit, quia antequam anima incorporaretur, habebat
puram rationem, quae in corporis coniunctione perturbatur. Et ostendit
W44:21-23　quomodo fiant similes mentis nostrae motus motibus firmamenti. *Confir-* 425
mato, scilicet *examine*, id est iudicio, *rationis ingeneratae*, id est cum ipsa
anima a deo creata. *Confirmato*, inquam, sic *examine, corrigant erraticos
motus suae mentis dum imitantur circumactionem*, id est rationabilem et
perfectum motum, *intelligibilis mundi*, repraesentatum nobis, *in aplano*, qui
sine errore mouetur. 430

W44:23　　　*Eadem.* Ostenso uisu necessario ad philosophiam, docet auditum ad idem
necessarium. Sunt autem hi duo sensus principales, quorum alter, id est uisus,
est euidentior, quia res praesentes acie sua comprehendit. Alter, id est
auditus, latior quia non solum de praesentibus, sed etiam de absentibus
instruit, uoce citatus. Ad hoc enim uocis sermo nobis datus est, ut qui melius 435
sentiret alteri indicaret, et auditus, ut minus sciens sapientem audiret.

47d　W44:26　　*Quantumque.* Docet quomodo auditus ualeat ad philosophiam: quia ualet
ad correctionem morum. Auditus enim consonantiis musicis, debemus in
moribus nostris uirtutum consonantia reformari. Licet enim anima secundum

413 similia] huiusmodi *O*　　haberi] habere *D*　　sed] scilicet *T*　　praetereo] praeterea
D M O: praeterita *P*　　417 tantum] tamen *P*　　ualet] ualeat *P*　　418 accipit] accepit *P*
dedisse] uel *T*　　420 rationabiles] rationabilis *O*　　422 non] *om. O*: uero *T*　　423
incorporaretur] incorporetur *P*　　425 mentis] menti *P*　　426 ingeneratae id est cum]
magis est tunc *O*　　427 creata] creaturae *D*　　Confirmato] Confirmamento *M O*:
Confirmat *P*　　inquam] in qua *M O T*　　428 imitantur *om. M*　　429 perfectum *om. T*
qui] quod *M T*　　431 necessario] medio *T*　　philosophiam] phisicam *O T*　　432 hi
om. O　　434 etiam] *om. M*: et *O T*　　435 instruit] instruitur *D P*　　uoce citatus]
vocitatus *T*　　enim *om. O*　　uocis *om. T*　　nobis *om. P*　　437 Quantumque]
Quantumcumque *D O T*　　438 correctionem] correptionem *M*　　439 consonantia
reformari] consonantiam reformare *T*

431-435 Cf. Cal., *Comm.* 267 (W272:5-10).　　438-443 Cf. Boethius, *De institutione
musica* 1.1 (ed. Friedlein, pp. 178-187).

consonantias sit compacta, tamen ipsae consonantiae ex corporum coniunc- 440
tione dissonae fiunt et reformandae sunt per exteriorem musicam. Et hoc est:
tota musica data est hominibus non ad delectationem, sed ad morum
compositionem.

W45:2-3   *Intensio modificata* uel inter duas cordas, uel inter pondera, uel inter
uoces, *et habens cognatas etc.* Talis armonia est commoda *prudenter utentibus* 445
W45:4-5   tali *Musarum munere.*

W45:5   *Quippe.* Probat quod satis sit commoda, quia dissonos motus animae
reuocat ad concordiam.

W45:7   *Rithmus.* Aliud genus auditus datum ad aures mulcendas ponit, quasi non
solum musicae consonantiae ualent ad morum compositionem, sed etiam 450
rithmus. Rithmus est aequalis numerus sillabarum et, secundum eius aequalitatem, statuenda est aequalitas in moribus nostris. Nota uoces per auditum
prodesse nobis tribus modis: scilicet intellectae, modulatae, numeratae.
Intellectae, id est sola significatione, nobis prosunt ad mutuam uoluntatem
intimandam. Modulatae etiam absque significatione prosunt ad concentum, 455
scilicet morum, qui in cantu notatur. Numeratae quoque prosunt ad parilitatem et conuenientiam, quae alteri ab altero exhibenda est, quod in rithmo
consideratur. Rithmus enim interpretatur numerus.

---

440 consonantias] consonantiam *T*   compacta] composita *T*   441 *post* et¹] ita *add. T*
sunt] fiunt *P*   442 hominibus *om. T*   delectationem] lectionem *P*   444 inter
pondera] interponenda *P*   445 cognatas] cognatos *O*   *post* utentibus] non *add. M O P*
447 *post* Probat] uel *add. P*   449 ad *om. T*   450 consonantiae] consonantiam *O*   451
Rithmus *om. P*   454 id est] in *T*   456 scilicet] sed *P*   456-457 morum...conuenien-
tiam *rep. P*   457 quod] quae *O*   rithmo] rithmum *O*   458 consideratur] considerandum est *T*

442-443 Cf. Cal., *Comm.* 267 (W272:17-24).   458 Cf. Isidorus, *Etymologiae* 1.39.3 (ed.
Lindsay): "rythmus ... qui Latine nihil aliud quam numerus dicitur."; Martianus Capella, *De
nuptiis* 9.966 (ed. Willis, p.372.14): "Nunc rhythmos, hoc est numeros, perstringamus."

<8>

<TRACTATVS DE PRIMORDIALI MATERIA>

47e W45:9 *Nunc quoniam.* Constituto sensili mundo, quia generatio eius absque hyle
esse non potuit, quae omni corpori ut materia praeiacet, de ea ingreditur
agere. Praemiserat enim tantum duo principia prima: deum scilicet et
archetipum. Sed de hyle parum uel nihil dixerat, quod modo supplet. Et
uocat hic hylen necessitatem, quia impossibile est aliquod corporeum sine ea   5
esse: seu sit materia ex qua fiant corpora, seu in qua fiant. Dicitur enim a
quibusdam hylen non esse principalem causam corporum, sed solas natiuas
formas quae obtinet uicem patris, quia sicut semen patris in aluo matris efficit
filium, ita formae natiuae uenientes in hylen generant corpora. Ipsa uero hyle
uicem obtinens matris necessaria fuit ad mundi generationem, ideoque dicitur   10
necessitas. Sed potest quaeri secundum hoc in quam materiam, ex qua fiat
aliquid, uenerint illae formae ad efficientiam corporum, cum hyle tantum sit
materia in qua fiant. Ad quod r<espondendum>: esse quamdam materiam
confusam in hyle creatam ex nihilo uel origine carentem quae, susceptis illis
natiuis formis, primo transiit in eliquata elementa, deinde, assumptis aliis, in   15
elementaria.
      Maior tamen usus habet ex hyle fieri omnia corpora, non in hyle, nisi sic
in hyle dicantur fieri, ut in cera statua, quae tamen est ex cera, quod ueri
similius est. Erit igitur hyle quasi pater, secundum hoc quod assumptis formis
transit in corpus; quasi mater, secundum hoc quod in se recipit formas. Et   20

---

1 Constituto] Constitutio *P*   sensili] sensibili *M*   eius *om. O*   2 quae] quia *O P*
praeiacet] praeiecit *P*   3 duo *om. P*   prima *om. O P*   deum] Ihesum *P*   et *om. P*
4 *post* archetipum] mundum *add. O T*   5 hic *om. M O*   quia] qui *T*   *post*
aliquod] corpus *add. T*   6 seu sit materia] sensili natura *T*   seu²] sensibilia *T*   7 *post*
causam] omnium *add. T*   8 formas *om. T*   *post* obtinet] etiam *add. M T*   obtinet
uicem patris] obtinent *O*   9 hyle] hilen *O*   10 *post* mundi] constitutionem uel *T*   11
secundum hoc] si haec *M*   materiam] naturam *T*   fiat] fiant *T*   12 uenerint] uenient
O: ueniant *P T*   hyle] ille *O*   13 *post* quod] est *add. T*   esse *om. T*   14 origine
carentem] originem *P*   15 natiuis *om. P*   transiit] transilit *P*: transit *T*   15-16
deinde...elementaria *om. T*   18 fieri *om. O*   18 statua] figura *P*   ex] in *P*   quod]
qui *T*   20 hoc *om. M O P*

4-5 Cf. Cal., *Comm.* 269 (W273:15).   8-11 pater] cf. *Timaeus* 50d (W48:16); mater] cf.
Timaeus 50d (W48:15), 51a (W49:8).

secundum quod pater, principalis causa erit corporum post deum et ideas;
secundum quod mater, secundaria causa.

W45:9   *Exceptis paucis* dicit propter quattuor elementa pura, de quibus nihil
dixerat. Et haec quattuor sunt *quae inuehit necessitas*, id est quae primo loco
hyle constituit. Vel dicatur hyle se ipsam inuehere, ut de ea dicendum sit.   25

3a W45:11-13   *Mixta.* Ponit causam quare dicendum sit de necessitate: quia *generatio
sensilis mundi constat mixta ex coetu intelligentiae et necessitatis*, non quod
intellectus admisceatur necessitati, sed operatur intellectus. Necessitas patitur
in se uel ex se operari, et hanc mixturam innuit cum subdit: *dominante
intellectu.* Et quia dominium aliud tyrannicae potestatis, aliud imperatoriae   30
sanctitatis, melior uero imperatoria sanctitas, ut illam accipiat. Subdit: *salubri
persuasione trahente*, ipso intellectu, *assidue rigorem*, id est in ordinationem,
ad optimos actus, id est ad ordinationem.

W45:13-14   *Itaque.* Et quia non uiolenter praecepit, igitur necessitas *uicta* paruit, et sic
constiterunt prima exordia, quae possunt dici uel quattuor pura elementa uel   35
haec quattuor elementaria ex illis coniuncta.

W45:15-16   *Si quis ergo.* Et quia ex hac necessitate constiterunt prima mundi exordia,
ergo si quis perfecte *mundi huius institutionem insinuaturus erit, hunc oportet
etc.* Erraticam causam uocat hylen, quia in ea ante informationem hanc et
discretionem omnia quasi fluctuando errabant.   40

W45:16   *Speciem* uocat eius proprietatem, scilicet quod naturaliter careat forma, uel
omni uel distincta. Ita distinguo secundum diuersos. Quidam enim dicunt
hylen prorsus fuisse informem, ita ut nullum nomen nec uerbum in sua ui de
ea possent dici, sicut nec substantia spoliata omnibus formis, scilicet inferiorum et suis. Sed cum dicitur hyle fuit materia pura et similia, ad remotionem   45
non secundum positionem aliquam hoc dicitur.

---

21 *post* pater] est *add. P*   22 causa *om. T*   24 inuehit] inuenit *O*   25 constituit]
constituet *P*   dicatur] dicant *O*   26 Mixta] Mixtam eadem *T*   27 constat] consistit
T   mixta] quattuor *M P*   non quod] numquam *D O*   28 patitur] operatur *P*   29
ex] in *T*   30 dominium] diuinum *M*   tyrannicae *in marg. dext. D*   31 *post* uero] est
add. T   post sanctitas] quam tirannica potestas *add. T*   32 in *om. O P*   ordinationem]
ordinem *P*   33 ordinationem] ordinem *P*   34 Et *om. T*   non *om. P*   uicta] iuncta
D   paruit] apparuit *P*   35 constiterunt] constituunt *D M P*   35-38 prima...erit *om.*
O   35 dici *om. P*   37 Et *om. T*   constiterunt] constituunt *D M P*   exordia]
eorum *D*: ex horum *P*   38 ergo] igitur *T*   40 omnia] certa *T*   41 uocat] uocant *D*
eius proprietatem] proprietatem eandem ylen *T*   scilicet] secundum *M: om. T   post*
naturaliter] omni *add. T*   forma] formam *D*   42 omni] omnium *T   post* uel] scilicet
T   distinguo] disiungo *M O P T*   43 nec] uel nullum *O:* uel *T*   44 possent] posset
O T   44-45 sicut...Sed *om. T*   44 sicut] sic *M   post* nec] de *add. O P*   formis]
uerbis *D*   45 hyle] hiles *O*

29-31 Cf. Cal., *Comm.* 270 (W274:16-18).   42-43 Pythagoras, Plato, Aristoteles, et
Stoici: cf. Cal., *Comm.* 280 (W284:11-14), 275 (W279:11-12), 283 (W286:1-2), 297
(W299:1).   43-44 Cf. *Timaeus* 48b-c (W45:24-26).

Alii dicunt hylen in priori statu consideratam multis affici formis—puritate, possibilitate, et similibus—sed non talibus quae distinguerent naturam corporum in ea latentem et confusam. Secundum hos igitur bene nomina et uerba quaedam in ui sua de ea enuntiantur. Nota etiam, secundum quod dicitur   50 erratica causa, ipsam hylen uideri non esse principalem causam huius mundi, quod concedimus, secundum quod supra determinatum est.

W45:16-17   *Quod ita,* id est quae demonstratio necessitatis, *fiet, si* recurramus *ad originem eorum quae implicant erroribus.* Implicita erroribus dicit haec quattuor elementa uisibilia, quia non habent permanentem figuram, sed fit ex   55 aquatico terrenum, et sic in ceteris. Horum originem accipit pura elementa,

W45:17-18   et *recursu facto ad* ea *perinde ut* se in *his quae ex mente sunt,* id est quae mens diuina instituit. Cum enim superius ageret de sensili mundo, recurrit ad intelligibilem.

48b   W45:21-22   *Nec naturam modo,* id est non tantum sincera elementa, quae scilicet non   60 permiscentur in se, quae etiam uocat *ueterem naturam, sed perpessiones,* quas scilicet patiebantur in hyle, ubi nullum eorum uim suam exercebat, quippe remotis inde adhuc natiuis formis, uel ibi existentibus, sed confusis.

W45:22   *Nullus.* Ideo de hyle et de puris elementis est nobis dicendum, quia nullus inde adhuc dixit.   65

W45:23-25   Sed *loquimur sic* de his mixtis et uisibilibus elementis, tamquam sciamus *quid sit* uerus *ignis.* Et ipsi etiam sciant quibus loquimur, dicentes ea esse *initia uniuersitatis,* id est sensilis mundi, *quae nec locum obtinet sillabarum.* Quia si uere uolumus examinare, sicut in constitutione uocis littera est primum elementum, secundum sillaba, dictio tercio loco constituitur, ita in   70 huius mundi constitutione hyle est primum elementum, secundum illa quattuor pura, tercium haec quattuor mixta.

---

48 possibilitate] passibilitate *D*   et similibus] etc. *T*   sed non talibus *om. T* distinguerent] distingueret *D*   50 Nota etiam] et *O*   53 ita *om. T*   demonstratio] determinatio *T*   *post* fiet] commode *suppl. T*   si] sed *M*   54 eorum] eius *O*   haec *om. T*   55 quia] que *T*   56 terrenum] terreum *M O P T*   57 et *om. T*   *post* recursu] dico *add. T*   ea] illa *T*   in his quae *om. M*   58 instituit] instruit *O*   ageret] egisset *T*   sensili] sensibili *D: corr. M*   recurrit] fecit recursum *T*   60 non[1] *om. M* scilicet] sunt *ut uid. in D*   61 quae] quod *T*   62 scilicet *om. T*   eorum *om. T* 64 de[2] *om. P*   65 inde *om. O*   66 uisibilibus] inuisibilibus *O*   70 constituitur] constituit *D M O P*   71 huius mundi] huius modi *O*: mundi *T*   72 *post* quattuor[1]] elementa *add. O*   haec] ibi *M*: elementum ista *T*

47-48 Thales, Empedocles, Aristoteles et al.: cf. Cal., *Comm.* 280 (W284), 282 (W285), 285 (W289:2-9).   50-52 Cf. 8.6-9 supra; cf. Cal., *Comm.* 271 (W275).   69-72 Cf. Cal., *Comm.* 272 (W276:8-14); Priscianus, *Institutiones grammaticae* 1.2.3, 2.1.1, 2.3.14 (ed. Hertz in *Grammatici Latini* 2:6, 44, 53).

8c W45:26   *Nostra igitur.* Quia dicturus erat quod illa quattuor pura elementa ex hyle
uel in hyle fierent, ne quaereretur an una sola forma an plures formarent hylen
ad illa quattuor corpora pura procreanda, uel ne quaereretur de forma mundi,   75
scilicet an esset una idea an plures, excusat se et dicit: non pertinere ad hoc
propositum, sed esse epopticam disputationem, id est supercaelestem. Haec

W45:26-27   uero disputatio phisica est, quod dicit: *de uniuersitatis uel initio uel initiis,* hoc
est an una idea an plures, uel an una sola natiua forma an plures, informent
hylen ad quattuor pura corpora generanda.   80

W45:27   *Non quo sit ullum impedimentum praeter inextricabilem difficultatem,* id est
W46:1-2   iuxta hoc, quod non possit extricari prae difficultate. Quasi: non ideo quod
haec difficultas mihi sit inextricabilis, sed ideo est impedimentum. Quia hoc
sermone instituto, scilicet phisicae, non possem peruenire *ad rei,* id est
initiorum, *explanationem,* quae pertinet ad epopticam disputationem. Vel sic   85
legunt quidam: nihil dicam de initiis, scilicet de elementis, *praeter inextricabi-*
lem difficultatem, id est praeter hylen. Quasi: non sic agam de aliis, ut taceam
de hyle, quae potest dici difficultas inextricabilis, quia uix uel non potest
diffiniri quid sit hyle.

W46:2-3   *Neque igitur.* Et quia sic instituto sermone, impossibile est, *igitur nec uos*   90
expectetis id, nec ego facere possum phisice agendo.

d W46:5   *In rebus imaginariis.* Nam ut sensilis est imago intelligibilis, ita rationes
de eo datae sunt imaginariae, quantum ad rationes intelligibiles *singulorum*
W46:7   per partes, *uniuersorum* in toto.

W46:7-8   *Deum ergo.* Laborat Plato ut instruat nos ad religionem, scilicet ut, cum   95
quid difficile incepturi sumus, deum *auxiliatorem* inuocemus, sicut facit
ingrediens procellas, *ante auspicium dictionis,* id est antequam incipiat. Ideo
ponit auspicium, quia sicut quod futurum est in auibus conspicitur, ita ipse
praeuiderat in animo quae dicturus erat.

---

73 erat *om. O   post* elementa] uel *add. P   74* quaereretur] quaererent *O   75*
quaereretur] quaererent *O   77* epopticam] epogticam *D M O P T*: *scrips.*: *cf. Cal., Comm.*
*272 (W277:5)   disputationem] dispositionem M   79 est om. O   informent] in formis
M: informet P   81 quo] quod O   82 quod¹ om. O   post extricari] et add. M   84
post sermone] ita suppl. T   85 explanationem] exempla P T   epopticam] epogticam
D M O P T: scrips.: cf. Cal., Comm. 272 (W277:5)   86 scilicet] sed O   de² om. T   87
difficultatem om. T   praeter om. O   88 dici om. P   90 quia om. O   nec] neque
T   91 facere] facile T   92 imaginariis] magnis D P   92-93 ita...intelligibiles hom.
D   95 ad om. O   95-96 cum quid] quod D   97 id est om. T   98 conspicitur]
conspicimus T   99 praeuiderat] praeuidebat M: praeuideat T*

---

77 epoptica disputatio] cf. Cal., *Comm.* 272 (W277:5-8), 127 (W170:10); uide den Boeft,
Calcidius on Demons, pp. 12-13.   85 Cf. 8.77 supra.   95-96 Cf. Cal., *Comm.* 273
(W277:10-11).

48e　W46:10-11　*Erit ergo initium tale*, quale dicam. *Eadem* res, id est imaginaria, scilicet　100
sensilis mundus, *magnificentius diuidetur*, id est in ampliori diuisione pone-
tur.

W46:11　　*Etenim.* Vere in ampliori, quia cum superius in bipertita, modo ponitur in
tripertita.

W46:15　　Mundum hunc uocat *secundae generationis*, non quod sit alius mundus　105
primae generationis, sed hic mundus, cum sit generatus, dicitur secundus in
dignitate.

49a　　　　*At uero tercium*, id est hylen, *minime diuisimus*, id est non possumus in
diuisione et ponuntur haec tria modo in diuisione: quod est aliud intelligibilis
mundus, aliud sensilis, aliud hyle.　　　　　　　　　　　　　　　　　110

W46:16-18　*At nunc.* Quantum ad superiorem tractatum sufficiebant superius duo
membra in diuisione, sed *nunc ratio impositura necessitatem*, id est ut de hyle
necessario tractetur. Philosophi est enim cuncta quae ad causam pertinent
diligenter inuestigare. *Videtur ire obuiam*, id est *manum conserere*: per simile
loquitur. *Aduersum fraudem*, id est hylen, *inexpugnabilem*, id est incompre-　115
hensibilem, *omni ratione* et ideo *omni eloquio.* Hylen ideo uocat fraudem,
quia nec sensu concipi secundum se nec uera ratione potest. Sensus enim non
credit rem incorpoream, cum uideat eam coloratam. Ratio non credit eam
corpoream, cum secundum propriam naturam nullam in ea inueniat corporum qualitatem. Et ideo uocat eam *inuolutam crassis tenebris*, id est magna　120
obscuritate.

W46:18-19　*Quam igitur.* Quia nec sensu nec ratione comprehenditur, *quam igitur etc.*
Vim hyles accipimus: quod omnes formas corporum in se recipiat, *naturam*
quod nullam habeat propriam.

W46:19-20　Et *est receptaculum omnium quae* in ea *gignuntur*, scilicet corporum, quia　125
formas superuenientes <recipit>, ut exinde fiant corpora.

W46:20　　*Atque hoc*, id est quod sit receptaculum et nutricula uerum est. Hic haerent
qui dicunt hylen esse materiam in qua, non ex qua, fiant corpora, sed frustra.

---

101 diuisione] diuinatione *O*　　101-102 ponetur] summetur *T*　　103 ponitur *om. O*
105 quod] quia *M*　　　mundus *om. D*　　107 dignitate] dignitatem *D*　　108 At] Atque
D　　possumus] ponimus *O*: posuimus *P T*　　*post* possumus] id est *add. D*　　109
diuisione] diuinatione *M*　　ponuntur] praeponuntur *O*　　modo in] in tali *T*　　quod] quia
T　　aliud] alius *T*　　110 aliud[1]] alius *T*　　111 nunc] uero *T*　　113 tractetur] tractatur
T　　Philosophi] Phisici *O*　　enim *om. O*　　cuncta] cum cuncta *M*: coniuncta *T*　　114
id est] idem *D P*　　118 *post* credit] esse *add. M P T*　　119-120 corporum] corporeum
M　　123 corporum] corporeas *T*　　naturam] natura *O*　　124 habeat] habet *D M T*
126 <recipit>] *scrips.*　　127-128 Atque...corpora *hom. P*　　127-128 uerum...mate-
riam *om. D*　　127 uerum] uera *O*　　128 qui] quidam *O*　　dicunt] dicentes *O*　　*post*
in qua] fiant *add. T*

103-104 Vide *Timaeus* 48e-49a (W46:11-16).　　113-114 Cf. Cal., *Comm.* 274 (W278:12).
127-128 Stoici: cf. Cal., *Comm.* 321 (W317:6-9).

Rectius enim aes dicitur nutrire formas quas recipit, ut fiat statua, uel etiam ipsam statuam, quam id in quo fabricatur statua. Sic et hyle.   130

49b W46:21-23 *Est tamen.* Dico *apertius* inde *dicendum,* sed *tamen arduum est* aperte dicere de ea, et ideo *magis, quod necesse est praeconfundi aciem mentis* loquendo *de igne* et *ceteris materiis,* id est de igneo et ceteris, *qui,* id est quomodo, *magis aquam etc.* Bene dicit praeconfundi, quia, quando uolumus ascendere ad hylen, in natura sua acceptam, oportet nos dicere de his   135
quattuor elementis concretis, in quorum erroribus praeconfunditur mens nostra. Cum unumquodque istorum ex quattuor puris elementis constet, semper tamen ex proximiori sibi nomen defendit, scilicet dicitur ignis in quo plus est de igne quam de ceteris. Vel praeconfunditur, dum putat: haec esse uera, quae non sunt uera elementa, cum permisceantur, ut ipse docet.   140

49c W46:27   *Eadem* glacies *ignita,* id est igne soluta, *et diffluens,* quia per nebulas
W47:1   transit in aerem, per aerem in ignem, et retrograde redit in terram.

W47:5-6 *Atque ita circuitu,* id est texendo et retexendo, scilicet transeundo in alia elementa, *fomentaque generationis,* quia unum ex alio generatur, *corporibus sibi inuicem mutuantibus,* scilicet iterum in se redeundo.   145

49d W47:8   *Quapropter,* id est quia extra puram essentiam accepta, sic permutantur.
W47:12   *Denique.* Quia nullam habent stabilitatem, non sunt digna designari pronominibus, quorum est meram substantiam significare in propria ui.

49e W47:13-14 *Fugiunt enim.* Vere non sunt designanda pronominibus, quia *nec expectant eam appellationem,* ad quam primo inuenta sunt pronomina. '*Hoc*' dicit ad   150
exprimendam eorum permutationem.

W47:14-15 *Igitur ignem.* Quia hoc igneum non est uerus ignis, propter permixtionem

129 quas *om. T*   129-130 uel...statua *hom. D*   129-130 uel etiam ipsam statuam *om.*
O   130 Sic et] Sicut *O*   131 tamen¹] enim *P*   *post* tamen¹] arduum *suppl. T*
arduum est] et *T*   132 quod] quam *M P*: quid *O*   133 id est¹ *om. O*   de igneo
et ceteris *om. O*   qui] quid *M*   134 aquam] aqua *D O P*: ad qua *M*   etc.] et *O*   135
nos] non omnes *O*   136 concretis] conexis *D*: et certis *T*   137 *post* Cum] in *add. T*
post istorum] mundi materiarum *add. T*   138 ex proximiori] proximioris *T*
scilicet] sed *O*   140 *post* uera] haec *add. O*   142 per aerem in ignem *om. O*
..trograde *def. T: cod. T usque ad finem scissus est*   143 circuitu *om. O T*   id est *om.*
T   144 ..ementa *def. T*   145-146 ...undo Qua...*def. T*   146 permutantur] permutatur
O   147 Quia *om. O*   nullam *def. T*   148 quorum] que *T*   ...stantiam significare
def. T   149 Fugiunt] Fugit *O*   150 ad quam primo *def. T*   primo] primum *P*
dicit] dixit *T*   151 exprimendam] explanendam *T*   permutationem] mutationem *T*
152 ignem...hoc *def. T*   Quia *om. M*   propter *om. O*

129-130 Cf. Boethius, *De trinitate* 2 (ed. Peiper, pp. 152.20-153.1).   147-148 Cf.
Priscianus, *Institutiones grammaticae* 12.4.15 (ed. Hertz, *Grammatici Latini* 3:585-586):
"Solam enim substantiam, non etiam qualitatem significant pronomina, quantum est in ipsius
prolatione uocis."; Cal., *Comm.* 325 (W320:8-13).

et instabilitatem, igitur ille ignis uerus putandus est *qui idem est et omne*, quasi hoc ipsum dico de omnibus elementis.

W47:16 *At uero*. Haec mutabilia non sunt designanda pronominibus, sed sola hyle 155 in qua soluuntur, *singula* corpora *pereuntia* secundum uariationem formarum. Quae ideo digna est designari pronominibus, quia semper eadem in sui natura consistit, nec ullam propriam habet qualitatem. Vel potest hoc referri ad pura elementa.

50a W47:19 *Porro*. Hyle, quia non recipit qualitatem semperque eadem est, digna est 160 designari pronominibus. *Porro*. Quodcumque *recipit qualitatem*, licet actu est immutabile, ut purus ignis et cetera pura, *uel etiam potest uerti in contrarias qualitates*, ut igneum et reliqua mixta, non puto designanda pronominibus. Vel secundum quod agetur de puris elementis '*illud*', sed *etiam uerti potest etc.* determinatio erit recipientium qualitatem. 165

W47:21 *Sed opinor*. Hoc dictum est de hyle, quod ipsa sola digna sit pronominibus designari. *Sed opinor* adhuc *apertius de eodem* dicendum.

W47:22 *Si quis enim*. Vere apertius, quia hoc modo, scilicet ostendendo quod, cum in hyle omnes formae ueniant, nulla est eius propria. Et ad hoc praemittit similitudinem de auro, scilicet quod, cum diuersae formae permutentur in eo, 170 W47:22-25 nulla potest dici eius propria. Et hoc est: *si quis cunctas formas et figuras*, id est cuncta corpora formata, *ex eadem materia sine intermissione reformet* 50b *in alias* formas; *tunc, si quis quaerat* ipsius formam, nulla potest *responderi* propria, sed sola materia. Vel interroganti de quolibet formato quid sit, non W48:1 respondebitur forma, sed materia. Chilinder est rotundae formae. 175

---

153 .gnis...putand..*def. T* *post* uerus] est *add. D* qui] quia *T* et omne] oratione *M* *post* omne] etc. *add. T* 154 hoc *om. T* ipsum] idem *P T* 155 Haec...sunt *def. T* *post* Haec] per *add. O* 156 pereuntia...uariationem *def. T* secundum] scilicet *M* 157 digna est] digna sunt *M*: *om. T* *post* pronominibus] dicitur *add. T* 157-158 .ui...habet *def. T* 159-160 ...menta...qualitat..*def. T* 161 designari *om. T* ...que...est *def. T* actu] actum *O* est *om. P* 162 immutabile] immutabilem *D P* et cetera] ceteraque *T* 162-163 uel...et *def. T* 163 reliqua] cetera *O T* 163-164 ...minibus...illud *def. T* 164 quod agetur] quod agitur *O*: agetur *P* 164-165 illud...qualitatem *in marg. sinist. M* 164 sed] secundum *O* uerti] conuerti *O* 165-166 ..cipientium...est *def. T* 167 designari...dicendum *def. T* 168-169 ostendendo...eius *def. T* 168 scilicet] *om. D*: apertius scilicet *T* quod] quia *D*: eo quod *P* 169 in *om. P* 170 auro...eo *def. T* cum] eum *D* 171-172 est...ex *def. T* 172-173 ...sione...potest *def. T* 172 intermissione] *lac. M* 174-175 materia...respondebitur *def. T* 175 respondebitur] responditur debita *O* *post* sed] sola *add. M* Chilinder...rotundae *def. T*

155-159 Cf. Bernardus Carnotensis: vide Ioannes Saresberiensis, *Metalogicon* 4.35 (ed. Webb, p. 205.24-27):

Non dico esse quod est, gemina quod parte coactum
   materie formam continet implicitam;
sed dico esse quod est, una quod constat earum;
   hoc uocat Idean, *illud* Acheus ilen.

8. DE PRIMORDIALI MATERIA   225

W48:2   *Eadem.* Adaptat praedictam similitudinem ipsi materiae, scilicet hyle, quam dicit recipere corpora cum recipit formas, quae ibi conficiunt corpora. Si insistis praedictam similitudinem, patet hylen esse materiam ex qua fiunt corpora.

W48:3   *Haec quippe.* Vere est similis ratio, quia *haec* hyle *minime recedit ex* 180 *propria conditione*, id est secundum se nullam habet formam.

W48:4   *Recipit enim.* Vere non recedit, quia, cum omnes formas recipiat, *ipsa informis remanet*, secundum propriam naturam, *intra gremium* hyles corpora formantur, et ibi ea *recipiuntur* per solas formas.

W48:5-6   *Estque usus etc.* Haec similitudo expressior est quam praedicta, cum sicut 185 cera est quiddam molle, sic et hyle quasi molle. Vel est omnino alia, cum in illa ageretur de interrogatione, hic nihil.

50c W48:8-9   *Quae uero ingrediuntur*, id est ipsa corpora, *mutant formas*, et ideo modo alia et alia apparent uel qualitates quae ingrediuntur mutant formas, id est se ipsas accendendo et recendendo.   190

W48:9-10   *Eademque quae introeunt et egrediuntur*, id est ipsae formae, *simulacra sunt* idearum quae uerum esse habent. *Formata*, id est procedentes ab illis, *miro modo*, sicut ostendemus, sed in parte non translata.

W48:12   *At uero* dixi quod ostendemus quomodo sint inde formata, sed *nunc* prius *trinum genus*, id est tres maneriae rerum sumendae sunt: *animo*, scilicet res 195 formata, quae est corpus, informis materia, scilicet hyle, et idea, quae semper manet eadem in mente diuina.

0d W48:14-16   *Decet ergo.* Quia posita sunt tria diuidentia, igitur doceamus quibus obtineant *similitudinem* singula: hyle obtinet uicem *matris*, at uero *unde obuenit*, id est archetipus mundus, uicem *patris*, non quod ideae commiscean- 200

---

176 Adaptat...hyle *def. T*   materiae] materiei *O*   177 corpora[1] *om. O*   177-178 corpora[1]...insistis *def. T*   177 conficiunt] consistunt *O*   178 praedictam similitudinem] praedicta similitudine *O*   178-180 ...tudinem...simili. *def. T*   180 *post* haec[2]] id est *add. O*   180-182 minime...enim *def. T*   182-183 ..cedit...propriam *def. T*   183-185 gremium...Estque *def. T*   184 *post* solas] scilicet *M*   185-186 Haec...quiddam *def. T*   186-187 sic...interrog... *def. T*   186 sic *om. M*   molle] hile *P*   187 hic *om. T*   188-189 Quae...se *def. T*   188 Quae] Quo *D O*   189 apparent] apparet *D*   190-192 ..cedendo et recedendo...sunt *def. T*   192-193 ..rum...ost... *def. T*   193-194 ...mus...for... *def. T*   194-196 .unc...for... *def. T*   194 prius] primum *D*   195 maneriae] materie *O*   196-197 est...mente *def. T*   196 scilicet *om. P*   197 in mente] manente *O*   diuina] dei *P*   198-200 Decet...uicem *def. T*   198 Decet] Docet *D*   diuidentia] diuidenda *O*   199 uero *om. D M P*   200 mundus *om. P*   200-201 non...natiuae *def. T*

---

193 Cf. Cal., *Comm.* 330 (W324:7-8).   195-197 Cf. Cal., *Comm.* 330 (W324:7-18). 195 maneriae] cf. Ioannes Saresberiensis, *Metalogicon* 2.17 (ed. Webb, p. 95.15-18); *Glose Willelmi de Conchis super Platonem* (ed. Jeauneau, p. 149 n.b).

tur hyle in efficientia sensilis, sed natiuae formae, quae sunt imagines
idearum. *Illi uero etc.*, id est sensili mundo danda est comparatio *prolis.*

W48:17   *Simul.* Hic agit contra Stoicos uolentes hylen unam propriam habere
formam, cui superuenirent aliae. Quod ostendit Plato non esse, quia cum
omnes recipiat formas, aliqua de superuenientibus esset illi uni formae similis,   205
quod non potest esse, cum id quod substernitur debeat esse dissimile ei cui
substernitur, sicut in pictura color qui substernitur, quem uocat infectionem,
dissimilis est omnibus superuenientibus. Et hoc est: *simul,* id est cum
praedictis de hyle, hoc *intelligendum* de ipsa, quod cum omnium formas
recipiat unam propriam non habet, nisi informitatem ei demus, quod est ibi: 210
nisi subiecto prius informi etc. Vel sic: non habet hyle unam propriam faciem,
nisi subiecto informi hoc est, sed potius dicatur informe gremium *corporum.*

50e   W48:21-22   *Etenim.* Vere non habet unam formam, quia si haberet unam, cum omnium
sit capax, hoc supple: *obueniet etc.*, id est contrarietas inter aliquam superuenientium et prius habitam formam occurreret. Et cum hoc sit, *discordabit etc.*,   215
quia duo contraria simul non reperiuntur. Cum deberet dicere: si unam
haberet, ponit aequipollentem, *si erit simile alicuius* superuenientium. Omnis
enim forma alicui debet esse simile. Vel probat id quod substernitur debere
esse *dissimile* omnibus superuenientibus, quia *si erit simile etc.*, discordabit
etc., quia duo similia in eodem concordare non possunt, ut album super   220
album non bene sedet. *Et<enim> cum quid obueniet dissimile,* id est
contrarium, prius habito, *discordabit etc.*

W48:23-25   *Ex quo.* Quia contrarietas proueniret uel quia gemina similitudo discorda-
ret, si una esset propria forma hyles, *ex quo fit, ut nullam habeat propriam.*

W49:1-3   *Vt qui.* Alia similitudo in medicina, quod nulla est propria forma hyles; *et*   225
qui materiis, item alia.

201-216 imagines...contraria *def. T*   202 etc. *om. P*   danda] data *P*   203 Simul. Hic]
Similis igitur *O*   204 superuenirent] superueniant *P*   206 esse *om. P*   208 simul]
similis *O*   209 quod] quia *M: om. O*   210 quod] quae *O*   211 *post* nisi] in *add. O*
hyle *om. P*   212 *post* informi] etc. *add. D*   213 *post*   unam] et *add. P*: formam *add. O*
cum *om. P*   214 contrarietas] contrarietates *P*   215 occurreret] occurret *M O*
216 reperiuntur] ceperunt *T*   216-217 Cum...simile *def. T*   217-432 ...tium...Prop-
terea... *def. T*   218 id] istud *O*   219 simile] dissimile *P*   221 Et<enim>] etiam *D*
M P: Et *O: scrips.: cf. W48:21*   222 contrarium] contrario *O*   223 proueniret] proueniet
P   similitudo] dissimilitudo *M*   225 quod] quia *M*

201-202 Cf. Ioannes Saresberiensis, *Metalogicon* 4.35 (ed. Webb, p. 205.15-19): "Ideas
tamen, quas post Deum primas essentias ponit, negat in seipsis materie admisceri aut aliquem
sortiri motum; sed ex his forme prodeunt natiue, scilicet imagines exemplarium, quas natura
rebus singulis concreauit."   203-204 Cf. Cal., *Comm.* 289-294 (W293-297).

<table>
<tr><td>1a W49:5-7</td><td></td></tr>
</table>

1a W49:5-7   *Sic ei*, id est hyle, quae *insignietur formis*, id est cui imprimuntur formae *omnium rerum*. *Nulla est tribuenda propria species*, quia *falsa opinione* tribuerentur, *figuris aeternae uitae*, id est idearum quae aeternaliter consistunt. Vocat hic formas quae in ipsa hyle fiunt, ubi, licet quaedam pereant, 230 tamen succedendo semper aliqua inueniuntur. Et ideo dicit eas manere *per saecula* uel propter archetipas quarum sunt imagines. Hoc dicit.

W49:7   *Ideoque*. Quia nullam habet propriam formam, igitur nec ignis nec terra. Vel quia sola hyle mater est omnium corporum, ideo nullum corporeum proprie dicitur mater.   235

W49:10-14   *Sed inuisibilem* appellamus eam positam *inter nullam et aliquam substantiam*. Vel nihil praedictorum appellandum dico esse matrem, *sed speciem*, id est naturam, *inuisibilem*. Corrigit quod dixit: *speciem et informem*, illam in quam speciem appellamus matrem, eam dico existentem *inter nullam etc.* Nulla non est, quia per adiunctionem formarum aliqua fit; aliqua non est, quia 240 secundum se formata non est, quod aperit cum subdit: *nec plane intelligibilem etc.* Plane intelligibilis non est, quia fit corpus; plane sensibilis non est, cum non sit corpus secundum se, sed talis est *quae ex his quae in ea commutantur*, id est ex corporibus intelligatur. Per corpora enim ista quodam modo sentitur et intelligitur hyle, sicut per indiuiduum res uniuersalis.   245

W49:14-15   *Ignis*. Docet quae in ipsa hyle commutentur, scilicet haec quattuor elementaria, quae quasi partes hyles considerantur. Et hoc est: *ignita pars hyles est ignis*. Hoc est hyle, si igniatur, id est afficiatur formis huius ignei fit ignis, id est igneum; si humectetur, fit aqua, id est aquaticum. *Terra quoque*, id est terreum, *et aer*, id est aerium, sunt partes hyles, *si forte* hyle *in se recipit* 250 *simulacra etc.* Simulacra horum accipit formas, quae, uenientes in hylen, procreant haec uisibilia quae proprie dicuntur simulacra idearum. Vel etiam haec uisibilia quattuor uocat simulacra archetiporum, quae non permutantur, cum ipsa permutentur in hyle. Videtur uelle Calcidius purum ignem et cetera

W49:16

---

227 insignietur] insignitur *P*   228 tribuenda *om. O*   229 figuris] figuras *M O P* 229-230 consistunt] consistit *M*   230 pereant] pereunt *O*   231 tamen *om. O* *post* succedendo] tum aliqua *add. O*   aliqua] aliquando *D*   Et ideo] etiam *O*   232 propter] per *O*   233 Quia *om. M*   *post* ignis] est *add. P*   235 proprie dicitur mater] dicit *O*   237-239 sed...matrem *in marg. dext. M*   237-239 id est...speciem *in marg. sinist. O*   238 inuisibilem] non usum *O*   239 quam speciem] qua specie *O*   241 aperit] ait *O*   intelligibilem *om. O*   242 sensibilis] sensilis *D*   244-245 intelligatur...et *hom. O*   245 hyle] hilen *D P*   246 Docet quae in ipsa hyle commutentur] quia ipsa commutentur *O*   commutentur] permutentur *D*   247 elementaria] elementa *O* 247-248 considerantur...Hoc est *om. O*   248 *post* hyles] id *add. D*   249 id est²] in *M*   251 simulacra *om. O*   253 haec *om. O*

254-256 Cf. Cal., *Comm.* 272 (W276:14-277:3), 337 (W330:2-6).

pura esse archetipa horum commixtorum, ignei scilicet et aliorum, et ipsum   255
purum ignem fieri ex intelligibili specie et hyle.

Sed debemus intelligere nec ea proprie archetipa dici, sed propter solam
puritatem et impermutabilitatem, ut forma Socratis dicitur idea ipsius, et
ipsum purum ignem ex hyle et natiua forma procreari. Nota secundum
quosdam hylen totam esse in singulis elementis, non per partes diuisam ad   260
modum uniuersalium rerum. Vnde dicit eam expertem, id est partibus
carentem, in suo statu attentam, sicut uniuersalia in uniuersali statu carent
partibus in quantitate.

Sed potest quaeri tunc quid sit, substantia scilicet an accidens? Patet non
esse accidens, cum sit materia corporum. Nec substantia uidetur esse, quia   265
nec generalissima, nec corpus, nec incorporeum. Generalissima non est, cum
non sit materia animae. Incorporeum non est, cum fiat corpus. Nec corpus
est, cum careat corporeitate, quia omnium forma. Item rem praedicamenta-
lem oportet eam esse, cum secundum Aristotelem omnium rerum multitudo
in decem locetur praedicamentis. Hyle uero res sit, sed praedicamentalis non   270
uidetur esse, cum nec singularis, nec communis. Singularis non est, quia
eodem tempore tota est in diuersis corporibus, utpote in Socratis corpore
tota, et in Platonis, et in similibus. Vniuersalis non est, cum nullum habeat
indiuiduum per quod actu existat. Ignis enim purus uel concretus, qui fit ex
ea, non est eius indiuiduum, et sic de aliis.   275

Ad quod r<espondendum>: hyle, quidem ante susceptionem etiam
natiuarum attenta, corpus est, quia est affecta corporeitate, ut forma substan-
tiali. Cum ergo auctoritas dicat eam esse informem et neget esse corpus, sic
accipe. Informis est, quia caret formis quae faciant eam sensibilem et quae
distribuant eam in elementa, quemadmodum quodlibet uniuersale dicitur   280
informe relatum ad inferiora, cum careat formis quibus redigitur in ea. Habet
tamen unumquodque formam uel accidentalem uel etiam substantialem. Ita

---

255 commixtorum] mixtorum *O*   256 purum *om. O*   et] id est *O*   257 proprie *om.*
P   258 forma] imago *M*   264 sit *om. D*   scilicet *om. O*   266 nec[1] *om. P*
266-267 cum non] cum *P*   268 omnium] omni *M P*   *post* forma] est *add. O*
270 locetur *om. O*   *post* praedicamentis] sit *add. O*   Hyle] Hiles *P*   praedicamentalis non] praedicamentaliter *P*   273 in similibus] similibus *O*   est *om. O*   274 uel]
et *O*   275 eius *om. O*   282 unumquodque] unamquamque *O*   uel[1] *om. M*   etiam
om. O

259-260 Cf. Cal., *Comm.* 281 (W285).   261 Vide *Timaeus* 51b (W49:15) et 53b
(W51:21).   264 Cf. Boethius, *In categorias Aristotelis* 1 (PL 64:170B1-2).   268-270 Cf.
Aristoteles, *Categoriae. Translatio Boethii* (ed. Minio-Paluello); Boethius, *In Isagoge Porphy-
rii. Editio secunda* 1.4 (ed. Brandt, pp. 143-146); Boethius, *De trinitate* 4 (ed. Peiper, p.
156.1-4); Cal., *Comm.* 226 (W241:10-14), 319 (W315:5-6).   278-279 Cf. Augustinus,
Confessiones 12.6 (ed. L. Verheijen, in *Corpus Christianorum: Series latina* 27, pp. 218-219).

hyle multis afficitur formis, nec distribuentibus eam, nec sensibilem facienti-
bus. Propter quod etiam dicitur non esse corpus, quia non est habilem ut
sentiatur. Cum autem sit corpus, erit species inanimati corporis contenta uno 285
indiuiduo, non excedenti legem aliorum indiuiduorum. Vel erit indiuiduum
solum sub una specie, excedens naturam aliorum in hoc quod eodem
tempore totum est in diuersis. Vel potest dici hylen talem essentiam esse,
quae per se quidem subsistat, sed praedicamentalis et dialecticae considera-
tionis immunem, scilicet nec substantiam uniuersalem nec indiuidualem 290
praedicamentaliter esse. Nec ideo minus omnium rerum praedicamentalium
intellige multitudinem in decem praedicamentis locari. Quod autem de
praedicamentalibus, id est uniuersalibus et indiuiduis, illud intelligendum sit
palam est, cum sint aliae res, ut homo mixtus ex anima et corpore, et similes
non habentes locum in praedicamentis, nisi forte per partes; sic et hyle habeat 295
ibi locum per ea quae constituit. Videtur tamen uelle Calcidius hylen esse in
omnibus praedicamentis diuersis respectibus, et hoc secundum Platonis
sententiam. Sed tunc quaereretur, sicut prius, an sit uniuersalis an singularis
res? Quorum neutrum uidetur esse.

Alii autem dicunt hylen esse quasi coagulatum globum cerae, qui sectus in 300
partes in diuersa transit corpora. Hyle enim, secundum hos, per partes
scinditur primo susceptione natiuarum formarum, et pars eius fit ignis, pars
terra, etc. Deinde per alias formas in alia et alia minuitur corpora. Sed
opponitur quod dictum est: eam carere partibus. Ad quod r<esponden-
dum>: partes quidem non habet in suo statu actualiter, cum confusum et 305
indiscretum quiddam sit, sed suscipere apta est formas per quas particulatim
diuiditur, et secundum hoc est quiddam indiuiduum sub quadam specie
inanimati corporis. Rursus secundum illos qui dicunt hylen esse materiam in
qua, non ex qua, fiant corpora, difficile est exprimere quid sit, nisi forte
iudicetur de ea secundum aliquem praedictum modum. 310

W49:17-18 *Estne.* Dixit quod tractatus esset instituendus de illis archetipis, et ecce sub
inquisitione ingreditur sic: an est solus noster ignis quem uidemus, an est
alius separatus ab illo. *Incommunicabilis,* id est qui nec a nobis uideatur nec

---

283 sensibilem] sensilem *O*   284 est *om. O*   285 inanimati] animati *P*   286 Vel] Et
M   287 *post* quod] in *add. O*   290 substantiam] substantialem *O*   294 ex] et ex *M*:
cum *O*   296 esse *om. P*   298 quaereretur] quaereretur *O*   299 neutrum *om. P*   esse
om. O   300 hylen *om. M*   301 in diuersa] diuersa *D*: indiuisa *O*   transit] trahit *O*
302-303 pars terra etc.] terra *D*   303 formas *om. O*   309 forte *om. M O P*   312
sic *om. O*   solus *om. M*   *post* noster] enim *add. M*   313 illo] illa *O*

296-298 Cf. Cal., *Comm.* 319 (W314-315).   300-301 Stoici: cf. Cal., *Comm.* 292
(W294-295), 289-291 (W293-294), 315 (W312).   308-309 Stoici: cf. Cal., *Comm.* 289
(W294:1-5), 321 (W317:6-9).

cuiquam corpori commisceatur, qualis est ille purus archetipus qui semper in
mente dei consistit. *Item ceterae species*, id est ideae terrae et aliorum, non   315
quod sint species praedicabiles, sed quarum similitudine consistant haec
sensibilia.

W49:23-24   *Quod quidem*, scilicet alia esse praeter haec quae uidemus, nec indiscus-
sum *relinqui placet, nec* multa uerba sunt apponenda, licet natura rerum, quae
est ampla, prolixum exigat tractatum.   320

51d W49:25   *At uero.* Non prolixe, sed compendiose et probabiliter inde disseram, quia
si quis etc.

W49:26   *Ipse igitur.* Quia discuti placet et operae pretium est, igitur meam ponam
sententiam.

W50:1   *Si intellectus.* Probat etiam praeter sensibilia esse intelligibilia hoc modo.   325
Si intellectus et opinio diuersae potentiae animae sunt, necesse est ea, quae
W50:2-3   istis comprehenduntur, esse diuersa. Et hoc est: *necesse est haec ipsa*, id est
intelligibilia, *per semet esse*, id est sine sensibilibus. Et hoc est quod subdit:
intellectu potius quam sensibus assequenda. Opinionem dicit, quam sumimus
ex persuasione sensuum. Quae, licet uera sit, sine ratione est et disciplina, nec   330
praestans rationem cur sic opinetur et quandoque falsis persuasionibus
mutatur. Confirmata tamen opinio fit ratio et firmata ratio fit intellectus.
Diuidit hic Calcidius intellectum in duo, scilicet in scientiam uel sapientiam
et recordationem. Scientiam uel sapientiam dicit de altis, ut de deo et ideis;
recordationem de his quae praeceptis artificialibus percipiuntur.   335
Opinionem quoque in duo diuidit: in credulitatem et aestimationem.
Credulitas de sensilibus, quae scilicet aliquo sensu percipiuntur; aestimatio
de fictis et imaginariis, et haec omnia mente discernimus.

51e W50:5-6   *Quippe.* Vere distant, quia in istis quod *alterum*, id est intellectum, *insinuet
nobis doctrina*, id est scientia intelligibilium; *alterum*, scilicet opinionem   340
insinuat persuasio sensuum. Alia differentia, cum dicit *alterum*, id est intellectus, *semper* est *cum uera* et certa *ratione*, quia numquam ratio de intelligibi-

---

314 commisceatur] misceatur *O*   archetipus *om. D*   315 Item] uere *O*   315-316 non
quod] numquam *M*   317 sensibilia] sensilia *O*   318 Quod] Quae *D*   haec *om. O*
319 natura] naturam *M*   323 igitur] ergo *O*   meam] in ea *D*   326 ea *om. O*   329
assequenda *om. O*   331 quandoque] quamquam *O*   332 mutatur] permutatur *O*   et
firmata ratio *om. O*   firmata] confirmata *D*   333 intellectum *om. O*   scientiam]
sententiam *D*   334 dicit *om. P*   altis] aliis *P*   post et²] de *add. P*   336-337
Opinionem...percipiuntur *in marg. dext. M*   336 aestimationem] existimationem *O*   337
aliquo] alio *M*   341 Alia] Altera *P*

329-330 Cf. Cal., *Comm.* 340 (W333:5-8).   333-338 Cf. Cal., *Comm.* 342
(W334:20-335:7).

libus permutatur. *Alterum*, id est opinio *sine ratione* certa, *item* differentia, *alterum*, id est intellectus, *nulla persuasione transducibile*, quia nulla persuasio diuertit intellectum a sua certa consideratione et ratione, *alterum*, id est 345 opinio, *deriuabile*, id est multis persuasionibus commutabile.

W50:9   *Quid quod.* Quarta differentia.

W50:10   *Quod cum ita sit*, scilicet quia intelligibilia semper sunt cum uera ratione, nec permutantur, *fatendum est esse speciem*, proprie intelligibilem, *semotam etc.* Et hic accipiuntur pura archetipa, quae consistunt in mente dei.   350

W50:14-15   *Porro quod ab hoc est secundum* ut corpus *sensile est etc.* Quidam hoc secundum uocant natiuas formas, quae dicuntur sensiles, quia ad hoc ducunt hylen, ut possit sentiri, et sustentabiles, quia ab hyle sustentantur.

W50:16-18   *Tercium genus est loci*, id est hyle quae dicitur locus, quia in eam descendunt natiuae formae, quibus recedentibus, hyle non interit. Sed ipsa 355 per se *sine sensu tangentis* est, cum sit incerta et infinita. Omne uero quod sentitur certum sit et finitum, *tangitur* non per se, sed per corpus, et ideo non sentitur a tangente proprie. *Adulterina* dicit, quia nec proprie corpus est, nec incorporeum. Vel *tangitur*, id est uidetur tangi, dum eius discernuntur colores, ut in tenebris de re aliquid opinamur, cum nihil uideamus.   360

W50:19   *Patimur quod somniantes*, id est decipimur, sicut illi putantes illam incorpoream habere determinatum locum, cum sine loco nihil possit sentiri.

W50:20   *Putamus enim.* Vere patimur quod somniantes, scilicet incertitudinem, quia nec sensu nec ratione eam comprehendimus.

W50:21   *Porro.* Quasi quis diceret: substantia quidem est sine sede et loco. Ad hoc 365 iste: *porro etc.* Nota hylen, id est siluam, nec intelligibile quid esse, ut ideae sunt, nec opinabile, ut natiuae, sed suspicabile. Suspicio uero est adulterina ratio.

W50:22   *Ob quam deprauationem*, id est quia non credimus esse quod in loco non est, *et alias consanguineas* deprauationes, id est quae ex sensibus ueniunt, 370 non *consistimus mente, in reputatione*, nedum in intelligentia, *uere existentis naturae*, id est hyles, quae uere existit, quia secundum propriam naturam

---

343-345 id...alterum *hom.* O   348-349 Quod...esse *om.* O   349 *post* speciem] id est *add.* M O   351 ab] ad O   352 sensiles] sensibiles D M P   353 sustentantur] sustentatur O P   354 est[1] *om.* O   eam] ea D   357 finitum] infinitum D M   364 nec ratione] neque ratione D   365 quidem] quid P   366 intelligibile] intelligibilem O quid] quod D: quidem O   367 opinabile] opinabilem O   suspicabile] suspicabilem O   *post* suspicabile] est *add.* P   369 Ob quam deprauationem] Obliqua O   371 consistimus] consistunt D M O P: *scrips.: cf.* W50:24   372 quia] quae P

351-353 Cf. Cal., *Comm.* 344 (W336:5-7).   359-360 Cf. Cal., *Comm.* 345 (W337:16-338:3).   365 Cf. Cal., *Comm.* 348 (W339:14-15).   366-368 Cf. Cal., *Comm.* 347 (W339:3-6).

eadem semper manet. *Somnia* uocat fallaciam sensuum et hyles inconstantiam.

52c W50:25-26   *Propriam nullam habet,* sed *formae,* id est formata, scilicet corpora, 375
W51:1   *transfigurantur ex alio ad aliud,* id est secundum diuersas formas. Existentem et peruigilem naturam quidam uocant hic deum et ideas, quae cum sensibus non habent societatem, quas quidam negant esse, quod accidit eis ex profundo sopore.

W51:2   *Suam substantiam nullam habet,* id est non est per se substantia in eodem 380 manens, et tamen aliquid est.

W51:3-4   *At uere.* Hyle non habet substantiam, cuius assertio firmatur plane, sed *assertio rerum uere existentium,* qua scilicet esse asseruntur, *firmatur perspicua luce rationis.* Vere existentes res accipit uel ideas uel etiam alias sic diuersas, quod unius natura non transeat in aliam, ut pura elementa. 385

W51:4-5   *Docens quidem.* Ostendit quomodo assertio confirmetur, scilicet *docens dum hoc erit aliud* ab illo et *illud aliud* ab isto, nec potest *consistere* in altero, id est quod alterius natura non transeat in aliud.

52d W51:5   *Nec simul idem unum,* id est cum uere existat aliquid unum non potest fieri duo diuersae naturae, ut lignum et aurum, quorum quodlibet, nec utrumque 390 esse potest nec mutari in alterum. Hyle uero haec omnia habet, quia cum sit unum, potest fieri duo, et cum hoc sit, potest fieri illud. Vt cum sit ignita, potest fieri aquatica, et esse utrumque.

W51:6   *Haec est mens.* Dixerat quod propriam daret sententiam, et ecce ponit eam, quasi: quidam uolunt tantum esse sensibilia, sed *mens est meae senten-* 395 *tiae,* id est meum iudicium, *haec tria fuisse existens,* id est archetipas formas, *locum,* scilicet hylen, *generationem,* id est natiuas. Et nota quoniam, licet ante constitutionem mundi omnes natiuae formae quae post in hylen uenerunt in ipsa hyle tantum potentialiter exstiterunt, illae tamen quae ipsam ad quattuor mundi elementa procreanda formabant, actualiter ante mundi exornationem 400 in ipsa constiterunt; non tamen ut carentes origine, ne sint plura principia prima quam tria: scilicet deus, hyle et ideae.

373 manet] remanet *P*   375 scilicet *om. P*   376 id est] scilicet *O*   382 uere] uero *D O*   383 qua] quas *D:* quia *O*   scilicet *om. D*   asseruntur] asserunt *O*   385 diuersas] diuisas *O*   386 quidem] quem *O*   387 illo...ab *hom. M*   389 id est *om. O* potest fieri] possit *O*   392 et...illud *om. O*   395 uolunt] dicunt *O*   tantum] tamen *O*   sed] haec *O*   meae *om. O*   397 natiuas] natiuitas *P*   licet *om. M*   399-400 exstiterunt...actualiter *om. O*   401 in ipsa *om. O*   constiterunt] constituunt *M*

376-379 Cf. Cal., *Comm.* 249 (W340:6-11).   389-391 Cf. Boethius, *Contra Eutychen et Nestorium* 6 (ed. Peiper, pp. 206.18-209.79).   394-395 Empedocles: cf. Cal., *Comm.* 350 (W341:12-13).   396-397 Cf. Cal., *Comm.* 350 (W341:14-16).   401-402 Cf. Cal., *Comm.* 307 (W308:14-309:2).

W51:7-8   *Igitur generationis.* Quia illa tria erant, ideo est mens meae sententiae,
ipsam *nutriculam*, id est hylen, quae formas in se uenientes, ut alienos filios,
nutrit, *uideri omniformem*, scilicet *modo humectatam etc.*   405

W51:9   *Passiones* accipit hic frigiditatem, siccitatem, et ceteras. *Humectatam* dicit,
non humectam, quia recipit formas per quas humectatur, nec habet eas ex se.

W51:10-12   *Quod tamen.* Licet dixerim omniformem eam uideri, tamen mens mea est
nihil eius esse aequale, id est nullam habere aequalitatem secundum formas,
ideo quod non instruatur, *priuatim*, id est secundum unumquodque elemen-   410
tum, *neque similibus uiribus neque aequatis potentiis*, sicut postea habuerunt.
Sed est mens mea fuisse eam *undique uergentem*, secundum habilitatem
suscipiendi formas, *et praeponderantem in pronum*, quia quae ibi erant uires
suas non exercebant, et quia adhuc praeponderat in pronum, secundum
terram addit, *et absonum*, id est ita quod ibi non fieret aliqua proportio, sed   415
turpis et dissona praeponderatio. Et mens mea est: *agitari* ipsam hylen,
agitari materiis ipsorum elementorum et quae elementa futura erant materiae
aliorum. Et mens mea est: ipsas *materias* sese *inuicem pulsare*, scilicet *pulsu
reciproco*, quia cum ignis natura esset supra ferri, impediebatur a terra, et cum
esset natura terrae ferri ad ima, impediebatur ab igne, et ita in ceteris. Nec   420
tamen actu ibi fuisse motum est intelligendum, sed quia contrariae res inde
processerunt, uidentur earum naturae, dum commixtae erant, inter se
pugnasse. Secundum quosdam tamen ibi erat motus, sed irrationabilis et
inordinatus, quia Plato dicit elementa ibi fluctuasse.

W51:13-14   *Ex quo fluctu*, id est quia ita reciproce et discorditer agitabantur, mens mea   425
est. Vel constat *turbatas materias in diuersa raptari et discerni a se*, secundum
eorum naturam. Ignis enim proprietas expetebat superiora, terrae uero
W51:15-17   inferiora. Bene similitudinem inducit: pistorium instrumentum accipit, ut
cribrum; machinam sub alia similitudine, ut uannum.

W51:18   *Dissimillima etc.* Hoc est duo extrema elementa, scilicet ignis et terra, licet   430
contrarias habeant qualitates omnino, tamen per duo media sociabantur.

---

403 Igitur] Qui *O*   405 uideri *om. D*   406 hic *om. M*   Humectatam] humectatem *M*
407 formas *om. O*   408 est *om. O*   413 erant] inerant *O*   414 pronum] pondere
O   418 pulsare] propulsare*M*   419-420 a...impediebatur *hom. D*   422-423
dum...tamen *loc. illegib. in P*   423 erat] erant *M O*   sed] scilicet *D P*   424 inordina-
tus] inornatus *O*   dicit...fluctuasse *loc. illegib. in P*   425 id est *om. O P*   agitabantur]
agebantur *O P*   425-426 mens...materias *loc. illegib. in P*   426 et discerni *om. O*   427
eorum] earum *M*   *post* ex] petebat...uero *loc. illegib. in P*   429 cribrum] cribum *M O*
430 Dissimillima] Dissimilia *O*   Hoc est] Haec *O*   431 habeant *om. P*   per...so-
ciabantur *loc. illegib. in P*

419-420 Cf. 7.27-28 supra.   423-424 Cf. Cal., *Comm.* 352 (W342-343).   427-428
Vide 7.27-28, 8. 419-420 supra.   429 uannus] cf. Dronke, *Fabula*, p. 22 n.2.

W51:19-20   *Proptereaque.* Quia dissimillima a se plurimum separabantur, propterea est
             mens mea ea *fuisse diuisa*, nondum tamen discreta uel exornata *ante mundi
             exornationem*, non tamen actu, secundum eorum naturam saltem.

53b W51:21   *Sed ubi.* Prius *inordinata*, ita fluctuabant, ut dictum est, *sed ubi placuit* 435
             artifici ea ordinare, *continuauit* ea, *non talia*, ante exornationem, *ut nunc
             sunt*, sed *quae praeferrent uestigia*, id est quae essent seminaria horum
             elementorum. Ipsa, dico, squalida et confusa, ut ea quibus deerat *diuina*
W52:1   *prospicientia*, id est exornatio, quasi ipsa deformitas accidebat eis pro defectu
             diuinae prouidentiae.   440

W52:1-2   *Nunc uero.* Quasi diceret: sed, postquam affuit operatrix, diuina prouiden-
             tia *sequebatur genituram etc.*

W52:3-4   *Nunc iam ordinationem*, scilicet quibus opportunitatibus inter se ordinen-
             tur et habitudinibus, *demonstrari conuenit nouo genere*, scilicet per quasdam
             proportiones arithmeticas, geometricas, armonicas, qui sunt gradus philoso- 445
53c   phiae. Dixi *nouo genere*, sed uobis cognito, qui in omni scientia perfecti estis.
             Hic innuit se uelle docere ueras et incommutabiles substantias quattuor
             principalium corporum, quod superius promiserat.

---

432 dissimillima] dissimilia *D M O*   a] apud *O*   433 mens mea] meam *T*   ea *om.*
T   434 eorum naturam *loc. illegib. in P*   435 fluctuabant] fluctuabantur *T*   436
ordinare] ordinate *O*   437 horum] omnium *P*: *def. T*   438 deerat] deerant *M*   439
quasi *def. T*   440 diuinae] dei *P*   441 operat... *def. T*   diuina] dei *ut uid. in cod. T*
443-444 ..dinetur et h... *def. T*   445 ...ricas armoni... *def. T*   armonicas] musicas
O   446 Dixi] Dico *D*   scientia] sapientia *M*   perfecti] profecti *O P*   446-447
estis...innuit *def. T*   447 incommutabiles] immutabiles *D*   448 promisera. *def. T*   *post*
promiserat] Finit *add. M*: Finit Liber *add. O*

444-446 Cf. Cal., *Comm.* 355 (W346:6).   447-448 *Timaeus* 53c-55c; cf. Cal., *Comm.*
335 (W345:21-22).

Appendix 1

<Notae Platonicae>

<1>
<cf. *Timaeus* 35b-36c>

Nota tres figuras in compositione animae depictas ad idem paene tendere. Interualla enim quae sunt in prima figura cum uellent impleri armonicis consonantiis (nec proportiones ipsae possent discerni integre in tam paruis numeris), facta est secunda figura, ut maioribus numeris doceatur, quod non poterat fieri in minoribus. Ponitur ergo VI loco unitatis; loco binarii XII; et sic nota in ceteris. Sed quia adhuc deerant numeri, in quibus semitonia discernerentur, inuenta est tercia figura et tantum pro suppletione hemitoniorum, quae tamen ibi per se non ostenduntur, sed in consonantiis, scilicet diatessaron et diapente, quarum consonantiarum proportionales numeri distincte ibi reperiuntur.

App. 1.1 D, M, T

1 compositione] corporee *T*   2 enim quae sunt in prima fig... *def. T*   3 discerni integre in tam *def. T*   4 ...ur quod...in min... *def. T*   5 Ponitur] ponuntur *M*   5-6 sic...deer *def. T*   6 discernerentur] dicit *et ras. T*   6-7 figura...hemitoniorum *def. T*   7 hemitoniorum] semitoniorum *M*   8 scilicet *om. T*   ...saron et...prop... *def. T*   9 distincte] distincti *M*

Cf. Cal., *Comm.* 33 (W82:4); 41 (W90:7); 48 (W98:2):

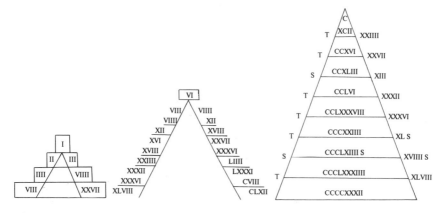

Cf. PL 90: 904A11-B9, p. 135 supra, et Lipsiensis Bibl. Univ. 1258, fol. 8r-v. "Secunda figura fere eadem est cum prima, sed ... ."

<2>

<cf. *Timaeus* 45d-46a>

Nota Platoni consentire Hebraicam philosophiam quae aliud uocat somnium, aliud uisum, aliud admonitionem, aliud spectaculum, aliud reuelationem. Somnium quippe dicunt quod ex reliquiis cogitationum animae exoritur; uisum quod ex diuina uirtute legatur; admonitionem cum angelicae bonitatis consiliis regimur et admone-
5   mur; spectaculum ut cum uidendum se offert caelestis potestas, aperte iubens aliquid aut prohibens; reuelationem quotiens ignorantibus sortem futuram imminentis exitii secreta panduntur.

App. 1.2 D, M, O, T

1 Nota ...som... *def. T*   quae] quod *D*   2 aliud admonitionem] alium admonitionem *T*   2-3 ...aculum...reliqu... *def. T*   2 *post* reuelationem] aliud *add. D M*   3 exoritur] oritur *T*   4 uirtute...bo... *def. T*   4 et] id est *T*   5 ...ectaculum...off... *def. T*   6 aut] uel *D O T*   reuelationem...imminenti... *def. T*   exitii] exitus *Cal., Comm. 256 (W265:11)*

Cf. Cal., *Comm.* 256 (W265:3-11)

<3>

<cf. *Timaeus* 36b-36c>

Nota in omni rotundo uel in uolubili posse considerari intelligibilem lineam, quasi per diametrum ductam in omnem partem, quae intelligitur immobilis, sicut axis in quo uoluitur rota. Firmamentum ergo, quamuis ab oriente in occidentem uoluatur, tamen secundum quod est uolubile aequaliter se habet ad omnem partem, et ita in
5   omnem partem potentialiter habet illam intelligibilem et immobilem lineam, quasi diametrum. Quae intelligibilis linea dicitur polus.

App. 1.3 D, M, T

1 Nota *def. T*   1-2 ...tundo...par... *def. T*   2 intelligitur] intelliguntur *D*   2-3 ...bilis...ori... *def. T*   4-5 tamen...potenti... *def. T*   5-6 et...polus *def. T*

Cf. pp. 97-98 supra et *Glosae* 6.54-57.

<4>

<cf. *Timaeus* 36d-e>

Nota caelum diuerso modo a philosophis accipi, scilicet: superficiem, quam Graeci yranon uocant, quae est limes uisus nostri, ultra quem scilicet nequit porrigi; speram etiam, quae dicitur aplanos; quicquid etiam a lunari globo surgit; communiter quicquid supra nos est, in qua regione nubila crescent, et aliquanto superius, ubi astra
5   sunt. Nam et pluuias de caelo dicimus manare, et stellas in caelo apparere; caelum quoque usurpantes omnem mundum dicimus. Animam ergo caeli siue mundi dicit

orsam a medietate usque ad extremitates mundani corporis et inde usque ad aliam
extremitatem, circumfusam cum globo corporis, operuisse totum eius ambitum, ut
infra et extra uitali uigore foueatur. Illud uero, quod a medio porrigi animam dixit,
10 quidam sic accipiunt, ut non tanquam a medio totius corporis facta dimensione
porrecta sit, sed ex ea parte membrorum uitalium in quibus uiuendi pontificium est
situm. Vnde et uitalia dicuntur. Non ergo a medietate corporis, quae terra est, sed
a regione uitalium, scilicet a sole, animae uigorem mundano corpori dicunt esse
infusum, siquidem terra immobilis, sol semper in motu. Si quis inaequalitatem
15 montium et uallium in terra opponat, terram non globum esse dicimus, sed
globosam, non pilam, sed pilae similem. Vel dicamus recte esse eam globum in
prima genitura sui, sed per exustiones et illuuiones huiusmodi tumores et deuexitates
concreuisse.

App. 1.4 D, M, T

1-2 Nota...limes *def. T*   2 quem...sper... *def. T*   3-4 etiam...cre... *def. T*   4-5
ubi...caelum *def. T*   5 *post* dicimus] uocat *exp.* D   6-7 ...pantes...medietate us... *def. T*
6 siue] sine D   7-8 mundani...cum *def. T*   8-9 ...is operuisse...foueatur *def. T*   10-12
a medio...Unde et *def. T*   10 non *om.* M   12-13 dicuntur...uigo... *def. T*   13-16
...dano...non pi... *def. T*   13 esse *om.* M   14 inaequalitatem] ineliqualitatem M
16-17 ...ae similem...per exusti... *def. T*   17-18 ...uiones...concreuisse *def. T*

1-6 Nota...dicimus: cf. Cal., *Comm.* 98 (W150:14-151:3)   6-9 Animam...foueatur: cf. Cal.,
Comm. 99 (W151:4-8)   9-14 Illud...motu: cf. Cal., *Comm.* 100 (W151:12-18)   14-16
Si quis...pilae: cf. Cal., *Comm.* 63 (W110:12-15)

<5>
<cf. *Timaeus* 39a>

Nota, dum planetae nituntur contra aplanon, tanta celeritate cotidianae uertiginis
eius rapi eos, ut non patiatur in eandem sedem unde progressae fuerant, ipsas
repraesentari, sed uel transire cogat uel leniore progressu non occurrere ad destinata,
et sic in spiram, non in circulum, redire coguntur.

App. 1.5 D, M

4 spiram] speram D

Cf. Cal., *Comm.* 106 (W161:7-12)

<6>
<cf. *Timaeus* 39d>

Nota uertentem annum innumeram annorum seriem comprehendere, quippe cum
errantium circuitus impares sint diuersisque temporibus cursus suos compleant,
praeterea latius aliae a medio mundi euagentur, aliae angustius ad austri septentrio-
nisque conuexa, celsiores uero aliae a terra sint, aliae proximiores terrae diuersosque

5 motus inter se agant, ut citae ultra progredientes tardioribus recedentibus, humilibus
   celsae, dextrae sinistris, sinistrae dextris occurrunt in unum. Completo hoc anno, ita
   ut prolixitas prolixitati, latitudo interuallorum latitudini, et profunditati conueniat
   profunditas; et omnes ab omnibus aequis distent diametris. Et sic opportunitas illa
   proueniat quae unam et eandem faciem repraesentet, quae fuit in initio mundi.

App. 1.6 D, M, T

1-2 Nota...diuersis *def. T*   2-6 cursus...sinistrae de... *def. T*   6-8 ...urrunt...opportun...
def. T   9 proueniat...mundi *def. T*   quae] quo *M*   et eandem] eandemque *M*

1-6 Nota...unum: cf. Cal., *Comm.* 118 (W163:4-12)   6-8 ita ut...profunditas: cf. Cal.,
Comm. 118 (W163:3-4)   8 omnes...diametris: cf. Cal., *Comm.* 118 (W163:14)
8-9 Et sic...mundi.: cf. Cal., *Comm.* 118 (W163:22-23)

<7>
<cf. *Timaeus* 45e-46a>

Platonica sententia est ignem interiorem per oculorum fenestras progredientem et
exteriori igni mixtum formari in corpore leuigato talem, qualem ille est a quo ignis
ille procedit. Aristoteles uero de hac re aliter sentit, siquidem asserit uisum non
posse adhaerere in corpore puro ac lubrico, ita ut in hispido et spisso, et ideo dicit
5 eundem uisum tanta celeritate reuerti, ut illum a quo procedit quasi retro intueatur.

App. 1.7 D, Lipsiensis Bibl. univ. 1258, fol. 8r, Guelferbytanus Bibl. Ducalis 4457,
          fol. 101v

2 igni *om. D*   mixtum] mixtam *D*   ignis *om. Guelferbytanus*   4 ac] et *Lipsiensis et Guelferbytanus*

Appendix 2

Witnesses to the Career of Bernard of Chartres

1 SIGNED DOCUMENTS

A

(ca. 1108; doc. no. 8 of the *Cartulaire de Saint-Jean-en-Vallée de Chartres*, ed. R. Merlet, Archives d'Eure-et-Loir, Collection de cartulaires chartrains, vol. 1, Chartres, 1906, p. 6; a gift of land by Ivo, son of Gaston of Rémalard, to Saint-Jean. One of the witnesses in a sequence of actions was:)

Bernardus subdiaconus

B

(1115; doc. no. 15 of the *Cartulaire de Saint-Jean-en-Vallée*, ed. Merlet, p. 10; a charter recording Bishop Ivo of Chartres's grant of a church to the monastery of Saint-Jean, contains the:)

<Signum Ber>nardi subdiaconi.

C

(1110-1115; doc. no. 12 of the *Cartulaire de Saint-Jean-en-Vallée*, ed. Merlet, p. 8; a donation of land by Bishop Ivo of Chartres to Saint-Jean, an act that was witnessed and approved by the assembled chapter, including:)

magister Bernardus

D

(29 November 1119; doc. no. 20 of the *Cartulaire de Saint-Jean-en-Vallée*, ed. Merlet, p. 14; an accord between the monasteries of Marmoutier and Saint-Jean which contains the:)

S<ignum> magistri Bernardi

E

(1119-1124; in *Un manuscrit chartrain*, ed. R. Merlet and A. Clerval, p. 196 [195-196]; the oath of the canons of Chartres on the matter of Gervais and his sons was signed by:)

Bernardus *scolae magister*

F

(1124; doc. 3.1 of the *Cartulaire de l'abbaye de Saint-Père de Chartres*, ed. Guérard, 2: 469, a list of witnesses only, and the same document in full [no. 119] in *Cartulaire de Saint-Denis de Nogent-le-Rotrou*, in *Saint-Denis de Nogent-le-Rotrou, 1031-1789*, ed. C. Métais, p. 243 [240-243], in which the monks of Saint-Père forsake any claim to the church of Saint-Denis of Nogent in favour of Cluny and receive the church of Brou and its lands in compensation. One of those present was:)

Bernardus cancellarius

G

(1119-1129; doc. 52 of the *Cartulaire de l'abbaye de Saint-Père de Chartres*, ed. Guérard, 2: 306; a document concerning Saint-Père and Alcherius de Medianello. Among the witnesses was:)

Bernardus cancellarius

2 VERSE

A1

(1127; Hugh of Saint-Victor, *Didascalicon* 3.12, ed. Buttimer, p. 61; notes and comments upon the so-called Six Keys of Learning:)

De disciplina
Sapiens quidam cum de modo et forma discendi interrogaretur:

Mens, inquit, humilis, studium quaerendi, uita quieta,
scrutinium tacitum, paupertas, terra aliena,
haec reserare solent multis obscura legendi.

Audierat, puto, quod dictum est: "Mores ornant scientiam," et ideo praeceptis legendi, praecepta quoque uiuendi, adiungit, ut et modum uitae suae et studii sui rationem lector agnoscat. Illaudabilis est scientia quam uita maculat impudica. Et idcirco summopere cauendum ei qui quaerit scientiam, ut non negligat disciplinam.

A2

(1159; John of Salisbury, *Policraticus* 7.13, ed. Webb, 2:145:)

Quae uero sint discendi claues, quae philosophantibus ad intuendam speciem ueritatis uiam eo tendentis expediunt, senex Carnotensis paucis expressit. Et, licet metri eius suauitate non capiar, sensum approbo et philosophantium credo mentibus fideliter ingerendum. Ait ergo:

Mens humilis, studium quaerendi, uita quieta,
scrutinium tacitum, paupertas, terra aliena,
haec reserare solent multis obscura legendo.

B1

(1159; John of Salisbury, *Metalogicon* 4.35, ed. Webb, p. 205:)

Bernardus quoque Carnotensis, perfectissimus inter Platonicos seculi nostri, hanc fere sententiam metro complexus est:

> Non dico esse quod est, gemina quod parte coactum
> materie formam continet implicitam;
> sed dico esse quod est, una quod constat earum;
> *hoc* uocat Idean, *illud* Acheus ilen.

B2

(1150-1175; a marginal gloss to *Timaeus* 49d-50a in MS Vatican, Archivio di San Pietro H. 51, fol. 11v, ed. Jeauneau, *Lectio*, p. 199:)

> Nec dic esse quod est gemina quod parte coactum
> Materie formam continet implicitam;
> Sed dic esse quod est una quod constat earum:
> Hanc uocat ydeam, *illud* Acheus ylen.

C

(1159; John of Salisbury, *Metalogicon* 4.35, ed. Webb, p. 206:)

Alibi quoque ait:

> Principium cui sola fuit diuina uoluntas,
> etas non frangit demoliturque uetustas.
> Dissoluit tempus quicquid producit ad esse;
> si non ad presens, constat quandoque necesse.
> Ergo super tali qui luget conditione,
> aut nichil aut minimum claret rationis habere.

3 DICTA

A

(1159; John of Salisbury, *Policraticus* 2.22, ed. Webb, 1:131; Bernard of Chartres used to quote Virgil, *Aeneid* 3.395 and 10.113 when things went wrong:)

Itemque poeticum, quo senex Carnotensis in angustiis fortunae frequentius utebatur:

> "Fata uiam inuenient, etc."

B

(1159; John of Salisbury, *Metalogicon* 3.4, ed. Webb, p. 136; the famous metaphor of the moderns as dwarfs seated on the shoulders of the giants of antiquity:)

Dicebat Bernardus Carnotensis nos esse quasi nanos gigantium humeris insidentes, ut possimus plura eis et remotiora uidere, non utique proprii uisus acumine aut eminentia corporis, sed quia in altum subuehimur et extollimur magnitudine gigantea.

C

(1159; John of Salisbury, *Metalogicon* 1.11, ed. Webb, p. 29. Bernard used to remind his listeners that there are three kinds of intellectual abilities:)

Horum tria sunt genera, sicut Carnotensis senex Bernardus frequenti colloquio suis auditoribus tradere consueuit. Aliud enim aduolans, aliud infimum, aliud mediocre est. Aduolans quidem eadem facilitate, qua percepit, recedit a perceptis, nec in aliqua sede inuenit requiem. Infimum autem sublimari non potest, ideoque profectum nescit; at mediocre, et quia habet in quo sedeat, et quia sublimari potest, nec de profectu desperat, et philosophantis exercitio accommodissimum est. Et in hac quidem specie naturam, opinor, artium fundamenta iecisse; usus enim huius studio inualescit.

D

(1159; John of Salisbury, *Metalogicon* 3.2, ed. Webb, pp. 124-125. Bernard of Chartres's comparison of "whiteness" to a pure virgin:)

Aiebat Bernardus Carnotensis quia *albedo* significat uirginem incorruptam, *albet* eandem introeuntem thalamum aut cubantem in thoro, *album* uero eandem, sed corruptam. Hoc quidem quoniam *albedo* ex assertione eius simpliciter et sine omni participatione subiecti ipsam significat qualitatem, uidelicet coloris speciem, disgregatiuam uisus. *Albet* autem eandem principaliter, etsi participationem persone admittat. Si enim illud excutias, quod uerbum hoc pro substantia significat, qualitas albedinis occurret, sed in accidentibus uerbi personam reperies. *Album* uero eandem significat qualitatem, sed infusam commixtamque substantie et iam quodammodo magis corruptam; siquidem nomen ipsum pro substantia subiectum albedinis, pro qualitate significat colorem albentis subiecti. Videbatur etiam sibi tam de Aristotile quam de multorum auctoritatibus niti. Ait enim: *Album* nichil aliud significat quam qualitatem. Multa quoque proferebat undique conquisita, quibus persuadere nitebatur res interdum pure, interdum adiacenter predicari, et ad hoc denominatiuorum scientiam perutilem asserebat. Habet hec opinio sicut impugnatores, sic defensores suos. Michi pro minimo est ad nomen in talibus disputare, cum intelligentiam dictorum sumendam nouerim ex causis dicendi. Nec sic memoratam Aristotilis aliorumue auctoritates interpretandas arbitror, ut trahatur istuc quicquid alicubi dictum reperitur.

4 THE MASTER AND HIS STUDENTS

A

(1159; John of Salisbury, *Metalogicon* 1.24, ed. Webb, pp. 53, 55-58:) Cap. 24. *De usu legendi et prelegendi; et consuetudine Bernardi Carnotensis et sequacium eius.*

... Sequebatur hunc morem Bernardus Carnotensis, exundantissimus modernis temporibus fons litterarum in Gallia, et in auctorum lectione quid simplex esset

et ad imaginem regule positum ostendebat; figuras gramatice, colores rethori-
cos, cauillationes sophismatum, et qua parte sui proposite lectionis articulus
respiciebat ad alias disciplinas, proponebat in medio; ita tamen ut non in
singulis uniuersa doceret, sed pro capacitate audientium dispensaret eis in
tempore doctrine mensuram. Et, quia splendor orationis aut a proprietate est,
id est, cum adiectiuum aut uerbum substantiuo eleganter adiungitur, aut a
translatione, id est, ubi sermo ex causa probabili ad alienam traducitur significationem, hec sumpta occasione inculcabat mentibus auditorum. Et quoniam
memoria exercitio firmatur, ingeniumque acuitur ad imitandum ea que audie-
bant, alios admonitionibus, alios flagellis et penis urgebat. Cogebantur exso-
luere singuli die sequenti aliquid eorum que precedenti audierant; alii plus, alii
minus; erat enim apud eos precedentis discipulus sequens dies. Vespertinum
exercitium, quod declinatio dicebatur, tanta copiositate gramatice refertum erat,
ut siquis in eo per annum integrum uersaretur, rationem loquendi et scribendi,
si non esset hebetior, haberet ad manum, et significationem sermonum, qui in
communi usu uersantur, ignorare non posset. Sed quia nec scolam nec diem
aliquem decet esse religionis expertem, ea proponebatur materia que fidem
edificaret et mores, et unde qui conuenerant, quasi collatione quadam, anima-
rentur ad bonum. Nouissimus autem huius declinationis, immo philosophice
collationis, articulus pietatis uestigia preferebat; et animas defunctorum com-
mendabat deuota oblatione psalmi qui in penitentialibus sextus est (Ps. 129)
et in oratione Dominica Redemptori suo. Quibus autem indicebantur preexerci-
tamina puerorum in prosis, aut poematibus imitandis poetas aut oratores
proponebat, et eorum iubebat uestigia imitari, ostendens iuncturas dictionum
et elegantes sermonum clausulas. Si quis autem ad splendorem sui operis
alienum pannum assuerat, deprehensum redarguebat furtum; sed penam sepis-
sime non infligebat. Sic uero redargutum, si hoc tamen meruerat inepta positio
ad exprimendam auctorum imaginem, modesta indulgentia conscendere iubebat, faciebatque, ut qui maiores imitabatur, fieret posteris imitandus. Id quoque
inter prima rudimenta docebat et infigebat animis, que in economia uirtus; que
in decore rerum, que in uerbis laudanda sint; ubi tenuitas et quasi macies
sermonis, ubi copia probabilis, ubi excedens, ubi omnium modus. Historias,
poemata percurrenda monebat diligenter quidem et qui uelut nullis calcaribus
urgebantur ad fugam; et ex singulis aliquid reconditum in memoria, diurnum
debitum diligenti instantia exigebat. Superflua tamen fugienda dicebat; et ea
sufficere que a claris auctoribus scripta sunt: siquidem persequi quid quis
unquam uel contemptissimorum hominum dixerit, aut nimie miserie, aut inanis
iactantie est, et detinet atque obruit ingenia, melius aliis uacatura; quod autem
melius tollit, eo usque non prodest, quod nec boni censetur nomine; omnes
enim cedas excutere et euoluere scripturas, etiam lectione indignas, non magis
ad rem pertinet quam anilibus fabulis operam dare. Vt enim ait Augustinus in
libro *De ordine*: Quis ferat imperitum uideri hominem qui uolasse Dedalum
non audierit; mendacem illum qui dixerit, stultum qui crediderit, impudentem
qui interrogauerit, non uideri? Aut in quo nostros familiares grauiter miserari

soleo, qui si non responderint quid uocata sit mater Euriali, accusantur inscitie; cum ipsi eos, a quibus interrogantur, uanos ineptos et curiosos non audeant appellare. Hec quidem ille eleganter et uere. Vnde inter uirtutes gramatici merito reputatum est ab antiquis, aliqua ignorare. Et quia in toto preexercitamine erudiendorum nichil utilius est quam ei quod fieri ex arte oportet assuescere, prosas et poemata cotidie scriptitabant, et se mutuis exercebant collationibus, quo quidem exercitio nichil utilius ad eloquentiam, nichil expeditius ad scientiam, et plurimum confert ad uitam, si tamen hanc sedulitatem regit caritas, si in profectu litteratorio seruetur humilitas. Non est enim eiusdem hominis litteris et carnalibus uitiis inseruire. Ad huius magistri formam preceptores mei in gramatica, Willelmus de Conchis et Ricardus, cognomento Episcopus, officio nunc archidiaconus Constantiensis, uita et conuersatione uir bonus, suos discipulos aliquandiu informauerunt. Sed postmodum, ex quo opinio ueritati preiudicium fecit, et homines uideri quam esse philosophi maluerunt, professoresque artium se totam philosophiam breuius quam triennio aut biennio transfusuros auditoribus pollicebantur, impetu multitudinis imperite uicti, cesserunt. Exinde autem minus temporis et diligentie in gramatice studio impensum est.

B

(1159; John of Salisbury, *Metalogicon* 1.5, ed. Webb, pp. 16-17. Among the lovers of learning in John's time were Gilbert of Poitiers, Thierry of Chartres, Abelard, and:)

itidem Willelmus de Conchis, gramaticus post Bernardum Carnotensem opulentissimus ...

C

(1157-1158; Otto of Freising, *Gesta Friderici I imperatoris* 1.52, ed. Waitz, p. 74. The course of Gilbert of Poitiers' education under a succession of masters:)

Iste enim ab adolescentia magnorum uirorum disciplinae se subiciens magisque illorum ponderi quam suo credens ingenio, qualis primo fuit Hylarius Pictauiensis, post Bernhardus Carnotensis, ad ultimum Anshelmus et Radulfus Laudunenses, germani fratres, non leuem ab eis, sed grauem doctrinam hauserat, manu non subito ferulae subducta, a scientia haut censura morum uitaeque grauitate discordante, non iocis uel ludicris, sed seriis rebus mentem applicarat.

D

(first quarter of the twelfth century; in the so-called Chartres Letter-Book, an anonymous letter from one at Orléans to Di<onysius> at Chartres that mentions master B<ernard>, Lucien Merlet, "Lettres d'Ives de Chartres et d'autres personnages de son temps, 1087-1130," *Bibliothèque de l'Ecole des chartes*, 16 (1855) 460 [no. 18]:)

Di., tanquam uni ex maximis amicis suis, in omnibus sapere et prosperari.

Memento, frater, semper omnia agere sapienter, et mihi amico tuo Aureliane manenti mitte libellos meos per istum probum hominem C., eo intersigno quod nos ambo inspiciebamus in dialectica mea aliquando aliqua nota que tu satis discernere ad transcribendum non poteras, preterea de gente mea nouas bene a fratre magistri B. exquisitas. Vale cum amica nostra matre tua.

E

(ca. 1117-1124; a letter in the Chartres Letter-Book generally assumed to have been sent by G<ilbert of Poitiers> to his master B<ernard>, ed. Merlet, "Lettres d'Ives de Chartres," p. 461 [no. 19]:)

Desiderantissimo atque karissimo domino ac magistro suo B., G. eius semper et ubique discipulus familiaris, cunctis philosophiam amplecti.

Quam ingentes tanto tamque excellenti magistro grates rependam, quas amoris flammas tue dulcedinis reminiscens concipiam, nullo adnisu pro uelle explicare preualeo, tue incomparabili scientie cogitandum relinquo. Quamuis etenim mihi in Aquitanie partibus scolas regenti hilari uultu fortuna arrideat, eo tamen dolore unice singulariter torqueor quoniam a tam preclari doctoris presencia abesse compellor. Siquidem tibi ea que in archanis philosophie tesauris hactenus implicata fuerant explicanti tota animi affectione optarem indeficienter assistere, ac de nitido atque inexhausto tue sapientie fonte, pro posse meo, indesinenter haurire. Corpore itaque ab excellentia tua separatus, animo uero, qui disiuncta coniungit, ac desiderii ardore unitus, quicquid boni, quicquid prosperitatis, quicquid scientie Dominus mihi uel concessit uel concessurum opinor, denique quicquid sum tibi post Deum attribuo, tibi ascribo, te ualere et letum esse sine fine exopto. Vale.

F

(ca. 1115-1124; a letter sent from Chartres by a student of master Bernard to his father, pleading for money; W. Wattenbach, "*Iter austriacum 1853*," *Archiv für Kunde österreichisches Geschichtsquellen* 14 (1855) 39-51; reedited by C.H. Haskins, *Studies in Mediaeval Culture*, Oxford, 1929; rpt. New York, 1958, p. 181:)

Miserere itaque pater, miserere, porrige manum egenti filio, subeat tibi paternus animus, non te deserat pietatis affectus, et per oratores qui ueniunt ad Sanctum Iacobum saltim IIII marcas argenti Carnotum ubi ego sub disciplina domini magistri Bernhardi dego mihi mittere studeas. In proxima uero Resurrectione sentenciis illis pleniter instructis repatriare studebo.

5 The Philosopher and His Followers

A

(1159; John of Salisbury, *Metalogicon* 2.17, ed. Webb, pp. 93-95; on Bernard, the belief in the Ideas and the *formae natiuae*, and the attempted reconciliation by Bernard and his followers of Aristotle with Plato. While Gilbert of Poitiers subscribed to the notion of the *formae natiuae*, it was Walter of Mortagne who emulated Plato and imitated Bernard of Chartres on the doctrine of the Ideas.:)

Ille <Gualterius> ideas ponit, Platonem emulatus et imitans Bernardum Carnotensem; et nichil preter eas genus dicit esse uel speciem. Est autem idea, sicut Seneca diffinit, eorum que natura fiunt exemplar eternum. Et quoniam uniuersalia corruptioni non subiacent, nec motibus alterantur, quibus mouentur singularia et quasi ad momentum aliis succedentibus alia defluunt, proprie et uere dicuntur esse uniuersalia. Siquidem res singule uerbi substantiui nuncupatione creduntur indigne, cum nequaquam stent et fugiant nec expectent appellationem; adeo namque uariantur qualitatibus, temporibus, locis, et multimodis proprietatibus, ut totum esse eorum non status stabilis sed mutabilis quidem transitus uideatur. Esse autem, inquit Boetius, ea dicimus que neque intentione crescunt neque retractione minuuntur, sed semper sue nature subnixa subsidiis sese custodiunt. Hec autem sunt quantitates, qualitates, relationes, loca, tempora, habitudines, et quicquid quodammodo adunatum corporibus inuenitur. Que quidem corporibus adiuncta mutari uidentur, sed in natura sui immutabilia permanent. Sic et rerum species transeuntibus indiuiduis permanent eedem, quemadmodum preter fluentibus undis motus amnis manet in flumine; nam et idem dicitur. Vnde illud apud Senecam, alienum tamen: Bis in idem flumen descendimus et non descendimus. He autem idee, id est exemplares forme, rerum primeue omnium rationes sunt, que nec diminutionem suscipiunt nec augmentum, stabiles et perpetue; ut, etsi mundus totus corporalis pereat, nequeant interire. Rerum omnium numerus consistit in his; et, sicut in libro *De libero arbitrio* uidetur astruere Augustinus, quia he semper sunt, etiamsi temporalia perire contingat, rerum numerus nec minuitur nec augetur. Magnum profecto est et notum philosophis contemplantibus altiora quod isti pollicentur; sed, sicut Boetius et alii multi testantur auctores, a sententia Aristotilis penitus alienum est. Nam et ipse huic sententie, sicut euidens est in libris eius, sepius aduersatur. Egerunt operosius Bernardus Carnotensis et auditores eius ut componerent inter Aristotilem et Platonem, sed eos tarde uenisse arbitror et laborasse in uanum ut reconciliarent mortuos qui, quamdiu in uita licuit, dissenserunt. Porro alius, ut Aristotilem exprimat, cum Gilleberto episcopo Pictauensi uniuersalitatem formis natiuis attribuit et in earum conformitate laborat. Est autem forma natiua originalis exemplum et que non in mente Dei consistit, sed rebus creatis inheret. Hec Greco eloquio dicitur *idos*, habens se ad ideam ut exemplum ad exemplar; sensibilis quidem in re sensibili, sed mente concipitur insensibilis; singularis quoque in singulis, sed in omnibus uniuersalis.

B

(1159; John of Salisbury, *Metalogicon* 2.20, ed. Webb, pp. 98,115; on the rejection of the Ideas and *formae natiuae* as universals. John remains unwilling to follow those who represent Plato's idealism, namely Augustine and the philosophers of John's own time, and hence Bernard of Chartres with whom he had already associated the Platonic doctrine of the Ideas:)

> Quare aut ab Aristotile recendendum est, concedendo ut uniuersalia sint, aut refragandum opinionibus que eadem uocibus, sermonibus, sensibilibus rebus, ideis, formis natiuis, collectionibus aggregant; cum singula horum esse non dubitentur.

> Vnde licet Plato cetum philosophorum grandem et tam Augustinum quam alios plures nostrorum in statuendis ideis habeat assertores, ipsius tamen dogma in scrutinio nequaquam sequimur.

C

(1159; John of Salisbury, *Metalogicon* 4.35, pp. 204-207; on Plato, Platonism, and the foremost Platonist of the age, Bernard of Chartres:)

> Plato quoque eorum que uere sunt et eorum que non sunt sed esse uidentur, differentiam docens, intelligibilia uere esse asseruit, que nec incursionum passionumue molestiam metuunt, non potestatis iniuriam non dispendium temporis, sed semper uigore conditionis sue eadem perseuerant. Vnde et eis post essentiam primam recte competet esse; id est firmus certusque status, quem uerbum, si proprie ponitur, exprimit substantiuum; temporalia uero uidentur quidem esse, eo quod intelligibilium pretendunt imaginem. Sed appellatione uerbi substantiui non satis digna sunt que cum tempore transeunt, ut nunquam in eodem statu permaneant, sed ut fumus euanescant; fugiunt enim, ut idem ait in Thimeo, nec expectant appellationem. Hanc autem ueram existentiam partiebatur in tria, que rerum principia statuebat; Deum, scilicet, materiam, et ideam; siquidem hec in sui natura immutabilia sunt. Nam Deus usquequaque immutabilis est; reliqua duo quodammodo immobilia, sed in effectibus ab inuicem uariantur. Materiam quippe aduenientes forme disponunt, et quodammodo motui reddunt obnoxiam; et item forme materiei contactu quadam ratione uariantur et, ut ait Boetius in Arismeticis, in uertibilem transeunt inconstantiam. Ideas tamen, quas post Deum primas essentias ponit, negat in seipsis materie admisceri aut aliquem sortiri motum; sed ex his forme prodeunt natiue, scilicet imagines exemplarium, quas natura rebus singulis concreauit. Hinc in libro *De trinitate* Boetius: Ex his formis, que preter materiam sunt, ille forme uenerunt, que in materia sunt et corpus efficiunt. Bernardus quoque Carnotensis, perfectissimus inter Platonicos seculi nostri, hanc fere sententiam metro complexus est:

> > Non dico esse quod est, gemina quod parte coactum
> > materie formam continet implicitam;
> > sed dico esse quod est, una quod constat earum;
> > *hoc* uocat Idean, *illud* Acheus ilen.

Et, licet Stoici materiam et ideam Deo crederent coeternam; alii uero, cum
Epicuro prouidentiam euacuante, ideam omnino tollerent; iste, cum illis qui
philosophantur, Deo neutram dicebat coeternam. Adquiescebat enim Patribus,
qui, sicut Augustinus testis est, probant quia Deus, qui omnia fecit de nichilo,
omnium creauit materiam. Ideam uero eternam esse consentiebat; admittens
eternitatem prouidentie, in qua omnia semel et simul fecit, statuens apud se
uniuersa que futura erant in tempore aut mansura in eternitate. Coeternitas
autem esse non potest, nisi in his que se nec natura maiestatis nec priuilegio
potestatis nec auctoritate operis antecedunt. Itaque solas tres personas, quarum
est una natura, potestas singularis, operatio inseparabilis, fatebatur esse coequa-
les et coeternus; nam in illis omnimoda parilitas est. Ideam uero, quia ad hanc
parilitatem non consurgit, sed quodammodo natura posterior est et uelut
quidam effectus, manens in archano consilii, extrinseca causa non indigens,
sicut eternam audebat dicere, sic coeternam esse negabat. Vt enim ait in
expositione Porphirii, duplex est opus diuine mentis, alterum quod de subiecta
materia creat aut quod ei concreatur; alterum quod de se facit et continet in se,
externo non egens adminiculo. Vtique celos fecit in intellectu ab initio, ad quos
ibi formandos nec materiam nec formam quesiuit extrinsecam. Alibi quoque ait:

> Principium cui sola fuit diuina uoluntas,
> etas non frangit demoliturque uetustas.
> Dissoluit tempus quicquid producit ad esse;
> si non ad presens, constat quandoque necesse.
> Ergo super tali qui luget conditione,
> aut nichil aut minimum claret rationis habere.

Quidam tamen, licet ab eterno concedant esse uera, ea tamen negant esse
eterna, dicentes nichil esse eternum, nisi quod uiuit, eo quod eternitas, teste
Augustino, status est interminabilis uite. Ex his patet placuisse Platonicis cum
Salomone omnia subsolana uana esse; et eas res dumtaxat esse ueras, que non
ut fantasmata euanescunt, sed statu substantie certa et semper eadem sunt.

D

(mid twelfth century; a marginal gloss from *Glosae* 5.35-44 to *Timaeus* 34c in
Oxford, MS Bodl. Auct. F.3.15, fol. 9ra, ed. Dutton, "The Uncovering," p. 208:)

Lege Bernardum et Calcidium et multas formas inuenies.

E

(mid twelfth century; a marginal gloss from *Glosae* 5.125-136 to *Timaeus* 35b in
Oxford, MS Bodl. Auct. F.3.15, fol. 9rb, ed. Dutton, "The Uncovering," p. 209:)

Hic lege Bernardum et adhuc inuenies.

F

(mid twelfth century; an anonymous *Accessus* to William of Conches's *Glosae in
Iuuenalem*, ed. Wilson, pp. 89-90. The author, possibly an *auditor* of William's
lectures, records a point regarding the content of the *accessus* on which William
differed from master Bernard:)

Sunt qui querendum existiment et in hoc et in aliis auctoribus cui parti philosophie subponantur. Magister uero Bernardus dicebat hoc non esse in auctoribus querendum cum ipsi nec partes philosophie nec de philosophia tractant. Magister Wilelmus de Conchis dicit auctores omnes, quamuis nec partes sint philosophie nec de ipsa agant, philosophie suponi propter quam tractant, et omnes illi parti philosophie suponi, propter quam tractant.

6 DEATH AND BEQUEST

A1

(1124-1130; an early version of the Necrology of Notre-Dame of Chartres, in Merlet and Clerval, *Un manuscrit chartrain*, p. 165, which gives the date of Bernard's death as 2 June:)

IIII NONAS JUNII

Obiit Bernardus, subdiaconus et cancellarius Sanctae Mariae, qui dedit huic ecclesiae libros suos.

A2

(*post* 1130; a later version of the Necrology of Notre-Dame of Chartres, ed. Lépinois and Merlet, in the *Cartulaire de Notre-Dame de Chartres*, 3:123:)

IIII NONAS JUNII

Obiit Bernardus, subdiaconus et cancellarius Sancte-Marie, qui dedit huic ecclesie XX^{ti}IIII^{or} uolumina librorum.

Appendix 3

A Finding List of Dependent Glosses

It is hoped that the third appendix will contribute to that process of identifying and sorting out *Timaeus* glosses that Edouard Jeauneau began in his pioneering work on William of Conches's glosses. So confusing and overgrown has the jungle of medieval *Timaeus* glosses seemed that it has hardly been possible to begin clearing it. With the identifications made by Jeauneau for William and those made here for Bernard, a few trees can now be dragged from the forest.

The third appendix lists every set of *Timaeus* glosses that is demonstrably dependent on the *Glosae super Platonem* of Bernard of Chartres. Every glossed copy of the *Timaeus* or lemmatic commentary hitherto identified has been compared against Bernard's. Only identical and nearly identical dependent glosses are listed below. In the left-hand column of the list the location of the gloss in question is cited by folio number and position on the page: whether it begins in the right margin (r.m), left (l.m.), top (t.m.), bottom (b.m.), or interlinear (int.). Each set of dependent glosses has been examined in sequence, though doubtless not all of the short interlinear glosses in some of the busier manuscripts have been caught. The right-hand column lists the passages of the *Glosae* drawn upon in two ways: a direct source and virtually identical passage is simply cited by section and line numbers of the above edition, while one that has been reworked, but which remains essentially the same or manifestly indebted to the *Glosae*, is preceded by cf.

The nature of the distinction drawn between the two categories of dependence can best be demonstrated by a few examples. In the first class we see:

App. 3.5
Bernard, *Glosae* 5.234-235:

id est bonam fortunam adepta est ab origine sua, quae diuina est, scilicet ab ipsa mente dei ...

Florence,
B.N. Conv.soppr. J.2.49, fol.13r int.

id est bonam fortunam adepta est ab origine sua, quae diuina est, scilicet ab ipsa diuina mente dei.

App.3.10
Bernard, *Glosae* 8.363-364:

Putamus enim. Vere patimur quod somniantes, scilicet incertitudinem, quia nec sensu nec ratione eam comprehendimus.

Olomouc,
Státní archiv CO 565, fol. 65r r.m.

Putamus. Et uere patimur quod somniantes, quia nec sensu nec ratione eam comprehendimus.

These two examples have been listed as direct correspondences, because, despite the addition or subtraction of a word or two, they are virtual copies of *Glosae* passages.

The next samples require closer comparison (cf.) because they reveal close, but not exact correspondences to *Glosae* passages.

App. 3.11
Bernard, *Glosae* 4.250-253:

Paris,
B.N. MS lat. 16579, fol. 20r l.m.

Quia facturus erat homines ad cognitionem sui conditoris, qui non starent sine solido, nec sine igne alter alterum uideret, nec rationabilem motum aplanos inspiceret, unde creatorem laudaret, et motus suae animae illi similes componeret, ideo posita sunt soliditas et ignis.

Ideo quia futuri erant homines ad cognitionem sui conditoris, qui non possent stare sine soliditate, et ideo posita est soliditas, et qui sine igne neque alter alterum uidere neque rationabilem motum aplanos posset inspicere, unde creatorem laudaret, et motus suae animae illi similes institueret, ideo positus est ignis.

App. 3.9
Bernard, *Glosae* 5.205-206:

Berlin, Staatsbibliothek
Latin quart. 202, fol. 10v r.m.

Vel per dextram intellige orientem, quia inde nobis omnia oriuntur, et ideo potior plaga est.

Atque exteriorem. Per dexteram partem notat orientem, quia nobis inde omnia oriuntur, et ideo potior pars est.

App. 3.12
Bernard, *Glosae* 7.128-129:

Pommersfelden, Gräflich Schönborn'-sche Bibliothek 76 (2663), fol. 29v l.m.

Nunc uero. Ostensa constitutione hominis in toto et deuiatione ex consensu sensuum, nunc membratim

Nunc. Quia constitutione hominis in toto et diximus, nunc per partes membratim dicamus.

In these cases the glosses are still dependent upon the *Glosae*, but they depart from their model at a number of specific points: by important word changes, substantial subtractions and additions of material, and a general reshaping of sentences. If the first category testifies to a strictly scribal reception, the second reflects the efforts of students and scribes as they reworked passages from the *Glosae* in their own copies of the *Timaeus*.

In listing the passages of the *Glosae*, the numbers (with lemmata incorporated) are used to bracket the passage at both ends. Thus, 5.31 ... 32 indicates the repetition of all the material in both of those lines; 5.31 anima ... 32, that the passage begins at "anima" in line 31 but runs to the end of line 32; 5.31 ... decebat 32, that it begins at the start of line 31 but ends in line 32 with the word "decebat"; 5.31 anima ..., that the passage begins in line 31 with "anima" and runs to the end of the line; and 5.31 ... corpore, that the passage begins at the start of the line but terminates with "corpore" in the same line. The lemmata of the *Glosae* in this listing are, for the most part, ignored or treated as blanks since the dependent glosses are already attached to the main text of the *Timaeus* in their manuscripts and, therefore, the dependent lemmata are understood.

LEMMATIC COMMENTARIES

1
Leipzig, Universitätsbibliothek Lat. 1258

Second half of the twelfth century. The lemmatic commentary on the Calcidian version of the *Timaeus* in fols. 1r-8r, which is followed by some notes on the *Timaeus* (fols. 8rb-8vb), draws extensively on the *Glosae*, though the scribe or glossator reworked many passages and added others. The MS was brought to light by P.O. Kristeller, *Iter italicum accedunt alia itinera. A Finding List*, vol. 3, p. 422.

1ra	3.45 Mos ... 46
	cf. 1.1 ... possent 4
1rb	cf. 2.2 Fuit ... suo 4
	cf. 2.15 id est ... uirtutem 16
	3.1 Volens ... suum 3
	cf. 3.6 Et ... habitas 7
	cf. 3.24 Nam ... operis 26
1va	cf. 3.30 fons ... est 39
	3.43 ... sententiae 45
	3.49 ... 50
	3.168 nota ... uoluitur 171
	3.210 ... 211
	4.6 id est ... caret 7
	4.8 ... semper.
	4.8 innuitur ... ingenitum 9
	cf. 4.12 ... opinabile 16
	4.22 ... 24
1vb	4.27 ... 64
2ra	4.69 ... semper est
	cf. 4.70 omne caelum ... temporis 73
	4.74 ... tempore 75
	4.81 ... est 82
	cf. 4.84 ... 87
	cf. 4.88 ... 89
	4.90 ... sunt 91
	4.92 Bene ... 93
	cf. 4.97 ... 99
	4.100 ... exemplum 102
	cf. 4.103 tunc ... 104
	cf. 4.105 ... 108
	4.109 ... archetipi 110
	cf. 4.110 exemplum ... inueniuntur 112
	cf. 4.112 ... differentiam 121
2rb	cf. 4.140 At ... mundum 147

cf. 4.154 quanto ... incerta 157
cf. 4.162 ... 163
4.165 ... imum. Vel 166
4.168 Hoc ... 169
4.170 ... 172
cf. 4.179 ... 180
4.181 ... 182
cf. 4.188 dicit ... exornasse 195
cf. 4.212 ... 214
4.215 ... 218
4.219 ... 223

2va   4.250 ... contraria 255
4.257 ... 259
4.289 hoc ... 290
4.291 in ... superet 293
cf. 4.302 ... 303
cf. 4.304 ... ceteris 308
4.318 ut ... 320
cf. 4.321

2vb   4.322 ... 323
4.335 ... posset 338
cf. 4.338 In ... eorum 346
4.356 ... 357
cf. 4.364 Haec ... 365

3ra   4.366 qui ... uolui 367
4.371 ... 373
4.374 ... etc. 376
cf. 4.381 aeque ... 383
5.1 ... constituit
5.8
5.14 ... ut
5.17 ... 24
cf. 5.25 ... animae 29
cf. 5.33 ... uires 35

3rb   cf. 5.50 ... 97
5.98 ... compositionis

3va   cf. 5.106 Eadem ... percipiuntur 108
5.110 ... 119
cf. 5.120 ... 124
5.125 ... denotatur 143
5.149

3vb   5.161 ... proportionem 165
5.170 ... epitritorum 172
cf. 5.179 ... terrenis 191

5.195 ... firmamentum 197
5.202 quia ... 203
cf. 5.205 per ... 206
5.207 ... 211
4ra   5.213 septem ... aplano 220
5.223 ... 224
5.229 Cum ... 232
5.234 auspicata ... uitae 236
cf. 5.238 ... 240
5.241 ... 244
5.245 ... est 250
5.253 ut ... sensibilia 254
5.258 ... 266
cf. 5.269 ... 273
4rb   5.276 ... 281
cf. 5.282 ... adaequaret 285
5.301 ... intelligibili
5.305 ratio ... simul 307
5.310 ... 312
5.316 ... tempore 317
cf. 5.319 ... 320
5.325 ... sequuntur 328
5.336 ... omnes 341
cf. 5.347 ... 348
5.349 ... aplanos 354
5.357 ... quia 358
5.363 Spira ... motu 367
cf. 5.379 ... 380
5.381 ... 382
cf. 5.383 ... annorum 386
cf. 5.389 ... sunt 390
5.391 nata ... stellarum 392
6.4 ... animalium
4va   6.5 ad ... 6
cf. 6.9 ... 12
6.16 Vel ... 17
cf. 6.18 ... 22
6.23 ... 25
6.27 Stipans ... 32
cf. 6.33 ... ratiocinantem 36
6.37 ... 40
6.44 ... 46
6.47 ... ex 49
6.50 ... polum 58

6.60 ... conseruatur 62
6.63 Antiquissimam ... 67
6.68 ... 72
4vb   6.73 ... 89
cf. 6.91 ... sit 93
5ra   6.93 facit ... 127
cf. 6.128 ... crediderunt 130
6.131 Rationes ... ueritatem 132
6.134 Necessarias ... 136
6.137 ... 138
6.139 ... beatitudinem 140
6.146 ... iubeo
6.149 Hic ... 151
6.158 ... textu 162
6.166 Faenus ... corpori
6.186 ... est 192
6.194 ... 197
5rb   cf. 6.200 ... 205
6.206 potest ... 209
cf. 6.210 ... 217
6.219 non ... corpus
6.225 ... egeritur 226
6.227 Oportebat ... 241
cf. 6.244 ira ... 245
6.246 ... 251
6.254 locus ... 255
6.256 deinceps ... 261
cf. 6.262 Sententia ... 269
5va   cf. 6.270 ... 273
6.274 non ... ceteris 277
6.281 ... auctori
6.283 primis ... stella 284
6.285 ... planetis 286
cf. 6.287 ... arare
6.289 ... 290
cf. 6.292 id est ... 293
7.1 ... 2
cf. 7.3 ... breuitatem 8
7.10 ... corporis
cf. 7.12 ... 16
7.17 ... opiniones 19
7.24 ... 25
7.26 ... moueri
7.27 ... fluitare 29

cf. 7.29 sine ... infusionem 31
7.33 ... uexari 35
cf. 7.38 Puer ... eliditur 40
7.46 propterea ... data 49
cf. 7.49 Sensus ... animae 51
cf. 7.60 ... opinioni 62

5vb   7.70 Testimonio ... ratione 71
cf. 7.74 ... est 75
7.97 ... est 99
7.104 ... erraticus 105
cf. 7.106 ... 107
7.109 id ... sensuum
7.87 Aristoteles ... uocat
7.113 ... 117

6ra   7.122 Perturbatio ...
7.123 ... intellectum 125
7.132 spectari ... 136
7.137 figuram ... 145
7.146 ... 156
cf. 7.157 ... 160
7.162 ... 163
cf. 7.169 ... 171
cf. 7.175 ... exterior 177

6rb   7.181 ... ignis
7.182 commentae ... 191
7.197 illi ... speciem 198
cf. 7.199 ... 200
7.203 ... imaginis
7.207 ... ibi
7.209 ... tangitur
7.212 ... 214
7.225 ... 227
7.228 id ... 232
cf. 7.235 fieret ... 239
7.242 ... 255
7.258 Somnia ... naturalia 259
cf. 7.263 ... detuitionem 264
7.264 Tuitio ... superficie 267
7.269 interius ... 285

6va   7.286 ... 289
7.292 Cum ... sinistra 297
7.299 ... est 302
7.305 ... transit 307
7.311 ... 316

cf. 7.317 ... 320

7.328 ... corpora 330

7.331 ... humanis 333

6vb   7.337 ... 350

cf. 7.351 id ... concupiscentiam 356

7.358 disserendum ... 359

7.363 de ... 366

7.367 ... 370

7.377 ... rebus 394

7.373 ... 376

7ra   7.397 ... 401

7.402 ... numerus 405

7.407 ... 410

7.412 officia ... possunt 413

cf. 7.415 ... 418

7.419 dati ... suae 420

7.423 ... 430

7.431 ... 434

7.437 ... musicis 438

7.444 ... 446

cf. 7.447 ... 448

7rb   7.449 non ... 458

cf. 8.7 hylen ... necessitas 11

cf. 8.23 ... 25

8.26 ... 33

8.34 ... 36

cf. 8.37 ... proprietatem 41

8.53 ... 59

cf. 8.60 ... 61

8.64 ... 78

cf. 8.79 an una ... 80

7va   cf. 8.81 ... disputationem 85

8.90 ... 91

8.95 ... 99

8.100 Eadem ... 102

8.103 in ampliori ... 107

cf. 8.108 ... 110

8.111 sufficiebat ... tractetur 113

8.116 Hylen ... 121

8.122 ... uerum est 127

8.131 ... ceteris 139

8.147 ... pronominibus 148

8.149 non ... pronomina 150

8.152 ... 153

8.155 ... qualitatem 158
8.161 Porro ... purus 162
8.163
8.166 ... 167
8.168 ... materia 174
7vb   8.175 Chilinder ...
8.176 ... corpora 177
cf. 8.180 ... 184
8.188 ... apparent 189
cf. 8.191 ... 193
cf. 8.194 ... animo 195
8.198 ... sensilis 201
cf. 8.208 simul ... 212
8.213 ... formam
8.227 ... inueniuntur 231
8.233
8.236 ... substantiam 237
8.246 ... commutentur
cf. 8.249 si ... idearum 252
8ra   cf. 8.254 Videtur ... 256
8.257 ... procreari 259
cf. 8.311 ... 317
8.318 ... apponenda 319
cf. 8.323 ... 324
cf. 8.325 ... 328
cf. 8.341 differentia ... 346
8.348 ... etc. 351
8.354 ... formae 355
8.357 tangitur ... incorporeum 359
8.363 ... 364
cf. 8.369 ... manet 373
8.375 ... formas 376
cf. 8.380 ... 381
cf. 8.382 ... 385
8.386 ... existat 389
8rb   8.389 aliquid ... 393
8.394 ... constiterunt 401
8.403 ... 405
8.406 ... et
8.408 ... pugnasse 423
cf. 8.425 ... inferiora 428
8.428 similitudinem ... cribrum 429
8.432 ... 434
8.435 sed ... exornatio 439

cf. 8.443 ... 446
Additional notes App. 1.7
    8vb   8.5 ... necessitas 11

2
Uppsala, Universitetsbiblioteket C. 620

Thirteenth century. The lemmatic commentary on the *Timaeus* found in this manuscript (fols. 81v-92r) has occasioned much interest since a transcription of it was first published by Toni Schmid, "Ein Timaioskommentar in Sigtuna," pp. 220-266. See Gregory, *Anima mundi*, pp. 15-16; *Glose Willelmi de Conchis super Platonem*, ed. Jeauneau, pp. 13-14; Jeauneau, *Lectio*, p. 150 n.1; Stock, *Myth and Science in the Twelfth Century*, p. 36 n. 42; Southern, *Platonism, Scholastic Method, and the School of Chartres*, pp. 16 n. 7 and 22-23; Dutton, "The Uncovering," pp. 201-202; and above pp. 19, 106.

The Uppsala commentary would appear, in final analysis, to reflect a compilation of various sets of glosses, among which those of Bernard of Chartres and William of Conches are the most prominent. The text as it stands reveals precisely the kinds of confusions one would expect a scribe to introduce as he attempted to transform the different layers of glosses found in the margins of a copy of the *Timaeus* into a lemmatic commentary: disordered and garbled glosses and dropped lemmata. The commentary in the Uppsala manuscript ends prematurely with a gloss on "gratiaeque expertem" from *Timaeus* 47e (W45:8).

82v	(Schmid 230.5-6)	3.43 ... sententiae 45
	(Schmid 230.7-8)	3.49-50
	(Schmid 230.12-13)	3.64 ... duplicis
	(Schmid 230.37-38)	3.148 senex ... transitorie 149
83r	(Schmid 233.3-8)	cf. 3.229 ... signum 233
83v	(Schmid 233.27)	3.267 ... uacabant
	(Schmid 233.30-32)	3.272 Timaeus ... mundi 274
	(Schmid 234.14-16)	4.12 ... semper 13
	(Schmid 234.29-31)	4.22 ... 24
84r	(Schmid 235.34-35)	4.90 ... sunt 91
	(Schmid 235.35-37)	cf. 4.92 Bene ... 93
	(Schmid 236.8-9)	4.100 ... quia
	(Schmid 236.15-20)	cf. 4.114 ... comprehendi 118
	(Schmid 236.23-24)	cf. 4.118 De ... naturas 121
	(Schmid 236.26-34)	4.130 Etiamsi ... mundum 147
85r	(Schmid 241.1)	4.223
85v	(Schmid 241.19-20)	4.289 est se ... 290
	(Schmid 241.20-22)	4.291 modus ... superet 293
	(Schmid 242.20-21)	4.354 id ... planum
86r	(Schmid 243.24-27)	cf. 5.33 ... significat 35

	(Schmid 243.27-32)	cf. 5.53 Per ... percipiuntur 56
	(Schmid 244.9-10)	5.98 ... genus 99
	(Schmid 244.24)	cf. 5.101 ex ... diuersa 102
	(Schmid 244.27-28)	cf. 5.106 coniugatione ... coniuncta
	(Schmid 244.28-30)	cf. 5.110 ... 111
86v	(Schmid 245.22-23)	5.126 Per ... animae 127
	(Schmid 245.24-25)	cf. 5.125 ... incorporeis
88r	(Schmid 251.16-18)	5.245 ... natura 246
	(Schmid 252.23-25)	cf. 5.285 Tempus ... serpens 286
88v	(Schmid 253.32-34)	cf. 5.326 Inferiores ... sequuntur 328
89r	(Schmid 255.16-18)	6.20 ... 22
	(Schmid 255.19-20)	6.24 Ideo ... 25

3
Glose Willelmi de Conchis super Platonem

William's glosses, which were composed in the second quarter of the twelfth century, bear a striking resemblance in choice of lemmata, examples and illustratons, way of reasoning, and some doctrines to those of Bernard. But, though William knew and was influenced by Bernard's *Timaeus* glosses, he does not directly copy them in his own treatment of the dialogue. Consequently, the following list of dependent passages can indicate only some literal points of contact between the two sets of glosses and not the much richer ground for a comparison of the philosophies of the two men. For a comparison in parallel columns of several specific glosses, see Dutton, "The Uncovering," pp. 203-205. The left-hand column below refers to Jeauneau's critical edition of William's glosses.

pp.	62.17-18	cf. 3.12 Inscripsit ... arrogantiam 14
	66.20	2.49 A minori
	66.28	cf. 2.51 Sollon ... communis 52
	67.6	cf. 2.57 id ... excusando
	68.6-7	cf. 2.64 in ... proprie
	73.28-29	cf. 3.49 ... 50
	76.3	3.60
	76.25	cf. 3.68 Gymnos ... se 69
	80.14	3.103 interrupit ... 104
	84.26	cf. 3.142 ... 143
	85.9-10	3.146 ... erant
	85.15	3.148 ... senex
	86.26-27	cf. 3.160 in perfectis ...
	94.14-15	cf. 3.201 Et ... 202
	96.9-10	cf. 3.232 Gades ... signum 233
	98.5	4.1 tractaturus ...

101.23	cf. 4.14 ratione ... 15
102.9-10	4.12 Alterum id ... semper 13
102.21	cf. 4.22 sensu ... quia
108.18-19	4.170 ... ergo et 171
109.14	4.90 omnia ...
111.16	cf. 4.100 ... exemplar
112.24-25	4.107 ratione ... operis 108
113.3-4	4.109 ergo est ... archetipi 110
114.21	4.145 imaginis ... intelligibilis 146
116.6	cf. 4.168 Hoc ... sacrum
117.22	cf. 4.169 dissolui ...
127.20	4.224 ... duo
136.17-18	cf. 4.319 et ... igne
137.21-22	4.332 sine ... diminutione
144.3-4	cf. 4.381 et ... 383
145.2-3	5.7 Unde ... 8
151.22-23	cf. 5.110 ... speciem 111
163.13	5.172 ex his ...
170.23-24	cf. 5.207 ... 208
175.25-26	cf. 5.267 ... imprimi 268
176.6	5.270 hilaratus ... ualde 271
176.9-10	cf. 5.272 Specimen ... 273
177.9	5.280 aeuo ... 281
185.1	cf. 5.363 Spira ...
185.13-14	cf. 5.362 Circulus ... ad
188.1-3	cf. 5.384 Perfectus ... annorum 387
200.15	6.126 Demon ... sciens 127
201.22-202.1	cf. 6.101 colendi ... Venerem 103
202.4	cf. 6.130 Et ... his 131
203.22-23	cf. 6.137 ... inuisibilia
208.13	6.158 faciam ... animam 159
219.3	cf. 6.272 congruas ... 273
227.11-12	cf. 7.19 saepe ...
227.12-13	cf. 7.39 complosionem ... eliditur 40
236.10-11	cf. 7.169 ... persona
234.12	7.189 leues ... planos
244.2-5	cf. 7.266 Intuitio ... 269
248.1	7.311 ... concaui
248.8-9	7.315 imago ... 316
248.19,22	cf. 7.324 dei ... summam 325
250.3	7.331 ... sciunt
250.21-22	cf. 7.338 igitur ... digniore 339
252.3-4	cf. 7.373 ... philosophiam 374
264.18-21	cf. 8.69 in ... 72

268.15	cf. 8.120 inuolutam ... 121
269.15-16	cf. 8.127 ... uerum est
274.21	cf. 8.175 Chilinder ...
274.23-25	cf. 8.176 ... 177
277.21-22	cf. 8.225 ... 226
278.22-23	cf. 8.225 nulla ...
286.18-19	cf. 8.371 uere ... hyles 372
288.28	cf. 8.429 ut uannum

GLOSSED COPIES OF THE *TIMAEVS*

Descriptions of the following manuscripts may be found in Waszink, "Praefatio," pp. cvii-cxxx, cxciii. Whereas Waszink assigned dates for the copies of the main text of the *Timaeus*, the dates provided below refer to the relevant glosses, which in some cases were added much later by a different scribe.

4

Oxford, Bodleian Auct. F.3.15, fols. 1r-19v

Mid twelfth century. On the glosses in this manuscript and their connection with Bernard's, see above pp. 10-14 and Dutton, "The Uncovering," pp. 206-210. The glosses in this manuscript were, for the most part, excerpted directly from the *Glosae*, though there are some slight reworkings and additions of simple one and two word glosses, particularly to *Timaeus* 17a-27d.

1ra	t.m.	cf. 2.15 id ... uirtutem 16
	int.	2.18 intrinsecam ... uirtute 20
	int.	2.26 ... amicitiam 27
	int.	cf. 2.32 quod ... 34
	int.	2.44 quia ... laudari
3ra	int.	cf. 3.134 ... ualetis
	int.	3.136 ... redderetis
3rb	int.	3.138 ... excusandi
4ra	l.m.	3.164 referebat ... meus
4v	t.m.	3.196 quasi ... conditam 203
6va	int.	4.14 ratione ...
	l.m.	4.22 fallitur ... comprehendit 23
7va	l.m.	4.212 ... 214
8rb	int.	4.326 uoluntate ... dissolui 327
	r.m.	4.332 id ...
8va	l.m.	4.340 ... esset
	int.	4.342

	int.	4.351 terra ...
	l.m.	4.356 ... 357
	l.m.	4.358 ... digeritur 359
	l.m.	4.363 quod ... 365
8vb	r.m.	4.366 ... 370
	int.	4.375 deum ... mansurum
	int.	4.382 in ... 383
	int.	4.384 ... oblique
	int.	4.385 id ... arcuatum
	int.	5.1 medietate ... rerum 2
	int.	5.4 ideo ... diffusam 5
	int.	cf. 5.15 ambitu ... 16
	int.	5.18 id ... firmamentum
	int.	5.22 plures ... contemperatur 23
	b.m.	5.21 propriae ... conueniente 22
9ra	l.m.	5.29 Licet ... corpus 31
	l.m.	5.35 Secundum ... rebus 44
	int.	5.88 tercium ... sensualem 90
	int.	5.101 ... locauit 105
	int.	5.112 Repugnant ... uirtutum 114
9rb	t.m.	5.120 ... 121
	int.	5.123 id ... 124
	int.	5.125 ... distinguntur 136
9va	l.m.	5.175 id ... semitonii 176
	l.m.	5.178
	l.m.	5.179 ... seriem 191
	int.	5.193 scilicet ... 194
	int.	5.195 ... firmamentum 197
	int.	5.200 ... irrationabilem 201
	int.	5.205 per ...
	int.	5.207 ... 208
9vb	t.m.	5.214 In ... notantur 215
	int.	5.209 ... 211
	int.	5.212 Vbi ... diuisa 213
	int.	5.217 non ... discurrunt 218
	int.	5.219 ferri ... aplano 220
	int.	5.223 ... 224
	int.	5.228 corrigit ... mundi 229
	int.	5.230 notat ... 232
	int.	5.233 non ... 237
	int.	5.242 notat ... symphoniae 243
10ra	int.	5.254 cognitando ... inuenerit
	l.m.	cf. 5.251 facile ... genera 252
	int.	cf. 5.252 ut ... uitia 253

	int.	5.258 ... 259
	l.m.	5.260 ... scientia 264
	int.	5.264 Circulus ... 266
	int.	5.267 ... 268
	int.	5.269 ... mentis 270
	int.	5.272 id ... 273
	b.m.	5.276 ... aeui 278
10rb	r.m.	5.284 ... 288
	int.	5.289 ... 297
	int.	5.298 quantum ... praeteritum 299
	int.	5.300 id ...
	int.	5.301 ... paruitatem 303
	int.	5.304 ad homines
10va	t.m.	5.306 ... 309
	l.m.	5.311 Reditus ... 315
	l.m.	5.317 notat ... 318
	int.	5.319 Quia ... 320
	l.m.	5.326 Inferiores ... sequuntur 328
	int.	5.336 de ...
	int.	5.337 ... 339
10vb	int.	5.341 locatae ... aplano 345
	int.	5.350 ex ... retorquente 351
	int.	5.362 Circulus ... descendens 364
11ra	l.m.	5.371 dum ... 373
	l.m.	5.377 ... 378
	int.	5.379 ... 380
	int.	5.381 ... uarietas
	l.m.	5.384 Perfectus ... annorum 386
	int.	5.389 ... stationaria 391
11rb	r.m.	6.5 id ... 6
	r.m.	cf. 6.11 Caeleste ... 12
	r.m.	6.13 ... animalis
	b.m.	6.14 Speciem ... elementis 16
11va	int.	6.20
	int.	6.26 in ...
	l.m.	6.23 planetas ... 25
	int.	6.31 pro ... 32
	l.m.	6.34 deuiet ... deorsum 35
	int.	6.37 ... exire 38
	l.m.	cf. 6.39 ... statu 42
	int.	6.45 quia ... 46
	int.	cf. 6.50 quia ... quaedam 52
11vb	int.	cf. 6.54 Polum ... antarcticum 55
	int.	6.68 ... animal 69

	int.	6.87 Haec ... agentis
	int.	6.88 quia ... multis
12ra	int.	6.91 ... modo
	l.m.	6.93 sententias ... credendum 95
	int.	6.131 quantum ... ueritatem 132
	int.	6.135 quantum ... auctoritatem
	int.	6.137 ... 138
12rb	r.m.	6.142 ... 143
	int.	6.144 hanc ... 145
	int.	6.146 ... feci
	int.	6.147 id ...
12va	int.	6.148 ... dii 149
	int.	6.152 ... 153
	int.	6.154 uestrum ... perfectos 155
	int.	6.156 ... 157
	l.m.	6.158 ... iusticiam
	int.	6.159 uniuersi ... hominum
	int.	6.160 uel ... animalium
	l.m.	6.163 textum ... suum 164
	l.m.	6.164 Cibum ... fructum 167
	l.m.	6.167 haec ... concupiscat 170
	int.	6.177 ... 178
	int.	6.181 ... diuerso
12vb	int.	6.192 quantum ... ideas
	int.	6.194 ... semente
	r.m.	6.200
	int.	6.203 Prima ... generatur 204
	int.	6.205 Secunda ...
	int.	6.207 eiusdem ... 209
	r.m.	6.218 Est ... corpus 219
	int.	6.221 masculum ...
	int.	cf. 6.225 ... frigus
	int.	6.226 per ... meatus
	int.	6.227 per ... etc.
13ra	t.m.	6.229 ... tale 231
	t.m.	6.227 Oportebat
	l.m.	6.272 scilicet ... 273
	r.m.	6.274 non ... contraxerant 275
13rb	int.	6.278 id ... homines
	r.m.	6.281 ... 282
	int.	6.287 ... uiuendi
	int.	6.289 ... 290
	int.	6.291
13va	t.m.	6.292 id ... uitiorum

	l.m.	7.1 ... 2
	l.m.	7.4 redibit ... constat 5
	l.m.	7.13 Circuitus ... 14
	l.m.	7.15 Hic ... 16
	l.m.	7.17 ... corpus
	int.	cf. 7.17 incrementum ... 18
	r.m.	7.19 ... esse 20
13vb	int.	cf. 7.24 ... corpus
	r.m.	7.46 ... passiones
	int.	7.48
	int.	7.50 ... etc.
	r.m.	7.51 id ... opinionem 52
	int.	7.55 id ... facientes 56
14ra	l.m.	7.84 ... uexentur 85
	int.	7.93 quando ... sensibus 94
	l.m.	7.95 quando ...
14rb	t.m.	7.102 ... 103
	int.	7.104 ... erraticus 105
	r.m.	7.106 ... 107
	int.	7.113 meatus ... 115
14va	t.m.	7.118 ... opinionem 120
	l.m.	7.132 id ... consilium 133
	l.m.	7.128 ... 131
14vb	r.m.	7.164 ... 166
	r.m.	cf. 7.167 ... 168
	r.m.	7.169 ... sensuum
15ra	t.m.	7.172 ... claritate solis 173
	int.	7.173 exterior ... oculorum 174
	l.m.	7.174 Vel ... 180
	int.	7.189 orbes ... 191
	int.	7.192 ... 194
15rb	int.	7.209 ... interponat 211
	int.	7.212 id ... repercussione
	r.m.	7.225 ... uisum 226
	l.m.	7.240 ... fiunt 241
	int.	7.252 ... animae 253
15va	l.m.	7.271 diuersis ... 279
	int.	7.290 ... rotundi
	int.	7.299 ... partium 300
	l.m.	7.305 ... 310
15vb	int.	7.311 ... concaui
	r.m.	7.323 id ...
16ra	int.	7.333 uere ... animae 334
	int.	7.354 iram ... rationis 355

	int.	7.355 id ... concupiscentiam 356
	int.	7.358 id ... appetitu 359
	int.	7.360 id ... 361
	int.	7.367 ... oculorum 369
	l.m.	7.369 dirigere ... 370
	int.	7.371 ... 372
	r.m.	7.373 quia ... philosophiam 374
	b.m.	7.341 Principalis ... concupiscentiam 342
16rb	int.	7.375 id ... 376
	r.m.	7.419 ideo ... rationabiles 420
16va	int.	7.421 dum ... 422
	int.	7.426 id ... creata 427
17ra	l.m.	cf. 8.70 ... 72
	b.m.	cf. 8.50 dicitur ... 51
17va	int.	8.143 ... elementa 144
	l.m.	cf. 8.155 ... qualitatem 158
17vb	r.m.	8.146
	int.	8.147 ... propria 148
	int.	8.150 ... pronomina
	r.m.	8.152 ... 153
18ra	t.m.	8.173 ... materia 175
	int.	8.175 rotundae ...
	l.m.	8.176 ... 179
	int.	8.188 ... apparent 189
	int.	8.191 id ... formae
18rb	int.	8.192 id ...
	r.m.	8.193 in ...
	r.m.	8.194 ... 197
	int.	8.199 hyle ... patris 200
	int.	8.202

5
Florence, Biblioteca Nazionale Conv. soppr. J.2.49, fols. 1r-27v

Second half of the twelfth century. Sparsely glossed until fol. 9r (*Timaeus* 28b), this manuscript contains at least three different sets of glosses, one of them copied in the thirteenth century and another in the fourteenth. A twelfth-century scribe, glossing in a small and regular script, drew directly and extensively from the *Glosae* or from an exemplar of the *Timaeus* that contained the same. There is almost no evidence here that Bernard's glosses were reworked or much changed. Moreover, this set of glosses preserves lemmata as though these were extracted directly from a lemmatic commentary along with its glosses.

6r	r.m.	3.229 ... paruae 235
6v	int.	3.344 ... falsum
	l.m.	3.245 ... 246
9r	int.	4.151 quae ... 153
	int.	4.142 id ... transitorium 144
	int.	4.154 ... gignitur 155
	int.	4.156 id ... intelligibilis 158
	int.	4.155 id ... essentiae 156
	r.m.	4.159 ... incertas 160
	r.m.	4.162 ... 163
9v	int.	4.166 ut ... finem
10r	int.	4.258 ... facere 262
10v	t.m.	4.288 ... superet 293
	l.m.	4.293 Congrua ... 296
	l.m.	4.302 ... sit 308
	int.	4.308 materia ... collata 309
	int.	4.310 ... 311
	l.m.	4.312 ... 313
	int.	4.314 soliditate ... altitudinem 316
	l.m.	4.317 duo ... igne 319
	int.	4.321
11r	int.	4.322 ... soluatur 328
	int.	4.332 id ... 334
	r.m.	4.335 ... 336
	r.m.	4.337 ... posset 338
	int.	4.340 ... 342
	int.	4.344 Regerit ... eorum 346
	int.	4.350 ... 351
	int.	4.352 ... 353
	int.	4.354 ... 355
	r.m.	4.356 ... 357
11v	l.m.	4.358 ... 361
	l.m.	4.362 ... cadauera 364
	l.m.	4.364 Haec ... 365
	l.m.	4.366 ... rediens 369
	l.m.	4.371 ... 373
	l.m.	4.374 ... prospicientia 378
	int.	4.381 leuem ... mouentem 382
	int.	4.384 ... 386
	int.	5.1 ... animam
	l.m.	5.2 per ... reposita 13
	int.	5.14 ... posuit
	int.	5.17 ... orbes 21
12r	t.m.	5.21 id ... 24

	r.m.	5.25 ... 30
	int.	5.31 ... 32
	r.m.	5.94 ... 97
	r.m.	5.86 ... eam 87
	r.m.	5.33 ... significat 35
	int.	5.100 quia ... natura 103
	int.	5.121
	int.	5.122 sumptae ... massa 123
12v	l.m.	5.148 Ex ... duodenarius 156
	l.m.	5.161 ... 169
	int.	5.170 sesquiterciis ... 171
	int.	5.174 complebat ... epogdois 175
	int.	5.178
	int.	5.193 ... 194
	int.	5.195 ... 199
	l.m.	5.200 ... loco 202
13r	t.m.	5.202 quia ... 203
	r.m.	5.207 ... 208
	int.	5.209 ... 211
	int.	5.212 ... planetarum
	int.	5.216
	int.	5.219 id ...
	int.	5.223 ... uelocitatem 224
	l.m.	5.225 ... uoluntate 226
	int.	5.226 Et ... constitutionem
	r.m.	5.230 Apto ... 232
	r.m.	5.227 Hic ... mundi 229
	r.m.	5.238 ... 240
	int.	5.234 auspicata ... 237
	r.m.	5.241 ... rationem 242
	r.m.	5.243 ... 244
13v	l.m.	5.260 ... scientia 262
	int.	5.268
	int.	5.270 ... laeticia 271
	int.	5.274 ... 275
	l.m.	5.276 ... 281
	int.	5.282 ... sensili 283
	int.	5.284 quia ... sensili
	int.	5.285 Tempus ... praeteritum 286
14r	t.m.	5.291 ... 297
	int.	5.298 ... praeteritum 299
	int.	5.300
	r.m.	5.301 ... 305
	r.m.	5.306 ... 309

	r.m.	5.310 ... notaretur 311
	r.m.	5.314 ... 315
	r.m.	5.321 ... 324
	int.	5.317 Per ... suum
	int.	5.319 ... 320
	r.m.	5.325
14v	l.m.	5.326 ... eo 331
	t.m.	5.336
	int.	5.337 ... 339
	int.	5.341 tam ... animalibus 344
	l.m.	5.347 ... 348
	l.m.	5.349 ... aplanos 354
	l.m.	5.362 Circulus ... descendens 364
	int.	5.361
	l.m.	5.368 Achantus ... 369
	int.	5.359 ut ... uideantur 360
	int.	5.370 ut ... solis 371
15r	int.	5.371 id ... illuminationem 375
	r.m.	5.375 Integer ... 380
	int.	5.381 ... 382
	r.m.	5.383 ... 388
	int.	5.389 ... 394
15v	l.m.	6.1 ... erant 4
	int.	6.7 ... 8
	int.	6.9 idearum ... rerum 10
	l.m.	6.11 Caeleste ... 12
	int.	6.14 Speciem ... 17
	l.m.	6.20 ... putantur 27
	int.	6.29 id ... eis 37
16r	t.m.	6.37 quia ... 46
	r.m.	6.47 ... his 49
	r.m.	6.51 ... habitant 54
	int.	6.65 ... 66
	int.	6.62 Deam ... deum 63
	int.	6.73 id ... persequi 77
	r.m.	6.68 ... 72
	int.	6.77 id ... 87
	r.m.	6.88 ... 89
16v	l.m.	6.90 ... aliorum 94
	int.	6.129 sumatur ... crediderunt 130
	l.m.	6.137 ... 138
17r	t.m.	6.139 opifex ... creationem 140
	t.m.	6.140 Hic ... attentos 141
	r.m.	6.142 ... 143

	int.	6.144 ... 145
	r.m.	6.146
	int.	6.148 rationem ... 151
	r.m.	6.152 ... 153
	r.m.	6.154 ... igitur
17v	t.m.	6.154 id ... 155
	l.m.	6.156 ... 157
	l.m.	6.158 ... impediunt 161
	int.	6.162 ... phisicam 166
	l.m.	6.163 uel ... suum 164
	l.m.	6.166 Faenus ... fructum 167
	int.	6.184 quia ... 185
	l.m.	6.177 ... 180
	int.	6.186 ... exercere 189
	l.m.	6.189 secundae ... 193
	int.	6.194 ... exponit 201
	int.	6.201 necessitatem ... incorporationis 202
	int.	6.203 Prima ... 205
	l.m.	6.206 ... 209
	int.	6.210 docuit ... 211
18r	t.m.	6.215 Hoc ... 217
	r.m.	6.212 ... posterius 214
	r.m.	6.218 ... corpus 219
	int.	6.221 masculum ...
	int.	6.223 Necessitate ... 225
	r.m.	6.226 ... etc. 227
	r.m.	6.228 Violentas ... tale 231
	r.m.	6.254 Contubernium ... beatam 257
	int.	6.262 ... Platonem 268
	r.m.	6.270 ... uitiis 271
	int.	6.272 congruas ... 273
	r.m.	6.274 ... uitia 277
18v	l.m.	6.281 ... 282
	int.	6.282 animandis ... stella 284
	int.	6.285 ... 293
	int.	7.5 id ... 7
	l.m.	7.12 ... apparata 13
	int.	7.13 Circuitus ... opinionem 14
19r	t.m.	7.15 Hic ... egestione 16
	int.	7.17 ... corpore 18
	int.	7.25 Hic ... infusionem 31
	r.m.	7.31 Quasi ... incorporatur 48
	int.	7.51 quod ... 59
	r.m.	7.60 ... opinionis 63

19v	int.	7.64 diuersis ... ratione 71
	l.m.	7.71 Ideo ... duplicis 74
	l.m.	7.79 id ... 101
	int.	7.102 ... 103
	int.	7.105 id ...
	l.m.	7.106 ... incorporationis 108
20r	t.m.	7.109 id ... 112
	t.m.	7.114 postquam ... 117
	r.m.	7.120 ita ... 122
	r.m.	7.128 ... 133
	int.	7.137 ... capiti 139
	r.m.	7.146 ... circulis 148
20v	t.m.	7.148 Potest ... 156
	t.m.	7.157 ... 163
	l.m.	7.164 ... 171
	l.m.	7.174 reddit ... 180
	int.	7.181 ... potestates 182
	l.m.	7.186 ... uoluerunt 187
	int.	7.188 id ... exteriori
21r	t.m.	7.188 Et ... 191
	r.m.	7.192 ... 194
	r.m.	7.195 ... 214
	r.m.	7.225 ... 233
	r.m.	7.234 ... locis 254
21v	t.m.	7.263 ... 285
	int.	7.286 ... resultant
	int.	7.287 ... diuerso 288
	int.	7.290 et ... latus 292
	l.m.	7.293 id ... 298
	int.	7.299 ... 304
	l.m.	7.305 ... 310
	int.	7.311 ... 316
22r	r.m.	7.317 ... 320
	r.m.	7.328 ... passiones 330
	r.m.	7.331 ... 336
	r.m.	7.337 ... corpore 339
	int.	7.351 disciplinae ... intelligatur 352
	int.	7.357 ... igitur 358
	int.	7.360 ... se 361
22v	l.m.	7.361 de ... 362
	l.m.	7.372 utilitate ... 376
	l.m.	7.397 ... 401
	int.	7.405 et ... 406
	l.m.	7.408 Per ... 410

	l.m.	7.415 ... actum 418
	int.	7.421 dum ... 422
	l.m.	7.423 ... Confirmato 426
23r	t.m.	7.426 id ... 430
	r.m.	7.431 ... 436
	r.m.	7.437 ... 443
	int.	7.444 inter ... etc. 445
	l.m.	7.447 ... 448
	r.m.	7.449 ... 458
	r.m.	8.1 ... in qua fiant 6
	int.	8.23 ... constituit 25
	r.m.	8.26 ... 33
23v	t.m.	8.34 ... 40
	l.m.	8.54 erroribus ... 59
	int.	8.60 ... mundi 68
	l.m.	8.69 ... 72
	l.m.	8.73 ... 80
	int.	8.82 Quasi ... initiorum 85
	int.	8.90
	int.	8.92 ... intelligibiles 93
24r	t.m.	8.95 ... procellas 97
	r.m.	8.97 Ideo ... 99
	int.	8.100 ... 104
	r.m.	8.105 ... 107
	int.	8.108 ... 110
	r.m.	8.111 ... 121
	l.m.	8.122 ... loquendo 133
	int.	8.139 praeconfunditur ... 140
24v	int.	8.141 ... 142
	int.	8.143 scilicet ... 151
	l.m.	8.152 ... igitur 153
	l.m.	8.155 ... soluuntur 156
	int.	8.154
	int.	8.156 singula ... formarum 157
25r	t.m.	8.160 ... recipit 161
	r.m.	8.166 ... designari 167
	int.	8.168 ... 175
	r.m.	8.176 ... 179
	int.	8.180 ... naturam 183
	int.	8.188 ... 192
25v	t.m.	8.194 ... 197
	l.m.	8.198 ... patris 200
	l.m.	8.203 ... simul 208
	l.m.	8.213 ... alicui 218

	l.m.	8.225 ... 226
	int.	8.227 ... rerum 228
	int.	8.229 id ... consistunt 230
	int.	8.232 propter ... imagines
26r	l.m.	8.233 ... 235
	int.	8.240 ... 245
	int.	8.246 ... aerium 250
	l.m.	8.305 partes ... sit 306
	r.m.	8.311 ... 317
	int.	8.318 ... 322
26v	t.m.	8.323 ... 324
	l.m.	8.325 ... sensibilibus 328
	l.m.	8.329 Opinionem ... mutatur 332
	l.m.	8.333 ... 338
	int.	8.339 ... 347
	int.	8.350 Et ... 353
	r.m.	8.354 ... formae 355
	int.	8.357 certum ... corpus
	int.	8.358 quia ... incorporeum
	l.m.	8.361 ... 364
27r	int.	8.370 deprauationes ... 374
	int.	8.375 ... formas 376
	int.	8.380 ... alterum 391
	int.	8.395 quidam ... existens 396
	int.	8.403 ... 407
	r.m.	8.408 ... ceteris 420
27v	t.m.	8.425 ... 429
	int.	8.432 ... 434
	int.	8.435 ... 440
	int.	8.443 ... philosophiae 446
	l.m.	8.447 Hic ... 448

6
London, British Library Royal 12.B.xxii, fols. 2r-9r, 36r-41v

Second quarter of the twelfth century. One set of glosses in this frequently faint and often illegible copy of the *Timaeus* is drawn directly from the *Glosae*. See Dutton, "The Uncovering," pp. 199-200 and n. 41, and above pp. 17-18.

2r	int.	2.15 Et ... uirtutem 16
	int.	2.22 hoc ... 28
	int.	2.38 liberalibus ...
	int.	2.41 a ...

	int.	2.47 morum ... persona
	int.	2.56 ... me 58
	b.m.	cf. 3.1 Volens ... intendit 2
	b.m.	3.45 Mos ... rebus 46
2v	int.	3.51 ... hominis 52
	int.	3.61 entibus
	int.	3.104
	int.	3.64 Quasi ... obedientibus 65
	int.	3.93 ... iudicatis
3v	t.m.	3.134 quia ... 137
6r	r.m.	cf. 4.27 factum
	r.m.	4.95 quia ... 96
	r.m.	4.100 ... optimus 101
	r.m.	4.110 exemplum ... exemplar 111
	r.m.	4.105 Repetitio ... probationis
	r.m.	4.109 ... archetipi 110
	r.m.	4.114 uellet ... naturas 121
6v	l.m.	cf. 4.164 ... 169
	l.m.	4.181 ... 182
7r	t.m.	4.258 ... duobus 263
	int.	4.318 ut ...
	r.m.	4.321
	int.	4.324 ... aeternus 325
	int.	4.322 conuenienti ... sociatam
	r.m.	4.331 ... indissolubilis
	r.m.	4.337 ... esset 340
7v	l.m.	4.358 ... digeritur 359
	l.m.	4.366 ... uolui 367
	l.m.	5.71 Merito ... 74
	l.m.	5.33 Plato ... significat 35
	l.m.	cf. 5.35 Secundum ... 40
	b.m.	5.58 ... 66
	b.m.	5.87 potest ... sensualem 90
	int.	5.87 igitur ... composuit
8r	t.m.	5.112 id ... percipitur 118
	int.	5.122 ut ... massa 123
	r.m.	cf. 5.126 Per ... 129
	r.m.	5.230 notat ... diffusam
8v	l.m.	5.246 Indiuidua ... hyle 247
	l.m.	5.269 ... mentis 270
9r	r.m.	5.319 Quia ... 320
	r.m.	5.363 Spira ... descendens 364
36r	r.m.	6.3 et iam ... 6
	r.m.	6.11 Caeleste ... 12

	r.m.	6.24 Ideo ... infixae 27
	int.	6.30 ... punctum 31
	r.m.	6.33 ... ratiocinantem 36
	r.m.	6.38 Quinque ... mouendi 42
	int.	6.45 dicit ... 46
	int.	6.48 quia ... retrogradae 49
	r.m.	6.54 Polum ... immobilis 57
	b.m.	6.69 se ... 72
	b.m.	6.63 Antiquissimam ... 67
36v	t.m.	6.82 colorem ... figuras 83
	int.	6.89
	l.m.	6.91 ... 104
	l.m.	cf. 6.105 ... dicit 107
	l.m.	6.136 Hic ... 136
	l.m.	6.137 ... 138
	int.	6.146 ... iubeo
37r	t.m.	6.262 Sententia ... uniuersitatem 268
	r.m.	cf. 6.187 ... est 192
	r.m.	cf. 6.194 Stellae ... 197
	r.m.	6.200
	r.m.	6.203 Prima ... 205
	int.	6.206 homini ... arbitrium
	r.m.	6.214 quae frux ... 217
	r.m.	6.228 Violentas ... 235
	r.m.	cf. 6.242 ... 245
	r.m.	6.247 Voluptas ... fuga 250
	int.	6.281 ideo ... peccarent 282
37v	int.	cf. 6.292 id ... 293
	l.m.	7.1 ... 2
	l.m.	7.33 ... egeruntur 34
	l.m.	7.84 quod ... possint 85
38r	t.m.	7.148 Potest ... 154
	int.	7.107 donari ...
	r.m.	7.140 ratio ... 145
38v	t.m.	cf. 7.173 claritate ... 180
	l.m.	7.187 intimus ... exteriori 188
	l.m.	cf. 7.240 naturam ... 250
	l.m.	cf. 7.263 ... 270
39r	t.m.	cf. 7.377 ... uiderit 385
	t.m.	7.397 ... cognitio 399
	r.m.	7.317 ... 320
	r.m.	7.337 ... 350
	int.	7.351 disciplinae ... intelligatur 352
	int.	7.400 quae ... 401

	int.	7.409 quaerimus ... 410
	r.m.	7.415 ... actum 418
	r.m.	7.431 ... 436
39v	l.m.	7.437 ... fiunt 441
	int.	7.444 ... uoces 445
	l.m.	cf. 8.1 ... 6
	l.m.	8.7 ... necessitas 11
	int.	8.37
	l.m.	8.41 ... forma
	int.	8.56 Horum ... 59
	l.m.	8.70 ... 72
	l.m.	8.73 ... supercaelestem 77
	int.	8.95 instruat ... religionem
	l.m.	8.98 sicut ... 99
	int.	8.101 id ... 102
40r	t.m.	8.109 aliud ... 110
	r.m.	8.116 Hylen ... potest 117
	int.	8.120 magna ... 121
	int.	8.123 accipimus ... 124
	r.m.	8.134 uolumus ... ceteris 139
	r.m.	8.155 ... qualitatem 158
	r.m.	8.160 ... 163
	r.m.	8.176 hyle ... 179
40v	int.	cf. 8.194 ... maneriae 195
	l.m.	8.212 sed ...
	l.m.	8.259 Nota ... elementis 260
	l.m.	cf. 8.254 Videtur ... procreari 259
41r	r.m.	8.325 ... diuersa 327
	r.m.	8.354 ... proprie 358
	int.	8.363 ... 364
	int.	8.358 dicit ... incorporeum 359
	r.m.	cf. 8.369 ... manet 373
	int.	8.388 alterius ...
	int.	cf. 8.389 ... 393
	r.m.	8.397 id ... constiterunt 401
	b.m.	8.408 ... praeponderatio 416
41v	t.m.	8.418 Et ... pugnasse 423

7
Vatican City, Biblioteca Apostolica Vaticana Vat.
Lat. 3815, fols. 1r-32v

Late twelfth century. A few of the marginal glosses in this lightly glossed copy of the *Timaeus* derive from the *Glosae*. There are few glosses after fol. 8r.

1v	t.m.	cf. 1.40 quod ... 63
2r	r.m.	2.51 Sollon ... sollemnis 52
	r.m.	3.30 unitas ... auditor 39
5v	l.m.	3.142 Cerimonides ...
6v	int.	cf. 3.139 egimus ... 140
	l.m.	3.165 referebat ... 166
7r	r.m.	3.168 ad ... 172
8r	r.m.	3.210 ... 211

8
London, British Library Add. 22815, fols. 4r-35r

Second half of the twelfth century. Several sets of glosses are to be found in this lightly glossed copy of the *Timaeus*, one of them drawn from William of Conches's glosses and another from Bernard of Chartres's. See Jeauneau, "Extraits des *Glosae super Platonem* de Guillaume de Conches dans un manuscrit de Londres," pp. 212-222 and Dutton, "The Uncovering," p. 200.

4r	int.	2.15 id ... uirtutem 16
13v	l.m.	4.8 Hic ... 11
	int.	4.65 Quasi ... fortunam 66
	b.m.	cf. 4.27 ... 28
	b.m.	4.6 id ... generatione 7
14r	r.m.	4.98 fundamenta ... 99
	int.	4.100 ... exemplar
	l.m.	cf. 4.101 Sin ... immutabile 102
	int.	4.103 mundi ... 104
14v	l.m.	cf. 4.114 ... comprehendi 118
16v	int.	4.332 id ... diminutione

9
Berlin, Staatsbibliothek Latin quart. 202, fols. 1r-22v

Second half of the twelfth century. A majority of the glosses in this manuscript are dependent on the *Glosae*, though many have been reworked. At least two scribes worked on the glosses, one of whom was also the scribe of the main text. The *Timaeus* is not glossed on fols. 13r-15r or fols. 18r-22r.

1r	int.	cf. 2.15 id ... omnem 17
	l.m.	cf. 2.21 ... 22
	l.m.	cf. 2.51 Sollon ... singulare 52
	l.m.	cf. 2.62 Res ... 65
1v	t.m.	cf. 3.1 Volens ... 9
	l.m.	cf. 3.23 ... 39

	r.m.	3.43 ... sententiae 45
	r.m.	3.49 ... 50
4r	r.m.	cf. 3.168 Et ... 172
7r	t.m.	cf. 4.6 ... 9
	r.m.	4.27 ... facit 61
	l.m.	4.62 Continuatio ... 64
	l.m.	4.21 sensu ... 24
	l.m.	4.69 ... 72
	l.m.	4.90 ... 93
	r.m.	4.97 ... immutabile 98
	r.m.	4.105 ... 108
7v	l.m.	4.105 ... 108 (*sic*)
	l.m.	4.114 ... eos 120
	l.m.	4.140 At ... mundum 147
	r.m.	4.162 ... 163
	l.m.	4.164 ... 172
	l.m.	cf. 4.183 ... exornasse 195
8r	r.m.	cf. 4.201 ... 208
	l.m.	cf. 4.209 ... 211
	r.m.	4.212 ... 214
	r.m.	4.215 ... 218
	r.m.	4.219 ... 223
8v	t.m.	4.250 ... 257
	l.m.	4.258 ... possent 259
	l.m.	4.291 ... superet 293
	l.m.	4.305 extima ... ceteris 308
	l.m.	4.317 partibus ... 318
	l.m.	4.322 ... 323
	r.m.	4.331 ... 336
	b.m.	4.328 quia ... 330
9r	r.m.	4.337 ... posset 338
	r.m.	cf. 4.338 dicit ... 339
	r.m.	cf. 4.340 ... eorum 346
	r.m.	4.356 ... eicitur 360
	r.m.	4.362 ... 365
9v	t.m.	4.375 res ... leuem 376
	t.m.	cf. 4.376 Vel ... 386
	l.m.	5.1 ... 8
	l.m.	5.14 ... 24
	r.m.	5.25 ... genita 27
	l.m.	cf. 5.33 ... 74
	r.m.	5.90 tercia ... sensualem
	r.m.	cf. 5.94 ... 97
10r	t.m.	5.120 ... 123

	r.m.	5.125 ... denotatur 143
	r.m.	5.161 ... proprtionem 165
	b.m.	cf. 5.179 ... firmamentum 197
10v	r.m	cf. 5.204 ... 206
	l.m.	5.207 ... 208
	l.m.	5.209 ... 211
	r.m.	5.212 ... 215
	l.m.	5.216 ... mouentur 219
	l.m.	cf. 5.225 igitur ... 232
	l.m.	5.245 ... sensibilia 254
	r.m.	5.238 ... rationem 242
11r	t.m.	5.242 Cum ... 244
	l.m.	5.258 ... 259
	r.m.	5.264 Cicrculus ... 266
	r.m.	5.260 ... scientia 264
	r.m.	5.269 ... 273
	r.m.	5.276 ... 281
	r.m.	5.284 ... adaequaret 285
	r.m.	cf. 5.301 ... 309
11v	l.m.	5.310 ... retrogradae 320
	l.m.	5.325 ... sequuntur 328
	r.m.	5.336
	l.m.	5.337 ... 339
	l.m.	5.340 ... omnes 341
	l.m.	cf. 5.347 ... 348
12r	r.m.	5.349 ... aplanos 354
	r.m.	5.357 ... punctum 364
	r.m.	5.379 ... 380
	l.m.	5.381 ... 382
12v	l.m.	5.383 ... annorum 386
	l.m.	5.389 ... stellarum 392
	r.m.	6.3 id ... animalium 4
	r.m.	cf. 6.5 ... animalia 7
	l.m.	6.9 ... sensili 11
	l.m.	cf. 6.13 ... 17
15v	l.m.	7.24 ... 25
	l.m.	cf. 7.33 ... uexari 35
	int.	7.35 Ita ... incurisset 38
	l.m.	7.49 Et ... diximus 51
	l.m.	cf. 7.54 ... statuentes 55
	l.m.	cf. 7.60 ... falsa 66
	l.m.	cf. 7.90 ... falsidicorum 91
	l.m.	7.74 ... dignior 75
	b.m.	7.91 inclinationes ... est 99

16r	r.m.	cf. 7.108 ... malum 111
	r.m.	7.113 ... 117
	r.m.	7.123 ... intellectum 125
	r.m.	7.128 ... capiti 139
16v	l.m.	7.139 duos ... 145
	l.m.	7.146 ... 154
	l.m.	cf. 7.155 ... 160
	r.m.	7.162 ... 163
	l.m.	cf. 7.167 ... 171
	l.m.	7.181 ... 185
	l.m.	7.186 ... 191
17r	r.m.	cf. 7.192 ... 204
	r.m.	cf. 7.205 ... 214
	r.m.	7.225 ... 227
	r.m.	7.240 ... incipiens 243
17v	l.m.	7.243 sic ... posteriora 250
	l.m.	7.263 ... appareat 266

10
Olomouc, Státní archiv CO 565, fols. 32r-66v

Thirteenth century. The glosses of this copy of the *Timaeus* were written by the scribe who transcribed the main text. He probably depended upon an exemplar in which portions of the *Glosae* had already been incorporated with some major and minor changes, and a few additions. On this manuscript, see Jeauneau, "Plato apud Bohemos," pp. 166-168.

33v	r.m.	cf. 3.76 Communes ... turpitudinem 88
37r	r.m.	3.168 nota ... 172
38r	r.m.	3.210 ... 211
44r	l.m.	4.219 ... illius 220
44v	l.m.	cf. 4.241 Proposuit ... causam 243
	int.	4.258 ... 259
45v	int.	cf. 4.337 ... posset 338
	int.	cf. 4.340 reputatione ... accessione 341
47r	r.m.	5.161 ... epogdoi 164
47v	r.m.	5.196 quia ... firmamentum 197
	int.	5.201 quia ... mouetur
48r	int.	cf. 5.210 debebat ... 211
	int.	cf. 5.231 sicut ... 232
48v	r.m.	5.260 ... scientia 264
49v	r.m.	5.310 ... notaretur 311
	r.m.	5.311 Reditus ... 312

50r	int.	5.349 ... aplanos 351
	r.m.	5.357 ... 358
51r	int.	6.20
	int.	6.23 ... fixas
	int.	6.30 ... currunt 32
51v	int.	6.33 moueantur ...
	r.m.	6.37 quia ... 38
	int.	6.44 quia ... ideo
	int.	6.47 ... errant
52v	r.m.	6.137 ... obtinebant
	int.	6.139 opifex ... beatitudinem 140
53r	int.	6.146 ... iubeo
53v	int.	6.187 ... exercere 189
54r	int.	6.205 Secunda ...
	r.m.	6.207 ideo ... 209
	r.m.	6.233 Sensus ... 235
	r.m.	6.247 Voluptas ... fuga 250
	int.	cf. 6.254 ... 255
54v	int.	6.270
	int.	6.272 scilicet ... lupus 273
	int.	6.280
	int.	6.281 ... peccarent 282
	int.	6.285 quae ... planetis 286
55r	r.m.	7.1 ... 2
55v	int.	cf. 7.38 Puer ... eliditur 40
	int.	7.47 per ... incorporatur 48
	r.m.	7.54 ... intellectum 55
	int.	cf. 7.55 id ... facientes 56
	r.m.	7.60 ... opinioni 62
	r.m.	7.90 ... deriuationes 92
56v	int.	7.113 ... circuitus 114
57r	r.m.	7.146 ... membra 147
57v	l.m.	7.184 ... 185
	int.	7.186 ... ipsos 187
	int.	7.189 congestos ... 191
58r	int.	7.207 ... repercussione
	int.	7.208 passionis ...
	r.m.	cf. 7.215 ... accidens 217
	int.	7.228 dissimile ... 229
	int.	7.235 fieret ... opercula 236
58v	l.m.	7.263 ... speculum 274
	int.	7.299 ... speculi
	int.	7.300 coniugationem ... ignis 301
	int.	7.302 quia ... coadunata

	int.	7.305 dextra ... sinistra 306
59r	l.m.	7.317 ... 320
	int.	7.351 id ... intelligatur 352
59v	int.	cf. 7.358 id ... 362
	r.m.	7.366
	int.	7.373 ... philosophiam 374
	int.	7.397 ... consideratione 398
60r	int.	7.415 ... actum 416
	r.m.	cf. 7.431 ... comprehendit 433
60v	int.	7.444 ... uoces 445
	int.	cf. 7.447 ... 448
	int.	8.23 ... dixerat 24
	int.	8.32 ordinationem ... praecepit 34
61r	int.	8.55 elementa ... terrenum 56
	int.	8.64 ... 65
61v	int.	8.101 ... 104
	int.	8.108 possumus ... diuisione 109
	int.	cf. 8.111 ... diuisione 112
	int.	8.116 Hylen ... potest 117
62v	int.	cf. 8.149
	int.	8.152 ... 153
	int.	8.160 ... pronominibus 161
63r	r.m.	8.176 ... similitudinem
	int.	8.180
63v	int.	8.198 ... similitudinem 199
	int.	8.210 nisi ... demus
	r.m.	cf. 8.213 ... contrarietas 214
	int.	8.223 ... proueniret
64r	int.	8.229 idearum ... consistunt 230
	int.	8.233
	int.	8.246 ... commutentur
	r.m.	8.311 ... inquisitione 312
64v	int.	cf. 8.323 ... 324
	r.m.	8.325 ... intelligibilia 328
	int.	8.344 nulla ... 346
65r	r.m.	8.354 ... formae 355
	r.m.	8.363 ... 364
65v	int.	8.382 ... substantiam
	int.	8.396 id est archetipas ... natiuas 397
	int.	8.403 ... nutriculam 404
	r.m.	8.408
66r	int.	8.425 ... est 426
	r.m.	8.432 ... diuisa 433
	int.	8.437 quae praeferrent ... seminaria

11
Paris, Bibliothèque Nationale lat. 16579, fols. 1r-53r

Late twelfth century. Perhaps a quarter of the glosses accompanying this amply
glossed copy of the *Timaeus* derive directly from the *Glosae*, while another quarter
have been substantially derived from it. The remaining glosses seem to reflect a close
reading of Calcidius' commentary. The glosses and the main text of the *Timaeus*
were written by the same scribe. Gérard d'Abbeville left the manuscript to the
Sorbonne in 1272.

2r	r.m.	2.16 circa ... uirtutis 17
	r.m.	cf. 2.24 Quasi ... 25
	int.	2.28 hoc ...
	r.m.	2.45 uitare ...
2v	l.m.	cf. 2.46 Quasi ... honorabas 49
	l.m.	2.59 quasi ... hunc 60
	int.	2.60 quia ... adiutores 61
	int.	2.62 primas ... Platonis 63
3r	r.m.	3.47 ... 48
3v	l.m.	cf. 3.52 Cuius ... dominantur 55
	int.	3.60 ... 63
4r	int.	3.64 ... naturae
	l.m.	cf. 3.67 per ... concordiam 68
	r.m.	3.70 ... 72
4r-5r		cf. 3.75 ... 101
5v	r.m.	3.108 ... 110
	int.	cf. 3.111
6r	l.m.	3.119 ... possunt 120
	r.m.	cf. 3.120 hoc ... 124
	int.	3.129 per ... deceptionis
6v	int.	3.132
	l.m.	cf. 3.134 ... uicem 135
	l.m.	3.136 ... 137
7v	int.	cf. 3.140 ... placeat 141
	r.m.	3.144 ... 147
8r	r.m.	3.148 senex ... 149
	l.m.	cf. 3.150 Hic ... 153
	r.m.	cf. 3.158 ... 163
9r	l.m.	cf. 3.167
9v	int.	3.178 nutrit ... 182
	r.m.	3.185 ... 187
	int.	3.184
10r	int.	3.191 ... etc.
	int.	3.192 gerundus ... informando 193

10v	l.m.	cf. 3.193 uestram ... 216
11r	int.	3.218 ... 219
	int.	3.220 ... etc.
	int.	3.222 ... 223
11v	int.	3.225 intellectum ... bonus 227
	l.m.	3.227 omnibus ... 228
	l.m.	3.229 ... columnas 233
	l.m.	3.233 Sciendum ... uicina 241
12r	int.	3.245 ... gentes
12v	int.	3.250 ... diluuio 251
	r.m.	cf. 3.252 ... 253
13r	r.m.	3.254 ... audieram 255
	l.m.	cf. 3.258 ... 260
	l.m.	cf. 3.261 ... aui 262
13v	l.m.	3.264 ... 265
	r.m.	cf. 3.267 ... uacabant
14r	int.	3.269 ... 270
	r.m.	cf. 3.272 ... 279
14v	int.	3.280
	int.	cf. 3.283 ... 284
15v	l.m.	cf. 4.16 opinione ... impeditur 20
16r	int.	4.75 habeat ... 76
16v	l.m.	4.94 ... habet 95
17r	l.m.	4.135 Itaque ... mundus 140
	l.m.	cf. 4.148 ... intelligibili 151
17v	l.m.	4.154 ... 158
	l.m.	4.159 ... 160
18r	l.m.	4.173 erat ... 174
	r.m.	cf. 4.175 ... 178
	l.m.	cf. 4.181 ... 184
	l.m.	4.185 ... perfectionis 186
	int.	4.187 ... commiscens 188
18v	r.m.	cf. 4.201 ex ... sentiente 206
	int.	4.200
19r	int.	4.216 id ... 218
	r.m.	4.219 ... 222
20r	t.m.	4.228
	int.	cf. 4.230 ... conueniret 231
	l.m.	cf. 4.250 ... ignis 253
	int.	4.253 Hic ... durum 254
	l.m.	4.291 qualitatibus ... molibus 292
20v	int.	4.300 ... iunguntur
	l.m.	4.312 ... 313
21r	l.m.	4.327 ... soluatur 328

21v	l.m.	4.335 ... hoc 336
	r.m.	4.337 ... posset 338
	l.m.	cf. 4.346 Nota ... est 349
	int.	cf. 4.350 distat ... 351
22r	l.m.	4.352 ... 353
	l.m.	4.356 ... 357
	l.m.	4.358 ... 361
22v	int.	4.369 Cardo ... 370
	l.m.	5.1 ... rerum 2
	l.m.	5.14 ... posuit
	int.	5.17 ... interiores 18
	int.	5.22 quia ... contemperatur 23
23r	l.m.	5.33 ... significat 35
	int.	5.53 Per ... 56
24v	int.	5.161 ... medietates
25r	l.m.	cf. 5.179 ... 183
	int.	5.196 quia ... firmamentum 197
25v	r.m.	5.212 ... diuisa 213
	int.	5.227 Hic ... mundi 229
	int.	5.230 Apto ... 232
26r	int.	5.234 id ... est 235
	int.	5.260 ... discernat 261
26v	int.	5.296 dicitur ... 297
27r	l.m.	5.290 istud ...
27v	l.m.	cf. 5.298 ... intelligibili 301
	l.m.	cf. 5.306 ... 309
	r.m.	5.304 quaecumque ... conditori 305
28r	r.m.	cf. 5.321 ... dicitur 324
	int.	cf. 5.328 sicut ... eo 331
28v	r.m.	5.363 Spira ... 369
29v	r.m.	5.381 ... 382
30r	l.m.	cf. 6.7 ... 8
30v	int.	6.9 idearum ... rerum 10
31r	t.m.	cf. 6.23 ... 25
	int.	6.29 id ...
32v	l.m.	cf. 6.132 quia ... sunt 134
	r.m.	6.134 Necessarias ... 136
	l.m.	6.95 Licet ... inhabitatas 106
33r	int.	6.137 ... 138
33v	int.	6.144 ... 145
34r	int.	6.169 iram ... concupiscat 170
34v	int.	6.156 ... 157
	l.m.	6.172 mortalia ... pereunt 173
	l.m.	6.177 ... 178

	l.m.	6.181 ... uitiorum 183
35r	r.m.	6.194 Stellae ... esset 196
		6.197 ut ...
	int.	cf. 6.200 ... progredientium 203
	int.	6.203 Prima ... 205
	l.m.	cf. 6.218 ... 219
35v	r.m.	cf. 6.233 Sensus ... 235
	r.m.	6.242 ex ... amamus 243
36r	l.m.	6.254 Contubernium ... 255
	r.m.	cf. 6.262 Sententia ... 269
36v	int.	6.274 ... contraxerant 275
	int.	cf. 6.279 ostensum ... 280
37r	int.	6.283 primis ... stella 284
	int.	6.285 ... incorporandae
	int.	6.287 ... similia
	l.m.	7.1 ... 2
38r	l.m.	7.38 Puer ... eliditur 40
	l.m.	7.43 ... 45
38v	l.m.	7.86 ... 89
	r.m.	cf. 7.54 ... statuentes 55
	r.m.	7.60 ... ei 62
39r	int.	7.90 anima ... sensuum 91
	r.m.	7.100 sicut ... 101
	l.m.	cf. 7.102 ... 103
39v	int.	7.105 ratio ...
40r	l.m.	cf. 7.118 ... illustrabuntur 122
	l.m.	7.125 unde ... 126
40v	int.	7.158 ubi ... offensio 159
	l.m.	cf. 7.164 ... 166
41r	r.m.	7.169 ... 171
	int.	cf. 7.183 ... exteriori
41v	r.m.	7.192 ... 204
42r	r.m.	cf. App. 1.2
	int.	7.234 ... coopertoria 235
	l.m.	7.240 ... somniorum 243
42v	int.	7.290 ... latus 292
	r.m.	7.307 Ne ... 310
43r	l.m.	cf. 7.317 ... 320
	r.m.	7.333 uere ... 336
	int.	cf. 7.326 Anima ... 327
43v	r.m.	7.337 ... secundaria 341
	l.m.	cf. 7.341 Principalis ... animae 345
	int.	7.354 id ... rationis 355
	r.m.	7.367 ... 370

	int.	7.373 ... philosophiam 376
44r	l.m.	7.397 ... logica 403
	l.m.	7.415 ... oculorum 416
44v	int.	7.423 ... perturbatur 424
45r	r.m.	cf. 8.4 Et ... necessitas 11
	r.m.	8.23 ... constituit 25
45v	r.m.	8.41 ... forma
46r	l.m.	cf. 8.76 non ... plures 78
	int.	8.82 non ... inextricabilis 83
46v	int.	cf. 8.92 ... 93
	r.m.	8.98 auspicium ... 99
	int.	cf. 8.100 ... 102
	r.m.	cf. 8.105 ... 107
47r	l.m.	8.113 Philosophi ... inuestigare 114
	int.	cf. 8.122 ... Vim 233
	int.	8.127 ... receptaculum
47v	int.	8.141 ... 142
	int.	8.143 ... retexendo
48r	t.m.	8.143 scilicet ... 145
	l.m.	cf. 8.147 ... 148
	int.	8.154
48v	l.m.	8.155 ... qualitatem 158
	l.m.	8.160 ... 163
	int.	8.172 ... materia 174
49r	int.	8.190
	l.m.	cf. 8.194
	l.m.	cf. 8.195 res ... 197
49v	l.m.	cf. 8.203 ... superuenientibus 208
	int.	cf. 8.208 id ... etc. 211
	int.	8.220 ... possunt
	int.	8.225 ... 226
50r	int.	8.259 Nota ... elementis 260
50v	int.	8.251 ... idearum 252
	int.	cf. 8.311 ... illo 313
	int.	8.315 id ... 317
	r.m.	8.254 Calcidius ... procreari 259
	int.	8.318 ... apponenda 319
51r	l.m.	8.325 ... diuersa 327
51v	l.m.	8.356 est ... 360
	l.m.	8.365 ... loco
52r	l.m.	8.363 ... 364
	int.	8.369 ... non est 370
	l.m.	8.375 ... formas 376
52v	int.	cf. 8.397 nota ... constiterunt 401

	int.	8.408 ... 411
	int.	cf. 8.420 Nec ... pugnasse 423
53r	t.m.	8.419 ... igne 420
	l.m.	cf. 8.430 ... 431
	int.	8.433 diuisa ...
	l.m.	cf. 8.437 ... exornatio 439
53v	int.	8.441 postquam ... 442
	int.	8.444 scilicet ... philosophiae 446

12
Pommersfelden, Gräflich Schönborn'sche Bibliothek 76 (2663), fols. 2r-39v

Last quarter of the twelfth century. On this manuscript, see above pp. 116-120. The text of the *Timaeus* and the glosses to it were written by the same late twelfth-century scribe who copied the *Glosae* later in the same manuscript. The glosses themselves, though reflective of the *Glosae*, must have been copied from some exemplar in which they had already been reworked. If such an exemplar also possessed a copy of the *Glosae*, one can begin to see how a glossator could freely excerpt passages from it.

	t.m.	2.44 quia ... laudari
2v	l.m.	2.45 uitare ...
	int.	2.59 quasi ... fruuntur 60
	int.	2.60 quia ... adiutores 61
	l.m.	2.62 primas ... digniora
	l.m.	2.63 Simulacrum ...
3r	r.m.	2.64 Causa ... 65
	int.	cf. 3.1 Volens ... 3
	r.m.	cf. 3.21 ... docebit 39
3v	l.m.	3.49 ... 50
4r	int.	cf. 3.67 per ... concordiam 68
	r.m.	cf. 3.70 ... publicae 71
8v	l.m.	cf. 3.167 ... subdita 168
	l.m.	cf. 3.175 ita ... 176
9r	r.m.	3.180 fama ... 182
	r.m.	cf. 3.185 ... 187
9v	l.m.	cf. 3.193 uestram ... 209
10r	t.m.	3.210 ... 216
	int.	3.218 apud nos ... uos
	int.	3.220 ... etc.
10v	l.m.	3.228 quia ...
	r.m.	3.227 ... bonus
	l.m.	3.229 ... signum 233
	l.m.	3.233 Sciendum ... insulam 241

11r	r.m.	3.244
	r.m.	3.245 ... gentes
	r.m	cf. 3.247 ... 248
11v	int.	cf. 3.252 ... 253
	l.m.	cf. 3.254 ... 256
12r	r.m.	cf. 3.258 ... uolebam
12v	l.m.	3.264 ... 265
	l.m.	3.267 ... disputationi
14r	r.m.	4.94 ... habet 95
15r	r.m.	4.148 ... intelligibili 151
15v	l.m.	4.177 perfectiora ... 178
	int.	4.183 ... 184
	int.	4.188 ... commiscens
17r	r.m.	4.312 ... 313
	r.m.	4.314 ... 315
17v	int.	cf. 4.335 ... 336
	int.	4.350 ... 353
18r	int.	4.369 Cardo ... 370
18v	l.m.	5.94 ... 97
19r	r.m.	5.118 Nota ... 119
	r.m.	cf. 5.151 quorum ... 160
19v	l.m.	cf. 5.197 obliquus ... 199
21v	int.	5.298 ... praeteritum 299
22v	l.m.	cf. 5.363 Spira ... contrarii 368
23r	int.	6.1 ... caeleste 2
25v	l.m.	6.144 ... 145
26r	int.	6.154 iuxta ... perfectos 155
	r.m.	6.156 ... 157
27r	int.	6.242 ... amamus 243
	r.m.	6.252 ... oportebat 253
28r	r.m.	7.26 ... moueri
	r.m.	7.38 Puer ... ignem 39
28v	int.	7.43 ... 45
29r	int.	7.105 ratio ...
29v	l.m.	7.118 ... illustrabuntur 122
	l.m.	7.125 unde ... 126
	l.m.	cf. 7.128 ... membratim 129
30r	int.	cf. 7.158 ubi ... offensio 159
	r.m.	cf. 7.164 ... 166
30v	l.m.	cf. 7.192 ... 193
31r	r.m.	7.205 ... 206
	int.	7.234 ... coopertoria 235
31v	int.	cf. 7.290 ... latus 292
	int.	7.307 Ne ... 310

32r	r.m.	7.333 uere ... intelligere est 334
	int.	7.336 in ...
34v	int.	cf. 8.92 ... 94
35r	int.	8.141 quia ... 142
35v	int.	8.143 scilicet ... 145
	int.	cf. 8.146
36v	int.	8.189 se ... 190
	int.	8.196 hyle ... 197
37r	int.	8.220 ... possunt
37v	int.	8.249 Terra ... 250
38r	r.m.	cf. 8.321 probabiliter ... placet 323
	r.m.	8.329 ... Quae 330
38v	l.m.	8.359 discernuntur ... 360
39v	l.m.	cf. 8.430 ... habeant 431
	l.m.	cf. 8.435 ... exornatio 439

13
Berlin, Staatsbibliothek Latin quart. 821, fols. 72r-105r

Fifteenth century. On this manuscript, see *Glose Willelmi de Conchis super Platonem*, ed. Jeauneau, pp. 42-43. One of the several sets of glosses on the *Timaeus* in
this manuscript reflects the *Glosae*. In general the selection of these glosses seems
to be related to those found in Pommersfelden 76 (2663), though here they are often
either truncated or expanded. The influence of Calcidius is also evident in the glosses
on the last part of the *Timaeus*.

72r	r.m.	2.45 uitare ...
72v	r.m.	2.59 quasi ... fruuntur 60
	int.	2.60 quia ... adiutores 61
	int.	2.62 primas ... digniora
	int.	2.63 Simulacrum ...
73r	t.m.	3.1 Volens ... Timaeo 3
	r.m.	3.49
78r	r.m.	cf. 3.167 ... subdita 168
	r.m.	cf. 3.175 ita ... 176
78v	l.m.	cf. 3.185 ... 187
79r	t.m.	cf. 3.193 uestram ... 209
	b.m.	3.210 ... 216
79v	r.m.	3.228 quia ...
	t.m.	3.229 ... signum 233
80r	r.m.	3.233 Sciendum ... uicina 241
	l.m.	3.244
	int.	cf. 3.245 ... gentes

80v	l.m.	cf. 3.252 ... 253
81r	r.m.	cf. 3.254 ... 256
	r.m.	cf. 3.258 ... uolebam
81v	l.m.	3.264 ... 265
	l.m.	3.267 ... disputationi
83r	int.	4.94 ... deum 95
83v	l.m.	4.148 ... intelligibili 151
84r	l.m.	4.181 ... 182
	int.	4.183 ... 184
	int.	4.188 ... commiscens
86r	t.m.	cf. 4.317 libratis ... igne 319
87r	b.m.	cf. 4.359 Stomachus ... 361
87v	t.m.	4.369 Cardo ... 370
88r	b.m.	5.94 ... 97
93r	r.m.	cf. 5.349 ... aplanos 351
93v	l.m.	cf. 5.383 ... etc. 384
97r	r.m.	cf. 6.228 Violentas ... tale 231
	int.	6.254 Contubernium ... hiemabant 255
	b.m.	cf. 6.258 redeat ... 261
99v	r.m.	cf. 7.118 ... illustrabuntur 122
102r	int.	7.351 disciplinae ... intelligatur 352
104r	l.m.	8.92 ... 94

14 and 15
(Vi) Vienna, Österreichische Nationalbibliothek 278, fols. 1r-84v
(Va) Vatican City, Biblioteca Apostolica Vaticana Vat. lat. 2063, fols. 1r-68v

Twelfth and fourteenth centuries respectively. Gregory, *Platonismo medievale*, pp. 88-91, noted that the *Timaeus* glosses contained in these two manuscripts were virtually identical. Va, it should be noted, lacks some of the glosses of Vi. Perhaps a quarter of the glosses in these manuscripts derive directly from the *Glosae*, but many of the remainder also seem influenced by the *Glosae*. As well the glossator-compiler of this set of glosses excerpted directly from Calcidius' commentary, especially towards the end of the *Timaeus*.

Vi 3v/Va 2v	cf. 3.1 Volens ... arrogantiam 14
Vi 4r/Va 3v	3.49
Vi 19v	3.229 ... 236
Vi 25r/Va 21r	cf. 4.164 ... 165
Vi 25v/Va 21v	cf. 4.12 ... atomi 23
Vi 26r/Va 21v-22r	4.27 ... 64
Vi 26v/Va 22r	4.81 ... 83
Vi 26v/Va 22v	cf. 4.85 probat ... 87
	cf. 4.88 ... 89

Vi 27r/Va 22v	4.69 ... 93
	4.95 quia ... 96
	4.97 ... immutabile 98
Vi 27v/Va 23r	4.100 ... optimus 101
	cf. 4.101 Si ... 104
Vi 28r/Va 23r	cf. 4.105 ... 108
	cf. 4.109 ... 113
	cf. 4.114 ... differentiam 121
Vi 28v/Va 24r	4.145 id ... intelligibilem 147
	4.152 quae ... 153
Vi 29r	cf. 4.164 ... 169
Vi 33v/Va 27v-28r	4.322 in ... aequilibrauit 324
Vi 33r/Va 28r	4.326 extra ...
	4.331 ... qualitates 332
Vi 34v/Va 28v	4.340 ... esset
	4.350 ... forma
	cf. 4.350 distat ... 351
	4.356 ... fecit
Vi 35r/Va 29r	4.358 ... spuma 360
	cf. 4.362 ... uiuebat
Vi 36r/Va 29v	5.6 idonea ... exercet 7
Vi 36r/Va 29v-30r	cf. 5.18 id ... dico 20
Vi 37r/Va 29v	cf. 5.58 ... inuenitur 60
Vi 37v/Va 30v	cf. 5.112 Repugnant ... 120
Vi 37v/Va 31r	5.122 ut ... massa 123
Vi 38r/Va 32r	cf. 5.161 ... medietates
	5.163 igitur ... limites 164
Vi 39r/Va 32r	5.171 duplorum ...
	5.174 Ita ... semitonii 176
Vi 39v/Va 32v	5.195 ... firmamentum 197
	5.201 quia ... 203
Vi 40r/Va 33r	5.214 In ... irrationabiles 216
Vi 41r/Va 33v	5.238 ... 240
	5.241 sententia ... symphoniae 243
Vi 42r/Va 34v	5.269 simulacrum ... mentis 270
	5.272 id ... 273
	5.276 ... 281
Vi 42v/Va 34v	5.284 ... sensili
Vi 43v/Va 35r	5.307 Ideo ... quia 308
Vi 44r/Va 36r	5.310 ... notaretur 311
Vi 44r/Va 36v	5.318 Contraria ... 320
Vi 44v/Va 36v	5.325
	5.337 ... 339
Vi 45r/Va 36v	5.340 ... singulae

	cf. 5.349 ... 358
Vi 46v/Va 38r	5.379 ... 380
	5.381 miranda ... 382
Vi 48r/Va 39r	6.11 Caeleste ... 12
	6.14 Speciem ... 17
Vi 48v/Va 39r	6.20 ... 22
	6.24 Ideo ... 25
Vi 48v/Va 39v	6.29 id ...
Vi 49r/Va 39v	6.37 dicit ... 38
Vi 49v/Va 40v	6.73 ... aliarum 76
Vi 50r/Va 40v	6.81 id ... figuras 83
Vi 50v/Va 40v	cf. 6.88 ... 89
Vi 51r/Va 40v	cf. 6.93 ponendo ... credendum 95
Vi 51r/Va 40v	cf. 6.105 ... 127
Vi 51v/Va 42r	6.135 Hic ... 136
	6.137 ... 138
Vi 54v/Va 44v	6.206 notari ... arbitrium 207
	cf. 6.203 Prima ... 205
	6.215 quia ... 217
Vi 55r/Va 44v	6.225
Vi 55r/Va 45r	6.228 Violentas ... tale 231
Vi 55r/Va 44v	cf. 6.236 ... 251
Vi 55v/Va 45r	cf. 6.262 Sententia ... 269
Vi 55r/Va 45v	cf. 6.270
Vi 56v/Va 45v	6.272 scilicet ... lupus 273
Vi 56v/Va 46r	6.283 primis ... descenderant 284
	6.287 ... arare
Vi 57r/Va 46v	7.1 ... 2
Vi 57v/Va 47r	7.12
Vi 58r/Va 47r	cf. 7.33 ... uexari 34
Vi 58r/Va 47v	cf. 7.38 Puer ... eliditur 40
Vi 60v/Va 49v	7.113 ... circuitus 114
Vi 61r/Va 50r	7.119 si ... concupiscentiam 120
Vi 62r	7.155 ... 156
Vi 62v/Va 50v-51r	7.140 Diuiditur ... 145
Vi 63r	7.184 In ... 185
Vi 63v/Va 51r	7.190 quia ... 191
Vi 64r/Va 52v	7.207 ... repercussione
	7.209 ... dirigitur 210
	7.212 id ... repercussione
Vi 64r/Va 52v	cf. 7.225 ... 227
Vi 64v/Va 52v-53r	7.228 id ... obscurato 231
Vi 64v/Va 51v-52r	cf. 7.263 ... 285
Vi 64v/Va 53r	7.258 Somnia ... naturalia 259

Vi 65r/Va 51v	7.240 ... posteriora 250
Vi 65v/Va 54r	cf. 7.300 Coitum ... est 302
Vi 66r/Va 54v	7.311 ... inspicientis 312
	7.313 deiecto ... imago 315
Vi 67r/Va 55r	7.332 ratio ... humanis 333
Vi 67r/Va 52v-53r	7.337 ... 350
Vi 67r/Va 55v	7.351 disciplinae ... intelligatur 352
Vi 67v/Va 55v	7.358 disserendum ... 359
	7.360 ... intelligenti 361
Vi 67v/Va 55r	7.368 Ministerium ... 370
Vi 68r/Va 56r	7.373 quia ... 374
	7.375 id ... 376
Vi 68r/Va 55v-56r	cf. 7.377 ... 396
Vi 68r/Va 56r	7.397 ... cognitio 399
Vi 68v/Va 56v	cf. 7.415 ... actum 416
Vi 69r/Va 56r	7.423 ... examine 427
Vi 69v	cf. 7.431 ... 436
	cf. 7.437 ... reformari 439
Vi 70r	7.444 ... uoces 445
	7.447 ... 448
	7.449 non ... sillabarum 451
Vi 72r	8.81 ... difficultate 82
Vi 72v/Va 59r	8.101 id ... 104
Vi 82v/Va 65r	8.389 unum ... duo 390

16
Wolfenbüttel, Herzog-August-Bibliothek Lat. 3614, fols. 113r-146v

Second half of the twelfth century. The scribe who copied the *Timaeus* added a few glosses derived from the *Glosae* to fols. 113r-v, but ceased glossing altogether after fol. 114v. Another scribe added a few glosses to fols. 118r and 119r.

113r	t.m.	1.52 elementa ... alterius 54
	t.m.	2.5 primam ... 9
	int.	2.44 quia ... laudari
113v	l.m.	2.56 si ... sapientem 58
	l.m.	cf. 2.62 Res ... Platonis 63

17
Admont, Stiftsbibliothek Cod. 514, fols. 1v-13v

Second half of the twelfth century. This lightly glossed copy of the *Timaeus* possesses a few glosses apparently dependent upon the *Glosae*.

6r	r.m.	4.305 Vel ... ceteris 308
	l.m.	cf. 4.358 ... digeritur 359
7r	t.m.	5.106 Eadem ... percipiuntur 108
	t.m.	5.105 Diuiduam ... coniuncta 106
	r.m.	5.126 Per ... 128
	r.m.	5.179 ... occidentem 187
7v	t.m.	5.230 Apto ... 232
	t.m.	5.276 ... aeui 278
8r	t.m.	5.349 laxiores ... retardantur 350

18
Leiden, Bibliotheek der Rijksuniversiteit B.P.L. 64, fols. 37r-54v

Second half of the twelfth century. Another sparsely glossed copy of the *Timaeus* in which there are a few reflections of the *Glosae*.

37r	r.m.	cf. 2.51 Sollon ... sollemnis 52
39v	l.m.	cf. 3.168 Et ... 172
42v	int.	4.181 ... 182
43r	int.	cf. 4.212 ... 214
44v	l.m.	5.134 Septem ... denotatur 143
45r	r.m.	5.179 ... terrenis 191

19
Avranches, Bibliothèque municipale 226, fols. 96r-113r

Second half of the twelfth century. The brief set of glosses in this manuscript was edited by Jeauneau in *Lectio*, pp. 212-225.

96r	*Lectio* 212.12	2.21 ... impossibilia
	Lectio 214.1-11	cf. 3.24 Nam ... notatur 34
96v	*Lectio* 214.12	cf. 3.34 Si ... docebit 39
97v	*Lectio* 217.21-22	3.136 hoc ... 137
101r	*Lectio* 221.16	4.95 quia ... 96
	Lectio 221.27-222.2	cf. 4.114 ... naturas 121
101v	*Lectio* 222.29	4.181 ... sui
	Lectio 222.31-34	cf. 4.189 ... exornasse 195

20
Cambridge, Trinity College R.9.23 (James 824), fols. 75r-92v

Fourteenth century. A mere trace of the *Glosae* is to be found in this modestly glossed twelfth-century copy of the *Timaeus*.

75r	l.m.	cf. 2.46 Quasi ... concordiam 47
	l.m.	2.48 Quasi ... honorabas 49
75v	l.m.	cf. 3.88 ... nuptias 89
76v	r.m.	3.108 ... 110
78v	l.m.	3.167 ... praeualendo 168
79v	l.m.	cf. 3.258.

Bibliography

1. Manuscripts Cited

Those manuscripts marked with an asterisk were
examined on microfilm, all others *in situ*

Admont, Stiftsbibliothek Cod. 514*
Avranches, Bibliothèque municipale 226*
Berlin, Staatsbibliothek Latin quart. 202*
Berlin, Staatsbibliothek Latin quart. 821*
Brussels, Bibliothèque Royale 5093*
Cambridge, Trinity College R.9.23 (James 824)
Durham, Cathedral Library C.IV.7
Florence, Biblioteca Nazionale Conv. soppr. J.2.49
Leiden, Bibliotheek der Rijksuniversiteit B.P.L. 64*
Leipzig, Universitätsbibliothek Lat. 1258*
London, British Library Add. 22815
London, British Library Arundel 339
London, British Library Royal 12.B.xxii
Munich, Bayerische Staatsbibliothek Clm. 540B
Olomouc, Státní archiv CO 565*
Orléans, Bibliothèque municipale 260 (216)
Oxford, Bodleian Library Auct. F.3.15
Paris, Bibliothèque Nationale lat. 16579
Paris, Bibliothèque Nationale nouv. acq. lat. 281
Pommersfelden, Gräflich Schönborn'sche Bibliothek 76 (2663)
Uppsala, Universitetsbiblioteket C. 620*
Vatican City, Biblioteca Apostolica Vaticana Vat. lat. 2063
Vatican City, Biblioteca Apostolica Vaticana Vat. lat. 3815
Vienna, Österreichische Nationalbibliothek 278
Vienna, Österreichische Nationalbibliothek 2376
Wolfenbüttel, Herzog-August-Bibliothek lat. 3614*
Wolfenbüttel, Herzog-August-Bibliothek lat. 4457*

2. Primary Sources

Abelard, Peter. *Historia calamitatum*, ed. J.T. Muckle. In "Abelard's Letter of
Consolation to a Friend (*Historia calamitatum*)." *Mediaeval Studies* 12
(1950) 163-213.

——. *Theologia christiana.* Ed. E.M. Buytaert. Corpus Christianorum: Continuatio Mediaevalis 12. Turnhout: Brepols, 1969.

Accessus ad auctores. Bernard d'Utrecht. Conrad d'Hirsau. Dialogus super auctores. Ed. R.B.C. Huygens. Leiden: Brill, 1970.

Adelard of Bath. *De eodem et diuerso,* ed. Hans Willner. In *Des Adelard von Bath Traktat De eodem et diuerso.* Beiträge zur Geschichte der Philosophie des Mittelalters 4.1. Münster: Aschendorff, 1903.

Apuleius. *De Platone et eius dogmate,* ed. Paul Thomas. In *Apulei Platonici Madaurensis opera quae supersunt,* vol. 3: *De philosophia libri,* pp. 82-134. 3rd ed. Stuttgart: Teubner, 1970.

Aristotle. *Categoriae vel praedicamenta.* Ed. Lorenzo Minio-Paluello. Aristoteles Latinus, vol. 1.1. Bruges: Desclée de Brouwer, 1961.

——. *De interpretatione vel Periermenias. Translatio Boethii.* Ed. Lorenzo Minio-Paluello. Aristoteles Latinus, vol. 2.1, pp. 1-38. Bruges: Desclée de Brouwer, 1965.

——. *Topica. Translatio Boethii.* Ed. Lorenzo Minio-Paluello. Aristoteles Latinus, vol. 5.1. Brussels: Desclée de Brouwer, 1969.

Augustine. *Confessionum libri xiii.* Ed. Lucas Verheijen. Corpus Christianorum: Series Latina 27. Turnhout: Brepols, 1981.

——. *De civitate dei.* Ed. B. Dombart and A. Kalb. Corpus Christianorum: Series Latina 47-48. Turnhout: Brepols, 1955.

——. *Retractationes.* Ed. Almut Mutzenbecher. Corpus Christianorum: Series Latina 57. Turnhout: Brepols, 1984.

[Bernard Silvester]. *The Commentary on Martianus Capella's 'De nuptiis Philologiae et Mercurii' Attributed to Bernardus Silvestris.* Ed. Haijo Jan Westra. Studies and Texts 80. Toronto: Pontifical Institute of Mediaeval Studies, 1986.

——. *The Commentary on the First Six Books of the 'Aeneid' of Vergil Commonly Attributed to Bernardus Silvestris: A New Critical Edition.* Ed. Julian Ward Jones and Elizabeth Frances Jones. Lincoln, Nebraska: University of Nebraska Press, 1977.

——. *Cosmographia.* Ed. Peter Dronke. Textus minores 53. Leiden: Brill, 1978.

Boethius. *De institutione arithmetica libri duo.* Ed. G. Friedlein. Leipzig: Teubner, 1867; rpt. Frankfurt: Minerva, 1966.

——. *De institutione musica libri quinque.* Ed. G. Friedlein. Leipzig: Teubner, 1867; rpt. Frankfurt: Minerva, 1966.

——. *In categorias Aristotelis libri quatuor.* PL 64: 159-294.

——. *In Isagogen Porphyrii commenta: editio secunda.* Ed. S. Brandt. Corpus scriptorum ecclesiasticorum latinorum 48. Vienna: Tempsky, 1906.

——. *Philosophiae consolatio.* Ed. Ludwig Bieler. Corpus Christianorum: Series Latina 94. Turnhout: Brepols, 1957.

——. *Opuscula sacra.* Ed. R. Peiper. In *Anicii Manlii Severini Boetii Philosophiae consolationis libri quinque accedunt eiusdem atque incertorum Opuscula sacra.* Leipzig: Teubner, 1871, pp. 147-218.

Calcidius. *Commentarius.* Ed. J.H. Waszink. In *Timaeus a Calcidio translatus commentarioque instructus,* pp. 53-346. Plato Latinus, vol. 4, ed. Raymond Klibansky. 2nd ed. London: The Warburg Institute, 1975.

Cartulaire de l'abbaye de Saint-Père de Chartres. Vol. 2. Ed. B. Guérard. Collection des cartulaires de France 2. Paris: Crapelet, 1840.

Cartulaire de Notre-Dame de Chartres. Ed. E. de Lépinois and L. Merlet. 3 vols. Chartres: Garnier, 1862-1865.

Cartulaire de Saint-Denis de Nogent-le-Rotrou, ed. C. Métais. In *Saint-Denis de Nogent-le-Rotrou, 1031-1789.* Archives du diocèse de Chartres 1. Vannes: Lafolye, 1895.

Cartulaire de Saint-Jean-en-Vallée de Chartres. Ed. René Merlet. Archives d'Eure-et-Loir. Collection de cartulaires chartrains 1. Chartres: Garnier, 1906.

[*Catalogi*]. *Catalogi Veteres librorum ecclesiae Cathedralis Dunelm. Catalogues of the Library of Durham Cathedral at Various Periods from the Conquest to the Dissolution ...* . Ed. James Raine. Publications of the Surtees Society 7. London: J.B. Nichols, 1838

——. *Mittelalterliche Bibliothekskataloge Deutschlands und der Schweiz,* vol. 2: *Bistum Mainz, Erfurt.* Ed. Paul Lehmann. Munich: Beck, 1928.

——. "Katalog der Bibliothek Hartmann Schedels." Ed. Paul Ruf. In *Mittelalterliche Bibliothekskataloge Deutschlands und der Schweiz,* vol. 3: *Bistum Augsburg,* pp. 807-839. Munich: Beck, 1932.

Cicero. *Partitiones oratoriae.* Ed. A.S. Wilkins. In *M. Tullii Ciceronis Rhetorica,* vol. 2. Oxford: Clarendon, 1903; rpt. 1955.

[Eriugena]. *Periphyseon* 1. Ed. I.P. Sheldon-Williams with Ludwig Bieler. In *Iohannis Scotti Eriugenae Periphyseon (De diuisione naturae).* Scriptores latini Hiberniae 7. Dublin: Dublin Institute for Advanced Studies, 1968.

——. Jean Scot. *Commentaire sur l'Evangile de Jean.* Ed. Edouard Jeauneau. Sources chrétiennes 180. Paris: Cerf, 1972.

Fulbert of Chartres. *The Letters and Poems of Fulbert of Chartres.* Ed. and trans. Frederick Behrends. Oxford: Clarendon, 1976.

Fulgentius, Fabius Planciades. *Mitologiae.* Ed. R. Helm. In *Fabii Planciadis Fulgentii V.C. opera.* Leipzig: Teubner, 1898.

[Garlandus of Besançon]. *Dialectica.* Ed. L.M. de Rijk. *Garlandus Compotista. Dialectica.* Assen: Van Gorcum, 1959.

Garnerius, bishop of Langres. *Sermones.* PL 205: 559C-828B.

Gilbert of Poitiers. *The Commentaries on Boethius by Gilbert of Poitiers.* Ed. Nikolaus M. Häring. Studies and Texts 13. Toronto: Pontifical Institute of Mediaeval Studies, 1966.

[Horace]. *Q. Horatii Flacci opera.* Ed. F. Klingner. 3rd ed. 1959: rpt. Leipzig: Teubner, 1970.

[Hugh of Saint-Victor]. *Didascalicon.* Ed. C.H. Buttimer. In *Hugonis de Sancto Victore Didascalicon De studio legendi: A Critical Text.* Studies in Medieval and Renaissance Latin 10. Washington: Catholic University Press, 1939.

Hyginus. *Fabulae.* Ed. Herbert J. Rose. Leiden: Sijthoff, 1933; rpt. 1967.

Isidore of Seville. *De natura rerum.* Ed. Jacques Fontaine. In Isidore de Seville, *Traité de la nature.* Bibliothèque de l'Ecole des Hautes Etudes Hispaniques, fasc. 28. Bordeaux: Féret et Fils, 1960.

——. *Etymologiae.* Ed. W.M. Lindsay. In *Isidori Hispalensis episcopi Etymologiarum sive originum libri xx.* 2 vols. Oxford: Clarendon, 1911; rpt. 1971.

Ivo, bishop of Chartres. *Decretum.* PL 161: 47-1022.

——. *Panormia.* PL 161: 1041-1344.

[Johannitius]. *Isagoge ad Techne Galieni,* ed. Gregor Maurach. In Maurach, Gregor. "Johannicius. *Isagoge ad Techne Galieni.*" *Sudhoffs Archiv* 62.2 (1978) 148-174.

John of Salisbury. *Entheticus Maior.* Ed. Jan van Laarhoven. In *John of Salisbury's Entheticus Maior and Minor,* vol. 1. Studien und Texte zur Geistesgeschichte des Mittelalters 17. Ed. Albert Zimmermann. Leiden: Brill, 1987.

——. *Metalogicon.* Ed. Clement C.J. Webb. Oxford: Clarendon, 1929 and Clement C.J. Webb. "Ioannis Saresberiensis Metalogicon: Addenda et Corrigenda." *Mediaeval and Renaissance Studies* 1 (London, 1941-1943) 232-236.

——. *Policraticus.* Ed. Clement C.J. Webb. 2 vols. Oxford: Clarendon, 1909.

——. *The Letters of John of Salisbury,* vol. 1: *The Early Letters (1153-1161).* Ed. W.J. Millor, H.E. Butler, revised by C.N.L. Brooke. London: Thomas Nelson, 1955. Vol.2: *The Later Letters (1163-1180).* Ed. W.J. Millor and C.N.L. Brooke. Oxford: Clarendon, 1979.

Lucan. *Bellum civile.* Ed. A.E. Housman. Oxford: Blackwell, 1927.

Macrobius. *Commentarii in Somnium Scipionis.* Ed. James Willis. Leipzig: Teubner, 1963.

——. *Saturnalia.* Ed. James Willis. Leipzig: Teubner, 1963.

Manegold of Lautenbach. *Liber contra Wolfelmum.* Ed. Wilfried Hartmann. Monumenta Germaniae Historica: Quellen zur Geistesgeschichte des Mittelalters 8. Weimar: Hermann Böhlaus, 1972.

Martianus Capella. *De nuptiis Philologiae et Mercurii.* Ed. James Willis. In *Martianus Capella.* Leipzig: Teubner, 1983.

Metamorphosis Goliae, ed. R.B.C. Huygens. In "Mitteilungen aus Handschriften. III: Die Metamorphose des Golias." *Studi Medievali* ser. 3, 3 (1962) 764-772.

Otto of Freising. *Gesta Friderici I imperatoris.* Ed. G. Waitz. 3rd ed. Monumenta Germaniae Historica: Scriptores rerum Germanicarum in usum scholarum. Hanover: Hahn, 1912.

Plato. *Timaeus a Calcidio translatus.* Ed. J.H. Waszink. In *Timaeus a Calcidio translatus commentarioque instructus,* pp. 1-52. Plato Latinus, vol. 4, ed. Raymond Klibansky. 2nd ed. London: The Warburg Institute, 1975.

——. *Platonis Timaeus interprete Chalcidio cum eiusdem commentario … .* Ed. J. Wrobel. Leipzig: Teubner, 1876.

——. *Timaeus a Cicerone translatus.* Ed. Remo Giomini. In *M. Tullii Ciceronis scripta quae manserunt omnia,* vol. 46: *De divinatione, De fato, Timaeus.* Leipzig: Teubner, 1975.

Porphyry. *Isagoge. Translatio Boethii.* Ed. Lorenzo Minio-Paluello. Aristoteles
    Latinus, vol. 1.6-7. Bruges: Desclée de Brouwer, 1966.
Priscian. *Institutiones grammaticae.* Ed. Martin Hertz. In *Grammatici latini* 2-3. Ed.
    H. Keil. 2 vols. Leipzig: Teubner, 1855-1859; rpt. Hildesheim: Olms, 1961.
Pseudo-Bede. *De mundi celestis terrestrisque constitutione.* Ed. and trans. Charles
    Burnett. Warburg Institute Surveys and Texts 10. London: Warburg Institute,
    1985.
——. Medieval additions to the above. PL 90: 904A11-910A2.
Rhetorica ad Herennium. Ed. F. Marx and W. Trillitzsch. Leipzig: Teubner, 1964.
Scriptores rerum mythicarum latini tres Romae nuper reperti. Ed. G.H. Bode. 2 vols.
    in 1. Celle: Schulze, 1834; rpt. Hildesheim: Olms, 1968.
Thierry of Chartres. *The Latin Rhetorical Commentaries by Thierry of Chartres.* Ed.
    Karin M. Fredborg. Studies and Texts 84. Toronto: Pontifical Institute of
    Mediaeval Studies, 1988.
[Varro]. *De lingua latina.* Ed. G. Goetz and F. Schoell. In *M. Terentii Varronis De
    lingua latina quae supersunt.* Leipzig: Teubner, 1910; rpt. Amsterdam:
    Hakkert, 1964.
[Virgil]. *P. Vergilii Maronis opera.* Ed. R.A.B. Mynors. Oxford: Clarendon, 1969;
    rpt. Oxford, 1972.
Walter of Mortagne. *Tractatus 'Quoniam de generali,'* ed. B. Hauréau. In *Notices et
    extraits de quelques manuscrits latins de la Bibliothèque Nationale* 5 (Paris,
    1892) 298-325.
William of Conches. *Commentum super Boethium* [in part], ed. J.M. Parent. In *La
    doctrine de la création dans l'école de Chartres,* pp. 124-136. Paris: Vrin, 1938.
——. *Glosae in Iuvenalem.* Ed. Bradford Wilson. In Guillaume de Conches, *Glosae
    in Iuvenalem.* Textes philosophiques du Moyen Age 18. Paris: Vrin, 1980.
——. *Glose Willelmi de Conchis super Platonem.* Ed. Edouard Jeauneau. In
    Guillaume de Conches, *Glosae super Platonem.* Textes philosophiques du
    Moyen Age 13. Paris: Vrin, 1965.
——. *Philosophia mundi,* ed. Gregor Maurach. In Wilhelm von Conches, *Philoso-
    phia.* Pretoria: University of South Africa, 1980. Also in PL 172: 39A-102A.

3. SECONDARY SOURCES

Alverny, Marie-Thérèse d'. "Maître Alain 'Nova et vetera'." In *Entretiens sur la
    renaissance de 12ᵉ siècle,* ed. M. de Gandillac and Edouard Jeauneau, pp.
    117-145. Paris: Mouton, 1968.
——. "Translations and Translators." In *Renaissance and Renewal in the Twelfth
    Century,* ed. Robert L. Benson and Giles Constable with Carol D. Lanham,
    pp. 421-462. Cambridge, Mass.: Harvard University Press, 1982.
Baltes, Matthias. *Die Weltenstehung des Platonischen Timaios nach den antiken
    Interpreten.* Philosophia antiqua: A Series of Monographs on Ancient Philo-
    sophy 30. Leiden: Brill, 1976.
Baswell, Christopher. "The Medieval Allegorization of the *Aeneid*: MS. Cambridge,
    Peterhouse 158." *Traditio* 41 (1985) 181-237.

Baeumker, Clemens. "Der Platonismus im Mittelalter." 1916; rpt. in *Platonismus in der Philosophie des Mittelalters*, ed. W. Beierwaltes, pp. 1-72. Wege der Forschung 197. Darmstadt: Wissenschaftliche Buchgesellschaft, 1969.

Beaujouan, Guy. "The Transformation of the Quadrivium." In *Renaissance and Renewal in the Twelfth Century*, ed. Robert L. Benson and Giles Constable with Carol D. Lanham, pp. 463-487. Cambridge, Mass.: Harvard University Press, 1982.

Benton, John F. "Philology's Search for Abelard in the *Metamorphosis Goliae*." *Speculum* 50 (1975) 199-217.

Bischoff, Bernhard. *Die südöstdeutschen Schreibschulen und Bibliotheken in der Karolingerzeit*, vol. 1: *Die bayerischen Diözesen*. Wiesbaden: Harrassowitz, 1960.

Boeft, J. den. *Calcidius on Demons (Commentarius Ch. 127-136)*. Philosophia antiqua: A Series of Monographs on Ancient Philosophy 33. Leiden: Brill, 1977.

———. *Calcidius on Fate: His Doctrines and Sources*. Philosophia antiqua: A Series of Monographs on Ancient Philosophy 18. Leiden: Brill, 1970.

Bolgar, R.R. *The Classical Heritage and Its Beneficiaries: from the Carolingian Age to the End of the Renaissance*. London: 1954; rpt. New York: Harper and Row, 1964.

Brisson, Luc. *Le même et l'autre dans la structure ontologique du 'Timée' de Platon: un commentaire systématique du 'Timée' de Platon*. Publications de l'Université de Paris X Nanterre, Lettres et Sciences Humaines: Série A: Thèses et travaux 23. Paris: Klincksieck, 1974.

Brooke, Christopher. "John of Salisbury and His World." In *The World of John of Salisbury*, ed. Michael Wilks, pp. 1-20. Studies in Church History, Subsidia 3. Oxford: Blackwell, 1984.

Brunner, Fernand. "Deus forma essendi." In *Entretiens sur la renaissance du 12ᵉ siècle*, ed. M. de Gandillac and Edouard Jeauneau, pp. 85-116. Paris: Mouton, 1968.

Burnett, Charles. "The Content and Affiliation of the Scientific Manuscripts Written at, or Brought to, Chartres in the Time of John of Salisbury." In *The World of John of Salisbury*, ed. Michael Wilks, pp. 127-160. Studies in Church History, Subsidia 3. Oxford: Blackwell, 1984.

Cambridge History of Later Greek and Early Medieval Philosophy. Ed. A.H. Armstrong. Cambridge: Cambridge University Press, 1967.

Cappuyns, Maïeul. *Jean Scot Erigène, sa vie, son oeuvre, sa pensée*. Louvain: Abbaye du Mont Cesar, 1933; Paris: Desclée de Brouwer, 1933; rpt. Brussels: Culture et Civilisation, 1964.

Catalogue général des manuscrits des bibliothèques publiques de France. Départements (Octavo series). Vol. 11: *Chartres*. Paris: Plon, 1890.

Catalogue général des manuscrits des bibliothèques publiques de France. Départements (Octavo series). Vol. 12: *Orléans*. Paris: Plon, 1889.

Châtillon, Jean. "Les écoles de Chartres et de Saint-Victor." In *La scuola nell'oc-*

cidente latino dell'alto medioevo, pp. 795-839. Settimane di studio del Centro Italiano di studi sull'alto medioevo 19.2. Spoleto: Presso la Sede del Centro, 1972.

Chenu, M.D. "Auctor, Actor, Autor." *Bulletin du Cange (Archivium latinitatis medii aevi)* 3 (1927) 81-86.

——. "Découverte de la nature et philosophie de l'homme à l'école de Chartres au XIIe siècle." *Cahiers d'histoire mondiale* 2 (1954) 313-325.

——. *Nature, Man, and Society in the Twelfth Century. Essays on New Theological Perspectives in the Latin West.* Ed. and trans. Jerome Taylor and Lester K. Little. Chicago: University of Chicago Press, 1968.

——. *La théologie au douzième siècle.* 3rd ed. Etudes de philosophie médiévale 45. Paris: Vrin, 1976.

Clerval, Alexandre. "Bernard de Chartres." *Les lettres chrétiennes* 4 (1882) 390-397.

——. *Les écoles de Chartres au Moyen Age (du Ve au XVIe siècle).* Paris: Garnier, 1895; rpt. Frankfurt: Minerva, 1965.

Colish, Marcia L. "Another Look at the School of Laon." *Archives d'histoire doctrinale et littéraire du Moyen Age* 53 (1986) 7-22.

Concordance of Boethius: The Five Theological Tractates and the Consolation of Philosophy. Ed. Lane Cooper. The Medieval Academy of America Publication 1. Cambridge, Mass.: Medieval Academy of America, 1928.

Cordoliani, A. "La *Logica* de Gerland de Besançon." *Revue du Moyen Age Latin* 5 (1949) 43-47.

Cornford, Francis MacDonald. *Plato's Cosmology. The 'Timaeus' of Plato Translated with a Running Commentary.* London: Routledge and Kegan Paul, 1937.

Courcelle, Pierre. *La Consolation de philosophie dans la tradition littéraire: Antécédents et Posterité de Boèce.* Paris: Etudes Augustiniennes, 1967.

——. *Late Latin Writers and their Greek Studies.* Trans. Harry E. Wedeck. Cambridge, Mass.: Harvard University Press, 1969.

Cousin, Victor. *Fragments philosophiques: philosophie scholastique.* 2nd ed. Paris: Ladrange, 1840.

——. *Fragments de philosophie du Moyen Age.* 2nd ed. Paris: Didier, 1856.

Dahan, G. "Une introduction à la philosophie au XIIe siècle: Le *Tractatus quidam de philosophia et partibus eius.*" *Archives d'histoire doctrinale et littéraire du Moyen Age* 49 (1982) 155-193.

Delisle, Léopold. *Catalogue des manuscrits du fonds de la Trémoïlle.* Paris: Champion, 1889.

——. "Notice sur plusieurs manuscrits de la Bibliothèque d'Orléans." *Notices et extraits des manuscrits* 31.1 (1884) 390-391.

Demimuid, Mauritius. *De Bernardo Carnotensi grammatico professore et interprete Virgilii.* Paris: Thesis, 1873.

Dickey, Mary. "Some Commentaries on the *De inventione* and *Ad Herennium* of the Eleventh and Twelfth Centuries." *Mediaeval and Renaissance Studies* 6 (1968) 1-41.

Dillon, John M. *The Middle Platonists: A Study of Platonism, 80 B.C. to A.D. 220.* London: Duckworth, 1977.

Dondaine, Antoine. "Abbréviations latines et signes recommandés pour l'apparat critique des éditions de textes médiévaux." *Bulletin de la Société internationale pour l'étude de la philosophie médiévale* 2 (1960) 142-149.

———. "Variantes de l'apparat critique dans les éditions de textes latins médiévaux." *Bulletin de la Société internationale pour l'étude de la philosophie médiévale* 4 (1962) 82-100.

Dronke, Peter. *Fabula. Explorations into the Uses of Myth in Medieval Platonism.* Leiden: Brill, 1974.

———. "Introduction." In *A History of Twelfth-Century Western Philosophy*, ed. Peter Dronke, pp. 1-18. Cambridge: Cambridge University Press, 1988.

———. "New Approaches to the School of Chartres." *Anuario de estudios medievales* 6 (1969) 117-140.

———. "Thierry of Chartres." In *A History of Twelfth-Century Western Philosophy*, ed. Peter Dronke, pp. 358-385. Cambridge: Cambridge University Press, 1988.

Duby, Georges. *The Three Orders: Feudal Society Imagined.* Trans. Arthur Goldhammer. Chicago: University of Chicago Press, 1980.

Dutton, Paul Edward, and Hankins, James. "An Early Manuscript of William of Conches' *Glosae super Platonem*." *Mediaeval Studies* 47 (1985) 487-494.

Dutton, Paul Edward, and Jeauneau, Edouard. "The Verses of the *Codex Aureus* of Saint-Emmeram." *Studi Medievali* ser. 3a., 24.1 (1983) 75-120.

Dutton, Paul Edward. "*Illustre ciuitatis et populi exemplum*: Plato's *Timaeus* and the Transmission from Calcidius to the End of the Twelfth Century of a Tripartite Scheme of Society." *Mediaeval Studies* 45 (1983) 79-119.

———. "The Uncovering of the *Glosae super Platonem* of Bernard of Chartres." *Mediaeval Studies* 46 (1984) 192-221.

Elferink, M.A. *La descente de l'âme d'après Macrobe.* Philosophia antiqua: A Series of Monographs on Ancient Philosophy 16. Leiden: Brill, 1968.

Elford, Dorothy. "Developments in the Natural Philosophy of William of Conches: A Study of the *Dragmaticon* and its Relationship to the *Philosophia*." Ph.D. diss. Cambridge University, 1983.

———. "William of Conches." In *A History of Twelfth-Century Western Philosophy*, ed. Peter Dronke, pp. 308-327. Cambridge: Cambridge University Press, 1988.

Ernout, A. and Meillet, A. *Dictionnaire étymologique de la langue latine: histoire des mots.* 4th ed. Paris: Klincksieck, 1959.

Evans, Gillian R. "John of Salisbury and Boethius on Arithmetic." In *The World of John of Salisbury*, ed. Michael Wilks, pp. 161-167. Studies in Church History, Subsidia 3. Oxford: Blackwell, 1984.

Ferruolo, Stephen C. *The Origins of the University: The Schools of Paris and their Critics, 1100-1215.* Stanford: Stanford University Press, 1985.

Findlay, J.N. *Plato: The Written and Unwritten Doctrines.* London: Routledge and Kegan Paul, 1974.

Flatten, Heinrich. "Die *materia primordialis* in der Schule von Chartres." *Archiv für Geschichte der Philosophie* 40 (1931) 58-65.

Fontaine, Jacques. *Isidore de Seville et la culture classique dans l'Espagne wisigothique.* 2 vols. Paris: Etudes Augustiniennes, 1959.

Forest, Aimé. "Le réalisme de Gilbert de la Porrée dans le commentaire du *De hebdomadibus.*" *Revue néo-scholastique de philosophie* 36 (1934) 101-110.

Fredborg, Karin Margareta. "The Commentary on Cicero's *De inventione* and *Rhetorica ad Herennium* by William of Champeaux." *Cahiers de l'Institut du Moyen-Age Grec et Latin* 17 (1976) 1-39.

Gagnér, Stern, *Studien zur Ideengeschichte der Gesetzgebung.* Uppsala: Almquist and Wiksell, 1960.

Garin, Eugenio. *Studi sul Platonismo medievale.* Florence: Felice le Monnier, 1958.

Gersh, Stephen. *Middle Platonism and Neoplatonism: The Latin Tradition.* 2 vols. Publications in Medieval Studies, The Medieval Institute, University of Notre Dame 23.1-2. Notre Dame: University of Notre Dame, 1986.

———. "Platonism—Neoplatonism—Aristotelianism: A Twelfth-Century Metaphysical System and its Sources." In *Renaissance and Renewal in the Twelfth Century,* ed. Robert L. Benson and Giles Constable with Carol D. Lanham, pp. 512-534. Cambridge, Mass.: Harvard University Press, 1982.

Giacone, Roberto. "Masters, Books and Library at Chartres According to the Cartularies of Notre-Dame and Saint-Père." *Vivarium* 12 (1974) 30-51.

Gibson, Margaret. "The *Opuscula sacra* in the Middle Ages." In *Boethius: His Life, Thought, and Influence,* ed. Margaret Gibson, pp. 214-234. Oxford: Blackwell, 1981.

———. "The Study of the *Timaeus* in the Eleventh and Twelfth Centuries." *Pensamiento* 25 (1969) 183-194.

Gilson, Etienne. *History of Christian Philosophy in the Middle Ages.* New York: Random House, 1955.

———. "Note sur les noms de la matière chez Gilbert de la Porrée." *Revue du Moyen Age Latin* 2 (1946) 173-176.

———. "Le platonisme de Bernard de Chartres." *Revue néo-scholastique de philosophie* 25 (1923) 5-19.

Giomini, Remo. *Ricerche sul testo del Timeo ciceroniano.* Studi e saggi 9. Rome: Signorelli, 1967.

Grabmann, Martin. *Die Geschichte des scholastischen Methode.* 2 vols. 1909-1911; rpt. Graz: Akademische Druck -u. Verlagsanstalt, 1957.

Greenslade, S.L. "The Contents of the Library of Durham Cathedral Priory." *Transactions of the Architectural and Archaeological Society of Durham and Northumberland* 11.5-6 (1965) 347-369.

Gregory, Tullio. "Abélard et Platon." *Studi Medievali* ser. 3a, 13 (1972) 539-562.

———. *Anima mundi. La filosofia di Guglielmo di Conches e la scuola di Chartres.* Pubblicazioni dell'istituto di filosofia dell'universita di Roma 3. Florence: Sansoni, 1955.

———. "L'idea della natura nella scuola di Chartres." *Giornale critico della filosofia italiana* 4 (1952) 433-442.

——. "Note sul platonismo della scuola di Chartres: la dottrina delle *specie native.*" *Giornale critico della filosofia italiana* 32 (1953) 358-362.

——. "La nouvelle idée de la nature et de savoir scientifique au XIIᵉ siècle." In *The Cultural Context of Medieval Learning*, ed. J.E. Murdoch and E.R. Sylla, pp. 193-218. Boston Studies in the Philosophy of Science 26. Dordrecht: Reidel, 1975.

——. *Platonismo medievale: studi e ricerche.* Studi storici, fasc. 26-27. Rome: Istituto storico Italiano per il medio evo, 1958.

——. "Le Platonisme du XIIᵉ siècle." *Revue des sciences philosophiques et théologiques* 71 (1987) 243-259.

——. "The Platonic Inheritance." In *A History of Twelfth-Century Western Philosophy*, ed. Peter Dronke, pp. 54-80. Cambridge: Cambridge University Press, 1988.

Hagendahl, Harald. *Augustine and the Latin Classics.* 2 vols. Studia Graeca et Latina Gothoburgensia 20.1-2. Goteborg: Acta Universitatis Gothoburgensis, 1967.

Halm, Karl Felix von and Laubman, G. *Catalogus codicum latinorum Bibliothecae regiae monacensis.* Vol. 1.1: *(Codices num. 2329 complectens).* Munich: Palm, 1868.

Hankins, James. "Plato in the Middle Ages." In *Dictionary of the Middle Ages*, ed. Joseph R. Strayer, 9: 694-704. New York: Charles Scribner's Sons, 1987.

Happ, Heinz. *Hyle. Studien zum aristotelischen Materie-Begriff.* Berlin: Walter de Gruyter, 1971.

Häring, Nikolaus. "*Auctoritas* in der sozialen und intellektuellen Struktur des zwölften Jahrhunderts." In *Soziale Ordnungen im Selbstverständnis des Mittelalters*, 2 vols., ed. A. Zimmermann, 2:517-533. Miscellanea Mediaevalia 12. Berlin: Walter de Gruyter, 1980.

——. "Chartres and Paris Revisited." In *Essays in Honour of Anton Charles Pegis*, ed. J. Reginald O'Donnell, pp. 268-329. Toronto: Pontifical Institute of Mediaeval Studies, 1974.

——. "Commentary and Hermeneutics." In *Renaissance and Renewal in the Twelfth Century*, ed. Robert L. Benson and Giles Constable with Carol D. Lanham, pp. 173-200. Cambridge, Mass.: Harvard University Press, 1982.

——. "A Hitherto Unknown Commentary on Boethius' *De hebdomadibus* Written by Clarenbaldus of Arras." *Mediaeval Studies* 15 (1953) 212-221.

——. "Zur Geschichte der Schulen von Poitiers im 12. Jahrhundert." *Archiv für Kulturgeschichte* 47 (1965) 23-47.

Hartmann, Wilfried. "Manegold von Lautenbach und die Anfänge der Frühscholastik." *Deutsches Archiv für Erforschung des Mittelalters* 26 (1970) 47-149.

Haskins, Charles Homer. *The Renaissance of the Twelfth Century.* 1927; rpt. New York: Meridian Books, 1957.

——. *Studies in Mediaeval Culture.* Oxford: Clarendon, 1929; rpt. New York: Frederick Ungar, 1958.

Hauréau, B. "Bernard de Chartres et Thierry de Chartres." *Académie des Inscriptions et Belles-Lettres. Comptes rendus des séances de l'année 1872*, 3ᵉ serie, 1 (Paris, 1873) 75-85.

——. "Maître Bernard." *Bibliothèque de l'Ecole des chartes* 54 (1893) 792-794.

——. "Mémoire sur quelques chanceliers de l'église de Chartres." *Académie des Inscriptions et Belles-Lettres, Paris. Mémoires* 31.2 (Paris, 1884) 63-122.

——. "Mémoire sur quelques maîtres du XIIe siècle, à l'occasion d'une prose latine publiée par M. Th. Wright." *Académie des Inscriptions et Belles-Lettres, Paris. Mémoires* 28.2 (Paris, 1876) 223-238.

Heimpel, Hermann. "Reformatio Sigismundi, Priesterehe und Bernhard von Chartres." *Deutsches Archiv für Erforschung des Mittelalters* 17 (1961) 526-537.

Hendley, Brian. "John of Salisbury and the Problem of Universals." *Journal of the History of Philosophy* 8 (1970) 289-302.

Histoire littéraire de la France.... Vol. 12. Paris: 1763; rpt. Paris: Palmé, 1869. Vol. 13. Rpt. Paris: Palmé, 1869.

Holmes, Urban T., Jr. "Transitions in European Education." In *Twelfth-Century Europe and the Foundations of Modern Society*, ed. M. Clagett, G. Post, and R. Reynolds, pp. 15-38. Madison: University of Wisconsin, 1966.

Hunt, Richard W. "The Introductions to the 'Artes' in the Twelfth Century." In *Studia mediaevalia in honorem admodum reverendi patris Raymundi Joseph Martin ordinis praedicatorum S. theologiae magistri LXXum natalem diem agentis.* Bruges: De Tempel, 1948, pp. 85-112; rpt. in R.W. Hunt, *The History of Grammar in the Middle Ages: Collected Papers*, ed. G.L. Bursill-Hall, pp. 117-144. Amsterdam: John Benjamins, 1980.

——. "Studies on Priscian in the Eleventh and Twelfth Centuries." *Mediaeval and Renaissance Studies* 1 (1941-1943) 194-231; rpt. in R.W. Hunt, *The History of Grammar in the Middle Ages: Collected Papers*, ed. G.L. Bursill-Hall, pp. 1-38. Amsterdam: John Benjamins, 1980.

Huygens, R.B.C. "Guillaume de Tyr étudiant: un chapitre (19.12) de son *Histoire* retrouvé." *Latomus* 21 (1962) 811-829.

——. "Mittelalterliche Kommentare zum *O qui perpetua...*" *Sacris Erudiri* 6 (1954) 373-427.

Indici e cataloghi. Vol. 8: *I codici Ashburnhamiani della R. Biblioteca Mediceo-Laurenziana di Firenze* 1.1. Ed. Caesare Paoli and Enrico Rostagno. Rome: Presso i principali librai, 1887.

Jacquart, Danielle. "A l'aube de la renaissance médicale des XIe-XIIe siècles: L'*Isagoge Johannitii* et son traducteur." *Bibliothèque de l'Ecole des chartes* 144 (1986) 209-240.

——. "Aristotelian Thought in Salerno." In *A History of Twelfth-Century Western Philosophy*, ed. Peter Dronke, pp. 407-428. Cambridge: Cambridge University Press, 1988.

James, Montague Rhodes. "List of Manuscripts formerly owned by Dr. John Dee with Preface and Identifications." *Supplements to the Transactions of the Bibliographical Society, 1921-1926*, pp. 1-40. London: Bibliographical Society, 1926.

Jeauneau, Edouard. "Berkeley, University of California, Bancroft Library MS. 2 (Notes de lecture)." *Mediaeval Studies* 50 (1988) 438-456.

——. "Bernard of Chartres." In *Dictionary of Scientific Biography*, ed. Charles Coulston Gillispie, 2: 19-20. New York: Scribner's Sons, 1970.

——. "Extraits des *Glosae super Platonem* de Guillaume de Conches dans un manuscrit de Londres." *Journal of the Warburg and Courtauld Institutes* 40 (1977) 212-222.

——. "Gloses et commentaires de textes philosophiques (IXe-XIIe s.)." In *Les genres littéraires dans les sources théologiques et philosophiques médiévales: définition, critique et exploitation: Actes du Colloque international de Louvain-la-Neuve, 25-27 mai 1981*, pp. 117-131. Louvain-la-Neuve: Publications de l'Institut d'Etudes Médiévales, 1982.

——. "Jean de Salisbury et la lecture des philosophes." In *The World of John of Salisbury*, ed. Michael Wilks, pp. 77-108. Studies in Church History, Subsidia 3. Oxford: Blackwell, 1984; rpt. in *Revue des Etudes Augustiniennes* 29 (1983) 145-174.

——. *'Lectio philosophorum': Recherches sur l'Ecole de Chartres.* Amsterdam: Hakkert, 1973.

——. "Nains et géants." In *Entretiens sur la renaissance du 12e siècle*, ed. M. de Gandillac and Edouard Jeauneau, pp. 21-52. Paris: Mouton, 1968.

——. *La philosophie médiévale.* 3rd ed. Que sais-je? 1044. Paris: Presses universitaires de France, 1975.

——. "Plato apud Bohemos." *Mediaeval Studies* 41 (1979) 161-214.

——. Review of Peter Dronke's edition of the *Cosmographia* of Bernardus Silvestris. *Medium Aevum* 49 (1980) 112-117.

Jolivet, Jean. "The Arabic Inheritance." In *A History of Twelfth-Century Western Philosophy*, ed. Peter Dronke, pp. 113-148. Cambridge: Cambridge University Press, 1988.

——. "Eléments pour une étude des rapports entre la grammaire et l'ontologie au Moyen Age." In *Sprache und Erkenntnis im Mittelalter*, ed. Jan P. Beckmann et al., pp. 135-164. Miscellanea mediaevalia 13.1. Berlin: Walter de Gruyter, 1980.

——. "Les rochers de cumes et l'antre de Cerbère. L'ordre du savoir selon le *Commentaire* de Bernard Silvestre sur l'*Enéide*." In *Pascua Mediaevalia. Studies voor Prof. Dr. J.M. De Smet*, ed. R. Lievens, E. Van Mingroot, and W. Verbeke, pp. 263-276. Louvain: Universitaire Pers Leuven, 1983.

Jungmann, J.A. *The Mass of the Roman Rite. Its Origins and Development (Missarum Sollemnia).* Trans. F.A. Brunner. Revised by C.K. Riepe. London: Burns and Oates, 1959.

Kenney, James F. *The Sources for the Early History of Ireland: An Introduction and Guide.* Records of Civilization, Sources and Studies 11. New York: Columbia University, 1929; rpt. Octagon, 1966.

Kenny, Anthony and Pinborg, Jan. "Medieval Philosophical Literature." In *The Cambridge History of Later Medieval Philosophy from the Rediscovery of Aristotle to the Disintegration of Scholasticism, 1100-1600*, ed. Norman Kretzmann, Anthony Kenny, and Jan Pinborg, pp. 11-42. Cambridge: Cambridge University Press, 1982.

Ker, N.R. *Medieval Libraries of Great Britain. A List of Surviving Books.* 2nd ed. London: Offices of the Royal Historical Society, 1964.

Keyt, David. "The Mad Craftsman of the *Timaeus.*" *The Philosophical Review* 80 (1971) 230-235.

Klibansky, Raymond. *The Continuity of the Platonic Tradition during the Middle Ages: Outlines of a Corpus Platonicum Medii Aevi.* London: The Warburg Institute, 1939; rpt. 1950; rpt. with a new preface and four supplementary chapters, London, 1981.

——. "Report by the General Editor on the Progress of the Corpus Platonicum Medii Aevi." In *University of London: The Warburg Institute Annual Report 1956-1957,* p. 13. London: Warburg Institute, 1957.

——. "The School of Chartres." In *Twelfth-Century Europe and the Foundations of Modern Society,* ed. M. Clagett, G. Post, and R. Reynolds, pp. 3-14. Madison: University of Wisconsin, 1966.

Knowles, David. *The Evolution of Medieval Thought.* New York: Random House, 1962.

Kristeller, P.O. *Iter Italicum accedunt alia itinera. A Finding List of Uncatalogued or Incompletely Catalogued Humanistic Manuscripts of the Renaissance in Italian and Other Libraries,* vol. 3: *(Alia itinera 1) Australia to Germany.* London: The Warburg Institute, 1983.

Kuttner, Stephan. "Gratian and Plato." In *Church and Government in the Middle Ages: Essays Presented to C.R. Cheney on His 70th Birthday,* ed. C.N.L. Brooke, D.E. Luscombe, G.H. Martin, and Dorothy Owen, pp. 93-118. Cambridge: Cambridge University Press, 1976; rpt. in Stephan Kuttner, *The History of Ideas and Doctrines of Canon Law in the Middle Ages.* London: Variorum Reprints, 1980.

Langlois, Charles. "Maître Bernard." *Bibliothèque de l'Ecole des chartes* 54 (1893) 225-250.

Lapidge, Michael. "The Stoic Inheritance." In *A History of Twelfth-Century Western Philosophy,* ed. Peter Dronke, pp. 81-112. Cambridge: Cambridge University Press, 1988.

Lehmann, Paul. *Mitteilungen aus Handschriften 5.* Sitzungsberichte der bayerischen Akademie der Wissenschaften: philosophisch-historische Abteilung 4. Munich: Bayerischen Akademie der Wissenschaften, 1938.

Lesne, Emile. *Histoire de la propriété ecclésiastique en France,* vol. 5: *Les écoles de la fin du VIIIe siècle à la fin du XIIe.* Lille: Facultés Catholiques, 1940.

Liebeschütz, Hans. "John of Salisbury and the Pseudo-Plutarch." *Journal of the Warburg and Courtauld Institutes* 6 (1943) 33-39.

——. *Mediaeval Humanism in the Life and Writings of John of Salisbury.* Studies of the Warburg Institute, 17. London: the Warburg Institute, 1950.

Linder, Amnon. "The Knowledge of John of Salisbury in the Later Middle Ages." *Studi Medievali* ser. 3a, 18.2 (1977) 315-366.

Liron, Jean. *Bibliothèque générale des auteurs de France,* vol. 1: *La bibliothèque chartraine ou le traité des auteurs et des hommes illustres de l'ancien Diocèse de Chartres.* Paris: Garnier, 1719; rpt. as *Bibliothèque chartraine,* Geneva: Slatkine, 1971.

Lowe, E.A. *Codices latini antiquiores,* vol. 2. 2nd ed. Oxford: Clarendon, 1935.

Lucenti, Paolo. *Platonismo medievale: contributi per la storia dell'Eriugenismo.* 2nd ed. Florence: La nuova Italia, 1980.

Luscombe, David E. "Bernard of Chartres." In *The Encyclopedia of Philosophy* 1: 305. New York: Macmillan, 1967.

———. *The School of Peter Abelard: The Influence of Abelard's Thought in the Early Scholastic Period.* Cambridge Studies in Medieval Life and Thought, new series 14. Cambridge: Cambridge University Press, 1969.

Maas, Paul. *Textual Criticism.* Trans. Barbara Flower. Oxford: Clarendon, 1958.

Madan, F. et al. *A Summary Catalogue of Western Manuscripts in the Bodleian Library at Oxford,* vol. 2.2. Oxford: Clarendon, 1937.

Manitius, Max. *Geschichte der lateinischen Literatur des Mittelalters,* vol. 3: *vom Ausbruch des Kirchenstreites bis zum Ende des zwölften Jahrhunderts.* Munich: Beck, 1931.

Marenbon, John. *Early Medieval Philosophy (480-1150). An Introduction.* London: Routledge and Kegan Paul, 1983.

———. "Gilbert of Poitiers." In *A History of Twelfth-Century Western Philosophy,* ed. Peter Dronke, pp. 328-352. Cambridge: Cambridge University Press, 1988.

Martin, Janet. "John of Salisbury as Classical Scholar." In *The World of John of Salisbury,* ed. Michael Wilks, pp. 179-202. Studies in Church History, Subsidia 3. Oxford: Blackwell, 1984.

Martin, T.H. *Etudes sur le Timée de Platon.* 2 vols. Paris: Ladrange, 1841; rpt. New York: Arno, 1976.

McKeon, Richard. "The Organization of Sciences and the Relations of Cultures in the Twelfth and Thirteenth Centuries." In *The Cultural Context of Medieval Learning,* ed. J.E. Murdoch and E.D. Sylla. pp. 151-192. Boston Studies in the Philosophy of Science 26. Dordrecht: Reidel, 1975.

Menhardt, Hermann. *Das älteste Handschriftenverzeichnis der Wiener Hofbibliothek von Hugo Blotius 1576. Kritische Ausgabe der Handschrift Series nova 4451 vom Jahre 1597 mit vier Anhängen.* Österreichische Akademie der Wissenschaften, philosophisch-historische Klasse, Denkschriften 76. Vienna: Rohrer, 1957.

Mensching, Eckart. "Zur Calcidius-Überlieferung." *Vigiliae Christianae* 19 (1965) 42-56.

Merlet, Lucien. "Catalogue des livres de l'abbaye de Saint-Père de Chartres, au XIe siècle." *Bibliothèque de l'Ecole des chartes* 15 (1853-1854) 263-270.

———. "Lettres d'Ives de Chartres et d'autres personnages de son temps, 1087-1130." *Bibliothèque de l'Ecole des chartes* 16 (1855) 443-471.

Merlet, Lucien and Merlet, René. *Les dignitaires de l'église Notre-Dame de Chartres: Listes chronologiques.* Archives du diocèse de Chartres 5. Chartres: Métais, 1900. Paris: Picard, 1900.

Merlet, René and Clerval, A. *Un manuscrit chartrain du XIe siècle.* Chartres: Garnier, 1893.

The Metalogicon of John of Salisbury. A Twelfth-Century Defense of the Verbal and Logical Arts of the Trivium. Trans. Daniel D. McGarry. Berkeley: University of California Press, 1962.

Mohr, Richard D. *The Platonic Cosmology.* Philosophia antiqua: A Series of Monographs on Ancient Philosophy 42. Leiden: Brill, 1985.

——. "Plato's Theology Reconsidered: What the Demiurge Does." In *Essays in Ancient Greek Philosophy III: Plato,* ed. John Anton and Anthony Preus, pp. 293-307. Albany: State University of New York Press, 1989.

Moreau, Joseph. "*'Opifex, id est Creator'*: Remarques sur le platonisme de Chartres." *Archiv für Geschichte der Philosophie* 56 (1974) 33-49.

Munk-Olsen, Birger. "L'humanisme de Jean de Salisbury, un Cicéronien au XIIe siècle." In *Entretiens sur la renaissance du 12e siècle,* ed. M. de Gandillac and Edouard Jeauneau, pp. 53-83. Paris: Mouton, 1968.

Mynors, R.A.B. *Durham Cathedral Manuscripts to the End of the Twelfth Century.* Oxford: Oxford University, 1939.

Nelson, Axel. "Ett citat från Bernard av Chartres." *Nordisk tidskrift för Bok-och Bibliotheksväsen* 17 (1930) 41.

Newell, John Howle. "The Dignity of Man in William of Conches and the School of Chartres in the Twelfth Century." Ph.D. diss. Duke University, 1978.

Nielsen, L.O. *Theology and Philosophy in the Twelfth Century. A Study of Gilbert Porreta's Thinking and the Theological Expositions of the Doctrine of the Incarnation during the Period 1130-1180.* Acta Theologica Danica 15. Leiden: Brill, 1982.

O'Donnell, J. Reginald. "The Meaning of 'Silva' in the Commentary on the *Timaeus* of Plato by Chalcidius." *Mediaeval Studies* 7 (1945) 1-20.

——. "The Sources and Meaning of Bernard Silvester's Commentary on the Aeneid." *Mediaeval Studies* 24 (1962) 233-249.

Opelt, Ilona. "Das Bild des Sokrates in der christlichen lateinischen Literatur." In *Platonismus und Christentum: Festschrift für Heinrich Dörrie,* ed. H.D. Blume and F. Mann, pp. 192-207. Jahrbuch für Antike und Christentum 10. Münster: Aschendorff, 1983.

Padoan, Giorgio. "Tradizione e fortuna del commento all'*Eneide* di Bernardo Silvestre." *Italia medioevale e umanistica* 3 (1960) 227-240.

Paré, G., Brunet, A., Tremblay, P. *La renaissance du XIIe siècle: les écoles et l'enseignement.* Publications de l'Institut d'Etudes Médiévales d'Ottawa 3. Paris: Vrin, 1933.

Parent, J.M. *La doctrine de la création dans l'école de Chartres.* Publications de l'Institut d'Etudes Médiévales d'Ottawa 8. Paris: Vrin, 1938.

Pepin, Ronald E. "The 'Entheticus' of John of Salisbury: a Critical Text." *Traditio* 31 (1975) 127-193.

Piper, A.J. "The Libraries of the Monks of Durham." In *Medieval Scribes, Manuscripts, and Libraries: Essays Presented to N.R. Ker,* ed. M.B. Parkes and Andrew G. Watson, pp. 213-249. London: Scolar, 1978.

Platonismus in der Philosophie des Mittelalters. Ed. Werner Beierwaltes. Wege der Forschung 197. Darmstadt: Wissenschaftliche Buchgesellschaft, 1969.

Pleticha, Eva. *Adel und Buch. Studien zur Geisteswelt des fränkischen Adels am Beispiel seiner Bibliotheken vom 15. bis zum 18. Jahrhundert.* Veröffentlichungen der Gesellschaft für fränkischen Geschichte, Reihe IX, Darstellungen aus der fränkischen Geschichte 33. Neustadt an der Aisch: Degener, 1983.

Poncelet, Roland. *Cicéron, traducteur de Platon: L'expression de la pensée complexe en latin classique.* Paris: Boccard, 1957.

——. "Deux aspects du style philosophique latin: Cicéron et Chalcidius, traducteurs du *Phèdre* 245c." *Revue des études latines* 28 (1950) 145-167.

Poole, Reginald Lane. *Illustrations of the History of Medieval Thought in the Departments of Theology and Ecclesiastical Politics.* London: Williams and Norgate, 1884.

——. *Illustrations of the History of Medieval Thought and Learning.* 2nd rev. ed. London, 1920; rpt. New York: Dover, 1960.

——. "The Masters of the Schools at Paris and Chartres in John of Salisbury's Time." *The English Historical Review* 139 (1920) 321-342; rpt. in R.L. Poole, *Studies in Chronology and History*, pp. 223-247. Oxford: Clarendon, 1934.

Quain, Edwin A. "The Medieval *Accessus ad auctores.*" *Traditio* 3 (1945) 215-264.

Regen, Frank. "Zu Augustins Darstellung des Platonismus am Anfang des 8. Buches der Civitas dei." In *Platonismus und Christentum: Festschrift für Heinrich Dörrie*, ed. H.D. Blume and F. Mann, pp. 208-227. Jahrbuch für Antike und Christentum 10. Münster: Aschendorff, 1983.

Riché, Pierre. "Jean de Salisbury et le monde scolaire de XIIᵉ siècle." In *The World of John of Salisbury*, ed. Michael Wilks, pp. 39-61. Studies in Church History, Subsidia, 3. Oxford: Blackwell, 1984.

Rist, John M. "Basil's 'Neoplatonism': Its Background and Nature." In *Basil of Caesarea: Christian, Humanist, Ascetic. A Sixteen-hundredth Anniversary Symposium*, ed. Paul Jonathan Fedwick, 1:137-220. Toronto: Pontifical Institute of Mediaeval Studies, 1981.

Robert, Ulysse. *Le cabinet historique: Moniteur des Bibliothèques et des Archives.* New series 1, 28th year. Paris: Champion, 1882.

Ross, David. *Plato's Theory of Ideas.* Oxford: Clarendon, 1951; rpt. 1963.

Scheffel, Wolfgang. *Aspekte der platonischen Kosmologie. Untersuchungen zum Dialog 'Timaios'.* Philosophia antiqua: A Series of Monographs on Ancient Philosophy 29. Leiden: Brill, 1976.

Schipperges, Heinrich. *Die Assimilation der arabischen Medizin durch das lateinische Mittelalter.* Sudhoffs Archiv für Geschichte der Medizin und der Naturwissenschaften. Beihefte. Heft 3. Wiesbaden: Steiner, 1964.

——. "Die Schulen von Chartres unter dem Einfluss des Arabismus." *Sudhoffs Archiv für Geschichte der Medizin und der Naturwissenschaften* 40 (1956) 193-210.

Schmid, Toni. "Ein Timaioskommentar in Sigtuna." *Classica et mediaevalia: Revue Danoise de philologie et d'histoire* 10 (1949-1951) 220-266.

Schulz, Dietrich Joachim. *Das Problem der Materie in Platos 'Timaios'.* Abhandlungen zur Philosophie, Psychologie, und Pädagogik 31. Bonn: Bouvier, 1966.

Shaw, F. "The Irish Glosses and Marginalia in Bodl. MS. Auct. F.3.15." *Proceedings of the Royal Irish Academy* 58, section C (1956) 17-20.

Sheldon-Williams, I.P. "An Epitome of Irish Provenance of Eriugena's *De diuisione naturae* (MS. Bodl. Auct. F.3.15)." *Proceedings of the Royal Irish Academy* 58, Section C (1956) 1-16.

Silverstein, Theodore. "*Elementatum*: Its Appearance among the Twelfth-Century Cosmogonists." *Mediaeval Studies* 16 (1954) 156-162.

Skemp, J.B. *Plato. Greece and Rome* New Surveys in the Classics 10. Oxford: Clarendon, 1976.

Smits, E.R. "New Evidence for the Authorship of the Commentary on the First Six Books of Virgil's *Eneid* Commonly Attributed to Bernardus Silvestris?" In *Non nova, sed nove: Mélanges de civilisation médiévale dédiés à Willem Noomen*, ed. M. Gosman and J. van Os, pp. 239-246. Groningen: Bouma's Boekhuis, 1984.

Southern, R.W. "Humanism and the School of Chartres." In R.W. Southern, *Medieval Humanism and Other Studies*, pp.61-85. New York: Harper Torchbooks, 1970; rpt. Oxford: Blackwell, 1984.

———. *Platonism, Scholastic Method, and the School of Chartres: The Stenton Lecture, 1978.* Reading: University of Reading, 1979.

———. "The Schools of Paris and the School of Chartres." In *Renaissance and Renewal in the Twelfth Century*, ed. Robert L. Benson and Giles Constable with Carol D. Lanham, pp. 113-137. Cambridge, Mass.: Harvard University Press, 1982.

Stauber, Richard. *Die Schedelsche Bibliothek. Ein Beitrag zur Geschichte der Ausbreitung der italienischen Renaissance, des deutschen Humanismus und der medizinischen Literatur.* Studien und Darstellungen aus dem Gebiete des Geschichte 6.2-3. Freiburg, Herdersche, 1908.

Stock, Brian. *Myth and Science in the Twelfth Century. A Study of Bernard Silvester.* Princeton: Princeton University, 1972.

Stokes, Whitley. "Irish Glosses and Notes on Chalcidius." *Zeitschrift für Vergleichende Sprachforschung* 29, Neue Folge 9 (1887) 372-380.

Struve, Tilman. "The Importance of the Organism in the Political Theory of John of Salisbury." In *The World of John of Salisbury*, ed. Michael Wilks, pp. 303-318. Studies in Church History, Subsidia 3. Oxford: Blackwell, 1984.

Sulowski, Jan Franciszek. "Studies on Chalcidius: Anthropology, Influence and Importance (General Outline)." In *L'homme et son destin d'après les penseurs du Moyen Age. Actes du premier Congrès international de philosophie médiévale. Louvain-Bruxelles 28 Août-4 Septembre 1958*, pp. 153-161. Louvain: Nauwelaerts, 1960.

Switalski, B.W. *Des Chalcidius Kommentar zu Plato's Timaeus: eine historisch-kritische Untersuchung.* Beiträge zur Geschichte der Philosophie des Mittelalters 3.6. Münster: Aschendorff, 1902.

Tabulae codicum manu scriptorum praeter graecos et orientales in Bibliotheca palatina Vindobonensi asservatorum, vols. 1-2 *(Cod. 1-2000-3500)*. Vienna: Gerold, 1864-1868; rpt. Graz, 1965.

Taylor, A.E. *A Commentary on Plato's Timaeus.* Oxford: Clarendon, 1927; rpt. 1962.

Thomson, Rodney. "John of Salisbury and William of Malmesbury: Currents in Twelfth-Century Humanism." In *The World of John of Salisbury,* ed. Michael Wilks, pp. 117-126. Studies in Church History, Subsidia 3. Oxford: Blackwell, 1984.

———. "What is the *Entheticus?*" In *The World of John of Salisbury,* ed. Michael Wilks, pp. 287-302. Studies in Church History, Subsidia 3. Oxford: Blackwell, 1984.

A Thousand Years of Irish Script: An Exhibition of Irish Manuscripts in Oxford Libraries Arranged by Francis John Byrne. Oxford: Bodleian Library, 1979.

Tweedale, Martin M. "Logic (i): From the Late Eleventh Century to the Time of Abelard." In *A History of Twelfth-Century Western Philosophy,* ed. Peter Dronke, pp. 196-226. Cambridge: Cambridge University Press, 1988.

Vernet, A. "Un remaniement de la *Philosophia* de Guillaume de Conches." *Scriptorium* 1 (1946-1947) 243-259; rpt. with additions and corrections in André Vernet, *Etudes médiévales,* pp. 143-159, 660-666. Paris: Études augustiniennes, 1981.

Viarre, Simone. "L'interprétation de l'*Enéide.* A propos d'un commentaire du douzième siècle." In *Présence de Virgile. Actes du Colloque des 9, 11, et 12 Décembre 1976 (Paris E.N.S., Tours),* ed. R. Chevallier, pp. 223-232. Paris: Société d'édition 'Les Belles Lettres', 1978.

Vlastos, Gregory. *Plato's Universe.* Seattle: University of Washington Press, 1975.

Walzer, Richard. *Greek into Arabic: Essays on Islamic Philosophy.* Oriental Studies 1, ed. S.M. Stern and Richard Walzer. Cambridge, Mass.: Harvard University Press, 1962.

Ward, J.O. "The Date of the Commentary on Cicero's *De inventione* by Thierry of Chartres (ca.1095-1160?) and the Cornifician Attack on the Liberal Arts." *Viator* 3 (1972) 219-273.

Warner, George Frederic, and Gilson, Julius P. *British Museum. Catalogue of Western Manuscripts in the Old Royal and King's Collections.* 2 vols. London: The Trustees, 1921.

Waszink, J.H. "Praefatio." In *Timaeus a Calcidio translatus commentarioque instructus,* pp. vii-cxciv. Plato Latinus, vol. 4. Ed. Raymond Klibansky. 2nd ed. London: The Warburg Institute, 1975.

———. "Die sogenannte Fünfteilung der Träume bei Chalcidius und ihre Quellen." *Mnemosyne* new series 3 (1942) 65-85.

———. *Studien zum Timaioskommentar des Calcidius,* vol. 1: *Die erste Hälfte des Kommentars (mit Ausnahme der Kapitel über die Weltseele).* Philosophia antiqua: A Series of Monographs on Ancient Philosophy 12. Leiden: Brill, 1964.

Watson, Andrew G. "Thomas Allen of Oxford and His Manuscripts." In *Medieval Scribes, Manuscripts, and Libraries: Essays Presented to N.R. Ker,* ed. M.B. Parkes and Andrew G. Watson, pp. 279-313. London: Scolar, 1978.

Wattenbach, W. *"Iter Austriacum* 1853." *Archiv für Kunde österreichisches Geschichtsquellen* 14 (1855) 39-51.

Weijers, Olga. "The Chronology of John of Salisbury's Studies in France (*Metalogicon* 2.10)." In *The World of John of Salisbury,* ed. Michael Wilks, pp. 109-116. Studies in Church History, Subsidia 3. Oxford: Blackwell, 1984.

Weisheipel, James A. "The Nature, Scope, and Classification of the Sciences." In *Science in the Middle Ages,* ed. David C. Lindberg, pp.461-482. Chicago: University of Chicago Press, 1978.

Welliver, Warman. *Character, Plot, and Thought in Plato's Timaeus-Critias.* Philosophia antiqua: A Series of Monographs on Ancient Philosophy 32. Leiden: Brill, 1977.

Westra, Haijo Jan. "Bernard of Chartres." In *Dictionary of the Middle Ages,* ed Joseph R. Strayer, 2: 189-190. New York: Scribner's Sons, 1983.

Wetherbee, Winthrop. "Philosophy, Cosmology, and the Twelfth-Century Renaissance." In *A History of Twelfth-Century Western Philosophy,* ed. Peter Dronke, pp. 21-53. Cambridge: Cambridge University Press, 1988.

——. *Platonism and Poetry in the Twelfth Century: The Literary Influence of the School of Chartres.* Princeton: Princeton University, 1972.

White, Alison. "Boethius in the Medieval Quadrivium." In *Boethius: His Life, Thought, and Influence,* ed. Margaret Gibson, pp. 162-205. Oxford: Blackwell, 1981.

Whitehead, Alfred North. *Adventures of Ideas.* 1933; rpt. New York: Free Press, 1967.

Wilamowitz-Moellendorff, U. von. *Platon.* 2 vols. Berlin: Weidman, 1919; rpt. 1959-1962.

Wilks, Michael. "John of Salisbury and the Tyranny of Nonsense." In *The World of John of Salisbury,* ed. Michael Wilks, pp. 263-286. Studies in Church History, Subsidia 3. Oxford: Blackwell, 1984.

Wilmart, André. *Analecta Reginensia: Extraits des manuscrits latins de la reine Christine conservés au Vatican.* Vatican, Biblioteca Vaticana Studi e testi 59. Città del Vaticano: Biblioteca Apostolica Vaticana, 1933.

Winden, J.C.M. van. *Calcidius on Matter: His Doctrine and Sources. A Chapter in the History of Platonism.* Philosophia antiqua: A Series of Monographs on Ancient Philosophy 9. Leiden: Brill, 1959; rpt. 1965.

Wulf, Maurice de. *History of Mediaeval Philosophy,* vol.1: *From the Beginnings to Albert the Great.* Trans. Ernest C. Messenger. New York: Longmans, Green, 1926.

Index of Manuscripts

Index of Words in the Text

References in this index are to the section and line numbers of the *Glosae super Platonem.*

5.387, 6.38, 6.42, 6.216, 7.138, 7.147, 7.166, 7.391-392
Apostolus 3.15
appellatio 6.149
appetitus 3.226, 6.176, 6.289, 7.343, 7.359
appositio 3.14
aqua 3.170, 4.57-58, 4.280-281, 4.318-320, 7.28, 8.249
arbitrium, liberum 6.206-207, 6.293
arbores 4.36, 5.78
archetipum 4.124, 4.232, 8.4, 8.253, 8.255, 8.257, 8.311, 8.350
archetipus 4.4, 4.6, 4.45, 4.110, 4.114-117, 4.123-125, 4.140, 4.377, 4.379, 5.247, 8.200, 8.232, 8.314, 8.396
arcticus 6.55-58
Aristoteles 5.72, 7.87, 8.269
arithmetica 1.63, 5.144
arithmeticus 8.445
armonia 5.143, 7.445
armonicus 8.445
arrogantia 3.14
ars 1.61, 6.165, 6.287, 7.412
artifex 8.436
arx 3.52-53
asinus 4.178, 6.273
assertio 8.382, 8.386
astronomia 5.146, 6.89
Athena 3.161
Athenae 1.27, 3.140, 3.186, 3.197-198, 3.202, 3.206-207
Athenienses 3.188, 3.248, 3.252, 3.277
Atlas 3.229-231
atomus 4.23
auctor 2.15, 3.11, 3.119, 4.31, 4.242, 6.207, 6.209, 6.281
auctoritas 6.95, 6.135, 8.278
auditor 3.34, 3.39
auditus 7.431-452
augmentum 7.348
Augustinus 3.88, 3.142
aures 7.449
aurum 8.170, 8.390
auspicium 8.98
auis 4.284, 7.211, 8.98
auus 3.79, 3.164, 3.191, 3.255, 3.262
axis 3.169-171

Bacchus 6.102
beatitudo 4.174, 6.140, 6.260, 7.2
beniuolus 2.9
binarius 3.30

blanditiae 6.134
brachia 7.162

cacodemones 5.244, 6.12, 6.123
cadauera 4.364
caduca 5.29, 5.42, 6.176, 6.185
caelestis 1.34, 6.11-13
caelum 4.24, 4.81, 5.295, 5.306, 6.24, 6.26
Calcidius 5.58, 6.89, 6.160, 6.167, 6.233, 6.264, 7.259, 8.253, 8.296, 8.333; archidiaconus 2.4
caligo 6.67
callide 2.57, 6.71
calodemones 6.12, 6.108
calor 3.167, 3.173, 3.176, 3.178, 4.50-51, 4.338, 6.225, 6.251
Calpe 3.229, 3.232
Cancer 5.323
cantus 7.456
Capricornus 5.323
caput 3.53, 6.191, 7.97, 7.137-139, 7.146, 7.149, 7.156-157, 7.170, 7.245, 7.279
carbo 7.19
cardo 3.50, 3.169-170, 4.369
carmen 3.146
Carmentis 3.184
caro 7.37
Cato 3.91
causa 4.40, 4.60, 4.64, 4.66, 4.122, 4.125, 4.133, 4.138, 4.166, 4.168, 4.170-171, 4.179, 4.243, 4.327-328, 6.49, 6.146, 7.32, 7.130, 7.164, 7.166, 7.174, 7.326, 7.328-329, 7.359, 7.369, 8.7, 8.21-22, 8.39, 8.51, 8.113
causatiua 4.40
centrum 4.370, 5.363
cera 8.18, 8.300
cerebrum 3.53
Ceres 6.102
Cerimonides 3.142
cerimonium 3.143
certamen 3.69, 4.168
certitudo 7.260
chilinder 8.175
choreae 6.74
Christus 2.30
cibus 4.358-359, 6.224-225
cimbala 4.298
circuitus 7.13, 7.54, 7.114
circulum 4.71, 5.212, 5.223, 5.321, 5.347-349, 5.361-363, 6.42, 6.56, 7.118, 7.148
circumactio 5.386-387, 6.76

circumlatio 7.346
ciues honesti 3.56
ciuitas 3.158, 3.163, 3.208, 3.214, 7.149-152
clades, publica 3.188
claritas 7.172-173
coaceruatio 7.10
coaequaeuus 5.277, 5.306-307
coaeternus 5.27, 5.301
cogitatio 6.52, 7.244, 7.247, 7.252, 7.256-259
cognitio 4.250, 7.384, 7.399
coitus 3.211, 7.300
colligamenta 7.10
color 6.82, 8.207, 8.360
columnae, aereae 3.233
comestio 6.227
commixtio 5.79, 5.85
commotio 6.232, 6.237
comparatio 3.146, 8.202
compendium 6.130
compositio 4.108, 4.327, 5.33, 5.51, 5.88, 5.98, 5.249, 5.304, 6.150, 7.443, 7.450
concentus 5.147, 7.455
conceptio 5.135
conceptus 7.144
conclusio 4.91
concordia 1.55, 2.47, 6.68, 7.448
concorditer 1.52
concretio 6.180-181, 7.348
concupiscentia 3.54, 6.170, 6.176, 6.190-191, 7.120, 7.154, 7.242, 7.250, 7.343, 7.354, 7.356, 7.363
conditio 3.264, 4.305
conditor 3.158, 4.250, 5.82, 5.186, 5.188, 5.190, 5.305, 7.72
conexio 3.31, 3.33, 4.281, 4.285
confusio 4.191
coniugatio 7.300
coniugium 5.131
coniunctio 6.172, 7.73, 7.237, 7.304, 7.349, 7.424, 7.440
conseruatores 1.49
consideratio 7.132, 7.377-381, 7.397, 7.411, 7.415-417, 8.289, 8.345
consilium 7.133
consonantia 3.28, 3.35, 5.142, 5.146, 7.74, 7.438-440, 7.450
consortium 6.150
constitutio 3.198, 3.201, 3.203, 5.225-226, 5.229, 6.13, 6.92, 7.128, 8.69-71, 8.398
consuetudinaria 1.12
consuetudo 3.73

contagio 5.77
contemplatio 7.378, 7.395
continuatio 4.5, 4.62, 4.121, 4.133, 4.245, 5.29, 5.86, 5.278, 6.210, 7.35, 7.417
contrarietas 8.214, 8.223
contuberniones 6.255
conuenientia 3.67, 7.457
conuentus 3.46, 3.259
conuiuium 3.1, 3.8, 3.22-23, 3.43-44, 3.273
cor 3.53, 5.3, 6.191, 7.151, 7.248
corda 7.444
corporeitas 8.268, 8.277
corporeus 4.27, 4.86, 5.126, 5.239-242, 7.317, 7.321, 7.329, 7.335, 7.338, 7.368, 8.5, 8.119, 8.234
corpulentus 4.247, 4.249, 4.256
corpus 1.58-59, 4.18, 4.49, 4.51-56, 4.127, 4.189-190, 4.237, 4.241, 4.313, 4.361, 4.369, 5.8, 5.11, 5.26, 5.31, 5.73, 5.78, 5.93, 5.97, 5.106, 5.109, 5.131-132, 5.210, 5.214, 5.228-231, 5.370, 6.14, 6.30, 6.110-111, 6.136, 6.161-175, 6.188, 6.204, 6.219, 6.224, 6.229-232, 6.234, 6.250, 6.260, 6.275-276, 6.284, 7.3-15, 7.24-47, 7.121-123, 7.129-131, 7.148, 7.160, 7.176, 7.178, 7.184-186, 7.199, 7.202, 7.207-208, 7.210-212, 7.219, 7.265, 7.268, 7.281, 7.309, 7.318-319, 7.330-359, 7.424, 7.440, 8.2-448
corpuscula 7.11
correctio 7.393, 7.438
corruptio 4.55-56, 4.59, 7.350
crater 6.179
creatio 1.34, 3.276, 5.38, 6.140
creator 1.35, 4.10, 4.252
creatura 1.35, 4.10, 4.177, 4.237
credulitas 8.336-337
cribrum 8.429
Critias, uetus 3.155
crus 7.162
cubus 4.255, 4.276
culpa 6.208
cultus 1.41, 3.102
cupiditas 6.238
currus 3.214
cursus 3.66, 4.373, 5.136, 5.195, 5.211, 5.312, 5.317, 5.320, 5.333, 5.348, 5.352, 5.365, 5.383, 6.25
custodes 6.115

dea 3.209
decollatio 2.30

decretum 6.201, 6.279
defectus 3.235, 8.439
defensio 3.90
defluxus 4.54
degeneres 3.107
delectatio 3.89, 7.442
delibatio 4.333
deliberatio 7.380
delinimenta 3.67
demon 6.126, 6.168
demonstratio 8.53
denarius 5.138-139
deprauatio 8.370
deriuatio 7.92
desiderium 5.181
desperatio 6.241
determinatio 8.165
detractatio 7.50
detuitio 7.264, 7.268-270
deus 1.13, 1.16, 3.52, 4.5, 4.9, 4.32-33, 4.38-39, 4.41, 4.77, 4.95, 4.105, 4.191, 4.194, 4.232, 4.234, 4.236, 4.238-240, 4.258, 4.280, 5.27, 5.45, 5.52, 5.81, 5.247, 5.268, 5.310, 6.27, 6.63, 6.99, 6.116, 6.133, 6.167, 6.260, 7.385, 7.427, 8.3, 8.21, 8.96, 8.315, 8.334, 8.337, 8.350, 8.402
dialectica 7.224
dialecticus 7.289
dialogus 3.7
diapason 3.29, 3.36, 3.38
diapente 3.29, 3.37
diatessaron 3.28, 3.37
difficilis 2.12, 2.14, 2.24-26, 2.35, 3.127
difficultas 2.5, 2.10, 2.13, 2.24, 8.82-83, 8.88
diffinitio 7.49
dignitas 5.135, 6.148, 6.207, 8.107
dii 2.59-60, 5.305, 6.97, 6.100, 6.103, 6.149, 6.292, 7.235
dilectio 1.14, 1.17, 1.36
diligentia 6.115
diluuium 3.175, 3.182, 3.185, 3.251, 6.132
dimensio 4.263, 4.272, 4.313, 4.316
diminutio 4.332, 7.348
disciplina 7.357, 8.330
discipulus 3.13, 3.18
discordia, ciuilis 3.151
discretio 7.222, 7.349, 8.40
discrimina 3.251
disiunctio 7.349
dispositio 6.82, 7.144, 7.148, 7.386

disputatio 3.43-44, 3.267, 8.78; epoptica 8.77, 8.85
dissolubilis 4.28, 6.142
dissolutio 4.328, 5.304, 7.4
distinctio 6.49
diuersitas 5.114
diuina 4.19, 5.41, 5.55, 6.174, 6.174, 7.2, 7.142, 7.332, 7.362, 7.378, 7.362, 7.382, 8.440
diuinitas 6.137, 6.151, 7.384, 7.399
diuisio 4.9, 4.12, 5.94, 5.127, 5.182, 5.213-214, 8.101, 8.109, 8.112
docilis 2.10
doctrina 3.87, 6.175, 7.119
dolor 6.241, 6.243, 6.247
dominium 7.147, 8.30
dominus 2.8
domus 3.78

effectus 2.32, 7.230
efficentia 8.12, 8.201
effluxio 4.55, 7.32, 7.35, 7.53
egestio 7.16
ego 3.275, 4.163, 6.154, 6.158, 6.169
Egyptus 3.150, 3.247
elementa 1.52, 4.50-52, 4.56, 4.98, 4.131, 4.193, 4.291, 4.299, 5.10, 6.16, 6.53, 7.4-5, 7.12, 8.15, 8.23, 8.35, 8.55-56, 8.60, 8.64-73, 8.86, 8.136-140, 8.144, 8.153, 8.159, 8.164, 8.260, 8.280, 8.385, 8.400, 8.410, 8.418, 8.424, 8.430, 8.438
elementaria 8.16, 8.36, 8.247
endelichia 5.73
epistula 2.8; ad Hebreos 3.15
epitritos 5.174-176
epogdous 5.172-175
epulum 3.4-5, 3.43, 3.108
equus 3.115
Erictonius 3.195, 3.197, 3.199, 3.210, 3.212, 3.225
Eris 3.215
essentia 4.7, 4.156, 5.60, 7.143, 8.146, 8.288
et hoc est 2.11, 2.15, 2.22, 4.68, 4.172, 4.186, 2.55, 5.176, 5.191, 5.258, 6.220, 6.274, 7.73, 7.101, 7.183, 7.250, 7.334, 7.374, 7.403, 7.419, 7.441, 8.171, 8.208, 8.247, 8.327-328; et cum hoc sit 8.215; et hoc fit 7.289
ethica 1.56, 3.124, 6.165
Euander 3.184

inuocatio 3.283
inuolucrum 3.1, 3.81, 5.50, 5.180
ira 6.169, 6.176, 6.244, 7.120, 7.152, 7.242,
    7.246, 7.248, 7.325, 7.342, 7.354,
    7.356, 7.363
iracundia 3.54, 6.244-245, 6.250
Isocrates, auctor 2.15
iter 7.90
iudicium 5.261, 5.264, 7.69, 7.141, 7.426,
    8.396
Iuppiter 5.359, 6.135
ius 3.278, 6.200
iussio 3.96, 3.100, 6.167
iusticia 1.2, 1.6, 1.11, 6.158, 6.167, 6.208;
    naturalis 1.13, 1.16, 1.21-22, 1.25-26,
    1.32-33, 1.35, 1.38-40, 1.42-43, 1.45,
    1.51, 1.54, 1.56, 2.59, 3.2, 3.6, 3.109-
    110, 3.118, 3.133, 3.135, 3.270, 4.1;
    positiua 1.10, 1.12, 1.15, 1.20, 1.22,
    1.27, 1.40, 1.45, 1.55, 3.2, 3.4, 3.47-48,
    3.108, 3.118, 3.133, 3.135; uis iusticiae
    1.5, 1.9, 1.35
iuuens 3.54

labor 3.65
lac 7.41
laeticia 5.271
lapis 4.363, 7.266; quadratus 4.300, 4.347
latinus 2.3, 2.39, 2.41-42, 2.59, 2.63
latitudo 4.316
latus 5.150, 5.155
lectio 5.48
lex 4.166-167, 4.369, 5.48, 5.304, 6.200-
    206, 6.210, 6.218, 6.222, 6.239, 6.282,
    8.286
liber 1.1, 1.20, 1.23, 1.46, 2.1, 2.5, 2.10,
    2.61, 2.63, 3.19, 3.179, 4.374, 6.105,
    6.96, 6.132
libertas, communis 3.99; publica 3.249
libido 7.248
lignum 4.363, 8.390
limes 5.134, 5.141, 5.148, 5.164, 5.167-
    168, 6.57-58
linea 5.197, 5.362, 6.54, 6.57, 6.80, 7.295
lineamenta 7.309
lingua 2.64
liquor 4.360, 7.188
lis 3.215
littera 3.94, 6.165, 7.351, 8.69; litterae pu-
    blicae 3.183
litus 3.243
localiter 3.129
locus 3.18, 3.217, 4.367, 5.202-203, 6.51,

6.61, 6.103, 6.190-192, 6.254, 7.147,
    7.141, 7.245, 7.248, 7.250, 7.290, 8.24,
    8.70, 8.296, 8.354, 8.362, 8.365, 8.369;
    nobilium 3.107
logica 1.57, 6.166, 7.382, 7.403
longitudo 4.316
lucrum 6.100
lucta 3.69
ludus 3.66
lumbi 3.55
lumen 7.205-206, 7.281, 7.321
luna 5.325, 5.328, 5.340, 6.16
lupus 6.273
luxuria 6.103

machina 8.429
Macrobius 1.46, 1.49, 4.238, 4.286
magister 3.3, 3.16, 3.18, 3.40-41
magnitudo 6.64
maiores 1.13, 7.149
mane 3.227
maneriae 8.195
mansio 5.298
manus 3.246-247
mare 3.230, 3.234, 3.241, 3.243-244
maritus 3.92
masculinus 3.158, 3.160
massa 5.121, 5.12, 5.178
mater 3.184, 3.210, 5.138, 8.8, 8.10, 8.20-
    22, 8.234-235, 8.237-239
materia 1.40, 1.44, 1.50, 3.1, 3.49, 4.196-
    197, 4.237, 4.243-244, 5.87, 7.14, 8.2,
    8.6, 8.11, 8.13, 8.45, 8.128, 8.174-178,
    8.196, 8.265-267, 8.308, 8.418
materialis 6.144
materialiter 5.34
meatus 6.226, 7.113
medicina 8.225
medietas 4.305, 4.312, 5.153, 5.156, 5.158,
    5.161-163
Mediterraneus 3.230, 3.236
membrum 4.12, 4.37, 5.95, 7.130, 7.135,
    7.147, 7.156, 7.238, 8.112
memoria 3.144, 3.179, 3.181, 3.256, 6.289
memoriter 3.145
mens 4.238, 5.76, 6.93, 7.392, 7.425, 8.136,
    8.338, 8.403, 8.408, 8.412, 8.418,
    8.425, 8.433; dei 4.238, 5.45, 5.235,
    8.315, 8.350; diuina 5.270, 8.57-58,
    8.197
mensis 7.387
mentio 6.93
mentum 7.279, 7.315

merces 3.71
merita 1.16
metus 6.242, 6.249
milites 3.75, 7.150
militia 3.72
millenarius 6.259
Minerua 3.141, 3.209, 3.215, 3.267, 5.138
ministerium 7.368-369
mites 3.63, 3.66
mixtura 5.81, 5.149
modus 1.42
molendinum 3.169
moles 4.292, 6.175
mollis 8.186
monachi 3.100
montanus 6.133
montes 3.230
moralitas 7.388
mos 1.6, 1.15, 1.37, 2.47, 3.13, 3.45, 3.68,
  3.276, 7.393, 7.438-439, 7.442, 7.450,
  7.452, 7.456
morbus 4.43
motio 6.230
motus 1.59-60, 4.191, 4.252, 5.2, 5.19,
  5.21, 5.183, 5.188, 5.201, 5.216-219,
  5.260, 5.265, 5.295, 5.314, 5.345,
  5.376, 5.388-390, 6.37-46, 6.65, 6.196,
  7.18, 7.27, 7.60, 7.75, 7.105, 7.114,
  7.121, 7.160, 7.165, 7.252, 7.256,
  7.292-294, 7.343-350, 7.359, 7.390-
  393, 7.419-420, 7.425, 7.429, 7.447,
  8.421-423
mulier 3.95, 6.219, 6.265
multiplicitas 5.118
multitudo 8.269, 8.292
mundus 1.9, 1.52, 2.60, 3.19, 3.38, 4.2, 4.4,
  4.27, 4.32, 4.35, 4.38, 4.44, 4.52-54,
  4.56, 4.59-60, 4.81, 4.88, 4.92, 4.96,
  4.100-101, 4.109, 4.119, 4.125, 4.130,
  4.140, 4.142-158, 4.171, 4.180, 4.194,
  4.208-212, 4.219, 4.242, 4.245, 4.324-
  325, 4.329, 4.344, 4.351, 4.365, 4.379,
  5.30, 5.92, 5.229, 5.239, 5.247, 5.272,
  5.278-282, 5.310, 6.1, 6.7, 6.62, 6.93,
  6.132, 6.146, 6.216, 8.1, 8.10, 8.51,
  8.58, 8.68, 8.71, 8.75, 8.101, 8.105-110,
  8.200, 8.202, 8.398, 8.400
munus 2.50, 2.56, 6.223, 7.418
musica 1.62-63, 3.67, 5.142, 5.146, 7.441-
  443, 7.450
musicus 3.25, 5.147, 7.438
mutabilia 8.155
mutatio 4.364, 6.86, 6.264

narratio 3.202
natio 3.181
natiua 7.2, 8.367, 8.397
natiuitas 3.195-196
natura 3.57, 4.28, 4.33, 4.35, 4.42, 4.78,
  4.121-122, 4.124, 4.213, 4.221-222,
  4.332, 5.6, 5.36, 5.41, 5.43, 5.46, 5.52,
  5.56, 5.61-63, 5.80, 5.107, 5.110, 5.115-
  116, 5.248-249, 5.279, 6.21, 6.36,
  6.113, 6.143, 7.56, 7.100-101, 7.175,
  7.224, 7.240, 7.263, 7.290, 7.299,
  7.382, 7.386, 7.399, 7.409, 8.48, 8.119,
  8.135, 8.158, 8.183, 8.238, 8.287,
  8.319, 8.372, 8.377, 8.385, 8.388-390,
  8.419-422, 8.427, 8.434
naturalis 3.210, 4.42, 4.359, 6.244, 7.151,
  7.242, 7.259-261
naturaliter 1.36, 5.143
nauis 4.382, 7.275
nebulae 8.141
necessitas 4.43, 4.326, 6.201, 8.5, 8.11,
  8.26-28, 8.34, 8.37, 8.53
negligentia 3.152
negotium 3.281
nexus 4.287, 4.291, 6.144, 7.72
Nilus 3.177
Nioba 3.187
nobiles 3.107
nolae 4.298
nomen 3.13-15, 3.154, 3.157-158, 4.82,
  5.200, 6.101, 7.321, 8.43, 8.50, 8.138
noticia 5.42, 6.72, 6.133
nouiter 3.182
nubes 6.22
nudus 3.68-69
numeratio 5.140
numerus 3.25-26, 3.29-30, 3.35, 4.262-264,
  4.271, 4.280, 4.292, 5.131-145, 5.232,
  6.186, 7.451, 7.458
nuptiae, communes 3.76, 3.89
nutricatio 7.120
nutricula 8.127

obedientes 3.65
obedientia 3.96, 3.100
obscuritas 8.121
obtrectatio 6.248
obtunsio 4.338
occiput 7.282
oceanus 3.230, 3.232, 3.234-235, 3.240
oculus 4.356, 6.71, 7.88, 7.172-204, 7.273,
  7.313, 7.323, 7.369, 7.373, 7.416,
  7.418-419

7.150, 7.242, 7.342, 8.43, 8.50, 8.62, 8.148, 8.413

uisibilia 4.222

uisus 5.224, 6.21, 6.26, 7.180, 7.197, 7.225-226, 7.236, 7.240-241, 7.263-265, 7.290-317, 7.371, 7.380, 7.384, 7.389-415, 7.431-432

uitalitas 6.267

uitium 5.63, 5.65-66, 5.112, 5.114, 5.215, 5.220, 5.253, 6.183, 6.269, 6.276, 6.278, 6.292, 7.115-116, 7.392

uitrum 7.270

uoluntas 2.52, 4.60, 4.179, 6.117, 6.145, 7.454

uoluptas 6.241-242, 6.247-248, 7.116

uolutio 7.387

uox 7.435, 7.445, 7.452, 8.69

Vulcanus 3.211, 3.215

uultus 7.169-170, 7.266-267, 7.278

zodiacus 5.198, 5.207

zona 5.198

General Index

Abelard 15, 35, 40-42, 44, 49, 59, 61, 91
accessus 47, 50, 52, 54, 60, 63-65, 96, 106
Adalbold of Utrecht 4
Adelard of Bath, *De eodem et diuerso* 68
anima mundi. See world-soul
Anselm of Laon 29, 43, 46
Apuleius 1, 62, 89
archetype 71, 74, 79, 86, 93, 101
Aristotle 1-3, 62, 75, 80, 87-89, 103; *Categoriae* 65, 80, 83
Atlantis 1, 51
atoms 68
Augustine 53, 58-60, 62-63, 91; *De ciuitate dei* 60, 63; *Confessiones* 62; *Retractationes* 63
authority 58, 62-63, 69

Bernard of Chartres 11, 16, 21-45; epithets of 25-33; his books 32-33, 249; the question of his Breton background 22-23, 40-41; dicta 37, 241-242; dwarfs and giants metaphor 37, 39, 49, 241; *Glosae super Platonem* 5-6, 9-21, 44, 44-96; his influence 6-8, 14, 96-108, 135, 246-297; methods of teaching 38-39, 41-43, 45, 57, 242-245; poetry 16, 36, 81-85, 90, 240-241; six keys of learning 36, 42, 57, 240; exemplum of the white virgin 83, 87, 100, 242
Bernard of Moëlan 22-23, 41-42
Bernard Silvester 22-23; his commentary on the *Aeneid* 8; *Cosmographia* 22
Bible 61; Genesis 86
bodies 71-80
Boethius 1, 5, 7, 18, 21, 36, 52, 62, 64-65, 69, 80-81, 87, 92, 97, 99, 101, 104; *Contra Eutychen* 65; *De institutione arithmetica* 65; *De institutione musica* 65; *In Isagogen Porphyrii commenta: editio secunda* 35, 65, 80; *Philosophiae consolatio* 65; *De trinitate* 65, 77, 90
boys 57, 62
Brisson, Luc 1-2

Calcidius 1-2, 19, 52, 55, 58, 62, 65-70, 80-82, 90; *Commentarius* 5-8, 11-13, 15, 18-19, 21, 39, 48, 51, 62, 67, 70, 75-79, 83-84, 89, 94, 97-98, 135; *Timaeus a Calcidio translatus* 6-7, 16, 105, 131-133
cathedral schools 15, 29, 56
Cato 64
causa totius prosperitatis 36
causes 52, 67, 73, 80, 85, 94, 106; erratic 76, 95; primary and secondary 20
Cerimonides 63
Chartres, cartularies 27-28, 239-240; letter-book 34, 244-245; necrology 27, 31-32, 249; school of 15-16, 25, 31, 35, 42
Chenu, M.-D. 55, 63, 73
children 65
Christ 61
Christianity 61
Cicero 1, 6, 52, 64
circle 65
city 66
Clerval, Alexandre 23-24, 27, 29-30, 32, 42
colour 83
commentators 48, 58
Constantine the African: *Pantegni* 14
constitutio mundi 53
Cornford, Francis 1-2
Cornificius and the Cornificians 38-40
Cousin, Victor 22
creation 73, 75, 81, 85-86, 94-96; *ex nihilo* 72-73, 86, 91-92, 94
creator 71
creature 71-74, 87

Demimuid, Mauritius 22
Demiourgos 72
demonology 66, 98-99
desire, birth of 66
disciplina 36-37, 57, 61
disputatio 56, 69
dreams 66
Dronke, Peter 17-19, 34

Thierry of Chartres 22-24, 33, 40-42
Thomas Aquinas 49
Timaeus of Locri 1-2, 54, 57
time 84-85, 92-94
Trinity 92-93, 104
trivium 48, 69
Tuilecnad 11-14, 17-18, 26-27, 46, 51

universals 74-75, 87-89, 95, 101
uniuersitas 5

vices 60
Virgil 39-40, 62, 64-65, 105, 241
virtues 36, 60
vision 98
Vulgrin, chancellor of Chartres 29-30, 32, 43

Walter of Mortagne 87, 102
Waszink, J.H. 17, 109, 131, 134
Wilamowitz-Moellendorf, U. von 1
William of Champeaux 15, 43, 46
William of Conches 1-2, 4, 15-16, 19-20,

24-25, 29, 35, 37-40, 43, 47, 49, 56,
58-59, 62-63, 66, 69-71, 91, 97, 102,
250; *Glosae super Priscianum* 47, 54;
Glose Willelmi de Conchis super Platonem
5-6, 8, 14, 19-20, 39, 48, 52-54, 69,
105-106, 132-134, 260-262, 278; *Philosophia mundi* 19-21, 97-99 ; *accessus* by
an unidentified author to the *Glosae in
Iuvenalem* attributed to William 54, 97,
248-249
William of Tyre 41
wise men 66
women, held in common 59, 62, 64
workers 66
works, the three types of 67, 71, 84, 97
world, archetypal 72, 74, 78; intelligible 74,
92-93; sensible 71, 74, 76-78, 85-86, 92,
94
world-soul 11-12, 17, 20, 65

Yaḥyā ibn ʿAdi 1